Madagascar

the Bradt Travel Guide

Daniel Austin
Hilary Bradt

edition
12

www.bradtguides.com

Bradt Travel Guides Ltd, UK
The Globe Pequot Press Inc, USA

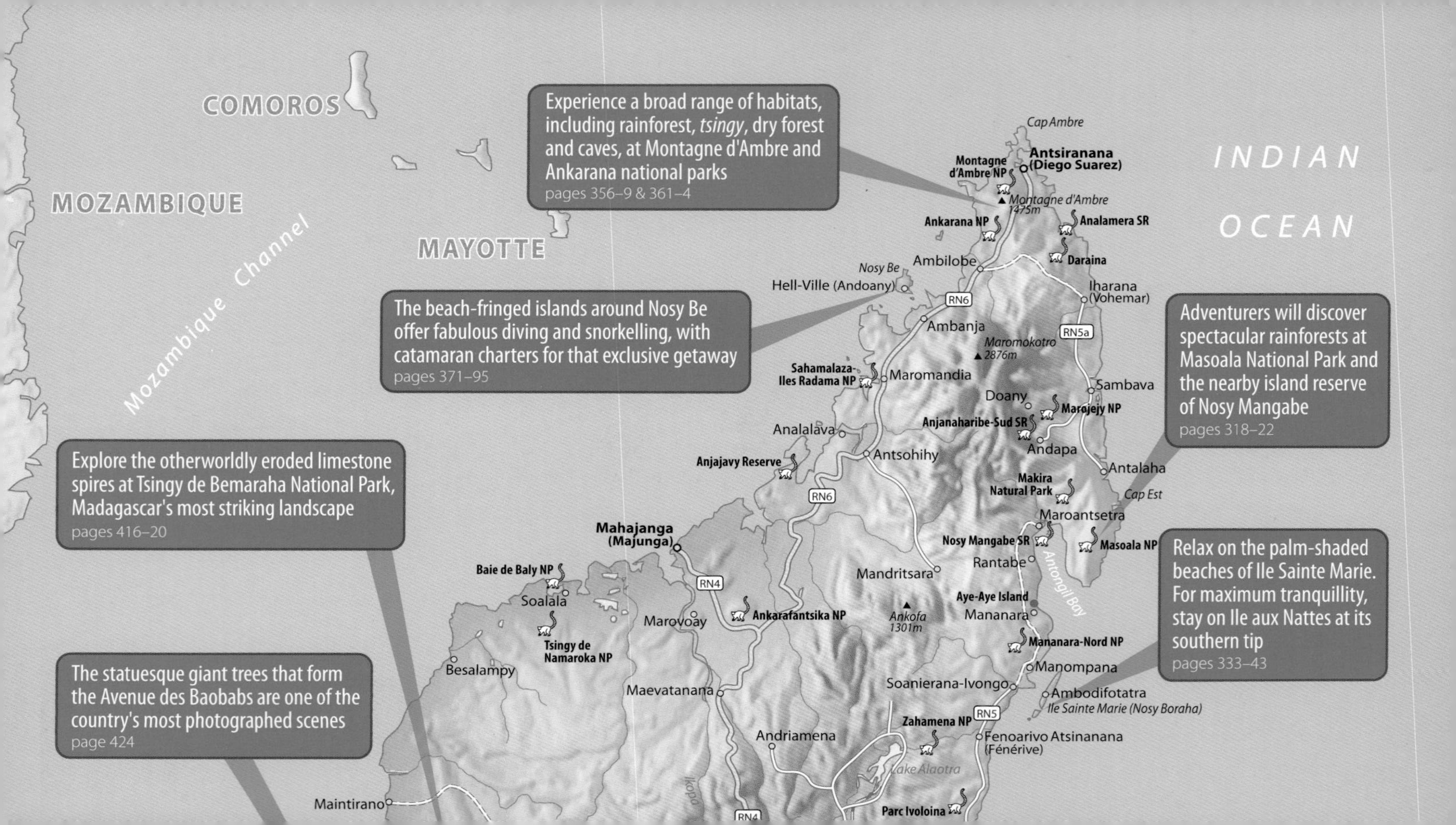

INDIAN OCEAN

COMOROS

MAYOTTE

MOZAMBIQUE

Mozambique Channel

Adventurers will discover spectacular rainforests at Masoala National Park and the nearby island reserve of Nosy Mangabe
pages 318–22

Relax on the palm-shaded beaches of Ile Sainte Marie. For maximum tranquillity, stay on Ile aux Nattes at its southern tip
pages 333–43

Experience a broad range of habitats, including rainforest, *tsingy*, dry forest and caves, at Montagne d'Ambre and Ankarana national parks
pages 356–9 & 361–4

The beach-fringed islands around Nosy Be offer fabulous diving and snorkelling, with catamaran charters for that exclusive getaway
pages 371–95

Explore the otherworldly eroded limestone spires at Tsingy de Bemaraha National Park, Madagascar's most striking landscape
pages 416–20

The statuesque giant trees that form the Avenue des Baobabs are one of the country's most photographed scenes
page 424

Cap Ambre

Antsiranana (Diego Suarez)
Analamera SR
Montagne d'Ambre 1475m
Montagne d'Ambre NP
Ankarana NP
Ambilobe
Iharana (Vohemar)
Daraina
RN5a
Sambava
Marojejy NP
Antalaha
Cap Est
Ambanja
RN6
Maromokotro 2876m
Doany
Andapa
Anjanaharibe-Sud SR
Maromandia
Makira Natural Park
Maroantsetra
Masoala NP
Nosy Be
Hell-Ville (Andoany)
Sahamalaza-Iles Radama NP
Antsohihy
Nosy Mangabe SR
Rantabe
Aye-Aye Island
Mananara
Mananara-Nord NP
Manompana
Ambodifotatra (Ile Sainte Marie)
Ile Sainte Marie (Nosy Boraha)
Analalava
RN6
Mandritsara
Soanierana-Ivongo
RN5
Fenoarivo Atsinanana (Fénérive)
Ankarafantsika NP
Ankofa 1301m
Andriamena
Zahamena NP
Lake Alaotra
Parc Ivoloina
MaroVoay
RN4
Maevatanana
Ikopa
Anjajavy Reserve
Mahajanga (Majunga)
Baie de Baly NP
Tsingy de Namoroka NP
Soalala
Besalampy
Maintirano

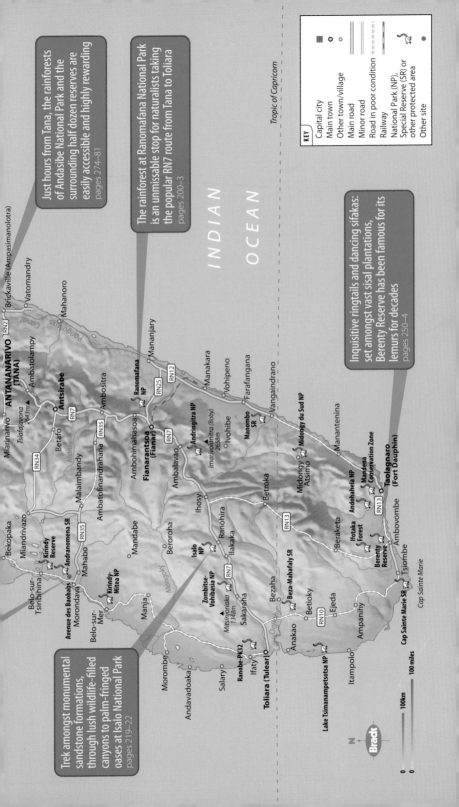

Just hours from Tana, the rainforests of Andasibe National Park and the surrounding half dozen reserves are easily accessible and highly rewarding pages 274–81

The rainforest at Ranomafana National Park is an unmissable stop for naturalists taking the popular RN7 route from Tana to Toliara pages 200–3

Inquisitive ringtails and dancing sifakas: set amongst vast sisal plantations, Berenty Reserve has been famous for its lemurs for decades pages 250–4

Trek amongst monumental sandstone formations, through lush wildlife-filled canyons to palm-fringed oases at Isalo National Park pages 219–22

INDIAN OCEAN

Tropic of Capricorn

KEY

■ Capital city
○ Main town
○ Other town/village
Main road
Minor road
Road in poor condition
Railway
National Park (NP), Special Reserve (SR) or other protected area
● Other site

Brickaville (Ampasimanolotra)
Vatomandry
RN2
Mahanoro
Ambatolampy
Mananjary
Mahanoro

ANTANANARIVO (TANA)
Miarinarivo
RN34
Tsiafajavona 2643m ▲
Antsirabe
RN7
Betafo
RN35
Malaimbandy
Ambositra
Ambohimahasoa
Fianarantsoa (Fianar)
Ranomafana NP
RN25
Manakara
Vohipeno
Farafangana
Vangaindrano

INDIAN OCEAN

Bekopaka
Miandrivazo
Belo-sur-Tsiribihina
Kirindy Reserve
Andranomena SR
RN35
Avenue des Baobabs
Morondava
Belo-sur-Mer
Kirindy-Mitea NP
Mahabo
Manja
Ambatofinandrahana
Ambalavao
RN7
Andringitra NP
Imarivolanitra (Boby) 2658m ▲
Olvohibe
Manombo SR
Midongy du Sud NP
Manantenina

Mandabe
Bereroha
Ihosy
Betroka
Mandabe
Isalo NP
Ranohira
Ilakaka
RN13
Midongy Atsimo
Mariena Conservation Zone
Andohahela NP
RN13
Taolagnaro (Fort Dauphin)

Morombe
Andavadoaka
Salary
Ranobe-PK32
Ifaty
Toliara (Tuléar)
Zombitse-Vohibasia NP
Mitsinjoriaka 1348m ▲
Sakaraha
RN7
Bezaha
Beza-Mahafaly SR
Betioky
RN10
Ejeda
Ampanihy
Beraketa
Ifotaka Forest
Berenty Reserve
Ambovombe
Anakao
Itampolo
Cap Sainte Marie SR
Tsiombe
Cap Sainte Marie

Pangalana Canal
Mania
Manandroro
Mangoky
Onilahy

N

0   100km
0   100 miles

Bradt

Madagascar
Don't
miss...

Rainforests
Ranomafana National Park is a fine
example of montane rainforest

(DA) pages 200–3

Avenue des Baobabs
These majestic trees make for a
curious and striking landscape

(DA) page 423

Lemurs
The ring-tail is the most famous of more than a hundred varieties of lemur, all endemic to Madagascar
(DA) pages 60–2

Beaches
Glorious uncrowded sandy beaches are easy to find
(DA) page 83

The chance to give something back
Responsible tourism and volunteering opportunities mean you can do your bit through numerous community and conservation projects
(DA) pages 131–44

Madagascar
in colour

above   Bad roads often get the better of *taxi-brousses*; here a pair of zebu is roped in to help pull one free (OR) page 98

left   The traditional *pousse-pousse* has largely been replaced by bicycle rickshaws, but tourists can still enjoy a ride in Antsirabe (DA) page 101

below   Pirogues — dugout canoes with an outrigger — are used by locals on the coast (DA) page 101

above   Madagascar's only tea plantation produces some 550 tonnes of tea each year (DA) page 208

right   Traditional *Antaimoro* paper is decorated with dried flowers (DA) page 210

below left   Sisal leaves are crushed then sun-dried for two days before being baled up for export (DA) page 250

below right   Open-pit mining for sapphires is back-breaking work (DA) page 223

left   The spiny forest of the arid southern region is a unique and extraordinary habitat (DA) pages 67–8

below   As an island, Madagascar has no shortage of ocean. There's something for everyone: from diving and snorkelling to windsurfing and kite-surfing; the diverse sea life includes dolphins, whales, turtles and myriad colourful reef fish (DA) page 81

bottom   The razor-sharp limestone karst pinnacles of the *tsingy* make for an otherworldly landscape. At Bemaraha, a walkway has been constructed to allow visitors to explore this stone forest (DA) pages 66–7

ABOUT THE AUTHORS

Daniel Austin's fascination with Madagascar began long before he managed to muster the funds to go and see the island first-hand, on what he planned to be a once-in-a-lifetime trip before submitting to the inevitability of getting a 'proper job'. Whether it was his aversion to such drudgery or the allure of Madagascar that was stronger than he expected isn't certain – perhaps both – but the trip changed the course of his life and he has returned every year for the decade and a half since, often for three months at a time. Now occupied full time with all things Malagasy, he leads small-group tours to the island (*www.danielaustin.co.uk*), gives occasional lectures on Madagascar, is secretary of the London-based Anglo-Malagasy Society (pages 137–8), founded the Madagascar Library (*www.madagascar-library.com*) and co-authored the other Bradt titles *Madagascar Wildlife* and *Madagascar Highlights*.

Hilary Bradt's career as an occupational therapist ended when potential employers noticed that the time taken off for travel exceeded the periods of employment. With her former husband George, she self-published her first guidebook in 1974 during an extended journey through South America. As well as running Bradt Travel Guides, Hilary worked for 25 years as a tour leader in Madagascar. Her in-depth knowledge of the country has brought her lecture engagements at the Royal Geographical Society, the Smithsonian Institution and on board expedition cruise ships, as well as numerous commissions for travel articles. She received an MBE in 2008 for services to the travel industry and a Lifetime Achievement Award from the British Guild of Travel Writers in 2009. She now lives in semi-retirement in Devon and is delighted to have handed over the hard graft of researching new editions to Daniel.

LOCAL CONTRIBUTOR

Based in Antananarivo, **Ony Rakotoarivelo** has been a major contributor to this guide since the seventh edition in 2001. In addition to this and working with Malagasy children's charity Ankizy Gasy, she is an independent travel consultant helping Anglophone tourists to plan their trips to Madagascar and sometimes guiding them herself. You can find her contact details on page 173.

Twelfth edition published September 2017
First published 1988
Bradt Travel Guides Ltd
IDC House, The Vale, Chalfont St Peter, Bucks SL9 9RZ, England
www.bradtguides.com
Print edition published in the USA by The Globe Pequot Press Inc,
PO Box 480, Guilford, Connecticut 06437-0480

ISBN: 978 1 78477 048 8 (print)
e-ISBN: 978 1 78477 513 1 (e-pub)
e-ISBN: 978 1 78477 414 1 (mobi)

British Library Cataloguing in Publication Data
A catalogue record for this book is available from the British Library

Photographs Daniel Austin (DA); Hilary Bradt (HB); FLPA: Jurgen and Christine Sohns
(JCS/FLPA); Nick Garbutt (NG); Elliott Hails (EH); Louise Jasper Gardner (LJ); Prodromos
Nikolaidis (PN); Ony Rakotoarivelo (OR); Mark Scherz (MS)
Front cover Ring-tailed lemurs (JCS/FLPA)
Back cover Malagasy girl at Marofandilia (DA)
Title page Avenue des Baobabs (DA); Tomato frog (DA); Traditional hut (DA)

Maps David McCutcheon FBCart.S
Illustrations Janet Mary Robinson, www.jmr.org.uk

Typeset by Ian Spick, Bradt Travel Guides
Production managed by Jellyfish Print Solutions; printed in India
Digital conversion by www.dataworks.co.in

Acknowledgements

First and foremost, our profuse thanks go to the in-country representative for this guidebook, Ony Rakotoarivelo, who sends us regular feedback on changes in Madagascar. Ony is not only a genius at tracking down any piece of information that we are struggling to find ourselves, but she also single-handedly took on the monumental task of calling to check the vast majority of the Malagasy phone number that appear in this book – and there's well over 3,000 of them!

Throughout these pages, 'boxes' written by specialists give the reader background information on a host of subjects. We owe a huge debt of gratitude to these experts for their invaluable contributions. Zoological material was provided by Nick Garbutt (mammals), Tara Clarke, Marni LaFleur, Kim Reuter and the late Alison Jolly (lemurs), Richard Jenkins, Paul Racey and Julie Hanta Razafimanahaka (bats), Duncan Murrell (whales), Jonathan Ekstrom (parrots), Devin Edmonds and Falitiana Rabemananjara (frogs), and Angus McCrae, Len de Beer and John Roff (invertebrates). Janet Mary Robinson is responsible for the delightful lemur illustrations that appear in *Chapter 3*. Clare and Johan Hermans, and Gavin Hart enthused on the wonders of Malagasy flora. Conservation issues were variously covered by Lanto Andrianandrasana, Chris Birkinshaw, Andrew Cooke, Rainer Dolch, Alasdair Harris, Richard Lewis, Kara Moses, Erik Patel, Lennart Pyritz, Jamie Spencer, Charles Welch and Anne Yoder. The expertise of Tim Ireland enriched the sections on geology and gemstones. Special thanks go to doctors Felicity Nicholson and Jane Wilson-Howarth for health and safety advice; Ailie Tam added background on HIV. Insights into history and politics came from John Grehan and Ambassador Timothy Smart, as well as former ambassador Sir Mervyn Brown who has lent his expertise since the very first edition. Wining and dining advice was provided by Carrie Antal and Christian Schiller. Specialists in traditional customs, crafts and social issues included Camilla Backhouse, Christina Corbett, Theresa Haine, Joseph Radoccia, Seraphine Tierney Ramanantsoa, Tess Shellard and Jo Shinner. Musicologist Paddy Bush offered his expertise with Derek Schuurman, who also authored sections on such diverse subjects as birds, fish and illegal logging. Janice Booth added her helpful tips on getting to grips with the Malagasy language. Specialist advice to mountain bikers was provided by Lex Cumber, Bill French and Julian Cooke. Divers will benefit from the input of Tim Healy, Liz Bomford and Rob Conway. Gordon Rattray contributed advice on travel for people with disabilities. Entertaining travellers' tales came from FRB, Chris Balance, Stephen Cartledge, Kelly Green, H and M Kendrick, Lee Miller, Toby Nowlan, Colin Palmer, Marko Petrovic, Suzy Pope, Robert Stewart, Ben Tapley and Nigel Vardy.

Many kind people living or working in Madagascar have helpfully provided updates or logistical support. Particular thanks in this regard go to Franco Andreone, Manitra Andriamialisoa, Lantohery Andrianantenaina, Haingo

Nomena Andriantahina, Sarobidy Andriantahina, Mickael Bashir, Richard Bohan, Edward Tucker Brown, Rachel Cowen, Viviane Dewa, Barry Ferguson, Velomasy Fidelis, Tsanta Fiderana Rakotonanahary, Louise Fox, Charlie Gardner, Julie Geels, Jaozandry Jenita Harilala, Laurence Ink, Louise Jasper-Gardner, Harriet and Mike Joao, Sian Jones, Ursula Kalo, AG Klei, Klaus Konnerth, Gary Lemmer, Fredel Mamindra, Brett Massoud, Eric Mathieu, Steve McDonald, Kerry O'Neill, Andry Petignat, Serge Rajaobelina, Soahary Ines Rajaonarivelo, Rindra Harimalala Rakotoarinjatovo, Ruth Rakotomanga, Harry Rakotosalama, Joshua Ralph, Njaka Ramandimbiarison, Justin Randrianarison, Nanja Raobison, Haja Rasambainarivo, Nivo Ravelojaona, Hanta Razafindrasoa, Miora Rivoarimino, Mark Scherz, Franz Stadelmann, Jacob ter Veen, Jacques Vieira and Pat Wright.

A small army of travellers have written in to share their experiences. Many took the time to write tremendously detailed trip reports for which we are extremely grateful. This book would not be as rich in detail without the eyes and ears of so many helpful readers. Thank you to Claire Aitken, Eric Arnold, Jorn Arnt, Alastair Cameron, Tiffany Coates, Davide Coles, Donal Conlon, Joan Curtis, Merel Dalebout, Roger Dawson, Jeffrey Deakin, Rory and Hannah Dillon, Andrew Eadie, Farnoush Farahji, Nicholas Fry, Jane Gamble, Rory Graham, Jim Haigwood, Zoe Hale, Hannah Hames, Jean Mickael Heil, Geoffrey Humble, Ariel Jacob, Peter Jones, Tehzoon Karmalawala, Chris Kean, Regina Kordt-Noerring, Marie Lauga, Daphne Levin, Heinrich Micheline, Sylviane Minnot, Fika Perié, Yasmine Piening, Aili Pyhälä, Gerda Rebel, David Robinson, Jim and Darlene Robinson, Juan Nicolás Rodríguez, Mark Rowlatt, Connie Scharf, Carol Snyder, Roberto Spanghero, Joanne Thibault, Yonina Tova, Carl VanderZanden, Nichola Vaughan, Anne Walker, Paul Whitehead, Stefan Wrobel and Jack Zektzer.

Last but not least, we are indebted to the Bradt team for their hard work on this edition, most especially editor Laura Pidgley who has done a sterling job catching our errors and oversights, as well as David McCutcheon – cartographer extraordinaire – who was, as ever, absolutely meticulous with the mapping.

FEEDBACK REQUEST AND UPDATES WEBSITE

At Bradt Travel Guides we're aware that guidebooks start to go out of date on the day they're published – and that you, our readers, are out there in the field doing research of your own. You'll find out before us when a fine new family-run hotel opens or a favourite restaurant changes hands and goes downhill. You can post your feedback and read updates from fellow travellers via our Madagascar forum at www.bradtupdates.com/madagascar or by clicking the feedback button on this book's Facebook page at bradtmadagascar. Alternatively, contact the office on 01753 893444 or e info@bradtguides.com or add a review of the book to www.bradtguides.com or Amazon.

Contents

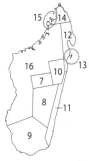

KEY TO MAP SYMBOLS

———————	Main road/other road	☆	Nightclub
======	4x4/track	e	Internet access
··········	Footpath	✝	Church/cathedral
—+—+—	Canal	☐	Cemetery
——▪——▪——	Railway	☪	Mosque
✈ ✈	Airport (international/domestic)	🦙	Zoological park
✈	Airfield	❀	Garden/botanical site
⊷—⊷	Pirogue/vedette ferry	🗼	Lighthouse
🚌	Taxi-brousse station, etc	⛴	Shipwreck
🚗	Car hire	✳	Scenic viewpoint
⛽	Filling station/garage	)))	Waterfall
🛈	Tourist information	◉	Cave
E	Embassy	○	Geyser/hot springs
🏛	Museum	⌐	Beach
🎭	Cinema/theatre	✔	Scuba diving
🏢	Historic building	♤	Isolated woodland feature
🏰	Castle/fort	♤	Isolated deciduous (inc baobab) feature
🗽	Monument/statue	▲	Summit (height in metres)
✉	Post office	●	Other place of interest
$ 🏧	Bank or bureau de change/ATM		Urban park
⊞	Hospital/clinic, etc		Urban market
✚	Pharmacy		Protected areas
			Forest reserves

LIST OF MAPS

NOTE ABOUT MAPS

Several maps use grid lines to allow easy location of sites. Map grid references are listed in square brackets after listings in the text, with page number followed by grid number, eg: [160 C3].

ATTENTION MADAGASCAR ENTHUSIASTS

For other books on Madagascar, check out Bradt's *Madagascar Wildlife*, *Madagascar Highlights* and *Madagascar: The Eighth Continent*. Go to www. bradtguides.com and key in MAD20 at the checkout for your 20% discount.

Introduction

Hilary Bradt

In 1975 I attended a slideshow in Cape Town given by a zoo collector who had just returned from a country called Madagascar. By the end of the evening I knew I had to go there. It wasn't just the lemurs; it was the utter otherness of this little-known island that entranced me. So I went, and I fell in love, and I've been returning ever since. Madagascar has brought me the best of times and the worst of times. I have exalted at the discovery of some of the strangest creatures in the world, laughed at the dancing sifakas and gushed over baby lemurs; I have snorkelled over multi-coloured coral and watched a lobster make its cautious way over the seabed; I have made the only footprints on a deserted beach overhung with coconut palms and swum in the sand-warmed sea in the moonlight. I have also endured the misery of 14-hour taxi-brousse journeys, the exhausting heat of the lowlands and the unexpectedly cold nights in the highlands. And I have been robbed on several occasions. Yet all I remember are the good times. A few years ago someone wrote to me: 'I went for the lemurs, but in the end it's the people I'll remember.' Me too. Even now, over 40 years since my first visit, this is still one of the poorest countries in the world, yet the overriding impression is of joy and laughter. I can hardly remember a time when I wasn't writing each new edition of this guide, and I never imagined that I would find someone to hand over to, but in 2006 I was contacted by Daniel Austin who had just finished a six-month exploration of Madagascar. For subsequent editions, he became lead contributor, then updater, and is now co-author who should take all the credit for the extraordinary amount of information in this book. Any gaps in his encyclopaedic knowledge are filled by Madagascar experts who have added their contributions as boxes to this book. Daniel's enthusiasm is inexhaustible: in numerous visits over the last decade or so, he has spent a total of 25 months travelling to every corner of this incredible island.

ACCOMMODATION PRICING IN THIS BOOK

Lists of accommodation present hotels in price bands according to the cost of a typical double room. Remember, prices change over time; prices given in this book are for guidance only.

Luxury	♛	Above 320,000Ar (£82/€94/US$105 and up)
Top end	€€€€€	190,000–320,000Ar (£48/€56/US$63 and up)
Upper range	€€€€	90,000–190,000Ar (£23/€27/US$30 and up)
Mid-range	€€€	40,000–90,000Ar (£10/€12/US$13 and up)
Budget	€€	18,000–40,000Ar (£5/€5/US$6 and up)
Penny-pincher	€	Below 18,000Ar

Part One

GENERAL INFORMATION

GEOGRAPHY
Full name Republic of Madagascar (*Repoblikan'i Madagasikara*)
Motto *Fitiavana, Tanindrazana, Fandrosoana* (Love, Fatherland, Progress)
Area 587,041km^2 (world's 4th-largest island; 2½ times the size of UK)
Capital city Antananarivo (Tana)
Major towns Fianarantsoa (Fianar), Antsirabe, Toliara (Tulear), Taolagnaro (Fort Dauphin), Toamasina (Tamatave), Mahajanga (Majunga), Antsiranana (Diego Suarez)
Main international airport Ivato Airport, Antananarivo (TNR)
Other main airports Antsiranana (DIE), Mahajanga (MJN), Morondava (MOQ), Nosy Be (NOS), Toamasina (TMM), Taolagnaro (FTU), Toliara (TLE)
Transport 5,613km paved roads; 854km railways; 432km navigable waterways

PRACTICALITIES
Public holidays 1 Jan, 29 Mar, Easter (movable), 1 May, Ascension (movable), Whit Monday (movable), 26 Jun, 15 Aug, 14 Oct, 1 Nov, 11 Dec, 25 Dec
Time zone 3 hours ahead of GMT (no daylight savings time observed)
Electricity 220 volts, European-style round-pin sockets
Currency Ariary (Ar; MGA)
International dialling code +261 (followed by 20 when calling landlines)
Internet domain extension .mg
Driving side Right
Visa Required by all tourists; available on arrival; max 90 days; see page 90

HUMAN STATISTICS
Population 25 million (2017 est); growing at 3% per year
Age structure 0–14yrs 40% of population; 15–64 yrs 57%; 65yrs & over 3%
Life expectancy Male 64 years; female 67 years
Poverty 81% live on less than US$1.25/day; 93% on less than US$2.00/day
Literacy 65% of over-15s can read and write
Official languages Malagasy, French
Religions Indigenous beliefs (52%), Christian (41%), Muslim (7%)

POLITICS AND ECONOMY
Leader President Hery Rajaonarimampianina (since January 2014)
GDP US$38bn (PPP); US$9.7bn (official ex rate); US$1,500 (per capita PPP)
Main agriculture Rice, coffee, vanilla, sugarcane, cloves, cocoa, cassava (tapioca), beans, bananas, peanuts, livestock products
Main exports Vanilla, cloves, nickel, cobalt, textiles, prawns, titanium and chromium ores, fish, cocoa beans, essential oils, precious stones
Main export partners France (18%), USA (12%), Germany (7%), China (6%), South Africa (6%), India (5%), Japan (5%), Belgium and Luxembourg (5%)
Main imports Petroleum, textiles, vehicles, rice, electronics, medicines, sugar, iron, paper, sulphur, cement, wheat
Main import partners China (21%), France (9%), India (6%), South Africa (5%)
Flag Horizontal bands of red and green alongside a vertical white band (the red represents sovereignty, the green stands for hope, and the white for purity)
Independence 26 June 1960 (from France)

1

The Country

GEOGRAPHY

A chain of mountains runs like a spine down the east-centre of the island descending sharply to the Indian Ocean, leaving only a narrow coastal plain. These eastern mountain slopes bear the remains of the dense rainforest which once covered all of the eastern section of the island. The western plain is wider and the climate drier, supporting forests of deciduous trees and acres of savannah grassland. Madagascar's highest mountain is Maromokotro, part of the Tsaratanana Massif, in the north of the island. In the south is the spiny forest.

CLIMATE

Madagascar has a tropical climate: November to March (summer/wet season) is hot with variable rainfall; April to October (winter/dry season) is mainly dry and mild.

Typically, southwest trade winds drop their moisture on the eastern mountain slopes and blow hot and dry in the west. North and northwest 'monsoon' air currents bring heavy rain in summer, decreasing southward so that the rainfall in Taolagnaro is half that of Toamasina. There are also considerable variations of temperature dictated by altitude and latitude. On the summer solstice of 22 December the sun is directly over the Tropic of Capricorn, and the weather is very warm. June is the coolest month.

Average midday temperatures in the dry season are 25°C (77°F) in the highlands and 30°C (86°F) on the coast. These statistics are misleading, however, since in June the night-time temperature can drop to near freezing in the highlands and it is cool in the south. The winter daytime temperatures are very pleasant, and the hot summer season is usually tempered by cool breezes on the coast.

Madagascar frequently suffers from cyclones, especially during February and March, primarily down the east coast (see box, page 4).

RAINFALL CHART

Region	Jan	Feb	Mar	Apr	May	Jun	Jul	Aug	Sep	Oct	Nov	Dec
Western	●	●	●	✳	✳	✳	✳	✳	✳	✳	✳	●
Central	●	●	●	●	✳	○	○	○	✳	✳	✳	●
Eastern	●	●	●	●	●	●	●	✳	✳	✳	✳	●
Northern	●	●	●	✳	✳	✳	✳	✳	✳	✳	✳	●
Northwestern	●	●	●	●	✳	✳	✳	✳	✳	✳	✳	●
Southwestern	●	●	✳	✳	○	○	○	○	✳	✳	✳	✳

● = rain　　✳ = driest months　　○ = fine but cool

The map and chart in this section highlight the driest and wettest months and regions, but remember: even in the rainiest months there will be sunny intervals, and in the driest there may be heavy showers. For more advice on the best months to visit Madagascar see page 75.

CYCLONES   *Daniel Austin*

Madagascar has always suffered from cyclones, which generally receive scant attention from the English-speaking media. In the decade to 2016 a total of 11 cyclones made landfall on the island (and a few more skimmed the coastline), collectively causing over 700 fatalities.

The 2006–07 cyclone season was a terrible one, with a chain of five – **Bondo, Favio, Gamede, Indlala** and finally **Jaya** – wreaking havoc across the island from December to April. Indlala was particularly destructive, resulting in 276 dead or missing after it struck the northeast coast. Then in 2008, **Ivan** was the worst of three to hit, causing devastation around Toamasina and Ile Sainte Marie, with 93 fatalities and some 190,000 rendered homeless. The following few years were somewhat calmer, with just five cyclones making landfall over the next eight seasons. In 2011, **Bingiza** destroyed over 25,000 houses and 36 schools but miraculously claimed just 22 victims. At least 33 more perished in 2012 at the hands of **Giovanna**, which wiped out two villages and damaged many more as it came ashore south of Toamasina. The next year, **Haruna** was unusual in striking the far south, where it claimed 36 lives and destroyed 70% of the town of Morombe. In 2014, despite being one of the most powerful cyclones on record, the aftermath of **Hellen** was remarkably limited and it dissipated rapidly on landfall, proving just how unpredictable these weather systems can be. By contrast the next season, a tropical storm called **Chedza** – not even strong enough to be classified as a cyclone – brought the worst flooding in living memory to Antananarivo, leaving 80 deaths and US$40 million of damage in its wake.

It is often said that Madagascar's cyclone season is January to March and its cyclone region is the northeast. In truth, although the northeast does suffer worst, cyclones strike all parts of Madagascar and can hit anytime from October to May.

But the risk to tourists is much less than you might imagine. Bear in mind that the majority of lives claimed by Madagascar's cyclones are lost at sea (109 of cyclone **Gafilo's** 363 victims in 2004 died in the sinking of a single ferry) and almost all of the buildings destroyed are huts constructed from natural materials rather than sturdy brick hotels. There is usually several days' warning and you can get regularly updated forecasts of the path of an approaching cyclone via www.usno.navy.mil/JTWC and www.wunderground.com/hurricane. Never embark on a boat journey if a cyclone may be approaching. In the unlikely event of being caught up in a severe cyclone, take shelter inside a strong building well away from the sea or any large trees.

To put the numbers of fatalities into perspective, for every one cyclone death in Madagascar, 89 people die from malaria and 58 more in road accidents. The real threat from a major cyclone is not in its direct casualties but the many thousands who will suffer in the months that follow as a result of the destruction of crops and infrastructure.

CLIMATIC REGIONS The **western** climate is dry tropical, with almost no rainfall from April to November. Towards its northern extremity, Mahajanga receives 140cm per year with around half the days from December to March seeing some rain. Further south, Morondava's annual rainfall is just 60cm and there are no more than seven or eight wet days per month even at the peak of the 'rainy season'. Daytime temperatures can be very hot although nights are cool from May to September.

The highlands, or **central climates** region can be cool: the capital city typically has daytime highs of around 27°C from October to April, falling to about 21°C in July. Night-time temperatures are about 11°C lower. Fianarantsoa's daytime temperatures vary between 17°C (July) and 25°C (November). The rainy season in this zone usually starts at the end of November, with two-thirds of days seeing some rain from December to March, and one-third for the rest of the year. Annual rainfall ranges from 80cm to 150cm.

Rarely does a week pass without rain in the tropical humid **eastern climate** zone. Annual rainfall ranges from 150cm in Taolagnaro to almost 500cm in parts of the Masoala Peninsula. The driest months are April to November, but December and January are also great times to visit. The risk of torrential rain and cyclones is highest in February and March. Typical daytime highs for this zone vary between 24°C (July and August) and 30°C (January).

The far **northern climate** is similar to the eastern zone, except for the area around Antsiranana, which has a microclimate that gets only 95cm of rain annually, with a long and reliable dry season from April to November and typical daytime temperatures reaching 30°C most of the year.

The **Sambirano climate** of the northwest is dominated by the Tsaratanana Massif. It is a small region that includes the island of Nosy Be and has a microclimate with frequent heavy rain alternating with sunshine. Annual rainfall is 200cm and the driest months are May to October. Daytime highs are typically in the high 20s year-round.

The driest of all is the semi-arid **southwestern climate**. Sometimes a year can pass with no rain at all in the extreme southwest. Toliara gets around 30cm a year, mostly in January and February. Daytime temperatures are typically 25–29°C, but nights can be quite cold, especially from June to August.

CLIMATIC REGIONS

A BRIEF HISTORY

THE FIRST EUROPEANS The first Europeans to sight Madagascar were the Portuguese in 1500, although there is evidence of earlier Arab settlements on the coast up to 800 years previously. There were unsuccessful attempts to establish

French and British settlements during the next couple of centuries but these failed due to disease and hostile local people. Hence a remarkably homogeneous and united country was able to develop under its own rulers.

By the early 1700s, the island had become a haven for pirates and slave traders, who both traded with and fought the local kings of the east and west coast clans.

THE RISE OF THE MERINA KINGDOM The powerful Merina Kingdom was forged by Andrianampoinimerina. Having succeeded to the tiny kingdom of Ambohimanga in 1787, by 1808 he had united the various Merina kingdoms and conquered the other highland tribes. In many ways the Merina Kingdom at this time paralleled that of the Inca Empire in Peru: Andrianampoinimerina was considered to have almost divine powers and his obedient subjects were well provided for. Each subject was given enough land for his family's rice needs, with some left over to pay a rice tribute to the king, and community projects such as the building of irrigation canals

ROBERT DRURY · *Hilary Bradt*

The most intriguing insight into 18th-century Madagascar was provided by the diary of Robert Drury, who was shipwrecked off the island in 1701 and spent over 16 years there, much of the time as a slave to Antandroy or Sakalava chiefs.

Drury was only 15 when his boat foundered off the southern tip of Madagascar (he had been permitted by his father back in Britain to go to India with trade goods). The shipwreck survivors were treated well by the local king but kept prisoners for reasons of status. After a few days they made a bid for freedom by seizing the king and some of his courtiers as hostages and marching east. They were followed by hundreds of warriors who watched for any relaxation in the guard; they were without water for three days as they crossed the burning hot desert and just as they came in sight of the River Mandrare (having released the hostages) they were attacked and many were speared to death.

For ten years Drury was a slave of the Antandroy royal family. He worked with cattle and eventually was appointed royal butcher, the task of slaughtering a cow for ritual purposes being supposedly that of someone of royal blood – and lighter skin. Drury was a useful substitute. He also acquired a wife.

Wars with the neighbouring Mahafaly gave him the opportunity to escape north across the desert to St Augustine's Bay, some 400km away. Here he hoped to find a ship to England, but his luck turned and he again became a slave, this time to the Sakalava. When a ship did come in, his master refused to consider selling him to the captain, and Drury's desperate effort to get word to the ship through a message written on a leaf came to nothing when the messenger lost the leaf and substituted another, less meaningful one. Two more years of relative freedom followed, and he finally got away in 1717, nearly 17 years after his shipwreck.

Ever quick to put his experience to good use, he later returned to Madagascar as a slave trader!

Some consider his diary to be a work of fiction, although Robert Drury is known to have existed. The places and events described correlate so well with reality, however, that it is almost certainly a genuine, if embellished, account. A ghost writer is thought to have been involved in preparing the diary for publication, and many scholars believe that to have been none other than Daniel Defoe. See page 443 for further reading on Robert Drury.

were imposed through forced labour (though with bonuses for the most productive workers). The burning of forests was forbidden.

Conquest was always foremost in the monarch's mind, however, and it was his son, King Radama I, who fulfilled his father's command to 'take the sea as frontier to your kingdom'. This king had a friendly relationship with Britain, which in 1817 and 1820 signed treaties under which Madagascar was recognised as an independent state. Britain supplied arms and advisors to help Radama conquer most of the rest of the island.

LONDON MISSIONARY SOCIETY To further strengthen ties between the two countries, the British Governor of Mauritius, which had recently been seized from the French, encouraged King Radama I to invite the London Missionary Society to send teachers. In 1818 a small group of Welsh missionaries arrived in Toamasina (Tamatave). David Jones and Thomas Bevan brought their wives and children, but within a few weeks only Jones remained alive; the others had all died of fever. Jones retreated to Mauritius, but returned to Madagascar in 1820, along with equally dedicated missionary teachers and artisans, to devote the rest of his life to its people. The British influence was established and a written language introduced for the first time (apart from ancient Arabic-script texts) using a few Roman letters.

'THE WICKED QUEEN' AND HER SUCCESSORS Radama's widow and successor, Queen Ranavalona I, was determined to rid the land of Christianity and European influence, and reigned long enough (33 years) to largely achieve her aim. These were repressive times for the Malagasy as well as foreigners. One way of dealing with people suspected of witchcraft or other evil practices was the 'Ordeal of *Tangena*' (see box, page 436).

It was during Queen Ranavalona's reign that an extraordinary Frenchman, Jean Laborde, arrived in Madagascar. Building on the work of the British missionaries he introduced the island to many aspects of Western technology. He remained in the queen's favour until 1857 – much longer than the other Europeans (see box, page 438).

The queen drove the missionaries out of Madagascar and many Malagasy Christians were martyred. However, the missionaries and European influence returned in greater strength after the queen's death and in 1869 Christianity became the official religion of the Merina Kingdom.

After Queen Ranavalona I came King Radama II, a peace-loving and pro-European monarch who was assassinated after a two-year reign in 1863. There is a widely held belief, however, that he survived strangulation with a silk cord (it was taboo to shed royal blood) and lived in hiding in the northwest for many years (see box, page 437).

After the death of Radama II, his widow Queen Rasoherina came to the throne, but the monarchy was now in decline and power shifted to the prime minister, who shrewdly married the queen. He was overthrown by a brother, Rainilaiarivony, who continued the tradition by marrying three successive queens and exercising all the power. During this period, 1863–96, the monarchs (in title only) were Queen Rasoherina, Queen Ranavalona II and lastly Queen Ranavalona III.

THE FRENCH CONQUEST Even during the period of British influence the French maintained a long-standing claim to Madagascar and in 1883 they attacked and occupied the main ports. The Franco-Malagasy War lasted 30 months, and was concluded by a harsh treaty making Madagascar a form of French protectorate. Prime Minister Rainilaiarivony, hoping for British support, managed to evade full acceptance of this status but the British government signed away its interest in the 1890 Convention of Zanzibar. The French finally imposed their rule by invasion in 1895. For a year the country was a full protectorate and in 1896 Madagascar became a French colony. A year later Queen Ranavalona III was exiled to Algeria and the monarchy abolished.

The first French governor general of Madagascar, Joseph Simon Gallieni, was an able and relatively benign administrator. He set out to break the power of the Merina aristocracy and remove the British influence by banning the teaching of English. French became the official language.

BRITISH MILITARY TRAINING AND THE TWO WORLD WARS Britain has played an important part in the military history of Madagascar. During the wars which preceded colonisation British mercenaries trained the Malagasy army to fight the French. During World War I, 46,000 Malagasy were recruited for the Allies and over 2,000 killed. In 1942, when Madagascar was under the control of the Vichy French, the British invaded Madagascar to forestall the possibility of the Japanese navy making use of the great harbour of Antsiranana (see box, pages 352–3).

In 1943 Madagascar was handed back to France under a Free French government. A Malagasy uprising against the French in 1947 was bloodily repressed (more than 89,000 are said to have died) but the spirit of nationalism lived on and in 1960 the country achieved full independence.

THE FIRST 40 YEARS OF INDEPENDENCE The first president, Philibert Tsiranana, was pro-France but in 1972 he stepped down in the face of increasing unrest and student demonstrations against French neocolonialism. An interim government headed by General Ramanantsoa ended France's special position and introduced a more nationalistic foreign and economic policy.

In 1975, after a period of turmoil, a military directorate handed power to a naval officer, Didier Ratsiraka, who had served as foreign minister under Ramanantsoa. Ratsiraka introduced his own brand of Christian-Marxism and his manifesto, set out in a 'little red book', was approved by referendum. Socialist policies such as the nationalisation of banks followed. Within a few years the economy had collapsed and has remained in severe difficulties ever since. Ratsiraka was nevertheless twice re-elected, though there were claims of ballot rigging and intimidation.

Albert Zafy defeated Ratsiraka in elections in 1993, but his time in office was to be short-lived. The constitution was revised but Zafy refused to accept the limitations on his presidential role and continued breaches of the constitution led to his impeachment in 1996. In the ensuing election former president Ratsiraka emerged the winner, and he promptly piloted through major amendments to the constitution restoring most of the dictatorial powers he had formerly enjoyed.

POLITICAL CRISIS OF 2002 The results of the 2001 elections were disputed, with victory being claimed by both Ratsiraka and his main rival, mayor of Antananarivo (Tana) Marc Ravalomanana. Ravalomanana installed his own ministers in government offices and Ratsiraka retreated with *his* government to his hometown of Toamasina. The world looked on as the farcical situation of one country with two presidents and two 'capital cities' descended into stalemate. In an attempt to gain the upper hand, Ratsiraka's supporters isolated Tana by dynamiting the bridges on the main transport routes into the city. The people of Tana faced a tenfold increase in the price of fuel and food staples. As the months passed, the blockade caused hardship, malnutrition and death. Flights were grounded and many businesses faced bankruptcy.

Eventually the balance of power shifted, Ratsiraka fled to France, and the international community recognised Ravalomanana as rightful president. Once

MADAGASCAR AND THE JEWS OF EUROPE   *John Grehan*

During the late 1930s, German Nazis and many European anti-Semites wanted to rid the continent of Jews. Their solution to the 'Jewish Question' was their wholesale deportation to Madagascar. What became known as 'The Madagascar Plan' was first discussed as early as November 1938, a year before the outbreak of World War II. (As Madagascar was a French colony one can only wonder at the degree of collusion between the French and German governments over this proposal.)

The annexation of Poland in 1939 brought yet more Jews under German administration. This led to a revival of The Madagascar Plan and prompted the President of the Academy of German Law – Hans Franc – to suggest that as many as three million Jews should be shipped to Madagascar. This would have meant the German occupation of the island and this was certainly discussed in 1940 within days of the fall of France. Indeed, Franz Rademacher of the German Foreign Office drew up firm arrangements for installing the Jews in Madagascar in September 1940, and he planned to visit the island to map out the details.

It was intended that the island would be under the authority of Heinrich Himmler though largely administered by the Jews themselves. Franc, in a speech in July 1940, even claimed that Jewish leaders had accepted The Madagascar Plan. But the Jews had been deceived if they thought that Madagascar had been chosen as the place for a sustainable Jewish homeland. Madagascar was to be a vast 'reservation' in which, because of the harsh climatic and agricultural conditions, the Jews would slowly die out. Some have gone even further and suggested that Madagascar was to be the place where the mass extermination of the Jews – with the gas chambers, ovens and all the associated paraphernalia of the death camps – would take place. Certainly the remoteness of Madagascar would have provided the Germans with privacy for conducting such atrocities.

Until well into 1941 The Madagascar Plan was Germany's stated 'Final Solution'. It was only when the Royal Navy's mastery of the seas made the plan impractical that exportation gave way to extermination and another, more terrible, Final Solution to the Jewish Problem took its place.

John Grehan is the author of The Forgotten Invasion *(see page 443).*

safely in office, he set about rebuilding the infrastructure, launching an ambitious road-building programme, and putting in motion a plan to triple protected areas. He is also credited with significant improvements in education, health and the reduction of corruption.

As a successful businessman, Ravalomanana understood well the importance of promoting foreign trade and investment; Madagascar's import and export markets increased massively during his presidency. But his business approach to politics was also to contribute heavily to his eventual downfall, as the line between his personal business interests and those of the country became increasingly blurred.

POLITICAL CRISIS OF 2009 Well into Ravalomanana's second term in office, the young mayor of Tana, Andry Rajoelina, made an unexpected challenge to his presidency. Angered by government actions against his radio and television network, Rajoelina mustered sufficient military and popular support to stage a *coup d'état*.

In a dramatic series of events in early 2009, demonstrations turned violent, stores were looted and the turning point came when guards opened fire on protesters outside the presidential palace, killing dozens. The Central Bank's coffers were raided by armoured military vehicles and at a crucial moment the French Embassy in Tana gave refuge to Rajoelina when it looked as if he might be arrested for fomenting violence and riot. Finally on 21 March 2009, in a huge ceremony in the capital, Rajoelina declared himself president of the so-called High Transitional Authority (HAT). Ravalomanana fled to mainland Africa when the HAT vowed to capture and imprison him. Most of the international community refused to recognise Rajoelina as the legitimate leader of Madagascar, freezing all non-humanitarian aid. Madagascar was suspended from both the African Union and the Southern African Development Community.

Despite the HAT's stated role being to keep order while swiftly organising democratic elections, few were surprised their first action was instead to rewrite the constitution. Thirty-five-year-old Rajoelina lowered the minimum age to stand for president from 40 to 35, and added a residency requirement for presidential candidates (thus rendering ineligible his only serious opponents – former presidents Ratsiraka, Zafy and Ravalomanana – by that time all living abroad). Crisis talks were repeatedly derailed and proposed election dates came and went over the next few years. Meanwhile, an impoverished Malagasy population became even poorer as economic output declined, foreign investment slowed to a trickle and tourist income fell.

A RETURN TO DEMOCRATIC RULE Eventually presidential elections went ahead at the end of 2013, with the two frontrunners – one considered to be a puppet of Rajoelina and the other of Ravalomanana – going head-to-head in a second round. Hery Rajaonarimampianina, who had been Rajoelina's finance minister in the HAT, narrowly won with 53% of the vote.

While election day itself ran smoothly and was declared free and fair by international observers, neither side played by the rules in the run-up to it and both accused the other of massive fraud. Eye-watering sums of money were spent on pre-election campaigning, including vast amounts of media time, and several helicopters were acquired for electioneering tours. One independent survey of 20,000 electors found nearly half had received gifts (such as T-shirts or money) from at least one party. Yet the origin of these funds is shrouded in mystery and many believe the only plausible source of such huge sums is the sale of illegally logged precious rosewood (see box, page 319).

Rajaonarimampianina assumed the presidency in January 2014, receiving brief international media attention for having the longest surname of any head of state in the world. The return to democracy opened the way for international aid to resume at long last, albeit more gradually than many would have liked. Rajaonarimampianina's time in office has not been without controversy. By the end of his second year he was already on his third prime minister and the parliament had attempted to impeach him on the grounds of 'constitutional violations and general incompetence', although this was quashed by the constitutional court. In April 2016 the prime minister and entire cabinet resigned following a widening rift with the president. There is growing frustration among the public at the perceived lack of progress, with the government seemingly preoccupied with infighting since its inception. Ravalomanana, who has since been allowed to return to the country, has announced his intention to stand in the 2018 elections, despite constitutional questions over his eligibility.

GOVERNMENT AND POLITICS

Madagascar is governed by a presidential system, but the powers of the president have varied under the different constitutions adopted over the last six decades. At independence the constitution was based closely on the French, with the president head of the government as well as head of state. Under the 'socialist revolution' (1975–91) Ratsiraka had virtually dictatorial powers, supported by large majorities for his party in the National Assembly. The strength of older left-wing parties prevented him from establishing a formal one-party state, but the constitution provided that only socialist parties could compete in elections. After his overthrow in 1991 the pendulum swung to a parliamentary constitution similar to the German or the British, with a largely ceremonial president and power vested in a prime minister elected by the National Assembly. But this was effectively destroyed by Zafy's refusal to accept the constitutional limits on his power, and when Ratsiraka subsequently returned to power he essentially reverted the constitution to its previous form.

Since colonial times the country has been divided for purposes of local government into six provinces, each consisting of hundreds of communes or municipalities with governors and prefects appointed by the central government.

An important factor in politics has been the coastal people's mistrust of the Merina who conquered them in the 19th century. The numerical superiority of the coastal people has ensured their dominance of parliament and government. When Ratsiraka was in trouble in 1991, and again in 2002, he stirred up coastal hostility to the Merina. However, the emergence of Ravalomanana as the first Merina elected president indicated that the coastal/plateau divide has become less significant.

ECONOMY

Since independence, Madagascar has declined from being modestly prosperous to becoming one of the poorest countries in the world. Around 93% of the population lives on less than US$2 a day. Under Tsiranana's post-independence government, a combination of careful management and political stability produced a steady growth in GNP and an improvement in living standards. However, from the late 1970s Ratsiraka's unwise policies of nationalisation and centralisation, coupled with a worsening of the terms of trade following successive oil-price shocks, led to the collapse of the economy. For 25 years the average GNP growth was zero so that, with the population doubling, living standards were halved. Reluctant recourse to the IMF and its policies of austerity and liberalisation led to some improvement in the late 1980s but the disruptions of successive political crises checked and sometimes reversed this recovery.

Madagascar has always had an adverse balance of trade, but in the post-independence days the deficit was modest and covered by various payments from France. The economic collapse under Ratsiraka greatly increased the deficit, and the country has since been dependent on massive support from the IMF, World Bank, EU and various bilateral donors led by France and the USA.

The local currency, the franc malgache, was maintained in parity with the French franc long after its real value had declined. In 2003 the franc was replaced by the ariary. Ravalomanana's abolition of a wide range of import taxes, designed to stimulate the economy, led in the short term to a rapid increase of imports without a corresponding rise in exports. The consequent increase in the trade gap caused a spectacular collapse of the currency in the first half of 2004, with the ariary losing over half its value.

France has long been Madagascar's biggest trade partner, and is still the recipient of almost a fifth of its exports. Some 29% of exports go to the rest of Europe. Exports to the USA increased hugely during the early 2000s, peaking at 36% of Madagascar's total sales, as a result of the African Growth and Opportunities Act (AGOA) that permitted some African states to export duty-free goods to the USA. Madagascar was suspended from AGOA following the coup and so that figure has now fallen to below 15%. Trade with China, on the other hand, is rapidly increasing: that portion of the export market has swelled tenfold to around 7% over the last decade.

The economy was always based on agriculture, with rice by far the largest crop, once providing enough to feed the population and even leave some over for export. But difficulties for rice growers and low official prices led to a reversion to a subsistence economy. Rice production accordingly failed to keep pace with the growing population so that the country now has to import a significant proportion of its needs, at considerable expense in foreign exchange.

The main cash crops for export are vanilla, cloves and dried legumes, as well as fruit such as lychees. Coffee was once a big earner, responsible for 19% of the country's export revenue in the mid-1990s, but the industry has since collapsed. Prawns, either fished or farmed along the west coast, have been a major export item over the last two decades, but now make up 2.5% of Madagascar's exports. Textiles and clothing make up a massive proportion of exports: officially some 25% in 2015.

The hitherto small mining sector has recently exploded with the discovery of large deposits of gems and minerals but, partly because of uncertainty about the future coupled with government corruption, the economy has not benefited as much as it should have. Nevertheless, revenue from exports of petroleum/mineral products, stone and metals rose more than tenfold between 2000 and 2015. Several major mining projects, principally for ilmenite, nickel and cobalt, have come online in the past decade, and plans to exploit other deposits are in the pipeline. Rises in global oil prices have also triggered interest in substantial reserves, which were hitherto uneconomical to extract.

The 2009 coup had a devastating effect on the country's economy. A World Bank report four years on emphasised how seriously the Malagasy have been impacted. If the economy had continued at its pre-crisis rate then GDP would have been 20% (US$8 billion) higher in 2013 than 2008. Instead, per capita incomes have been stagnant for more than a decade.

Tourism Much hope has been invested in tourism, and with an impressive doubling of visitor figures in seven years things were looking promising until the 2009 coup virtually stopped the industry in its tracks. Six years later, tourism numbers had recovered to 244,000, just 65% of their 2008 peak, despite a 66% increase in hotel capacity over the same period. This rapid development has been encouraged by a wildly optimistic government target to entice a million annual tourists by 2020.

According to 2015 statistics, the sector was directly responsible for creating over 39,000 jobs in hotels, restaurants and tour agencies, and contributed €527 million to the economy.

In the same year, visitors were primarily French (47%) and Italian (17%) – the latter figure up hugely from just 3.5% in 2012. Brits and Germans were each about 2.5% of the total, with a further 7.4% hailing from the rest of Europe. Some 4.2% originated in the USA or Canada, and 0.9% in Australia or New Zealand. Only 4.1% came from mainland Africa (half of whom from South Africa) but 5.3% were from other Indian Ocean islands and 2.9% from China. The average length of stay is 21 days.

2

People and Culture

ENIGMATIC ORIGINS

The consensus is that the first people arrived in Madagascar some 1,500–2,000 years ago (although one recent archaeological study found evidence supporting a possible human presence around 4,000 years ago). This is quite remarkable when you consider that modern man is thought to have originated just across the water in West Africa nearly a quarter of a million years previously and to have spread across all continents by ten millennia ago.

What is more surprising still is that the Malagasy people's origins are believed to be in Indonesia. Could it really be that the first settlers arrived not from the west across the 420km-wide Mozambique Channel but from the east across 7,300km of ocean? The idea seems preposterous yet the evidence overwhelmingly supports it.

It did not escape the notice of the first European visitors that many Malagasy look distinctly Asian. And it was at least 400 years ago that strong resemblances between the Malay and Malagasy languages were spotted. Later a 20th-century Norwegian missionary and linguist, Otto Christian Dahl, traced the language's roots to a dialect spoken in a small area alongside the Barito River in southern Borneo, finding 77% of the vocabulary to be the same or similar.

For some time, experts assumed this migration must have taken place in stages around the northern coastline of the Indian Ocean, but there is a worrying lack of archaeological and other evidence to support the theory. Then in 1985 a replica vinta boat was constructed by a team using the traditional methods of the time and it was successfully sailed without modern navigational instruments directly across the ocean from Indonesia to Madagascar, proving that such a crossing could have been possible. It took them 65 days. Certainly the Austronesians of the time are well documented as able seafarers, having colonised many remote Pacific islands such as Rapa Nui, Hawaii and the Marquesas, so perhaps it is not such a stretch to imagine they could reach Madagascar.

Researchers have only recently developed the tools to analyse historical migrations through genetics. A fascinating paper based on studies of mitochondrial DNA and published in 2012 showed that the most likely scenario was that Madagascar was founded 1,200 years ago by a group of southeast Asians that included approximately 30 women. This backed up the findings of a linguistic study the year before that had looked at variations in speaking across the island and concluded that the earliest dialect was that spoken around Farafangana on the southeast coast some 1,350 years ago. The location of the landing site lends more weight to the theory that the colonisers came across the Indian Ocean rather than from the African direction. Archaeobotanists have also turned their attentions to this puzzle: in 2016 scientists studying charred seeds from archaeological excavations in Madagascar found that the crops people were growing and

13

consuming around a thousand years ago were predominantly species native to Asia. It seems probable that they were brought by the original settlers.

But one enigma remains. The people of the Barito River basin, to whose language Malagasy was convincingly traced, lived inland and were not skilled seafarers like their coastal cousins. How could it be that they were the ones to reach Madagascar? We don't know but some interesting hints are emerging. An international team of geneticists testing the Malagasy origins in 2015 found relatively weak links to Borneo; instead it seems that many of the first settlers were from other Indonesian islands, including Sulawesi, Maluku and Sumda. One can only wonder how this mixture of colonisers led to today's Malagasy population. Perhaps there was a class divide, with the Borneans in charge, taking care of negotiations and organisation (and thus their dialect eventually dominated) while a working class of boatmen from other parts of Indonesia were responsible for the sailing and ultimately, on arrival, most of the procreating (such that their genes eventually dominated).

This already complex story is complicated further by significant waves of immigration from Africa in later centuries (the new genetic studies indicate most present-day Malagasy have around two-thirds African genes) along with influences from other Indian Ocean islands and Arabia that have left their mark in the form of certain local customs clearly derived from Islam and a smattering of words with Arabic roots. The two-continent origin of the Malagasy is easily observed, from the highland tribes who most resemble Indonesians, to the African type characterised by the Bara or Makoa in the south. In between are the elements of both races which make the Malagasy so varied and attractive in appearance. Thus there is racial diversity yet considerable cultural uniformity.

BELIEFS AND CUSTOMS

The Afro-Asian origin of the Malagasy has produced a people with complicated and fascinating beliefs and customs. Despite the various tribes or clans, the country shares not only a common language but a belief in the power of dead ancestors – *razana*. This cult of the dead, far from being a morbid preoccupation, is a celebration of life since the dead ancestors are considered to be potent forces that continue to share in family life. If the razana are remembered by the living, the Malagasy believe, they thrive in the spirit world and can be relied on to look after their descendants in a host of different ways. These ancestors wield considerable power, their 'wishes' dictating the behaviour of the family or community. Their property is respected, so a great-grandfather's field may not be sold or changed to a different crop. Calamities are usually blamed on the anger of razana, and a zebu bull may be sacrificed in appeasement. Large herds of zebu cattle are kept as a 'bank' of potential sacrificial offerings.

Belief in tradition, in the accumulated wisdom of the ancestors, has shaped the Malagasy culture. Respect for their elders and courtesy to all fellow humans is part of the tradition. But so is resistance to change.

SPIRITUAL BELIEFS At the beginning of time the Creator was Zanahary or Andriananahary. Now the Malagasy worship one god, Andriamanitra, who is neither male nor female.

Many rural people believe in 'secondary gods' or nature spirits, which may be male or female, and which inhabit certain trees, rocks (known as *ody*) or rivers. People seeking help from the spirit world may visit one of these sites for prayer. Spirits are also thought to possess humans who fall into a trance-like state, called

FADY AND THEIR ORIGINS

THE INTRUDERS AND THE GEESE During the rule of King Andrianampoinimerina, thieves once attempted a raid on the village of Ambohimanga. The residents, however, kept geese which caused a commotion when the intruders entered the compound, thus alerting the people who could take action. Geese are therefore not eaten in this part of Madagascar.

THE BABY AND THE DRONGO Centuries ago the communities of the east coast were persecuted by pirates who made incursions to the hills to pillage and take captives. At the warning that a pirate band was on its way the villagers would flee into the jungle. When pirates approached the village of Ambinanetelo the women with young children could not keep up with the others so hid in a thicket. Just as the pirates were passing them a baby wailed. The men turned to seek the source of the cry. It came again, but this time from the top of a tree: it was a drongo. Believing themselves duped by a bird the pirates gave up and returned to their boats. Ever since then it has been *fady* to kill a drongo in Ambinanetelo.

THE TORTOISE AND THE POT A Tandroy man put a tortoise in a clay pot of boiling water to cook it, but the tortoise kicked so hard that the pot shattered to smithereens. The man declared that his descendants would never again eat tortoise because it broke his pot.

tromba by the Sakalava and *bilo* by the Antandroy. Some clans or communities believe that spirits can also possess animals, particularly crocodiles.

The Malagasy equivalent of the soul is *ambiroa*. When a person is in a dream state it can temporarily separate from the body, and at death it becomes an immortal *razana*. Death, therefore, is merely a change and not an end. A special ceremony usually marks this rite of passage, with feasting and the sacrifice of zebu. The mood of the participants alternates between sorrow and joy.

Fady The dictates of the razana are obeyed in a complicated network of *fady*. Although fady is usually translated as 'taboo' this does not truly convey the meaning: these are beliefs related to actions, food, or days of the week when certain acts are risky. Fady vary from family to family and community to community, and even from person to person.

The following are some examples related to actions and food among the Merina: it may be fady to sing while you are eating (violators will develop elongated teeth); it is also fady to hand an egg directly to another person – it must first be put on the ground; for the people of Andranoro it is fady to ask for salt directly, so one has to request 'that which flavours the food'. A fady connected with objects is that the spade used to dig a grave should have a loose handle since it is dangerous to have too firm a connection between the living and the dead.

Social fady often involve the days of the week. For example, among the Merina it is fady to hold a funeral on a Tuesday, or there will be another death. Among the Tsimihety it is fady to work the land on Tuesdays; Thursday is also a fady day for some people, both for funerals and for farming.

A fady is not intended to restrict freedom but to ensure happiness and an improved quality of life. That said, however, there are some cruel fady which

Christian missionaries have been trying, over the centuries, to eliminate. One is the taboo against twins among the Antaisaka people of Mananjary. Historically twins were killed or abandoned in the forest after birth. Today this is against the law but still persists and twins may not be buried in a tomb. Catholic missionaries have established an orphanage in the area for the twins born to mothers torn between social tradition and maternal love. Many mothers who would otherwise have to suffer the murder or abandonment of their babies can give them to the care of the Church.

Many fady benefit conservation. For instance the killing of certain animals is often prohibited, and the area around a tomb must be left undisturbed. Within these pockets of sacred forest, *ala masina*, it is strictly forbidden to cut trees or even to burn deadwood or leaf litter. In southeast Madagascar there are *alam-bevehivavy* (sacred women's forests) along a stretch of river where only women may bathe. Again, no vegetation may be cleared or damaged in such localities.

For an in-depth study of the subject get hold of a copy of *Taboo* (see page 444).

Vintana Along with fady goes a complex sense of destiny called *vintana*. Broadly speaking, vintana is to do with time – hours of the day, days of the week, etc – while fady usually involve actions or behaviour. Each day has its own vintana which tends to make it good or bad for certain festivals or activities. Sunday is God's day; work undertaken will succeed. Monday is a hard day, not a good day for work although projects undertaken (such as building a house) will last; Tuesday is an easy day – too easy for death so no burials take place – but all right for *famadihana* (exhumation) and light work; Wednesday is usually the day for funerals or famadihana; Thursday

---

is suitable for weddings and is generally a 'good' day; Friday, *zoma*, is a 'fat' day, set aside for enjoyment, but is also the best day for funerals; Saturday, a 'noble' day, is suitable for weddings but also for purification.

As an added complication, each day has its own colour. For example Monday is a black day; a black chicken may have to be sacrificed to avoid calamity, dark-coloured food should not be eaten and people may avoid black objects. Tuesday is multicoloured, Wednesday brown, Thursday black, Friday red, Saturday blue, and Sunday white.

Tsiny and tody Additional forces shaping Malagasy morality, in addition to fady and vintana, are *tody* and its partner *tsiny*. Tody is somewhat similar to the Hindu/Buddhist karma. The word means 'return' or 'retribution' and indicates that for any action there is a reaction. Tsiny means 'fault', usually a breach of the rules laid down by the ancestors.

A reprint of a 1957 book on the subject (in French) – *Le Tsiny et le Tody* – can be found in Antananarivo's bookshops.

After death Burial, exhumation and second burial are the focus of Malagasy beliefs and culture. To the Malagasy, death is the most important part of life, when a person abandons their mortal form to become a much more powerful and significant ancestor. Since a tomb is for ever whilst a house is only a temporary dwelling, it follows that tombs should be more solidly constructed than houses.

Burial practices differ among the various tribes but all over Madagascar a ritual known as *sasa* is practised immediately after a death. The family of the deceased go to a fast-flowing river and wash all their clothes to remove the contamination of death.

shroud is left on and the new one put on top. There are three new silk shrouds for my mother which have been donated in remembrance and gratitude. The belief is that she won't be cold and the top shroud befits her, being of top-quality silk with beautiful, delicate embroidery. This is the time to touch her, give her something, talk to her. Her best friend is there, making sure that my mother is properly wrapped, as the ritual has to follow certain rules. Lots of touching as silent conversation goes on, giving her the latest news or family gossip, and asking for her blessing. Perfume is sprinkled on her and wishes made at the same time.

Flowers are placed on the bodies. The feeling of togetherness and love is so strong. This occasion is not just for the immediate family, but for cousins, and cousins of cousins, uncles and aunts and everybody meeting, bonded by the same ties.

Photographs of the dead person are now put on top of each body. A huge feast and celebration begins. We lift the bodies, carrying them on our shoulders. We sing old rhymes and songs and dance in a line, circling the tomb seven times, moving the body on our shoulder and making it dance with us.

The bodies have to be back inside the tombs by a precise time and the tomb is immediately closed after a last ritual cleaning. This moment of goodbye is very emotional. When next the tomb is opened it will not be for happiness but grief, for a burial. Famadihana happens only once every seven or ten years.

It has been a very special day for me. This famadihana brought so much joy, a strong sense of belonging and identity, and gave a spiritual feeling that death is not an end but an extension into another life, linked somehow with this one. *Misaotra ry neny* ('Thank you Mum').

Funeral practices vary from clan to clan. The Antankarana (in the north) and Antandroy (south) have 'happy' funerals during which they may run, with the coffin, into the sea. An unusual ritual, *tranondonaky*, is practised by the Antaisaka of the southeast. Here the corpse is first taken to a special house where, after a signal, the women all start crying. Abruptly, after a second signal, they dance. While this is happening the men are gathered in the hut of the local chief from where, one by one, they go to the house where the corpse is lying and attach money to it with special oil. The children dance through the night, to the beat of drums, and in the morning the adults wrap the corpse in a shroud and take it to the *kibory*. These tombs are concealed in a patch of forest known as *ala fady* which only men may enter, and where they deliver their last messages to the deceased. These messages can be surprisingly fierce: 'You are now at your place so don't disturb us any more' or 'You are now with the children of the dead, but we are the children of the living'.

More disturbing, however, is the procedure following the death of a noble of the Menabe Sakalava people. The body may be placed on a wooden bench in the hot sun until it begins to decompose. The bodily fluids which drip out are collected in receptacles and drunk by the relatives in the belief that they will then take on the qualities of the deceased.

If a Merina dies away from home, their body will be brought back by vehicle. Look out for cars adorned with a Malagasy flag. If the flag is on the left side, the body is being taken to the tomb; if it is on the right, the family are returning from the ceremony.

It is after the first burial, however, that the Malagasy generally honour and communicate with their dead, not only to show respect but to avoid the anger of the razana who dwell in the tombs. The best-known ceremony in Madagascar is the famadihana ('turning of the bones') by the Merina and Betsileo people. This is a joyful occasion which occurs about every seven years after the first burial, and provides the opportunity to communicate with and remember a loved one. The remains of the selected relative are taken from the tomb, rewrapped in a new burial shroud (*lambamena*) and carried around the tomb a few times before being replaced.

During the bone-turning ceremony the corpse is spoken to and informed of all the latest events in the family and village. Generous quantities of alcohol are consumed amid a festive atmosphere with much dancing and music. Women who are trying to conceive take small pieces of the old burial shroud and keep these under their mattresses to induce fertility.

By law a famadihana may take place only in the dry season (June–September). It can last up to a week and involves the family in considerable expense. Visitors fortunate enough to be invited to one will find it a strange but very moving occasion; it's an opportunity to examine our own beliefs and rituals associated with death. For an account of what famadihana means to a sophisticated London-based Merina woman, see the box on pages 16–17.

Variations of famadihana are practised by other tribes. The Menabe Sakalava, for example, hold a *fitampoha* every ten years. This is a royal famadihana in which the remains of deceased monarchs are taken from their tomb and washed in a river. A similar ritual, the *fanampoambe*, is performed by the Boina Sakalava further north.

HEALERS, SORCERERS AND SOOTHSAYERS The 'wise men' in Malagasy society are the **ombiasy**; the name derives from *olona-be-hasina* meaning 'person of much virtue'. Traditionally they were from the Antaimoro clan and were the advisers of royalty: Antaimoro ombiasy came to Antananarivo to advise King Andrianampoinimerina and to teach him Arabic writing.

The astrologers, **mpanandro** ('those who make the day'), work on predictions of vintana. There is a Malagasy proverb, 'Man can do nothing to alter his destiny'; but the mpanandro will advise on the best day to build a house, or hold a wedding or famadihana. Though nowadays mpanandro do not have official recognition, they are present in all levels of society. A man (or woman) is considered to have the powers of an mpanandro when he has some grey hair – a sign that he is wise enough to interpret vintana. Antandroy soothsayers are known as *mpisoro*.

The Malagasy have a deep knowledge of herbal medicine and all markets display a variety of medicinal plants, amulets and talismans. The Malagasy names associated with these are *ody* and *fanafody*. Broadly speaking, ody refers to fetishes such as sacred objects in nature, and fanafody to herbal remedies (nowadays it is used for medicine of all kinds, as in the word for a pharmacy: *fivarotam-panafody*, literally 'medicine shop'). Travellers will sometimes come across conspicuous ody in the form of stones or trees which are sacred for a whole village, not just for an individual. Such trees are called *hazomanga* ('excellent tree') and are presided over

TOMB ARCHITECTURE AND FUNERARY ART   *Hilary Bradt*

The style of tombs defines the different tribes better than any other visible feature, and also indicates the wealth and status of the family concerned.

MERINA In early times burial sites were near valleys or in marshes. The body would be placed in a hollowed-out tree trunk and sunk into the mud at the bottom of a marsh. These *fasam-bazimba* marshes were sacred. Later the Merina began constructing rectangular wooden tombs, mostly under the ground but with a visible structure above. In the 19th century Frenchman Jean Laborde had a profound effect on tomb architecture: tombs were built with bricks and stone. It was his influence which led to the elaborate structure of modern tombs, which are often painted with geometric designs. Sometimes the interior is lavishly decorated.

SAKALAVA During the Vazimba period, the Sakalava tombs were simple piles of stones. With the introduction of cement, a step design was added. At a later stage, wooden stelae, *aloalo*, were placed on the tombs facing east. These were topped with carvings, often of a most erotic nature. Since Sakalava tombs are for individuals and not families, there is no attempt at maintaining the stelae as it is believed that only when the wood decays will the soul of the buried person be released.

Tomb construction commences only after the person's death and can take up to six weeks, the body meanwhile being kept in a house. While a tomb is under construction, many zebu are sacrificed to the ancestors. The Sakalava call their tombs *izarana*, 'the place where we are separated'.

ANTANDROY AND MAHAFALY The local name of these tombs is *fanesy* which means 'your eternal place'. Zebu horns are scattered on the tomb as a symbol of wealth (on Sakalava tombs, zebu horns are only a decoration, not an indication of status). The Antandroy and Mahafaly tombs have much the same architecture as those of the Sakalava, but are more artistically decorated. The Mahafaly aloalo bear figures depicting scenes from the person's life, and the entire length is often carved with intricate designs.

by the mpisoro, the senior man of the oldest family in the village. Another type of ody is the talisman, *aoly*, worn for protection if someone has transgressed a fady or broken a promise. Aoly are sometimes kept in the house or buried. *Ody fitia* are used to gain love (white magic) but sorcerers also sell other forms of ody for black magic and are paid by clients with either money, zebu or poultry (a red rooster being preferred).

Mpamonka are witch doctors with an intimate knowledge of poison and *mpisikidy* are sorcerers who use amulets, stones and beads (known as *hasina*) for their cures. Sorcerers who use these in a destructive way are called **mpamosavy**.

On their death, sorcerers are not buried in tombs but are dumped to the west of their villages, barely covered with soil so that feral dogs and other creatures can eat their bodies. Their necks are twisted to face south.

THE WAY IT IS... Visitors from the West often find the beliefs and customs of the Malagasy merely bizarre. It takes time and effort to understand and respect the richness of tradition that underpins Malagasy society, but it is an effort well worth making. Leonard Fox, author of *Hainteny*, sums it up perfectly:

> Whoever has witnessed the silent radiance of those who come to pray... at the house of Andrianampoinimerina in Ambohimanga and has experienced the nobility, modesty, unobsequious courtesy, and balanced wholeness of the poorest Merina who has remained faithful to his heritage can have no doubt as to the deep integrative value of the Malagasy spiritual tradition.

MALAGASY SOCIETY

MARRIAGE AND CHILDREN The Malagasy have a strong sense of community which influences their way of life. Just as the ancestors are laid in a communal tomb, so their descendants share a communal way of life, and even children are almost considered common property within their extended family. Children are seldom disciplined but learn by example.

Marriage is a fairly relaxed union and divorce is common. There is no formal dowry arrangement or bride price, but a present of zebu cattle will often be made. In rural communities the man should bring his new wife home to his village (not vice versa) or he will lose face. You often see a young man walking to market wearing a comb in his hair – advertising his quest for a wife.

Most Malagasy have only one wife, and exceptions are becoming fairly rare. But men have been known to have more than ten wives and over 100 children. So long as the man is wealthy enough to provide housing for all his family, this arrangement seems to work surprisingly well, with each wife working to support her own children, and a head wife to whom the others defer.

THE VILLAGE COMMUNITY Malagasy society is a structured hierarchy with two fundamental rules: respect for the other person and knowing one's place. Within a village, the community is based on the traditional *fokonolona*. This concept was introduced by King Andrianampoinimerina when these councils of village elders were given responsibility for, among other things, law and order and the collection of taxes. Day-to-day decisions are still made by the **fokonolona**.

Rural Malagasy houses are traditionally aligned north–south and generally have only one room. Furniture is composed of mats, *tsihy*, often beautifully woven. These are used for sitting and sleeping, and sometimes food is served on them.

THE MALAGASY *LAMBA*   Joseph Radoccia

The *lamba* is the most distinctive item of traditional Malagasy clothing, and among one of the island's most vibrant forms of artistic expression. There are many types of lamba, each with its own role in Malagasy culture. The Merina highlanders have a long tradition of hand weaving; lamba are the fruit of this tradition. However, the variety most often encountered is not handwoven, but rather the machine-manufactured *lamba hoany*.

This, the category designated for everyday use, is a large decoratively printed rectangular cotton cloth. Some feature brilliantly hued patterns surrounding a central medallion; others, printed in two or three colours, depict a rural or coastal scene within an ornate border. You may also find some with images of Malagasy landmarks, the annual calendar, or historic events. A consistent feature of the various styles of lamba hoany is one essential recurring element that makes each unique: in a narrow box along the bottom you will find a Malagasy proverb or words of wisdom. For this reason the lamba hoany are often referred to as 'proverb cloths'.

As you travel the island you will discover that this seemingly simple wraparound cloth is adapted for many purposes. It is an invaluable essential for almost every citizen of rural Madagascar. As clothing, it is worn in coastal regions as a sarong, while in the highlands lamba are draped around shoulders as shawls for added warmth in the evening chill. Everywhere the lamba hoany is employed as a sling to carry a child on a mother's back or rolled up to cushion the weight when carrying a large basket on one's head. You may also encounter a lamba used as a light blanket, curtains in a window or door, and on occasion as a wall-hanging or tablecloth.

You can purchase a lamba at almost any market. The souvenir vendors usually carry a few, but you will find a much wider selection and better prices with the textile merchants. The widest choice is to be found at the fabric stores just north of the Analakely market pavilions in Antananarivo. Take your new purchase to a tailor in the market to have the edges hemmed.

Also noteworthy is the *lambamena* (literally 'red cloth', although not necessarily red in colour). These are handwoven from the silk of an indigenous Malagasy silkworm and used primarily as burial shrouds in funerary ceremonies. If you prefer a traditional handwoven lamba, a nice colourful selection can be found at the Anosy flower market in Tana.

Joseph Radoccia is an artist and Malagasy art enthusiast who visits Madagascar frequently to paint. See his lamba-inspired paintings at www.radoccia.com.

There are often fady attached to tsihy. For example you should not step over a mat, particularly one on which meals are eaten.

Part of the Malagasy culture is the art of oratory, **kabary**. Originally kabary were the huge meetings where King Andrianampoinimerina proclaimed his plans, but the word has now evolved to mean the elaborate form of speech used to inspire and control the crowds at such gatherings. Even rural leaders can speak for hours, using highly ornate language and many proverbs; a necessary skill in a society that reached a high degree of sophistication without a written language.

The market plays a central role in the life of rural people, who will often walk as far as 20km to market, even with no intention of selling or buying but simply to

Camilla Backhouse

During my year working in Madagascar I was particularly struck by the wonderful array of different hats worn there. Market stalls were piled high with hats of all shapes, colours and sizes.

Little had been noted about Malagasy headwear until the missionaries came in the early 19th century. At that time, few hats were worn as a person's hairstyle was regarded as more important and a sign of beauty. People from each region of Madagascar had different ways of plaiting their hair and they would often incorporate shells, coins or jewels. Oils and perfumes were massaged into the hair – the richer people used *tseroka*, a type of castor oil mixed with the powdered leaf of *ravintsara*, which produced a nutmeg scent, while the poorest population were satisfied with zebu fat.

The chiefs wore simple headdresses but it was not until the Europeans came that hats became more popular. Although plaiting and the art of weaving were already very well established, there was little evidence of woven hats. The cutting of hair was introduced in 1822 which may have changed the Malagasy attitudes – to cover an unplaited head certainly would not be any detriment to its beauty. Initially hats were worn by the wealthy. Chiefs could be seen wearing caps made of neatly woven rushes or coarse grass and the people of Antananarivo began to wear hats of more costly and durable material (often imported). It was Jean Laborde in the 1850s who started the industry of hat-making and helped increase production.

In each region the hats vary: they use different plant fibres depending on what grows locally, different weaves and occasionally dyes. The colours used are not the vegetable or plant dyes I had imagined but imported from China. The fibres are usually from palms (raffia, *badika*, *manarana*, *dara*), reeds (*penjy*, *harefo*) or straw. Some of the best regions that I came across for seeing weaving were near Lake Tritriva (straw), Maroantsetra (raffia), Mananjary (*penjy*, *dara*), Mahsoabe near Fianarantsoa (*badika*) and Vohipeno (*harefo*).

The ways of preparing the fibres for weaving differ, but in general they are dried, flattened and then, if necessary, stripped into thin fibres using a sharp knife. Some are woven into strips which are eventually machined together, while other regions use a continuous weave method to make the entire hat. The latter can be extremely complicated and is an amazing art to watch. The weaver will place their foot on the central part of the woven circle and gradually intertwine hundreds of different fibres into position. One of my lasting memories was spending time in Maroantsetra where they make the most beautiful crochet-style raffia hats. Women sit on palm mats outside their houses weaving, while children play, plait hair or busily prepare food for the next meal. Occasionally the hats are blocked (shaping a crown or brim over a wooden block). There are places in the capital where they heat steel blocks on a fire and then press the woven hat into a trilby style for example. This was a fascinating sight to see as normally these blocks are electrically heated.

The variety of hats is astounding. It can take a day for a woman to weave a hat, and this can be a main source of family income. If you are interested in getting a Malagasy hat, it is worthwhile getting to know a weaver so they may be able to make one large enough for the *vazaha* head!

catch up on the gossip or continue the conversation broken off the previous week. You will see well-dressed groups of young people happily making their way to this social centre. Often there is a homemade tombola, and other outlets for gambling.

FESTIVALS AND CEREMONIES Malagasy Christians celebrate the usual holy days, but most tribes or clans have their own special festivals.

Ala volon-jaza This is the occasion when a baby's hair is cut for the first time. Among the Antambahoaka in the south the haircut is performed by the grandparents. The child is placed in a basin filled with water, and afterwards bathed. Among the Merina the ceremony is similar but only a man whose parents are still alive may cut a baby's hair. The family then have a meal of rice, zebu, milk and honey. Coins are placed in the bowl of rice and the older children compete to get as many as possible.

Circumcision Boys are usually circumcised at the age of about two; a baby who dies before achieving this milestone may not be buried in the family tomb.

The operation itself is often done surgically, but in some rural areas it may still be performed with a sharpened piece of bamboo. The foreskin is not always simply discarded. In the region of the Antambahoaka it may be eaten by the grandparents, and in Antandroy country it could be shot from the barrel of a gun!

Different clans have their own circumcision ceremonies. Among the Antandroy, uncles dance with their nephews on their shoulders. But the most famous ceremony is *sambatra*, which takes place every seven years in Mananjary. The next one will happen in 2021.

Tsangatsaine This is a ceremony performed by the Antankarana. Two tall trees growing side by side near the house of a noble family are tied together to symbolise the unification of the tribe, as well as the tying together of the past and present, the living and the dead.

Fandroana This was the royal bath ceremony which marked the Malagasy New Year. These celebrations used to take place in March, with much feasting. While the monarch was ritually bathed, the best zebu was slaughtered and the choicest rump steak presented to the village nobles. The day was the equivalent of the Malagasy National Day, but the French moved this to 14 July, the date of the establishment of the French Protectorate. This caused major resentment among the Malagasy as effectively their traditional New Year was taken from them. After independence the date was changed to 26 June to coincide with Independence Day. Nowadays, because of the cost of zebu meat and the value attached to the animals, the traditional meat has been replaced by chicken, choice portions again being given to the respected members of the community. In the absence of royalty there is, of course, no longer a royal bath ceremony.

ETHNIC GROUPS

The different clans of Madagascar are based more upon old kingdoms than upon ethnic grouping. Traditions are changing: the descriptions below reflect the tribes at the time of independence, rather than in the more fluid society of today. The groups may differ but a Malagasy proverb shows their feeling of unity: *ny olombelona toy ny molo-bilany, ka iray mihodidina ihany*; 'men are like the lip of the cooking pot which forms just one circle'.

There are traditionally said to be 18 ethnic groups but some subgroups, such as the Vezo and Zafimaniry (officially belonging to the Sakalava and Betsileo respectively) are often treated as distinct groups.

ANTAIFASY ('PEOPLE OF THE SANDS') Living in the southeast around Farafangana, they cultivate rice, and fish in the lakes and rivers. Divided into three clans, each with its own 'king', they generally have stricter moral codes than other tribes. They have large collective burial houses known as kibory, built of wood or stone and generally hidden in the forest.

ANTAIMORO ('PEOPLE OF THE COAST') These are among the most recent arrivals and live in the southeast around Vohipeno and Manakara. They guard Islamic tradition and Arab influence and still use a form of Arab writing known as *sorabe*. They use verses of the Koran as amulets.

ANTAISAKA Centred south of Farafangana on the southeast coast but now fairly widely spread throughout the island, they are an offshoot of the Sakalava tribe. They cultivate coffee, bananas and rice – but only the women harvest the rice. There are strong marriage taboos among them. Often the houses may have a second door on the east side which is used only for taking out a corpse. They use the kibory, communal burial house, the corpse usually being dried out for two or three years before finally being put there.

ANTAMBAHOAKA ('THOSE OF THE PEOPLE') The smallest tribe, they are of the same origin as the Antaimoro and live around Mananjary on the southeast coast. They have some Arab traits and amulets are used. They bury in a kibory. Mass circumcision ceremonies are carried out every seven years.

ANTANDROY ('PEOPLE OF THE THORNS') Traditionally nomadic, they live in the arid south around Ambovombe. A dark-skinned people, they wear little clothing and are said to be frank and open, easily roused to either joy or anger. Their women occupy an inferior position, and it is fady for a woman to milk a cow. The villages are often surrounded by a hedge of cactus plants. Until recently they ate little rice, their staples being maize, cassava and sweet potatoes. They believe in the *kokolampo*, a spirit of either good or bad influence. Their tombs are similar to those of the Mahafaly tribe. Sometimes it is fady among them for a child to say his father's name, or to refer by name to parts of his father's body. Thus he may say 'what he moves with' for his feet or 'the top of him' for his head.

ANTANKARANA ('THOSE OF THE ROCKS') Living in the north around Antsiranana (Diego Suarez), they are fishermen or cattle raisers whose rulers came from the Sakalava dynasty. Their houses are usually raised on stilts. Numerous fady exist among them governing relations between the sexes in the family; for example a girl may not wash her brother's clothes. The legs of a fowl are the father's portion, whereas among the Merina, for instance, they are given to the children.

ANTANOSY ('PEOPLE OF THE ISLAND') The island is a small one in the Fanjahira River. They live in the southeast, principally around Taolagnaro (Fort Dauphin). Their social structure is based on clans with a 'king' holding great authority over each one. There are strict fady governing relationships in the family. For example, a brother may not sit on or step over his sister's mat. As with many

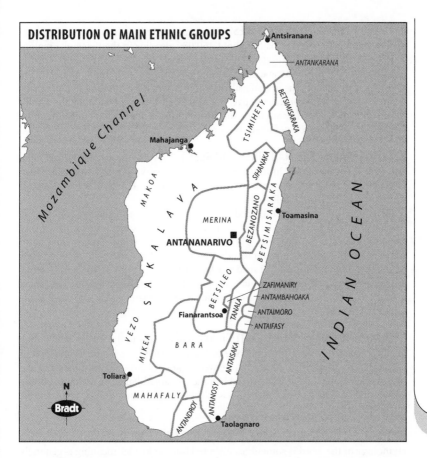

DISTRIBUTION OF MAIN ETHNIC GROUPS

Antsiranana

ANTANKARANA

Mozambique Channel

TSIMIHETY

BETSIMISARAKA

Mahajanga

MAKOA

SIHANAKA

SAKALAVA

BEZANOZANO

MERINA

ANTANANARIVO

BETSIMISARAKA

Toamasina

INDIAN OCEAN

VEZO

BETSILEO

ZAFIMANIRY

ANTAMBAHOAKA

MIKEA

TANALA

ANTAIMORO

Fianarantsoa

ANTAIFASY

BARA

ANTAISAKA

Toliara

MAHAFALY

ANTANOSY

ANTANDROY

Taolagnaro

N

Bradt

other tribes there are numerous fady regarding pregnancy: a pregnant woman should not sit in the doorway of the house; she should not eat brains; she should not converse with men; people who have no children should not stay in her house overnight. Other fady are that relatives should not eat meat at a funeral and the diggers opening a tomb should not wear clothes. When digging holes for the corner posts of a new house it may be fady to stand up so the job must be performed sitting down.

BARA Originally in the southwest near Toliara, these nomadic cattle raisers now live in the south-central area around Ihosy and Betroka. Their name has no special meaning but it is reputed to derive from an African (Bantu) word. They may be polygamous and women occupy an inferior position in their society. They attach importance to the *fatidra* or 'blood pact'. Cattle stealing is regarded as proof of manhood and courage, without which a man cannot expect to get a wife. They are dancers and sculptors, a unique feature of their carved wooden figures being eyelashes of real hair set into the wood. They believe in the *helo*, a spirit that manifests itself at the foot of trees. In the past a whole village would move after somebody died owing to the fear of ghosts. They use caves in the mountains for burial. It is the custom to shave the head on the death of a near relative.

BETSILEO ('THE MANY INVINCIBLES') They are centred in the south of the *hauts plateaux* around Fianarantsoa but about 150,000 also live in the Betsiboka region. They are energetic and expert rice producers, their irrigated, terraced rice fields being a feature of the landscape. Famadihana was introduced to their culture by the Merina at the time of Queen Ranavalona I. It is fady for the husband of a pregnant woman to wear a *lamba* thrown over his shoulder. It may be fady for the family to eat until the father is present or for anyone to pick up his fork until the most honourable person present has started to eat.

BETSIMISARAKA ('THE MANY INSEPARABLES') They are the second-largest tribe and live on the east coast in the region between Nosy Varika and Antalaha. They cultivate rice and work on vanilla, coffee and lychee plantations. Their clothes are sometimes made from locally woven raffia.

Originally their society included numerous local chiefs. The *tangalamena* is the local official for religious rites and customs. The Betsimisaraka have many superstitious beliefs: *angatra* (ghosts), *zazavavy an-drano* (mermaids), and *kalamoro*, little wild men of the woods, about 65cm high with long flowing hair, who like to slip into houses and steal rice from the cooking pot. In the north coffins are generally placed under a shelter, in the south in tombs. It may be fady for a brother to shake hands with his sister, or for a young man to wear shoes while his father is still alive.

BEZANOZANO ('MANY SMALL PLAITS') The name refers to the way in which they do their hair. They were probably one of the first tribes to become established in Madagascar and now live in an area between the Betsimisaraka lowlands and the Merina highlands. Like the Merina, they practise famadihana. As with most of the coastal tribes their funeral celebrations involve the consumption of considerable quantities of *toaka* (rum).

MAHAFALY ('THOSE WHO MAKE TABOOS' OR 'THOSE WHO MAKE HAPPY') The etymology of the word is sometimes disputed but the former meaning is generally regarded as being correct. They live in the southwest desert area around Ampanihy and Ejeda. They are farmers, with maize, sorghum and sweet potatoes as their chief crops; cattle rearing occupies a secondary place. They kept their independence under their own local chiefs until the French occupation and still keep the bones of some of their old chiefs – this is the *jiny* cult. Their villages usually have a sacrificial post, the hazomanga, on the east side where sacrifices are made. Some of the blood is generally put on the foreheads of the people attending.

The tombs of the Mahafaly attract a great deal of interest. They are big rectangular constructions of uncut stone rising a metre above the ground and decorated with *aloalo* (sculpted wooden posts) and the horns of the cattle slain at the funeral feast. The burial customs include waiting for the decomposition of the body before it is placed in the tomb. It is the practice for a person to be given a new name after death.

The divorce rate is very high and it is not at all uncommon for a man to remarry six or seven times. It is often fady for children to sleep in the same house as their parents. Their *rombo* (similar to the *tromba* of the Sakalava) is the practice of contacting various spirits for healing purposes.

MAKOA The Makoa are descended from slaves taken from the Makua people of Mozambique and, although sometimes classified as Vezo, they maintain a separate identity. Typically of larger stature than most Malagasy, Makoa men were

Vazimba is the name given to the earliest inhabitants of Madagascar, pastoralists of the central plateaux who were displaced or absorbed by later immigrants. Once thought to be pre-Indonesian aboriginals from Africa, it is now generally accepted that they were survivors of the earliest Austronesian immigrants who were pushed to the west by later arrivals.

Vazimba come into both the legends and history of the Malagasy. Vazimba tombs are now places of pilgrimage where sacrifices are made for favours and cures. It is *fady* to step over such a tomb. Vazimba are also thought to haunt certain springs and rocks, and offerings may be made here. They are the ancestral guardians of the soil.

often employed by the French as policemen and soldiers, thus reinforcing their distinction from other Malagasy.

MERINA ('PEOPLE OF THE HIGHLANDS') They live on the hauts plateaux, the most developed area of the country, the capital being 95% Merina. They are of Malayo-Polynesian origin and vary widely in skin colour, with straight hair. They used to be divided into three castes: the Andriana (nobles), the Hova (freemen) and the Andevo (serfs); but legally these divisions no longer exist. Most Merina houses are built of brick or mud; some are two-storey buildings with slender pillars, where the people live mainly upstairs. Most villages of any size have a church – probably two: Catholic and Protestant. There is much irrigated rice cultivation, and the Merina were the first tribe to have any skill in architecture and metallurgy. Famadihana is essentially a Merina custom.

MIKEA The term refers not so much to a tribe as to a lifestyle. They subsist by foraging in the dry forests of the west and southwest. Various groups along the west coast are called Mikea, although their main area is the Mikea Forest between Morombe and Toliara. The Mikea are Malagasy of various origins, having adopted their particular lifestyle (almost unique in Madagascar) for several reasons, including fleeing from oppression and taxation exerted on them by various powers.

SAKALAVA ('PEOPLE OF THE LONG VALLEYS') They live in the west between Toliara and Mahajanga and are dark-skinned with Polynesian features and short curly hair. They were at one time the largest and most powerful tribe, though disunited, and were ruled by their own kings and queens. Certain royal relics remain – typically being kept in the northeast corner of a house. The Sakalava are cattle raisers, and riches are reckoned by the number of zebu owned. There is a record of human sacrifice among them up to the year 1850 at special occasions such as the death of a king. The tromba (trance state) is quite common. It is fady for pregnant women to eat fish or to sit in a doorway. Women hold a more important place among them than in most other tribes.

SIHANAKA ('PEOPLE OF THE SWAMPS') Their home is the northeast of the old kingdom of Imerina around Lake Alaotra and they have much in common with the Merina. They are fishermen, rice growers and poultry raisers. Swamps have been drained to make vast rice fields cultivated with modern machinery and methods. They have a special rotation of fady days.

2

ST MARIANS   The population of Ile Sainte Marie is mixed. Although Indonesian in origin there has been influence from both Arabs and European pirates.

TANALA ('PEOPLE OF THE FOREST')   These are traditionally forest dwellers, living inland from Manakara, and are rice and coffee growers. Their houses are usually built on stilts. The Tanala are divided into two groups: the Ikongo in the south and the Menabe in the north. The Ikongo are an independent people who never submitted to Merina domination, in contrast to the Menabe. Burial customs include keeping the corpse for up to a month. Coffins are made from large trees to which sacrifices are sometimes made when they are cut down. The Ikongo usually bury their dead in the forest and may mark a tree to show the spot.

Some recent authorities dispute that the Tanala exist as a separate ethnic group.

TSIMIHETY ('THOSE WHO DO NOT CUT THEIR HAIR')   The refusal to cut their hair (to show mourning on the death of a Sakalava king) was to demonstrate their independence. They are an energetic and vigorous people in the north-central area and are spreading west. The oldest maternal uncle occupies an important position.

VEZO (FISHING PEOPLE)   Sometimes recognised as a separate tribe, the Vezo are historically a clan of the Sakalava. They live on the coast in the region of Morondava in the west to Faux Cap in the south. They use dugout canoes fitted with one outrigger pole and a small rectangular sail. In these frail but stable craft they go far out to sea (see page 414). The Vezo are also noted for their tombs, which are graves dug into the ground surrounded by wooden palisades, the main posts of which are crowned by erotic wooden carved figures.

ZAFIMANIRY A clan of some 15,000 people distributed in about a hundred villages in the forests between the Betsileo and Tanala areas southeast of Ambositra. They are known for their woodcarvings and sculpture. Their houses, which are made from vegetable fibres and wood with bamboo walls and roofs, have no nails and can be taken down and moved from one village to another.

LANGUAGE

The Indonesian origin of the Malagasy people shows strongly in their language which is spoken, with regional variations of dialect, throughout the island. Malagasy is a remarkably rich language, full of images, metaphors and proverbs. Literal translations of Malagasy words and phrases are often very poetic. 'Dusk' is *maizim-bava vilany*, 'darken the mouth of the cooking pot'; the very early hours of the morning are referred to as *misafo helika ny kary*, 'when the wild cat washes itself'. The richness of the language means that there are few English words that can be translated into a single word in Malagasy, and vice versa. An example given by Leonard Fox in his book on the poetry of Madagascar, *Hainteny*, is *miala mandry*. *Miala* means 'go out/go away' and *mandry* means 'lie down/go to sleep'. Together, however, they mean 'to spend the night away from home, and yet be back in the early morning as if never having been away'!

Learning, or even using, the Malagasy language may seem a challenging prospect to the first-time visitor. Place names may be very long (because they usually have

People and Culture   LANGUAGE   2

> ### SOME MALAGASY PROVERBS
>
> *Tantely tapa-bata ka ny foko no entiko mameno azy.*
> This is only half a pot of honey but my heart fills it up.
>
> *Mahavoa roa toy ny dakam-boriky.*
> Hit two things at once like the kick of a donkey.
>
> *Tsy midera vady tsy herintaona.*
> Don't praise your wife before a year.
>
> *Ny omby singorana amin' ny tandrony, ary ny olona kosa amin' ny vavany.*
> Oxen are trapped by their horns and men by their words.
>
> *Tondro tokana tsy mahazo hao.*
> You can't catch a louse with one finger.
>
> *Ny alina mitondra fisainana.*
> The night brings wisdom.
>
> *Aza manao herim-boantay.*
> If you are just a dung beetle don't try to move mountains.
>
> *Aza midera harena, fa nitera-dahy.*
> Do not boast about your wealth if you are a father.
>
> *Ny teny toy ny fonosana, ka izay mamono no mamaha.*
> Words are like a parcel: if you tie lots of knots you will have to undo them.

Once you've thrown out the idea that you must speak a foreign language correctly or not at all, and that you must use complete sentences, you can have fun with only a few words of Malagasy. Basic French is understood almost everywhere, but the people warm instantly to any attempts to speak 'their own' language.

If you learn only three words, choose **misaotra** (thank you), pronounced 'mi*sow*tr'; **veloma** (goodbye), pronounced 've*loom*'; and **manao ahoana** (pronounced roughly 'manna *own*er'), which is an all-purpose greeting. If you can squeeze in another three, go for **tsara** (good); **azafady** (please); and **be** (pronounced 'beh'), which can be used – sometimes ungrammatically, but who cares?! – to mean big, very or much. Thus *tsara be* means very good; and *misaotra be* means a big thank you. Finally, when talking to an older person, it's polite to add **tompoko**. This is equivalent to *madame* or *monsieur* in French. If your memory's poor, write the vocabulary on a postcard and carry it round with you.

In a forest one evening, at dusk, I was standing inside the trunk and intertwining roots of a huge banyan tree, looking up through the branches at the fading sky and a few early stars. It was very peaceful, very silent. Suddenly a small man appeared from the shadows, holding a rough wooden dish. Old and poorly dressed, probably a cattle herder, he stood uncertainly, not wanting to disturb me. I said '*manao ahoana*' and he replied. I touched the bark of the tree gently and said '*tsara*'. '*Tsara*,' he agreed, smiling. Then he said a sentence in which I recognised *tantely* (honey). I pointed questioningly to a wild bees' nest high in the tree. '*Tantely*,' he repeated quietly, pleased. I pointed to his dish – '*Tantely sakafo?*' Yes, he was collecting wild honey for food. '*Tsara. Veloma, tompoko.*' I moved off into the twilight. '*Veloma*,' he called softly after me. So few words, so much said.

Another day, in Antananarivo, a teenage girl was pestering me for money. She didn't seem very deserving but wouldn't give up. Then I asked her in Malagasy, 'What's your name?' She looked astonished, eyes suddenly meeting mine instead of sliding furtively. 'Noro.' So I asked, very politely, 'Please, Noro, go away. Goodbye.' Nonplussed, she stared at me briefly before moving off, the cringing attitude quite gone. By using her name, I'd given her dignity. You can find that vocabulary in the language appendix on page 440.

'What's your name?' is probably the phrase I most enjoy using. Say it to a child and their eyes grow wider, as a timid little voice answers you. Then you can say '*manao ahoana*', using the name, and you've forged a link. Now learn how to say 'My name is…' and you're into real conversation!

When I'm in Madagascar I still carry a copy of the language appendix of this guidebook in my bag. It's dog-eared now, and scribbled on. But it's my passport to a special kind of contact with friendly, gentle and fascinating people.

a literal meaning, such as Ranomafana: 'hot water'), with seemingly erratic syllable stress. However, as a courtesy to the Malagasy people you should learn a few Malagasy words. You will find a basic Malagasy vocabulary in *Appendix 2* and a recommended phrase book in *Appendix 3*.

3

Natural History

INTRODUCTION

Isolated for 65 million years, Madagascar is the oldest island on earth. As a result its natural history is unique. There are over 200,000 species on the island, living in habitats ranging from rainforests to deserts and from mountain tops to mangrove swamps. The residents are as unique as they are diverse – a list of Malagasy species reads like a hurried appendix tagged on to the end of a catalogue of the world's wildlife. Eight whole plant families exist only on Madagascar, as do more than a thousand orchid species, many thousands of succulents, countless insects, hundreds of species of frog, around 420 kinds of reptile, five families of birds and 220 different terrestrial mammals, including an entire branch of the primate family tree, the order to which we ourselves belong.

This magnificent menagerie is the product of a spectacular geological past. About 167 million years ago Madagascar was a landlocked plateau at the centre of the largest continent the earth has ever seen: Gondwana. This was during the age of the reptiles at about the time when flowering plants were beginning to blossom and primitive mammals and birds were finding a niche among their giant dinosaur cohabitants. With a combination of sea-level rises and plate movements Gondwana

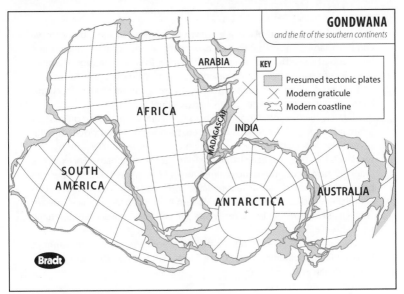

GONDWANA
and the fit of the southern continents

KEY
▢ Presumed tectonic plates
✕ Modern graticule
🗺 Modern coastline

ARABIA

AFRICA

MADAGASCAR

INDIA

SOUTH
AMERICA

ANTARCTICA

AUSTRALIA

Bradt

subsequently broke apart. Madagascar, still attached to present-day India, drifted away from Africa. Then, around the time of the mass dinosaur extinction, Madagascar broke completely free, setting itself adrift as one of the earth's great experiments in evolution.

Some of the plants and animals present on the island today are the results of adaptation from the original, marooned Gondwana stock. Ancient groups such as the ferns, cycads, palms and screw pines, and primitive reptiles such as the boas and iguanids, are descendants of this relic community. Yet the magic of Madagascar is that a select band of species has enriched the community by arriving *since* the break-up. Flying, swimming, journeying as seeds or riding the floodwaters of the East African rivers in hollow trunks, wave after wave of more recent plants and animals came from over the horizon during a period of 100 million years, bringing with them the latest adaptations from the big world beyond. Colonisers, such as the lemurs and carnivores, may have had a helping hand from a partial land-bridge which is thought to have appeared from beneath the waves of the Mozambique Channel about 40 million years ago.

Yet, whatever their mode of transport, upon landfall each species spread outwards in every direction, through the tremendous range of habitats, changing subtly as they encountered new environments, frequently to the extent that new species were formed. This evolutionary process is termed **adaptive radiation** and it results in the creation of an array of new species found nowhere else.

The patterns in the island's diversity tell us something of the timing of these colonisations. A large number of unique succulent plants indicates an early arrival from Africa in the dry west, followed by a radiation eastward ending in the rainforests. On the other hand, the two Malagasy pitcher plants found in the east probably arrived at about the same time as people, and from the same direction.

From this great evolutionary melting pot has emerged the bewildering array of animals and plants that bless Madagascar today; most are unique to the island and countless still await discovery.

SCIENTIFIC CLASSIFICATION   *Daniel Austin*

Millions of animals and plants are known to science but most do not have common names. Those that do may have many common names, or the same name could be used for multiple plants or animals. To avoid confusion, scientists use scientific names (sometimes called 'Latin names'). These are unambiguous and universal across languages, which is why we often use them in this book. For those unfamiliar with the system, here is a brief explanation.

All life is divided into kingdoms including Plantae (plants) and Animalia (animals). Each of these groups is divided, then further subdivided, through several levels of classification, right down to individual species. The bottom two levels (genus and species) together form the scientific name. For example, mankind belongs to the genus *Homo* and species *sapiens*. Our species can be written as *Homo sapiens* (abbreviated to *H. sapiens*). Sometimes species are further divided into subspecies. Modern humans belong to a subspecies (also called *sapiens*) so to be really specific we refer to ourselves as *Homo sapiens sapiens*.

You will encounter scientific names for plants and animals throughout this book, particularly where there is no universally accepted English common name.

BIODIVERSITY In recognition of its massive wealth of endemic flora and fauna, Madagascar has been designated a Biodiversity Hotspot by Conservation International – and as hotspots go, Madagascar is considered one of the hottest.

Biodiversity Hotspots cover less than 1% of the earth's surface, yet are home to well over half of its plant and animal species. Although it is not entirely understood why Madagascar has so many species, two factors have helped: it is near to the Equator and it contains an astonishing array of habitats. The tropical climate is a perfect host to the processes of life – far more living things survive within the tropics than in cooler regions – and the habitat variety provides greater opportunity for animal and plant variation.

GEOLOGY With information from Tim Ireland

The story of Madagascar's astonishing natural history begins millions of years ago. The island's geology raises plenty of interesting questions – many still unanswered – and attracts geologists and mining companies from around the world. Madagascar comprises three main geological terranes: a **crystalline core** comprising the central highlands, a **sedimentary shelf** that flanks this core on the west, and dispersed **volcanic edifices**.

The **crystalline core** dates to the Late Proterozoic, 900–550mya (million years ago), a period long before the evolution of complex life, and before the assembly of the continents as we know them. Yet these rocks contain tiny crystals of zircon which testify to a far greater antiquity (2,600mya). It is thought that this zircon records the formation of a continent that would later become part of Gondwana. Other continental masses also existed, several that would later become the northern continents, and one that would split and become South America and Africa.

Two of these (Australia-Antarctica-India-Madagascar and South America-Africa) had been drifting slowly closer together until they collided 690mya, just as the first large multicellular marine creatures were beginning to evolve. During such collisions the edges of the continents crumple and sheets several kilometres thick are thrust over each other forming mountain ranges. The so-called Mozambique Belt of mountains was immense, extending 7,000km from present-day Kenya down to Antarctica, with Madagascar right at the centre.

The rocks buried during mountain-building are recrystallised and partially melted under the intense pressure and heat. The central highlands of Madagascar are just a small part of the exhumed roots of this vast and ancient mountain belt, consisting of recrystallised rocks such as gneisses, granulites, migmatites and granites. The ramparts of the Mozambique Belt then stood sentinel, slowly eroding but largely unchanged, for several hundred million years, while soft-bodied life in the oceans experimented with the idea of greater progression.

The **sedimentary shelf** began to form early in the Palaeozoic (500mya), as macroscopic organisms with external skeletons evolved and diversified explosively. The old mountain belt had been eroded down near to sea level, and the waning of an ice age caused flooding of the land. Across the world, life evolved dramatically towards a climax of plant productivity in the Carboniferous (320mya) and then shivered through its most severe ice age and most catastrophic extinction only 30 million years later (96% of marine species vanished). That ice age scraped all evidence of the preceding sedimentation from Madagascar and the geological record there is reset, beginning with gravel and boulder deposits laid down as the glaciers retreated. In the middle Permian (270mya) the southern continents were still assembled as one supercontinent – Gondwana – in which Madagascar was a

Madagascar is famed for its bizarre and unique wildlife today, but many of the island's most fascinating animal inhabitants have long since disappeared.

A number of remarkable fossil discoveries have been made in recent years. In the south, scientists unearthed two prosauropods (herbivorous dinosaurs) that dated back 230 million years, making them not only the earliest fossils ever to be found in Madagascar, but strong contenders for the title of the *world's* oldest.

Another unusual find was of a very strange blunt-snouted, herbivorous crocodile in northwest Madagascar, dating from the late Cretaceous (97–65 million years ago). Prior to the discovery of this beast (*Simosuchus clarki*) experts had believed ancient crocodiles to resemble more closely those alive today.

In 2001 a new species of dinosaur was named *Masiakasaurus knopfleri* after the lead guitarist of Dire Straits because whenever they played his music they struck lucky finding fossils! *M. knopfleri* was a ferocious little bipedal carnivore (the genus name comes from the Malagasy for 'violent') whose larger cousin *Majungatholus atopus* was discovered by the same team from the State University of New York, Stony Brook. This lived around 70–65 million years ago and is believed to have been cannibalistic. An examination of distinctive marks on the fossilised bones suggests that they could only have been caused by the teeth of the same species, though it is still a matter of debate whether the victim was alive at the time. Cannibalism has been documented in only one other species of dinosaur.

In 2013, a new species of dinosaur was announced after archaeological work in the far north. The 3½m-long *Dahalokely tokana*, whose scientific name is Malagasy for 'lonely little bandit', was thought to have lived some 90 million years ago.

Until very recently, Madagascar had a flourishing megafauna (a word used to refer to all large animals). When humans first settled on the island, they would have been greeted with great forests populated by huge tortoises, dwarf hippos and lemurs the size of gorillas. Around 17 extinct species of lemur are known – all larger than the largest living species – and all thought to have died out.

Perhaps the most amazing of Madagascar's extinct animals is still fresh in Malagasy folklore. Tales of this creature were passed along to Marco Polo who wrote extravagantly of an awesome bird, the giant roc, capable of carrying off an elephant. This majestic animal was, in fact, the flightless elephant bird. Standing over 3m tall, it would have made an ostrich seem like a goose. The largest, *Aepyornis maximus*, weighed in at more than 500kg and is thought to have been the largest bird ever to have lived. Sadly, like the famous dodo of neighbouring Mauritius, it was driven to extinction by humans in the last few centuries.

The roc as visualised in 1598

central part without identity, bound on the west by present-day Africa, the east by India and the south by Antarctica.

Gondwana began to split apart soon after, towards the modern continental distribution. As a continent divides, rifts form, gradually becoming seas, then oceans. The rocks of the sedimentary shelf record 100 million years of deposition spanning that cycle for the rift separating Madagascar from Africa. The earliest sediments are mixed glacial, river and lake deposits that contain a fossil flora common to all the modern southern continents. Later, the land was inundated and marine carbonates were deposited in this new shallow sea preserving the remains of some primitive fish. During the Triassic (240–210mya) the landscape was uplifted and terrestrial gravels and sands were deposited, including those exposed in Isalo National Park. A major rise in sea level followed, and from this time until after the demise of the dinosaurs (63mya) fossil-bearing limestone sedimentation dominated in the growing Mozambique Channel. These sediments today make up the Bemaraha Plateau and the *tsingy* landscapes of western Madagascar. The shallow marine ecosystems were characterised by a great abundance of ammonites, and today the sedimentary carbonates of west Madagascar are an incredible repository of these fossils. Uplifting occurred again 50–30mya as a major eastern rift developed between India and Madagascar, ending sedimentation on the shelf.

The **volcanic edifices** of Madagascar are less obvious than the volcanoes responsible for the islands of the Comoros, Réunion and Mauritius. They are widespread in the north and along the east coast, and inland they make up the Ankaratra Massif, Itasy highlands and Montagne d'Ambre. Underwater volcanic activity began during the Cretaceous (120mya) and has persisted off the north coast up to the present day. The lavas and intrusive rocks produced have a bizarre and unique chemistry. The most recent major volcanic activity occurred less than 2mya, giving rise to Nosy Be, where modern hot springs testify to the island's relative youth. There are suggestions that the volcanic focus is moving southeast towards Madagascar; the volcanic record in the island is potentially far from over.

Significant **landscape evolution** has occurred over the last 40 million years. Since India began to head northeast, the rift between Africa and Madagascar stabilised and mountains were regenerated by activity on major NNE- and NNW-oriented faults. These orientations can be recognised across the country bounding smaller sedimentary basins and mountain ranges, and most noticeably control the strikingly linear geometry of the east coast. The centre and east were uplifted more than the west, providing the basis for the modern shape of the island. Completely emergent for the first time for several hundred million years, land plants and animals proliferated and evolved towards the island's present flora and fauna. Local lake and river deposits developed in the lowlands and erosion cut back the highlands. In the centre and east, the entire marine record was stripped away, revealing the crystalline core and resulting in undulating dome-like mountains, such as Pic d'Imarivolanitra. In the west the sedimentary rock was eroded flat to near sea level. Tectonic activity in the last million years has again uplifted the Malagasy terrain, and this ancient erosional surface now defines the plateaux of the west, including Bemaraha.

HUMAN COLONISATION The final chapter starts when people arrived (page 13) and began a dramatic demonstration of how humans can affect geological processes. Reduction in primary forest since the colonisation of Madagascar has indisputably influenced the shape of the land. Soils once stabilised by deep root systems became susceptible to erosion, and the sediment load in the rivers increased. In the 50 years to 1945, 40m of clay was deposited in the delta of the Betsiboka River at

3

Mahajanga, immensely more than the underlying sedimentary record suggests was usual prior to deforestation. Ubiquitous hillside scars (called *lavaka*) are the inland testimony to this accelerated redistribution of material from highlands to coast, an inexorable environmental response to deforestation that is sending the Malagasy highlands towards eventual peneplanation (flattening) at an incredible rate. Even with an average annual erosion of 1mm taking place continuously, Madagascar will be reduced to near sea level in a geologically short three million years.

FLORA

Madagascar and its adjacent islands harbour some 13,000 species of flowering plants of which a staggering 89% are endemic. Although some other regions of the world (such as the Tropical Andes, Indonesia and Brazil) have more plant species, they have substantially lower rates of endemism, typically below 50%. Madagascar is the world's number one floral hotspot for an area its size. The fortuitous break from Africa and Asia at a time when the flowering plants were just beginning to diversify allowed many groups to develop their own lineage, supplemented occasionally by the later colonisations of more advanced forms.

FERNS AND CYCADS Ferns were in their heyday before Gondwana was even formed. Their best efforts were the impressive **tree ferns**, which had large spreading fronds sprouting from a tall, scaly stem. These structures created vast forests in all warm, humid areas during the Carboniferous, 350mya. Although they eventually lost ground to seed-bearing plants during the age of the dinosaurs, it is a credit to their design that they are still abundant and successful. Indeed the soft, symmetrical foliage of ferns very much epitomises the lushness of hot, wet places. It's true that they have been relegated to a life in the shade of more recently evolved plants, but here they excel, out-competing all others.

Although some species are present in dry habitats, the vast majority of Madagascar's ferns decorate the branches and trunks of the eastern rainforests. One eye-catching species is the huge **bird's nest fern** (*Asplenium nidus*) which adorns many large trunks with luxuriant balconies of leaves. The ancient tree ferns (*Cyathea* spp) that once supplied the forest canopy are still present on its floor, contributing to the prehistoric atmosphere of the forest.

Often mistaken for a tree fern, the **cycad** (*Cycas* spp) is in fact one of the original seed-bearing plants. The evolution of seed propagation eventually led to the flowering plants that currently dominate all of the world's habitats, marking the end of the ferns' reign on earth. Resembling a tree fern with palm-like leaves, the single Malagasy representative of the genus, *Cycas thouarsii*, is found only in the eastern rainforests. Look closely at its cone: it holds seeds which, 30mya, became the most significant single plant adaptation in the history of life.

CARNIVOROUS PLANTS There are two species of insect-eating **pitcher plant** (*Nepenthes* spp), a genus which otherwise lives only in Asia. In Madagascar's eastern wetlands they poke out of the marsh beds like triffids planning an ambush. One of their leaves wraps upon itself to create a trumpet-shaped fly trap, which then serves up trace elements, from the flies' remains, unobtainable from the mud below. There are also five species of **sundew** (*Drosera* spp), which possess leaves covered in sticky red tentacles that are capable of wrapping around and ensnaring any insects that become stuck to them before secreting a cocktail of enzymes to digest the prey. The semi-aquatic **corkscrew plant** (*Genlisea margaretae*) also has members of the animal kingdom on its menu. It feasts on minute microfauna caught by underground traps formed from highly modified leaves. Also present are several types of **bladderwort** (*Utricularia* spp), a group of unusual organisms that lack the distinction between root, leaf and stem organs found in most flowering plants. They are covered in vacuum-filled bladders recognised as among the most sophisticated structures in the plant kingdom. Each bladder has a small trapdoor sealed with a soft membrane that is connected to a hair trigger. When disturbed by a tiny creature, this levers open the membrane causing the partial vacuum to suck the prey inside before the door snaps shut again – all in less than a hundredth of a second. The cell then sets about extracting nutrients from its unfortunate inmate by means of digestive juices, before cleaning and repriming itself within a matter of hours.

SUCCULENTS *With information from Gavin Hart*
In Madagascar, wherever rainfall is below about 40cm a year, succulents reign. The entire southwest of the island is dominated by their swollen forms. Further north they decorate the natural rock gardens of Isalo, Itremo and the countless outcrops on the central plateau. They also appear within the sparse dry forests of the west, among the stony chaos of the *tsingy* (see box, page 416), and even venture on to the grasslands and into the rainforests. About 150 succulent species occur in Madagascar, distributed widely across the island.

Euphorbia This is one of the largest genera of flowering plants with more than 2,000 species worldwide. Almost 500 are succulent species occurring predominantly in Africa and Madagascar. They have diversified into countless different forms, from bushes resembling strings of sausages, and trees sprouting smooth leafless green branches, to spiny stalks emerging from swollen underground tubers. Many species shed their leaves at the start of the dry season, but when present they are swollen with water and shining with wax. To replace the leaves they often yield wonderful flowers and in so doing brighten up the landscape.

E. milii lines the streets of many towns. These are small shrubby plants with spiny stems (hence the common name: crown of thorns) and a few terminal leaves. The most dominant feature, however, is the bright red bracts surrounding the flowers which produce a blaze of colour from the mass plantings.

All euphorbias have white milky sap which is toxic, may burn on skin contact, and can cause temporary blindness, so caution is urged in handling these plants.

Pachypodium This genus contains five species from southern Africa and about 20 from Madagascar. The Malagasy pachypodiums have an unusual flower structure in that the stamens are covered by a segmented cone which must be penetrated to achieve pollination. They vary from tree-like species to caudiciforms (stem succulents) with white, red or yellow flowers. They are mostly quite spiny when young but tend to lose their spines as they mature.

The bizarrely compressed *P. brevicaule*, which has been likened to a sack of potatoes, has most of its large mass beneath the ground. *P. lamerei* – widespread in the southwest – is the most common species in cultivation. *P. rutenbergianum* is widely distributed from the mid-west coast to the north and is the largest species, reaching up to 15m tall with a heavily branched crown.

Didiereaceae The most intriguing plants in Madagascar are the Didiereaceae of the arid southwest: they are an entire family of bizarre plants found nowhere else on earth. They look similar to cacti, but their tiny deciduous leaves – and the immense

Madagascar is home to more than a thousand different species and varieties of orchid, of which well over three-quarters are endemic. They have adapted to every possible habitat, including the spiny forest and the cool highland mountain ranges, but their highest density is in the wet forests of the east. The best time for seeing them in flower is the rainy season from January to March. Some of the most memorable orchids are to be found in the eastern coastal area, which is the habitat of large *Angraecum*, *Eulophiella* and *Cymbidiella* species. Many are epiphytes living on tree branches or trunks; anchored by their roots they scramble over their host collecting moisture and nutrients, but they are not parasites.

A. eburneum can be seen in flower mainly from May to September, its thick leathery leaves forming a half-metre-wide fan shape; the flower stems reach above the leaves carrying a number of large greenish-white flowers. Like many Malagasy orchids the blooms are strongly scented and white in colour to attract pollinating moths at night.

The comet orchid, *A. sesquipedale*, is one of the most striking. It flowers from June to November and the plants are similar to *A. eburneum* but are more compact. Individual flowers can be 26cm across and over 30cm long including the lengthy nectary spur, characteristic for the angraecoid orchids, at the back of the flower. The flower was described by Charles Darwin at the end of the 19th century when he predicted that there would be a moth with a very long tongue that could reach down to the nectar at the bottom of the spur. This idea was ridiculed by his contemporaries, but in 1903 – more than two decades after his death – he was proved right: a hawk-moth with a proboscis of over 30cm (*Xanthopan morganii praedicta*) was discovered, and it has recently been caught on film pollinating this orchid.

Aeranthes plants look similar to *Angraecum*. Their spider-like greenish flowers are suspended from long thin stems, gently nodding in the breeze.

Eulophiella roempleriana, which can reach almost 2m tall, is now very rare. One of the few remaining plants can be seen on Ile aux Nattes, off Ile Sainte Marie. The large, deep pink flowers are well worth the pirogue trip to the island. A few more of these plants survive in the reserves around Andasibe and Ranomafana. They normally flower from October onwards.

thorns that protect them – indicate that they are not (cacti don't have thorns; their spines are modified leaves). Of this family's four genera, **Alluaudia** contains six species, **Alluaudiopsis** and **Didierea** each contain two species and **Decaryia** just one.

The octopus trees (*Didierea* spp) are the most famous members of this group. Species vary greatly in form and flower colouration within the family. *Alluaudia ascendens* is the largest, growing initially as a single stem, but then branching from the base forming massive V-shaped plants 10–15m tall with white to reddish flowers. *Alluaudia comosa* also branches from the base, but forms a wide, flat-topped shrub 2–6m tall. The spines are up to 2cm long and white flowers cover the ends of its shoots. The beautiful *Alluaudiopsis marnieriana* grows to 4m and has the most colourful flowers of the whole family – up to 3cm across and bright crimson.

Aloe About 450 species of this genus occur in southern and eastern Africa and Madagascar. Over a hundred are recognised in Madagascar but there are distinct differences between African and Malagasy species. Even though aloes are known

Cymbidiella orchids are also very striking; they flower from October to January. *C. pardalina*, with its huge crimson lip, cohabits with a staghorn fern, while *C. falcigera*, with black-spotted yellow flowers, prefers the exclusive company of the raffia palm.

The highlands, with their cooler and more seasonal climate, are inhabited by numerous terrestrial orchids, growing in soil or leaf litter; underground tubers produce deciduous leaves and flower stems – not dissimilar to temperate orchids.

Eulophia plantaginea is a relatively common roadside plant; large colonies can sometimes be found, especially in boggy areas. *Cynorkis* can also be seen along the roads. Many are terrestrials, others grow on wet rock or in swamps. The most common highland species is *C. ridleyi*. Epiphytes such as *Angraecum* and *Aeranthes* can still be found in the few remaining pockets of forest in the highlands.

Aerangis plants are instantly recognisable by their shiny, dark green foliage. The flowers superficially resemble those of *Angraecum* but they are often much smaller, carried on elegant racemes, and their scent is exquisite. The plants are commonly seen in the wet shade of the rainforest reserves of Andasibe and Ranomafana. *Jumellea* are again similar but have a narrower, folded-back single flower on a thin stem.

Bulbophyllum orchids are easily missed by the untrained eye; their rounded, plump pseudo-bulbs are often seen on moss-covered trees. They are always worthwhile to investigate: small gem-like blooms may be nestled among the foliage.

Oeonia with its huge white lip and two red dots on its throat can be found rambling among the undergrowth. The apparently bare higher peaks of the *hauts plateaux* also contain a very specialised community of orchids. The thick-leaved, sun-loving angraecoids and *Bulbophyllums*, known as lithophytes, share the rock faces with succulents.

One of the best and easiest places to see orchids – including *Angraecum*, *Cymbidiella* and *Gastrorchis* – is in the grounds of hotels and private gardens, but one must be aware that these domestic collections may contain the odd foreign interloper. Orchids from the Orient and South America are brought in as pot plants, the flowers often being bigger and brighter than those of the natives.

Note that orchids are covered under CITES regulations and export permits are required to transport any plants out of Madagascar.

as low-growing plants, some species have stems to raise their broad foliage above the ground. The largest aloes have stocky 3m stems covered in untidy dead scales which sport huge succulent leaves and, in June and July, a large red inflorescence. *A. divaricata* is a fast-growing species common in the southwest. Its single or branched stems are 2–6m long with narrow blue-grey leaves and red-brown marginal teeth, scattered along the whole length. Highly branched inflorescences of up to 1m bear coral-red flowers. *A. suzannae* is unique among aloes in being a night-bloomer; flowers open before midnight and close the following morning. Its flowers (which only appear after ten years or so) are pollinated by the souimanga sunbird and Madagascar white-eye as well as by bats and mouse lemurs.

Kalanchoe The genus *Kalanchoe* contains around 130 species of succulent perennials distributed through Africa, Madagascar, Arabia and Asia – with 63 occurring in Madagascar. The most well known is the panda plant (*K. tomentosa*), a shrub with dense rosettes. The species are highly variable in form (from low leafy

Unlike animals, plants cannot escape harsh environments. The plants of Madagascar's dry southwest have therefore had to adapt to tolerate strong sunlight, high temperatures and – most restrictive of all – desiccation. These high demands have produced unusual-looking and fascinating plant species called **xerophytes**.

All xerophytes have deep root systems to acquire what little water there is available. Their leaves are usually small and covered in hairs, and much of their photosynthesis is done by the green stems. This design lowers the surface area of the plant and traps still air adjacent to the leaf, reducing water loss – the key aim. In addition to desiccation, overheating is as much a problem for plants as it is for animals. Xerophytes have therefore evolved various techniques to minimise heating: usually they have their narrowest edge facing the sun and they often add grey pigments to their leaves to deflect the harsh rays of midday.

The most extreme adaptations for a dry life are to be seen in the **succulents**. This general term describes all xerophytes which store water in their waxy leaves, roots or stems. Water is a valuable commodity in a dry habitat, and one that must be protected from thirsty grazers, so succulents usually employ toxins or spines as a defence. This is evident in many of the island's spectacular plants, not least the octopus trees of the spiny forest.

succulents to tall tree-like plants), leaf shape, size and colour. *Kalanchoe* flowers have parts in multiples of four – four connected petals forming a tube, four sepals, four carpals and eight stamens – whereas most other Crassulaceae flowers have parts in multiples of five. In Madagascar the largest species (eg: *K. arborescens*, *K. beharensis*, *K. grandidieri*) tend to be restricted to the semi-arid south and southwest, while the smaller species occur mostly in the more humid areas up to 2,000m.

Adenia There are more than a hundred species of *Adenia* in the passionflower family. Most are deciduous vines, climbing with the aid of tendrils, extending from a swollen stem base. They are usually dioecious (either male or female) with inconspicuous creamy greenish flowers and fruit that's often vividly coloured.

Uncarina An endemic genus of a dozen species in the Pedialaceae family, *Uncarina* plants are deciduous shrubs or small trees up to 8m tall with a substantial underground tuber. Flowers may be yellow, white, pink or violet, and the fruits are large capsules covered with numerous, ferociously hooked thorns, which aid dissemination by attaching to the hairy coats of animals.

Cyphostemma More than 300 species are in this genus (a minority of which are succulent) in the Vitaceae family. Twenty-four occur in Madagascar. *C. sakalavense* is bottle-shaped with a stem up to 3m tall. It can be found on the limestone rocks of the *tsingy* in northwest Madagascar.

Senecio This is a genus of leaf succulents, existing essentially as a collection of swollen leaves sprouting from the earth. The leaves are often ornamental, tinged with terracotta and bearing harsh spines, but also display showy red flowers during times of drought.

PALMS Madagascar is home to one of the world's richest palm floras. There are around 200 species – three times more than in the rest of Africa put together – and 189 of these are found nowhere else.

A lack of large herbivores in Madagascar has left its palms – with no need for defences – spineless and without poisons. Pollination is mostly by bees and flies, but some have tiny flowers to entice unknown insect guests. For seed dispersal lemurs are often employed. Ring-tailed, black, red ruffed and brown lemurs all assist in scattering the seeds. The bright colours of some fruits serve to attract birds and forest pigs, while the handful of African palms, which normally use elephants as dispersers, presumably make do with zebu.

The dominance of species with Asian relatives betrays the fact that Madagascar severed with India millions of years *after* it broke away from African shores.

The species present range from the famous to the recently discovered, from dwarf to giant, and almost all have intriguing characteristics. One palm has led to a Malagasy word entering the English language – the **raffia palm** (*Raphia farinifera*). The fibres from its leaves are woven into hats, baskets and mats. Of the dozens of new palm species discovered in recent years, one is worth particular attention: *Ravenea musicalis*, the world's only **water palm**. It starts life underwater in only one of Madagascar's southeastern rivers. As it grows, it surfaces, eventually bears fruit, and then seeds. Its discoverer named it *R. musicalis* after being charmed by the chimes of its seedpods as they hit the water below. There are other riverside palms in Madagascar adapted to tolerate the recurrent floods of the island's lowland rainforest, but none as perfectly as the musical water palm.

Another unusual group is the **litter-trapping palms**. The crown of their leaves is arranged like an upturned shuttlecock, sprouting at first from the forest floor, and then gaining height as the stem grows from below. Its watertight crown catches leaves falling from the canopy, perhaps to obtain trace minerals, but no-one knows for sure. A strange consequence of this growth is that the roots of other plants, which originally grew through the soil into the crown by mistake, later dangle down from its heights as alabaster-white zigzags.

Although the vast majority of palms live among the hardwoods of the lowland rainforests, there are species which brave the more arid environments, notably the **feather palms** (*Chrysalidocarpus* spp) which nestle in the canyons of Isalo National Park and stand alone among the secondary grasslands of the west.

False palms The word 'palm' is often used rather liberally. The **travellers' palm** (*Ravenala madagascariensis*), symbolic of Madagascar, is not a palm at all (see *Trees* below). In fact it is in the same family as the bird of paradise flower (Strelitziaceae). Another is the **Madagascar palm**, which is actually a spiny succulent *Pachypodium lamerei* (page 37). And then there are **pandan palms** or screw pines (*Pandanus* spp), which consist of untidy grass-like mops that awkwardly adorn rough branches periodically emerging from their straight trunks. Common in both rainforests and dry forests there are some 90 species, only one of which is found elsewhere, placing the country alongside Borneo for pandan diversity.

TREES Until the arrival of humans, Madagascar is thought to have been largely cloaked in forest. There remain examples of each of the original forests, but vast areas have become treeless as a result of *tavy* (slash-and-burn agriculture; see box, page 67) and soil erosion.

Most of the remaining **evergreen trees** form the superstructure of the rainforest. They are typically 30m high, with buttressed roots, solid hardwood trunks and vast canopies. There can be up to 250 species of tree in a single hectare of lowland rainforest, but from the ground they all look very similar. To identify a species, botanists must often wait for flowering, an event that is not only extremely difficult to predict, but also one that takes place 30m high, out of sight.

One notable and obvious tree is the **strangler fig** (*Ficus* spp), which germinates up in the canopy on a branch of its victim, grows down to the floor to root, and encircles and constricts its host leaving a hollow knotted trunk. The Malagasy prize the forest hardwoods; one canopy tree is called the 'kingswood' because its wood is so hard that, at one time, any found were automatically the property of the local king.

The only evergreen species to be found outside the rainforest are the **tapia tree** (*Uapaca bojei*), the nine species of **mangrove tree** and some of the **succulent trees** in the extreme southwest where sea mists provide water all year round. In tolerating the conditions of west Madagascar, these evergreens have borne their own unusual communities.

The rest of Madagascar's trees are **deciduous**, losing their leaves during the dry season. The taller dry forests of the west are dappled with the shadows of **leguminous trees** such as *Dalbergia* and *Cassia*, characterised by their long seedpods and symbiotic relationships with bacteria which provide fertilisers within their roots. Sprawling **banyan figs** (*Ficus* spp) and huge **tamarind trees** (*Tamarindus indica*) create gallery forest along the rivers of the west and south, yielding pungent fruit popular with lemurs. In drier woodland areas Madagascar's most celebrated trees, the **baobabs** (*Adansonia* spp), dominate.

One last species deserves a mention. The **travellers' palm** (*Ravenala madagascariensis*) is one of Madagascar's most spectacular plants. It is thought to have earned its name from the relief it affords thirsty travellers: water is stored in the base of its leaves and can be released with a swift blow from a machete. Its elegant fronds are arranged in a dramatic vertical fan, which is decorative enough to have earned it a role as Air Madagascar's logo. Its large, bulbous flowers sprout from the leaf axils and, during the 24 hours that they are receptive, are visited by unusual pollinators – ruffed lemurs. The lemurs locate flowers which have just opened, and literally pull them apart to get at the large nectary inside. Keeping a lemur fed puts quite a demand on the tree, but it produces flowers day after day for several months, and during this time the lemurs eat little else. The travellers' palm is perhaps the only native species to have benefited from tavy agriculture – it dominates areas of secondary vegetation on the central plateau and east coast.

This secondary rainforest that grows back after tavy is called *savoka*. Aside from the travellers' palm, these areas of savoka are sadly dominated by foreign tree species which will eventually infest all returning forest, changing Madagascar's rainforest communities forever. A handful of native plants have managed to compete with these exotics but relatively few animals live in this vegetation.

Baobabs The baobab – a freak among trees with its massively swollen trunk and sparse stubby branches – is emblematic of Madagascar. This is the motherland of baobabs. Of the nine species found worldwide, six grow exclusively in Madagascar. The others (one in Australia and two in mainland Africa) are believed to have originated from seedpods that were swept away from Malagasy shores around 10mya and survived the ocean crossings. One of the African species can be seen in Madagascar today, for it was introduced by Arab traders as street planting in towns.

The reason for the baobab's extraordinary girth – sometimes exceeding 30m – is that it is well adapted to inhospitably dry conditions. It is capable of taking up and storing water from sporadic downpours very efficiently, its porous wood acting like a huge sponge. No doubt inspired by the great size of some specimens, claims have been made that these giants can live for many thousands of years. It is difficult to be certain because unlike other trees baobabs do not produce growth rings, but recent radiocarbon dating suggests that the very oldest may be 900 years old, with most significantly younger.

Baobabs have large, showy flowers that open at dusk and are receptive for one night only. Pollinators include fruit bats, fork-marked lemurs, giant mouse lemurs, sunbirds, bees and hawk-moths.

Species of baobab Even to the expert eye, baobab species can be tough to identify. Their form is highly dependent on environmental factors meaning there can be massive variation within one species.

Found between Morombe and Belo-sur-Tsiribihina, **Adansonia grandidieri** is the most majestic and famous species and may reach 30m in height. The best-known specimens form the Baobab Avenue near Morondava. These trees would once have been surrounded by dense forest, but today their isolated silhouettes can be seen for miles across the flat, featureless rice fields. Unlike these smooth, columnar giants, the same species in the spiny scrub at Andavadoaka is quite knobbly and almost spherical, often reaching little more than 3m in height.

Typically with a tall, straight trunk and grey bark around the crown, *A. za* is the most widespread species, with a range covering much of western and southern Madagascar. It is found further inland than the others, most notably around Zombitse, presumably because it is more tolerant of the cooler climate. The fruits are ovoid rather than round and have peculiarly swollen stalks.

Preferring sandy soil, *A. rubrostipa* (formerly *A. fony*) is the smallest species. It grows along much of the west coast, from Itampolo almost as far north as Mahajanga. In the spiny forest it assumes a bottle shape, but at Kirindy it is taller and more slender. The fruits are rather thin-walled and do not carry far without breaking open. This may explain why clusters of them are often found growing in relatively high concentrations. Identifying features include serrated leaf edges and reddish-tinged bark.

Restricted to a few sites in the extreme north of Madagascar, the rare *A. suarezensis* is characterised by its horizontal branches and smooth red bark.

Rarer still, *A. perrieri* is sometimes called the rainforest species for it shuns the drier habitats where its siblings thrive. It occupies a specialised niche on the sheltered banks of small streams running down from Montagne d'Ambre. It is the largest of the three northern baobabs, and with just a few dozen specimens remaining it is also one of the rarest trees in the world.

The most variable of the baobabs is *A. madagascariensis*, found along the northwest coast from Mahajanga to Antsiranana. Given favourable soil and water conditions, such as at the east entrance to Ankarana, it may reach an imposing 20m in height, while on the nearby karst the same species is squat and pear-shaped. The bark is pale grey and the flowers dark red. The fruits are smaller, rounder, less furry, and narrower-stalked than in other species.

The African baobab, *A. digitata*, is an introduced species but has become naturalised in several parts of Madagascar. The best-known specimen grows in the middle of a road at the western side of Mahajanga, where it has a role as a traffic island! This is the fattest tree in the country with a circumference of nearly 21m.

Uses and conservation Baobabs provide a number of resources for humans. The seeds are eaten and used for cooking oil; the bark is used to make rope and roofing materials; and the leaves are fed to cattle, as is the wood in times of drought.

3

Baobab wood is neither strong enough for building nor particularly good for burning, so the trees tend to be left standing when the surrounding forest is cleared. Removal of the bark does little damage since baobabs possess the rare ability to regenerate it. Mature trees are even quite resistant to fire and so rarely succumb to the regular burning of undergrowth carried out to stimulate new grazing.

Nevertheless, the long-term outlook for the Malagasy baobabs is bleak. Half of the species are listed as endangered and all are recognised as threatened by habitat loss. The main problem is that there is virtually no new growth. Deprived of the protection afforded by the surrounding forest, those seedlings that escape burning are promptly devoured by zebu. Furthermore, two species (*A. grandidieri* and *A. suarezensis*) are thought to depend on animals to disperse their seeds. But since no living Malagasy creature is known to eat the fruit of the baobab, it can only be assumed that these seed dispersers are now extinct – very bad news indeed for the future of these species.

If these trees were allowed to die out it would be a terribly sad loss. But the impact penetrates much deeper than that. Baobabs provide food, support and homes for a plethora of creatures, both directly and indirectly, including lemurs, bats, birds, insects, geckos, humans and even other plants and fungi. Treat these majestic giants with respect and remember that many are honoured as *faly* (sacred) – so try to ask permission before you take photos.

Baobab fruit was legally authorised as a food in Europe and the USA in 2009. An NGO called Pink Forest (*www.pinkforest.org*) aims to promote their conservation by giving them economic value. They describe it as a 'superfruit', the dry pulp of

THE VALUE OF THE FLORA

Many Malagasy plants crop up in garden centres throughout Europe. Familiar to horticulturalists are the **dragon tree** (*Dracaena marginata*), **crown of thorns** (*Euphorbia milii*), **Areca palm** (*Dypsis lutescens*), **flamboyant tree** (*Delonix regia*) and **Madagascar jasmine** (*Stephanotis floribunda*) of bridal bouquet fame. Other natives are valued for their uses rather than their aesthetic qualities. There has been interest in Madagascar's various **wild coffees** (Rubiaceae family), not least because many are naturally caffeine-free.

The **Madagascar rosy periwinkle** (*Catharanthus roseus*) is a champion of those who campaign to conserve natural habitats. The plant has a long history of medicinal use the world over. In India, wasp stings were treated with juice from the leaves; in Hawaii, the plant was boiled to make a poultice to stop bleeding; in China, it was considered a cough remedy; in Central and South America, it has also been used in homemade cold remedies to ease lung congestion, inflammation and sore throats; in the Caribbean, an extract of the flower was used to treat eye infections; and in the Philippines it was used to treat diabetes during WWII. It was the last of these that brought it to the attention of pharmaceutical companies, who carried out trials in the 1950s, ultimately leading to its use in chemotherapy. Since the early 1960s, two alkaloids called vinblastine and vincristine extracted from the rosy periwinkle have proved effective in the treatment of leukaemia and lymphomas.

There are certainly many other plants with equally life-saving chemical properties yet to be found, but the rate of forest destruction may be driving these to extinction before we have a chance to appreciate them or even discover the species at all.

which has six times as much potassium as banana, three times more calcium than milk, ten times more antioxidants than goji berries, 15 times the vitamin C levels of pomegranate and three times more magnesium than apricots – as well as proven cosmetic and hair-care properties.

FOREIGN INVADERS In common with many islands around the globe, Madagascar has suffered from accidental and intended introductions of alien species. Sometimes referred to as weeds, because they do not really belong there, they can cause havoc.

Out-competing native species, sharp tropical grasses from South America permanently deface the burnt woodlands of the west. And their populations explode because zebu do not find these exotic species appetising. Where thick forest is cleared, fast-growing *Eucalyptus* and *Psidium* trees step in. The trumpet lily (*Datura* spp) is now rampant in localised areas. Another growing problem is the rubber bush (*Calotropis procera*), which is native to tropical Africa and Asia; this has become the dominant plant in some areas around Antsiranana. It either suffocates competitors with its dense growth or poisons the soil with its toxins. In drier areas, superbly adapted and profoundly damaging prickly pear cacti spread from the nearby sisal plantations and flourish where there was once spiny forest.

Needless to say, the native animal populations, unable to adapt to these invaders, also suffer – and this, perhaps even more than the endangerment of plant species, has prompted action from conservation bodies.

FAUNA

Compared with the breathtaking ecosystems of mainland Africa, Madagascar's fauna has far more subtle qualities. A combination of ancient Gondwana stock and 65 million years of isolated evolution has created a haven for a plethora of strange and unusual creatures. Here are a seemingly random collection of animal groups that had the opportunity to prove themselves in the absence of large predators and herbivores. The resulting 180,000 species, existing in habitats from rainforests to coral reefs, bring human opportunity too: for numerous truly unique wildlife encounters.

INVERTEBRATES There are well over 150,000 species of invertebrate in Madagascar, the majority in the eastern rainforests. To spot them turn over leaves and logs on the forest floor, peer very closely at the foliage or switch on a bright light after dark. Although perhaps creepy, and undeniably crawly, they do contribute substantially to the experience of wild areas on the island and – provided you can suppress the spine shivers – your mini-safaris will be hugely rewarding.

It is a difficult task to pick out the most impressive invertebrates, but notable are the hugely oversized **pill millipedes** that roll up when threatened to resemble a striped golf ball. Among the forest foliage are superbly camouflaged **praying mantises**, **net-throwing spiders** that cast their silk nets at flyers-by, and **nymphs** and bugs of all shapes, colours and adornments. Among the leaf litter there are spectacular striped and horned **flatworms**, the otherworldly **ant lions** (see box, page 411) and vast numbers of wonderful **weevils**, the most spectacular being the bright red giraffe-necked weevil (most easily seen at Ranomafana). The species gets its name from the male whose tremendously long neck is almost three times the length of his body!

One invertebrate whose presence will not be welcomed by most visitors is the **leech**, but it is a more fascinating creature than you might at first imagine; turn to the box on page 330 to discover why.

There are around 300 species of **butterfly** in Madagascar, two-thirds of which are endemic to the island. The most eye-catching are the heavily patterned swallowtails, and the nymphalids with their dominant blue and orange liveries. Many nymphalids are effectively four-legged, their front pair being considerably reduced and folded out of sight for reasons that are not fully understood. Madagascar's **moths** are significantly older in origin and are probably descendants of the Gondwana insects marooned on the island. This explains the diversity – 4,000 species – including many groups active during the day, filling niches that elsewhere are the realm of butterflies. Most dramatic is the huge yellow comet moth (*Argema mittrei*) with a wingspan of up to 25cm, and the elaborate urania moths (*Chrysiridia* spp), which look just like swallowtails decorated with emeralds. A very close relative is found in the Amazon rainforest.

Across the island, huge **golden orb-web spiders** (*Nephila madagascariensis*) string together massive webs often extending between trees and telephone wires.

CURIOUS ARACHNIDS
Len de Beer & John Roff

LOOKING LIKE... You're walking through a patch of forest and stop to photograph an unusual flower, when you notice some thoughtless bird has relieved itself on a leaf you were about to lean on. You're about to wipe it off when you have a hunch that you should look closer. What looked like a bird dropping turns out to be a fine specimen of *Phrynarachne* – a specialised crab spider that spends its time sitting on top of a leaf looking like poo. Some even emulate the scent of urine and faeces.

Why? Flies delight in landing on faeces and other choice decomposing substances; bird droppings are a fine source of nutrition for forest flies. Bird-dung crab spiders like *Phrynarachne* take full advantage of this, waiting on leaves or other prominent surfaces for hungry flies to come and investigate the latest tempting blob of excrement. Once the fly is within reach, the spider seizes it with lightning speed and administers a deadly bite.

A FREAK BACK FROM THE DEAD In 1881 a spider hunter with the charming moniker of Octavius Pickard-Cambridge was staring at a 'fossil' that had come crawling out of the substrate as if to proclaim: 'Ha! You thought I had gone!' in much the same way that Prof J L B Smith would later stare at the resurrected coelacanth as it received instant worldwide recognition as a living fossil.

The archaea – or pelican spider – has languished in obscurity, a victim of its small size, northern hemisphere bias and irrational arachnophobia. The archaeid spiders with their giraffe necks and cannibalistic natures were first described from Baltic amber in 1854. Imagine Octavius's rapture when 27 years later, on an expedition to the dripping escarpments of the Red Isle, archaea tiptoed back into the list of species with which humans are privileged to share the earth.

'Bizarre' seems too mild an adjective for an arachnid that does not build a web, has massively elongated, spiked jaws that can extend outward at right angles, and stilt-like legs that enable it to hover over its prey. The fact that the victims are exclusively other spiders just adds to the archaea's mystique. Living archaeids have only been found on the southern land masses of Madagascar, Africa and Australia, yet more evidence that these places were once a continuous continent. Is it a coincidence that both archaea and the coelacanth are associated with an island renowned for the freakier designer labels of creation that so fascinate us?

BUGS, DRUGS AND LEMURS   *John Roff & Len de Beer*

A couple of fascinating stories have emerged from Madagascar concerning the relationship between bugs and drugs – and both involve lemurs.

The first relates to lemur hygiene. In 1996 black lemurs were being studied at Lokobe on Nosy Be as part of research into seed dispersal. A mature female was observed to grab a millipede (*Charactopygus* sp), bite it and rub the juices of its wounded body vigorously over her underside and tail. While enacting this strange ritual she half closed her eyes and salivated profusely with a silly grimace on her primate face. She was seen to do this a second time and it is speculated that the toxins in the millipede serve to protect her against parasites such as mosquitoes. Or maybe she just needed a fix?

In a relationship that goes the other way, the golden bamboo lemur – a species unknown to science until 1984 – has developed a startling specialism. These furry honey-coloured characters avoid competition with other resident species of lemur at Ranomafana by feeding exclusively on the shoots of *Cephalostachyum viguieri* – a giant bamboo that contains about 150mg of cyanide per kilogramme of fresh shoots. In so doing each individual consumes 12 times the theoretical lethal dose for a primate of its size per day – that's enough cyanide to kill three grown men. High concentrations of this deadly chemical are found in its dung and it turns out that this is the exclusive food source of a very specialised rainforest dung beetle. It is currently not known how either creature manages to survive this poisonous diet, but one thing is fairly certain: were the golden bamboo lemur to become extinct, the fascinating beetle that relies on its toxic excrement would follow suit.

Fortunately they prefer to do this well above head height. Their silk is so strong that it can be woven into fabric and Queen Victoria was the recipient of a pair of Malagasy spider silk stockings. More recently, British textile designer Simon Peers and US entrepreneur Nicholas Godley (*www.godleypeers.com*) spent eight years weaving one shawl and one cape from this naturally golden thread. The incredibly ambitious project required the silk of more than a million wild *Nephila* spiders, which were caught, 'milked' (or should that be 'silked'?) and then released by a team of some 80 people. It was woven using labour-intensive traditional methods into the two exquisite garments, which went on to be exhibited at New York's American Museum of Natural History and the V&A Museum in London.

Other arachnids in Madagascar include **scorpions** and **tarantulas**, though neither is frequently encountered.

FISH *With information from Derek Schuurman*
Freshwater species The inhabitants of Madagascar's abundant lakes, marshes, estuaries, rivers and mountain brooks have been as much isolated by history as those of the land. The most interesting species are the **cichlids** with their huge variety, colourful coats and endearing habits of childcare – they protect their young by offering their mouths as a retreat in times of danger. Other Malagasy species demonstrate the parental instinct, a feature rare in fish. Some of the island's **catfish** are also mouth-brooders, and male **mudskippers** in the mangroves defend their nest burrows with the vigour of a proud father.

Another major group is the **killifish**, which resemble the gouramis found in pet shops. Specialised **eels** live high up in mountain brooks, and blind **cave fish** are to be found in the underground rivers of western Madagascar, in some cases surviving entirely on the rich pickings of bat guano. The one problem with the island's fish is that they are not big and tasty. Consequently many exotic species have been introduced into the rivers and are regularly on display in the nation's markets. These new species naturally put pressure on the native stock and, as is so often the story, the less-vigorous Malagasy species have been all but wiped out. The main culprit seems to be the Asian snakehead (*Channa* spp). North Koreans farmed them in Madagascar in the 1980s, but following the first floods they spread to all the major lakes. The snakehead is a voracious predator and has severely reduced populations of endemic fish wherever it occurs. The other predatory fish which has decimated indigenous species is the largemouth bass, *Micropterus salmoides*.

Marine species More robust are the marine species to be found swimming off the island's 4,800km of coastline. Madagascar is legendary for its **shark** populations and a quick dip off the east coast should be considered carefully. On the opposite side, the Mozambique Channel is the most shark-infested stretch of water in the world, both in terms of number of species and number of individuals. However, swimming on this west coast is generally safe because the inshore waters are mostly shallow and protected by fringing **coral reefs**. Much of this reef is in good condition and bursting with life, outdoing even the Red Sea for fish diversity. The reefs are host to a typical Indo-Pacific community of clownfish, angelfish, butterflyfish, damselfish, tangs, surgeonfish, triggerfish, wrasse, groupers, batfish, blennies, gobies, boxfish, lionfish, moray eels, flutefish, porcupinefish, pufferfish, squirrelfish, sweetlips and the moorish idol.

Scuba-diving in Madagascar can therefore be very rewarding; see page 81 for practical information.

FROGS Stop and listen to the sounds of the rainforest. You may think those mysterious chirps, squeaks and clicks are birds and insects, but in most cases you would be wrong: the dominant sound in the Malagasy rainforest is often the frog chorus. Frogs are the only amphibians in Madagascar – no toads, newts or salamanders here – but with some 315 species already described (and at least 220 more in the pipeline, at various stages of the formal description process) they outnumber Madagascar's lemurs, chameleons and snakes combined.

All but three are endemic and they come in all colours and sizes, including some camouflaged like moss and bark. In contrast, the eye-catching **mantellas** exhibit dramatic colours to warn predators that they contain alkaloid toxins. Another frog it would be wise to avoid eating is the aptly named tomato frog. When attacked these obese, bright red frogs gum up the predator's mouth with a thick gluey substance secreted from their skin.

Each December, for just three or four days, *Aglyptodactylus* frogs gather in huge numbers to mate. Males (and sometimes also females) turn a bright canary yellow for the occasion. With tens of thousands of individuals gathered in a single marshy pool the noise of their croaking is deafening. After this colourful orgy each female will produce a clutch of up to 4,130 eggs. At the other end of the spectrum, green climbing mantellas lay just one egg at a time and exhibit unusual levels of paternal care in defending it.

New frog species are constantly being discovered in Madagascar, with at least 75 described in the last decade. But for many it is a race against extinction. Some 140 of Madagascar's frog species are considered threatened by extinction, 20 critically so.

Recently, an influx of exotic **Asian black-spined toads** came to light around Toamasina. This large species is similar to the cane toad that has caused untold ecological damage after being introduced to Australia to control pests in 1935. It is not known for sure how the black-spined toad reached Madagascar but a publicly leaked internal email from the Director of Corporate Social Responsibility for the Ambatovy mining project – with operations based at the heart of the outbreak – showed not only were they already aware of the problem in February 2014, but that they thought it was 'entirely possible... given the lax customs quarantine measures' that their company was responsible, adding 'this could cause quite some reputational damage'.

The toad looks set to spread across the island wreaking environmental havoc: it's a hardy, highly adaptable species that breeds prolifically; its toxic skin secretions pose a threat to native predators and even smaller predators may be poisoned by the eggs or tadpoles. The toad is voracious, feeding on insects, molluscs, centipedes, millipedes and scorpions as well as smaller frogs, reptiles and rodents. Even endemic species that would neither be consumed nor poisoned by the toads could still suffer from competition for resources with these invaders, or fall victim to foreign pathogens spread by them. For now it seems that the outbreak is still relatively localised – albeit numbering several million individuals – but experts looking into the feasibility of an eradication programme are not optimistic.

REPTILES The unique evolutionary history of Madagascar is typified by its reptiles. There are around 400 endemic species, representing 96% of the island's reptilian population. Some are derived from ancient Gondwana stock, many of which are more closely related to South American or Asian reptiles than to African ones. There are also large groups of closely related species marking the radiations that stemmed from African immigrations in more recent times. This is illustrated most dramatically by the **chameleons**. Madagascar is home to about half the world's chameleon species including the smallest and the largest. With impressive adaptive dexterity, they have dispersed throughout the habitats of the island to occupy every conceivable niche.

The family Chamaeleonidae is represented in Madagascar by four genera, the true chameleons – *Calumma* and *Furcifer* – and the little stump-tailed chameleons, *Brookesia* and *Palleon*. Unlike the true chameleons, their short tail is not prehensile.

Similar in their success have been the **geckos**. The hundred or so gecko species in Madagascar seem to be split between those that make every effort imaginable to camouflage themselves and those that go out of their way to stick out like a sore thumb. The spectacular **day geckos** (*Phelsuma* spp) sport dazzling emerald coats emblazoned with Day-Glo orange blotches intended for the attentions of the opposite sex and competitors. Once in their sights they bob their heads and wave their tails as if an extra guarantee of visibility is needed. In contrast a magnificently camouflaged **leaf-tailed gecko** (*Uroplatus* spp) could easily be resting on a tree trunk right under your nose without being noticed. With its flattened body, splayed tail, speckled eyes, colour-change tactics and complete lack of shadow, you may remain ignorant of its presence unless it gets nervous and gapes its large, red tongue in your direction.

A quiet scuttle on the floor of a western forest may well be a **skink**, while louder rustlings are likely to be one of the handsome **plated lizards**. However, the most significant disturbances, both in the forest and the academic world, are made by the **iguanids**. This group of mostly large lizards is primarily found in the Americas but no evidence of their presence has ever been discovered in Africa. The question of how some came to be in Madagascar is still a matter of debate.

THE THREAT OF CHYTRID FUNGUS

Devin Edmonds & Falitiana Rabemananjara

Large-scale mass die-offs of amphibians have been observed worldwide during the last three decades. The cause remained a mystery until a pathogenic fungus called *Batrachochytrium dendrobatidis* was discovered in 1998. When this microscopic chytrid fungus enters a new environment it can have devastating effects, causing numerous species to become extinct or decline dramatically.

The chytrid fungus was originally detected in Madagascar in 2010, first in the Makay Massif then later at sites as spread out as Ankarafantsika, Ranomafana and Ankaratra. Previous tests at these sites were negative, suggesting the fungus may have arrived only recently.

The future for Malagasy frogs seemed grim with news of chytrid's arrival. As a safeguard, a biosecure captive-breeding facility was established in Andasibe by Association Mitsinjo to ensure the survival of the most threatened species, and a nationwide surveillance strategy was implemented by the Chytrid Emergency Cell. These initiatives are part of the Sahonagasy Action Plan, the national strategy for amphibian conservation.

However, trepidation has gradually turned to cautious optimism as there has been little sign of disease actually impacting Malagasy frogs, for reasons that are yet to be fully understood.

You can help by reporting observations of any dead, dying or sick amphibians via www.sahonagasy.org and www.amphibians.org. And please help slow the spread of the disease by cleaning and drying all hiking and camping gear between sites; the fungus will die if completely dried out or heated above 40°C.

Devin Edmonds (e dedmonds@lemurreserve.org) works with Association Mitsinjo. Falitiana Rabemananjara is Coordinator of the Chytrid Emergency Cell.

Madagascar's four **boas** are in the same boat. They exist only as fossils in Africa, supplanted by the more stealthy pythons, but they do have distant relatives in South America. Most often seen are the Madagascar tree boas, recently split into eastern and western species (*Sanzinia madagascariensis* and *S. volontany* respectively), which although decorated in the same marbled glaze, vary in colour from orange or green (when juvenile) to grey and black, brilliant green or brown and even blue. The Madagascar ground boa and Dumeril's ground boa (*Acrantophis madagascariensis* and *A. dumerili*) are the largest of all but typically very placid – their scientific name comes from the Greek 'akrantos' meaning lazy. Of the remaining species of snake, the metre-long **Madagascar hog-nosed snake** (*Leioheterodon madagascariensis*), in its dazzling chequer-board of black and yellow, is one of the most frequently encountered, usually gliding across a carpet of leaves on the lookout for frogs.

Despite the fact that none of the island's snakes poses a danger to humans, the Malagasy are particularly wary of some species. The blood-red tail of one harmless tree snake (*Ithycyphus perineti*), known to the Malagasy as **fandrefiala**, is believed to have powers of possession. It is said to hypnotise cattle from up high, then drop down tail-first to impale its victim. Similar paranormal attributes are bestowed on other Malagasy reptiles. The chameleons, for example, are generally feared by the Malagasy, and when fascinated *vazaha* go to pick one up, this is often met with surprised gasps from the locals. Another reptile deeply embedded in the

Everybody thinks they know one thing about chameleons: that they change colour to match their background. *Wrong!* You have only to observe the striking Parson's chameleon, commonly seen at Andasibe, staying stubbornly green while transferred from boy's hand to tree trunk to leafy branch, to see that in some species at least this is a myth. Most chameleons are cryptically coloured to match their preferred resting place (there are branch-coloured chameleons, for instance, and leaf-coloured ones) and some do respond to a change of surroundings, but their abilities are mainly reserved for expressing emotion. An anxious chameleon will darken and grow stripes and an angry chameleon, faced with a territorial intruder, will change his colours dramatically. The most impressive displays, however, are reserved for sexual encounters. Enthusiastic males explode into a riot of spots, stripes and contrasting colours, while the female usually responds by donning a black cloak of disapproval. Only when feeling receptive will she present a brighter appearance.

Chameleons use body language more than colour to deter enemies. If you spot a chameleon on a branch you will note that his first reaction to being seen is to put the branch between you and him and flatten his body laterally so that he is barely visible. If you try to catch him, he will blow himself up, expand his throat, raise his helmet (if he has one) and hiss. His last resort will be to bite, jump, or try to run away. Fortunately they must be the slowest of all lizards, are easily caught, and pose for the camera with gloomy resignation (who can resist an animal that has a constantly down-turned mouth like a Victorian headmistress?). This slowness is another aspect of the chameleon's defence: when he walks, he moves like a leaf in the wind. In a tree, his best protection is to keep completely still. He can do this by having feet shaped like pliers and a prehensile tail so he can effortlessly grasp a branch, and eyes shaped like gun-turrets which can swivel 180° independently of each other, enabling him to view the world from front and back without moving his head.

There is often a striking colour difference between males and females. Many males have horns (occasionally used for fighting) or other nasal protuberances. You can also recognise the male by the bulge of the scrotal sac beneath the tail.

The chameleon achieves its colour change with a transparent epidermis, then three layers of different coloured cells. The cells are under control of the autonomic nervous system, expanding and contracting according to a range of stimuli. Change of colour occurs when one layer is more stimulated than others, and patterning when one group of cells receives maximum stimulation.

In the early 17th century there was the firm conviction that chameleons subsisted without food. A German author in 1609 mentioned the chameleon living 'entirely on air and dew' and Shakespeare refers several times to the chameleon's supposed diet of air. Perhaps at that time no-one had witnessed the tongue flash out through the bars of its cage to trap a passing insect. This tongue is as remarkable as any other feature of this extraordinary reptile. It was formerly thought that the club-shaped tip was sticky, but researchers discovered that captive chameleons had been catching much larger prey (lizards intended to coexist as cage-mates) than should be possible by this method. A high-speed video camera showed that a chameleon is able to use a pair of muscles at the tip of its tongue to form a suction cup milliseconds before it hits its prey. The whole manoeuvre takes about half a second.

folklore is the **Nile crocodile** which, although threatened throughout the island, takes on spiritual roles in some areas (see *Lake Antanavo*, page 359). A number of Madagascar's **tortoises** are severely threatened with extinction. Captive-breeding programmes at Ankarafantsika are currently successfully rearing the ploughshare and flat-tailed tortoises, and further south the Beza-Mahafaly reserve is protecting the handsome radiated tortoise. Four species of freshwater **turtle** inhabit the western waterways, the only endemic species being the big-headed or side-necked turtle, now also being bred at Ankarafantsika. Beyond, in the Mozambique Channel, there are **sea turtles** (hawksbill, loggerhead, olive ridley, leatherback and green turtles), many of which nest on Madagascar's remoter beaches. Sadly it is estimated that local fisheries are catching up to 16,000 turtles a year in the southwest alone, despite the practice being illegal. Even more concerning are recent reports of Chinese mafia plundering the west coast for turtles in vast numbers.

BIRDS *With information from Derek Schuurman*
Madagascar's scoresheet of birds is surprisingly short: of 294 species recorded there, only 210 regularly breed on the island. However, half of these are endemic, including five endemic families and 37 endemic genera, rendering Madagascar one of Africa's top birding hotspots.

Key endemics include the three rail-like **mesites** – the brown mesite in the rainforests, the white-breasted mesite in the western dry woods and the sub-desert mesite in the southwestern spiny bush. A similar allocation of habitats is more generously employed by the ten species of **coua**, which brighten forests with their blue-masked faces. Six species are ground-dwellers, occupying roles filled elsewhere by pheasants and roadrunners. Difficult to see are the **ground-rollers**, which quietly patrol the rainforest floor in their pretty uniforms. One member of the family, the long-tailed ground-roller, inhabits the southwestern spiny bush. The two **asities** resemble squat broadbills, to which they are related. In the eastern rainforests, the **sunbird-asities** appear as flashes of blue and green in the canopy, their down-turned beaks designed for the nectaries of canopy flowers.

Beak variation is remarkable among Madagascar's most celebrated endemic family, the **vangas**. All species have perfected their own craft of insect capture, filling the

Derek Schuurman

To see a fair spectrum of the endemics, divide your time between rainforest, spiny forest and dry deciduous forest. Add wetlands if time permits. During a stay of two or three weeks, you should be able to tick off most of the island's sought-after 'lifers'. Here are some birding hotspots:

EASTERN RAINFOREST Rainforest birding is best from mid-September to January. Around **Andasibe** you can see most of the broadly distributed rainforest endemics. Specials include collared nightjar, red-fronted coua, Rand's warbler, coral-billed nuthatch vanga and Tylas vanga. In rank herbaceous growth, look for Madagascar wood rail, white-throated rail and Madagascar flufftail. At **Mantadia** the pitta-like, scaly (rare) and short-legged ground-rollers occur, as do velvet asity, common sunbird-asity and brown emutail. Two wetlands nearby, **Torotorofotsy** and **Ampasipotsy**, hold Madagascar rail, Madagascar snipe, grey emutail and Madagascar swamp warbler. **Ranomafana** is best known for ground-rollers (pitta-like and rufous-headed especially) as well as brown mesite, yellow-browed oxylabes, Crossley's babbler, grey-crowned greenbul, forest rock thrush and Pollen's vanga. Velvet and common sunbird-asities are plentiful. On high ridges, look for yellow-bellied sunbird-asity, brown emutail and cryptic warbler. Birding in **Masoala** is exceptional. Specials include brown mesite, red-breasted coua, scaly ground-roller and the helmet and Bernier's vangas. The extremely rare Madagascar serpent eagle and Madagascar red owl have a stronghold here but both are highly elusive.

WESTERN TROPICAL DRY DECIDUOUS FORESTS An outstanding birding locality year-round, **Ankarafantsika** holds most of the western specials, including white-breasted mesite, Coquerel's coua, Schlegel's asity and Van Dam's vanga. Several other vangas (sickle-billed, rufous, Chabert's, white-headed, blue and rufous) abound. Raptors include the Madagascar fish eagle, Madagascar harrier-hawk and Madagascar sparrow-hawk. You can also find Madagascar crested ibis and Madagascar pygmy kingfisher. In the **Betsiboka Delta** look for Humblot's heron, Madagascar teal, Madagascar white ibis and Madagascar jacana.

TRANSITION FOREST A seriously unmissable experience year-round, **Zombitse** is included in all birding itineraries for the Appert's greenbul. It also holds an impressive variety of other endemics, such as giant and crested couas. Look out for Madagascar partridge, Madagascar buttonquail, Madagascar sandgrouse, greater and lesser vasa parrots, grey-headed lovebird, Madagascar green pigeon, Madagascar hoopoe, Thamnornis warbler, common newtonia, common jery, long-billed green sunbird, white-headed and blue vangas, and Sakalava weaver.

SPINY FOREST Birding in this zone is excellent year-round; start just before daybreak. The spiny bush at **Ifaty** is home to some extremely localised birds, notably sub-desert mesite, long-tailed ground-roller, Lafresnaye's vanga and Archbold's newtonia. Look for running coua, sub-desert brush-warbler, banded kestrel and Madagascar nightjar. On the lower coral ragg scrub around **St Augustine's Bay** and **Anakao**, you will find Verreaux's coua, littoral rock thrush and the recently described red-shouldered vanga. At puddles along the road look for Madagascar plover.

Natural History **FAUNA**

3

niches of various absent African bird groups, which they may resemble superficially. Vangas often flock together or with other forest birds, presenting a formidable offensive for local invertebrates. Most prominent is the sickle-billed vanga which parallels the tree-probing habits of Africa's wood hoopoes. The heavily carnivorous diet of shrikes is adopted by – among others – the hook-billed vanga and the dramatic, blue-billed helmet vanga, which resembles a small hornbill. Other vangas mimic nuthatches, flycatchers and tits. In short, if *The Beagle* had been caught by the West Wind Drift and Darwin had arrived in Madagascar instead of the Galapagos, the vangas would certainly have ensured that his train of thought went uninterrupted.

Malagasy representatives of families found elsewhere make up the bulk of the remaining birdlife. Herons, ibises, grebes, ducks and rails take up their usual positions in wetlands, including endemics such as the endangered Madagascar teal of some western mangroves, and the colourful Madagascar malachite kingfisher. Game birds include the attractive Madagascar partridge and Madagascar sandgrouse. The impressive Madagascar crested ibis, Madagascar blue and green pigeons and tuneful vasa parrots occupy the various strata of vegetation. More colourful birds include the grey-headed lovebird, Madagascar bee-eater, Madagascar paradise flycatcher, Madagascar hoopoe, Madagascar red fody dressed in scarlet during the breeding season (October to March), souimanga and long-billed green sunbirds, and the crested drongo with its black plumage, forked tail and silly crest. The four rock thrushes look like European robins in morning suits. The confiding endemic Madagascar magpie robin sports black-and-white attire and flirts fearlessly with humans.

The Madagascar kestrel is joined by other **raptors** such as the banded kestrel, the exceptionally handsome Madagascar harrier-hawk, Frances's sparrow-hawk, Madagascar buzzard, Madagascar cuckoo-hawk and seven species of owl. The two endemic eagles – the critically endangered Madagascar fish eagle of the west coast and the Madagascar serpent eagle of the northeastern rainforests – are among the world's rarest raptors. Like the Madagascar red owl, the serpent eagle had managed to escape detection for several decades and was feared extinct, until both species were found thriving discreetly in various rainforest sites. The ultra-rare Sakalava rail was also recently rediscovered in the Mahavavy Delta, which holds a small breeding population.

In 2011, a new species, the **tsingy wood rail**, was described from a dry forest in the central west. But the most sensational avian news to emerge from Madagascar in recent years was the discovery in 2006 of fewer than two dozen **Madagascar pochards** living on a remote northern lake, Lake Matsaborimena. This diving duck had not been seen alive since 1992. Monitoring revealed that the chicks were not surviving so experts launched an emergency rescue plan. A local hotel was commandeered as a temporary centre for the incubation and hatching of eggs. Durrell Wildlife Conservation Trust successfully reared 23 chicks from wild-collected eggs and then in early 2012 the first 18 captive-bred ducks were hatched as part of an ambitious breeding programme. By 2016, there were 80 living at their facility. A suitable wild habitat has been identified and is being restored with a view to commencing a release programme by 2018.

MAMMALS Madagascar's land mammals are the prize exhibit in the island's incredible menagerie. They exist as an obscure assortment of primates, insectivores, carnivores, bats and rodents, representing the descendants of parties of individuals who, curled up in hollow trunks or skipping across temporary islands, accidentally completed the perilous journey from eastern Africa to the island beyond the horizon at different times over the last 100 million years. Once established, they gradually spread through the diverse habitats of their paradise island, all the time evolving and creating new species.

THE AYE-AYE   *Hilary Bradt*

The strangest lemur is the aye-aye, *Daubentonia madagascariensis*. It took a while for scientists to decide that it was a lemur at all: for years it was thought to be a peculiar type of squirrel. Now it is classified in a family of its own, Daubentoniidae. The aye-aye seems to have been assembled from the leftover parts of a variety of animals. It has the teeth of a rodent (they never stop growing), the ears of a bat, the tail of a fox and the hands of no living creature, since the middle finger is like that of a skeleton. It's this finger which so intrigues scientists, as it shows the aye-aye's adaptation to its way of life. In Madagascar it fills the ecological niche occupied elsewhere in the world by woodpeckers. The aye-aye evolved to use its skeletal finger to winkle grubs from under the bark of trees. The aye-aye's fingers are unique among lemurs in another way – it has claws not fingernails (except on the big toe). When searching for grubs the aye-aye taps on the wood with its finger, its enormous ears pointing like radar dishes to detect a cavity. It can even tell whether this is occupied by a nice fat grub. Another anatomical feature of the aye-aye that sets it apart from other primates is that it has inguinal mammary glands. In other words, its teats are between its back legs.

Although destruction of habitat is the chief threat to this fascinating animal's survival, it is also at risk because of its supposedly evil powers. Rural people believe the aye-aye to be the herald of death. If one is seen near a settlement it must be killed, and even then the only salvation may be to burn down the village.

'I WANT TO SEE AN AYE-AYE' A glimpse of Madagascar's weirdest lemur is a goal for many visitors. And many go away disappointed. When weighing up whether to try to see one in the wild or to settle for a captive animal, you should bear in mind that the aye-aye is a rare, nocturnal and largely solitary species. Most of its waking hours are spent foraging for food in the upper canopy; only occasionally does it descend to the ground. So even in the reserve of Nosy Mangabe, which was created for aye-ayes, you will be lucky to see two distant shining eyes retreating from your torch beam.

It is the most widespread of all lemurs, occurring in most of the national parks, yet it is so rarely sighted that even most full-time forest guides have never seen one. These days, the best chances of a truly wild sighting are at Daraina or Fontenay Nature Park (page 357). Alternatively, there are semi-wild aye-ayes living on the tiny eponymous island at Mananara (see page 312). But both places can be challenging to get to so seeing caged animals might be your only practical option. In theory Tsimbazaza zoo in Antananarivo has a day-to-night house (allowing you to see the creatures awake in daytime) but in practice it is rarely open nowadays and conditions here have deteriorated terribly. A far better option is Ivoloina Park near Toamasina. The park is not routinely open during the aye-ayes' active hours, but dusk visits are possible if you book in advance (see page 307).

Outside Madagascar, 13 zoos have aye-ayes, often in night-reversed cages. These include ZSL London, Bristol and Jersey (the late Gerald Durrell's zoo) in the UK and Duke Lemur Center in North Carolina, USA. Since the first captive birth in 1992 at Jersey, 97 have been born across a dozen zoos. There are presently 20 in the European breeding programme, 26 in the USA and nine in Japan.

Diurnal (day-active) lemurs are the largest and easiest to identify. They are usually found in groups of between three and 12 individuals. In many of the island's renowned wildlife locations two or more species can been seen relatively easily.

Ring-tailed lemur

RING-TAILED LEMUR (*Lemur catta*) Instantly recognisable by its banded tail. More terrestrial than other lemurs and lives in troops of up to 20 animals in the south and southwest, notably in Anja Park, Isalo, Andohahela and Andringitra national parks, and Berenty Reserve.

RUFFED LEMURS (genus *Varecia*) Large lemurs commonly found in zoos but difficult to see in the wild. There are two species and both live in eastern rainforests: the black-and-white ruffed lemur is found sporadically in pristine areas and can sometimes be seen in Mantadia and Ranomafana national parks, and on Nosy Mangabe, while the red ruffed lemur is restricted to Masoala and Makira.

TRUE LEMURS (genus *Eulemur*) All are roughly cat-sized, with long noses, and live in trees. A confusing characteristic is that males and females of most species have somewhat different markings and coat colours. The well-known black lemur (*E. macaco*), from northwest Madagascar, notably Nosy Komba and Lokobe, is perhaps the best example. Only males are black; females are chestnut brown. Visitors to Ranomafana and Mantadia often see

Black-and-white ruffed lemur

red-bellied lemurs (*E. rubriventer*); males have white tear-drop face-markings, while females have creamy white bellies. In far northern reserves crowned lemurs (*E. coronatus*) are common: males are sandy-brown, females are grey, and both sport triangular crowns.

The species of brown lemur present the ultimate challenge, but fortunately their ranges do not overlap, so locality helps identification. In most cases males are more distinctively marked and look quite different from females which tend to be uniformly brown. Two neighbouring male brown lemurs have beautiful cream or white ear-tufts and side whiskers: Sanford's brown lemur (*E. sanfordi*) is found in far northern reserves, while the white-fronted brown lemur (*E. albifrons*) occurs in the northeast and males have bushy white heads and Santa Claus-like side whiskers. Further south you will find common brown lemur (*E. fulvus*) in both the east (eg: Andasibe-Mantadia National Park) and the

Collared brown lemur

northwest (eg: Ankarafantsika). Red-fronted brown lemurs (*E. rufus*) live in the southeast and southwest. The males of the two variations of collared brown lemur (*E. collaris* and *E. cinereiceps*) unsurprisingly have distinctive tufty fur collars and both occur in far southeastern areas, but the latter has an extremely restricted range and is very rare.

BAMBOO LEMURS (genera *Hapalemur* and *Prolemur*) Smaller than the true lemurs, with short muzzles and round faces. They occur in smaller groups (one to four animals), cling to vertical branches, and feed mainly on bamboo. You may see the commonest species, grey bamboo lemur (*H. griseus*), in several eastern parks including Marojejy, Andasibe-Mantadia and Ranomafana. The very much rarer golden bamboo lemur (*H. aureus*) and greater bamboo lemur (*P. simus*) are, realistically, only seen at Ranomafana.

Grey bamboo lemur

INDRI (*Indri indri*) The largest lemur and the only one with virtually no tail. This black-and-white teddy-bear lemur is unmistakable, having a characteristic eerie wailing song. It is seen in and around Andasibe.

Indri

SIFAKAS (genus *Propithecus*) Sifakas belong to the same family as the indri, and have characteristic long back legs. Some sifakas (pronounced *shee*fahk) are the famous dancing lemurs that bound upright over the ground and leap spectacularly from tree to tree.

The commonest sifakas are mainly white and are quite unmistakable. Verreaux's sifaka (*P. verreauxi*) shares its southern habitat with the ring-tailed lemur, while its cousin the Coquerel's sifaka (*P. coquereli*), which has chestnut-maroon arms and legs, is seen at Ankarafantsika in the northwest. You may also see the stunningly beautiful diademed sifaka (*P. diadema*) in Mantadia and the rich chocolate-coloured Milne-Edwards' sifaka (*P. edwardsi*) at Ranomafana.

Verreaux's sifaka

Because they are generally smaller than the diurnal lemurs (sometimes *very* tiny) and active primarily after dark, the various types of nocturnal lemur are often more challenging to identify. However, night walks in Madagascar's forests are safe and very exciting as you can never really be sure what you might discover. Two types of nocturnal lemur – sportive lemurs and woolly lemurs – often helpfully sleep or doze in the open during the day so are regularly seen by tourists.

Brown mouse lemur

MOUSE LEMURS (genus *Microcebus*) This group are the smallest of all primates: the most minuscule is Madame Berthe's mouse lemur (*M. berthae*) which could sit in an egg cup and weighs 30g. As a group these are the most abundant type of lemur and are generally common in virtually all native forests types; they even survive in some forest fragments where other lemurs have disappeared. There's now quite a number of species (21 at the last count), which makes accurate identification confusing and difficult. The easiest places to see them are Andasibe-Mantadia and Ranomafana national parks in the east and Ankarafantsika, Ankarana and Berenty reserves in drier areas.

DWARF LEMURS (genera *Cheirogaleus*, *Mirza* and *Allocebus*) Dwarf lemurs are mostly squirrel-sized and run along branches in a similar fashion. Some, like the fat-tailed dwarf lemur (*C. medius*), become dormant during the winter, sleeping in tree holes and surviving on reserves of fat stored in their tails. Dwarf lemurs from the genus *Cheirogaleus* have distinctive dark spectacle-like rings

Greater dwarf lemur

Eastern fork-marked lemur

around their eyes which helps identification. Giant dwarf lemurs (genus *Mirza*) are unusual as they are sometimes predatory and eat baby birds, frogs, lizards and even small snakes. For a long time it was through the hairy-eared dwarf lemur (*A. trichotis*) was exceedingly rare; it now turns out to have been overlooked and is actually quite widespread; it can even be seen in Andasibe-Mantadia National Park. It is about the size of a large mouse lemur, but look out for its distinctive ear-tufts.

FORK-MARKED LEMURS (genus *Phaner*) These lemurs prefer to live high in the canopy so are often rather difficult to see and identify. Their distribution is also somewhat sporadic. Perhaps the best places to look are the dry western forests such as Kirindy and Zombitse. The dark fork markings on the face are highly distinctive.

SPORTIVE LEMURS (genus *Lepilemur*) Sportive lemurs mostly spend the day in tree holes from which they peer drowsily. Their name is something of a misnomer as they are rarely particularly energetic, even at night. They cling vertically to tree trunks and, after dark, their high-pitched calls are often a feature of the forests they inhabit. Recently scientists have described many new species (the genus now contains 26 species) and in appearance they are often very similar. The best guide for identification is locality.

Small-toothed sportive lemur

WOOLLY LEMURS (genus *Avahi*) Woolly lemurs also adopt a vertical posture and are similar in size to sportive lemurs, but have round, owl-like faces and conspicuous white thighs. They often sleep in the tangled branches of trees. Many park guides use 'woolly lemur' and 'avahi' interchangeably as the common name. One recently described species is named after British comic actor John Cleese: Cleese's woolly lemur (*A. cleesei*) is currently known only from Tsingy de Bemaraha National Park.

Western woolly lemur

AYE-AYE (*Daubentonia madagascariensis*) This gargoyle of a lemur is Madagascar's most bizarre mammal. Many people think aye-ayes are small, but in fact they are larger than a domestic cat and have huge bushy tails. However, it is their face and hands that make them unique; with teeth like a rabbit's, ears like a bat's and fingers like Edward Scissorhands' there is nothing else to compare. Once thought to be on the brink of extinction but now known to be quite widespread (albeit at low densities), it is theoretically possible to see one in many reserves. The chances are extremely slight but you could get lucky. For more on the aye-aye, see the box on page 55.

Aye-aye

Biologists often refer to Madagascar as a museum housing living fossils. This is because almost all the mammals on the island today closely resemble groups that once shone elsewhere but have since been replaced by more advanced species. Although evolution has certainly occurred on the island, it seems to have plodded on with less momentum than back in Africa. Hence, while their cousins on the mainland were subjected to extreme competition with the species that were to develop subsequently, the Malagasy mammals were able to stick more rigidly to their original physiques and behaviours.

The word 'cousins' is especially poignant when applied to the lemurs, for across Africa primate evolution was eventually to lead to the ascent of humankind. How opportune then for an understanding of our own natural history that one of our direct ancestors managed to end up on this island sanctuary and remain, sheltered from the pressures of life elsewhere, relatively true to its original form for us to appreciate 35 million years later.

Lemurs Lemurs are to a biologist what the old masters are to an art critic: they may not be contemporary, but historically they are very important and they are beautiful to look at. Lemurs belong to a group of primates called the prosimians, a word which means 'before monkeys'. Their basic body design evolved about 40–50

BATS	Julie Hanta Razafimanahaka & Richard Jenkins, Madagasikara Voakajy

Bats make a significant contribution to tropical diversity but in Madagascar they have only recently received the concerted attention of biologists. New species continue to be discovered. Over ten new endemic bats have been described since 2004, bringing the total to some 43 species (31 of which are thought to be endemic) with others still in the process of being formally described. The megachiropterans (fruit bats) are represented by three endemic species (*Pteropus rufus*, *Eidolon dupreanum* and *Rousettus madagascariensis*); they feed on flowers, fruits and leaves. Seven families of insectivorous microchiropterans are also found in Madagascar, including the endemic family of sucker-footed bats (genus *Myzopoda*).

Bats are threatened by habitat loss, persecution (as fruit-crop pests and unwanted house guests), hunting (bushmeat) and roost-site disturbance. They are not protected under Malagasy law and only populations inside reserves or at sacred sites receive any protection. Madagasikara Voakajy is currently working to create five new protected areas to safeguard fruit bat roosts. Many species are gregarious and roost in cavities (eg: caves, tree holes, roofs) or on vegetation.

Madagasikara Voakajy is a Malagasy conservation organisation dedicated to conserving the island's bats and their habitats. Our experts study all aspects of bat ecology and operate a conservation awareness campaign. There are many bat roosts that remain unknown to conservationists and we would very much like to hear from anyone who finds a bat cave or tree roost not mentioned here (e *voakajy@voakajy.mg*; *www.madagasikara-voakajy.org*).

The Madagascar flying fox *P. rufus* is large (wingspan 1.2m) and forms colonies of up to 5,000 individuals. It makes short flights during the day and excellent viewing rewards patient observers. Good tourist sites to see them include Berenty, Nosy Tanikely, Nosy Mangabe, the mangroves near Anjajavy, and a number of new protected areas near Lake Alaotra. The Madagascar straw-coloured bat *E. dupreanum* is best seen in the Grotte des Chauve-Souris at Ankarana or flying around rock overhangs at Cap Sainte Marie. Adventurous types can visit Ankorabe.

million years ago. With stereoscopic colour vision, hands that could grasp branches, a brain capable of processing complex, learned information, extended parental care and an integrated social system incorporating a wide range of sound and scent signals, the lemurs were the latest model in evolution's comprehensive range of tree-dwelling mammals. Their reign lasted until about 35 million years ago, when a new model – the monkey – evolved. Monkeys were superior in a number of ways: they were faster, could think more quickly, used their vision more effectively and were highly dexterous. Their success rapidly drove the less adaptable prosimians to extinction across most of the world. A few stowaways managed to take refuge in Madagascar, a corner of the world never reached by more advanced primates (until the recent arrival of humans). Today we see the results of 35 million years of leisurely evolution. The single ancestral species has adapted into around 111 recognised varieties and instead of gazing at inanimate rocks we have the luxury of being able to watch, hear and smell the genuine article.

Smell is an extremely important aspect of lemur lives. Through scents, lemurs communicate a wide range of information, such as who's in charge, who is fertile, who is related to whom and who lives where. They supplement this language with a vocal one. Chirps, barks and cries reinforce hierarchies in lemur societies, help to defend territories against other groups and warn of danger. Socially the lemurs show

The smallest Malagasy fruit bat, *R. madagascariensis*, lives in caves and a large colony is resident at the aforementioned Ankarana Cave. It is also a flagship species for the new protected area at Ambatofotsy. They betray their presence by noisy chattering and reflective orange eyeshine. The best time to view fruit bats is during June and July when the kapok trees are flowering in the west. All three species flock to these trees at night to feed on nectar and can be observed in torchlight at close quarters.

The circuits at Tsingy de Bemaraha offer the chance of seeing some roosting microchiropterans. Other reserves with bat caves include Ankarana, Anjohibe, Tsingy de Namoroka and Tsimanampetsotsa. House-roosting bats can be seen at dusk as they emerge to feed; a good site to watch this is at the post office in Andasibe. Mauritian tomb bats can be seen in a rock crevice on the Manambolo circuit at Tsingy de Bemaraha and also roosting on tree trunks in the campsite at Ankarafantsika.

There is a roost site of *E. dupreanum* at Cap Sainte Marie that can be seen from one of the tourist trails as it passes a deep valley. The bats are sometimes active in the day and can be seen flying between different rock overhangs.

There is a *P. rufus* roost on Nosy Atafana, an offshore island in the marine reserve.

Madagasikara Voakajy can advise on how to visit the new protected area of Analalava near Lake Alaotra dedicated to the conservation of *P. rufus* (motorbike or 4x4 required).

Bats are sensitive to disturbance while roosting. Always ask advice from your guide and use common sense: avoid handling bats, avoid shining bright lights at roosting bats, keep quiet at roosts and don't try to provoke resting bats into flight. Bats are key species in Madagascar's fragile environment; they disperse seeds over vast distances and pollinate trees such as baobabs. They tend to be vilified by most people, eaten by some and ignored by the rest. By showing a genuine interest in bats when you visit protected areas you can help Madagasikara Voakajy and its partners to raise bats on to the conservation agenda.

a great variety of organisational skills and the strategy used by each species is largely dependent on the nature of their diet. The small, quick-moving, insectivorous lemurs such as the mouse lemurs and dwarf lemurs are nocturnal and largely solitary except during the mating season when they pair up with a member of the opposite sex. Literally surrounded by their insect food, they require only small territories, hence they never cover large distances and spend their entire lives in the trees. A different way of life is led by the larger leaf-eating species such as the indri. In a rainforest there is no shortage of leaves; however, as a food source leaves are poor in nutrients, so each lemur needs to consume a large amount. Leaf eaters therefore tend to collect in small groups, together defending their territory of foliage with scents and often loud calls which in the dense forests are the best forms of communication.

Their sex lives vary, but most of these species have family groups in which a single male dominates. The most social lemurs on the island are those with a more varied diet concentrating on fruit, but also including seeds, buds and leaves. These include the ring-tailed lemur, ruffed lemur and true lemurs. The diet of these species requires active foraging over large areas during the day, so in order to defend their expansive territory, and to protect themselves in daylight, these lemurs form troops. The societies are run by matriarchs, who organise the troop's movement, courtship and defence. But there are also whole groups of males, which often separate for week-long excursions away from the home base. Usually operating in more open country, these lemurs use a wide range of visual signals to accompany their scents and sounds, making them particularly entertaining to watch.

Perhaps the most entertaining of all is the ring-tailed lemur. Among lemurs it forms the largest and liveliest troops. Each troop typically stirs at dawn, warms up with a period of sunbathing and then, guided by the matriarchs, heads off to forage, breaking at noon for a siesta. The troop moves along the ground, each individual using its distinctive tail to maintain visual contact with the others. If out of eyesight, the troop members use the catlike mews that prompted their scientific name, *Lemur catta*. By dusk they return to the sleeping trees which they use for three or four days before moving on. In the April breeding season the males become less tolerant of each other and engage in stink fights where, after charging their tails with scent from glands on their wrists, they waft them antagonistically at opponents. Similar aggressive interactions occur when two troops of ring-tails meet, sometimes leading to serious injury or death, but usually one side backs down before it reaches this stage.

Even for a keen naturalist, sorting out Madagascar's 111-plus species and subspecies of lemur can be challenging. The illustrated layman's guide on pages 56–9 should help you put names to faces. The first box covers diurnal (day-active) species; the second describes the nocturnal ones more likely encountered on a night walk.

Tenrecs Employing one of the most primitive mammalian body plans, the tenrecs have been able to fill the vacancies created by an absence of shrews, moles and hedgehogs, and in doing so have diversified into about 34 different species. Five of these are called the spiny tenrecs, most looking just like hedgehogs, some with yellow and black stripes. However, the largest, the tailless common tenrec (*Tenrec ecaudatus*), has lost the majority of its spines. Not only is this species the largest insectivore in the world at 1.5kg, but it can also give birth to enormous litters which the mother feeds with up to 24 nipples. The 26 species of furred tenrecs are mostly shrew-like in stature, although three species look and act more like moles, and one has become aquatic, capturing small fish and freshwater shrimps in the fast-flowing streams of the *hauts plateaux*.

Rodents Highly successful elsewhere, rodents have made little impression on Madagascar. There are 25 or so species, most of which are nocturnal. The easiest to see is the red forest rat (*Nesomys rufus*) which is active during the day. The most unusual are the rabbit-like giant jumping rat (*Hypogeomys antimena*) from the western forests and the two tree-dwelling *Brachytarsomys* species which have prehensile tails.

BATGIRL GOES MISSING   *Paul Racey*

The sucker-footed bats belong to Madagascar's only endemic bat family, Myzopodidae, which was thought to contain just a single species until a second was described in 2007. Both the eastern and western sucker-footed bats have a distinctive appearance, with upper lips extending beyond the lower, large broad ears and adhesive pads on their thumbs and soles.

Mahefa Ralisata and I studied the eastern sucker-footed bat at Kianjavato in southeast Madagascar, where they live around a coffee research station. We fitted tiny radios to bats that we caught in mist nets set across forest trails. By following the radio signals, we learned where the bats were feeding – among coffee plantations, over rice paddies and in open spaces in degraded forest.

The signals also led us to the bats' roosts in the central leaves of travellers' trees (*Ravenala*). Each month, this charismatic tree produces one new leaf, which starts as a tightly coiled tube. As it begins to unfurl, it forms a gradually widening tube in which the bats roost, head up, holding on to the smooth surface with their adhesive pads. Once the leaf opens completely, it no longer provides protection and the bats must find another at the right stage of development. Despite searching banana trees and caves, we only ever found the bats roosting in these young *Ravenala* leaves.

Our study received a huge boost when we were joined by Likely, a guide who was able to free-climb the trees. He would fit a large bag over the unfurling leaf and lower it to the ground, whereupon we would discover as many as 53 bats sheltering within. Through netting trails and checking roosts we caught about 300 individuals, some several times. As the years passed, a curious pattern emerged: every last bat we found was male. Seven years came and went but not once did we find a female.

We know the females must be nearby because juvenile males arrive at our study site twice a year, and young bats can't fly long distances. Such extreme sexual segregation is unprecedented in mammals, so why do these females live apart? The honest answer is nobody yet knows; I don't have a credible hypothesis. And as for where the females are hiding, that is still a mystery too. Unfortunately satellite tags tiny enough to be fitted to a 10g bat haven't yet been developed (and the range of radio tags is too limited to track males going in search of mates) so for now the location of the females' secret hideaway remains a tantalising enigma.

Paul Racey (e p.a.racey@exeter.ac.uk) has worked in Madagascar for more than 25 years. He has some 300 academic papers to his name, as well as an endemic Malagasy bat species named after him. He has received recognition for his outstanding achievements in bat studies from both the UK Bat Conservation Trust and the North American Society for Bat Research.

Carnivores The island's ten carnivores were long thought to be civets and mongooses, but only quite recently has it been shown that they belong to a separate family (Eupleridae) all descended from a single ancestor. The largest, the fossa (*Cryptoprocta ferox*), is very catlike with an extremely long tail which assists balance during canopy-based lemur hunts. This extremely shy creature is quite widespread but rarely seen – except at Kirindy (see pages 420–1). The size of a chubby cat, the striped civet (*Fossa fossana*) hunts in the eastern rainforests for rodents, and a third, very secretive animal, the falanouc (*Eupleres goudotii*) inhabits the northeastern rainforests where it lives almost entirely on earthworms. Each of Madagascar's forest types plays host to mongoose-like euplerids. There are six species in all, the most commonly seen being the ring-tailed mongoose (*Galidia elegans*) which varies in colour but is typically a handsome, rusty red.

Bats Possessing, among mammals, the unique gift of flight, it is perhaps surprising that only a quarter of Madagascar's bats can also be found beyond its shores. There are three species of fruit bat which are active during the day, very noisy, large and unfortunately often on the Malagasy menu. If the fruit bats look like flying foxes (their alternative name), then the 40 species remaining are not unlike flying mice. These are nocturnal, prefer moths to figs and find them by echolocation. They tend to have shell-like ears and distorted noses. It is known that some moths outwit these bats by chirping back at them in mid-flight, scrambling the echo and sending the aggressor off into the night.

Marine mammals At least 37 marine mammals are known from the waters of Madagascar including, most famously, the **humpback whale**. Antongil Bay marks the northern extent of their migrations. The whales calve just beyond the coral reefs in July and August, and after this period migrate south as far as the Antarctic coast to feed. **Dugongs** (sea cows) are extremely rare. The Vezo of the west coast share their fishing grounds with an abundance of **dolphins**, and regard them as kin. If a dolphin is discovered dead they wrap it in shrouds and bury it with their ancestors.

In 2015, scientists working around Nosy Be announced several sightings of **Omura's whale**. Although this species had been described in 2003, it had hitherto

---

SEX AND THE FOREST   *Hilary Bradt*

It's a jungle out there! I don't know what it is about Madagascar, but when it comes to male equipment the animals seem to be more interestingly and excitingly endowed here than anywhere else in the world. For starters there's the parrot that does it with a golf ball (see box, pages 408–9), but the fossa puts even that eye-watering performance in the shade. For a few days each year the females are penetrated by the largest penis in proportion to its size of any mammal. This impressive member is supported by a baculum, or penis bone, which enables the lucky fellow to perform for up to 6 hours at a time. To the female, size definitely does matter, and if her fellow isn't up to scratch she'll disengage and try someone else.

While size is everything to the parrot and fossa, reptiles such as chameleons go one better. One and one makes two, or a hemipenis. The two penes (yes, that really is the plural) are like a key: they only fit the female of the species, thus avoiding the risk of trying to get off with the wrong lady.

been known only from dead carcasses in Japan. The team was able to confirm this surprising identification after spending three years gathering video footage, hydrophone recordings and DNA samples.

MADAGASCAR'S ECOSYSTEMS

Madagascar's amazing array of habitats is the result of the effects of ocean currents, prevailing winds and geological forces. Rain is heaviest in the north and east, and lightest in the south and west. Rainfall is the single most significant factor in creating habitat characteristics, so a complex spectrum of habitat types has resulted within a relatively small area. Madagascar's geology brings further variety by creating undulating coastlines, broad riverbeds and estuaries, shallow ocean shelves for coral reefs, high mountainous slopes and plateaux, a wealth of soil types and even bizarre limestone 'forests' riddled with caves. These various habitats house a wealth of ecosystems, the most important of which are described below.

RAINFORESTS The spine of mountains which border the central plateau forces the saturated air arriving from over the Indian Ocean to drop its moisture on to the east coast of the island. Madagascar's rainforests therefore form in a distinct band adjacent to the east coast where the continuous rainfall is high enough to sustain the evergreen canopy trees. Known as the Madagascar Sylva, this band of forest – now seriously fragmented by deforestation – extends inland only as far as the mountain range, so it is broadest in the northeast. The southern end of the range near Taolagnaro (Fort Dauphin) forms a unique but fragile divide between the evergreen rainforest to the east and the arid spiny forest beyond.

Littoral rainforest (sea level) Very little of Madagascar's unique coastal, or littoral, rainforest remains. Rooted in sand, washed with salty air, battered by cyclones and bordering lagoons and marshes, coastal forests harbour a very unusual community. The architecture of the forest is similar to the more widespread lowland forest, but the plants are different: they are salt-tolerant and highly efficient at extracting water and nutrients from the shallow, porous sand beneath. *Good example: Tampolo Forestry Station.*

Lowland rainforest (0–800m) Most of the rainforest in Madagascar is lowland – that is, below around 800m. This type of forest is hot and sticky, with humidity at 100% and annual rainfall of up to 500cm. The forest canopy is 30m above the ground, with few trees emerging beyond this level. Butterflies flutter as monstrous beetles and myriad ants and termites patrol the forest floor.

Lemurs skip among the branches and lianas which serve as highways between the forest floor and the world above. Preying on the lemurs, the fossa is at home among the canopy branches, while above the leaves birds of prey and fruit bats patrol. Tenrecs and forest birds rummage through the leaf litter, and the Madagascar striped civet and mongooses wait to pick off any unsuspecting prey. *Good examples: Masoala, Nosy Mangabe and the lower parts of Marojejy.*

Montane rainforest (800–1,300m) As altitude increases and air temperature drops, the tree species of the lowland rainforests give way to those more able to tolerate the cooler conditions. These species have lower canopies and are the foundation of the montane rainforest. The change from lowland to montane forest is a gradual one influenced by a number of factors. In southern Madagascar, montane forest occurs lower down; in the warmer north lowland forest may continue up to around 900m.

Once in true montane forest the landscape is very different. Not only is the canopy lower and the temperature much cooler, the understorey is far more dense. Tree ferns and bamboos litter the forest floor and there is a tight tangle of trunks, roots and woody lianas, all sporting furry lichens and lines of bright fungi.

Montane reserves are excellent places to spot mammals and birds, including many lemur species. *Good examples: Ranomafana, Andasibe-Mantadia, Montagne d'Ambre and parts of Marojejy.*

Cloudforest (above 1,300m)
The forest beyond 1,300m has an even lower canopy and is characteristically thick with ferns and mosses. It is properly called high-altitude montane rainforest, but because it is often cloaked in mists it is also known as cloudforest. The low temperatures slow down decomposition, creating waterlogged peaty soils in valleys. Termites cannot live at these altitudes, so large earthworms and beetles take their place as detritivores. The canopy can be as low as 10m, and in places the understorey gives way to a thicket of shrubs. Mosses, lichens and ferns inhabit every branch and stone, and cover the floor along with forest succulents and *Bulbophyllum* orchids. *Good examples: Marojejy and Andringitra.*

DRY DECIDUOUS FOREST
The magnificent dry forests of the west once covered the vast lowland plain west of the hauts plateaux. Now only a few patches remain, sharing the coast with the mangroves, bordering the largest rivers of the south and dotted about the plains near Isalo and inland from Mahajanga. The forest supports far fewer species than the eastern rainforests but has higher levels of endemism. The trees are less densely arranged and the canopy is typically 12–20m high.

The canopy leaves are shed during the seven or eight months of the dry season and a carpet of leaves begins to accumulate on the forest floor shortly after the rains stop in May. These decompose creating a thick humus layer in the soil. During this dry period much of the wildlife goes to ground, quite literally: amphibians and insects bury themselves in the soil to await the return of the rains.

Sifakas, sportive lemurs, brown lemurs and the ubiquitous mouse lemurs are particularly in evidence. Vangas live in the canopy and tuneful vasa parrots make territories in the understorey. The deep litter layer is home to tenrecs, tortoises, boas and hog-nosed snakes. Fossas and mongooses regularly run along their patrol trails, sometimes pursuing their prey up into the canopy. *Good examples: Kirindy, Ankarafantsika and Berenty.*

INSELBERG AND *TSINGY* COMMUNITIES
In the west, where the underlying rocks are exposed, localised communities of specialised plants and animals develop. Since rain simply drains off – or through – the rocks, all the residents must be tolerant of desiccation. Magnificent *Euphorbia*, *Aloe*, *Kalanchoe* and *Pachypodium* species grip on to tiny crevices, bringing foliage and flowers to the rock face. The insects, birds and lemurs rely on these for sustenance, only retreating in the heat of the day to rest beneath the trees in nearby canyons.

Plants and animals are also to be found among the knife-edge pinnacles of the spectacular limestone karst massifs known as *tsingy* (see page 416). These bizarre eroded landscapes enable a complex mosaic of communities to live side by side. The towering pinnacles which sport the succulents are in fact the ornate roofs of extensive cave systems below. These caves are inhabited by bats and rodents, with

TAVY   *Jamie Spencer*

Slash-and-burn farming, *tavy* in Malagasy, is to blame for the permanent destruction of the rainforest. Even those practising tavy agree with this. They also respect the forest and they can see that tavy greatly jeopardises the future for the next generations. So why destroy what you love and need?

One answer to a very complex question is the practical need. In Madagascar poverty is extreme and there are few options. Life's priority is to feed your family and children. Rice, the food staple, is grown both on the flat ground in sustainable paddy fields, and on the steep slopes of slashed and burned forest. Cyclones often wash away much of the paddy rice crop and wipe out the earth dams and irrigation waterways built at great cost and effort. Some farmers have invested a lifetime's savings employing labour for their construction. So if floods strike, people rely on the hill rice. Fertility in these fields is not replenished as in paddies where nutrients are carried in the water. The soil quickly becomes unproductive so new slopes must be cut after a few years.

The cultural explanation for tavy is less obvious. The people of 'my' village, Sandrakely, are Tanala. The forest is their world and to survive in this surprisingly harsh environment they clear the land with fire – the ancient agricultural technique brought by the original immigrants from Indonesia. In more recent history the Tanala were forced into the forest by warring neighbours and colonial occupants of more fertile areas.

As the traditional means of survival and provision, tavy can be seen as central to society's make-up and culture. The calendar revolves around it, land ownership and hierarchies are determined by its practice, and politics are centred on it. It is the pivot and subject of rituals and ceremonies. The forest is the domain of the ancestors and site of tombs and religious standing stones. Tavy is an activity carried out between the living and the dead: the ancestors are consulted and permit its execution to provide for the living. The word tavy also means 'fatness', with all the associations of health, wealth and beauty.

If they have the choice, many are happy to pursue sustainable agricultural alternatives, so Feedback Madagascar is ready to help them. But the practical and cultural context must always be respected. The alternatives must be rock solid when people's lives are at stake and to be truly enduring they must be accommodated within the culture by the people themselves. It is they who understand the problems and know the solutions that are acceptable. They must not be forced.

Jamie Spencer is the founder of Feedback Madagascar; see page 140.

millions of insects and arachnids feeding on the bat guano and each other. Blind cave fish share these dark subterranean rivers with lurking cave crocodiles.

This diverse habitat supports numerous birds and mammals. It has even been claimed that Ankarana has the highest density of primates on earth. *Good examples: Isalo, Ankarana, Bemaraha and Namoroka.*

SPINY FOREST Whenever photographers wish to startle people with the uniqueness of Madagascar they head straight for the spiny forest. Its mass of tangled, prickly branches and swollen succulent trunks creates a habitat variously described by naturalists as 'a nightmare' and 'the eighth wonder of the world'. Stretching in a band around the southwest coast from Morombe to Taolagnaro, the spiny forest is the only primary community able to resist the extremely arid environment. All the plants here are beautifully adapted to survive on the sporadic rainfall, sometimes going without water for more than a year. The otherworldly landscape of this community is a result of the dramatic and striking forms of tall *Aloes*, broad-leaved *Kalanchoe* 'trees', octopus trees, *Pachypodium*, *Euphorbia*, endemic orchids and palms – all extremely specialised to withstand the harsh dry conditions.

The most evident animal life, aside from reptiles and desert arthropods, are the groups of sifakas which somehow avoid the vicious spines of the *Didierea* as they leap from one trunk to another. *Good examples: Berenty, Ifaty, Beza-Mahafaly and along the road from Taolagnaro to Ambovombe.*

WETLANDS Wetlands everywhere are regarded as important habitats – and Madagascar has no fewer than nine sites on the Ramsar List of Wetlands of International Importance. The plants here are terrestrial species adapted to tolerate waterlogging. Lakes, swamps and marshes all over the island are popular with birds, attracted by the shelter and materials of the reeds and rushes, and the sustenance to be gained from the insect life. On open water and lagoons near the coast, large flocks of flamingos gather, accompanied in their feeding by various waders.

But in Madagascar it is not only birds that make their homes among the reeds. In the reed beds of Lake Alaotra, a rare species of bamboo lemur, the Alaotran gentle lemur, has given up bamboo for papyrus to become the world's only reed-dwelling

DURRELL WILDLIFE CONSERVATION TRUST
Richard Lewis

Durrell Wildlife Conservation Trust is an international conservation charity with its headquarters in Jersey, Channel Islands. Established by the visionary conservationist and renowned author Gerald Durrell in 1963, the organisation has pre-eminent expertise in hands-on management of endangered species and a global reputation for its work through its field conservation projects, captive breeding, reintroduction and research. Durrell currently has 45 conservation projects in 12 countries, as well as an extensive programme of research, training, conservation and breeding of endangered species.

Since Durrell began working in Madagascar in the early 1980s, with the signing of the first accord with the government in 1983, we have grown to become one of the country's conservation leaders with projects in nine major sites and a dedicated team of over 45 local staff. Our core mission is saving the rarest species in Madagascar from extinction. We have developed a range of methods to do this that include supporting local human communities to sustainably manage critical habitats, both for people and for wildlife.

It was the ploughshare tortoise, or *angonoka*, that first brought us to Madagascar. It was restricted to a tiny range within the dry bamboo scrub of Baly Bay, and its habitat was rapidly disappearing. Through extensive collaboration with local communities, and the creation of the Baly Bay National Park, we were able to reduce the pressures on the habitat. We also set up a captive-breeding programme as a safety net for the species – the first of its kind in Madagascar. This programme has now introduced 80 animals back into the wild, and in 2011 we reached a major milestone, seeing the first babies of these released animals. Unfortunately, the *angonoka* has now become one of the most highly prized

primate. Lakes and waterways also play host to sometimes-sacred populations of crocodiles. *Good examples: Tsimanampetsotsa, Lake Alaotra, Lake Ampitabe, Lake Ravelobe and Ankarafantsika.*

MANGROVES Where trees dominate the wetlands instead of grasses, there are swamps. The most important of these are the mangrove swamps. Madagascar possesses the largest area of mangroves in the western Indian Ocean – about 330,000ha. The aerial roots of their characteristic salt-tolerant trees are alternately submerged and exposed twice daily with the tide. Some of the trees get a head start in life by germinating their seeds while still on the parent tree.

Mangroves are important and rich ecosystems. They support a wealth of bird species, which feast on the swarms of insects above the water and shoals of fish below. Many marine fish and crustaceans use mangroves as a nursery, coming in from the open sea to mate, breed and rear their young in relative safety. However, mangroves are now under threat in Madagascar. *Good examples: Mangoro (south of Anakao), Katsepy, Marovoay and Morombe.*

CORAL REEFS Madagascar has about 1,000km of coral reefs. Most of the species they support come from a community of globetrotting fish, corals and invertebrates, which crop up wherever the environment is just right.

The 1,600km difference in latitude between north and south Madagascar results in a subtle temperature gradient. The slightly cooler waters of the south are dominated by different corals and other species from those found in the north.

3

reptiles in the illegal pet trade and so poaching has become the dominant threat, once again making the species potentially the most threatened tortoise in the world. With local and international partners, the *angonoka* will remain one of our highest-priority species for years to come.

Following the rediscovery in 2006 of the Madagascar pochard, which was then presumed extinct, Durrell collaborated with the Wildfowl and Wetlands Trust, the Peregrine Fund, Asity and the Malagasy government to initiate a long-term programme to restore the species (see page 54). A dedicated breeding centre was built in 2011 in the town of Antsohihy and a candidate release site has been identified. Our field teams are now working to establish a release programme and also restore a wetland as a sustainable resource for local communities.

Much of what Durrell does in Madagascar involves working with local communities to identify ways to sustainably manage and protect natural resources, both to improve their well-being and to reduce the loss of habitat or direct persecution of threatened species. Currently we are working with these communities to develop local monitoring teams who check for signs of illegal practices in their forests and apply local rules designed and enforced by community structures. We have initiated the largest community-led monitoring programme in Madagascar and it is proving to be very effective.

At Lake Alaotra, Madagascar's largest inland lake and rice cultivation area, this community approach has led to the protection of the Alaotran gentle lemur, found only at this site and the only primate in the world wholly reliant on a wetland habitat. The Lake Alaotra area is one of three sites in Madagascar where Durrell is leading the development of community-led new protected areas.

The continental shelf surrounding Madagascar also contributes to diversity. A sharp drop-off on the east coast limits fringing reef growth, while the west coast's vast and shallow shelf – spreading out under the Mozambique Channel and warmed by the Agulhas Current – is much better suited to coral reef development. Along this coast there are fringing and barrier reefs sporting remote cays and a wealth of fish and invertebrates. Loggerhead, green and hawksbill turtles cruise the underwater meadows between reefs and nesting beaches, and from July to September migrating humpback whales use the warm waters of eastern Madagascar for breeding. *Good examples: Ile Sainte Marie, islands off Nosy Be, Ifaty, Anakao and Lokaro.*

CONSERVATION

AN AGE-OLD PROBLEM The early colonisers in Madagascar brought with them a culture dependent on rice and zebu cattle. Rice was the staple diet and zebu the spiritual staple, the link with the ancestors. Rice and zebu cannot be raised in dense forest, so the trees were felled and the undergrowth burned.

Two hundred or so years ago King Andrianampoinimerina punished those of his subjects who wilfully deforested areas. The practice continued, however. In 1883, a century later, the missionary James Sibree commented: 'Again we noticed the destruction of the forest and the wanton waste of trees.' The first efforts at legal protection came as long ago as 1927 when ten reserves were set aside by the French colonial government, which also tried to put a stop to the burning. Successive governments have tried – and failed – to halt this devastation.

Since independence in 1960, Madagascar's population has quadrupled to 25 million and the remaining forest has been reduced by half. Only about 10% of the original cover remains and an estimated 2,000km² is destroyed annually – not by timber companies (although there have been some culprits) but by impoverished peasants clearing the land by the traditional method of tavy (slash-and-burn; see box, page 67), and cutting trees for fuel or to make charcoal. However, Madagascar is not overpopulated; the population density averages only 42 people per square kilometre (compared with 654 in neighbouring Mauritius and 420 in England). The pressure on the forests is because so much of the country is sterile grassland. Unlike in neighbouring Africa, this savannah is lifeless because Malagasy animals evolved to live in forests; they are not adapted to this new environment. Change in Madagascar's vegetation is by no means recent, for scientists have identified that the climate became much drier about 5,000 years ago. But humans have catalysed the process.

THE RACE AGAINST TIME Madagascar has more endangered species of mammal than any other country in the world. The authorities are well aware of this environmental crisis: as long ago as 1970 the director of scientific research made this comment in a speech during an international symposium on conservation: 'The people in this room know that Malagasy nature is a world heritage. We are not sure that others realise that it is *our* heritage.' Resentment at having outsiders make decisions on the future of their heritage without proper consultation with the Malagasy was one of the reasons there was little effective conservation in the 1970s and early 1980s. This was a time when Madagascar was demonstrating its independence from Western influences. Things changed in 1985, when Madagascar hosted a major international conference on conservation for development. In partnership with WWF, the government evaluated all protected areas in the country, then numbering 37 (2% of the island), and developed a strategy to provide people living near the reserves with economically viable alternatives to exploiting them. These original protected areas are

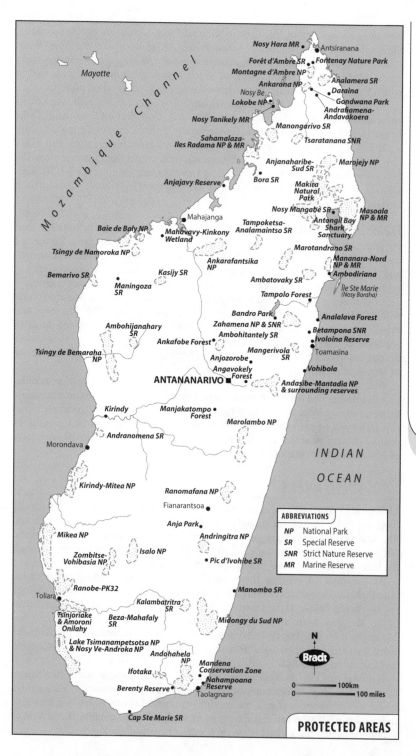

Mozambique Channel

INDIAN

OCEAN

Nosy Hara MR • Antsiranana
Forêt d'Ambre SR • Fontenay Nature Park
Montagne d'Ambre NP
Ankarana NP • Analamera SR
Daraina
Nosy Be • Gondwana Park
Lokobe NP • Andrafiamena-Andavakoera

Nosy Tanikely MR
Sahamalaza-Iles Radama NP & MR
Manongarivo SR
Tsaratanana SNR

Anjanaharibe-Sud SR
Marojejy NP
Anjajavy Reserve
Bora SR
Makira Natural Park

Nosy Mangabe SR
Masoala NP & MR
Baie de Baly NP
Mahavavy-Kinkony Wetland
Tampoketsa-Analamaintso SR
Antongil Bay Shark Sanctuary

Mahajanga

Tsingy de Namoroka NP
Marotandrano SR
Mananara-Nord NP & MR
Ambodiriana
Île Ste Marie (Nosy Boraha)

Bemarivo SR
Kasijy SR
Ankarafantsika NP
Ambatovaky SR

Maningoza SR
Tampolo Forest

Bandro Park
Analalava Forest
Ambohijanahary SR
Zahamena NP & SNR
Betampona SNR
Ankafobe Forest
Ambohitantely SR
Ivoloina Reserve

Mangerivola SR
Toamasina
Anjozorobe
Mangerivola SR
Tsingy de Bemaraha NP
Angavokely Forest
ANTANANARIVO ■
Andasibe-Mantadia NP & surrounding reserves
Vohibola

Kirindy
Manjakatompo Forest
Marolambo NP
Andranomena SR

Morondava •

Kirindy-Mitea NP
Ranomafana NP
Fianarantsoa •

Anja Park
Mikea NP
Andringitra NP
Zombitse-Vohibasia NP
Isalo NP
Pic d'Ivohibe SR

Ranobe-PK32
Manombo SR
Toliara •
Kalambatritra SR
Tsinjoriake & Amoroni Onilahy
Beza-Mahafaly SR
Midongy du Sud NP
Lake Tsimanampetsotsa NP & Nosy Ve-Androka NP
Andohahela NP
Mandena Conservation Zone
Ifotaka
Nahampoana Reserve
Berenty Reserve
Taolagnaro
Cap Ste Marie SR

Mayotte

N

Bradt

| 0 | 100km |
| 0 | 100 miles |

ABBREVIATIONS

NP	National Park
SR	Special Reserve
SNR	Strict Nature Reserve
MR	Marine Reserve

PROTECTED AREAS

now the responsibility of Madagascar National Parks, which was established under the auspices of the Environmental Action Plan (EAP) sponsored by the World Bank. Among their successes has been the establishment of a number of new national parks and several Debt for Nature swaps, in which international debts are cancelled in return for some of Madagascar's repayments going into conservation projects.

Numerous projects in Madagascar are funded by conservation NGOs and other agencies including Conservation International, Coopération Française, Duke Lemur Center, Durrell Wildlife Conservation Trust, German Primate Centre – DPZ, GTZ and KfW (German government), Madagascar Fauna and Flora Group, Margot Marsh Biodiversity Foundation, Missouri Botanical Garden, The Peregrine Fund, UNDP (United Nations Development Programme), UNESCO, USAID (US Agency for International Development), Wildlife Conservation Society and WWF.

EXPANSION OF PROTECTED AREAS In a dramatic announcement in 2003, the then president Marc Ravalomanana promised to triple the area of Madagascar's protected reserves. Deforestation, he said, had taken its toll. 'We can no longer afford to sit back and watch our forests go up in flames. This is not just Madagascar's biodiversity; it is the world's biodiversity. We have the firm political will to stop this degradation.'

A programme was launched to identify areas in need of protection, and to create wildlife corridors connecting existing parks (see box, page 277). The new and existing protected areas are now grouped into the System of Protected Areas of Madagascar (SAPM) which has three major objectives: to conserve Madagascar's unique biodiversity; to conserve its cultural heritage; and to enable sustainable use to help alleviate poverty.

Well aware of the widespread international acclaim this protection-tripling promise had earned his predecessor, current president Hery Rajaonarimampianina made a similar pledge in 2014 to triple Madagascar's *marine* protected areas. While this move will be extremely beneficial if seen through appropriately, it is a rather smaller commitment that Ravalomanana's and has failed to win him the same level of recognition from the international community.

PROTECTED AREAS

CATEGORIES The main types of protected area are those managed by Madagascar National Parks. These are: national parks, special reserves and strict nature reserves. The first two categories are generally open to tourism. There is little difference between national parks and special reserves from a tourist point of view, although the latter typically have less-developed visitor infrastructure.

At the time of writing there are 26 national parks: Andasibe-Mantadia, Andohahela, Andringitra, Ankarafantsika, Ankarana, Baie de Baly, Tsingy de Bemaraha, Nosy Hara (marine), Isalo, Kirindy-Mitea, Lokobe, Mananara-Nord, Marojejy, Marolambo, Masoala-Nosy Mangabe, Midongy du Sud, Mikea, Montagne d'Ambre, Tsingy de Namoroka, Ranomafana, Sahamalaza-Iles Radama, Nosy Tanikely (marine), Lake Tsimanampetsotsa, Nosy Ve-Androka, Zahamena and Zombitse-Vohibasia.

National parks in Madagascar are very different from those in North America or even Europe. They are not huge areas of wilderness with a network of hiking trails where you can wander at will, but carefully controlled places which you may visit only with a guide who will require you to stick to prescribed circuits. If you want to get off the beaten track, don't try to do it within a national park.

There are a dozen or so special reserves, of which Ambohitantely, Analamera, Anjanaharibe-Sud, Andranomena, Beza-Mahafaly, Cap Sainte Marie and Manombo are described in this book.

Many new areas coming under protection include some vast corridors along the eastern rainforest belt such as the recently established Makira Natural Park. As yet, many still have very limited infrastructure for handling tourist visits.

There are also an increasing number of private reserves and NGO-run protected areas which welcome tourists. These include Ambodiriana Reserve, Analalava Forest, Andrafiamena-Andavakoera, Anja Park, Anjajavy Reserve, Anjozorobe, Ankafobe, Mitsinjo's Analamazaotra and Torotorofotsy, Bandro Park, Berenty Reserve, Daraina, Fontenay Nature Park, Gondwana Private Park, Ifotaka Community Forest, Ivoloina Park, Kirindy Reserve, Mahavavy-Kinkony Wetland Complex, Mandena Conservation Zone, Manjakatompo Forestry Station, Maromizaha, Nahampoana Reserve, Tampolo Forestry Station, Tsinjoriake Protected Area, Vohibola and Vohimana.

PERMITS The cost of permits to visit the national parks and special reserves increased sharply at the end of 2015. The prices here are for adult foreign tourists, but there are concessions for children (*25,000Ar/day at all parks*), residents, nationals and researchers. Isalo and Ankarana national parks are classified as 'Exceptional' and cost 65,000Ar (about £16/€19/US\$20) per day. The 'Flagship' parks of Andohahela, Ankarafantsika, Tsingy de Bemaraha, Lokobe, Montagne d'Ambre, Nosy Hara and Ranomafana charge 55,000Ar daily (£14/€16/US\$17). The remaining parks and reserves cost 45,000Ar per day (£11/€13/US\$14). There are no longer discounted multi-day permits, except at Isalo where four days costs 200,000Ar.

In theory, half of this entrance fee goes to Madagascar National Parks and half to the nearby communities, but locals have been complaining for some time that they don't receive the promised money anymore. Permits are always available at the park entrance (be sure to get a receipt) but you may wish to visit the office in Antananarivo or see www.parcs-madagascar.com.

GUIDES It is obligatory to be accompanied by a guide in all national parks and special reserves. Note that the permit price does not include their fee. Guide prices vary from park to park but a list of agreed rates is normally on display at each park entrance. Additionally it is usual to tip your guide for good service (see page 96).

Private reserves run by other organisations normally also require you to take a guide, although the entrance permit and guide fee are usually combined into a single fee often charged on a per-circuit basis.

ASISTEИTRAVEL

Madagascar Differently

Tour Operator & DMC
Bespoke & Luxury vacations throughout Madagascar
www.asisten-travel.com
info@asisten-travel.com
Tel : +261 (20) 22 577 55

fb.com/asistentravel   @asistentravel

4

Practical Information

WHEN TO VISIT

Read the section on climate (page 3) before deciding when to travel. Broadly speaking, the dry months are in the winter between April and September, but rainfall varies enormously in different areas. Try to avoid July/August and the Christmas/New Year period when popular places are crowded. January to March is the rainy season when some more remote places get cut off by the swollen rivers, particularly in the north and west. However, the off-peak season can be rewarding, with cheaper international airfares and accommodation and fewer other tourists. September is nice, but frequently windy in the south. April and May often have lovely weather, and the countryside is green after the rainy season.

Keen naturalists have their own requirements: botanists may want to go in February when many of the orchids are in flower, and herpetologists will prefer the spring/summer because reptiles are more active – and brightly coloured – during those months. Bear in mind that giant jumping rats, dwarf lemurs, tenrecs and some reptiles are less active and so harder to see during the cool dry months of June to September. Our favourite months to visit Madagascar are October and November, when the weather is usually fine but not too hot, the jacarandas are in flower, the lemurs have babies, and lychees are sold from roadside stalls in the east.

CHOOSING A TRIP TO SUIT YOU

When planning a holiday most people consider only their interests and how much they are prepared to spend, but in order to ensure that you enjoy Madagascar it is important also to take care in matching the trip to your personality.

WHAT SORT OF PERSON ARE YOU? The catch-22 of tourism in Madagascar is that the type of person who can afford the trip is often the type least suited to cope with the Malagasy way of life. In our culture those with assertiveness and efficient organisational skills have success in business, and thus the income to finance exotic travel. Such people often find Madagascar unbearably inefficient and frustrating and would benefit most from a tailor-made tour with a vehicle and driver.

Frequently, the happiest travellers are either those who choose to travel on a low budget or those who can let go and adopt the attitude of one elderly woman on a group tour who said 'I'm going to give up thinking; it doesn't work in Madagascar.' It doesn't, and she had a great time!

It will undoubtedly be a trip you'll never forget; choose wisely from the options below to ensure that's for the right reasons.

The luxury package Four-star hotels and better are no longer unusual in Madagascar; over the past decade many splendid options have been popping up across the country. Luxury-seekers will have no problem planning their tour around the new upmarket boutique hotels. A handful of fly-in hotels even shield you from the realities of Madagascar by whisking you off to their resort by private plane.

Cruising On a ship you know that you will sleep in a comfortable bed each night and eat familiar food. It is thus ideal for the adventurous at heart who are no longer able to take the rigours of land travel. **Expedition cruise** ships typically carry only a hundred or so passengers and can be the only way to reach some remote offshore islands. Try Noble Caledonia (*www.noble-caledonia.co.uk*), Zegrahm Expeditions (*www.zegrahm.com*), Silversea (*www.silversea.com*), or Hapag-Lloyd Cruises (*www. hl-cruises.com*).

For **regular cruising** – a more affordable but less personal experience, with typically one or two thousand passengers aboard – contact Costa (*www.costacruises.co.uk*), Fred Olsen (*www.fredolsencruises.com*), Oceania (*www.oceaniacruises.com*), Holland America Line (*www.hollandamerica.com*), or Crystal (*www.crystalcruises.co.uk*).

Group travel Typically group tours are small, with 8–14 people. It's usually a lot of fun, ideal for single people who do not wish to travel alone, and if you choose the tour company and itinerary carefully you will see a great deal of the country, gain an understanding of its complicated culture and unique wildlife, and generally have a great time without the need to make decisions. But you do need to be comfortable relinquishing the decision-making.

Tailor-made tours This is the ideal option for a couple or small group who are not restricted financially, especially if time is the main limitation. It is also the best choice for people with special interests or who like things to run as smoothly as possible. You will be the decision maker and will choose where you want to go and your preferred level of comfort, but the logistics will be taken care of.

Either organise your tailor-made trip through a tour operator in your home country, in which case you will have the benefit of legal protection if things go wrong, or contact some Malagasy tour operators. Let them know your interests, the level of comfort you expect, and whether you want to cram in as much as possible or concentrate on just a few centres. Operators specialising in tailor-made tours are listed later in this chapter.

Semi-independent travel You can save money by dealing directly with a tour operator in Madagascar. Many are listed later in this chapter. Most local operators have a good understanding of tourists' needs and give impressive service. The downside is that they aren't bonded, so if things go wrong you won't be protected.

Perhaps the ideal do-it-yourself trip is to hire a local driver/guide and vehicle when you arrive in Antananarivo (Tana). This way you are wonderfully free to stop when you please and stay where you wish; see pages 90 and 173.

Independent travel Truly independent travellers usually have a rough idea of where they want to go and how they will travel but are open to changes of plan dictated by local conditions, whim and serendipity. Independent travellers are not necessarily budget travellers. Those who can afford to fly to major towns, then rent a vehicle and driver, can eliminate a large amount of hassle and see everything they set out to see – providing they set a realistic programme.

The majority of independent travellers use public transport and stay in mid-range or budget hotels. They are exposed to all Madagascar's joys and frustrations and most seem to love it. The key here is not to try to do too much, and to speak at least some French.

The seriously adventurous
Madagascar must be one of the very few countries left in the world where large areas are not yet detailed in a guidebook. A study of the standard 1:2,000,000 map of Madagascar reveals some mouth-watering possibilities, and a look at the more detailed 1:500,000 maps confirms the opportunities for people who are willing to walk or cycle. Or drive. During five decades, two of our most adventurous correspondents, Valerie and John Middleton, have travelled all over Madagascar by 4x4 in pursuit of their caving and botanical interests. Having a focus helps, especially when explaining your presence to bemused locals.

Serious adventurers will need to plan their trip beforehand with the FTM regional maps. These can be bought at their office in Tana (page 171) or theoretically obtained by mail order (*www.ftm.mg*).

Throughout this book there are quotes from people who have headed into Madagascar's least explored corners, sometimes after a lot of preparation and sometimes on a whim. Not everyone is courageous enough to step or pedal into the unknown like this, but in fact it's one of the safest ways to travel: the Malagasy that you meet will invariably be welcoming and hospitable.

Travelling alone
To travel alone may be a matter of choice or necessity. The trick is to make the necessity into choice by revelling in the opportunity to get close to the local people and to immerse yourself in their culture.

Lone travellers need to be prepared for the long evenings. Robert Bowker found nights at national parks particularly lonely: 'Dinner is early, and after that nothing to do but go to your bungalow. Take a powerful torch and lots to read. I got through a fair number of crossword puzzles. Also take music.'

Another issue with solo trips is that parks and reserves will be expensive unless you team up with other travellers, because guide fees are usually the same for one person as for a group of four. The economy of scale applies to hiring a 4x4 or boat. You have a choice, then, of going to the more popular areas, with a greater chance of finding travel buddies along the way, or heading off the beaten track, where you'll find the prices lower, locals friendlier and discover a more genuine traditional culture. For more on solo travel, see pages 127–9.

Family travel
It is becoming more practical to travel in Madagascar with children. For specific advice on this refer to page 129.

Travelling with a disability
With careful planning and help from a local tour operator, wheelchair users can see something of the landscape and wildlife. See page 129 for general advice.

Working holidays and volunteering
There is a growing interest in paying to be a volunteer in a scientific or community project. This is an excellent way of 'giving something back' while enjoying a learning experience which will stay with you much longer than the normal holiday memories. There are also some opportunities to work as a volunteer for local charities or NGOs. You will need to fund your airfare and some costs, and in some cases will only be accepted if you have a particular skill. For details of organisations that accept 'voluntourists', see pages 137–44.

If you are thinking of taking a bike to Madagascar, do it; you'll love it. On most of the roads you will be more comfortable than anyone in motorised transport. The simplicity and strength of the humble bike will get you virtually anywhere, bring you closer to the wonderful people of the island and allow you to see things that you would miss if you travelled any other way.

If you intend to cycle between the major centres and in the more developed parts of the island, then you can plan as for touring but in tough conditions. You will need a mountain bike as the tarred roads can be broken, especially after rains, and there are many unmade roads. You should carry a good supply of spares and tools, some food and plenty of container capacity for water, though you probably will find enough to eat and drink in most areas, as well as places to stay. If you plan to go into more remote areas and to tackle the smaller roads, then here are some tips.

THE BIKE What you need to think is simplicity, strength and self-sufficiency. Don't take it if it can't be fixed with the tools you carry yourself, or with a hammer by a Malagasy mechanic. Fit a new chain and block, carry spare spokes, brake blocks, cables, inner tubes and take plenty of oil (the dust is unbelievable). Go with the strongest wheels you can afford, and the fattest tyres you can fit (1.95in/50mm minimum). You can pick up cheap bike parts in the larger towns. Bill adds: 'Take at least two dozen patches for punctures, a chain riveter, a few dozen plastic cable ties plus ten Jubilee clips.'

ON THE BIKE Lex: 'Forget panniers unless you are staying on good roads. A 20–35-litre backpack held away from your back with mesh for ventilation is ideal: it's more flexible, stays with you at all times, and you do get used to it. A rear rack with a rack bag is a good addition, and allows you to carry heavy tools/food/water away from your back.' Bill: 'Only front panniers break off, they tend not to survive Malagasy roads. Sturdy back panniers are necessary – tie them together so you don't lose them on bumpy roads; a backpack makes you more tired.'

CLOTHING You need two sets, one for cycling and one for socialising/resting. If you are going to explore the deserts, I advise the 'Beau Geste' style of hat with peak on front, and flap on back. General-purpose shorts, with cycling short inners underneath (two pairs minimum) are ideal. Also take leather cycling gloves (artificial materials disintegrate with the sweat and the heat); footwear of the trainer/walking boot variety is ideal, again go for natural materials; lightweight socks, with a clean set of underwear spare at all times. I find an Arabic scarf a fantastic all-purpose bit of kit: sleep under it, dry yourself with it, use it as a picnic blanket or head covering for dust storms, etc. Bandanas are a useful addition and keep the sweat out of your eyes. Just think tough kit for your contact points on the bike, and breathable kit everywhere else. The rule to apply for your clothing is 'one set wet, one set dry'. At night consider a clean T-shirt/vest with a cotton or similar shirt, and lightweight trousers. Finally, take a lightweight fleece as it can get cold at night, and some sort of windbreaker/waterproof shell.

PERSONAL HYGIENE Take a good first aid kit, and Savlon for your backside. My colleague on our 3,000km Madagascar adventure had golf-ball-sized boils on his behind for three–four weeks as a result of a) lots of saddle time, b) sweat, c) lack of 'arse discipline' (as we called it). Apply Savlon liberally, and if you get the chance to wash, take your time and be particular down below. Anti-fungal creams are a good idea as well. Take rehydration salts, Imodium-type pills and laxatives. Your body will not know what's hit it, and you never know how it will react. Salt pills are useful as well. Remember to drink as much as you can at night. Take water purifiers.

REMOTE TOWNS When pulling into a town/village, think of riding right the way through it first, to select your likely bar/bunkhouse, and then cycle back to it. You don't want to miss the heavenly spot 500m up the road because you pulled over early. If in doubt look for a village elder. If you are really remote, the locals will often run away, but just wait and the relevant person will find you. You may not always be able to buy food. If you do buy food in remote villages make sure you give the womenfolk the money, not the men. Bear in mind villagers will often offer you food, and as result go without themselves.

RIDE ROUTINE Be moving before sunrise if you're in the desert: 05.00 is about right. If you can finish your riding for the day by 11.00–12.00, that's perfect, but be realistic. Don't ride in the middle hours of the day unless you really have to. Just find or make some shade and rest. You'll probably be exhausted by then anyway, but after a short while you should be able to put in 6–8 hours' riding per day. Rest days are vital, and give you the benefit of time in great places.

FOOD Carry two days' rations if you can, because you just never know when you may have to spend a night out. Try peanuts, raisins, dates, processed cheese, salt, couscous, muesli with powdered milk and boiled sweets. Take some with you or pick them up in one of the larger towns. This food stash will supplement your basic rice diet, which soon becomes boring, and lacks the calories required for hard riding. Otherwise, watch where the locals eat and don't be afraid of the roadside stands; they are fantastic. Carry a lightweight stove.

CAMPING Strangely in Madagascar camping is viewed as suspicious behaviour by many rural communities. Where possible avoid it. However, you need to carry a sleeping bag and mat anyway, so a poncho or tent will allow you the flexibility to camp out should you need to, or just take a mozzie net if in the dry season. Best advice: try not to be too obvious or you will attract a lot of unwanted attention.

SECURITY As a rule Madagascar is a very safe place, but on a bike you are exposed. Your best defence is learning some of the language, using humour and keeping some small-denomination notes handy. In remoter areas you may go several days between banks, so you will have to carry cash – though your costs will be low. Spread it around: hide some in your bike etc. Have photocopies of documentation on you, as well as originals. Leave details in the capital, and inform your national consulate or someone of an approximate return date. If in trouble, don't raise your voice, and negotiate calmly with the head man, be patient, and keep smiling.

NAVIGATION Even the best maps available in Madagascar are inaccurate. Rely on local knowledge when navigating the minor roads. If you are travelling cross-country, good compass work and the ability to read the terrain is essential. Again local knowledge and the ability to stay calm when lost are essential.

SPECIAL INTERESTS

Trekking and hiking Trekking in the truest sense, where your gear is carried by porters to a different campsite each night, is only really possible in a small number of places, such as Isalo or Marojejy. There are also excellent hiking possibilities at Andringitra and Ankarana, but note that you must always be accompanied by a guide in national parks.

Many of Madagascar's 'roads' are overgrown tracks, and ideal for hiking. There are a couple of well-known routes, the Smugglers' Path and the Trans-Masoala Trail, as well as a network of one-day and multi-day trails between the Zafimaniry villages.

Geocaching This is an outdoor recreational activity in which participants hunt for 'hidden treasure' using GPS co-ordinates and clues obtained online. Dating back to 2000, it is a modernised and globalised version of the letterboxing pastime famously practised on Dartmoor in the UK since 1854. The treasure usually takes the form of a concealed watertight box containing a small logbook for discoverers to sign. The chosen locations are often local beauty spots, so that geocaching is really just a great excuse and motivation to hike in nature.

Worldwide around 3 million geocaches are hidden. The activity is in its infancy in Madagascar, with just a dozen or so across the island so far (including Tana, Ile Sainte Marie pirate cemetery, Ivoloina, Bemaraha, Antalaha, Ifaty, Andringitra, Mananjary, Ankarana, Nosy Be and Nosy Tanikely). If you enjoy geocaching, why not help to expand this pastime in Madagascar by hiding one of your own while there and registering it in the online index? More information about both hunting for and placing geocaches may be found at www.geocaching.com.

Running Trail running, ultramarathons, marathons and fun runs have become very popular in Madagascar in recent years. Several are becoming regular annual events. Dates are spread from March to December; search online to find upcoming runs. Recent events include: Nosy Be Trail (25/50km), Isalo Raid (3/22/42/80km), Les Foulées d'Antsiranana (15km) and Marathon de Diego Suarez (22/42km), all of which are organised by RandoRun Océan Indien (e *randorunoi@gmail.com; www.randorunoi.com*); Ultra-Trail des Ô Plateaux (4/10/30/65/135km) operated by UTOP (e *info@utop.mg; www.utop.mg*); Trail de l'Ile Rouge (135km) by Africa Trek & Run (*http://africa.trekandrun.free.fr*); Rain Forest Run (12km) from Ivoloina Park (*www.parcivoloina.org*); and Trail d'Ibity (2/12/30km) organised by Naoxime Sports (e *naoximesports@gmail.com*).

Mountain biking By cycling under your own muscle power, you won't be delayed by bad roads and breakdowns, and you will have more time to appreciate fully the communities and landscapes you pass through. Bill and Nina French, who have made two trips in Madagascar by bicycle, recommend the following routes: Manompana–Mananara (52km with some very difficult stretches), the Masoala Peninsula, Ambalavao–Fianarantsoa, Manakara–Sahasinaka, Ranomafana–Fianarantsoa, Fianarantsoa–Soatanana–RN42, Lac Tritriva–Marinanpona and Ambatolampy–Antananarivo.

For advice on cycling, see the box on pages 78–9. RandoRun (see *Running* above) organises an annual 300km mountain-biking event in the southeast.

Climbing Rock-climbing centres are Andringitra (pages 211–14) and the Antsiranana area, including French Mountain (page 351) and Nosy Hara (page 355). Those interested in tree climbing should see pages 176, 267, 278 and 348.

You might be surprised to learn that BEAL, one of the world's leading manufacturers of quality climbing equipment, manufactures their rope in Madagascar. But don't expect to pick up a bargain on your trip: they are only licensed for export, not to sell locally. BEAL supports a reforestation project at Andringitra with a commitment to plant one tree for every rope sold – no small promise when you consider they produce 8 million metres per year!

Caving Madagascar has some fabulous caves, and several expeditions have been mounted to explore them. Caving is not a popular Malagasy pursuit, however, so cavers should take particular care to explain what they are doing and get the necessary permits for exploring protected areas. An experienced local tour operator will help with the red tape.

The best karst areas are in the north and west: **Ankarana** (the best explored and mapped area, with more than 100km of subterranean caves), **Narinda** (where the longest cave is over 5km), **Bemaraha**, the **Mikoboka Plateau** (north of Toliara, with pits to a depth of 165m) and the **Mahafaly Plateau** (south of Toliara). For those with experience, cave diving is possible at **Tsimanampetsotsa**.

Diving The best and most exciting diving is among the islands of the northwest, centred on Nosy Be. Some outstanding marine biodiversity is found around the spectacular Radama and Mitsio archipelagos, but to reach them really requires a few days on a liveaboard. You may see humpback whales and dolphins from the boat, even whale sharks if you're lucky. The area is also extraordinarily good for nudibranchs. Ile Sainte Marie also has good dive sites, although visibility is often more limited. The southwest used to offer very good diving but these days overfishing and silting have taken their toll and the diving is a shadow of what it used to be.

With the cooler waters of August and September you would be best with a hood or a sweat, but the rest of the year a 3–5mm suit will do. For more details, see the boxes on pages 82–3 and 124.

Watersports In addition to scuba-diving, Madagascar offers an impressive array of world-class sites for surfing, windsurfing, kitesurfing and sea kayaking. Sport fishing can be organised from Nosy Be.

River trips There are some splendid rivers, particularly in the west. Some offer the perfect means to pass through otherwise inaccessible areas of the country. The range includes extended calm-water floats to exciting white-water sections. See page 433 for a description of the western rivers. Close to the capital there are some great

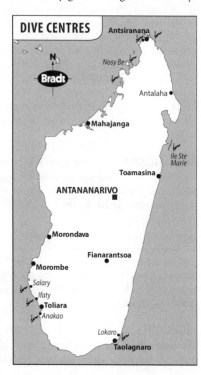

NORTH Composed principally of coral reefs, lagoons, mangroves and an abundance of small islands. One of the richest in marine life of all the regions. Important species seen in this area include whale sharks, turtles and manta rays. Due to the variety of sites and beauty of this region, tourism is well established and is supported by several hotels and dive centres which offer diving and snorkelling excursions.

Sites: *Islands and coral reefs:* Archipelago of Nosy Mitsio including Ilots des Quatres Frères, Nosy Hara, Nosy Be, Nosy Manitse and Nosimborona, Nosy Ratafanika, Nosy Iranja, Nosy Haramy and Nosy Milomboka, Nosy Faho, Nosy Mangabe, Nosy Tanikely, islands of the Baie d'Emeraude (Nosy Antaly-Be, Nosy Suarez, Nosy Lava), Nosy Lowry and Nosy Ankao. Continental shelf from Nosy Be to Antsiranana (sites with specific coral and topographic formations). *Mangroves and estuaries:* Ambanja and Antsiranana.

WEST Characterised by extensive beaches, several rocky rivers and large estuaries supporting extended mangroves. Most of this region's small islands and coral reefs are seldom visited. Its coast offers enormous potential for quality dive tourism. Hotels and dive centres are limited.

Sites: *Islands and coral reefs:* Kirindy-Mitea coast and small islands, and Barren Islands. *Mangroves and estuaries:* Tsiribihina, Betsiboka, Mahajamba, Manambolomaty and Mahavavy estuary.

SOUTHWEST Composed of a variety of habitats including large areas of mangroves and vast lagoons lined with endless beaches. Some of the most notable sites are located within one of the largest coral reef systems in the world stretching over 150km from the coastal town of Toliara northward. Tourism is well developed in this region, where access to various marine sites is assured.

Sites: *Islands and coral reefs:* Mikea coastal reef, islands and lagoons, Toliara's Grand Récif (frontal reef wall and pools), Nosy Ve and reefs, and Nosy Manitse.

white-water trips on the highland rivers coming off the plateau. Many of these offer medium and extreme white-water runs to challenge rafters and kayakers of all skill levels.

Birdwatching There are several tour operators that specialise in birding trips. Twitchers travel with such a different focus from other wildlife fans that it's well worth going with a like-minded group and an expert tour leader. See the box on page 53 for full details on the best birding places.

HIGHLIGHTS AND ITINERARIES

One of the hardest decisions facing the first-time visitor to a country as large and diverse as Madagascar is where to go. Even a couple of months is too short to see *everything*, so itineraries must be planned according to interests and the level of comfort desired.

HIGHLIGHTS
Wildlife The flora and fauna is undoubtedly the island's number one selling point for tourism. There are now several dozen national parks, special reserves

Continental shelf from Toliara to Morombe (sites with specific coral and topographic formations).

SOUTHEAST Composed principally of rocky shoreline with some isolated coral reefs supporting Madagascar's largest lobster fishery. There are a few good dive sites which benefit from both a diverse and picturesque coastline. Tourism is being developed, offering opportunities for diving.
Sites: *Coral and rocky reefs:* Lokaro to St Luce. *Offshore:* humpback whales.

EAST Composed of long beaches divided by rivers running down from the rainforest. There are some patches of coastal forest and a semi-natural canal network known as the Pangalanes. Diving opportunities are limited along this coast, which is well known for its spices and rainforest.
Sites: *Islands:* Nosy Fonga and Dombala, and Nosy Faho. *Wetland:* Pangalanes Canal and coastal forest.

NORTHEAST Composed of a diverse range of habitats from rocky shores to long sandy beaches and impressive coral reefs circling several small islands. This is an important area for humpback whales breeding during the winter months. The coastline is located near some of Madagascar's most impressive rainforests.
Sites: *Islands, wrecks and reef:* Ile Ste Marie (coastal wrecks and reef), Nosy Atafana (attached to Mananara-Nord National Park), Masoala Marine Reserve and Cap Est reef. *Offshore:* humpback whales (Ile Ste Marie and Antongil Bay).

Tim Healy is an environmental consultant, BBC correspondent and keen diver based in Madagascar for nearly 20 years. He is compiling information for a dive and snorkelling guide; if you would like to support his project, let us know.

and private or community-administered protected areas that have nearby tourist accommodation, maintained trails and trained guides.

Scenery Most recommended for views are the central highlands between Fianarantsoa and Ambalavao, Andringitra, Isalo and Andohahela national parks, Avenue des Baobabs (near Morondava), Tsingy de Bemaraha, Ankarana, Montagne d'Ambre and the Andapa region.

Beaches Madagascar's best beaches are the blue lagoons along the west coast, but some people are disappointed because of the shallow water (it is often impossible to swim at low tide). There are beautiful beaches on the east coast but strong currents and sharks are a risk in many parts. The very best beaches are in remote areas such as Anjajavy, the islands around Nosy Be, Ile Sainte Marie and south of Toliara.

Nightlife Nowadays there are many modern clubs and bars in Tana and other cities. The people of southern Madagascar are the most outgoing on the island, with good discos in Taolagnaro, Toliara and almost every village in-between. Nosy Be – and specifically Ambatoloaka – has the most famous nightlife among tourists, but the place has become synonymous with sex tourism.

Museums If you know where to look there's a handful of fascinating little museums dotted around, often in quaint dusty backrooms. In and around the capital, there is a city museum called Tana of Yesteryear, a pirate museum, a gemstone and mineral museum, an art and archaeology museum and the royal museum of Andafiavaratra Palace (closed at the time of writing). The historic site of Ambohimanga is a museum in itself, and there are small ethnographic exhibitions at the other royal hills of Ilafy, Ambohidrabiby and Antsahadinta.

Further afield, you will find the national police museum in Moramanga, Fort Flacourt military museum in Taolagnaro, Fianarantsoa Diocese Museum, Museum of the Androy at Berenty, CEDRATOM ethnological museum of Toliara university, Mahajanga's Akiba cultural history museum, the museum of Jean Laborde at Mantasoa, Ambositra royal palace museum and Barday history museum near Mahajanga. Toamasina has a city and port museum, a regional museum, and a museum of art and culture. Those interested in marine environments may like to visit the Museum of the Sea in Tulear, CNRO oceanographic museum on Nosy Be, and ReefDoctor's marine museum at Ifaty. In addition, there are interpretation centres at several parks and reserves – including Isalo, Andasibe, Masoala, Ankarafantsika, Tampolo Forest and the Arboretum d'Antsokay.

Lastly, while not intended as a museum, history fans might like to take a stroll past Tana's fire station on Rue Reallon. It is like taking a step into the past with an incredible assortment of old fire engines, donated by developed countries when they became obsolete.

Traditions and tombs Your tour operator may be able to organise a visit to a *famadihana* (only in the highlands between June and September) – an unforgettable experience. Merina tombs can be seen easily between Tana and Antsirabe, but the most intriguing and interesting tombs are those of the Mahafaly in the Toliara region.

ITINERARIES The mistake everyone makes initially when planning a trip to Madagascar is trying to cram too much into their itinerary. There is so much to see and do, but this is a vast island with poor transport infrastructure. Let's put it in perspective: driving flat out from dawn to dusk with no stops, it would take you seven days to get from one end to the other, in a good vehicle, in the dry season! Whether you're organising your trip independently or looking for ideas before approaching a tour operator to tailor-make your itinerary, this section is designed to help you to make the most efficient use of your precious time in Madagascar.

To appreciate the challenges in designing a workable itinerary, you first need to understand the basic geography of the country's transport connections. Madagascar's road network is like a spider, with the capital city (where virtually all the international arrivals come in) right at the centre, the only major roads trailing off radially, like legs, to various points around the coast. Consequently, it is not possible to travel in a loop. Whichever direction you go from Tana, you will typically either have to retrace your steps or take a domestic flight to get back, unless you're up for several days of ambitious off-roading.

The trouble with building a lot of domestic flights into your plan is not only that they are very expensive, but also that they are unreliable; an itinerary that includes multiple flights is very likely to be disrupted by at least one last-minute cancellation or schedule change. The other difficulty with flights is that they suffer the same limitation as the roads in that the routes generally start or end in Tana; you cannot fly between the south and north of Madagascar without a change in the capital (typically necessitating an overnight stay). The upshot is that if your visit is less than about 15 days long then, realistically, you will need to choose between the north and the south – or be prepared to spend a very significant proportion of your trip travelling.

Below are outlined half a dozen routes carefully chosen to optimise your time and let you experience as big a cross section of Madagascar's treasures as possible. These can be mixed and matched to build an itinerary that fits the time you have available.

Southern route (RN7)   This route follows the 925km Route National 7 for its full length from Tana to Toliara, passing through the domains of the Merina, Betsileo, Zafimaniry and Bara ethnic groups, ending up among the Vezo, Mahafaly and/or Mikea. You will see an excellent range of habitats and landscapes, from rice paddies and rainforests to savannah and spiny bush, which is why this is the most popular tourist route. It is best done with a 4x4 and driver. You can incorporate as a side trip the day-long train journey from Fianarantsoa to Manakara (but cancellations and major delays are very common so don't try to include this in a tight itinerary). Doing the RN7 in this direction means you can finish with some rest and relaxation on the beaches of Anakao or Ifaty before flying back to Tana. The advantages of going in the reverse direction are that you could get a good deal on a vehicle (lots of them drive back to Tana empty because most tourists travel the RN7 southward) and, having got the flight out of the way at the start, you won't risk missing your onward flights from Tana due to an unexpected schedule change.

Allow 7–14 days for this route. See *Chapter 8* and *Chapter 9* for full details.

Southeast (Anosy region)   Because of the terrible state of the roads in the deep south, the Anosy region is effectively disconnected from the rest of the country (fittingly Anosy means 'island') so, unless you have plenty of time, stamina and an adventurous spirit, you will have to fly into and back out of Taolagnaro. But the area is worth it, with some excellent hotels, surfing spots, and top wildlife-viewing opportunities – including Berenty, where oh-so-many lemur documentaries have been filmed.

The southeast makes a good add-on to the southern route, as it's possible to fly direct from Toliara to Taolagnaro. Allow 3–6 days to see the area. More information is on pages 250–64.

The west (Menabe region)   Reachable by road (700km from Tana), river trip or flight, the Menabe area holds some real treasures. From Morondava, you'll pass the famous Baobab Avenue and Kirindy Forest, with its fossa and jumping rats, on your way to the striking limestone pinnacles of Tsingy de Bemaraha. The road is only passable in a 4x4, and only from around May to November.

Allow 4–8 days. Full details are on pages 415–27.

Eastern route (RN2)   Following Route National 2 from Tana will take you to Toamasina, Madagascar's main port. Around the halfway point, if you wish, you can switch your car for a boat and float the rest of the way along the Pangalanes Canal. Having reached the ocean, you can continue to Ile Sainte Marie, which boasts a plethora of palm-shaded beaches and a pirate cemetery. Even if you don't want to follow this whole route, most people do the first 136km section as far as Andasibe, where there is a cluster of spectacular rainforest reserves.

For the whole route, including Andasibe, the canal and Ile Sainte Marie, allow 6–12 days. See *Chapter 10*, *Chapter 11* and *Chapter 13* for full details.

The north (Diana region)   The far north boasts some incredible parks and reserves, paradise islands, and exceptional diving. But Antsiranana is about

1,200km from Tana by road (with relatively little to do *en route*) so people generally fly. The suggested route is to visit Montagne d'Ambre and Ankarana national parks then head southeast to Ankify, the crossing point to Nosy Be. On and around this island there are some top hotels; activities include diving, snorkelling, fishing, sunbathing and even catamaran charters. There is an airport on Nosy Be with regular connections back to Tana.

Allow 6–12 days for the north. More information is in *Chapter 14* and *Chapter 15*.

The northeast (SAVA region) This is another area that is not connected to the rest of the country by proper roads, but which rewards those prepared to expend the effort to get there. Resilient types who aren't in a rush could enter from the north via a horrendous road or from the south by a day-long boat journey; otherwise the only option is to fly in to Sambava or Antalaha. The main highlight in this vanilla-growing region is Marojejy, a mountain national park that is home to rare white silky sifakas. Daraina, where you will find another rare sifaka species, also warrants a visit.

Allow 5–10 days for the SAVA region. Details are on pages 321–31.

TOUR OPERATORS

UK ATTA (*African Travel and Tourism Association; www.atta.co.uk*) has a comprehensive listing for Madagascar, separated into different interests. The organisation **Responsible Travel** (*www.responsibletravel.com*) promotes ethical tour operators. Specialist operators are listed below; note that some of their websites classify Madagascar under Africa while on others you will find it listed under Indian Ocean.

Aardvark Safaris ☏01980 849160/020 8150 7216; e mail@aardvarksafaris.com; www. aardvarksafaris.com. Exclusive tailored holidays & honeymoons.

Abercrombie & Kent ☏01242 547760; e info@ abercrombiekent.co.uk; www.abercrombiekent. co.uk. Luxury itineraries.

Africa & Beyond ☏0161 789 8838; e enquiry@ africaandbeyond.co.uk; www.africaandbeyond. co.uk. Manchester-based family business.

Africa Travel ☏020 7843 3500; e info@ africatravel.co.uk; www.africatravel.co.uk. Wildlife & beach tours.

Audley Travel ☏01993 838250; e africa@ audleytravel.com; www.audleytravel.com. Tailor-made safaris.

Cox & Kings ☏020 3813 9321; e info@ coxandkings.co.uk; www.coxandkings.co.uk. Luxury travel agency.

Explore! ☏01252 884289; e sales@explore. co.uk; www.explore.co.uk. Small-group wildlife tours.

Gane & Marshall ☏01822 600600; e info@ ganeandmarshall.co.uk; www.ganeandmarshall. com. Tailor-made holidays.

G Adventures ☏020 7243 9870; e experience@ gadventures.com; www.gadventures.co.uk. Small-group trips for thrill-seekers & adventurers; wildlife & culture focus. See ad, 2nd colour section.

Imagine Africa ☏020 7622 5114; e info@ imagineafrica.co.uk; www.imagineafrica.co.uk. Tailor-made itineraries.

Natural World Safaris ☏01273 691642; e sales@naturalworldsafaris.com; www. naturalworldsafaris.com. Tailor-made, small-group & family trips for naturalists.

Naturetrek ☏01962 733051; e info@naturetrek. co.uk; www.naturetrek.co.uk. Specialist trips inc lemurs & endemic flora.

Okavango Tours & Safaris ☏07721 387738; e info@okavango.com; www.okavango.com. Long-established specialists in Africa & Indian Ocean.

Pioneer Expeditions ☏01202 798922; e info@pioneerexpeditions.com; www. pioneerexpeditions.com. Adventure travel.

Rainbow Tours ☏020 7666 1276; e info@ rainbowtours.co.uk; www.rainbowtours.co.uk. Experts in tailor-made trips with emphasis on wildlife, birding, culture & community tourism. See ad on the inside of the front cover.

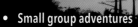

Madagascar Awaits

When you explore Madagascar, you'll get it all –
bustling local life and a natural world teeming with
colour. And with G Adventures, you can give back
to both while having the adventure of a lifetime.

G Adventures

gadventures.co.uk

Reef & Rainforest Tours `01803 866965; e mail@
reefandrainforest.co.uk; www.reefandrainforest.co.uk.
Wide variety of wildlife & adventure tours.
Safari Consultants `01787 888590; e bill@
safariconsultantuk.com; www.safari-consultants.
co.uk. Specialists in the south & central regions.
Steppes Travel `01258 787507; e enquiry@
steppestravel.co.uk; www.steppestravel.co.uk.
Ethical wildlife travel.
Sunbird `01767 262522; e sunbird@
sunbirdtours.co.uk; www.sunbirdtours.co.uk.
Group tours for birders.

Tribes Travel `01473 890499; e enquiries@
tribes.co.uk; www.tribes.co.uk. Tailor-made
holidays. See ad, page 114.
The Ultimate Travel Company `020 3733
5356; e enquiry@theultimatetravelcompany.co.uk;
www.theultimatetravelcompany.co.uk. Upmarket,
personalised journeys.
Wildlife Worldwide `01962 302086;
e reservations@wildlifeworldwide.com; www.
wildlifeworldwide.com. Tailor-made wildlife tours inc
some where you can get hands-on with scientists.
World Odyssey `01905 731373; e info@world-
odyssey.com; www.world-odyssey.com. Luxury
itineraries.

USA Of the operators listed above under *UK*, the following also have offices in the
USA: **Aardvark Safaris** (`858 523 9000`), **Abercrombie & Kent** (*www.abercrombiekent.
com*), **Cox & Kings** (*www.coxandkingsusa.com*), **Explore!** (*www.exploreworldwide.
com*), **Imagine Africa** (*www.imagineafrica.com*), **Natural World Safaris** (`866 357
6569`), **Steppes Travel** (`855 203 7885`) and **World Odyssey** (`800 868 5194`). Also
with a US number is South Africa-based **Jenman Island Safaris** (`866 487 4323`).
These are the US-based specialists:

Cortez USA `800 854 1029/858 755 5136;
e info@cortez-usa.com; www.cortez-usa.com.
Experienced operator; caters for all travellers from
nature lovers to honeymooners.
Field Guides `512 263 7295/800 728 4953;
e fieldguides@fieldguides.com; www.fieldguides.
com. Professionally guided birding tours.
Mountain Travel Sobek `888 831 7526;
e sales@mtsobek.com; www.mtsobek.com.
Private group adventure travel & custom tours.

Terra Incognita Ecotours `855 326 8687;
e info@ecotours.com; www.ecotours.com.
Specialists in responsible travel.
Wilderness Travel `510 558 2488/800 368
2794; e africa@wildernesstravel.com; www.
wildernesstravel.com. Group adventures & small
ship cruises.

SOUTH AFRICA

Birding Africa `021 531 4592; e info@
birdingafrica.com; www.birdingafrica.com. Expert-
led birding & wildlife trips.
Destinations A Buzz `011 467 5713; e janet@
destinationsabuzz.co.za; www.destinationsabuzz.
co.za. Honeymoons & general, adventure &
specialist trips.
Jenman Island Safaris `021 683 7826;
e enquiries@jenmansafaris.com; www.
travel2madagascar.com. Fishing trips, yacht
charters & romantic getaways.
MadagasCaT Charters & Travel `021 200
0173/079 149 6438; e info@madagascat.co.za;

www.madagascat.co.za. Specialised exclusively
in Madagascar; tailor-made tours & catamaran
charters. Exceptional personal service.
Nomad Tours `021 426 5445; e marketing@
nomadtours.co.za; www.nomadtours.co.za.
Adventure & standard itineraries.
Pulse Africa `011 325 2290; e info@
pulseafrica.com; www.pulseafrica.com. Tailor-
made personalised holidays. See ad, page 114.
Starry Starry Nights `011 706 5959; m 082
777 1104; e conradhennig@mweb.co.za; www.
starry-starry-nights.com. Luxury tailored trips;
wildlife focus.

AUSTRALIA AND NEW ZEALAND Abercrombie & Kent has representation in
Australia (*www.abercrombiekent.com.au*); **Terra Incognita Ecotours** can be

contacted free from Australia (✆ *1800 790 704*) and New Zealand (✆ *0800 452 872*); and **Jenman Island Safaris** has an Australian line (✆ *1800 140 835*). These specialists are based in Australia:

Adventure Associates ✆ 02 6355 2022; e mail@adventureassociates.com; www.adventureassociates.com. A range of 9–21-day itineraries. See ad, 2nd colour section.

Adventure World ✆ 1300 295 049; e info@adventureworld.com.au; www.adventureworld.com.au. Mix-'n'-match itineraries to all regions.

Heritage Destinations ✆ 02 4228 3887; e info@heritagedestinations.com.au; www.heritagedestinations.com.au. Custom individual & expert-led small-group tours.

Wildlife Safari ✆ 1800 998 558; e info@wildlifesafari.com.au; www.wildlifesafari.com.au. Luxury wildlife tours.

MADAGASCAR Most reputable Malagasy agencies belong to the trade association **GOTO Madagascar** (Groupement des Opérateurs du Tourisme de Madagascar; *www.go2mada.com*) and/or the one for receptive tour operators: **TOP** (Tours Operators Professionnels Réceptifs de Madagascar; *www.top-madagascar.com*).

Below are listed some of the most active tour operators in Madagascar. See page 110 for an explanation of phoning Malagasy numbers from abroad.

ASISTEN Travel ✆ 22 577 55; e info@asisten-travel.com; www.asisten-travel.com. Highly recommended 100% Malagasy operator specialised in anglophone tourism. See ad, page 74.

Authentic Madagascar Tours ✆ 24 241 32; m 033 11 343 20/033 37 980 80/033 37 980 76; e info@authentic-madagascar-tours.com; www.authentic-madagascar-tours.com. Cultural, wildlife & trekking tours; also yacht cruises. See ad, 2nd colour section.

Boogie Pilgrim ✆ 22 248 37/47; m 033 12 441 27/032 02 375 42; e contact@boogiepilgrim-madagascar.com; www.boogiepilgrim-madagascar.com. Tours of every sort, even by helicopter. Emphasis on sustainable tourism.

Cactus Tours ✆ 22 018 25; m 034 15 057 57; e info@cactus-madagascar.com; www.cactus-madagascar.com. Many types of tours, especially birding, cycling & cultural. See ad, 3rd colour section.

Corporate Adventures ✆ 22 311 64; e info@corporateadventures.mg; www.corporateadventures.mg. A fairly new tour operator from the same company that makes Dzama rum! Their speciality is Land Rover adventures.

Dodo Travel ✆ 22 690 36; e info@dodotravel.com; www.dodotravel.com. Leaders in tailored trips to the Indian Ocean islands.

Encounter Madagascar (Océane Aventures) ✆ 22 312 10; e info@encountermada.com; www.oceane-aventures.com. Adventure tours, cultural experiences & vehicle hire. See ad, 3rd colour section.

Espace Mada m 032 11 301 72/033 11 301 72/034 05 828 45; e espacemada@espacemada.com; www.espacemada.com. Western zone experts with own boats for river trips. See ad, 2nd colour section.

Evasion Sans Frontière ✆ 22 616 69; e info@mada-evasion.mg; www.mada-evasion.com. Specialists for the north & Nosy Be.

GassiTours m 032 41 991 00/033 06 021 48; e gassitours@gmail.com or contact@gassitours.com; www.gassitours.com. Run by enthusiastic local guide Belaza.

Gondwana Explorer ✆ 22 296 96; e info@gondwanaexplorer.com; www.gondwanaexplorer.com. Long-established & reliable.

Holidays Madagascar ✆ 22 222 93; e europe@holidays-mada.com; www.holidays-mada.com. Tours highlighting community & biodiversity. See ad, 2nd colour section.

Island Continent Tours m 033 15 254 96/032 07 254 96; e info@ictours.mg; www.ictours.mg. Reputable Malagasy-Belgian operator & vehicle hire company. See ad, 2nd colour section.

Kijana Tours ✆ 22 649 14; m 034 61 314 37; e kijana.net@moov.mg; www.kijana-tours.com. Running culture & nature tours since 2006 with a sustainability theme.

Le Voyageur ✆ 22 435 21/26 405 80; e voyageur@madagaskar.travel; www.madagaskar.travel. Tailor-made & specialist trips. Swiss-owned.

MAD Caméléon ✆ 22 630 86; m 032 07 344 20; e info@madcameleon.com; www.madcameleon.com

com. Reliable & efficient. Specialities inc river trips & trekking.

Mada Bluesky Tours m 033 03 026 94/034 07 762 02; e contact@mada-bluesky-tours.com or salama_deo@yahoo.fr; www.mada-bluesky-tours. com. Antsirabe-based operator offering tailored tours nationwide. See ad, page 114.

Mada Expeditions m 032 86 614 68/032 40 377 77; e contact@mada-expeditions.com; www. mada-expeditions.com. Tour operator, 4x4 hire & sea kayaking.

Mada Viaggi & Turismo 22 551 31/553 88; m 032 07 670 44; e tourisme@mada-viaggi-turismo.com; www.mada-viaggi-turismo.com. Professional service for tours, from ecotourism to relaxation. See ad, 2nd colour section.

MadaBotanik m 032 02 628 56; e christophe. quenel@yahoo.fr; www.madabotanik.com. Specialists in tours with a flora focus.

Madagascar Airtours 22 241 92/627 99; e airtours@madagascar-airtours.com; www. madagascar-airtours.com. Offering all types of tour since 1968, inc birding, botanical, caving, fishing & adventure.

Madagascar Discovery Agency 22 351 65/367 55; e mda@mda.mg; www.madagascar-discovery.com. Experienced tour organiser & luxury hotel operator.

Madagascar Endemics m 034 07 247 07; e contact@mer-madagascar.com; www.mer-madagascar.com. Enthusiastic experts on wildlife tours. See ad, 2nd colour section.

Madagascar Expedition Agency 22 261 14; e mea@moov.mg; www.tourmadagascar.com. Natural world discovery.

Madagascar Explorer 22 223 23; e info@ madagascar-explorer.net; www.madagascar-explorer.net. Founded by an Italian almost 30 years ago; bespoke tours nationwide. See ad, 2nd colour section.

Madagascar Green Tours m 032 04 364 27/033 04 351 17; e info@madagascar-green-tours.com; www.madagascar-green-tours.com. Antsirabe-based so main focus is south/central tours, inc birding & river trips. See ad, page 113.

Madagascar Mozaic Tour m 034 01 913 19/034 45 629 50; e contact@madagascar-mozaic-tour.com; www.madagascar-mozaic-tour. com. Excellent tailor-made trips for wildlife, photography & adventure. See ad, 2nd colour section.

Madagascar Natural Tours m 034 15 000 30; e madanaturaltours@gmail.com or info@madagascar-natural-tours.com; www. madagascar-natural-tours.com. English-speaking ecotourism specialists. See ad, page 182.

Madagascar Tour Guide m 032 52 503 65; e info@madagascar-tour-guide.com; www. madagascar-tour-guide.com. Camping, biking, birding, river trips & more. Even visits to Zahamena & Lake Alaotra. See ad, page 394.

Madagascar Tour Rental m 033 07 206 38/034 06 843 86; e mclocation@gmail.com; www. madagascar-tour-rental.com. Guided 4x4 tours. See ad, page 435.

Madagascar Touring 26 413 36; m 034 85 009 82/034 79 739 49/034 18 594 06; e infos@madagascaradventures.com; www. madagascaradventures.com. Culture, adventure & wildlife tours. See ad, page 435.

Madagascar Tourism Expeditions 22 365 15; m 032 02 278 94; e info@madagascar-tourism-expeditions.com; www.madagascar-tourism-expeditions.com. Professional operator. See ad, page 113.

Madagascar Visit Company m 033 18 081 77/034 73 440 45; e lovasson@yahoo.fr; www. madagascar-visite.com. Run by enthusiastic & reliable English-speaking guide Lova Emadisson; tailored tours by 4x4 & river. See ad, page 113.

Madamax 22 351 01; m 032 04 130 41; e madamax@madamax.com; www.madamax.com. Adventure sports, climbing, trekking, canoeing & white-water rafting. See ad, page 144.

Makay Tours e contact@makay-tours.com; www.makay-tours.com. Young English-speaking team with a focus on responsible tourism.

Malagasy Tours 22 356 07; m 034 49 627 24/034 49 356 07; e contact@malagasy-tours. com; www.malagasy-tours.com. Custom tours inc specialised botanical itineraries, trekking, birding & lemurs. See ad, 2nd colour section.

Mercure 22 237 79; m 032 05 221 55; e mercure@mercure-voyages.com; www.mercure-voyages.com. Reliable operator founded in 1972; 4x4 & bus hire.

Mora-Travel 22 020 12; m 032 07 115 11; e info@moratravel.com; www.moratravel.com. Dutch-owned operator offering flexible itineraries since 2000. See ad, 2nd colour section.

Moto Tour Madagascar m 032 11 028 52; e contact@moto-tour-madagascar.mg; www.

4

moto-tour-madagascar.mg. Specialists in 7- to 15-day motorbike trips, on & off road.

MTV Tours ✆26 405 43; **m** 032 42 545 14/033 06 763 31; **e** info@madagascar-visit-tours.com; www.madagascar-visit-tours.com. Many destinations & activities. See ad, 3rd colour section.

Ortour **m** 032 07 704 64/034 05 704 64; **e** ortour@gmail.com; www.ortour.com. Trustworthy operator of package & tailor-made trips. Trekking a speciality. See ad, 3rd colour section.

PRIORI ✆22 625 27; **e** priori@moov.mg; www.priori.ch. Swiss-owned & reliable. They also run a Madagascar information centre in Switzerland (*www.madagaskarhaus.ch*). See ad, 2nd colour section.

Ramartour ✆22 487 23; **m** 032 02 133 68/033 14 978 81; **e** info@ramartour.com; www.ramartour.com. Personal service from a dedicated & enthusiastic Dutch-Malagasy couple. See ad, page 113.

Remote River Expeditions ✆95 523 47; **m** 032 47 326 70; **e** info@remoterivers.com; www.remoterivers.com. Morondava-based specialists in river trips & custom themed tours. See ad, 4th colour section.

Roadtrip Madagascar **m** 033 02 804 23; www.roadtripmadagascar.com. Hire of 4x4s (self-drive or with driver) equipped with camp gear. See ads, pages 73, 114 & 2nd colour section.

SETAM Madagascar ✆22 298 07; **e** setam@iris.mg; www.setam-madagascar.com. Experienced operator of traditional tours.

Sobeha **m** 034 09 385 48/033 02 789 45; **e** infosobeha@gmail.com; www.sobeha.net. All kinds of tours inc by bike. See ad, 2nd colour section.

TAMàNA **m** 034 20 660 02; **e** info@tamana-tours.com; www.tamana-tours.com. Responsible tourism to all corners of the island.

Touramada **m** 032 52 262 18; **e** info@touramada.com; www.touramada.com. Adventure, climbing, kitesurfing & diving experts with their own 18m schooner.

Universal Trading Tourisme ✆22 411 30; **e** tourisme@universal-madagascar.com; www.universal-madagascar.com. Italian-owned with a fleet of 4x4s & minibuses.

Urlaub auf Madagaskar **m** 033 12 048 92; **e** kontakt@urlaub-auf-madagascar.com; www.urlaub-auf-madagascar.com. Experienced English-speaking operator especially recommended for tailored specialised, themed or family trips. Based not far from Antananarivo airport, they also have a beautiful quiet guesthouse, Villa Sibylle, for clients. See ad, 2nd colour section.

Visit Mada Tours **m** 033 11 319 24; **e** visitmadatours@gmail.com; www.madagascar-tour.com. Tours, car rental, canoeing, trekking & river trips. See ad, page 182.

Za Tours ✆22 424 22; **e** zatour@iris.mg; www.zatours-madagascar.com. Experienced & conscientious operator able to tailor tours to a wide range of interests: birding, entomology, history, diving, etc. See ad, 2nd colour section.

FIND YOUR OWN GUIDE If you're on a tight budget, you could skip the middleman and seek out a guide yourself. It's a riskier option since you must trust their word that they are knowledgeable and reliable, but it's a great way of keeping costs down while ensuring your money benefits the real Malagasy people. There are several websites designed to hook travellers up with freelancers and willing locals; the main ones with members in Madagascar are Who's My Guide (*www.whosmyguide.com*), Tours By Locals (*www.toursbylocals.com*), ShowAround (*www.showaround.com*), Viator (*www.tourguides.viator.com*) and Shiroube (*http://shiroube.com*).

RED TAPE

VISAS Visa rules are the same for all nationalities. Every foreign tourist requires one and they are easy to obtain at the airport on arrival, although if you prefer you can get it in advance of your trip at the Malagasy embassy in your country (this option may be more expensive).

There are three categories: **up to 30 days** (80,000Ar/€24/US$26), **31–60 days** (100,000Ar/€29/US$33) and **61–90 days** (140,000Ar/€41/US$46), payable in cash in euros, dollars or ariary. Fees are fixed in ariary so the foreign currency amounts may vary with exchange rate fluctuations. Extension of a 90-day visa is not possible under normal circumstances, but if you exit (to Mauritius or Réunion, say) you can come back immediately and get a fresh 90-day visa on your return.

MADAGASCAR'S EMBASSIES AND CONSULATES ABROAD For details of Madagascar's foreign diplomatic missions, you can refer to www.madagascar-consulate.org. Until such time as the London embassy reopens, Brits should contact the one in Belgium or France. The main foreign embassies in Madagascar are listed on page 174.

GETTING THERE AND AWAY

BY AIR It can be cheaper to book through an agency or flight metasearch site such as Google Flights (*www.google.com/flights*), Skyscanner (*www.skyscanner. net*), Expedia (*www.expedia.com*), Kayak (*www.kayak.com*), Opodo (*www.opodo. com*), Cheapflights (*www.cheapflights.co.uk*), eBookers (*www.ebookers.com*) or STA Travel (*www.statravel.co.uk*) rather than contacting airlines direct.

From the UK There are no direct flights to Madagascar from the UK. **Air France** (*www.airfrance.com*) flies from several UK cities via Paris three times a week. **Kenya Airways** (*www.kenya-airways.com*) is generally a cheaper option with flights from London Heathrow via Nairobi most days, but sometimes with long connections. Although generally a more expensive option, **South African Airways** (*www.flysaa.com*) is a reliable operator to Johannesburg, from where you can connect through to Tana or Nosy Be with their regional partner **Airlink** (*www.flyairlink.com; see ad, 2nd colour section*). The last single-stop option from London is via Mauritius with **Air Mauritius** (*www.airmauritius.com*) but this can entail a lengthy stopover. As of 2015, the multi-award-winning **Turkish Airlines** (*www.turkishairlines.com*) offers a comfortable alternative route from various points in the UK via Istanbul four times a week at surprisingly competitive rates, but note that the plane makes a brief stop in Mauritius before reaching Tana. The very lowest prices from London are often found on the three-hop route via Abu Dhabi and Mahé with **Air Seychelles** (*www.airseychelles.com*) – the first leg of which is operated by their codeshare partner Etihad.

From Europe Air Madagascar (*www.airmadagascar.com*) flies direct between Paris and Tana most days, taking 10½ hours, sometimes with a stop in Marseille. Air Mad is represented in the UK by Aviareps (*www.aviareps.com*). The airline was blacklisted by EU airspace in 2011 but the ban was finally lifted in 2016. It should be noted that the safety concerns that resulted in the embargo were over the condition of the aircraft previously being used rather than any serious incident (Air Mad has had just one fatal accident since 1970, and that was a 19-seater 33 years ago; for comparison, in the same period Air France had nine fatal accidents while British Airways had two). **Corsair** (*www.corsair.fr*) connects Paris with Tana once a week and is usually cheaper than Air France, but makes a brief stop in Réunion *en route*.

From most other European countries, it is necessary to transit via one of the aforementioned hubs (Paris, Istanbul, Nairobi, Mauritius or Johannesburg). From Italy, **Air Italy** (*www.meridiana.it*) operates weekly flights direct to Nosy Be from Milan. And as of late 2016, **LOT Polish Airlines** (*www.lot.com*) runs a Warsaw–Tana connection.

From other Indian Ocean islands The tourist boards of the Indian Ocean islands have started to engage on a co-operative marketing strategy under the brand 'the Vanilla Islands', leading to a recent increase in flight links across the region. You can fly

4

with Air Madagascar from Mauritius, Réunion, Mayotte and the Comoros. **Air Austral** (*www.air-austral.com*) connects the main five Malagasy airports with Mauritius and Réunion. **Air Mauritius** also flies to Tana from Mauritius and **Air Seychelles** connects Tana to the Seychelles twice a week (Air Madagascar has a codeshare on this route). **Comores Aviation International** (*www.comoresaviation.com*) links Anjouan and Moroni with Tana and Mahajanga and another Comoroan company, **AB Aviation** (*www.flyabaviation.com*), also flies from Moroni to these two Malagasy destinations. **EWA Air** (*www.ewa-air.com*) has routes from Mayotte to five cities in Madagascar.

From Africa Kenya Airways flies daily to Tana and Airlink connects Johannesburg to both Tana and Nosy Be. AB Aviation links Dar-es-Salaam in Tanzania to Antananarivo via a brief stop in Moroni (Comoros).

From the USA and Canada Madagascar is about as far from California as it is possible to be so fares from North America are typically expensive, but it is worth investing some time in checking out all the options as there are some very good deals. The cheapest options most often go via Paris or Johannesburg.

From Australia One option is to go via Johannesburg and pick up a flight with Airlink from there. But it usually works out cheapest to take Air Mauritius from Perth to Madagascar via Mauritius, or via Abu Dhabi and Mahé with Air Seychelles.

BY SEA
From other Indian Ocean islands The *Mauritius Trochetia* has passenger cabins and sometimes plies the Toamasina–Mauritius route via Réunion (4 days); contact Mauritius Shipping for details (*www.mauritiusshipping.net*). A ferry called *Maria Galanta* operates between Mahajanga and Maroni/Mutsamudu in the Comoros. The 18-hour crossing costs €115 one way. Reservations can be made directly with the operator (*www.sgtm.com*) or through their representative in Mahajanga (\ *62 231 29*; m *034 15 085 47/032 04 822 39*).

From mainland Africa There are no passenger boats crossing the Mozambique Channel to Madagascar, but many people sail their own yachts from Durban. It takes six or seven days to reach Anakao.

EXPORT RESTRICTIONS There is a 2kg limit on vanilla pods for passengers departing Madagascar. Other allowances are 400,000Ar in local currency, 1kg of gemstones, 1kg of coffee, 1kg of pepper and, bizarrely, 1kg of onions. Certificates are required to take out of the country any precious woods, precious stones, precious metals, or animal or vegetable material. Take receipts for your purchases to the mining, forestry, veterinary and phytosanitary kiosks inside Ivato airport before departure.

WHAT TO TAKE

This section gives you some guidance on what to consider packing. The ideal content of your travel bags depends significantly on the level of accommodation you will be staying in and how you will be travelling. Items essential to one traveller might be dead weight to another, so nobody will need *everything* listed here.

LUGGAGE A **soft bag or backpack** is more practical than a hard case. Backpackers should consider buying a rucksack with a zipped compartment to enclose the straps when using them on airlines. Or bring a lightweight **rucksack bag**, which protects the straps, gives added security, and may also double as a rain cover.

CLOTHES There is quite a difference between summer and winter temperatures, particularly in the highlands and the south where it is distinctly cold at night between May and September. A fibre-pile **jacket** or a body warmer is useful in addition to a light **sweater**. In June and July a scarf can give much-needed extra warmth. At any time of the year it will be hot during the day in low-lying areas, and very hot between October and March. Layers of clothing – **T-shirt**, sweatshirt, light sweater – are warm and versatile, and take less room than a heavy sweater. Don't bring jeans, they are too heavy and too hot. Lightweight cotton or cotton-mix **trousers** are much more suitable. At any time of year you will need a light **shower-proof jacket**, and during the wet season, or if spending time in the rainforest, appropriate rain gear and perhaps a small **umbrella**. A light cotton jacket is always useful for breezy evenings by the coast. Don't forget a **sunhat** and **sunglasses**. Be aware that military-style clothing is officially forbidden; we have never heard of birders with camouflage outfits getting into trouble but it would be wise to avoid wearing such gear in sensitive areas such as airports.

For footwear, **trainers** and sandals are usually all you need. **Sports sandals** which strap securely to the feet are better than flip-flops. **Hiking boots** are necessary for Marojejy and may be required in places like Ankarana, Andringitra and Isalo but are not necessary for the main tourist circuits.

Give some thought to beachwear if you enjoy snorkelling. You may need an old pair of trainers or some diving booties to protect your feet from coral and sea urchins, and a T-shirt and shorts to wear while in the water to prevent sunburn.

TOILETRIES Although you can buy just about everything in Madagascar, imported goods can be very expensive, especially products like **sunscreen**. Bring **moist wipes** for freshening up, and **antibacterial hand gel**. When used regularly, especially after shaking hands or handling money, this is a real help in preventing traveller's diarrhoea. **Dental floss** is excellent for repairs as well as for teeth.

Don't take up valuable space with a towel; all hotels provide them. If you want to bring your own, then pack a **sarong** (or buy a *lamba* on arrival; see page 21). It is more absorbent than you'd think, very lightweight, incredibly fast-drying (which can be really useful), and more multi-purpose than a towel: you can lie on it on the beach, sleep under it, use it for shade, hang it up for a bit of privacy to change behind, or wear it like a skirt.

MEDICAL ITEMS For detailed advice on what to put in your **medical kit**, see *Chapter 5*. In addition to any regular medication and other personal items like contact lenses, you must not forget your **malaria prophylaxis**. It is impossible to understate how vital it is to be properly protected against mosquitoes. DEET-based **repellents** are by far the most effective but need to be at least 20% concentration (ideally 50%) and can damage synthetic fabrics and plastics. Some natural alternatives have been shown to work but require far more frequent reapplication. For hotel rooms, pyrethrum coils which burn slowly are available cheaply all over Madagascar. Plug-in repellents work in a similar way. Most hotels in areas with mosquitoes have effective screening or provide nets. If you are staying in budget hotels you should consider bringing your own **mosquito net**, as even if one is provided it is likely to have rips. Hotel rooms rarely have hooks to hang nets from, so a free-standing type may be more practical (though more expensive). A couple of **bungee cords** with hooked ends can be useful for rigging up a hanging net.

Camping and backpacking gear Basic camping gear gives you the freedom to travel adventurously. You will need some sort of cover to protect your backpack from dirt: either buy a custom one or use a rice sack from a Madagascar market.

In winter (June to August) a lightweight **sleeping bag** will keep you warm in cheap hotels with inadequate bedding. A sleeping bag liner plus a light blanket (buy on arrival) are ideal for the summer months (September to May).

An **air-mattress or pillow** gives added comfort on hard seats or pads your hips when sleeping out. One of those horseshoe-shaped travel pillows lets you sleep sitting up (which you'll need to do on *taxi-brousses*).

A lightweight **tent** allows you to strike out on your own and stay in national parks and on deserted beaches. It will need to be well ventilated. Tent designs that can be erected without pegs are strongly advised, as many sheltered tent pitches at campsites have wooden floors which pegs cannot be driven into.

Bring a lightweight **camping stove** if you will be spending a lot of nights under canvas. Standard gas canisters can be sourced in the capital but are hard to find elsewhere. There are always fresh vegetables for sale in the smallest village so bring some stock cubes to make vegetable stew. Take your own **mug and spoon** so you can enjoy roadside coffee without the risk of a cup rinsed in filthy water, and market yoghurt without someone else's germs on the spoon. Don't forget a **water bottle** and **water purifiers** (see page 118).

HANDY ITEMS FOR BUDGET TRAVELLERS Bring a small roll of insulating tape or **gaffer tape** which can be used for all manner of things, including patching up the inevitable holes in the mozzie nets at cheap hotels. **Blu-tack** is equally versatile; bring enough to make a plug for your sink, to stop doors banging or to hold them open. **Penknives** and **scissors** are very useful, a **rubber wedge** will secure your hotel door at night, and a **combination padlock** has many uses. A **light tarpaulin** and a length of **strong cord** also have multiple uses, as do **Ziploc plastic bags**.

Earplugs are just about essential if you are a light sleeper, to block out not only the sounds of the towns but those of enthusiastic nocturnal animals when camping in reserves. A large **handkerchief or bandana** is handy for mopping your streaming face or protecting your neck from the sun or your hair and lungs from dust.

ELECTRICAL AND PHOTOGRAPHIC EQUIPMENT The mains voltage in Madagascar is 220V. Outlets are European-style plugs with two round pins. Note that increasingly upper-end eco-hotels in remote locations are using solar power; such lodgings usually do not have power sockets in the rooms (but batteries can always be charged at reception).

Don't forget to pack a **small torch**, a **headlamp** for night walks and a travel **alarm clock** (or mobile phone with that facility). You won't forget your **camera** but think carefully about all the **camera accessories** you may need: memory cards, spare batteries, data cables, flash, cleaning kit, tripod, etc. You may also want to take **binoculars**.

AA batteries, although sold everywhere, are almost universally of poor quality, which will not be a problem for low-drain applications such as alarm clocks or small torches, but may not work at all in a digital camera. Bring good **rechargeable batteries** from home. It may be useful to pack a solar **charger** as well as a plug-in one.

BOOKS, ETC You will probably want to take a **notebook and pens**, not only if you like to keep a travel journal but also for noting names of places and species you photograph and the contact details of new friends you make.

Give some thought to ways of interacting with the locals; a Malagasy **phrase book** provides lots of amusement as you practise your skills, and a pocket French dictionary could help you get by off the main tourist trail. Keen naturalists may need **field guides** – although many of them are impractically heavy to take with you. See *Appendix 3* for recommended books.

Bring enough general **reading material** (English-language books are not easy to find) and maybe a clip-on reading light for nocturnal bibliophiles. **Playing cards** and other **travel games** will help fill quiet evenings or, if you prefer to lie on the beach and enjoy the night sky, why not take a **star chart** for the southern hemisphere?

And lastly, remember your **guidebook**, naturally!

GIFTS This is a difficult area. In the past tourists have handed out presents to children and created the tiresome little beggars you will encounter in the popular areas (if you don't now know the French for 'pen' or 'sweets', you soon will). They have also handed T-shirts to adults with similar consequences. For more on this subject see *Chapter 6*. There are, however, plenty of occasions when a gift is appropriate. Giving money in return for services is entirely acceptable so in rural areas it's best to pay cash and refrain from introducing a new consumer awareness. In urban areas or with more sophisticated Malagasy people, presents are a very good way of showing your appreciation for kindness or exceptional service. If you want to contribute something a little more intellectually satisfying, here is a suggestion from Dr Philip Jones of Money for Madagascar: 'I was asked several times for an English Grammar, so any such books would be valued gifts. If visitors take a French–English dictionary, why not leave it in Madagascar?'

The most deserving of your gifts are the hard-pressed charities working to make life bearable for those struggling most in Madagascar. Why not contact one of the many organisations mentioned in *Chapter 6* and elsewhere in this book to see if there are any urgently needed items you can take out to them?

MONEY

It is easy to find places to exchange **foreign cash** in euros or US dollars but somewhat harder to change pounds. Exchange rates are typically better at bureaux de change than banks, but do shop around (we have seen variations of up to 20% between the rates of different offices just within Ivato airport). The ideal denomination is €20/50 or US$20/50, because high-value notes are generally not accepted (owing to fears of counterfeits) while there is often a worse exchange rate for low-value notes. They may also refuse to exchange old (pre-2006) or dog-eared notes. Most banks in the major towns will also accept euro/dollar **travellers' cheques**.

Large hotels now usually take **credit cards** – mainly Visa, but MasterCard acceptance is catching up; nobody takes American Express. Credit and debit cards may be used to draw cash at most banks. Branches of BFV and BOA banks only accept Visa, and BNI takes both. Almost all banks in Tana and the major towns now have **ATMs**, and increasingly even in smaller towns. BNI machines dispense a maximum of 385,000Ar per withdrawal; for BFV the limit is 300,000Ar.

If you need cash in a hurry there are **Western Union** offices at most banks and post offices across Madagascar. Money can be transferred from home in a few hours, or in minutes if your nearest and dearest are willing to go to a Western Union office with cash (*www.westernunion.com*).

THE CURRENCY In 2003, the *franc malgache* (FMG) was replaced by the ariary (Ar). But only urban centres have fully adapted to the 'new' currency; in rural areas the locals still quote prices in the old FMG. One ariary is equal to 5FMG.

Banknotes in circulation range from 100Ar to 10,000Ar, with the introduction of a new 20,000Ar note announced as we went to press. Smaller denomination coins exist down to 1Ar, although tourists rarely encounter these.

The ariary floats against hard currencies and the exchange rate changes frequently. For this reason many upper-range hotels quote their prices in euros. Approximate exchange rates as of 2017: £1 = 4,050Ar, €1 = 3,450Ar, US$1 = 3,225Ar.

HOW MUCH WILL IT COST? The airfare is the most expensive part of your trip. Once there, you will find Madagascar can be a relatively cheap country for accommodation, food and public transport. Fuel prices are equivalent to those in Europe, however, so car hire is not cheap, and domestic flights are definitely pricey. Travelling by *taxi-brousse*, and eating and sleeping like the locals, a couple can keep general costs below £25/€30/US$33 per day. Note that couples can travel almost as cheaply as singles, since most budget and mid-range hotels charge by the room.

Costs quickly mount up if you are visiting many national parks or reserves. You must pay the park permit fee plus the cost of a guide, which together can total £75/€88/$99 per day for a couple at some of the flagship sites.

Save money by being sensible about where you buy bottled water; upmarket hotels can charge up to ten times the supermarket price (and similarly for beer). Purify your own water (see page 118) to avoid this expense entirely.

TIPPING This is a tricky subject on which to give universal advice and one that consistently causes anxiety in travellers. Tipping is normal for guides, drivers, porters, etc who have performed their duties impressively. In restaurants, a tip of 5% is plenty. Baggage handlers at airports and some hotels are masters of the disappointment act. They may feign offence at the amount if they think you are new to Madagascar, but a tip of 500–1,000Ar is ample for carrying luggage. Taxi drivers do not expect a tip.

Forest guides should be tipped according to their service. There is no obligation to tip, but those enthusiastic guides who have done well in spotting animals, speak good English, and have shown themselves to be knowledgeable about the flora and fauna might expect to be rewarded with a gratuity of 2,000–20,000Ar (€1–6) per day.

The hardest tipping question is how much to pay the guides and drivers who have spent several days with you and given excellent service. The answer here is to keep in mind the cost of living in Madagascar and tip proportionately: a fully qualified government schoolteacher has a starting salary of €80 per month but the best can earn three times that with experience; community teachers, who are less qualified but make up 70% of the teaching staff in Malagasy schools, get no more than €30 a month.

Give tips in ariary rather than foreign currency and do try to ensure that the people who work behind the scenes, such as cooks and cleaners, also get rewarded.

GETTING AROUND

BY ROAD 'If I make roads, the white man will only come and take my country. I have two allies: *hazo* [forest] and *tazo* [fever],' declared King Radama I. Coping with the 'roads' is one of the great travel challenges in Madagascar. It's not that the royal decree has lasted 200 years but there's a third ally that the king didn't mention – the weather. Torrential rain and cyclones destroy roads almost as fast as they are constructed.

Taxi-brousse is the generic name for public transport in Madagascar. *Car-brousse*, *camion-brousse*, *taxi-be* and *kat-kat* are also used, but they all refer to the 'bush-

Every visitor has a *taxi-brousse* story or two. Here are a few sent in by readers over the years.

At about 10 o'clock the two of us went to the taxi-brousse station. 'Yes, yes, there is a car. It is here, ready to go.' We paid our money. 'When will it go?' 'When it has nine passengers.' 'How many has it got now?' 'Wait a minute.' A long look at notebooks, then a detailed calculation. 'Two.' 'As well as us?' 'No, no, including you.' It finally left at about 7 o'clock. (Chris Ballance)

After several hours we picked up four more people. We couldn't believe it – the driver had to sit on someone's lap! (Stephen Cartledge)

I was jammed in behind a very sick soldier, who spent most of the journey with his head out of the window spewing lurid green bile like something from a horror movie. After 20 minutes we had to stop at a roadside stall to buy mangoes. Since I was now on the sunny side of the vehicle the temperature of my shirt rose to what, had it been made of polyester, would have been melting point. Our next stop was Antsirabe where we were surrounded by apple vendors. All and sundry went absolutely berserk. I hadn't seen so many apples since… since we left Ambositra. At about 5pm the radio was turned on so we could listen to two men shouting at each other at a volume which would have caused bleeding of the eardrums in Wembley Stadium. At about 6pm it started to get decidedly brisk, and since the ailing squaddie in front of me showed no sign of having rid himself of toxic enzymes I now had to endure an icy blast in my face. Our next stop was for grapes. We now had enough fruit on board to start a wholesale business in Covent Garden, and I was a bit tetchy. (Robert Stewart)

We eventually made it after an eventful 4-hour taxi-brousse journey which entailed the obligatory trawl around town for more passengers, selling the spare tyre shortly after setting off, a 30-minute wait outside the doctor's as the driver wasn't feeling very well, and all of us having to bump-start the vehicle every time we stopped to pick anyone up. (H & M Kendrick)

I woke up nice and early to get my taxi-brousse to Mahamasina from Diego. I clambered on to a nice new minibus, eager to hit the open road. There was one other passenger. We cruised around for 3 hours, frequently changing drivers, trying to get more customers. In this time our driver got into three fights, one lasting half an hour. There was even a painful-looking tug-of-war with passengers to persuade them to use their taxi-brousse. (Ben Tapley)

Our journey from Morondava to Antsirabe began with nine sweaty hours of east-coast heat, then rapidly became teeth-chatteringly cold as we climbed up to the *hauts plateaux* in the middle of the night. Sat alongside the driver we wondered why he kept leaning across us to fiddle with the seal around the windscreen. We understood when, after bumping across miles of pot-holes, the window worked its way loose and eventually slipped out of its frame entirely. Unable to push it back into place, the driver attempted to tie it with rope. This was unsuccessful, so it fell to me to hold the windscreen in place for the rest of the journey! We barely raised an eyebrow when later in the journey the side door fell off. (Daniel Austin)

On one memorable trip from Fianar to Tana the back three seats were stacked high with crates of chicks which chirped noisily for the full 10 hours. In addition to the breakdowns we've come to expect, we drove through a fire, came close to colliding with at least one oncoming vehicle, dodged an exploding tyre from the truck in front, and a chicken lost its life under our wheels. (Kelly Green)

taxis' which run along virtually every road in the country. These have improved a lot in recent years, especially along tourist routes.

Red-and-white 'milestones' mark out 1km intervals along main roads. These markers, known as Points Kilométriques (PK), are numbered starting from a major town (usually Tana). PK numbers are given throughout this book to specify points on major routes.

Taxi-brousse If you're prepared for the realities, an overland journey can be very enjoyable and gives you a chance to get to know the Malagasy. Taxi-brousses are generally minibuses with about 14 seats, which operate on all roads that are in good enough condition. For rougher roads there are several more rugged varieties on the theme.

Vehicles typically leave from the *gare routière* (bus station) on the side of town closest to their destination, although some towns have one combined station. You should try to go there a day or two ahead of your planned departure to check times and prices, and reserve a seat. Buy from a kiosk, not a middleman, and make sure you get a receipt. You should only have to pay half the fare as a deposit.

Arriving at a big taxi-brousse station can be a scary experience. You are likely to get mobbed by touts demanding to know where you are going. Keep an eye on your luggage; it's not likely to be stolen, but touts often take bags hostage by loading them on to their preferred vehicle before you've even decided which company you want to travel with. Just head determinedly for one of the kiosks and talk directly to the official at the desk. Most stations have numerous offices of different companies, but prices should be standard across them all. Not all companies offer all destinations.

Come prepared for a long wait. Taxi-brousses do sometimes leave on time, but as they never depart until they are full it can be hours before you set off.

If you want to reserve a particular seat, check they write your name on their seat plan when you book. Choose your seat carefully. The two seats upfront may be the most comfy and usually the only ones with seat belts, but sitting next to the driver you'll be punched in the leg each time he changes gear (no good if you want to sleep) and these seats can get hot as they are above the engine. The row directly behind the driver has the best leg room.

Tourists are occasionally charged for luggage that is strapped on to the roof, but you are entitled to 20kg or so for free, so refuse politely. If you have a very large quantity of luggage then a fee is reasonable, but you should not pay more than about 10,000Ar per 50kg of extra stuff.

On overnight journeys (best avoided for security reasons; see page 125), come prepared for cold even if it's sweltering at the time of departure. On the winding roads of the highlands, motion sickness can be a problem, so take precautions if you are prone. Drivers stop to eat, but usually drive all night. If they do stop during the night most passengers stay in the vehicle or sleep on the road outside.

BY AIR Air Madagascar (*www.airmadagascar.com*) started its life in 1962 as Madair, a name that was so mocked that they changed it within a year. Although previously quite a reliable airline, their operations have recently reached a state of such disarray that a reversion to their original name might seem appropriate. It is now 90% owned by the government, employs around 2,000 staff and runs a fleet of 11 planes.

Since 2011, last-minute time changes and cancellations have become not just commonplace but almost normal on domestic routes; one traveller reported that of 12 domestic flights he booked over a six-month period, only two went ahead at the expected time. Flights not only get cancelled or delayed but also brought forward, with several readers telling us they were notified at the last moment that

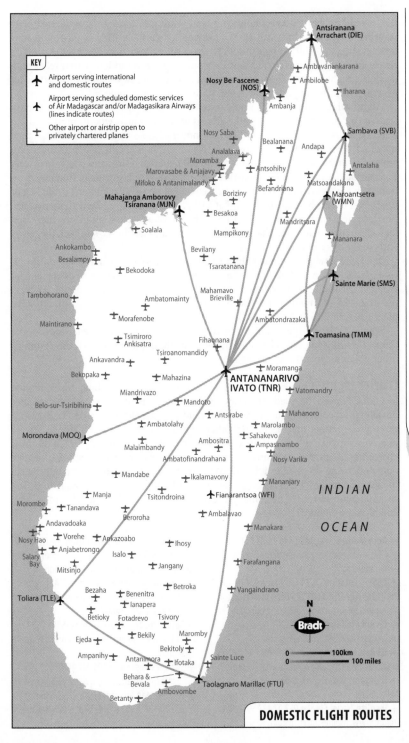

KEY

✈ Airport serving international and domestic routes

✈ Airport serving scheduled domestic services of Air Madagascar and/or Madagasikara Airways (lines indicate routes)

+ Other airport or airstrip open to privately chartered planes

Antsiranana Arrachart (DIE)
Ambavanankarana
Nosy Be Fascene (NOS)
Ambilobe
Iharana
Ambanja
Sambava (SVB)
Nosy Saba
Bealanana
Andapa
Antalaha
Analalava
Moramba
Antsohihy
Matsoandakana
Marovasabe & Anjajavy
Befandriana
Maroantsetra (WMN)
Mifoko & Antanimalandy
Boriziny
Mananara
Mahajanga Amborovy Tsiranana (MJN)
Besakoa
Mandritsara
Soalala
Mampikony
Bevilany
Sainte Marie (SMS)
Ankokambo
Tsaratanana
Besalampy
Bekodoka
Mahamavo Brieville
Tambohorano
Ambatomainty
Ambatondrazaka
Morafenobe
Toamasina (TMM)
Maintirano
Tsimiroro Ankisatra
Fihaonana
Ankavandra
Tsiroanomandidy
Moramanga
Bekopaka
Mahazina
ANTANANARIVO IVATO (TNR)
Vatomandry
Miandrivazo
Mandoto
Belo-sur-Tsiribihina
Antsirabe
Mahanoro
Ambatolahy
Marolambo
Morondava (MOQ)
Sahakevo
Malaimbandy
Ambositra
Ampasinambo
Ambatofinandrahana
Nosy Varika
Mandabe
Ikalamavony
Mananjary
Manja
Tsitondroina
Fianarantsoa (WFI)
INDIAN
Morombe
Tanandava
Ambalavao
Andavadoaka
Beroroha
Manakara
OCEAN
Nosy Hao
Vorehe
Ankazoabo
Ihosy
Salary Bay
Anjabetrongo
Isalo
Farafangana
Mitsinjo
Jangany
Betroka
Vangaindrano
Bezaha
Benenitra
Toliara (TLE)
Ianapera
Betioky
Fotadrevo
Tsivory
Ejeda
Bekily
Maromby
Bekitoly
Ampanihy
Antanimora
Ifotaka
Sainte Luce
Behara & Bevala
Taolagnaro Marillac (FTU)
Ambovombe
Betanty

N
Bradt

0 ——— 100km
0 ——— 100 miles

DOMESTIC FLIGHT ROUTES

they would be flying several hours, or even a full day, sooner than planned. One traveller was woken by a call at 04.00 saying his early-evening flight would now be departing at 06.00, so he must go to the airport immediately! Given Air Mad's recent unreliability, it is inadvisable to arrange any travel itinerary that relies on a domestic flight departing on time, without any contingency plan. Constructing an itinerary with two flights on the same day is asking for trouble.

Flights which are said to be fully booked at the office may in fact have empty seats, so it can be worth going to the airport well in advance, where empty seats are filled on a first-come-first-served basis. Conversely, passengers who check in late may find their seats resold, so always arrive in good time. Officially passengers are advised to arrive 2 hours before the scheduled departure time, and check-in at least an hour before to guarantee their tickets are not released for resale. Passengers on domestic flights are limited to one checked bag of up to 20kg and one cabin bag of up to 6kg. Excess baggage is charged at €1/kg. Arriving at the gate with an oversize or overweight cabin bag incurs a €10 penalty. They have also significantly increased fees and penalties for date changes, cancellations and no shows, so check the terms and conditions carefully.

In 2015, a new airline called **Madagasikara Airways** (*www.madagasikaraairways. com*) launched, adopting the *ankoay* – Madagascar fish eagle – as its official emblem. At the time of writing they have just a single 30-seat Embraer aircraft, operating 25–30 flights per week to nine destinations across the island, but have plans to expand their fleet soon.

See the map on page 99 for the current domestic routes of these airlines. At the time of writing the typical cost of flying from the capital to one of the country's other major airports (one way) is about €250.

Charter flights Private aircraft can be the only way of reaching many remote locations if days of off-road driving are to be avoided. They can give you much greater flexibility; scheduled flights serve only around a dozen airports across Madagascar, but there are more than a hundred other airstrips and helipads available to private planes (see map, page 99). With scheduled domestic flights often in such disarray, chartering an aircraft can sometimes be the only solution. Stories abound of tour operators being dropped in it by Air Mad and being left with no choice but to take the huge financial hit and lay on a charter flight to get their clients from A to B. The main operators are listed here; many also do medical evacuations, aerial photography and pleasure flights.

✈ **Aero Marine** m 032 11 444 44/033 11 444 44; e aeromarine.com@gmail.com; www. aeromarine.mg

✈ **ASSIST Aviation** ✆ 24 106 11; m 034 07 185 98/034 07 187 30/034 07 185 86; e aviation.dg@ assistgroup.mg or aviation.ops@assistgroup.mg

✈ **CivAIR Madagascar** ✆ 22 261 14; e civair@ moov.mg; www.civairmadagascar.com

✈ **GS Aviation** m 032 11 019 04/032 11 020 05; e sar@gs-aviation.com; www.gs-aviation.com

✈ **Heliquip** e chris@heliquip.net; www. heliquip.net

✈ **Insolite Travel Fly** m 032 07 427 50; e itf@ itf.mg; www.insolite-travel-fly.com

✈ **Madagascar Transport Aériens (MTA)** m 034 03 355 35/032 07 090 09; e mtransair@ moov.mg or mta@mta.mg; www.mta.mg

✈ **Mission Aviation Fellowship (MAF)** ✆ 24 524 57; m 032 11 656 05; e mad-office@maf.org; www.maf-madagascar.org

✈ **Service et Transport Aériens (STA)** ✆ 22 230 34; e stacommercial@gmail.com; www.sta-aviation.com

✈ **Sky Services** m 032 05 217 40/033 37 217 40; e infos@skymada.com; www.skymada.com

✈ **Trans Ocean Airways (TOA)** ✆ 22 538 38; m 032 05 536 36/034 02 411 48; e toa@toa.mg; www.toa.mg

BY BOAT The Malagasy are traditionally a seafaring people and, in the absence of roads, their stable outrigger canoes are used to cover quite long sea distances. Pirogues without outriggers are used extensively on the rivers and canals of the watery east. Quite a few adventurous travellers use pirogues for sections of their journeys. Romantic though it may be to sail in an outrigger canoe, it can be both uncomfortable and, at times, dangerous.

Ferries and cargo boats known as *boutres* travel to the larger islands and down the west coast. River journeys are popular as a different way of seeing the country (pages 433–5).

BY RAIL After years of deterioration, Madagascar's rail system has seen some improvement over the past two decades. Passenger services now run a few times a week between Fianarantsoa and Manakara (page 208) and between Moramanga and Toamasina (page 265).

TRANSPORT WITHIN CITIES Most cities have very cheap **buses** but few foreigners use them because of the difficulty in understanding the route system. For the adventurous, it is a great way to get around Tana and mix with the locals, but they are always crowded so not recommended if you have luggage. Visit the tourist office kiosk in Antaninarenina to see a map of the routes. **Taxi** rates have gone up in recent years because of rising fuel prices, but they are still reasonable. They have no meters, so you must agree on the price before you get in. In some towns (but not the capital) there are official set rates.

Pousse-pousses (**rickshaws**) were introduced into Madagascar by British missionaries who wanted to replace the traditional palanquin due to its association with slavery. Pulled by a running man, they are a Madagascar speciality seen in the flatter towns, although *cyclo-pousses* (**pedal rickshaws**) and **tuk-tuks** (auto rickshaws) have now almost entirely replaced them.

Many Western visitors are reluctant to sit in comfort behind a ragged sweating barefoot man, and no-one with a heart can fail to feel compassion. However, this is a case of needing to abandon our own cultural hang-ups: these men need work. Bargain hard (before you get in) and make sure you have the exact money. Traveller Les Parkes observes: 'the carriages in Manakara are cleverly designed to look comfortable but have a metal bar cunningly placed to bear against your vertebrae; those in Toliara are large and sumptuous by comparison and incorporate no such torture device; the cyclo-pousses have a fringe which annoyingly restricts your vision but on the plus side they are faster'.

HIRING, BUYING OR BRINGING YOUR OWN TRANSPORT Reader Tim Ireland puts it succinctly: 'The great pity is watching so many magnificent landscapes tear past your eyes as you strain your neck trying to get a better view past 15 other occupants of a taxi-brousse.' He goes on to recommend a mountain bike as the perfect means of transport, but a hired vehicle will achieve the same flexibility.

Car hire Generally cars come with chauffeurs (providing a local person with a job and you with a guide/interpreter); self-driving is rare and generally more expensive. A few days on Madagascar's roads will cure you of any regret that you are not driving yourself. A few agencies do rent vehicles without drivers. Adventurous souls who are tempted by this must be sure to check the vehicle over thoroughly before departure, get as much information about the intended route as possible (including where the fuel stops are), and avoid driving after dark at all costs.

A British driving licence is technically valid in Madagascar, but you would be safer to get an International Driving Permit. These are available in the UK for £5.50 from the AA, RAC and certain Post Office branches.

Reader Paul Kolodziejski has this questionable advice for self-drivers: 'Stopping at police checkpoints seems to be optional. There are a lot and I did stop at one but it was a big waste of time. So from then on whenever I was waved to stop, I just waved back pretending I was replying in greeting. I never had any problems.'

There are car-hire outfits in most towns. Tourist offices and hotels have details; local tour operators can organise vehicles too. Hire prices including fuel and driver are around €85 per day for a saloon car or €120 for a 4x4. Taxi drivers will often agree to a full-day hire for around €60.

Note that bringing your own car to Madagascar is costly, complex and risky.

Motorbike Reader Tiffany Coates purchased a motorcycle at the start of her three-month visit and found it gave her great freedom: 'It's easy to find somewhere safe to park overnight (even inside a dining room or reception), you rarely get stopped at police checkpoints, fuel consumption is very reasonable, you can go anywhere (even along footpaths, like the locals do) and it is the best vehicle for the road conditions encountered in Madagascar.' We later learned that she had been so inspired by her trip that two years later she ended up organising a biker tour, leading nine international riders the length of the island in 17 days.

Bicycle The French for mountain bike is 'VTT'. Bikes can be hired in most major towns. Alternatively, you can bring your own bike (see box, pages 78–9) or buy one there.

ACCOMMODATION

For all hotel categories, rates are normally quoted *per room* in Madagascar, with the notable exceptions of the Nosy Be and Ile Sainte Marie areas where the more expensive ones tend to quote prices *per person*. There is a tourist tax, *vignette touristique*, of 600–3,000Ar per room per night. This is often absorbed into the price but may be additional to rates quoted. Many places are open to negotiating discounted prices for stays of several nights, particularly outside of the peak season. Except at the top hotels, breakfast is rarely included in the price and, when it is, it is commonly just bread and coffee. Note that the word *hotely* refers to a simple local restaurant rather than accommodation (but some do also have basic rooms).

Outside the towns, accommodation is usually in bungalows which are often constructed of local materials and are quiet, atmospheric and comfortable. Urban hotels are reliant on the municipal water and electricity supplies, which are very unreliable in some areas, and many do not have backup generators – so always keep a torch handy!

Most mid-range and budget hotels will do your washing for you at a very reasonable price. This gives employment to local people and is an important element of responsible travel. In upper-range and top-end hotels laundry can be disproportionately expensive.

HOTEL CATEGORIES: WHAT YOU GET FOR YOUR MONEY
Luxury The top hotels and lodges are truly luxurious. They are almost all foreign-owned, but many show a good sensitivity to the needs of the local people. One such French owner explained that as foreigners their conscience dictates that they do not appear as neocolonials and so they go out of their way to contribute to community-based projects.

Top end These are either a cut above the average upper-range hotel or are in an expensive part of Madagascar, such as Nosy Be or the capital city, where all prices are higher.

Upper range These are very comfortable hotels which can be found in all major towns and tourist centres. They have all the trappings that upmarket tourists expect: TV, minibar, Wi-Fi, etc. They will have en-suite bathrooms and restaurants with good food. The larger ones are popular with groups, so check the listed number of rooms if you're looking for a more intimate atmosphere.

Mid-range These are often just as clean and comfortable, and most have at least some en-suite rooms. There will be no TV beaming international satellite channels into your bedroom, but you should have comfortable beds. The hotels are often family run and very friendly.

Budget and penny-pincher In early editions these were described as 'exhilaratingly dreadful at times' until a reader wrote: 'We were rather disappointed by the quality of these hotels... We found almost all the beds comfortable, generally acceptably clean, and not one rat. We felt luxuriously cheated!' However, the following description from Rupert Parker of a hotel in Brickaville should gladden the masochistic heart: 'It is a conglomeration of shacks directly beneath the road bridge. The rooms are partitioned-off spaces, just large enough to hold a bed, in a larger wooden building. The partitions don't reach to the ceiling and there is only one light bulb for all the rooms; the hotel manageress controls the switch. Not only can you hear everyone's conversation and what they're up to, but when there is a new arrival, at whatever time of the night, the light comes on and wakes everyone up – that is if you've managed to ignore the rumbling and revving of trucks as they cross the bridge above you, or the banging on the gate announcing the new arrival. Suffice to say the toilet and washing facilities are non-existent.' It would be rather a shame if they've improved it in the intervening years!

Such hotels certainly give the flavour of how Madagascar used to be, and in remote areas you will still find the occasional sagging double bed and stinking hole toilet. Most of the budget hotels in this book are clean, friendly and excellent value. In a very out-of-the-way place you will pay as little as £1.55/€1.25/US$1.75 for the most basic room. For this you get a bed and maybe a candle, mozzie coil and ripped mozzie net. In small towns, about £7.00/€8.25/US$9.25 would be average for a room with a shared toilet.

ACCOMMODATION PRICING IN THIS BOOK

Lists of accommodation present hotels in price bands according to the cost of a typical double room. The key below can also be found on page ix.

Luxury	👑	Above 320,000Ar (£82/€94/US$105 and up)
Top end	€€€€€	190,000–320,000Ar (£48/€56/US$63 and up)
Upper range	€€€€	90,000–190,000Ar (£23/€27/US$30 and up)
Mid-range	€€€	40,000–90,000Ar (£10/€12/US$13 and up)
Budget	€€	18,000–40,000Ar (£5/€5/US$6 and up)
Penny-pincher	€	Below 18,000Ar

Airbnb This online service (*www.airbnb.com*) allowing individuals to rent out their rooms is gaining popularity. There are some 650 listed rental properties in Madagascar at the time of writing.

CouchSurfing and other cost-free hosts CouchSurfing (*www.couchsurfing.org*) is a service that connects budget travellers with local hosts willing to let them stay for free. The motivation is usually the opportunity to meet interesting new friends or practise language skills. The movement has not taken off to a great extent in Madagascar, but it does exist: at the time of writing there are about 600 registered members in the country of whom a few dozen are actively accepting guests. The vast majority live in the capital.

Alternative services on a similar theme include Hospitality Club (*www. hospitalityclub.org*), BeWelcome (*www.bewelcome.org*), Global Freeloaders (*www. globalfreeloaders.com*) and Tripping (*www.tripping.com*).

Solo travellers in particular should exercise caution as occasionally hosts register with these services in search of more than just friendship.

Camping Campsites are a relatively new phenomenon in Madagascar. There is a growing number, mainly at national parks and other reserves. Such camping is usually under a thatched shelter on a wooden platform (or sometimes sand). Tents can be hired at some sites but if you bring your own make sure it is a free-standing design since you can't drive tent-pegs into the platform. Wild camping outside of designated campsites is unusual so try to seek permission before doing so.

EATING AND DRINKING

FOOD Eating well is one of the delights of Madagascar. Wherever you go you will find freshly prepared, original dishes at independent outlets and complete escape from ever-growing global homogenisation; in Antananarivo, you are nearly 1,000km from the nearest McDonald's (Réunion) and well over 2,000km from any Starbucks (Jo'burg). The international hotels do serve international food, usually with a French bias, but frequently offer Malagasy-inspired dishes too. Smaller hotels serve local food which is almost always excellent, particularly on the coast where lobster, crayfish, shellfish and other seafood predominates. Meat lovers will enjoy the zebu steaks. Incredible food can be found in the unlikliest of places (see box, page 420) but in remoter areas, hotels tend to offer a set menu. This can cost as little as £1.00/€1.20/US$1.35. At the upper end you can expect to pay around £15/€18/US$20 for that special treat. There is generally not much variation in price between typical tourist restaurants.

Independent travellers on a tight budget will find Chinese restaurants in nearly every town; these are almost always good and reasonably priced. *Soupe chinoise* is available nearly everywhere, and is filling, tasty and cheap. The Malagasy eat a lot of rice, but most restaurants also cater to foreign tastes. Away from the tourist routes, however, most dishes are accompanied by a sticky mound of rice – sometimes embellished with small stones, so chew with caution!

If you're in Tana in December, don't miss the MadaSakafo Malagasy food festival (*www.madasakafo.com*).

Local specialities For a real Malagasy meal, eat at a *hotely*. These are often open-sided shacks where the menu is chalked up on a blackboard: *henan-omby* (beef), *henan-borona/hen'akoho* (chicken), *henan-kisoa* (pork), *trondro* or *henan-drano/hazan-drano* (fish), all served with *vary* (rice). Other dishes include *tsaramaso* (rice with beans and pork), *vary sosoa* (rice pudding/porridge) and *koba* (rice ground

In the highlands, *laoka* (a catch-all word for whatever accompanies the obligatory mound of rice) are often vegetables, pulses or animal proteins in tomato-based sauces flavoured with pork, while coastal dishes reflect even more variety, adding coconut sauces and a wider range of seafood. The historic influence of Islam in coastal areas means zebu meat may be substituted for pork (often *fady*).

In the north, steak or poultry *au poivre vert* (creamy green peppercorn sauce) and poultry or seafood *à la vanille* (vanilla sauce) blend French and local influences. In Mahajanga the speciality is *khimo* (curried ground beef), while near Morondava *kabaro* (lima beans with curry or coconut) are a filling alternative to meat. On the coast you can try treats such as *godro-godro* (cardamom-coconut pudding), *boatamo* (coconut cookies) or *mokary* (a coconut-flavoured *mofogasy*; see below), or spice up your dishes with tart *lasary* – a chutney-like condiment of lemon, mango or papaya sold in a colourful array of recycled bottles at roadside stands. While in the highlands, you can try other lasary made of tomato (*voatabia*), peanuts (*voanjo*), mango (*manga*) or vegetables (*legioma*) in a curried vinaigrette, or tuck into a bowl of scrumptious, peanut-flavoured *voanjobory* (bambara groundnuts with pork).

Under the 19th-century Merina monarchy, New Year was celebrated with rich and distinctive dishes. Among these were *tatao* (boiled rice, honey and milk) and *jaka* (beef conserved in clay pots for a year). The main seven dishes have become iconic of highland cuisine: *romazava* (beef stew; see box, page 106), *varanga* (fried slivered beef) and *sesika* (a sort of poultry blood sausage), as well as pork with *ravitoto* (shredded cassava leaves), *vorivorin-kena* (beef tripe), *amalona* (stuffed eel) and *vorontsiloza* (turkey) – a staple of highland celebrations, especially weddings and Christmas.

Certain foods are also traditionally associated with specific life events. At a *famadihana* it is customary to eat *vary be menaka* – rice prepared with beef and lots of fatty pork. After the birth of a baby, thinly sliced strips of pan-fried smoked beef called *kitoza* are traditionally prepared to help the new mother regain her strength. She may also be offered *ro-patsa*, a bouillon made of potato and tiny dried shrimps believed to aid in nursing – although its reputation for restoring health and vitality makes it a popular home remedy for any ill.

Madagascar's array of doughnut-like treats is surprisingly diverse in flavour and texture. In the highlands, rice is used to make sweet *mofogasy*, savoury *ramanonaka* and half-sweet *mofo grefy*, as well as rice-flour doughnut rings (*menakely*) or balls (*mofo baolina*). Savoury ones are made from chopped greens (*mofo anana*), chilli sauce (*mofo sakay*), various veggies or prawns. The more common sweet ones are made from baguette (*makasaoka*), banana (*mofo akondro*), pumpkin (*mofo voatavo*), sweetcorn (*mofo katsaka*), sweet potato (*mofo bageda*), cassava (*mofo mangahazo*) or yam (*bokoboko*).

Most laoka involve some sort of sauce or juice to flavour the rice. You can find almost anything curried (*au curry*) or in coconut milk (*au coco* or *voanio*), and if no sauce is specified then expect something mild and tomato-based. *Ritra* means 'simmered in its own juices'. Green and red *sakay* (chilli sauce) are usually available on the side to spice things up to your taste. You will find more basic food vocabulary for decoding Malagasy menus on pages 104 and 441. *Mazotoa homana!*

with peanuts and banana, wrapped in a banana leaf and served in slices). For a more detailed rundown of Malagasy cuisine, see the box on page 105.

Along with the meat or fish and inevitable mound of rice comes a bowl of watery liquid. This is a stock to be spooned over the rice or drunk as a soup, and not – as one reader discovered to his embarrassment – a finger bowl!

Thirst is traditionally quenched with *ranovola* obtained by boiling water in the pan in which the rice was cooked. It has a slight flavour of burnt rice, and since it has been boiled for several minutes it is safe to drink.

For do-it-yourself meals there is a great variety of fruit and vegetables, even in the smallest market. A selection of fruit is served in most restaurants, along with raw vegetables or *crudités*. From June to August the fruit is mostly limited to citrus and bananas, but from September there are also strawberries, mangoes, lychees, pineapples and loquats, to name but a few. As an extra-special treat in late summer you may come across the purple mangosteen.

From October you will find corossol. This is the French name for what is called soursop in English, although you may never have heard of it. Closely related to the pawpaw, it has lightly spiky green skin and a light-coloured edible pulp that has been likened to a mixture of strawberry and pineapple, with a hint of lemon and a creaminess akin to banana or coconut. One fruit typically weighs 2kg, but exceptionally may exceed 6kg. The fresh juice is especially delectable.

Slices of coconut are available especially on the coast where coconut milk is a popular and safe drink, and toffee–coconut/peanut nibbles are sold on the street, often wrapped in paper from school exercise books. There are some good, locally produced cheeses and Malagasy yoghurt is excellent. Chocaholics should keep their eyes peeled for Chocolate Robert – available in several varieties.

Vegetarian food Madagascar is becoming more accustomed to *vazaha* vegetarians. With patience you can usually order meatless dishes anywhere, even at

CHOOSING MALAGASY WINE   *Christian Schiller*

Malagasy wine tends to be of good table wine quality, not more. The main grape varieties are traditionally Petit Bouchet, Villardin, Chambourcin and Varousset for *vins rouges* (reds) and Couderc Blanc for *vins blancs* (whites). Little known in the world of fine wine, these so-called French-American hybrid grape varieties have the advantage of being robust, but do not match the *Vitis vinifera* varieties – such as Riesling, Chardonnay, Merlot and Pinot Noir – for elegance and refinement. *Vitis vinifera* varieties dominate worldwide wine consumption, but there is increasing interest in French-American hybrids in the 'green' movement.

Currently seven producers in Madagascar make wine with French-American hybrid grapes. Each winemaker produces one or more brands, each of which typically comes as *vin rouge*, *vin gris* (white wine made from red grapes), *rosé* and *vin blanc*. In addition, you find *vin blanc moelleux*, a white wine with noticeable remaining sweetness. All these wines are non-vintage (NV) wines.

Antsirabe Viticulteur-Encaveur Chan Fao Tong, a first-wave Chinese winemaker, produces the best wine from hybrid grapes: **NV Grand Cru d'Antsirabe**. It comes as **Rouge Alicante** (medium-bodied), **Rouge Seyve Villard** (earthy), **Rose Viala** (good summer wine), **Gris de Gris** (goes well with Malagasy food) and **Blanc Couderc** (medium-bodied, dry).

Another interesting wine producer is Lazan'i Betsileo, a large co-operative created in Fianarantsoa in 1971. Supported by Swiss development aid, they used to make the best wine of the country. Quality has suffered since that funding project was terminated, but they are now trying hard to get back on track, with some success. Lazan'i Betsileo offers one wine, **NV Haute Matsiatra**, which comes as **Rouge** (medium-bodied), **Rouge Primeur** (lighter), **Gris** (my favourite Malagasy food wine), **Blanc** (dry, fruity) and **Blanc Moelleux** (medium sweet white).

In a new development, there is now one winery that is radically different from the others. Owned and run by Pâquerette and Jean Allimant, Clos Nomena exclusively uses noble *Vitis vinifera* grapes. From 2001, they set up a five-year experimental vineyard in Ambalavao and the four grape varieties that showed the most promising results were selected to be grown commercially. With the first wines released in 2011, the eponymous **Clos Nomena** label now includes a **Blanc Sec** (dry, fruity, crisp), a **Rosé** (great aperitif wine) and a **Rouge** (medium bodied, elegant, lingering finish). They are available in a few of Tana's top restaurants and some special shops but at considerably higher prices than traditional Malagasy wines.

Dr Christian Schiller is a member of the International Federation of Wine and Spirits Journalists and Writers and runs a daily wine blog (www.schiller-wine. blogspot.com). He previously worked for the IMF in Tana.

a small *hotely*. The problem tends to be communicating what you do and don't eat; once this is clear, most kitchens can offer some vegetarian options. *Tsy misy hena* means 'without meat' and *tsy oman-kena aho* means 'I don't eat meat'.

DRINK The most famous drink, Three Horses Beer, known universally as THB (*www. star-thb.com*), is wonderful on a hot day. Or a cold day, for that matter. Available in bottles, cans or occasionally on draught, it has 5.4% alcohol. Star Brewery also produces THB Fresh, a light shandy. For years Star effectively held a monopoly on the Malagasy **beer** market, but a number of competitors have appeared in the past few years. Ambatolampy-based Skol (*www.skol.mg*) produces the eponymous Skol, as well as Libertalia Original, Phoenix, a THB Fresh equivalent called Skol Panache and – as of 2013 – Guinness too. Castel Beer is now also widely available. Both THB and THB Fresh have won gold awards at the prestigious Monde Selection in Belgium.

It is not well known in the rest of the world that Madagascar produces **wine**. It is not world class, but some is very pleasant; see the box on page 107 for advice on picking a reasonable one. A rather nice **aperitif** is Maromby (the name means 'many zebu') and Litchel, made from lychees, is good. Based in Nosy Be, the Vidzar company (*www.dzama.mg*) has made **rum** since 1982; their premium products under the Dzama brand have won awards worldwide. Cheap rum, or *toaka gasy*, is plentiful everywhere; and fermented sugarcane juice, *betsabetsa* (east coast), or fermented coconut milk, *trembo* (north), make a change. *Rhum arrangé* – rum flavoured with various fruits or spices – is found in most locally run *hotels*. The best cocktail is *punch coco*, with a coconut milk base, a speciality of the coastal areas.

The most popular **mineral water** is called Eau Vive, but other brands are available. **Soft drinks** including Coca-Cola, Sprite and Fanta are also available (made under licence by Star Brewery) as well as a ginger beer marketed under the name Stoney Ginger. The locally produced *limonady* sadly bears no resemblance to lemons; a very sweet brand called Bonbon Anglais describes itself as a 'sublimely flavoured drink'.

Malagasy **coffee** is all right if taken black, but often only condensed milk is available (one quickly regresses to childhood and surreptitiously spoons the condensed milk not into the coffee but directly into the mouth). If you prefer unsweetened white coffee it might be better to bring your own powdered milk. Caffeine addicts who don't get along with the local coffee can find Nescafé sachets in the supermarkets. The locally grown **tea** is available in both green and black, the best quality being reserved for export. A nice alternative is *thé citronelle* – lemongrass tea.

PUBLIC HOLIDAYS

The Malagasy take their holidays seriously. There are often parades with speeches and an air of festivity. When an official holiday falls on a Tuesday or Thursday, the neighbouring Monday or Friday may be declared a bridge holiday, making a long weekend. Banks and certain other businesses often take a half-day off on the day preceding a holiday. The following public holidays are observed:

1 January	New Year's Day
29 March	Commemoration of 1947 rebellion
March/April (movable)	Easter Monday
1 May	Labour Day
May (movable)	Ascension Day
May/June (movable)	Whit Monday

26 June	Independence Day
15 August	Feast of the Assumption
14 October	First Republic Day
1 November	All Saints' Day
11 December	Fourth Republic Day
25 December	Christmas Day

SHOPPING FOR SOUVENIRS

You can buy a huge variety of handicrafts in Madagascar. Most typical of the country are woodcarvings, a great variety of raffia work, crocheted and embroidered tablecloths and clothes, leather goods, carved zebu horn, Antaimoro paper (with embedded dried flowers) and marquetry. The choice is almost limitless, and it can all be seen in the handicrafts markets and shops in Tana and throughout the country. Good quality cotton T-shirts bearing Malagasy designs and slogans are produced by the Baobab, Maki, Carambole and Fosa labels.

In the south you can buy attractive heavy silver bracelets that are traditionally worn by men. In the capital, and the east and north (including Nosy Be), you will be offered vanilla pods, peppercorns, cloves and other spices, and honey. Almost anywhere you can find shops selling lambas. Delightful little toy cars and other vehicles constructed from scrap tin cans are among the most colourful wares in the craft markets. You may also see wooden toy trucks for sale by the roadside south of Tana. Musical instruments are represented by the *djembe* drum and the *valiha*. Both are sold in full-size and scaled-down souvenir versions.

Madagascar is a rewarding place for gem-hunters, with everything from amethyst, aquamarine, citrine and garnets to beryl, sapphire, topaz and tourmaline. The centre for gems is traditionally Antsirabe but they are for sale in many towns. If you buy uncut stones bear in mind the cost of having them cut at home – better to have it done in Madagascar, if you have time. The solitaire sets using semi-precious minerals are typical and most attractive.

BUYING ETHICALLY Not all handicrafts and souvenirs are to be encouraged. Many items made from animal products should be avoided for conservation reasons and you could even get into serious trouble for trying to take some out of the country. Do not buy products from endangered species. These include tortoise shell, turtle shell, snakeskin, sea shells, coral and – of course – live animals. The mounted bodies of butterflies and other insects are likely to come from wild-caught specimens too, so are best avoided unless you are sure of the source.

Other prohibited items include endemic plants without a permit and any genuine article of funerary art. Most bones or fossils cannot legally be taken out of the country, including subfossil elephant bird eggshell fragments (often on sale reconstructed into complete eggs) – however, ammonites and petrified wood are not a problem. Crocodiles are farmed commercially so their skins may be sold legally; products made from zebu horn are also fine.

The dilemma of wooden carvings is less clear-cut. Most carved souvenirs are made from palisander, rosewood or ebony – all slow-growing precious woods that are being illegally logged from Madagascar's forests at an alarming rate. But these carvings provide employment and income for many poor families, and the quantity of wood used for making souvenirs is minuscule compared with the hundreds of tonnes of timber being illegally exported to China to make furniture. You may therefore feel that, on balance, small carved items are not unethical.

Be sure to obtain receipts for wood and stone items and anything expensive. On departure you should take your receipts for any minerals or large ammonites to the Ministry of Mines desk at the airport to obtain an export permit. Botanical material should be declared at the neighbouring phytosanitary desk.

BARGAINING Haggling is expected in markets and with street sellers, but not generally in shops. It can be a controversial subject for travellers in poor countries like Madagascar, where the typical tourist could easily be hundreds of times richer than the locals. Hard bargaining over a few pennies that would bring little gain to wealthy buyers may make a world of difference to the sellers struggling to feed their families. On the other hand, it is not beneficial for the local economy in the long run if tourists routinely pay over the odds for goods, and such behaviour tends to change local attitudes to foreigners for the worse.

The answer is to strike a balance. Before beginning negotiations over the price of an item, try to establish what a sensible price would be. Haggling, when done with courtesy and good humour, is an enjoyable way of engaging with locals. Keep in mind that your goal is to reach a mutually agreeable price, not to eliminate their profit. And in the case of handicrafts remember that the best workmanship should be rewarded, otherwise you will only encourage production of cheap-quality products in future.

ARTS AND ENTERTAINMENT

MUSIC Malagasy music is distinctive and justly famous; see the box opposite. Finding good live local music is a hit-and-miss affair when travelling. Often your best bet is to look out for posters advertising concerts, regularly put up near the *gare routière*. CDs of Malagasy music are widely available in Tana.

TELEVISION AND CINEMA The better hotels have CNN and sometimes BBC World, but the satellite channels available are mainly in French. Much of the output on local channels comprises music videos. Cinemas show films dubbed into French.

COMMUNICATIONS

TELEPHONES
Making calls The seven-digit phone numbers given in this guide (marked with a ❭ symbol) are landline numbers. The ten-digit numbers are mobile/cellphone numbers, which all begin 03 and are indicated by an m symbol in this book.

The international dialling code for Madagascar is +261. When calling a **landline**, you must also add 20. Thus to phone Air Madagascar (❭ 22 222 22) from abroad, you would dial +261 20 22 222 22. To call a **mobile number** from abroad, simply replace the initial 0 with +261.

When making an international call out of Madagascar, the international prefix (represented by +) is 00, as is standard across most of Europe, Africa and Asia.

Mobile phones Mobiles/cellphones are very popular in Madagascar. Nowadays network coverage is good, reaching most places that tourists are likely to go. Operators claim their basic 2G coverage reaches 85% of the population, with 3G available in 150 towns, and 4G now being rolled out. You can buy a SIM card at the airport (or in any town) for next to nothing and call rates are reasonable too, so if you're going to be in Madagascar for more than a week or so it would probably

Derek Schuurman & Paddy Bush

Like everything else in Madagascar, the island's music portrays characteristics from other parts of the world but the end result is uniquely Malagasy.

Justin Vali (Justin Rakotondrasoa) – a Merina from the *hauts plateaux* – is today the country's best-known Malagasy musician outside of his country. Apart from Vali, other Malagasy musicians who have enjoyed success abroad include D'Gary, who has a huge following in Canada and USA; Regis Gizavo; Jojoby, the King of Salegy, who is once again performing after a near-fatal car accident; the band Tarika, which was highly rated in an international *Time* magazine poll a few years ago; and Mahaleo, the Malagasy version of the Beatles, who have been going strong since the 1970s.

Many Western instruments have found their way into Malagasy music. It is not uncommon to see accordions in particular, but also clarinets and certain brass instruments, being played at the colourful *hira gasy* events. On the other hand, visit a vibrant nightclub and you'll see contemporary musicians belting out thumping dance tracks using modern electric and bass guitars and synthesisers.

The national instrument is the *valiha*, which belongs to the family of tube and box zithers. This fascinating instrument goes back generations in Justin Vali's family, who both make and play it. The original or 'ancestral' form of valiha is constructed from certain rare species of bamboo, known as *volo* ('hair from the ground' – a wonderful way to describe bamboo). Valiha are of great spiritual significance and have been played for centuries in ceremonies sacred to the *razana* (ancestors).

The valiha is thought to have arrived some 2,000 years ago from southeast Asia, where various forms of the instrument are still to be found in the Borneo and Philippines region. In these areas it is also an instrument of the spiritual world, being used in ceremonies to appease animistic forest spirits.

The bamboo from which the valiha is made must be cut during the three-day period during a full moon, which is when the plants are apparently free of certain insects – otherwise months later they will emerge from eggs laid inside and destroy the instrument. (I have seen this happen when a friend tried to import a huge consignment of valiha, only to have them ruined by the insects; we were forced to make an enormous bonfire of hundreds of contaminated valiha!)

The valiha has a royal heritage: according to Justin Vali, King Radama II was a superb composer. During his reign Queen Victoria gave him a piano, which resulted in the standardising of valiha-tuning into diatonic form – called *lalandava* ('straight road') – corresponding to the white notes on a keyboard. One of the most legendary players of the instrument, Rakotozafy, built himself a *marovany*-like valiha out of sheet iron, and today his music is still widely played on radio.

The marovany, unlike the tube valiha, appears to have African origins. It is tuned in a very different way and is played in the coastal regions where the African influence is more apparent than in the highlands. If you happen to be in the right places in Madagascar, searching for recordings of Malagasy music, and you want to hear phenomenal marovany players, ask for Madame Masy, Bekamby, Daniel Tomo or Albi, to name a few of the best.

Musician, producer and music critic Paddy Bush is one of very few Westerners to have mastered playing the marovany and valiha. He has performed with Justin Vali.

be worth getting one (especially considering that making/receiving calls using a foreign mobile is typically many times more expensive).

There are four operators: **Orange** (numbers starting with 032), **Airtel** (033), **Telma** (034) and **bip** (039). Orange is the most popular but Airtel and Telma have now overtaken in terms of speed, reliability and coverage in many areas. Calls to phones with the same operator are much cheaper than to a different network, so if you envisage mainly communicating with certain specific people then pick the same network as them. For reasons of economy, many Malagasy have three numbers: one for each network. If you are going to be staying in Madagascar for a while and want to do the same, consider taking a multi-SIM phone.

Top-up cards are available in shops everywhere. Values range from 1,000Ar to 100,000Ar, but you will have to go to an Orange/Airtel/Telma shop for the higher-value recharge cards; in small villages 2,000Ar might be the biggest you can find.

Emergency numbers The emergency telephone number for **police** is ❯ 17 or 117. For the **fire service**, the emergency number is ❯ 18 or 118. There is no general emergency number for medical assistance, but you will find numbers for local hospitals and medical services throughout this guide. For consular assistance, see the contact details of embassies on page 174.

INTERNET Cybercafés are established in all towns. Be warned that the keyboards are usually the French AZERTY layout, not the QWERTY type used in the UK, USA and some other parts of the world. This can be intensely frustrating if you are normally a fast typist. These days most decent hotels and restaurants have free Wi-Fi.

If you will be taking a laptop to Madagascar with you, then you can purchase a 3G+ USB 'key' for internet access from any of the mobile operators (see *Mobile phones* above). This device is a small dongle which contains a SIM card and plugs into your computer's USB port, giving you internet access wherever there is mobile signal. It is not often fast but is usually more than enough for checking email. They cost about €12 and access is charged according to the amount of data used: 250MB (typically valid for 7 days) costs around €4 and 1GB (30 days) about €12.

MAIL AND COURIER SERVICES The mail service is unpredictable; more often than not it is reasonably efficient, with letters taking about two weeks to reach Europe and a little longer to North America. Stamps are quite expensive. There are post offices even in small towns, with some 220 branches around the country.

Parcel carrier Colis Express has some 70 branches across Madagascar and is an efficient way of sending domestic packages. Internationally they hook up with DHL, which also has its own offices in major towns, and there is a FedEx agency in Tana (see page 172).

If you need to order something online from a company in Europe that doesn't offer a courier service to Madagascar, try the PackYellow forwarding service (*www. packyellow.com*).

BUSINESS HOURS

Most businesses open 08.00–noon and 14.00–18.00. In the hottest towns, there may be a 3-hour lunch closure. Banks are generally open until 16.00 and closed at weekends, though the largest towns normally have one bank that opens Saturday morning.

5

Health and Safety

With Dr Felicity Nicholson

BEFORE YOU GO

Sensible preparation will go a long way to ensuring your trip goes smoothly. Particularly for first-time visitors to Africa, this includes a visit to a travel clinic to discuss matters such as vaccinations and malaria prevention. A list of recommended travel clinic websites worldwide is available at www.itsm.org, and other useful websites for prospective travellers include www.travelhealthpro.org.uk and www.netdoctor.co.uk/travel. The Bradt website now carries a health section (*www.bradtguides.com/africahealth*) to help travellers prepare for their African trip, elaborating on most points raised below, but the following summary points are worth emphasising:

- Make sure you have **insurance** covering the cost of helicopter evacuation and treatment in Réunion or Nairobi, which offer more sophisticated medical facilities than are available in Madagascar. For advice on specialist insurance, see the box on page 124 for scuba divers and page 129 for the elderly or people with disabilities.
- Make sure all your **immunisations** are up to date. A **yellow fever** certificate is required from travellers coming from yellow fever areas, but there is no risk from this disease in Madagascar itself.
- The biggest health threat is **malaria**. There is no vaccine against this dangerous mosquito-borne disease, but malarone, mefloquine (Lariam) and doxycycline are reasonably effective preventative drugs against the strains found in Madagascar.
- Madagascar is classified as a high-risk country for **rabies**, so vaccination is advisable, which involves three doses taken over a minimum of 21 days. This is particularly important if you intend to have contact with animals, or are likely to be 24 hours away from medical help. See also box, page 120.
- Anybody travelling away from major centres should carry a **personal first aid kit**. Contents might include a good drying antiseptic (eg: iodine or potassium permanganate), Band-Aids, aspirin or paracetamol, antifungal cream (eg: Canesten), ciprofloxacin or norfloxacin (for severe diarrhoea), antibiotic eye drops, tweezers, a digital thermometer and a needle-and-syringe kit with an accompanying letter from a healthcare professional. Also remember your suncream, insect repellent, mosquito net, anti-malarial prophylaxis and contraceptives, as appropriate.
- Don't forget any **personal medicine** for existing health issues, including regular medication and preventative treatments for conditions such as allergies or asthma (specialist medications can be hard to find in-country).

With less than a week left until the end of my seven months in Madagascar I fell ill with a serious infection. About a fortnight earlier, I had scratched a mozzie bite on my ankle just a bit too vigorously and it had turned septic. I treated it with antiseptic powder and covered it with plasters and it almost healed. So I went out with it uncovered and while I was engaged in conversation the infernal flies found the minute spot and had a feast.

Next day I found I could hardly walk because the infection had spread to the muscle. I obtained some antibiotics and had a good dressing put on it. By evening the whole foot had ballooned and looked quite frightening. The next two days I spent mainly in bed because even sitting put me in great discomfort. I had high fever and couldn't eat. But with my visa running out and my flight back booked I had to get to Antananarivo. The two-day road journey from Vangaindrano was out of the question so I flew from Farafangana via Taolagnaro to the capital. The Air Mad steward helpfully folded down the seat in front so I could keep my leg up. I was very impressed with how quickly I was provided with a wheelchair at both Taolagnaro and Ivato without even having asked.

My flight back to Paris was the following evening but an 11-hour flight in a sitting position was completely out of the question and, having no insurance, I didn't want to pay for extra seats. So I decided to stay in Madagascar for treatment. The infection was already creeping up the leg and an enormous sausage-like blood blister now spanned the whole length of the foot. The first doctor that saw me at the clinic where I was taken was so fascinated by the sight that the first thing he did was to take out his mobile phone to take pictures! I was given a bed in a room on my own. Everything was wonderfully clean and new. The following day an old, greying doctor performed an operation under local anaesthetic to remove the worst infected tissue. He told me that he'd studied neonatal surgery at Great Ormond Street Hospital.

Despite large doses of intravenous antibiotics the infection spread up as far as my knee and it was four or five days before it showed signs of receding. Meanwhile the big blood blister had burst, dried and formed a large scab which the doctor now wanted to remove (under general anaesthetic) because it was sealing in the infected tissue underneath. I became scared, both about having an open wound covering half my foot, as well as the expense of the operation, and decided to risk the flight back to Paris. I had spent a week in hospital, at the end of which the infection had been successfully driven down and confined to the foot and my body temperature was brought down to normal. I paid only about £200.

The people looking after me all this time were a Slovenian missionary priest, a French nun who took care of my expiring visa and I'm especially grateful to the parishioners of Père Pedro, who took me to this hospital and provided me with a *guarde* (a personal carer, as is normal practice in Malagasy hospitals). Before I was discharged the nurses took pains over my dressing saying: 'We don't want people to think we're underdeveloped'! The awful treatment I was later to get from the *vazahas* at Charles de Gaulle airport where I waited 3 hours for a wheelchair made me wonder who was the more developed.

At the end the parishioners took me to the airport in their Land Rover ambulance. I lay on the stretcher in the back and there were children on both sides singing all the way there. It had been worth staying in Madagascar just for that experience!

MALARIA AND OTHER MOSQUITO-BORNE DISEASES Tablets do not give complete protection from malaria (though it will give you time to get treatment if it does break through) and there are other insect-borne diseases in Madagascar so it is important to protect yourself from being bitten. The *Anopheles* mosquitoes that spread malaria usually bite from dusk to dawn, so it is wise to dress in long trousers and long-sleeved shirts, and to cover exposed skin with insect repellent especially in the evenings. In most countries, malaria transmission is rare in urban environments, but it does occur around Antananarivo because rice fields are so close to the city. Most hotels have screened windows or provide mosquito nets, but bring your own freshly impregnated net if staying in cheap hotels. Check the walls of your room for mosquitoes at bedtime and consider burning mosquito coils overnight.

The symptoms are fevers, chills, joint pain, headache and sometimes diarrhoea – in other words the symptoms of many illnesses including flu. Malaria can take as little as seven days to develop but consult a doctor if you develop a flu-like illness within a year of leaving a malarial region. The life-threatening complication of cerebral malaria will become apparent within three months and can kill within 24 hours of the first symptoms (extreme shaking, fever and sweating; seizures; impaired consciousness; and neurological abnormalities).

The combined medicine artemether and lumefantrine, available in Malagasy pharmacies under the name Coartem, is an effective treatment for uncomplicated infections by the most serious strain of malaria.

Mosquitoes also pass on Rift Valley fever, elephantiasis, dengue and other serious viral fevers. By avoiding mosquito bites you also avoid illness, as well as those itching lumps which so easily become infected. Once you've been bitten, tiger balm or calamine lotion will help stop the itching.

TRAVELLER'S DIARRHOEA Diarrhoea is very common in visitors to Madagascar, and you are more likely to suffer from this if you are new to tropical travel. The oral Dukoral cholera vaccine may give partial protection against traveller's diarrhoea although it is not licensed in the UK for this use. Tourists tend to be obsessed with water sterilisation but, contrary to popular belief, diarrhoea usually comes from contaminated food, not water. So, particularly if you have a sensitive stomach or haven't travelled much before, you should avoid ice cream, ice, salads, fruit with lots of crevices such as strawberries, uncooked foods and cooked food that has been hanging around or has been inadequately reheated. Sizzling hot street food is likely to be far safer than the food offered in buffets in expensive hotels, however gourmet the latter may look. Remember: *peel it, boil it, cook it or forget it!*

The way to the quickest recovery from traveller's diarrhoea is to reduce your normal meals to a few light or high-carbohydrate items, avoid milk and alcohol, and drink lots of clear fluids. You need to replace the fluids lost down the toilet, and drinks containing sugar and salt are best. Add a little sugar to a salty drink (such as Marmite or Oxo) or salt to a sugary one (such as non-diet Coca-Cola). Sachets of rehydration mixtures are available commercially but you can make your own by mixing four teaspoons of sugar and a quarter-teaspoon of salt into a glass of boiled and cooled water. Drink two glasses of this every time you open your bowels – more often if you are thirsty. If you are in a rural area drink young coconut water or *ranovola* (rice water).

Once the bowel has ejected the toxic material causing the diarrhoea, the symptoms will settle quite quickly and you should begin to feel better again after

5

24–36 hours. If you pass blood or slime, seek medical advice as soon as possible; this is likely to be a form of dysentery requiring antibiotics to treat.

You might not have the luxury of taking it easy for a couple of days if you are on a fixed itinerary, so if a long bus journey or flight is anticipated you may wish to take a blocker such as Imodium – but if you are tempted to do that it is better to take an antibiotic with it. Take one dose of ciprofloxacin (500mg) and a second dose 10–12 hours later with plenty of water. If this does not stop the diarrhoea then you need to seek medical help as more treatment may be needed. It works in about 80% of cases.

Water sterilisation Most traveller's diarrhoea comes from uncooked, inadequately cooked or reheated contaminated food rather than from water. Even so, it is best to take care with what you drink. Bringing water to the boil kills all microbes that are likely to make you ill so tea, coffee or *ranovola* (rice water) are safe. Mineral water, although widely available, causes a litter problem and can be quite expensive. To sterilise tap or stream water, there are several options: **chlorine-based tablets** (very effective but have an unpleasant taste and take at least 30 minutes to work fully); **silver-based tablets** (tasteless but less effective and also take time); battery-powered or USB-chargeable **ultra-violet purifiers** such as SteriPEN (very fast and proven to eliminate 99.9% of bacteria and viruses), or just take a travel **immersion heater** (boiling is the most reliable of all the methods but requires a power outlet).

TAPEWORM There is a high prevalence of tapeworm in zebu, so eat your steaks well done. If you do pass a worm, this is alarming but treatment can wait.

BILHARZIA (SCHISTOSOMIASIS) This is a nasty, debilitating disease which is a problem in much of lowland Madagascar. The parasite is carried by freshwater snails and is caught by people who swim or paddle in clean, still or slow-moving water (not fast-flowing rivers) where an infected person has defecated or urinated. The parasite may cause 'swimmer's itch' when it penetrates the skin. Since it takes at least 10 minutes for the tiny worm to work its way through your skin, a quick wade across a river, preferably followed by vigorous towelling off, is low risk. If you think you may have been exposed to the disease, ask your doctor to arrange a blood test when you get home. This should be done more than six weeks after the last contact with infected water. Bilharzia is cured with a single dose of Praziquantel.

SEXUALLY TRANSMITTED INFECTIONS These are common in Madagascar and Aids is on the increase. If you enjoy nightlife, male or female condoms will make encounters less risky.

RABIES Rabies is feared wherever it occurs – and it occurs in Madagascar. However, there are highly effective vaccines. The virus can be carried by any mammal, and the commonest route of infection is from a dog bite. It is plausible that lemurs could pass on rabies (see box, page 120) and bats can certainly carry it. Unfortunately, most rabid animals do not look mad or froth at the mouth so it is important to assume that any mammal bite could be dangerous. Acting fast is key to survival. There is no time to 'wait and see'; by the time symptoms become apparent, the victim is doomed and the mode of death is terrible.

After any animal bite, scratch or a lick even over intact skin, vigorously clean the wound with plenty of soap under running water for at least ten full minutes. Then flood the wound with strong antiseptic or alcohol. Get the wound dressed – but

Accurate statistics for rates of HIV are particularly hard to come by in Madagascar as a result of low levels of testing and a historical lack of data collection. According to recent government and WHO estimates, prevalence among vulnerable groups is thought to be between 1.0% and 1.8%. That this figure is notably lower than other African countries may be partially attributed to the island's geographical isolation.

However, social indicators suggest that Madagascar could well be following in the footsteps of mainland Africa, with low condom use (around 2% among women in rural communities), the relative prevalence of polygamous relationships and partners, and high birth rates (see box, page 139).

In the southeast region of Anosy, indicators suggesting the likelihood of an HIV epidemic are all too apparent. Almost 90% of the population lives below the poverty line, illiteracy is as high as 80% and malaria, bilharzia, typhoid and respiratory diseases are widespread. HIV prevention efforts in the regional capital of Taolagnaro (Fort Dauphin) were initiated during the development of the Rio Tinto ilmenite mine which briefly caused a boom in migration.

HIV testing in the town is low, but indications are that infection levels have risen by around 64% in the last four years. In 2010 the first child was diagnosed with the virus. Other factors which increase the likelihood of the spread of HIV are underage sex and marriage (from as young as 12) and low levels of sexual health knowledge. Sex work is common and considered culturally acceptable among both men and women; acceptance is as high as 90% among impoverished groups. There are strong *fady* around the discussion of sex and access to information is typically low. Another indicator used to predict potential or actual levels of HIV is the prevalence of sexually transmitted diseases, which are estimated by doctors to be around 40% in the town.

The Malagasy government has responded to the threat of HIV with the implementation of a national strategy as part of the country's development plan. This has involved the establishment of regional HIV/Aids Task Forces to co-ordinate community-based activities in prevention, counselling, treatment and aftercare. However, as a result of the 2009 political crisis, withdrawal of international funding and restructuring of governmental ministries, co-ordination has completely collapsed.

The youth representative for the Anosy HIV/Aids Task Force, Azafady, began HIV prevention efforts in 2006. A pilot study was conducted, from which a major three-year behaviour change programme in the town was developed, followed by a specialised maternal HIV prevention project in 2010. During this time, Azafady (now called SEED Madagascar) managed to increase HIV knowledge among young people by an average of 25% and has distributed over 65,000 condoms as well as information, education and communication materials. This has been achieved through local peer group educators and the implementation of a range of community-based activities including focus groups, home visits, the first antenatal group, school workshops, film screenings, sport and culture events, and mass mobilisations.

The biggest community mass mobilisation is the well-established World Aids Day street carnival, held annually on 1 December and supported by diverse community groups. It is an extremely uplifting and enjoyable celebration well worth visiting Taolagnaro for.

Health and Safety   SPECIFIC HEALTH ISSUES

5

When I was leading a trip in Madagascar a few years ago one of my group was bitten on the forearm by a female ring-tailed lemur. The animal was carrying a baby and was startled. It bit in self-defence. The skin was broken and there was a small amount of bleeding. In the days that followed, Susanne and I agonised about the possibility of rabies and what to do about it.

We asked advice from a local hotel manager who reassured her that there was almost no possibility of the lemur being rabid. I felt the same way so Susanne decided to wait until she returned to Germany, but the uncertainty spoiled the rest of her trip. Even the tiniest chance of catching rabies is too terrible to contemplate – and she couldn't stop contemplating it.

She saw her doctor 18 days after the bite and was started on a course of injections. Rather than being reassuring, her doctors told her that she'd left it much too late, and that she would not know for three months whether or not she would get rabies – and die. Of course she is fine now, but what *should* we have done?

I've talked to several people about this dilemma. What is the likelihood of an infected animal surviving long enough to bite a human? Lemurs tame enough to bite a tourist are found only in private reserves where dogs are excluded. Even if a rabid dog did get into the reserve would it be able to catch a lemur? And if it did catch one, would it inflict a bite which infected the animal but didn't kill it? The likelihood seems very small.

The late Alison Jolly, who studied lemurs for more than 50 years, said: 'I have never heard of anyone catching rabies from a lemur. I think that the chances are so small that I wouldn't dream of getting rabies shots after a lemur bite – except in one circumstance. If the lemur was hand-raised, either a current pet or a pet released into the wild, it may attack a human without provocation. In that case you get a deep bite with no warning. It probably is just misguided "normal" behaviour, treating you as one of its own species, but you can't be sure, so I would get shots. A bite in self-defence, though, isn't worth bothering about.'

Dr Jane Wilson-Howarth adds: 'I have now been involved in quite a number of cases of tourists who have been bitten overseas and then are badly scared by the prospect of the disease and finding clinical services abroad. Increasingly I encourage travellers to pay out for the jabs before they travel.'

not stitched – and seek post-bite jabs immediately. Tetanus jabs and sometimes antibiotics may be needed to treat wound infection.

If you have not had pre-exposure rabies vaccine then you need to get rabies immunoglobulin as soon as possible and five doses of rabies vaccine over the next 28 days. Rabies immunoglobulin is in global short supply so is very unlikely to be available in Madagascar meaning you would need to evacuate to get it. Those who have had the full three-dose pre-exposure vaccine will only need two more doses of vaccine and no longer need the rabies immunoglobulin. Travel-health insurers and embassies may be able to advise on the nearest source of vaccine and immunoglobulin.

CHOLERA Although it has a fearsome reputation, cholera doesn't usually make healthy people ill. It takes the debilitated, poor and half-starved of famine or conflict zones, or it is present along with other gastro-intestinal infections. Cholera is avoided in the same way as other 'filth-to-mouth' diseases and – if there are symptoms – it can be treated with the usual oral rehydration fluids (see page 117).

PLAGUE Occasionally it pops up in the media that Madagascar and Congo are the last bastions of **bubonic plague**, or Black Death – the disease that killed some 25 million in the Middle Ages. In the years 2010–15, Madagascar saw 2,404 cases (representing 74% of all cases worldwide), of which a fifth were fatal. However, this does represent a significant decline since a peak of 1,214 cases in 2004. In any case, travellers need not be concerned; those at risk live among rats in squalid conditions, such as in prisons and slums. The rarer but deadlier **pneumonic plague** is of a little more concern because it is capable of human-to-human transmission, so it would be wise to avoid a village that has had a recent outbreak.

FOOT PROTECTION Wearing shoes or sandals even on the beach will protect the feet from injury and parasites. Old trainers (running shoes) worn when you are in the sea will help you avoid getting coral or urchin spines in the soles of your feet and give some protection against venomous fish spines. Diving booties will protect from coral but not venomous fish. See page 238 for first-aid advice following encounters with marine nasties.

THE NASTY SIDE OF NATURE
Animals Malagasy terrestrial **snakes** are back-fanged, and so are effectively non-venomous. **Sea snakes**, although venomous, are easy to see and are rarely aggressive. However, if you are bitten then seek immediate medical treatment; try to keep the bitten part as still and as low as possible to slow the spread of venom. Large **spiders** can be dangerous, and the innocuous-looking black widow is found in Madagascar. Navy digger **wasps** have an unpleasant sting, but it is only **scorpions** that commonly

> **A DOCTOR CALLS**   *Hilary Bradt*
>
> It was only a scratch. I mopped the blood from my shin, cursed Madagascar's thorns and the fact that I was wearing shorts, and ignored it. The flies gathered and I brushed them away when I remembered to.
>
> A few days later it was the evening of our farewell dinner. Tomorrow I would take the long flight home and I was worried about my leg. It was now very hot, red and swollen. Lalaina, our guide, was at hand so I showed it to him and we agreed that I should get a doctor to look at it. By that time it was after 17.00 and we'd be leaving for our dinner at 19.30. The hotel had a list of English-speaking doctors (the embassy would have been my first point of call if I'd been travelling independently) and within an hour a very competent doctor and her assistant were in my hotel room examining my leg. She prescribed dressings and antibiotics, and sent Lalaina off to the pharmacy. All sorted. He arrived back in time for me to have the leg and myself dressed in time for dinner. The visit cost €25 and the medication €16. Lalaina had used the doctor's car (with driver) for the trip to the pharmacy. 'We had to have the red lights on,' he said 'otherwise we would never have got back in time for the dinner'. The traffic was terrible.
>
> Good to know he has his priorities right. Me too; without those antibiotics things could have got nasty. €40 well spent and another positive experience in the land of positives.

GETTING JIGGY ON MY BIRTHDAY   *Kara Moses, primatologist*

My 26th birthday was one I'll never forget. Friends at Durrell threw me a very Malagasy party: much local food, music, dancing and of course rum.

The next morning, my *actual* birthday, I blearily awoke in the sweltering heat with a pounding head and searing pain in my right foot. Washing away the dirt revealed three large white lumps, each with a black dot at the centre: the dreaded *parasy* (jiggers) that I'd been having nightmares about. These parasitic fleas burrow beneath the skin, periodically laying and releasing eggs through a hole.

Fidy volunteered to dig them out and gathered a disturbing array of equipment: sewing needles, scissors, candles and, to my bewilderment, a bottle of brake fluid. Miles from the nearest town, this was the best antiseptic available. I swallowed hard and prepared myself for the ordeal, wondering if there was any rum left over.

Closer inspection revealed my foot to have, in fact, *five* new residents. My stomach churned. For what seemed like an eternity, Fidy hacked at my foot, gleefully singing *Happy Birthday to You*, while I fought back tears and vomit. They were the biggest one's he'd ever seen, Fidy announced, adding that they must have been there at least a month, hidden under the permafilth covering my feet. With number three out, I took a breather, consoling myself we were over halfway. Then he discovered yet another two.

Once they were all finally removed (and burnt on the candle with a satisfying pop), the seven sore, gaping holes were steeped in brake fluid. I spent the rest of my birthday dousing the entire camp with insecticide. From then on I religiously washed and inspected my feet daily, deferring for a second opinion at the slightest mark, much to the amusement of all. '*Parasy?*' I'd ask fearfully. '*Tsy misy parasy,*' they'd laugh, and I'd breathe a sigh of relief.

cause problems because they favour hiding places where one might plunge a hand without looking. If you sleep on the ground, isolate yourself from these creatures with a mat, a hammock or a tent with a sewn-in ground sheet.

Scorpion and **centipede** stings are very unpleasant and worth avoiding. Scorpions often come out after rain. They are nocturnal but they like hiding in small crevices during the day. People camping in the desert or the dry forest may find that a scorpion has crept into the pocket of a rucksack – despite taking the sensible precaution of suspending their luggage from a tree. Scorpion stings are very painful for about 24 hours.

Leeches can be a nuisance in the rainforest, but are only revolting, not dangerous (Aids is not spread via leeches). They are best avoided by covering up, tucking trousers into socks and applying insect repellent (even on shoes – but beware, DEET dissolves plastics). Once leeches have become attached they are best not forcibly removed or their mouthparts may remain causing the bite to itch for a long time. Either wait until they have finished feeding (when they will fall off) or encourage them to let go by applying a lit cigarette, a bit of tobacco, chilli, salt or insect repellent. The wound will bleed a great deal and may easily become infected if not kept clean. For more on leeches see the box on page 330.

Beware of strolling barefoot on damp, sandy riverbeds and areas of beach where locals defecate. This is the way to pick up **jiggers** (see box, above). Jiggers are female sand fleas, which resemble maggots and burrow into your toes and soles to incubate their eggs. Remove them using a sterilised needle, by picking the top off the boil they make and teasing them out (this requires some skill, so it is best to ask a local for help). Disinfect the wound thoroughly to avoid infection.

Plants Madagascar has quite a few plants which cause skin irritation. One of the worst is a climbing legume with pea-pod-like fruits that look furry. This 'fur' penetrates the skin as thousands of tiny needles, which must be painstakingly extracted with tweezers. Prickly pear fruits have the same defence. Relief from the secretions of other irritating plants is obtained by bathing. Sometimes it is best to wash your clothes as well, and immersion fully clothed may be the last resort!

MEDICAL KIT

Apart from personal medication taken on a regular basis, it is unnecessary to weigh yourself down with a comprehensive medical kit, as many of your requirements will be met by Malagasy pharmacies. Expeditions and adventurous travellers should contact a travel clinic.

PERSONAL FIRST AID KIT A minimal kit contains a good drying antiseptic (eg: iodine or potassium permanganate, *not* antiseptic cream); a few small dressings (Band-Aids); aspirin or paracetamol; antifungal cream (eg: Canesten); ciprofloxacin or norfloxacin for severe diarrhoea; tinidazole for giardia or amoebic dysentery; antibiotic eye drops for sore, 'gritty', stuck-together eyes (conjunctivitis); and fine-pointed tweezers (to remove caterpillar hairs, thorns, splinters, coral, etc). Also take an alcohol-based hand rub or a bar of soap in a plastic box, condoms or femidoms as appropriate, and travel sickness pills. Don't forget your suncream, insect repellent, anti-malarial tablets, and permethrin spray if you're not taking your own impregnated bed net.

SAFETY

The Institute for Economics and Peace produces an annual Global Peace Index, ranking the world's countries from the most dangerous to the calmest based on 23 indicators – from political instability, terrorist activity, violent crime and murder rates to firearms availability, size of the police force, and levels of conflict. In the 2016 list, Madagascar ranked third-most-peaceful among Africa's 54 nations (after Mauritius and Botswana), and even surpassed the UK, France and the USA. While such statistics don't tell the whole story, it is reassuring to know that Madagascar is an overwhelmingly peaceful nation.

Before launching into a discussion on crime, it's worth reminding readers that by far the most common cause of death or injury while on holiday is the same as at home: road accidents. Violence is rare in Madagascar and most visitors return home after a crime-free trip, with fond memories of touchingly honest locals. But this is one area where being forewarned is forearmed: there are positive steps that you can take to keep yourself and your possessions safe.

BEFORE YOU GO You can enjoy peace of mind by making some preparations before you leave home. Make photocopies of all your important documents (passport, visa, airline ticket, travellers' cheques, credit cards, emergency phone number for stolen cards, and travel insurance details including emergency hotline number). Leave one set of copies with a friend or relative at home and keep another in your

Madagascar has some truly wonderful underwater opportunities but divers need to be cautious. Until recently there was no hyperbaric recompression chamber in the country and diving casualties had to be evacuated at great risk by air, but thankfully that changed in 2015. Divers Alert Network (*www.diversalertnetwork.org*) offers comprehensive diving insurance.

If you are going to dive in Madagascar you should be an experienced diver, taking responsibility for your own dives. Madagascar is not suitable for newly qualified PADI open-water divers. It is essential to dive within guidelines and take your own computer so you do not depend blindly on the local dive leaders. Do not dive with any outfit that does not carry oxygen on the boat. Make sure you ask about this; your life may depend on it.

There are no regulations in Madagascar and dive operators are not obliged to provide good quality octopus rigs, or to service equipment regularly, or indeed to carry out any of the 'housekeeping' that is required to provide safe diving. If you can manage it, bring your own equipment. Also make sure that you are conservative with your dive profiles and take an extra-long safety stop on ascending.

Don't be afraid to ask about safety issues. You are not being a wimp. I had a 'bend' in Madagascar in 2003. If my instructor had not been equipped with oxygen, I would be dead. As it was, he didn't have enough and I now have mild but permanent neurological injuries. Don't let them tell you there are no accidents in Madagascar; I was that statistic and I feel sure I'm not the only one.

main luggage, in case your hand luggage with the originals goes missing. A simpler alternative is to send all of these details to a web-based email account or upload them to cloud storage. It is also useful to have a list of contact numbers for your closest friends and family in case your mobile gets damaged, lost or stolen. Leave your valuable-looking jewellery at home; you do not need it in Madagascar. Likewise your fancy watch. Lock your bag when travelling by plane or *taxi-brousse*. Make or buy a lockable cover for your backpack (some double as handy rain covers).

CRIME PREVENTION Despite a degradation in security in Madagascar since the 2009 coup, violent crime against tourists is still incredibly rare. The response to a potentially violent attack is the same as anywhere: if you are outnumbered or the thief is armed, do as they say.

But you are *far* more likely to be robbed by subterfuge. In crowded places, razor-slashing of backpacks and pockets is not uncommon. Try to avoid bringing a bag to such places and keep your money and passport in a moneybelt or neck pouch. Women have advantages here: the neck pouch can be hooked over their bra so no cord shows at the neck and a moneybelt beneath a skirt is safe since it needs an unusually brazen thief to reach for it! If you must have a bag, make sure it is difficult to cut, and that it can be carried across your body so it cannot be snatched. Passengers in taxis may be the victims of robbery while in heavy traffic: the thief reaches through the open window and grabs your bag. Keep it on the floor by your feet.

The most common mistakes first-timers to Madagascar make are wearing jewellery ('But I always wear this gold chain'), carelessness with valuables ('I just put my bag down while I tried on that blouse'), and expecting thieves to look shabby ('But he was such a well-dressed young man').

Attacks on vehicles, especially taxi-brousses, have become more commonplace than a few years ago, but there is no evidence that tourists are specifically targeted. The *malaso* (bandits; sometimes also called *dahalo*, although technically that word refers specifically to cattle rustlers) who carry out these attacks can be quite vicious, cunning in their methods of ambush, and merciless in stripping every passenger of all their belongings. In one particularly horrific 2016 attack north of Ifaty, 20 armed *malaso* ambushed a taxi-brousse and murdered all but one of the 32 occupants, including 10 children. Fortunately the risk is easily mitigated, because almost all such attacks are carried out under the cover of darkness. Travelling at night, even close to major towns, is inadvisable. Indeed many car-hire companies now forbid their vehicles to be driven at night outside urban centres.

CARRYING YOUR PASSPORT Foreigners are required to have their passport on them at all times. If you prefer to leave yours in a safe place in your hotel room when you go out, carrying a photocopy is permitted but it must be an *authorised* copy. Take a photocopy of your passport (photo page and visa page) to any commune office or police station. They will compare it to the original then for a nominal fee they will add their official stamp confirming they are identical. It is a bit of a hassle, but losing your passport is worse.

If you are stopped without your passport or an authorised copy on you, a corrupt police officer may well demand an on-the-spot 'fine' of however much he thinks he can get away with. By law you may request to be taken to a police station where you will pay a fee of around €1 and be made to sign a form agreeing to produce your documents at the station within a couple of days.

TIPS FOR AVOIDING ROBBERY

- Remember that most theft occurs in the street not in hotels; leave your valuables hidden in a locked bag in your room or in the hotel safe.
- If you use a hotel safe at reception, make sure your money is in a sealed envelope that cannot be opened without detection. There have been cases of the key being accessible to all hotel employees, with predictable results.
- If staying in budget hotels, bring a rubber wedge to keep your door closed at night. If you can't secure the window put something like a metal water bottle on the sill; it will fall with a loud clatter if someone tries to enter.
- Pay particular attention to the security of your passport.
- Carry cash in a moneybelt, neck pouch or deep pocket. Wear loose trousers with zipped pockets. Keep emergency cash (dollars/euros) in a very safe place. Keep a small amount of cash in a wallet that you can give away if threatened.
- Divide up cash and cards so they are not all in one place. Keep photocopies of important documents in your luggage.
- Remember, what the thief would most like to get hold of is money. Do not leave it around (in coat pockets hanging in your room, in your hand while you concentrate on something else, in an accessible pocket while strolling).
- In a restaurant never hang your bag on the back of a chair or lay it by your feet (unless you put your chair leg over the strap). When travelling in a taxi, put your bag on the floor by your feet.
- For thieves, the next best thing after money is clothes. Avoid leaving them on the beach while you go swimming (in tourist areas) and never leave swimsuits or washing to dry outside your room near a public area.

As Her Majesty's Ambassador to Madagascar, I have overall responsibility for the British Embassy in Antananarivo. This includes overseeing our political, prosperity, consular, cultural, visa and communication work.

Key priorities for the embassy include **security** in which we work with a variety of partners to promote democracy, rule of law and good governance; **assisting British nationals** in Madagascar (see below); **prosperity**, supporting new and existing British businesses; and **development**, encouraging sustainable development (particularly on health, sanitation, food security and education) and long-term protection of biodiversity.

HOW WE CAN HELP YOU The embassy can assist British nationals living or travelling in Madagascar in the event of a serious situation arising. This may include illness, hospitalisation, death, missing persons, natural disasters, civil unrest, terrorist incidents, child abduction, kidnapping, rape, assault and other serious crimes. We will attempt to contact you within 24 hours of being informed that you have been detained. We can contact family or friends for you in times of distress as well as providing details of local lawyers, interpreters, doctors and funeral directors as necessary. We can also provide information about transferring funds.

The embassy provides documentary services (such as birth/death registration and help with marriage or civil partnership documents) and can also issue temporary replacements for travel documents, such as lost or stolen passports. Contact details for foreign embassies in Madagascar are on page 174.

HOW WE ARE UNABLE TO HELP YOU We cannot help you enter the country if you do not have a valid passport. Nor can we ensure your safety and security or get you preferential treatment in prison or hospital. We are unable to give legal advice, translate documents, make business arrangements on your behalf, pay bills or give you money, make travel bookings for you, or find you work or accommodation. We are unable to investigate crimes, carry out searches for missing persons, get you out of prison, prevent the local authorities from deporting you, interfere in court proceedings or get involved in private disputes over property, employment, commercial or other matters.

HOW YOU CAN HELP YOURSELF We encourage all British nationals (residents and visitors) to check our Travel Advice on Madagascar (*www.gov.uk/foreign-travel-advice/madagascar*) and to follow us via Facebook (🇫 *fcotravel*) and Twitter (🐦 *@fcotravel*) for the latest information.

We also suggest you make sure your passport is valid with emergency contact details up to date; take out comprehensive travel insurance or have in place an overseas health plan; leave copies of your passport, insurance and flight details with family and friends; take enough money for your trip and some backup funds; make sure you bring any necessary medication; and check your vaccinations are up to date.

But remember, the vast majority of visits to Madagascar are trouble free. Please do tell us if you think we need to amend our travel advice or if you have any suggestions. Your advice and comments matter to me.

Timothy Smart was appointed HM Ambassador to Madagascar in 2012.

- Bear in mind that it's impossible to run carrying a large piece of luggage. Items hidden at the bottom of your heaviest bag will be safe from a grab-and-run thief. Pass a piece of cord through the handles of multiple bags to make them one unstealable unit when waiting at a taxi-brousse station.
- Avoid misunderstandings – genuine or contrived – by agreeing on the price of a service before you set out.
- But above all, enjoy yourself. It's preferable to lose a few unimportant things and see the best of Madagascar than to mistrust everyone and ruin your trip!

WHAT TO DO IF YOU ARE ROBBED Have a little cry and then go to the police. They will write down all the details then send you to the chief of police for a signature. It is likely to take all day (indeed, one reader who had his possessions taken from a bungalow in Antsohihy in 2014 says he spent *five* days with the police writing reports), and will remind you what a manual typewriter looks like, but you will need the certificate for your insurance. If you are in a rural area, the local authorities will do a declaration of loss.

If your passport has been stolen or you have been the victim of a serious crime, you should also contact your embassy or consulate. The box opposite details the circumstances under which the British Embassy will assist British citizens, and how they can and cannot help. This information applies broadly to all embassies.

WHAT TO DO IF YOU ARE ARRESTED Being taken into police custody is unsettling at the best of times, so in a foreign land where you understand neither the laws nor the language it can be a terrifying experience. In this unlikely event, the police must explain why you are being arrested. You will be taken to a police station where a statement will be taken, usually in French; you are not obliged to sign anything you do not fully understand. Guilty or not, you have the right to insist your embassy be notified. Within 24 hours they should visit you to ensure you are being treated appropriately, furnish you with the details of reputable English-speaking lawyers, and, with your permission, can notify family and friends of your predicament.

ADVICE FOR SPECIFIC TYPES OF TRAVELLER

Solo travellers (and single-sex groups) face their own issues when travelling. In this section there are suggestions for women and men, gay and lesbian travellers, families travelling with young children, and infirm or disabled people.

WOMEN TRAVELLERS Foreign ladies travelling without male company are likely to encounter a few local men who think it's worth trying their luck. A firm refusal is usually sufficient. Try not to be too offended; think of the image of Western women that the average Malagasy male is shown via the cinema or TV. A woman Peace Corps volunteer gives the following advice for women travelling alone on taxi-brousses: 'try to sit in the cab, but not next to the driver; if possible sit with another woman; if in the main body of the vehicle, establish contact with an older person, man or woman, who will then tend to look after you'. Common advice is to wear a ring and say you are married, which most readers report to be effective in Madagascar, although reader Phoebe Mottram notes that most men are undeterred if you say you have a husband who is back home. Her advice is to perfect your story in advance, for example that your husband works in Madagascar and you are just on your way to meet him. She adds that being young,

5

I had a fantastic time travelling alone for a few weeks in rural Madagascar! Making a journey between Soanierana-Ivongo and Maroantsetra I'd expected to be left with overwhelming impressions of beautiful coastlines, an extraordinary ecosystem, improbable fauna and near-impossible transport conditions. I wasn't disappointed! Just as special though were the warmth and hospitality of the Malagasy people.

I'd landed in Antananarivo with the doubtful benefit of four months' (poorly) self-taught French and only the vaguest idea of an itinerary, having booked the flight on a whim to satisfy a long-standing but uninformed curiosity about the island. In an almost *vazaha*-free area I must have been quite a novelty but I learnt a few words of Malagasy and tried to take an interest in everything – although after attempting to de-husk rice grains with a giant (2m) pestle and mortar, I decided that this was best left to the experts!

Travelling alone is perhaps nobody's ideal but I really wouldn't have missed the experience for the world, at least in this part of the world; I was constantly touched by the friendship and companionship extended by local people. My limited linguistic skills were no bar to laughter and camaraderie in the back of a *camion*, as our lurching vehicle threw us among the sacks of rice, flour and sugar, the cooking pots and tomatoes, while the beer crates crashed alarmingly on shelves just above our heads… although it was sometimes difficult to see each other through the diesel fumes! My (all male) companions on this journey were unfailingly charming, lowering a plank which I used to enter and exit more easily as we made the numerous stops required to rebuild bridges and take on/offload people, poultry and produce… and I found this pattern of courtesy and kindness repeated again and again in so many situations as I progressed via 4x4s and ferries, pirogues, on foot, by boat and even, briefly, on the back of a motorbike.

I should have at least one cautionary tale to tell of an intimidating experience – but I haven't! I enjoyed myself far more than I'd anticipated and am left humbled by the simple humanity of the people who made this possible. I never felt unsafe and while eating in *hotelys* or having bread and coffee from a roadside stall would generally find people willing to chat.

Having said that, it was a relief to speak English when happy chance found me a travelling companion. Perhaps the solo experience might have been more uncomfortable among the groups of *vazaha* present in the more touristy areas. But if you're thinking of seeing Madagascar alone – do it! I found that the rural Malagasy respond with relief to someone who trusts them and will make you welcome. If you're in a tourist area, try to find a like-minded *vazaha* to enjoy it with – and don't forget to exchange email addresses; sharing the memories afterwards is as important as living them.

female and alone worked in her favour in the vast majority of situations, as locals would be less wary of making friendly contact and more willing to look out for you and make sure you are all right.

Reader Tiffany Coates took a solo motorbike trip around some of Madagascar's remotest corners: 'I met incredible people and had the most amazing time. Travelling by motorcycle made me much more approachable in the eyes of local people and it was a great ice-breaker.' Lone travellers, both male and female, seem to have a better time well off the beaten track; see the box above.

MEN TRAVELLERS In tourist spots, particularly in beach resorts, lone male travellers may find themselves pursued or harassed. Prostitutes are ubiquitous and beautiful, but venereal disease is common, and prostitutes have been known to drug a tourist's drink to render him unconscious then rob his possessions.

Authorities clamp down hard on sex tourism, especially with underage girls. Considering the risks you would be foolish to succumb to temptation.

TRAVELLING WITH CHILDREN The Malagasy people are very child-friendly although facilities typically are not. Travelling with children in Madagascar should not be undertaken lightly, but with the right preparation it can be a fun and rewarding experience.

Family travel needn't break the bank. Under-fives travel free on taxi-brousses. On domestic flights, there are discounts for youngsters. Many places offer reduced prices for children and most hotels have family-size rooms costing not much more than a double.

High chairs and cots are generally only found in top-end establishments and not commonly outside of the capital. But you will always find staff to be accommodating – offering to store baby formula in the chef's fridge or helping to organise a babysitter.

Imported supplies such as baby food, nappies (diapers) and wipes are available in supermarkets in Antananarivo. Jumbo Score also stocks baby carriers, bottles, clothing and other accessories, but they are generally rather poor quality. Don't rely on finding any of these goods outside the capital.

Expats Len and Sonja de Beer, who lived for years in Madagascar with their three youngsters, advise stocking up well on snacks before a trip (although safe bottled water is available everywhere) and point out that kids often get car sick on the winding roads of the highlands – so bring travel sickness tablets and keep plastic bags to hand.

If you'll be walking in national parks, it is useful to have some means of carrying young children when they get tired. 'Even in towns, strollers are almost entirely useless – much better to invest in a good kid carrier/backpack to tote your little one around the island. And if you plan to travel by car, you will want to bring a car seat' (Kyle & Monika Lussier).

Always take care to protect children adequately from the sun, keep them hydrated, use mosquito repellent, and bring a mozzie net for night-time (those provided by hotels are often snagged or ripped) especially if your infant is too young to take malaria prophylaxis. Hotels will help you find a doctor if you need one, but for serious emergencies keep in mind that you may need to return to Antananarivo to find reliable medical care.

Finally, Len and Sonja note that their children do not enjoy being called *vazaha*: 'you need to prep kids on the fact that they will look different and be stared at'.

TRAVELLERS WITH A DISABILITY It is not easy to find disabled-friendly accommodation in Madagascar. An increasing number of the higher-end hotels are beginning to offer one or more 'accessible rooms' but what they mean by this varies widely as there is no effective Malagasy legislation that sets a standard.

The only tour operator we are aware of explicitly catering to accessible tours in the country is France-based Dominique Dumas (\+33 663765791/+33 473908869; e *d.dum2@wanadoo.fr*). They use specially adapted vehicles on the road and for forest visits they have all-terrain one-wheeled chairs known as Joëlettes. As long as you are clear about your specific needs, though, you will find many local operators willing to work with you to tailor-make a suitable itinerary.

At airports, there should always be help available, including wheelchairs, but if you cannot walk at all you may need to be manhandled – without an aisle chair – to and from the aircraft. Public transport is generally very crowded with no concessions to disabled travellers. So, in general, a hire car would be preferable; most are of the 4x4 variety and come with a driver who, although not specifically trained in this skill, will usually be willing to assist you in and out of the vehicle as required. Keep in mind that distances are great and roads often bumpy, so if you are prone to skin damage you need to take extra care (bring a pressure-relieving cushion and pads as necessary). Stops with proper toilets can be few and far between, so if this is an issue then be very clear about your needs at the planning stage.

Although the majority of Madagascar's wildlife highlights are not disabled-friendly, there are two outstanding exceptions. The luxurious Anjajavy resort has villas, of which one is officially accessible (see pages 408–9), and Berenty (pages 250–4) has broad, smooth, well-maintained forest paths. The ideal route for a disabled traveller would be RN7 from Antananarivo to Toliara by hired car and driver. For lemurs try Lemurs Park (page 177).

Everywhere in Madagascar, pavements and paths are frequently unsurfaced or uneven, steps often irregular, and open drains are not uncommon, so wheelchair users and visually impaired travellers need to be aware of these challenges.

Across most of the country, clinics and pharmacies are often basic and poorly stocked. Make sure you can fully explain your particular medical requirements and have your own supplies of any essential medication and equipment with you. Travel insurance with no upper age limit and for people with pre-existing medical conditions can be purchased from Age UK (☏ 0800 389 4852; www.ageuk.org).

GAY AND LESBIAN TRAVELLERS Madagascar is one of the few African countries where homosexuality is not a crime, although the age of consent is higher: 21 (as opposed to 14 for heterosexual sex). There is general societal discrimination – and no laws prohibiting such discrimination – but travellers are unlikely to suffer open hostility. Public displays of affection are nevertheless best avoided. Little exists in the way of a gay 'scene' (La Caverna in Antananarivo's Isoraka district is the only place we know of that explicitly promotes itself as a gay bar).

6

Madagascar and You

RESPONSIBLE TOURISM

In recent years there has been a welcome shift of attitude among visitors to developing countries, from focusing on what they can get out of their trip to how they can give something back. This chapter addresses those issues, and suggests ways in which you can help this marvellous, yet sometimes tragic, country.

THE MALAGASY WAY Communication succeeds only when the participants end up attaching the same meaning to the message being conveyed. Such meanings, however, are heavily dependent on subtle underlying assumptions which can differ greatly from culture to culture. Consequently – even when there is no language barrier – miscommunication is likely when members of different cultures interact. Indeed, the traditional Malagasy way of thinking can differ so greatly from Western viewpoints that anthropologist Øyvind Dahl wrote a whole book on the resulting misunderstandings: *Meanings in Madagascar: Cases of Intercultural Communication*.

So unconsciously ingrained are our concepts of time, fairness, respect, responsibility, gratitude, and so on that the behaviour of someone operating on a different set of values can leave us utterly baffled. We must not be too quick to dismiss such unexpected behaviour as the mark of an idiot or interpret it as being deliberately devious.

Tolerance and the fear of causing offence is an integral part of Malagasy social relationships. So if a tourist expresses anger in a way that is entirely appropriate in his own culture, it may be counter-productive. Deeply unsettled, the person at the receiving end may giggle in response, exacerbating the situation. If you are patient, pleasant and keep your temper, your problem will be solved more quickly. Avoid being too dogmatic in conversation; non-confrontation and indirectness are the norms.

Imagine an American in a bar, who calls out 'Hey, can I get a beer over here!' and a Brit at the next table who ushers over the barman to say 'I wonder if it might be possible to see a menu when you get a free moment'. This may be exaggerating the stereotypes a little, but the point is clear: this Brit thinks the American rather rude while the American finds the Brit quaintly polite, yet in reality both customers may be acting equally politely in the context of their own cultural norms. Now crank up the politeness-o-meter a couple of notches further, and *voilà*: you have the Malagasy.

Be plentiful in your thanks and praise to minimise the chance of causing offence. Smiling goes a long way in conveying your satisfaction too. And notice how people stoop in deference, often with one arm extended to convey the message 'Excuse me, may I come through?'

Respect for hierarchy is strong in Malagasy culture and independent thought is not encouraged by employers in the same way as in the West. Picture the scene: it's early morning in a simple Malagasy hotel. There is just one breakfast option: bread,

The question I'm most often asked by journalists is how do I deal with the dilemma of encouraging people to fly halfway across the world while knowing that this contributes to carbon emissions and global warming? I reply that to me it's no dilemma...

Not long ago, I was the lecturer on board a cruise ship. Yes, a long flight then a ship which also contributed its share of CO_2 – so thumbs down for that. But in my lectures I described the work done by the Ivoloina Park and the charity HELP in Toamasina, and invited passengers to see the work for themselves. Afterwards some told me it was one of the highlights of the trip, and the outcome was a combined on-the-spot donation of about US$1,500. In my experience this sort of generosity is not unusual once people can see for themselves the work done in Madagascar in conservation and educating the next generation.

The budget travellers' contribution is equally valuable because they bring goodwill and an enthusiasm for breaking down cultural barriers. The backpackers who contribute their stories and philosophies to this book may be the politicians or businessmen and women of the future. Their experiences in Madagascar will help inform the decisions they make as leaders.

And even those visitors who simply enjoy Madagascar, relaxing on the beaches, visiting the national parks, buying handicrafts and gaining a little understanding of what makes the average Malagasy tick, have made a contribution to the economy of the country.

So, although I admire those conscientious people who are prepared to make the sacrifice of not flying, I think they're wrong. The best way to save Madagascar is to go there – and that means taking a plane. If you want to offset your carbon emissions do it by contributing to one of the reforestation programmes in Madagascar. See pages 179, 278, 286, 323 and 410 for details.

butter, jam and coffee for a fixed price. So you order one, but you're not thirsty so you tell the waitress not to bother with the coffee. She nods shyly and soon brings your food. But as you tuck in, she returns without making eye contact and delivers a cup of coffee to the table, leaving you wondering what went wrong in this simple exchange; you're sure your French isn't *that* bad! Is this girl stupid?

Seen from her perspective, she was put in an impossible situation: there is no price set for a breakfast without coffee. By deviating from the prescribed menu you might demand to pay less, then she would risk getting in trouble with her boss later. On the other hand, she would also feel very rude telling you that you must pay for a coffee you didn't receive.

Sometimes a little reflection reveals the reasons behind the failure to produce the expected service, but sometimes you just have to tell yourself 'Well, that's the way it is'. After all, you are not going to be able to change Madagascar, but Madagascar may change you.

CONSIDER THE ENVIRONMENT Part of responsible tourism is relinquishing some of our normal comforts. Consider this: fuel-wood demand in Madagascar far outstrips supply. Wood and charcoal are the main sources of energy, and the chief users are city dwellers. In rural areas, tourist establishments may be the main consumers.

Do you still feel that hot water is essential in your hotel? Another source of energy is hydro-electric power, so drought – as is common in these times of climate change – causes electricity cuts. So think before leaving the air conditioning and lights on when absent from your room.

One of the keys to responsible tourism is ensuring that as much as possible of the money you spend on your holiday remains in Madagascar. Independent travellers should try, whenever possible, to stay at small hotels run by Malagasy. Tourists on an organised tour will probably find themselves in foreign-owned hotels, but can do their bit by buying handicrafts and perhaps donating to local charities.

SHOPPING Give some thought to buying ethical souvenirs. You will find a list of products to avoid on page 109, along with some guidance on haggling appropriately. Advice on tipping is on page 96.

WASTE DISPOSAL Madagascar has no mechanised recycling plants. Instead, the poorest of the poor scavenge the rubbish dumps for clothes, containers and suchlike. In rural areas rubbish is simply dumped on the beach or on wasteland and burned. Wherever possible take your non-biodegradable rubbish home with you, or at least back to the city. Batteries in particular must be taken home and disposed of properly. The exception is plastic bottles: rural people in Madagascar need all the containers they can get for carrying or storing water or other liquids (or even using as plant pots – see box, page 281) so you can give your empty water bottles to villagers. In parallel with recent laws introduced in many other countries, Madagascar banned lightweight plastic bags in 2015.

TREAD SOFTLY *Alasdair Harris, Blue Ventures*

Madagascar's coastal environments comprise some of the most ecologically sensitive areas of the country. Visitors should be aware of the intrinsic effect that their presence and activities will have on local habitats and plan their holiday in a way that minimises impact on the environment.

When trekking, try to avoid sensitive habitats and vegetation types, reducing the impact of your movement and access to and from campsites. All waste should be sorted and disposed of sensibly. In arid environments such as the southwest, keep freshwater use to a minimum.

Swimmers, snorkellers and divers should avoid all physical contact with corals and other marine life. Divers should take care to avoid damaging reefs by maintaining good buoyancy control to avoid accidental contact or stirring up sediment.

In coastal hotels and restaurants, seafood is commonly caught to order, regardless of the sustainability of the catch. In some tourist areas it is not uncommon to see critically endangered species such as the humphead or Napoleon wrasse served up in a restaurant. Shellfish should not be bought out of season, since this can have devastating consequences for populations.

The marine curios trade is equally driven by tourism and visitors must refrain from purchasing shells. In Toliara alone, almost 150 species of gastropods are exploited for the ornamental shell trade. Several of these – notably the magnificent helmet shell and the cowries – are now threatened with extinction. Similarly, the exploitation of sea turtles is increasingly focused at the tourist market, turtle shells now fetching staggering prices in markets and *bijouteries*.

TOURIST POWER We can sometimes be too cautious about making our feelings felt because so often the hotel management is only trying to please us. But by expressing their views, tourists can help shape a more ethical tourism industry. If a smart new hotel proudly states that they use the valuable – and highly endangered – hardwoods such as rosewood or palisander for their furniture or floors, you could get into a conversation with the owner about sustainability.

There is, of course, a big difference between complaining about bad service and informing the management about a shift in tourist values. Your disapproval of illegally kept pet lemurs (page 141) should be expressed tactfully, and your views about sustainable tourism need even more care. Your green views won't be shared by all tourists and it's not a conversation you can have in a hurry when paying your bill. Take some time to discuss it over a drink.

PHOTOGRAPHY Lack of consideration when taking photos used to be the most common example of irresponsible tourist behaviour – one that each of us has probably been guilty of at some time. It is so easy to take a sneaky photo without first establishing contact with the person, so easy to say we'll send a print of the picture and then not get around to it, so easy to stroll into a market or village thinking what a wonderful photo it will make and forgetting that you are there to experience it. What has changed is the genuine delight most people – especially kids – get in seeing the photo on the digital camera's monitor. So, although the rules remain that you should not to take people's photos without permission, these days it is rare to receive a negative response. Always establish contact first with a greeting and a mimed question about whether you may take a photo. Give consideration to the offence caused by photographing the destitute. Be cautious about paying your way to a good photo; often a smile or a joke will work as well, and sets no precedent. And if you do want to send a print of the photo – and it will give huge pleasure if you do (see box opposite) – be sure to note the address and honour any promise to send copies. In rural areas without a postal service, your guide (if you are in a group) may be able to locate the person in his or her next trip.

THE EFFECTS OF TOURISM ON LOCALS The impact of foreigners on the Malagasy was noted as long ago as 1669 when a visitor commented that formerly the natives were deeply respectful of white men but were changed 'by the bad examples which the Europeans have had, who glory in the sin of luxury in this country'.

In developing countries, tourism has had profound effects on the inhabitants – some good, some bad. Madagascar inspires a particular devotion and an awareness of its fragility, both environmental and cultural. Wildlife is profiting from the attention given it and from the emphasis on ecotourism. For the people, however, the blessings may be very mixed: some find jobs in the tourist industry, but for others the impact of tourism has meant that their cultural identity has been eroded, along with some of their dignity and integrity. Village antagonisms are heightened when one or two people gain the lion's share of tourist revenue, leading in some cases to murder, and hitherto honest folk have lapsed into corruption, alcoholism or thievery.

BEGGARS Whether or not to give to professional adult beggars is up to you. But it is important to make up your mind before you hit the streets so you can avoid standing there rifling through a conspicuously fat wallet for a low-denomination bill. Keep in mind that for every genuinely needy person with the brazen confidence to ask a stranger for cash, there are a thousand more too shy or too proud. Giving to

'PLEASE SEND ME A PHOTO'   *Hilary Bradt*

It is not always easy to keep a promise. Of course we *intend* to send a print after someone posed cheerfully for the photo, but after we get home there are so many other things to do, so many addresses on scraps of paper. I now make sure to honour my promises. Here's why.

Many years ago, I was checking my group in to a Nosy Be hotel when the bellboy asked if he could speak to me. He looked nervous, so suspecting a problem with the bookings I asked him to wait until everyone was in their rooms. When we were alone he cleared his throat and recited what was obviously a carefully prepared speech: 'You are Mrs Hilary Bradt. Ten years ago you gave your business card to the lady at Sambava Voyages and she gave it to a schoolboy who wrote to you. But you were away so your mother answered the letter. She wrote many letters. My name is Murille and I am that boy. And now I want to talk to you about Janet Cross and Brian Cross and Andrew and…' There followed a list of every member of my family. As I listened, incredulous, I remembered the original letter. 'We love England strongly,' he wrote, 'especially London, Buckingham, Grantham, Dover…' I remembered passing it to my mother saying I was too busy for such a correspondence but maybe she'd like to write. She kept it up for several years, answering questions such as 'How often does Mrs Hilary go to Grantham and Dover?' and she sent a photo of the family gathering at Christmas, naming every member on the back of the photo.

This brought an indignant letter from a cousin. 'I have seen your photo. It is a very nice one. I asked Murille if he would lend it for one day only because we all study English so we must have photo of English people more to improve this language, but he refused me strongly because they are only his friends not mine…'

Murille brought out the treasured photo. It had suffered from the constant handling and tropical heat and was peeling at the edges. He wanted to trim it, he explained, 'but if I do I will have to cut off a bit of your mother's beautiful chair and I can't do that.'

Later that year I sent Murille a photo album filled with family photos. I never heard from him again – that's the way it is in Madagascar – but the story has a twist to its tail. I returned to Sambava 12 years after the original visit, and found myself addressing a classroom of eager adult students of English and their local teacher. Searching for something interesting to say, I told them about the time I was last in their town and the series of letters between Murille and my mother. And I told them about the cousin who also wrote to her. 'I think his name was Patrice,' I said. The teacher looked up. 'I'm Patrice. Yes, I remember writing to Janet Cross…'

a reputable charity is a much fairer way of making sure your donation is distributed among those in need.

The unintentional effect of giving sweets, pens, money or whatever to begging children can be seen in any popular resort. Kids trail after you, grabbing your hands and beseeching you for gifts. Many tourists are simply worn down by their persistence and give in, thus perpetuating the problem. Reader Bill French offers the following advice: 'Just don't give anything. Ignore their begging and change the subject – sing, play, do tricks or just chatter away. These are skills you have to work on.'

GIVING PRESENTS This is a subject often discussed among experienced travellers who cannot agree on when, if ever, a present is appropriate. Gifts of money are quite normal in exchange for a service among the Malagasy. For example, if a family invites you to share their meal or hosts you overnight, they would expect not to be left out of pocket even though they may not explicitly ask for payment. But unsolicited presents are usually given for self-gratification more than real generosity, and that one thoughtless act can change a village irreparably. Shyly inquisitive children turn into tiresome beggars, and ambitious young men into scoundrels. So it is perhaps better to give gifts only where you are sure they are deserved.

OFF THE BEATEN TRACK Travellers venturing deep into uncharted territory will want to do their utmost to avoid offending the local people, who are usually extremely warm and hospitable. With the many *fady* varying from area to area, it is impossible to know exactly how to behave, although outsiders are normally considered exempt from the consequences of infringing a local fady. It is advisable to take a guide in far-flung areas, at least for communication as many isolated peoples speak only Malagasy.

On arrival in a remote village you should ask for the *président du fokontany* and explain why you are there. Adventurous readers Valerie and John Middleton write: 'you will never cease to be amazed at how helpful he will wish to be once your purpose is understood and perhaps even more importantly the authority of his backing confers a considerable degree of protection'. He will show you where you can sleep (sometimes a hut is kept free for guests; sometimes someone will be moved out for you) and probably provide you with a meal.

Philip Thomas, a social anthropologist who has conducted research in the southeast, points out how tourists may unwittingly cause offence: '*Vazaha* sometimes refuse hospitality, putting up tents and cooking their own food. But in offering you a place to sleep and food to eat the Malagasy are showing you the kindness they extend to any visitor or stranger, and to refuse is a rejection of their hospitality and sense of humanity. You may think you are inconveniencing them, and this is true, but they would prefer that than if you keep to yourselves as though you were not people (in the widest sense) like them. It may annoy you that it is virtually impossible to get a moment away from the gaze of the Malagasy, but you are there to look at them and their activities, so why should there not be a mutual exchange?'

NEW FRIENDS Visitors who have spent some time in Madagascar and have befriended a particular family often find themselves in the 'more and more and more' trap. The foreigner begins by expressing appreciation of the friendship by sending a gift. A request for a more expensive gift follows. And another one, until the luckless *vazaha* feels that he or she is seen as a bottomless cornucopia of goodies. The reaction is a mixture of guilt and resentment.

Understanding the Malagasy viewpoint may help you to come to terms with these requests. You may be considered as part of the extended family, and family members often help support those who are less well off. You will almost certainly be thought of as fabulously wealthy, so it is worth dispelling this myth by giving some prices for familiar foodstuffs at home and explaining that you have a family of your own that needs your help. Don't be afraid to say 'no'.

Be cautious about giving your name and address to locals with whom you have only a passing acquaintance. Women may be surprised – and possibly delighted – to receive a letter declaring undying love, but it's just possible that this comes with a few strings attached.

But of course new friendships can be hugely rewarding for all concerned. We know of a few travellers who have translated their wish to help the Malagasy into airfares to visit their home country. This is not to be undertaken lightly – the red tape from both governments is horrendous – but it is a gesture that will never be forgotten.

HOW YOU CAN HELP

There are countless organisations doing good in Madagascar, mainly through community and conservation projects. Any of them would welcome even a modest financial donation and some can make use of certain donated items, such as clothes, books or medical supplies. You can also give your time and energy to several charities as a volunteer. Working holidays and voluntourism opportunities range from a single day of your holiday to a several-month placement for those on a gap year or career break. Of the organisations listed below, those which accept volunteers are indicated by the ✋ symbol.

SELECTED CHARITIES AND OTHER ORGANISATIONS The organisations listed alphabetically in this section mostly have projects at multiple sites across Madagascar or are engaged with the country on a general basis; many more local charities can be found in the relevant regional chapters in *Part Two*.

Access Madagascar Initiative ✋ (e *info@accessmadagascar.org; www. accessmadagascar.org*) This UK-based non-profit organisation was founded to continue The Dodwell Trust volunteer programme. AMI works to help children, young people and communities through shared development projects and access to education, including teaching English, training teachers and building classrooms and libraries. There are opportunities for hands-on experience in teaching English, working with children, conservation work, medical electives and more. Groups and families with children are also welcome to apply.

Akany Avoko Faravohitra (e *contact.avoko@gmail.com; www.avokofaravohitra. com*) Not to be confused with Akany Avoko in Ambohidratrimo (although when founded in the 1960s they were affiliated), this inspiring home for vulnerable girls is located in a large house in central Tana. It can accommodate up to 40 children aged 5–18, usually victims of abuse or those with behaviour issues, drug problems, or who are in trouble with the law. AAF takes care of all aspects of the girls' lives and their rehabilitation. They welcome donations of supplies or money; or you can sponsor a girl via Mad13 Development Trust (page 142).

Andrew Lees Trust/Andry Lalana Tohana (*www.andrewleestrust.org*) The UK-based ALT was set up in 1995 and in 2010 achieved a long-term goal of launching a fully Malagasy NGO (Andry Lalana Tohana) to carry its work forward. The trust develops social and environmental education projects in the south to increase access to information and education that empowers local populations to improve food security, reduce poverty and manage natural resources more sustainably. ALT's Project Radio broadcasts vital information and delivers education to nearly a million isolated rural listeners.

Anglo-Malagasy Society (*www.anglo-malagasysociety.co.uk*) The UK-based AMS holds meetings in London three or four times a year with speakers on a diverse range of Malagasy topics, followed by a delicious Malagasy buffet. Its detailed quarterly newsletter keeps members informed of news and developments from the island. Membership is inexpensive, especially for students, and non-members are welcome at events.

Ankizy Gasy – Children of Madagascar Foundation ✋ (m +261 34 52 118 96/+261 33 37 097 34; e volunteer@childrenofmadagascar.com; www. childrenofmadagascar.com) Based in Ambohidratrimo, near the capital's airport, this foundation supports 260 local kids through educational and nutritional sponsorship. It welcomes volunteers willing to teach or organise activities. See ad, page 282.

Arboretum d'Antsokay ✋ (e info@antsokayarboretum.org; www.antsokayarboretum. org) This splendid arboretum near Toliara (see page 232) does valuable work to protect rare species and welcomes donations and assistance from volunteer ecotourists.

Blue Ventures ✋ (e madagascar@blueventures.org; www.blueventures.org) This multi-award-winning organisation, with field projects mainly along the west coast, has had great successes in marine conservation projects and wide-ranging community work from education to family planning schemes. The volunteering programme is universally praised and the scientific research to which it contributes wins regular international acclaim. Staff-to-volunteer ratios are high, scientific training is rigorous and PADI scuba-diving training is included. Flexible expeditions of 3–12 weeks or more are offered. See also the boxes on pages 133, 139, 431 and 432.

Centre Fihavanana (Streetkids Centre) (☎ +261 20 22 299 81; m +261 34 13 459 91; e bpfihavanana@blueline.mg) Run by the Sisters of the Good Shepherd, about 300 children aged 3–12 are taught, undernourished babies are fed, their destitute mothers given training in childcare, teenagers learn basic skills and handicrafts, and elderly people come for company and care. Food is taken to over 300 women and youngsters in prison. The centre also has a scheme which provides bicycles for young men who need them to earn a living. And a group of women do beautiful embroidery from home, providing income both for them and for the centre. They accept donated supplies, clothing and cash, and can give donors a tour of the centre. See page 176.

Conservation Fusion (e conservationfusion@gmail.com; www.conservationfusion. org) Focusing primarily on Madagascar, this new organisation aims to provide the tools to empower local people to find innovative solutions to help themselves. Its work particularly includes projects with schools that highlight biodiversity issues.

Conservation International (www.conservation.org) CI is one of the most active conservation organisations in Madagascar. Its current projects include establishing the 425,000ha Ankeniheny–Zahamena Corridor as a protected area, enabling nearby communities to manage their forest resources more effectively for both sustainable livelihood and biodiversity conservation, increasing local capacity in child and maternal health, and improving access to family planning and reproductive health services.

CPALI ✋ (e info@cpali.org; www.cpali.org) This US-Malagasy partnership takes a community-centred approach to conservation and helps build sustainable silk-producing livelihoods to lift people out of poverty in northeast Madagascar (page 315). The project accepts volunteers. You can also support their work by donating via their website or ordering some of their extraordinarily fine silk products, from

FAMILY PLANNING *Tess Shellard, Blue Ventures*

Most visitors to Madagascar quickly notice just how many children there are. With a large unmet need for family planning services, the total population is doubling every 20 years. While working with remote Vezo fishing communities, Blue Ventures recognised the need to address this issue if their hard work to conserve their coastal resources was to have any chance of success.

A British-based GP, Vik Mohan, began conducting research in the village of Andavadoaka to develop a clearer picture of the pressures the community was facing. He found girls were having their first pregnancy soon after puberty and that some families had as many as 16 children. Many more were struggling to provide for themselves. One in five children in the region died before their fifth birthday.

Surveys discovered that the local women were desperate for better information about sexual health and better access to contraception. Anyone wanting to access family planning had to walk 50km through dense, spiny forest. There was clearly a huge unmet need for sexual and reproductive health services.

In 2007, Mohan opened the region's first family planning clinic in Andavadoaka. The response was overwhelmingly positive: 20% of all women of reproductive age attended, requesting contraception. Couples were empowered to choose the number and spacing of their births for the very first time, and so the project came to be known as Safidy ('freedom to choose').

To get the word out, a play about sexually transmissible infections was performed using humour and recognisable local stereotypes to make this sensitive topic entertaining and accessible. The play, *Captain Kapoty* ('Condom'), was performed again a month later to a packed audience on the beach and a competition held for the community to create their own plays.

This initiative was seen as an unusual move for a marine conservation charity but integrating these areas of work offered real hope for the Vezo of finding a way to live more healthily and sustainably, and to improve their food security. Crucially it also helped the Vezo to develop their resilience to climate change.

Over the next few years, Blue Ventures' integrated PHE (Population, Health and Environment) programme grew to include strands on maternal and child health, as well as water, hygiene and sanitation. Blue Ventures offered opportunities for the Vezo women to become economically active for the first time by farming sea cucumbers and seaweed, enabling them to create their own path out of poverty and become less reliant on finite natural resources.

Local women were trained to travel between villages and distribute contraception, water purifying solution, diarrhoea-treatment kits and antenatal medication. By using community-based distribution alongside more traditional clinics, the programme was able to grow to reach more than 20,000 people across 50 remote communities along Madagascar's southwest coastline.

The health of the villagers was improving and the community was becoming more resilient. The proportion of women using contraception increased more than fivefold from 10% to 55% between 2007 and 2013, while the general fertility rate fell by over a third. Every three months Blue Ventures reaches over 5,000 people through educational tours featuring a variety of integrated health and conservation topics.

This award-winning integrated approach led to Sir David Attenborough describing the project as 'a model for everyone working to conserve the natural life-support systems of our troubled planet'.

scarves and hats to placemats, cushions and even jewellery (*www.wildsilkmarkets. com*).

The Dodwell Trust (e *dodwellandhobbs@gmail.com; www.dodwell-trust.org*) This British-registered charity founded by explorer and broadcaster Christina Dodwell in 1995 runs a learning centre and primary school for disadvantaged children in Ampefy, and collaborates with projects for community development and reforestation. The charity's long-running volunteer programme is now managed separately by Access Madagascar Initiative (page 137).

Duke Lemur Center (*www.lemur.duke.edu*) This world-leading lemur research centre in North Carolina has launched an initiative in northeast Madagascar called SAVA Conservation. Its community-based approach to biodiversity conservation includes an extensive environmental education programme with educational visits to Marojejy National Park for local student groups as well as a teacher-training scheme. The centre promotes sustainable livelihoods, reforestation projects and, of course, wild lemur research and conservation. See the box on page 329.

Durrell Wildlife Conservation Trust (*www.durrell.org*) Since the 1980s, this Jersey-based charity has been working in Madagascar with a core mission to save the rarest species from extinction. It is now one of the biggest conservation organisations in the country, with projects at nine sites and a team of more than 45 local staff. See box, pages 68–9.

Feedback Madagascar (e *info@feedbackmadagascar.org; www.feedbackmadagascar. org*) This small but highly effective Scottish charity has worked to alleviate poverty and environmental degradation in the highlands for more than 20 years. It has dozens of project sites in the Fianarantsoa province focusing on improving primary health care and primary education, promoting natural resource management and developing income-generating schemes. It is currently working on revitalising the silk industry, community forest management and adult literacy programmes. Feedback occasionally has volunteer openings; contact the charity for details.

Frontier (*www.frontier.ac.uk*) This organisation takes paying volunteers for their marine research, wildlife conservation and medical and teaching programmes lasting 1–12 weeks. Although often accused of focusing too much on glossy marketing and too little on producing work of genuine worth, we know of several former volunteers and most report having a fantastic time. Unfortunately we are also aware of former volunteers whose grievances ended up in court.

Hope for Madagascar (e *hopeformadagascar@comcast.net; www.hopefor madagascar.org*) This US charity seeks volunteers with previous experience of living abroad and teaching English. Besides providing English lessons, the charity builds schools, distributes school supplies and runs village development projects. It aims to build a new school every two years and provides scholarships to ensure students can attend.

Lambas for Lemurs (e *lambasforlemurs@gmail.com; www.lambasforlemurs.com*) Set up by US/Canadian zoologists, this programme promotes primate conservation in Madagascar. You can support their cause by buying their locally made *lamba* (sarongs), featuring mongoose lemur designs, via their website.

Marni LaFleur, Kim Reuter & Tara Clarke

Caged, tethered or free-ranging pet lemurs are commonly encountered at tourist sites. Hoteliers and others capitalise on lemurs' inherent appeal to lure in business, sometimes charging for the opportunity to feed or take photos with the animals. There's no doubt of the attraction of these cute-and-cuddly characters, but you should consider carefully whether to support these places.

Lemurs are protected by national and international laws, and only a dozen or so sites in Madagascar hold official permits to keep them. Pet lemurs are almost invariably wild-caught and suffer extremely high mortality – just 30% survive their first six months of captivity. Many of these social animals are kept alone in poor conditions and fed inappropriate diets including bananas, fish, rice and beer. More than 28,000 lemurs are thought to have been kept illegally between 2010 and mid-2013, including some critically endangered species. Coupled with the threats from bushmeat hunting and deforestation, this is seriously impacting wild populations.

Sadly even some of the few authorised captive facilities in Madagascar treat their animals poorly. Please support only those facilities that put animal welfare first. You can recognise these as the lemurs will be free-ranging (or in large enclosures) and appear healthy. The staff should not allow direct contact between visitors and animals; by law, you must remain 2m away from any lemur. Guides might offer treats to entice them to come close or jump on to you – encouraging this behaviour puts both you and the animals at risk of disease transmission or injury.

Some facilities – even legal ones – capture new animals from the wild whenever theirs die. Before supporting an establishment that keeps lemurs, it is important to understand why they are doing so, where the animals came from, and if their well-being is properly catered for. When challenged about keeping these pets, hoteliers often claim they are rescued orphans or confiscated pets that are being rehabilitated for release. Alas there is rarely any truth in these excuses.

HOW YOU CAN BE A LEMUR ALLY Never pay for photos with or of illegal pet lemurs; never feed or interact with them; do not support businesses or individuals that keep lemurs illegally; and don't share photos of people touching lemurs as this perpetuates the belief that they make good pets. Finally please report any pet lemurs you encounter in Madagascar to the Pet Lemur Survey (*www. petlemursurvey.com*). It's anonymous and all feedback supports our research into this growing problem.

Drs Marni LaFleur and Tara A Clarke are the co-directors of Lemur Love (see below), which is collaborating with the Pet Lemur Survey overseen by Dr Kim Reuter.

Madagascar and You HOW YOU CAN HELP

6

Lemur Love (e *info@lemurlove.org; www.lemurlove.org*) This US-based non-profit organisation established in 2012 conducts and disseminates scientific research on wild ring-tailed lemur populations and wild-caught former pet lemurs in Madagascar (see box above). They also collaborate with the Pet Lemur Survey to improve the plight of these creatures.

Mad13 Development Trust (*info@mad13.org.uk; www.mad13.org.uk*) This charitable trust was set up to administer the legacy of a huge 2013 UK Scouting expedition to Madagascar, which delivered numerous community sanitation and water improvements. Support their ongoing projects in Madagascar or sponsor a vulnerable girl at local partner Akany Avoko Faravohitra (see page 137) via their website.

Mada Clinics (e *imadaclinics1@gmail.com; www.madaclinics.org*) Mada Clinics operates two healthcare centres in the north and has also established a rural school. It offers volunteers the chance to work in the clinics, help in the school, and has assisted them in setting up a biodiversity project near Ankarana. Volunteer positions are for a minimum of two weeks and the charity is especially keen to hear from those with medical experience.

Madagascar Biodiversity Partnership (e *MBPweb@madagascarpartnership. org; www.madagascarpartnership.org*) Founded in the USA in 2010, MBP aims to protect Malagasy forests through research, education and outreach. There are volunteer places on its reforestation, lemur reintroduction, sustainable energy and drinking water projects.

Madagascar Fauna and Flora Group (e *tim@savethelemur.org; www. madagascarflorafauna.org*) MFG is an international consortium of zoos and other conservation organisations co-operating to protect Malagasy wildlife. Its projects focus on captive breeding, community education, agricultural experimentation, training and veterinary services. The group manages Betampona Reserve and Ivoloina Park (page 307). The latter takes volunteers to help in its model farm station and zoo, usually for three-month placements.

La Maison d'Aïna (*www.lamaisondaina.org*) This NGO was founded in 2002 by the parents of a nine-year-old girl who passed away that year and in whose memory the charity is named. Based in Tana, they aim to improve the living conditions of underprivileged families and children by providing nutritional and medical assistance, family planning, counselling, education and training. Find out about donating and child sponsorship on their website.

Mar Y Sol (*www.shopmarysol.com*) Formerly called MadImports, this socially responsible company works with Malagasy artisans to produce fine-quality fair-trade handbags and hats from raffia and other local materials. The sale of these products (mainly in the USA) supports community development and helps preserve traditional craft skills.

MICET (+261 20 22 55 790; e *micet@moov.mg*) This is the Madagascar branch of the Institute for the Conservation of Tropical Environments. The best first point of contact for any researchers interested in doing fieldwork in the parks and reserves, MICET offers advice and logistical support to foreign students working across the country.

Mission Aviation Fellowship (e *mad-office@maf.org; www.maf-madagascar. org*) MAF is a Christian organisation whose mission is to fly light aircraft to isolated areas to help people in need. It provides logistical support to numerous NGOs and also carries out medical evacuations, flying to 83 airstrips at the last count –

a number that is likely to increase as runway construction in remote locations is another of their activities.

Money for Madagascar (e *info@moneyformadagascar.org; www.moneyformadagascar. org*) This long-established and well-run Welsh charity funds a large number of projects to help destitute children, vulnerable women and girls, families escaping poverty and communities in ecological hotspots, as well as providing disaster relief. It only funds projects that have been planned and initiated by Malagasy people. MfM describes its approach as 'no frills': their wholly volunteer staff works from home to keep overheads low, allowing donations to be channelled to where they are needed. Donations may be made via the charity's website, where there is also a shop selling 'alternative' gifts.

MOSS (e *obackhouse@btinternet.com; www.mossuk.net*) The Madagascan Organisation for Saving Sight was set up in 1993 by ophthalmologist Oliver Backhouse and his wife after their research showed that 70% of adult blindness in Madagascar is treatable and a staggering 90% of childhood blindness is preventable. MOSS is currently engaged in a number of projects, including cataract quality improvement, paediatric ophthalmology and various medical training schemes. The organisation also specialises in connecting volunteers with appropriate ophthalmic medical student elective placements, undergraduate and postgraduate research projects and direct work programmes.

Operation Wallacea (*www.opwall.com*) Opwall runs biological and conservation management research programmes in nine remote locations worldwide, including Madagascar. Groups of student volunteers team up with academics in the field to carry out biodiversity or social and economic surveys at the study sites, which go on to inform scientific research. Trips last 2–6 weeks with a choice of start dates each year.

Opt in (*www.optin.uk.net*) The Overseas Partnering and Training Initiative was set up to share the knowledge and skills of healthcare staff with hospitals in developing countries, providing training that results in sustained improvements. Currently the initiative has three projects in Madagascar. Volunteers mostly come from the Leeds teaching hospitals, but other medical professionals with relevant experience are also encouraged to apply.

Peace Corps (*www.peacecorps.gov*) The volunteering programme run by the US government aims to help people in foreign countries and promote bilateral understanding. At the time of writing, 130 Peace Corps volunteers are serving in Madagascar's far-flung corners and new openings often come up. The programme is open to all Americans over 18.

People and Places (e *enquiries@travel-peopleandplaces.co.uk; www.travel-peopleandplaces.co.uk*) Specialising in responsible volunteering in a dozen countries, including Madagascar, this social enterprise aims to match volunteer skills with local project needs.

Population Services International (*www.psi.org*) PSI is dedicated to improving health by focusing on serious challenges such as lack of family planning, HIV/Aids, barriers to maternal health, and the greatest threats to children under five, including malaria, diarrhoea, pneumonia and malnutrition.

ReefDoctor (e *info@reefdoctor.org; www.reefdoctor.org*) This UK-based marine conservation NGO carries out coral-reef research in southwest Madagascar with the help of volunteers. Placements are available for a minimum of three weeks. PADI scuba training is provided for non-divers.

SEED Madagascar (e *info@seedmadagascar.org; www.madagascar.co.uk*) This British-Malagasy charity works in the southeast of Madagascar, aiming to break the cycle of poverty and environmental degradation. Projects focus on sustainable improvements in community health, increasing food security and household income in order to reduce poverty of marginalised communities, facilitating sustainable use of natural resources, and providing vital education, water and sanitation infrastructure. The charity accepts volunteers for conservation, community development and English-teaching roles for 2–10 weeks.

Water Aid (*www.wateraid.org*) Based in the UK, this NGO's vision is a world where everyone has access to safe water and sanitation. Since 1999, it has been working in Madagascar, where the majority of the population does not have these vital services. Projects span five of the country's 22 regions.

Wildlife Conservation Society (*www.wcs.org*) New-York-based WCS has a wide range of conservation projects, most notably management of the new Makira Natural Park, near Masoala, funded by the sale of forest carbon credits. Nearby, its marine conservation project helped create Madagascar's first law overseeing whale-watching operations to ensure ecotourism generates revenue for locals while keeping whales safe. It also works in the south to protect radiated tortoise habitat and the Toliara barrier reef.

World Challenge Expeditions (*www.world-challenge.co.uk*) This organisation specialises in adventurous educational trips for school and student groups, including Madagascar expeditions of 21–28 days.

WWF Madagascar (e *wwfrep@moov.mg; www.wwf.mg*) For more than half a century WWF has been in Madagascar helping local communities manage natural resources, promoting renewable energy, fighting deforestation and bush-fires, protecting rare species and helping to establish protected areas. A Youth Volunteer and Internship Programme for ages 20–27 operates three to six-month placements ranging from coral reef and wetland management to forest and community projects. The WWF seeks creative individuals who can write, take photos, make videos, or find other innovative ways to inspire others.

Part Two

THE GUIDE

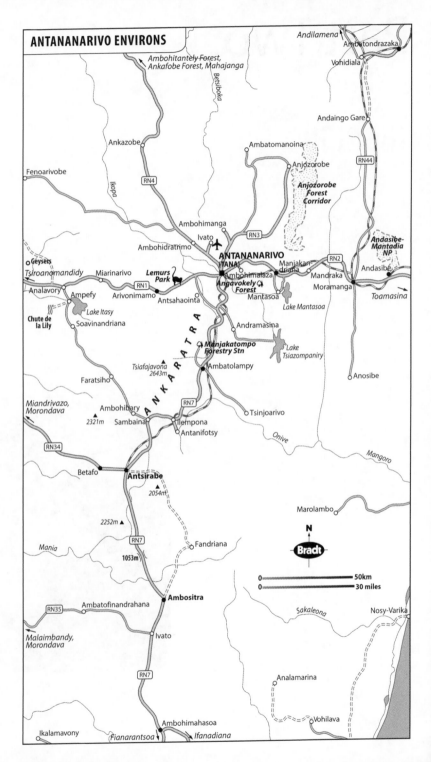

ANTANANARIVO ENVIRONS

Andilamena
Ambatondrazaka
Vohidiala
Ambohitantely Forest,
Ankafobe Forest, Mahajanga
Betsiboka
Andaingo Gare
Ankazobe
Ambatomanoina
RN44
Anjozorobe
Fenoarivobe
Ikopa
RN4
Anjozorobe
Forest
Corridor
Ambohimanga
Andasibe-
Mantadia
NP
Geysers
Ivato
RN3
Tsiroanomandidy
Ambohidratrimo
Manjakan-
driana
Andasibe
Miarinarivo
ANTANANARIVO
(TANA)
Mandraka
Lemurs
Park
RN2
RN1
Ambohimalaza
Mandraka
Analavory
Ampefy
Arivonimamo
Angavokely
Forest
Moramanga
Chute de
la Lily
Lake Itasy
Antsahaointa
Mantasoa
Toamasina
Soavinandriana
Lake Mantasoa
Andramasina
A N K A R A T R A
Manjakatompo
Forestry Stn
Lake
Tsiazompaniry
Tsiafajavona
2643m
Ambatolampy
Anosibe
Faratsiho
Miandrivazo,
Morondava
Ambohibary
2321m
RN7
Tsinjoarivo
Sambaina
Ilempona
Onive
RN34
Antanifotsy
Mangoro
Betafo
Antsirabe
2054m
Marolambo
2252m
N
RN7
Bradt
Fandriana
1053m
Mania
0 ____ 50km
0 ____ 30 miles
RN35
Ambatofinandrahana
Ambositra
Sakaleona
Nosy-Varika
Malaimbandy,
Morondava
Ivato
Analamarina
RN7
Vohilava
Ikalamavony
Ambohimahasoa
Fianarantsoa
Ifanadiana

7

Antananarivo and Area

Looking down from the plane window as you approach Antananarivo you can see how excitingly different this country is. Clusters of red clay houses and steepled churches stand isolated on the hilltops overlooking a mosaic of green and brown paddy fields. Old defence ditches, *tamboho*, form circles around villages or estates, and dotted in the empty countryside are the white concrete Merina tombs from where the dead will be exhumed in *famadihana* ceremonies.

Most people stay no more than a day or so in Tana (as Antananarivo is often called), but there is plenty to see in the city and the surrounding *hauts plateaux*. A week would not be too long to experience the cultural, historical and natural sites which lie within a day's excursion from the capital. The kingdom of Imerina thrived for over a century before French colonisation, so it is here that the rich and fascinating history and culture of the Merina people are best appreciated.

HISTORY

At the end of the 16th century the Merina king Andrianjaka conquered a Vazimba town called Analamanga, built on a great rock thrusting above the surrounding plains. He renamed it Antananarivo and ordered his palace to be built on its highest point. With its surrounding marshland ideal for rice production, and the security afforded by its position, this was the perfect site for a Merina capital city.

In the 18th century there were two centres for the Merina kingdom: Antananarivo and Ambohimanga. The latter became the more important and around 1787 Ramboasalama was proclaimed king of Ambohimanga and took the name of Andrianampoinimerina. By his death in 1810 the central plateau was firmly in control of the Merina and ably administered through a mixture of old customs and new. Each conquered territory was governed by local princes, answerable to the king, and the system of *fokonolona* (village communities) was established. From this firm foundation the new king, Radama I, was able to conquer most of the rest of the island.

Antananarivo means 'city of the thousand', supposedly because a thousand warriors protected it. By the end of the 18th century Andrianampoinimerina had taken Antananarivo from his rebellious kinsman and moved his base there from Ambohimanga. From that time until the French conquest in 1895 Madagascar's history centred around the royal palace or *rova*, the modest houses built for Andrianjaka and Andrianampoinimerina giving way to a splendid palace designed for Queen Ranavalona I by Jean Laborde and later clad in stone by James Cameron. The rock cliffs near the palace became known as Ampamarinana ('the place of hurling') where Christian martyrs met their fate at the command of the queen.

There was no reason for the French to move the capital elsewhere: its pleasant climate made it an agreeable place to live, and plenty of French money and planning went into the city we see today.

IVATO AIRPORT AREA

Almost all visitors to Madagascar enter the country through Ivato Airport, which is also the hub for domestic flights, so your itinerary is likely to include at least a couple of nights in Tana. Tourists are increasingly opting to stay in hotels near to the airport rather than venturing into the city – a journey which can take 45–60 minutes or more during the 'rush hour' (which nowadays lasts much of the day). Staying close to the airport can be a wise choice given Air Madagascar's current tendency to change domestic flight times at the 11th hour.

Ivato and the neighbouring areas around Lake Ambohibao (Lake Mamamba) to the south of the airport have developed into a thriving district in its own right, separated from the main city of Tana by a broad band of rice paddies. For convenience, we have therefore separated Tana into the Ivato Airport area (this section) and the rest of the city (pages 155–77).

ARRIVING IN MADAGASCAR The fairly small airport is divided into two sections – international and domestic – by a small corridor. There are a few souvenir shops, money-changing facilities, a couple of places to eat, a tourist-office kiosk and booths for the various cellphone networks where you can buy a cheap local SIM card for your mobile phone (see page 110).

On arrival from abroad the procedure is as follows:

1 Fill in a landing card if you haven't already (usually these are handed out on the plane as part of a little booklet about Madagascar). The questions are straightforward, but be ready to say where you'll be staying the first night.
2 After passing the health desk ('santé'), if you already have your visa, join the left-hand immigration queue. Otherwise go to the 'stamps for visa' kiosk and pay the appropriate amount for the required duration (see page 90 for prices) then proceed to the no-visa immigration queue.
3 When your passport is handed back to you, check the visa carefully; mistakes are not uncommon, especially with visas for more than 30 days.
4 Your luggage should shortly arrive on the baggage carousel (if not, see *Lost luggage* opposite). Porters will be insistent in aiding you and will expect a tip. Be firm in declining if you don't need their assistance.
5 There are trolleys to take your bags through customs. Show your passport to the inspector who will usually ask what is inside and may want to check. Some travellers have been asked to pay money at this point; don't fall for this ruse.
6 Just as you think there cannot possibly be any more passport checks, there is one more – and then you're free.

Porters and agents The porters at Ivato are very assertive. Be on your guard and, unless you need help, insist on carrying your own stuff. They are well aware that new arrivals are unlikely to have any small change and will often ask for euros, feigning disappointment on being given anything less than a small fortune. Remember even a single €1 coin is five or ten times the usual porter's tip in Madagascar, so if you need their services try to have some low-value ariary currency to hand. If you are being met by a tour operator you won't need a porter, so be firm.

You may also be approached by freelance guides offering to organise trips. Some travellers have reported these 'guides' disappearing with their money, never to be heard from again. Most are reputable, but exercise caution and avoid handing over cash upfront to agents not working out of the office of a proper tour agency.

Changing money There are BOA and BNI banks with ATMs, and a SOCIMAD bureau de change (⊕ *24hrs*) which almost invariably has the most favourable exchange rates (avoid B€$t Change – the first bureau de change as you emerge from arrivals; its rates are never the 'b€$t' and in fact for sterling can be as much as 20% 'wor$€' than SOCIMAD's). Think carefully before changing a large amount of cash at once; just €300 will give you a thick wad of at least a hundred banknotes in ariary. There are plenty of places to change more money later in the city centre (page 171).

Lost luggage If your luggage doesn't arrive, there is a relatively efficient procedure: at the lost-luggage kiosk near the baggage carousel, fill in a form and they'll phone your hotel when the bag arrives. Ask for a phone number so you can find out if your luggage has been traced yet. Depending on the policy of your airline, your bag may be delivered to your hotel once it materialises, otherwise you will have to collect it from the airport yourself (or nominate someone to collect it on your behalf but they will need a notarised letter of permission from you). Some airlines use a system that allows you to track your bag's recovery online.

LEAVING MADAGASCAR You must exchange or spend any unwanted ariary before passing through security; the souvenir shops, bar and cybercafé in the international departure lounge accept only euros and dollars.

TRANSPORT TO THE CITY CENTRE (16KM) A comfortable airport shuttle bus service run by **ADEMA** (m *032 07 062 56/032 07 063 02*) runs to the city centre after most major flights and will make request stops at any hotels *en route*. It leaves from outside Domestic Arrivals and costs a fixed rate of 14,000Ar (so for nearby hotels taxis may be a cheaper option, especially if there's more than one passenger).

Most mid- and upper-range hotels offer airport transfers. Otherwise official **taxis** should cost no more than 50,000Ar (you may be shown an 'official' price card indicating a higher rate but you can haggle), although beyond the airport perimeter you can find taxis willing to take you for 30,000Ar. The trip can take as much as an hour, although 20 minutes is possible when the roads are clear (late evenings and Sundays). For a fraction of the price, experienced travellers can take the red-and-white **local bus** to Soarano. It stops at the road junction about 100m from the airport, costs 500Ar, and you can pay for an extra seat for your luggage.

WHERE TO STAY Most hotels offer airport transfers, often included in the room price.

Luxury

🏠 **Relais des Plateaux** [150 B4] (42 rooms) Antanetibe, Ivato; ✆ 22 441 18/22 441 22; m 032 05 678 91/032 05 678 92/032 05 678 93; e reservation@ relais-des-plateaux.com; www.relais-des-plateaux. com. En-suite rooms with AC/heater, minibar, safe, sat-TV & Wi-Fi. Children's playground, heated pool,

massage, good restaurant & helpful staff. Airport transfers inc. Credit cards accepted.

Top end €€€€€

🏠 **A&C** [150 C2] (172 rooms & 15 bungalows) Ivato; ✆ 22 449 06/22 449 17/22 484 02; m 034 02 449 06/034 02 449 18/034 02 449 23; e a.c_hotel@live.fr; www.hotel-ac.mg. Recently

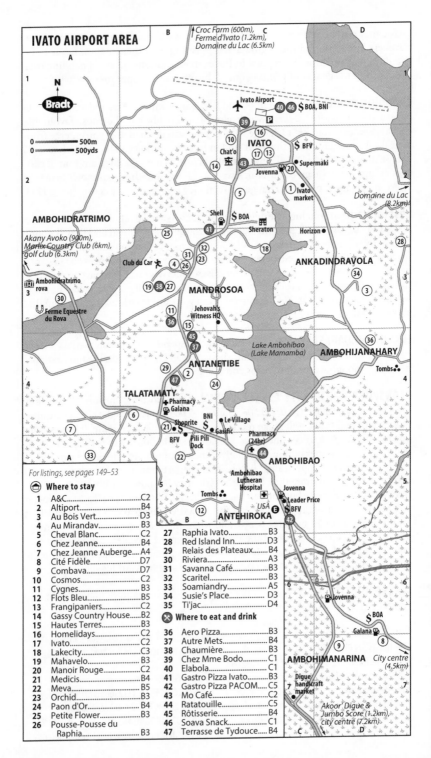

IVATO AIRPORT AREA

Croc Farm (600m),
Ferme d'Ivato (1.2km),
Domaine du Lac (6.5km)

N

Bradt

0 ———— 500m
0 ———— 500yds

Ivato Airport

40 46 $ BOA, BNI

39

10   IVATO

Chat'o $ BFV

14   17 13

43   Supermaki

Jovenna   20

1   Ivato market

5   Domaine du Lac (8.2km)

AMBOHIDRATRIMO

Akany Avoko (900m),
Marlix Country Club (6km),
golf club (6.3km)

Shell $ BOA

41   Sheraton   Horizon   28

25

32   18   ANKADINDRAVOLA

31   23

Club du Car   4   26   34   3

19 38 27   MANDROSOA

Ambohidratrimo rova

30

11   Jehovah's Witness HQ

Ferme Equestre du Rova

36   15

45   Lake Ambohibao   36
37   (Lake Mamamba)

AMBOHIJANAHARY

29   ANTANETIBE   Tombs

47   2

TALATAMATY   24

Pharmacy   Galana

6   Shoprite   BNI   Le Village

7   21   Gasific

BFV   Pili Pili   Pharmacy (24hr)
Dock

33   22   44   AMBOHIBAO

Ambohibao Lutheran Hospital

Tombs   Jovenna

12   USA   Leader Price

ANTEHIROKA   42 $ BFV

For listings, see pages 149–53

⊖ Where to stay

1	A&C	C2
2	Altiport	B4
3	Au Bois Vert	D3
4	Au Mirandav	B3
5	Cheval Blanc	C2
6	Chez Jeanne	B4
7	Chez Jeanne Auberge	A4
8	Cité Fidèle	D7
9	Combava	D7
10	Cosmos	C2
11	Cygnes	B3
12	Flots Bleu	B5
13	Frangipaniers	C2
14	Gassy Country House	B2
15	Hautes Terres	B3
16	Homelidays	B3
17	Ivato	C2
18	Lakecity	C3
19	Mahavelo	B3
20	Manoir Rouge	C2
21	Medicis	B4
22	Meva	B5
23	Orchid	B3
24	Paon d'Or	B4
25	Petite Flower	B3
26	Pousse-Pousse du Raphia	B3
27	Raphia Ivato	B3
28	Red Island Inn	D3
29	Relais des Plateaux	B4
30	Riviera	A3
31	Savanna Café	B3
32	Scaritel	B3
33	Soamiandry	A5
34	Susie's Place	D3
35	Ti'jac	D4

✗ Where to eat and drink

36	Aero Pizza	B3
37	Autre Mets	B4
38	Chaumière	B3
39	Chez Mme Bodo	C1
40	Elabola	C1
41	Gastro Pizza Ivato	B3
42	Gastro Pizza PACOM	C5
43	Mo Café	C2
44	Ratatouille	C5
45	Rôtisserie	B4
46	Soava Snack	C1
47	Terrasse de Tydouce	B4

AMBOHIMANARINA   City centre (4.5km)

Digue handicraft market

Akoor' Digue & Jumbo Score (1.2km), city centre (7.2km)

$ BOA   Galana

9   8

Jovenna

expanded hotel complex with swimming pools, spa, hammam, sauna, jacuzzi, gym, boutiques & quite possibly Madagascar's 1st multi-storey car park. Dbl & family rooms with AC, TV, minibar & Wi-Fi.

🏠 **Au Bois Vert** [150 D3] (27 rooms) Ankadindravola; `22 447 25; m 034 02 447 26; e boisvert@moov.mg; www.auboisvert.com. Very pleasant & quiet setting in a 3ha stand of tall trees. Attractive en-suite bungalows with Wi-Fi & swimming pool nestled among gardens. Restaurant with inside & outside dining is generally highly praised.

🏠 **Hautes Terres** [150 B3] (22 rooms) Ivato; m 032 41 356 98; e leshautesterres-hotel@iris.mg; www.leshautesterres-hotel.com. Comfortable but rather overpriced en-suite rooms with minibar, Wi-Fi, TV, AC & safe.

🏠 **Orchid** [150 B3] (68 rooms) Mandrosoa; `22 442 03/22 442 05; m 033 21 025 03; e orchid.hotel@moov.mg; www.orchidhotelantananarivo.net/uk. Handy location with quiet rooms but described as soulless by more than one reader. Chinese restaurant of variable quality overlooks pool & nice view.

🏠 **Paon d'Or** [150 B4] (260 rooms) Antanetibe; `22 451 76; m 032 08 838 61; e paonhotel@aliyun.com; www.hotelpaondor.com. Chinese resort of 54 large luxurious villas built as presidential accommodation for the 2009 African Union Summit.

🏠 **Petite Flower** [150 B3] (5 rooms) Mandrosoa; m 032 04 021 95/034 64 528 90/034 87 269 97; e fonzysd95@hotmail.fr or petiteflower.guesthouse@gmail.com. This delightful new Malagasy-French-run guesthouse opened in 2015 & has colourful stylish décor throughout. The bright spacious rooms have large comfy beds & en-suite facilities, some with bath. Restaurant, bar & swimming pool.

Upper range €€€€

🏠 **Combava** [150 D7] (12 rooms) `23 584 94; m 032 11 584 94/032 11 584 95; e combava@terra.mg; www.hotel-combava.com. Not only is each room named after a different spice or fragrance of Madagascar, but that product inspires the décor of each unique room. Spacious rooms & suites with AC, TV, Wi-Fi, kitchenette & some with terrace. Excellent restaurant.

🏠 **Gassy Country House (IC Hotel)** [150 B2] (22 rooms) Ivato; m 032 11 144 64/033 07 144 64/034 07 144 64; e info@gassycountryhouse.mg or info@ichotel.mg; www.ictours.mg; see ad, 3rd colour section. En-suite family rooms with sat-TV, AC, Wi-Fi, minibar & veranda overlooking rice paddies. Good restaurant & large swimming pool. Owned & run by Belgian-Malagasy tour operator Island Continent Tours (see page 88).

🏠 **Lakecity** [150 C3] (9 rooms) Mandrosoa; m 032 63 223 23 (manager)/033 11 078 96 (manager)/034 76 358 73 (reception); e lakecity-hotel@harenabusiness.com; www.lakecityhotel-mada.com. A smart lakefront boutique hotel. Rooms have sat-TV, AC, minibar, safe, desk & en-suite facilities; 6 also have balcony with lake view. Restaurant, bar & elegant swimming pool.

🏠 **Meva** [150 B5] (6 rooms) Talatamaty; m 032 42 896 62; e booking@mevaguesthouse.com; www.mevaguesthouse.com. New B&B in the home of Malagasy-Dutch couple Jonah & Wendy, who also run tour operator Ramartour (page 90) & can organise fascinating cultural visits of 1–3 days around the capital. En-suite rooms with kettle & Wi-Fi. Airport transfers inc.

🏠 **Red Island Inn** [150 D3] (10 rooms) Ambohibao; m 032 63 223 23 (manager)/034 76 358 73/034 79 751 00 (reception)/034 97 685 22; e redislandinn-hotel@harenabusiness.com; www.redislandinn-hotel.com. Under same ownership as Lakecity (above), it has a restaurant, bar, pool, gym & view over rice paddies. Rooms with sat-TV, AC & Wi-Fi.

🏠 **Susie's Place** [150 D3] (4 rooms) Ambodirano; m 034 53 106 04; e info@susiesplacebb.com; www.susiesplacebb.com; see ad, 3rd colour section. Homely B&B run by welcoming Malagasy-Dutch family. Wi-Fi.
Also in this category:

🏠 **Mahavelo** [150 B3] www.hotel-antananarivo.com

🏠 **Savanna Café** [150 B3] e savannacafe@yahoo.fr

Mid-range €€€

🏠 **Au Mirandav** [150 B3] (10 bungalows) Mandrosoa; `22 459 16; m 033 12 062 57/034 22 459 16; e mirandav@moov.mg; www.madadecouverte.com/aumirandav. Family atmosphere. All bungalows have en-suite bathrooms; some have sat-TV. Meals available with advance notice.

Cheval Blanc [150 C2] (32 rooms) Ivato; m 032 62 367 36; e auberge@chevalblanc. mg; www.cheval-blanc-madagascar.com. Long-established hotel with en-suite sgl & dbl rooms set in a pleasant garden. TV lounge with Wi-Fi. Restaurant with live music nightly & buffet on Sun. Airport transfers inc. Visa & MasterCard accepted.

Chez Jeanne [150 B4] (12 rooms) Talatamaty; m 032 02 643 97/033 17 494 18/034 74 170 93; e chezjeanne@moov.mg or ihasiniaina@yahoo.fr or skst@moov.mg; www. chezjeanne.net. Simple sgl & dbl rooms with Wi-Fi; some en suite. There are also several small self-catering apartments.

Cosmos [150 C2] (5 rooms) Ivato (next to airport); 22 448 49/24 794 61; e info@lecosmos-hotel-ivato.com; www.lecosmos-hotel-ivato.com. Simple but welcoming hotel on the doorstep of the airport: less than 400m from the terminal car park.

Cygnes [150 B3] (8 rooms) Mandrosoa; 22 452 98; m 032 41 361 48. Sgl & dbl rooms with Wi-Fi. Malagasy & Creole cuisine.

Flots Bleu [150 B5] (14 rooms) Ambohibao; 26 238 99; m 032 02 609 51/033 11 417 66; e bonjour.flotsbleustana@gmail.com or lesflotsbleu_tana@blueline.mg; www.hotel-lesflotsbleu-antananarivo.com. Spacious en-suite rooms with TV. Restaurant, bar, pizzeria, pool, massage & Wi-Fi.

Homelidays [150 C2] (5 rooms) m 033 92 352 35/034 02 814 96; e ortegawilly@gmail.com; www.ivato-home-holidays.com. A mere 300m from the airport car park, this little guesthouse has en-suite dbl rooms & family rooms with shared facilities. Simple but friendly & an unbeatable location if you want to be within walking distance of the terminal. Wi-Fi.

Ivato [150 C2] (29 rooms) Imotro, Ivato; 22 445 10; m 034 12 445 10; e ivatotel@ moov.mg; www.ivatohotel.com. Friendly, clean & comfortable. Dbl, twin & family rooms with safe, Wi-Fi & hot showers. Restaurant Sel et Poivre specialises in Malagasy & Chinese food. Arrival airport transfer inc. Visa accepted.

Manoir Rouge [150 C2] (25 rooms) Ivato; m 032 05 260 97; e manoirrouge@gmail.com; www.hotel-manoirrouge-madagascar.e-monsite. com. Popular hotel with wide range of affordable rooms from budget dorm beds to 6 en-suite rooms that are in the main building dating to 1931. Also 3 self-catering apartments for longer stays. Nice garden (camping permitted), restaurant, massage & bike hire. Inbound airport transfer inc.

Medicis [150 B4] (19 rooms) Talatamaty; 22 441 64/22 441 65/22 441 66; m 034 36 890 60; e lemedicishotel@gmail.com or lemedicishotel@yahoo.fr; www.lemedicishotel. com. Sgl, dbl, twin & family rooms with minibar, sat-TV, Wi-Fi & private bathrooms.

Raphia Ivato [150 B3] (11 rooms) Mandrosoa; 22 452 97; m 034 06 257 76; e hotelraphia@moov.mg; www.hotelsraphia. com. En-suite rooms colourfully refurbished. Tennis court & trampoline! Restaurant Basmati is particularly noted for its *sambo* (samosas).

Riviera [150 A3] (6 rooms & 4 bungalows) Mandriambero; 24 782 70; m 032 04 702 63/034 17 385 10; e rivieragarden@gmail.com. Spacious rooms in a calm lakeside spot; better known for its restaurant.

Soamiandry [150 A5] (13 rooms) Ankadivory, Talatamaty; m 032 43 943 77/034 19 464 15; e soamiandry@gmail.com or soamiandry@yahoo.fr. Family-run B&B. Joshua & Fara go out of their way to help guests. Garden with pool.

Ti'jac [150 D4] (7 rooms) Ambohijanahary; m 032 02 153 35; e clara.tijac@gmail.com or tijactana@gmail.com; www.le-ti-jac.com. Named after the jackfruit tree in the garden, this guesthouse has en-suite rooms with Wi-Fi & 2 self-catering apartments. Food if ordered in advance.

Also in this category:

Altiport [150 B4] e altiresthotel@gmail. com

Chez Jeanne Auberge [150 A4] www. chezjeanne.net

Cité Fidèle [150 D7] e lacitefidele@gmail. com

Frangipaniers [150 C2] e frangipaniers@ gmail.com

Pousse-Pousse du Raphia [150 B3] www. hotelsraphia.com

Scaritel [150 B3] e scaritelhotel@gmail. com

✖ **WHERE TO EAT AND DRINK** Hotels **Combava** and **Au Bois Vert** are very good options for eating. There are also restaurants at Croc Farm, the golf club, Marlix

Country Club, Club du Car, Chat'o and Ferme d'Ivato, details for all of which are in the next section. With advance notice, Akany Avoko and Domaine du Lac can serve meals too.

✖ **Aero Pizza** [150 B3] Maibahoaka, Ivato; ☎ 22 482 91. Pizzas for eat-in, take-away or delivery.

✖ **Autre Mets (Bistrot 21)** [150 B4] Antanetibe; m 032 03 707 11; 🄵 lautremets; ⏲ 08.00–14.30 daily & 18.00–22.00 Fri/Sat. Low-carb French-style meat & seafood dishes.

✖ **Chaumière** [150 B3] ☎ 22 489 64. Popular for its Réunionais specialities.

✖ **Chez Mme Bodo** [150 C1] m 032 07 940 37/033 09 903 25. Simple eatery just outside airport compound.

✖ **Elabola** [150 C1] Ivato airport (upstairs in international terminal). Snacks & meals with a runway view.

✖ **Gastro Pizza Ivato** [150 B3] m 032 40 904 07/033 14 300 16/034 06 786 35; www.lagastronomiepizza.com. Pizzas & fast food at low prices.

✖ **Gastro Pizza PACOM** [150 C5] m 033 32 156 30/034 37 797 53; www.lagastronomiepizza.com. Branch opposite US embassy.

✖ **Mo Café** [150 B3] m 034 55 272 58/034 55 272 59; e mocafeivato@gmail.com; ⏲ Mon–Sat 15.00–22.00, closed Sun. Friendly family-run place with Mauritian-influenced menu.

✖ **Ratatouille** [150 C5] Ambohibao; m 034 41 731 32. Famous for its bread & sandwiches. Pizzas also very good.

✖ **Rôtisserie** [150 B4] Antanetibe, Ivato; ☎ 23 584 94; m 032 11 222 07/032 11 584 94; e combava@terra.mg. Inspired menu made with fresh organic food.

✖ **Terrasse de Tydouce** [150 B4] Antehiroka, Rte d'Ivato; ☎ 24 522 51; m 033 11 336 99; e tydouce@freedsl.mg. Cosy restaurant serving French cuisine.

🖵 **Soava Snack** [150 C1] Ivato airport (domestic terminal). Simple snacks & sandwiches.

WHAT TO SEE AND DO In this section are the attractions in the immediate vicinity of the airport. If you have more than half a day to spare, you should also see pages 174–7 for things to do in the rest of Tana.

Croc Farm [150 B1] (⏲ daily 09.00–17.00; entry 10,000Ar, under-8s free) As its name suggests, this is a working farm, raising crocodiles for leather, meat and other products. But the 3ha park is also a zoo, home to lemurs, fossa, chameleons, tortoises and parrots, sadly not all kept in the best of conditions. Crocs of every size are top of the bill with many hundreds in residence. Croc Farm also informs visitors about the threats faced by the few wild crocs left in Madagascar and local superstitions surrounding them. For an unusual culinary experience, try grilled crocodile in vanilla sauce – or cooked some other way – at the restaurant **Coco d'Iles Taverne** (non-croc dishes also available) overlooking the main lake.

Ferme d'Ivato [150 B1] (☎ 23 584 94; m 032 11 584 94/032 11 584 96; e combava@terra.mg; www.lafermedivato.com; ⏲ Tue–Sun for lunch) Located 1.5km past the Croc Farm turning, this organic farm produces fruit, veg, meat, eggs, cheese, yoghurt and essential oils. Visitors can get a tour, and the produce is served in a modest on-site restaurant (as well as at Combava Hotel and Rôtisserie restaurant, which are under the same ownership).

Domaine du Lac [150 B1] (m 032 28 597 44/032 67 301 20; e info.lacmada@gmail.com or domainedulac@ymail.com; ⏲ daily 09.00–17.00; entry 10,000Ar) This lakeside botanical garden with 500 plant species also has a small zoo with tortoises, chameleons, snakes, frogs, tenrecs and free-ranging sifakas. Food can be served if booked in advance. Although it's located just 1km from the end of

the runway, to get there you have to drive 9km around the airport in the direction of Croc Farm.

Next door is a B&B called **Patrakala** (m *032 58 615 67/032 40 151 78;* e *etspatrakala@yahoo.fr*) which offers fishing, canoeing and tours of their farm.

Ambohidratrimo Rova [150 A3] One of Tana's 12 sacred hills (see page 177), Ambohidratrimo boasts good views towards the city and some reconstructed royal tombs, sadly recently damaged in a fire. The tombs, including that of local 12th-century ruler King Ratrimo after which the hill takes its name, are just a 500m walk from the main road.

Ferme Equestre du Rova [150 A3] (*Villa Fahafinaretana, Ambodisaha, Ambohidratrimo;* m *032 07 039 04/033 08 765 68;* e *fedrova@gmail.com*) This farm offers horse-riding around the northern outskirts of Tana, including the Ambohidratrimo *rova* close to which it is situated, as well as lessons for first-time riders.

International Golf Club du Rova [150 A3] (*PK 21, RN4;* ✆ *22 011 90;* m *032 11 011 90*) Constructed in the 1950s, this 18-hole 72-par 6,670-yard (6,100m) golf course a few minutes north of Ambohidratrimo has many slopes and doglegs. Inexpensive lessons and caddy services are available but booking is advised. It also has a swimming pool and clubhouse restaurant.

Marlix Country Club [150 A3] (✆ *22 351 01;* e *marlix.madagascar@gmail.com*) Just opposite the golf club, this adventure park offers an aerial runway, tree-top assault course, water zorbing, paintballing, horse-riding and 18-hole minigolf.

Akany Avoko Ambohidratrimo [150 A3] (m *034 22 441 58;* e *director@ akanyavoko.com; www.akany-avoko.blogspot.com*) A visit to this halfway house and orphanage offers an insight into their work helping disadvantaged girls of Tana. Why not schedule a visit on your last day to donate your leftover ariary, clothes or medical supplies? A café is run by the older girls as part of a professional education programme. Book tours and meals at least a day ahead.

Club du Car [150 B3] (✆ *22 447 02;* e *clubhousecar@gmail.com;* **f** *clubducar;* ⊕ *daily 08.00–17.00*) Five minutes or so from the airport, this sports and leisure complex has a swimming pool, tennis courts, volleyball and massage centre. Those in Tana for a while can also enrol in classes including water aerobics, martial arts, Zumba – and even drawing and Malagasy language lessons.

Branch Office of Jehovah's Witnesses [150 C3] (*Mandrosoa;* ✆ *22 448 37;* m *033 02 448 37;* ⊕ *Mon–Fri 07.30–11.00 & 13.00–16.00*) The Madagascar headquarters of Jehovah's Witnesses runs eye-opening 1-hour tours of their impressive operation, which supervises the activity of about 600 congregations, produces audio and video recordings in their modern studios, and handles distribution of almost a million books and brochures each month.

Chat'o [150 C2] (✆ *22 033 33;* ⊕ *daily 09.00–18.00; entry adults 5,000Ar, children 15,000Ar*) This is an amusement park with a swimming pool, bouncy castle, merry-go-round, laser tag games and a restaurant. It's very near the airport; good for keeping kids occupied during long flight delays.

ANTANANARIVO CITY

From the right place, in the right light, Antananarivo is one of the most attractive capitals in the developing world. In the evening sunshine it has the quality of a child's picture book: brightly coloured houses stacked up the hillsides with mauve jacarandas and purple bougainvillea against the dark blue of the winter sky. Red crown-of-thorns euphorbias stand in rows against red clay walls, rice paddies are tended right up to the edge of the city, clothes are laid out on canal banks to dry, and zebu carts rumble along the roads on the outskirts of town. It's all deliciously foreign and can hardly fail to impress the first-time visitor as he or she drives in from the airport. During the dry season the sun is hot but the air pleasantly cool, for the altitude is between 1,250m and 1,450m.

Sadly, for many people this wonderful first impression does not survive a closer acquaintance. Tana can seem squalid and dangerous, with conspicuous poverty, persistent beggars and pollution from heavy traffic.

The geography of the city is both simple and confusing. It is built on two ridges which meet in a 'V'. On the highest hill, dominating all the viewpoints, is the queen's palace or *rova*. Down the central valley runs a broad boulevard, Avenue de l'Indépendance, known as Avenue de la Libération before 1960 (as several old signs on its buildings still attest), and initially called Avenue Armand Fallières after the 1906–13 French president when work began on its arcades in 1935. It terminates at the grand colonial railway station, opened in 1910 and now beautifully restored as a small shopping precinct. It narrows at the other end to become Rue du 26 Juin. To escape from this valley means climbing steps if you are on foot, or driving through a tunnel if you are in a vehicle.

It is convenient to divide central Tana into the two main areas most often wandered by visitors: Av de l'Indépendance and the side streets to its southwest (districts Analakely and Tsaralalana, or the **lower town**), and the smarter area at the top of the steps leading up from Rue du 26 Juin (districts Antaninarenina and Isoraka, or the **upper town**). Of course there are lots of other districts but most tourists will take taxis to these rather than going on foot.

GETTING THERE AND AWAY BY ROAD The *gares routières* (bus stations) for national *taxi-brousses* are sited on the outskirts of the city and should cost about 10,000Ar to reach by taxi from the centre. Although there is some overlap of destinations served by each station, the main three are **Ampasampito**, 4km east of the centre, the starting point for trips east (Moramanga and Toamasina); **Ambodivona**, just north of Andravoahangy craft market, where you will find services heading north (Mahajanga and Antsiranana) and also some east; and **Fasan'ny Karana** on RN4, 1km west of its junction with RN7, which serves the south of the country (Fianarantsoa and Toliara) and the west.

Numerous travellers have reported being cheated at Fasan'ny Karana station; so be on your guard against overcharging. A favourite scam is for them to draw your attention to Malagasy small print on your ticket that says '*ny zaza 5 taona…*', explaining that this means there is a €5 fee for bags, or there is a 5kg luggage limit. In reality the text states that kids under 5 travel free! This station is also notorious for sellers lying to customers (Malagasy and *vazaha* alike) about expected departure times and the number of empty seats remaining.

GETTING AROUND Traffic jams and pollution are major problems in Tana. Traffic is often gridlocked on the narrow, hilly streets so it makes sense to avoid vehicular transport when possible. Get to know the city on foot during the day (but carry nothing of value); use taxis for long distances, unknown destinations and always at night.

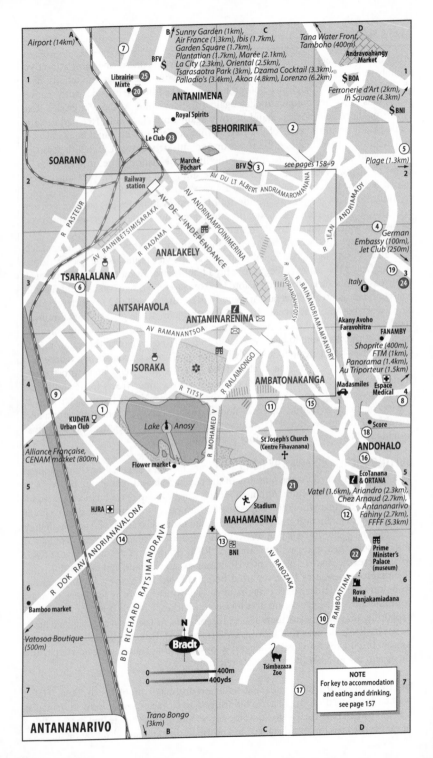

ANTANANARIVO

ANTANANARIVO
For listings, see pages 161–7

🛏 Where to stay

1	Carlton	A4
2	Chez Aïna	C2
3	Cristal	C2
4	Evergreen	D3
5	Grégoire	D2
6	Ile Bourbon	A3
7	Jardin d'Antanimena	B1
8	Lemur Hostel	D4
9	Lemurien Blanc	A4
10	Lokanga	D6
11	Lotus Bleu	C4
12	Maison Vue Royale	D5
13	Manoir	C6
14	Motel d'Antananarivo	B6
15	Niaouly	C4
16	Relais de la Haute Ville	D5
17	Relais des Pistards	C7
18	Résidence du Rova	D5
19	Vahiny	D3

Off map

Akoa	B1
Ariandro	D5
Garden Square	B1
Ibis	B1
Lorenzo	B1
Panorama	D4
Sunny Garden	B1
Tamboho	D1
Trano Bongo	B7
Vatel	D5

✖ Where to eat and drink

20	Cattleya	B1
21	Gastro Pizza Mahamasina	C5
22	Grill du Rova	D6
23	Mille Feuilles	B2
24	Montparnasse	D3
25	Villa Vanille	B1

Off map

Au Triporteur	D4
Chez Arnaud	D5
Dzama Cocktail	B1
Marée	B1
Oriental	B1
Palladio's	B1
Plantation	B1

Taxis are easily recognised by their cream colour. Tough bargainers will pay no more than 8,000Ar for a short trip (more after dark). Taxis do not have meters so agree the price before you get in. The taxis that wait outside posh hotels are more expensive but also more reliable than those cruising the streets. Check the fare with the hotel receptionist if you think you are being ripped off. The cheaper option is to take one of the battered old vehicles which wouldn't dare go near a hotel and you have the extra bonus of watching the street go by through the hole in the floor, or being pushed by helpful locals when it breaks down.

The advantage of having no meters is that if the driver gets lost (not unusual) you won't pay any more for the extra journey. Tana's taxi drivers are usually honest and helpful, and can be trusted to get you to your destination – eventually.

Local buses are *much* cheaper (usually 500Ar per journey), but sorting out the routes can be a challenge. There is a route map at the tourist information kiosk in Antaninarenina but, with some 70 lines operating, your best bet is to ask helpful locals to point you to the right bus.

ORIENTATION
Analakely and Tsaralalana (lower town)
Av de l'Indépendance is a broad boulevard (grassed in the centre) with shops, snack bars and hotels along each side. **Soarano railway station** stands proudly at one end, and dominated over the whole avenue until 2010 when a grand **town hall** was constructed halfway along, displacing it as the most imposing architectural feature.

This is not a street for strolling; there are too many persistent beggars, street vendors and pickpockets (whose attacks have become quite brazen of late) so walk briskly. Tsaralalana is a more relaxing area of side streets to the south of Av de l'Indépendance (although maps do not indicate the steep climbs involved if you go too far). Walk down Rue Indira Gandhi, past Le Grand Mellis, to the cumbersomely named Place du 19 Mai 1946. Beyond it is Hôtel Taj and the very popular Sakamanga Hotel. A couple of souvenir shops are here and, at the top of the road, is BioAroma, which sells beauty products and herbal remedies. But to avoid this steep climb to Isoraka you could double back on one of the parallel streets to Av de l'Indépendance.

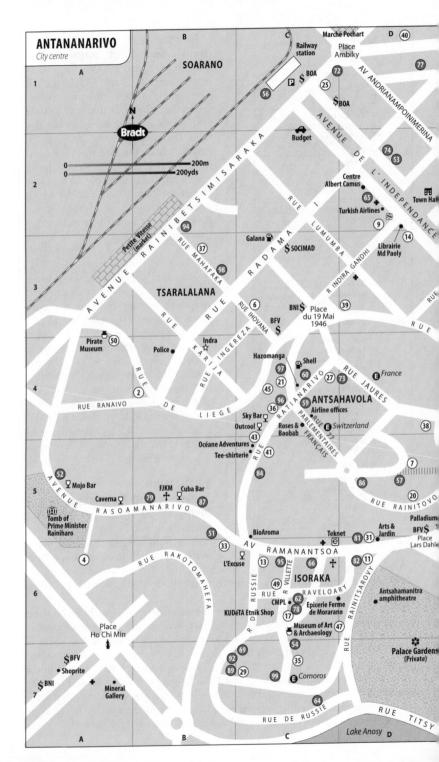

ANTANANARIVO
City centre

SOARANO

Railway station

Marché Pochart

Place Ambiky

AV ANDRIANAMPOINIMERINA

BOA

Budget

AVENUE DE L'INDEPENDANCE

Centre Albert Camus

Town Hall

Turkish Airlines

RUE LUMUMBA

Librairie Md Paoly

RUE RADAMA I

Galana

SOCIMAD

Petite Vitesse (market)

RUE MAHAFAKA

AVENUE RAINIBETSIMISARAKA

R INDIRA GANDHI

TSARALALANA

BNI

Place du 19 Mai 1946

BFV

RUE IHOVANA

RUE INGEREZA

Pirate Museum

Police

Indra

Hazomanga

Shell

France

RUE JAURES

RUE DE LIEGE

RUE RANAIVO

RUE KARIJA

RUE RATIANARIVO

ANTSAHAVOLA

Airline offices

Switzerland

RUE PARLEMENTAIRES FRANÇAIS

Sky Bar
Outcool
Roses & Baobab
Océane Adventures
Tee-shirterie

Mojo Bar

AVENUE RASOAMANARIVO

Tomb of Prime Minister Rainiharo

Caverna

FJKM

Cuba Bar

RUE RAINITOVO

Palladium
BFV
Place Lars Dahle

RUE RAKOTOMAHEFA

BioAroma

Teknet

Arts & Jardin

AV RAMANANTSOA

L'Excuse

RUE RUSSIE

R VILLETTE

ISORAKA

RUE RAVELOARY

Place Ho Chi Min

R DE RUSSIE

CMPL

KUDéTA Etnik Shop

Epicerie Ferme de Morarano

Museum of Art & Archaeology

RUE RAINITSAROVY

Antsahamanitra amphitheatre

BFV
Shoprite

BNI

Mineral Gallery

Palace Gardens (Private)

Comoros

RUE DE RUSSIE

RUE TITSY

Lake Anosy

200m
200yds

N

Bradt

158

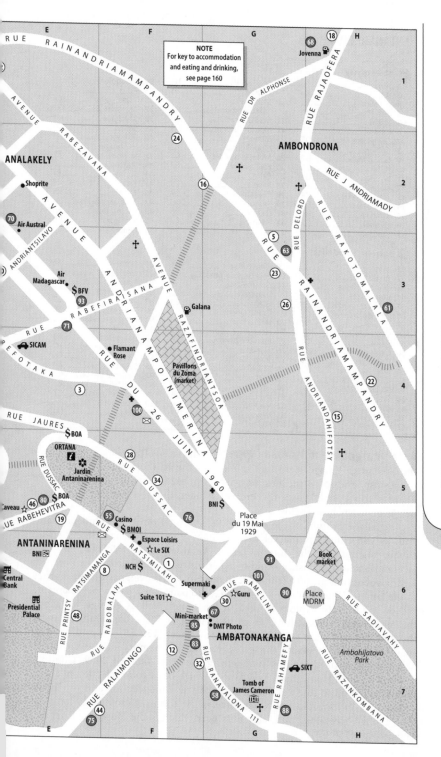

NOTE
For key to accommodation
and eating and drinking,
see page 160

ANTANANARIVO *City centre*
For listings, see pages 161–7

Antaninarena and Isoraka (upper town)
This is the Islington of Tana; or the Greenwich Village. Here are the jewellers, the art shops and craft boutiques, the atmospheric hotels, the inexpensive guesthouses and a little-known museum. There is also a public garden where, in October, the jacaranda trees drip their nectar on to the heads below.

Start at the bottom of the steps by Select Hotel on Av de l'Indépendance and, as you climb up, marvel that so many men can make a living selling rubber stamps. At the top is **Jardin Antaninarena** [159 E5] with its jacarandas and rose bushes – and benches for relaxing. Nearby is Le Buffet du Jardin where you can sip a fruit juice in the sun. Cross over, past the post office, to the famous Hôtel Colbert – a good place to pause for a pastry or ice cream.

Now it's time to explore Isoraka. A 30-minute walk is enough to take in the main sights. From the Colbert head towards Place Lars Dahle, passing the **Presidential Palace** (Ambohitsorohitra Palace) [159 E6]. Stop to note the small monument opposite the gates, erected in memory of the dozens of protesters shot dead on this spot during the *coup d'état* of 2009. Continue towards Radama Hotel and Arts & Jardin, which has a good selection of crafts, then turn left on to Rue Raveloary. Cross the next intersection and you'll pass a very nice little restaurant: Chez Sucett's. At the next crossroads look out for a bronze 'tree' hung with clay pots near which is the **Museum of Art and Archaeology** [158 C6].

WHERE TO STAY

Luxury ♔

🏠 **Carlton** [156 A4] (171 rooms) Rue Pierre Stibbe; ☎ 22 260 60; e contact@carlton. mg or reservation@carlton.mg; www.carlton-madagascar.com; see ad, 3rd colour section. Popular with businessfolk, this 17-storey ex-Hilton hotel has 5-star rooms & many on-site offices, shops, restaurants & bank. Also swimming pool, tennis court, gym, hammam, jacuzzi & casino. Lovely views over Lake Anosy.

🏠 **Colbert** [159 F6] (124 rooms) 29 Rue Ratsimamanga; ☎ 22 202 02; m 034 80 973 04; e colbert@moov.mg; www.hotel-restaurant-colbert.com. In a prime location in the upper town it offers an indoor pool, sauna, spa, gym, cybercafé, bar, decadent patisserie & 3 restaurants. Standard rooms & suites have AC, sat-TV, desk, minibar, safe & en-suite shower or bath.

🏠 **Lokanga** [156 D6] (6 rooms) Rue Dr Ralarosy; ☎ 22 235 49; m 034 14 555 02; e contact@lokanga-hotel.mg; www.lokanga-hotel.mg. Lovingly renovated 1930 townhouse a stone's throw from the rova, highly praised by countless readers. Rooms each have different character based on themes from Malagasy history & furnished with antiques passed down through the half-Malagasy proprietor's family. Rooms are en suite with balcony, minibar, safe & Wi-Fi. Tall guests should request one with a larger bed; avoid top-floor rooms if you have difficulty with steep steps. Restaurant closed to public on Mon.

🏠 **Maison Gallieni** [159 H4] (4 rooms) Faravohitra; ☎ 22 313 45; m 032 11 274 00; e maisongallieni@maisongallieni.com; www.maisongallieni.com. Gorgeous B&B perched on a hillside near Faravohitra cathedral overlooking central Tana. The grand building was built in 1879. Once Madagascar's 1st bank & now home to the Monacan ambassador, it has been refurbished with a stylish modern interior. Immaculate spacious rooms with AC, TV & Wi-Fi. Library & heated swimming pool.

🏠 **Maison Vue Royale** [156 D5] (5 rooms) Andoalo; m 034 20 388 38; e chantsiry@yahoo.fr or maisonvueroyale@gmail.com; www.vueroyale.com. A new B&B with splendid views across the city. En-suite dbl & twin rooms with AC, TV, Wi-Fi, balcony & safe. B/fast inc.

🏠 **Tamboho** [156 D1] (30 rooms) Tana Waterfront, Ambodivona; ☎ 22 693 00; m 032 07 693 00; e info@hoteltamboho.com; www.hoteltamboho.com. Attractive hotel sited within the secure Tana Water Front complex (see page 170), overlooking a 400m-long lake with good birdwatching. Small heated outdoor pool & good restaurant. Rooms in 2 sizes, all with AC, sat-TV, safe, Wi-Fi & en-suite bathroom. B/fast inc.

Top end €€€€€

🏠 **Ibis** [156 B1] (174 rooms) Rte des Hydrocarbures, Ankorondrano; ☎ 23 555 55; www.ibis.com. Located 4km north of the city centre, this 7-floor glistening spaceship of a hotel was the Ibis group's 835th, but 1st in Madagascar. Spacious comfy rooms with TV, minibar, Wi-Fi & safe. Spa with massage, sauna, gym & hammam.

🏠 **Louvre** [159 E5] (85 rooms) 4 Pl Philibert Tsiranana; ☎ 22 390 00; m 032 05 390 00; e reservation@hotel-du-louvre.com; www.hotel-du-louvre.com. Expanded in 2009, facilities inc spa, gym, jacuzzi, hammam, pool & massage. Rooms on 6 floors around central 'vertical garden'; all with AC, sat-TV, safe, Wi-Fi, kettle/coffee maker & en-suite facilities. Suites have unusual design with glass bathroom in the centre. B/fast inc. Restaurant Le 313 is named after the original height of the Eiffel Tower in metres!

🏠 **Palissandre** [159 G3] (46 rooms) 13 Rue Andriandahifotsy; ☎ 22 605 60; e clercvion@hotel-palissandre.com or resapalissandretana@hotel-palissandre.com; www.hotel-palissandre.com. All comforts, good food, lovely views & central location. Rooms are en suite with AC, sat-TV, Wi-Fi, minibar & safe. Bar, massage, pool & gym.

🏠 **Pavillon de l'Emyrne** [158 C7] (12 rooms) 12 Rue Rakotonirina; ☎ 22 259 45/22 259 46; m 032 05 368 29/033 02 566 38/034 11 334 01; e reservation@pavillondelemyrne.com; www.pavillondelemyrne.com. This charmingly restored 1930s house is quiet despite its central position, near plenty of restaurants. Regularly praised by readers as characterful with very genuine staff. Rooms have TV, AC/heater, minibar & Wi-Fi.

🏠 **Tana Hotel** [159 E5] (31 rooms) 4 Rue Rabehevitra; ☎ 22 313 20/22 313 26; e tanahotel@

moov.mg; www.tana-hotel-madagascar.com. Smart new hotel in upper town with modern décor. Rooms offer AC, sat-TV, minibar, Wi-Fi & safe. Proximity to 2 nightclubs means it's not the quietest spot at w/ends.

🏠 **Varangue** [159 E6] (9 rooms) 17 Rue Ratsimamanga; 📞 22 251 74/22 273 97/22 552 30; m 032 05 273 97/033 05 273 97/034 05 273 97; e varangue@moov.mg; www.hotel-restaurant-lavarangue-tananarive.com. Charming traditional Creole-style home with fascinating décor: bar decorated lavishly with antiques. Comfortable en-suite rooms with fan, heating, safe, TV, kettle & minibar. Wi-Fi. Exceptional but pricey restaurant (*closed Sun*).

Also in this category:

🏠 **Hôtel de France** [159 E3] e contact@siceh-hotels.com

🏠 **Sunny** [159 E7] 📞 22 257 70

🏠 **Sunny Garden** [156 B1] www.sunnymada.com

Upper range €€€€

🏠 **Belvédère** [158 A6] (27 rooms) Av Rasoamanarivo; 📞 22 321 10; m 034 16 950 79/034 79 866 38; e hotelbelvedere@ymail.com; www.hotel-antananarivo-belvedere.com. Attractive en-suite rooms, many with great views; also 2 self-catering apartments. Decent restaurant serving Malagasy & Italian specialities.

🏠 **Central** [158 C3] (52 rooms) Rue Ihovana; 📞 22 222 44; e contact@centralhoteltana.mg; www.centralhoteltana.mg. Rooms furnished in modern style with AC, minibar, Wi-Fi, sat-TV & safe. Buffet b/fast inc.

🏠 **Chalet des Roses** [158 D5] (38 rooms) 13 Rue Rabary; 📞 22 642 33/24 803 49; m 032 50 328 26; e hotel@chaletdesroses.com or restaurant@chaletdesroses.com; www.chaletdesroses.com. Stylish Italian-owned hotel-restaurant; dbl & family rooms with ceiling fan, minibar, safe, desk & Wi-Fi.

🏠 **Cristal** [156 C2] (22 rooms) Behoririka; 📞 22 670 58; m 034 05 670 58; e contact@hotelcristalmadagascar.com; www.hotel-cristal-madagascar.com. Smart décor with AC, Wi-Fi & sat-TV. Helpful staff & good food.

🏠 **Karibotel** [158 D3] (25 rooms) 26 Av de l'Indépendance; 📞 22 629 31; m 033 15 629 32/033 15 629 35; www.karibotel.mg. Clean, comfortable rooms with safe, TV & bath/shower;

some with balcony. Restaurant Papangoo offers international & Malagasy dishes.

🏠 **Lapasoa** [158 C6] (12 rooms) 15 Rue de la Réunion; 📞 22 611 40; m 032 07 611 40; e info@lapasoa.com or resa@lapasoa.com; www.lapasoa.com. Tastefully decorated rooms with sat-TV, safe & Wi-Fi. B/fast in KUDéTA restaurant downstairs.

🏠 **Les 3 Métis** [159 H1] (25 rooms) Antaninandro (opposite Jovenna); 📞 22 231 06/22 359 83; m 033 05 520 20; e infos@les-trois-metis.com; www.les-trois-metis.com. A charming colonial house built in 1913 by a rich raffia exporter. En-suite rooms with sat-TV, minibar & safe. Restaurant, bar & Wi-Fi.

🏠 **Radama** [158 D6] (16 rooms) 22 Av Ramanantsoa; 📞 22 319 27; e contact@radama-hotel.com or radama@moov.mg or resa@radama-hotel.com (reservations); www.radama-hotel.com. Good hotel in excellent location, but rooms rather dated; they have TV, minibar, AC, Wi-Fi & some with balcony.

🏠 **Raphia** [159 F7] (7 rooms) Rue Ranavalona III, Ambatonakanga; 📞 22 253 13/22 339 31; e hotelraphia@moov.mg; www.hotelsraphia.com. Nice hotel with views over Lake Anosy from upper floors. Simple rooms with Wi-Fi; some en suite. Restaurant Jardin du Raphia serves Indian food.

🏠 **Ribaudière** [159 F5] (17 rooms) 18 Rue Dussac; 📞 24 263 12; m 032 02 411 51; e laribaudiere@moov.mg; www.hotel-laribaudiere.com. Centrally located hotel; very comfortable rooms with sat-TV, safe, AC, Wi-Fi & impeccable bathrooms.

🏠 **Rova Hotel** [158 C7] (17 rooms) 45 Rue Dr Villette; 📞 22 292 77; m 032 11 292 77/033 15 292 77; e infos@rovahotel.com or resa@rovahotel.com; www.rovahotel.com. Smart en-suite dbl & family rooms with sat-TV, safe, minibar & Wi-Fi. Car rental.

🏠 **Sakamanga** [158 C4] (32 rooms) Rue Ratianarivo; 📞 22 358 09; m 032 02 668 34; e contact@sakamanga.com or saka@malagasy.com; www.sakamanga.com. Tana's most popular tourist hotel decorated throughout with interesting historic artefacts. Rooms en suite with fan, safe, sat-TV & Wi-Fi; some with AC & minibar. Booking is essential.

🏠 **Trano Bongo** [156 B7] (12 rooms) Tanjombato; 📞 22 461 32/22 461 33; e contact@trano-bongo-hotel.com. The contemporary design of this new hotel is inspired by Malagasy royal residences. Situated south of the city, it's well placed to make an early start on the RN7, so you don't have to spend the 1st hour fighting through traffic jams. Rooms have AC, sat-TV, minibar & Wi-Fi. The restaurant specialises in game inc wild boar.

Also in this category:

🏠 **Akoa** [156 B1] www.akoahotel.com
🏠 **Brajas** [159 G3] www.hotelbrajas.com
🏠 **Chez Aïna** [156 C2] www.chez-aina.com
🏠 **Evergreen** [156 D3] www.hotel-evergreen. com
🏠 **Garden Square** [156 B1] www. gardensquarehotel.com
🏠 **Grand Mellis** [158 D2] www.hotel-mellis. com
🏠 **Grégoire** [156 D2] www.hotel-gregoire. com
🏠 **Chez Lorenzo** [156 B1] e lorenzo@moov.mg
🏠 **Manoir** [156 C6] e lemanoir@moov.mg
🏠 **Palm** [158 C4] www.hotelantananarivo.com
🏠 **Panorama** [156 D4] www.panorama-tana. com
🏠 **Pergola** [159 G6] www.hoteldelapergola. com
🏠 **Résidence du Rova** [156 D5] www. residence-antananarivo.com
🏠 **Vatel** [156 D5] www.vatel.mg

Mid-range €€€

🏠 **Aina Hotel** [159 F6] (13 rooms) 17 Rue Ratsimilaho; m 034 22 630 51; e ainahotel@ gmail.com; www.ainahotel.com. This 5-floor hotel has en-suite dbl & trpl rooms with Wi-Fi, AC, safe & sat-TV; 1 with bath. Also a studio with kitchenette.
🏠 **Anjary** [158 B4] (108 rooms) 89 Rue de Liège; ℓ 22 279 58; e resatana@anjary-hotel. com; www.anjary-hotel.com. Good-value rooms of varying size/category, some with AC, Wi-Fi & safe. Spa & massage available. Good restaurants & snack bar.
🏠 **Ariandro** [156 D5] (5 rooms) Andohanimandroseza; ℓ 22 273 78; m 033 11 882 57/034 01 689 47; e ariandroco@yahoo.fr. Nestled in a secluded corner of southeast Tana, this beautiful guesthouse is especially recommended for creative or artistic folk. Individually decorated with the Malagasy owners' own artworks, the en-suite rooms overlook a central courtyard. Wi-Fi available. Also an apartment with kitchenette.

🏠 **Artistes** [159 E4] (17 rooms) Ambatomena; m 034 64 879 31; e hoteldesartistes@yahoo. fr; www.hoteldesartistes-tana.com. A quiet yet centrally located spot. En-suite rooms with safe, sat-TV & Wi-Fi.
🏠 **Karthala** [159 H4] (9 rooms) 48 Rue Andriandahifotsy; ℓ 22 248 95/22 272 67; m 032 02 956 99/033 11 971 56; e contact@le-karthala. com or le_karthala@yahoo.fr; www.le-karthala. com. A traditional Malagasy home in a secluded spot, a short (but steep) walk from the city centre. Readers routinely praise the warm welcome & good rates, but slate the mediocre b/fast.
🏠 **Lemur Hostel** [156 D4] (4 rooms) Rue Andrianaivoravelona, Antsahabe; m 032 66 091 20; e info@lemurhostel.com; www.lemurhostel. com. Recently opened hostel with male, female & mixed dorms; also a couple of private rooms with shared facilities. Wi-Fi. Kitchen for guests' use. B/fast inc. Free walking tours.
🏠 **Madagascar Underground** [158 D5] 18 Rue Rainitovo; ℓ 22 214 50; m 034 29 909 07; e madagascarunderground@gmail.com; www. madagascarunderground.com. Backpacker hostel run by a French-Australian couple; great vibe & Mexican restaurant. Private rooms & dorms with triple bunks.
🏠 **Mirador (Chez Francis)** [159 G3] (11 rooms) Rue Andriandahifotsy; ℓ 22 613 65; m 032 04 301 25 (manager)/032 26 742 75; e hotelchezfrancis@yahoo.fr or sebastienbarneoud@gmail.com; www.hotel-chezfrancis.com. Recently taken over by a young couple, Sébastien & Gina, this super little place has long been a backpacker favourite. Splendid views over Tana from back rooms. Clean en-suite rooms with TV.
🏠 **Relais de la Haute Ville** [156 D5] (9 rooms) Rue Pierre Rapiera; ℓ 22 604 58; m 034 05 133 16/034 14 604 58; e rhv@moov.mg. An old colonial house on the way to the rova. Comfortable rooms with sat-TV, internet & minibar. Good restaurant with Malagasy & European food.
🏠 **Relais des Pistards** [156 C7] (7 rooms) Rue Fernand Kasanga; m 032 29 471 65/032 67 813 13 (manager); e pistards@freedsl.mg. A friendly hotel with sgl & dbl rooms (some en suite). Excellent food.
🏠 **Shalimar** [158 B3] (25 rooms) 5 Rue Mahafaka; ℓ 22 260 70 (restaurant). Rooms with AC & TV. Some with shower/bath. Its restaurant

offers mainly Indian cuisine; reader Les Parkes highly recommends the royal couscous.

🏠 **Sole** [158 D3] (42 rooms) 32 Rue de Liège; \22 289 89; e resa@solehotel.mg; www.solehotel-mada.com. Rooms of various sizes with sat-TV & Wi-Fi. Massage.

🏠 **Tana-Jacaranda** [158 D6] (7 rooms) 24 Rue Rainitsarovy; \22 562 39/22 694 63; m 032 07 056 51/034 22 562 39; e tana-jacaranda@tana-jacaranda.com; www.tana-jacaranda.com. Simple clean sgl, dbl & twin rooms; some en suite. Guesthouse run by friendly couple Noro & Rodin. Use of kitchen & dining room with wonderful views. Free Wi-Fi. Good rates for solo travellers & long stays.

Also in this category:

🏠 **Glacier** [159 E3] www.hotel-glacier.com
🏠 **Ivotel** [159 F7] e sitivotel@moov.mg
🏠 **Jardin d'Antanimena** [156 B1] www.aujardintana.com
🏠 **Jean Laborde** [158 C6] m 032 02 692 85
🏠 **Lémurien Blanc** [156 A4] e lemurienblanc@gmail.com
🏠 **Lotus Bleu** [156 C4] www.lelotus-bleu.com
🏠 **Mad'Delices Hotel** [158 D6] \22 226 41
🏠 **Motel d'Antananarivo** [156 B6] www.motelanosy.com
🏠 **Muraille de Chine** [158 C1] e muraille@moov.mg
🏠 **Pavé** [159 F5] www.lepavehotel.com
🏠 **Riad** [158 B6] www.leriadtana.com
🏠 **Shanghai** [158 D4] www.shangai-hotel.com
🏠 **St Ange** [158 D1] www.st-ange.fr
🏠 **St Antoine** [158 C5] www.hotelstantoine.e-monsite.com

🏠 **St Pierre** [159 E1] www.hotelsaintpierre.biz
🏠 **Suncity** [158 C5] www.suncityhotel-mada.com
🏠 **Taj** [158 C4] e hoteltaj@moov.mg
🏠 **Vahiny** [156 D3] www.chambre-madagascar.com
🏠 **Villa Isoraka** [158 C6] www.villa-isoraka.net
🏠 **White Palace** [158 A4] e whitepalacetana@gmail.com

Budget €€

🏠 **Ile Bourbon** [156 A3] (9 rooms) 12 Rue Benyowski; \22 279 42. Réunionais-owned Creole-style house with dbl & trpl rooms; good ambience. Sat-TV & Wi-Fi. 'Excellent,' reports Franz Stadelmann on the food, 'quality/price very well balanced.'

🏠 **Isoraka** [158 D6] (7 rooms) 11 Av Ramanantsoa; \22 355 81; m 034 49 992 22; e hotel@isoraka.com. Simple backpacker hotel owned by Sakamanga. Bright sgl & dbl rooms with safe & fan, mostly quite small; some en suite.

🏠 **Lambert** [159 G2] (23 rooms) Ambondrona; \22 229 92; e hotellambert@yahoo.fr. Basic but clean, convenient, good value & popular; be prepared to climb a lot of stairs!

🏠 **Moonlight** [159 F2] (10 rooms) 62 Rue Rainandriamampandry; \22 268 70; m 034 06 265 15; e hasinaherizo@yahoo.fr. This old Malagasy house retains much of its former charm; recommended by several readers. Good for lone travellers (cheap sgl rooms & dorm beds).

🏠 **Niaouly** [156 C4] (18 rooms) \22 627 65; e hotel.niaouly@yahoo.fr; www.niaouly.com. Simple clean en-suite rooms & great city views.

✖️ **WHERE TO EAT AND DRINK** Most of the hotels listed on the previous pages serve food, and some are famous for their restaurants. Offering one of the best culinary experience in Tana, the **Varangue's** dining room is an elegant and intimate space – so, despite the high prices, booking is essential. Nearby **Villa Isoraka** is a trendy venue with a menu spanning French, Malagasy, Tex-Mex and pizzas.

At Sakamanga, **Le Saka** is a perennial favourite for evening dinner among tourists and expats alike, while buffet lunch is served in the tranquil surroundings of **L'Espace Jardin** every day. **Le 313** at the Louvre is good value and centrally located, with live music most Friday nights. If you want to experience local food then **Tatao**, the restaurant at Radama Hotel, specialises in Malagasy cuisine. The **Ribaudière** restaurant has a very pleasant garden dining area and serves nicely presented, delicious French food. Fantastic Indian dishes are available at Anjary's seventh-floor **Terrasse Exotique** restaurant, with a Bollywood ambience.

Fans of seafood should not miss **L'Aquarium**, one of the two restaurants at Grégoire; better fish dishes are not to be found anywhere in Tana, they say.

More central and with great city views, **La Table des Hautes Terres** at the Palissandre is a classy place, where the fish is also particularly recommended and there is live music some nights (Wed/Fri/Sun). For even more magical views across Tana, head to the restaurant terrace at **Lokanga**.

The Carlton has several eateries: **Café Charly** serves creative French cuisine and has an extensive wine list, while **La Terrasse** is a more relaxed affair; for a lighter bite try **Le Bistrot**, or **Oasis de Tana** in a poolside garden setting. More popular because of its central location is the Colbert, which has three restaurants: the smart **Taverne** specialises in French gastronomy; **La Fougère** with its outside terrace is great for lunch; and **Le Cellier** is a more intimate space for evening dining with good wine.

Special treat

✕ Carré [158 C4] Rue des 77 Parlementaires; m 032 60 498 00; e lecarretana@hotmail.fr; ⏰ Mon–Sat noon–23.00. Swish new lounge bar & restaurant specialising in sushi & European food.

✕ Chez Arnaud [156 D5] 21 Rue Rabozaka; ☎ 22 221 78; ⏰ Tue–Sun 11.30–14.30 & 18.00–22.00, Mon closed. This hidden gem is tucked away 4km southeast of the city centre and serves excellent mainly French cuisine in an unpretentious setting. Also many pizza & pasta dishes.

✕ Chez Mariette [159 H3] 11 Rue Rakotomalala, Faravohitra; ☎ 22 216 02. With more than 50 years' experience under her belt, Madagascar's most legendary native chef serves beautifully prepared traditional cuisine, inc veritable feasts based on Merina royal banquets of old. No Malagasy you meet will fail to be awestruck when you say you've dined at Mariette's. Opening hours are irregular, generally only for pre-booked parties.

✕ Citizen [158 C7] 12 Rue Rakotonirina; m 034 05 720 60; e citizentana@yahoo.fr; www.citizentana.mg; ⏰ daily except Sun eve. French-style haute cuisine with a pretty terrace looking out over Lake Anosy. Good choice for a special occasion. Also has 3 top-end rooms.

✕ Hédiard [158 D4] 14 Rue Jaures; ☎ 22 283 70; m 034 47 484 54; ⏰ Mon 09.00–18.00, Tue–Fri 09.00–22.00, Sat 09.00–20.00, Sun closed. Elegant restaurant serving classy French food, sushi & decadent desserts. Many French wines.

✕ KUDéTA [158 C6] 15 Rue de la Réunion; ☎ 22 281 54/22 611 40/22 677 85; m 032 07 281 55/032 07 611 40; e info@kudeta.mg; ▪ kudetamadagascar. Chic modern restaurant & lounge bar, always busy with an international clientele. Beautifully presented food. Wi-Fi.

✕ Le B' [158 B5] 72 Av Rasoamanarivo; ☎ 22 316 86; m 032 04 630 32/034 02 383 94; e lebresto@gmail.com; ⏰ daily noon–15.00 & 18.00–midnight. High-quality, stylish bar, lounge & restaurant. Standard menu is Indonesian inspired, but regular theme evenings feature Japanese, Caribbean, Hawaiian & other cuisines.

✕ Plantation [156 B1] Rue Ravoninahitriniarivo, Ankorondrano; ☎ 22 335 01; m 032 82 699 30; e laplantation.contact@gmail.com or laplantation.restaurant@gmail.com; ⏰ daily noon–14.30 & Tue 19.00–22.00. North of the city centre, next to Ibis. Reliably good restaurant either to take lunch out in the serene garden or a romantic dinner inside.

✕ Rossini [158 C6] Av Ramanantsoa; ☎ 22 342 44/22 555 00; m 034 05 015 88; e legrand@moov.mg or lerossini@moov.mg. Fancy French joint with good but overpriced food; reportedly popular with ostentatious types & high-ranking military. Live music Fri/Sat.

✕ Villa Vanille [156 B1] Pl Antanimena; ☎ 22 205 15; ⏰ 11.30–23.00. A fine century-old Tana house specialising in Creole food & vanilla recipes; also couscous, pizza & seafood. Good wine list with impressive number of Malagasy labels. Music every eve. Highly recommended (especially for soufflé).

Regular dining

✕ Arirang (Coréen) [158 B5] Av Ramanantsoa; ☎ 24 271 33; m 032 02 323 90 (manager). Popular authentic Korean restaurant with excellent food at good prices.

✕ Au Bistrot (Old No 7) [158 A5] 12 Av Rasoamanarivo; e aubistrot.restaurant@gmail.com or old7Bar@gmail.com; ⏰ Mon 18.00–02.00, Tue–Thu 11.00–02.00, Fri/Sat 11.00–05.00. Doner kebabs, tapas, waffles, pancakes & other snacks; shisha pipes. Also a fantastic bar that describes itself as the first Jack Daniel's bar in the Indian Ocean.

✗ Boussole [158 C7] 21 Rue Dr Villette; ☎ 22 358 10; m 032 07 605 03; e laboussole@moov.mg; ⓕ La Boussole Madagascar; ⏰ daily 10.30–22.30. Stylish restaurant-bar with charming patio for outdoor dining. Excellent French food & snacks. Especially lively Fri eve. Wi-Fi.

✗ Buffet du Jardin [159 F5] Pl de l'Indépendance, Antaninarenina; ☎ 22 338 87; e lebuffet@moov.mg; www.lebuffetdujardin-antananarivo.com. Relaxed brasserie in Jardin Antananarenina, recently taken over by the Colbert, convenient for a fast-food lunch, beer or coffee. Regular live music.

✗ Café de la Gare [158 C1] 1 Av de l'Indépendance (at Soarano railway station); ☎ 22 611 12; m 032 07 090 50; e info@cafetana.com; ⓕ cafedelagaretana; ⏰ Mon–Sat 09.00–23.00, Sun 11.00–22.00. Lively restaurant-bar with fantastic atmosphere & fast Wi-Fi. Limited choice of food but worth visiting at least for a drink/pastry & to use the kooky toilets built in a converted railway carriage!

✗ Carnivore [159 G7] 66 Rue Ratsimilaho; ☎ 22 241 98; m 032 05 125 04/032 29 292 01/034 05 125 04/034 07 241 98; e lecarnivore@yahoo.fr; www.le-carnivore.com; ⏰ daily noon–15.00 & 19.00–02.00. Trendy new steakhouse & bar modelled on famous Nairobi restaurant of same name. Broad range of meat dishes from chicken, lamb & pork to liver, kidney & crocodile. The all-you-can-eat concept makes it great value as long as you arrive hungry.

✗ Chez Sucett's [158 C6] 23 Rue Raveloary; ☎ 22 261 00; e chezsucetts@moov.mg; ⏰ daily except Sun lunch. Pleasant, small restaurant with extensive menu of Creole food & some unusual dishes. Once a beacon of excellence, quality has dipped slightly but you can still eat very well for a good price.

✗ Fat Boys [158 C6] 4 Rue de la Réunion; http://fatboys.loyalpanda.com; ⏰ Mon–Thu 10.00–21.00, Fri/Sat 10.00–22.00, Sun 10.00–20.00. Fast-food joint offering burgers, pizzas & a few more inventive items, inc something called 'crunchy banana'. A loyalty card scheme awards free gifts to the regulars, after whose eventual physique the establishment is presumably named.

✗ Fatapera [159 G6] Rue Ramelina, Ambatonakanga; m 033 15 088 21/033 15 088 91; e fatapera@madafood.com or madafood@moov.mg; www.madafood.com/fatapera; ⏰ 10.00–22.00 (restaurant), 07.00–22.00 (snack

bar). Covered & outdoor seating. An underrated establishment with tremendous dishes & fast friendly service.

✗ Foie Gras de Tana [158 C7] 29 Rue de Russie; m 032 07 924 83/033 11 239 49/034 07 924 83/034 11 239 49; e coin_foiegras_tana@yahoo.fr; ⏰ Mon–Sat 09.00–18.00. As you would expect from the name they serve a range of foie-gras-based dishes, as well as selling the product in jars.

✗ Glacier [159 E3] This 1933 hotel has been a prostitutes' hang-out for years but is lively & fun, with live music most nights from 20.00. It has 3 restaurants. The brasserie upstairs is quite civilised & has a great view of the avenue.

✗ Little India [159 E5] Rue Rabehevitra, Antaninarenina; m 032 78 161 12/034 71 909 06. Don't be put off by the dingy entrance passage or bland décor: the food in this Indian restaurant is tremendous. Wi-Fi.

✗ Minou [159 F7] Rue Ratsimilaho; ☎ 22 288 62; ⏰ 08.00–late. Very good restaurant with inexpensive, tasty Malagasy, Chinese & European dishes.

✗ Nerone [159 F6] 28 Rue Ratsimilaho; ☎ 22 231 18; ⏰ daily noon–14.00 & 19.00–22.00. Rather mediocre Italian food, considering the upmarket prices. Extensive menu. Sometimes live music.

✗ Oriental [156 B1] Ivandry; m 033 87 111 11/034 42 111 11; e lorientaltana@gmail.com; ⏰ daily 10.30–midnight. Don't be misled by the name; this is a Mediterranean restaurant specialising in Lebanese & Greek dishes. Praised by several readers.

✗ Ozone [158 B5] 58 Rue Rasoamanarivo; m 033 64 136 46/034 01 042 56; ⏰ daily 10.30–15.00 & 18.30–midnight. Thai restaurant with extensive menu & take-away. Reliable food & good prices but rather garish décor & loud TV. Live music 20.00–22.00 except Sun.

✗ Petit Verdot [159 G7] 27 Rue Rahamefy; ☎ 22 392 34/24 386 55; e lemanoir@moov.mg; ⏰ Mon–Fri 11.30–15.00 & 18.00–23.00, Sat 18.00–23.00, Sun closed. The long-time favourite among expats, this intimate 3-level bistro offers reliable French cuisine at great prices, especially the lunchtime set menu. Huge wine list. Seafood casserole every Sat eve. Booking advised.

✗ Pourquoi Pas [158 B7] 31 Rue de Russie, Isoraka; m 032 65 943 20; e serge.dupuis0951@orange.fr; ⏰ Tue–Sat. A simple & cosy French-run bistro with all the usual dishes at reasonable prices. Very welcoming owners.

✗ Tana Saïgon (Zebu Original Bistrot) [158 C7] 28 Rue du Dr Villette; m 034 44 006 01/034 44 006 02; ◷ Mon–Thu 10.00–22.30, Fri–Sat 10.00–23.30, Sun closed. A superb traditional Malagasy house with indoor & outdoor dining areas. As the name suggests, the speciality is steak (inc 'zeburgers') but other international dishes are on the menu too. Wi-Fi.

✗ Tsiky [159 G6] 12 Rue Ramelina; ✆ 22 283 87; m 032 02 679 01; e rakotoson.dany@gmail.com or tsikytraiteur@gmail.com; http://sites.google.com/site/tsikytraiteur. Lovely Malagasy eatery with some French dishes on the menu too.
Also in this category:

✗ Au Triporteur [156 D4] e atipikjeanluc@gmail.com

✗ Canela [158 D5] m 032 03 060 05

✗ Cattleya [156 B1] m 034 70 941 76

✗ ChillOut Café [159 G3] e chilloutcafetana@gmail.com

✗ Fleuve Rouge [159 H1] e lefleuverouge@gmail.com

✗ Gastro Pizza Analakely [159 E2] www.lagastronomiepizza.com

✗ Gastro Pizza Mahamasina [156 C5] www.lagastronomiepizza.com

✗ Grand Orient [158 C1] m 032 03 399 99

✗ Grill du Rova [156 D6] ✆ 22 627 24

✗ Jasmin [159 F5] ✆ 22 342 96

✗ Jonquille [158 D1] ✆ 22 206 37

✗ Marée (Chez Nari) [156 B1] m 032 02 692 67

✗ Medina [158 D6] www.lamedinatana.com

✗ Montparnasse [156 D3] ✆ 22 217 16

✗ Orion [158 D5] e restaurant.orion@hotmail.fr

✗ Palladio's [156 B1] ✆ 22 539 49

✗ Relais Normand [158 B2] ✆ 22 207 88

✗ Taj Mahal [158 B3] ✆ 22 309 02

Snack bars and cafés

⊐ Blanche Neige [158 D1] 15 Av de l'Indépendance; ◷ closed Mon. Tremendous ice cream & pastries.

⊐ Dzama Cocktail [156 B1] Ivandry; ✆ 22 434 10; m 032 03 234 10; www.dzamacocktailcafe.com. Chic bar & café owned by the Dzama rum emporium.

⊐ Honey [158 D2] 13 Av de l'Indépendance; ◷ closed Tue. Very good for b/fast & ice cream. Also cakes & milkshakes.

⊐ Infinithé Anosy [159 E7] ✆ 22 328 50; m 032 03 888 88/034 75 888 88; e anosy. infinithe@gmail.com. With branches in Ivandry & near Lake Anosy, this minimalist café is open for b/fast & lunch only.

⊐ Mad'Delices [158 D6] 29 Av Ramanantsoa, Isoraka; ✆ 22 226 41; ◷ 06.30–23.00. Cosy eatery with mainly Malagasy menu, luscious pastries & ice cream. Long opening hours. Great for b/fast.

⊐ Mille Feuilles (Maison de la Presse) [156 B2] Rue Rasamimanana, Behoririka; ✆ 22 231 93/22 267 76; ◷ Mon–Fri 08.30–noon & 14.00–17.30. A new bookshop café.

⊐ Phare [158 B7] 14 Rue de Belgique; ✆ 26 323 28; m 032 86 856 84; e lephare@orange.mg; ◷ daily 11.30–15.00 & 18.30–22.00 except Mon/Sun lunch & Mon/Tue eve. Pancakes & waffles in infinite variety are to be found at this intimate venue; also salads & desserts.

⊐ Planète [159 G6] Filling burgers, fries & sandwiches for hungry tourists.

⊐ Potinière [159 E3] 35 Av de l'Indépendance. Patisseries & tea shop near the Air Mad office.

⊐ Saka Express [158 C4] Rue Ratianarivo; ✆ 24 334 39; m 032 41 412 57/033 02 175 40. Cheap décor but big portions of filling food.
Also in this category:

⊐ Carrefour du Voyageur [158 C4] m 032 07 168 54

⊐ Duo [158 D2] m 032 63 490 38

⊐ Mystic [158 C5] ⨍ mystic.mythique

⊐ Shalimar Snack [158 C4] m 032 11 546 75

⊐ Tropique [159 F4]

NIGHTLIFE Many of the hotels and restaurants also have lively bars. Most of the cocktail bars and clubs hold themed nights, parties, gigs and special events, so ask around to find out where is the place to be on a particular night – or check Facebook where venues often post details of their upcoming programmes.

Tana loves novelty so club venues tend to get frequent makeovers; chances are by the time you read this, one or two of the places listed below will have been relaunched under a new name.

☆ **Caverna** [158 A5] ⏰ Mon–Sat 14.00–late. Opened in 2012, this lively venue styles itself as a straight-friendly gay bar with dancing, cocktails & karaoke.

☆ **Cuba Bar** [158 B5] Isoraka; m 032 91 837 72/032 98 108 81; e maheclark5@gmail.com; f Cuba bar tana; ⏰ 18.00–02.00. New lounge bar with snacks & cocktails, opened at the start of 2016.

☆ **KUDéTA Urban Club** [156 A4] ☎22 677 85; m 032 07 281 55; e info@kudeta.mg; ⏰ 10.00–late. Located by Carlton Hotel, this club & cocktail bar hosts DJs, live concerts & regular parties & events.

☆ **L'Excuse** [158 C6] Isoraka; e rhumerielexcuse@gmail.com; f L'excuse. Friendly atmosphere with wooden barrels as tables. Big range of *rhums arrangées*; also cocktails & snacks.

☆ **Mojo Bar** [158 A5] Rue Rasoamanarivo; e contact@lemojo.mg; ⏰ daily 18.00–04.00. Popular stylish cocktail bar; often has live music.

☆ **Outcool** [158 C4] Rue Ratianarivo; ☎22 553 77; m 033 12 126 24. Small internet café & bar with very friendly Malagasy owner.

☆ **Sky Bar (Tana Arts Café)** [158 C4] Rue Ratianarivo; m 032 28 579 34; f SKY BAR; ⏰ Mon/Thu 10.00–midnight, Fri/Sat 10.00–02.00, Sun 17.00–23.00. Stylish new cocktail bar with regular BOGOF happy-hour promotions & live music.

♀ **Caveau** [159 E5] Rue Rabehevitra; ☎22 343 93; ⏰ daily 22.30–04.00. Dating from 1949 this iconic underground club attracts all walks of life. Varied music inc Malagasy.

♀ **Guru** [159 G6] Rue Ramelina; ☎24 301 61. Regular nightclub.

♀ **In Square** [156 D1] Ambatobe (nr French School); m 034 07 066 40; e insquare.lounge@gmail.com; ⏰ Mon–Wed 10.00–22.00, Thu–Sat 10.00–02.30. Restaurant & club with themed nights, stand-up comedy & karaoke, about 7km northeast of the city centre.

♀ **Indra** [158 B4] 8 Rue Ingereza; ⏰ daily. Sweaty '90s-style disco.

♀ **Jet Club** [156 D3] Rte Circulaire, Antsakaviro; m 034 93 622 39; e jetclub.mg@gmail.com; ⏰ Thu–Sat 20.00–04.00. New in 2012, it's a modern bar, lounge & nightclub in neon colours. Cocktails, sorbets & Wi-Fi available.

♀ **Le Club (Le Bus)** [156 B2] Rue Rainizanabololona; ☎22 691 00; m 032 04 666 66/032 04 792 45; f LeClubAntanimena; ⏰ Fri/Sat 22.00–05.00. Restaurant, bar & large discotheque, considered the best clubbing spot in Tana. Very modern & professional set-up, attracting a young crowd; has the best DJs & latest music.

♀ **Le SIX** [159 F6] 13 Rue Ratsimilaho; m 033 15 666 66/034 42 666 66; e lesix@moov.mg; f Le six; ⏰ Fri/Sat 22.00–08.00. Fashionable club with comfy lounge & ambience much loved by 30-somethings, but prostitutes are much in evidence. Generally Western music but many themed evenings. Pizza at all hours.

♀ **Palladium (Buddha Club)** [158 D5] 8 Rue Rabehevitra; ☎24 317 76; e palladium.mcar@yahoo.fr. Centrally located discotheque.

♀ **Plage** [156 D2] Betongolo. To the east of the city. Popular with local youngsters so packed at w/ends.

♀ **Suite 101 (Phoenix/Pandora)** [159 F6] 1 Rue Rabobalahy, Antaninarenina; m 032 11 101 31; e lasuite101@gmail.com; f La Suite 101; ⏰ Mon–Sat. After a couple of years' closure it struggled to reinvent itself, but reopened in 2013 with sophisticated décor & cocktail bar.

ENTERTAINMENT If you are in Tana for a while, find out what's on by picking up the latest *No Comment* or *Tana Planète* – regular free booklets that can be found in hotels and restaurants. You can also drop into the **Centre Albert Camus** [158 D2] on Av de l'Indépendance to pick up a programme of concerts and films. Films are dubbed into French.

For a truly Malagasy experience go to a performance of *hira gasy* (see box, page 186). There are regular weekend performances at Anosibe and Andavamamba, southwest of Lake Anosy (contact the tourist information office for details). It's an exciting and amusing day out with food and drink stalls. Have plenty of small-denomination notes ready to support the best performers.

SHOPPING Note that bargaining is expected only in markets. It is neither customary nor appropriate to bargain in most shops.

FANORONA: THE NATIONAL GAME   *Hilary Bradt*

Stroll around Tana – or anywhere in Madagascar – and you may come across groups of men and boys clustered round a board marked with squares and criss-crosses. Usually the 'board' is scratched in the earth. They are playing a game unique to Madagascar: *fanorona*. It is a game of strategy; in its simplest version it has some similarities to draughts/chequers but for advanced players it is more like chess. Carved fanorona boards can be purchased at the Andravoahangy craft market.

Handicrafts markets While traditional Malagasy handicrafts are available at boutiques across the city, you will find a wider selection and better prices at the artisan markets. Most noteworthy are the embroidery, basketry, woodcarving, minerals and stiff leatherwork. Items made from raffia are common, as is carved zebu horn and the unique Antaimoro paper embedded with pressed flowers.

The most centrally located handicrafts market is at **Marché Pochart** [156 B2], near Soarano railway station. A second one, accessible from Rue Ramananarivo in **Andravoahangy** [156 D1], has a particularly good selection of carved games, including solitaire, chess and the traditional Malagasy *fanorona* (sellers can provide a rule sheet). It is about 30 minutes' walk northeast of the centre. Heading out of the city towards the airport you cannot miss the roadside **Digue** market [150 C7], which also has an impressive range of wares. And on the east side of Tana in District 67ha is the **CENAM** [156 A5] market with its 'artisan village'. There's also a **bamboo market** at Anosibe [156 A6].

Other markets Most of the handicrafts markets above are parts of larger general markets, which are always intriguing to explore. You cannot walk far in Tana without coming upon a market – and indeed often the streets *in-between* are filled with illicit street sellers, their wares laid out on a sheet.

In the centre, **Marché Pochart** [156 B2], and the **Pavillons du Zoma** [159 F4] at the southern end of Av de l'Indépendance, are both particularly active on Fridays (*zoma* is Malagasy for 'Friday'). They sell everything from fruit and veg to chicken heads and frog legs, as well as items like stationery and clothes. To the west of the station is **Petite Vitesse** [158 A3], where you will find a section selling medicinal plants. **Mahamasina** (market day Thursday) hosts another bustling bazaar on the western side of the stadium [156 C5]. And a colourful **flower market** is held daily to the south of Lake Anosy [156 B5]; on Thursdays there are bargains galore at a **secondhand market** in the same area.

Souvenirs and gifts The best-quality goods are sold in specialist shops. There are numerous boutiques, particularly in the Isoraka district of the upper town. You will also find several **Baobab Company**, **Maki** and other franchises that specialise in T-shirts. High-quality handicrafts are produced and sold at the **Fihavanana** orphanage [156 C5] – see page 176. Here are a few worth checking out:

Arts & Jardin [158 D6] 26 Av Ramanantsoa Isoraka. Sells a good range of crafts.
BioAroma [158 C5] 54 Av Ramanantsoa. A huge selection of their own brand of natural remedies, essential oils, cosmetics & beauty products.

Epicerie Fine de la Ferme de Morarano [158 D6] Rue Raveloary; e lafermedemorarano@yahoo. fr; www.lepicerie.fine.la.ferme.de.morarano.over-blog.com; ⊕ Mon–Sat 09.00–18.00. A fantastic range of top-quality jams, chutneys, spices, oils &

teas from a farm in Ambatolampy. They also sell essential oils, massage oils & cosmetics.

Ferronnerie d'Art Andranobevava; ☏22 407 28; m 033 11 337 42; e ferodar101@gmail.com; ⓕ Ferronnerie d'art Antananarivo; ⊕ Mon–Fri 08.00–17.30, Sat 09.00–17.00. Original products in metal & stone.

150F Alasora; m 032 42 374 35/034 28 953 35; e finfitfan@yahoo.fr. Short for 'Finoana, Fitiavana, Fanantenana, Fahasoavana' ('Belief, Love, Hope, Grace'), this inspiring metalwork workshop employs an almost entirely disabled staff & has built a school on-site for their children. The practical & decorative products are on sale in the showroom.

Flamant Rose [159 F4] Rue du 26 Juin 1960. A wide selection of crafts & especially art.

Gasific [150 B4] ☏22 695 53/22 444 24; m 032 04 116 88; e sales@centpourcent.mg; ⊕ Mon–Fri 09.00–17.00. Model-making workshop specialised in ships. Part of handicraft company Cent Pour Cent, which employs 120 craftsmen.

Hazomanga [158 C4] Rue Ratianarivo. A great little craft boutique, centrally located.

Le Village [150 C4] Ambohibao (nr airport); www.ships-models.com. They make scale models of every type of ship imaginable inc replicas of some famous ones. Prices €100–1,500. They can arrange shipping (no pun intended) so no need to worry how to get your purchase home in one piece. Visits to the workshop are interesting too.

Lisy Art Gallery [156 D4] Rte de Mausolée (nr Hôtel Panorama) A delightful shop; very large & excellent range of Malagasy souvenirs.

Mineral Gallery Fiaro Bldg, Ampefiloha; ☏22 297 63/24 148 03; m 032 07 268 62; e mineral. market@gmail.com; www.madagascargemstones. com. All kinds of Malagasy minerals, gemstones & ammonites.

Pili Pili Dock (Madépices) A huge range of beautifully presented gifts inc handmade soap, spices, *rhum arrangé* & dried Malagasy cuisine is available from 3 outlets: Talatamaty [150 B5] ☏26 299 42), La City (m 034 50 608 78) & Tana Water Front (m 034 20 912 07).

Roses & Baobab [158 C4] Rue des 77 Parlementaires Français; m 032 40 615 60/033 14 699 90; e art@rosesetbaobab.com; www. rosesetbaobab.com; ⊕ Mon–Sat 09.00–19.00. High quality carvings, paintings & other work by local artists.

Royal Spirits Rue Rev Callet, Behoririka; ☏22 616 27; www.royalspirits-madagascar.com; ⊕ Mon–Fri 08.00–noon & 14.00–18.00, Sat 08.00–noon & 14.00–17.30. Stocks most Malagasy wine and rum labels (as well as imported alcohol).

Soarano station [158 C1] 1 Av de l'Indépendance. Shops inside the refurbished railway station sell soaps, candles, spices, scarves & pricey but top-quality artwork, mainly paintings, sculptures & marquetry.

Tee-shirterie [158 C5] Rue Ratianarivo. Large selection of Madagascar-themed T-shirts.

Vatosoa Boutique Ilanivato. This is the place for exquisite *lamba*. In the same block is Lambamena Boutique.

Shopping centres, supermarkets and supplies

Madagascar's first truly modern shopping mall, **La City**, opened in 2012 at Alarobia – 3km north of the city centre [156 B1]. It has a food court, coffee shops, underground car park, kids' play centre, escalators, 52 outlets selling international brands – everything you would expect. Although aimed more at expats seeking home comforts, it also offers some shops and services for tourists: there is a Shoprite supermarket, bank, bureau de change, Orange/Airtel/Telma outlets, massage centre and Air Madagascar office with considerably shorter waiting times and longer opening hours than at their city-centre headquarters. The mall is open every day (⊕ *Mon–Sat 09.30–19.30, Sun 09.30–13.30*). Another opened in 2016 on the road to the airport: **Akoor' Digue** [150 D7] has among other outlets a supermarket, banks, a pharmacy and several eateries. A smaller shopping complex at Ambodivona (2km north of the city centre) is **Tana Water Front** [156 D1] with about 30 upmarket shops, a Shoprite supermarket, a new food court upstairs and an excellent hotel. It is open every day except Sunday (⊕ *Mon–Sat 09.00–18.30*).

If, instead of handicrafts or T-shirts, your family and friends would prefer consumable gifts such as Malagasy tea, chocolate, spices, beer or wine (see page 107 for advice), visit a supermarket for a broad selection at good prices. Tana now has more than a dozen supermarkets. They are also great for stocking up on supplies before heading off somewhere remote. **Shoprite** is a South African supermarket chain with six branches in Tana: in addition to the two mentioned above, they can be found behind the town hall [158 D2], near Lake Anosy [158 A7], near Panorama Hotel [156 D4] and not far from the airport [150 B4]. A Réunion-based company operates one **Score** supermarket and three **Jumbo Score** hypermarkets. These are at Antsahabe [156 D4], Ankorondrano, Tanjombato and at Akoor' Digue. The best-quality (and priciest) food is to be found at the French chain **Leader Price**, which has outlets in Ankorondrano, Tanjombato and opposite the American Embassy [150 C5]. Branches of a new chain of mini-markets called **Supermaki** have been springing up across the capital lately.

For camping, backpacking and other outdoor equipment, visit **CS Events** (*Rte du Mausolée, Andrainarivo;* ℡ *22 413 82;* e *csevents-madagascar@blueline.mg; www.csevents-madagascar.com;* ⊕ *Mon–Fri 08.00–12.30 & 13.30–18.00, Sat 08.00–13.00*). They sell tents, sleeping bags, rucksacks, binoculars, GPS, torches, camp stoves, penknives, first aid kits, hammocks, mosquito nets, walking poles and more. It is not cheap, but they stock quality brands (Garmin, Petzl, Coleman, etc) that you will not find elsewhere in Madagascar.

Books and maps Good bookshops include **Librairie Md Paoly** [158 D2] on Av de l'Indépendance and **Librairie Mixte**, which has recently moved to Victoria Plaza in Antanimena [156 B1]. In Isoraka, **CMPL** [158 C6] specialises in academic books but also has many books about Madagascar. For imported books (mainly French) try **Espace Loisirs** [159 F6] at 11 Rue Ratsimilaho and **Des Livres et Nous** at Tana Water Front. Bibliophiles should also explore the secondhand **book market** [159 H6] at the top of Rue du 26 Juin 1960.

Assorted maps may be found at many of the above, but the best selection is undoubtedly at **FTM** [156 D4] (*Rte Circulaire, Ambanidia;* ℡ *22 229 35;* e *ftm@moov.mg; www.ftm.mg;* ⊕ *Mon–Fri 08.00–16.00*). They publish a series of 12 folded 1:500,000 maps, together covering Madagascar (17,000Ar each) as well as more detailed maps at 1:100,000 (16,000Ar each) and, for certain parts of the country, 1:50,000 (17,000Ar each). Typically about 80% of the maps are kept in stock; others can be printed to order with a few days' notice, but the cost is higher.

MONEY There are countless banks across Tana, most now with 24-hour ATMs that take either Visa or MasterCard. The majority open Monday to Friday from 08.00 till 16.00. The BFV at 20 Rue Ranarivelo [156 C2] opens Saturday morning; and the BFV at 33 Av de l'Indépendance [159 E3] stays open until 17.00 and is the only bank open all day Saturday. **Western Union** services are available at nearly all branches of BFV, BOA and post offices. The best exchange rates are to be found at the bureaux des changes such as SOCIMAD [158 C3] and NCH-Change [159 F6].

COMMUNICATIONS
Internet Almost all Tana's hotels and restaurants now have free Wi-Fi. If you need a cybercafé, the best option is **Teknet** [158 C6] (*32 Av Ramanantsoa, Isoraka;* ℡ *22 313 59; www.teknetstore.com*). There are good computers in the business centre upstairs at the **Colbert** [159 F6], but it's expensive. The **Outcool** bar [158 C4] has several computers plus additional sockets for laptops.

Post offices The main post offices are the one opposite the Colbert [159 F6] (☺ *Mon–Sat 07.00–15.00*), which has a philately kiosk where you can buy attractive stamps, and another opposite the Pavillons du Zoma [159 F4].

Couriers Colis Express is the option for sending parcels and documents nationally. Of a dozen offices in Tana the most central is at 11 Rue Ratianarivo [158 C4] (✆ 22 272 42). DHL is based in Ivandry (✆ *22 428 39*; m *034 42 177 52/034 42 177 77*; e *cs.mg@dhl. com*; ☺ *Mon–Fri 08.00–18.00, Sat 08.00–noon*). And the agent representing FedEx is a company called **InterEx**, with their office in Ankorondrano (✆ *22 321 16*).

TRANSPORT AND TRIP PLANNING
Airline offices

✈ **Air Austral** [159 E3] 23 Av de l'Indépendance; ✆ 22 303 31; e tananarive@air-austral.com

✈ **Air France** Tour Zital (5th floor), Rte des Hydrocarbures, Ankorondrano; ✆ 23 230 23/01/16; e mail.tana@airfrance.fr or mail.cto.tnr@airfrance. fr; ☺ Mon–Fri 08.30–17.00, Sat 08.30–12.30

✈ **Air Madagascar** [159 E3] 31 Av de l'Indépendance; ✆ 22 222 22/510 00; e commercial@airmadagascar.com; ☺ Mon–Fri 07.30–17.00, Sat 08.00–11.00

✈ **Air Madagascar** [156 B1] La City, Alarobia; m 034 02 222 10; ☺ Mon–Sat 09.00–19.00, Sun 09.00–13.00

✈ **Air Mauritius** [156 D1] Tana Water Front; m 032 05 620 36; e contact-mada@airmauritius.com

✈ **Corsair** [158 C1] 1 Av de l'Indépendance (railway station); ✆ 22 633 36/24 261 36; e corsairfly@corsairfly.mg; ☺ Mon–Fri 08.30–17.00, Sat 08.30–noon

✈ **Interair** [156 A4] Carlton Hotel; ✆ 22 224 06/52; e interair@moov.mg; ☺ Mon–Fri 08.00–17.00, Sat 08.30–12.30

✈ **Kenya Airways & Airlink** [158 C4] Rue des 77 Parlementaires Français; ✆ 22 359 90/22 457 33; m 032 05 359 90; e ovah@rogers-aviation. com; ☺ Mon–Fri 08.30–12.30 & 13.30–17.30, Sat 08.30–noon

✈ **Madagasikara Airways** La City, Alarobia; ✆ 22 493 69; [mob] 032 05 970 07; e ankoay@ madagasikaraairways.com

✈ **Madagasikara Airways** Zoom bldg, Ankorondrano; ✆ 22 236 12; m 032 05 970 03/034 05 970 03

✈ **Turkish Airlines** [158 D2] 22 Av de l'Indépendance; m 032 11 520 51/032 11 520 52; e contact@turkishairlines-madagascar.com; ☺ Mon–Fri 09.00–17.00, Sat 09.30–11.30

Vehicle hire

🚗 **Budget** [158 C2] 4 Av de l'Indépendance; ✆ 22 611 11; m 034 05 811 13/032 05 811 13; e budget@madauto.mg; www.budget.mg. Car, 4x4 & bus hire.

🚗 **Europcar** ✆ 23 336 47/23 273 33; e europcar@moov.mg; www.europcar.com/ location/madagascar. Online booking.

🚗 **IC Cars & Motos** m 034 07 254 96; e info@ iccars.mg; www.iccars.mg. Reliable vehicle hire & tours based nr airport.

🚗 **Just In Madagascar** m 032 07 532 19/032 77 316 84; e justinmadagascarcarrental@ gmail.com or justinmadagascar@gmail.com; ✱ justinmadagascar. Transfers & vehicle hire with English-speaking drivers. See ad, 3rd colour section.

🚗 **Mada3 Carent** m 033 08 298 67/034 46 433 96; e mada3_carent@yahoo.fr. 4x4 hire run by Zéphyrin Zanarison.

🚗 **Madagascar on Bike** ✆ 22 484 29; m 033 11 381 36; e manfred@madagascar-on-bike.com; www.madagascar-on-bike.com. German-owned motorbike hire & tours.

🚗 **Madagascar Visit Company** m 033 18 081 77/034 73 440 45; e lovasson@yahoo.fr; www. madagascar-visite.com. 4x4 hire & guided tours. See ad, page 113.

🚗 **Madauto** ✆ 23 254 54; ✱ Madauto – Madagascar Automobile. Renault, Nissan, Honda & Lada 4x4s.

🚗 **Océane Aventures** [158 C4] 22 Rue Ratianarivo; ✆ 22 312 10; e info@oceane-aventure.mg; www.oceane-aventures.com. Saloon, 4x4, minibus & bus hire.

🚗 **SICAM** [159 E4] 17 Rue Rabefiraisana; 📞22 229 61; e sicam@cfao.com. Hertz partner in Madagascar.

🚗 **Soa Car** 📞24 370 17; m 032 28 919 23/034 37 097 98; e soacar.location@gmail.com; www.soacar-madagascar.com. 4x4 & van hire.

🚗 **Tanalahorizon** e info@tanalahorizon.com; www.tanalahorizon.com. Tour operator with reliable vehicles & good rates.

🚗 **Tanyah Tours** 📞22 392 41; m 032 04 493 73; e contact@tanyah-tours.com; www.tanyah-tours.com. Minibus & 4x4 hire.

🚗 **Traces** 📞23 350 35; m 032 88 345 23; e traces.madagascar@gmail.com; www.traces-locationmoto-madagascar.com. Experienced motorbike hire operation inc guided off-road tours.

🚲 **MBike** m 034 05 912 90; e serviceclient. mbike@mbike.mg or mbike@mbike.mg; www.mbike.mg. They rent & sell bicycles & cycling gear; also provide bike maintenance, run bike-riding lessons, organise cycling events & have extensive information on biking routes around Tana.

Local fixers, guides and drivers A local guide or fixer can take a lot of hassle out of planning an independent trip. Here are some, mainly recommended by readers.

Dyna Rasolomananarivo
www.dynamadagascar-guide-tour.com; 🔲 dyna.rasolomananarivo. Experienced & reliable driver-guide.

Elian Andriamanantena m 032 29 099 43; e madagascarguide@yahoo.com. Exuberant & knowledgeable guide for history around Tana.

Hasina Rasolofonjatovo e hasina505@yahoo.fr. English-speaking driver & fixer.

Jeannie Claudia Randrianasolo m 033 11 500 17/034 01 221 33; e rjeannieclaudia@yahoo.fr. English-speaking guide with good knowledge of the city's history & architecture.

Liva m 032 07 551 46; e heriliva@freenet.mg or aheriliva@gmail.com. English-speaking guide & driver.

Marius m 032 04 600 09; e rama7466@hotmail.fr. Reliable driver.

Ony Rakotoarivelo m 033 11 872 86/034 01 188 17; e onyrakoto19@gmail.com. Very enthusiastic guide & trip-planner based in the Ivato airport area; she speaks excellent English. See also page i.

Patrick Randrianarison e patrickrandrianarison@ymail.com. Reliable driver-guide.

Solofonirina Pierrot Randriamampionona 📞22 697 27; m 032 40 699 66; e gasikaraviaggi@moov.mg. Organises tours.

Thierry m 032 07 560 96; e larissarakotondrahanta@yahoo.fr. English-speaking driver with 4x4.

MEDICAL ASSISTANCE If you need medical care, here are some clinics and dentists you can contact for help. Tana has hundreds of pharmacies but many carry only limited products; a few of the best-stocked ones are listed below. To find the current out-of-hours pharmacy rota, check local TV, newspapers or look online at www.moov.mg/pharmacie.php.

➕ **Assistance+** m 032 07 801 10; e commercial@assistanceplus.mg; www.assistanceplus.mg. Medical assistance & 24hr emergency evacuations.

➕ **Espace Medical** [156 D4] Ambodivona; 📞22 625 66; m 034 02 009 11; e esmed@moov.mg; www.espacemedical.mg. Complete medical service inc 24hr emergency clinic, X-ray, home/hotel visits, ambulance & air evacuation.

➕ **Médical Plus** Ankaditoho; 📞22 567 58; m 032 04 602 05. 24hr home/hotel visits & ambulance service.

➕ **Polyclinique d'Ilafy** 📞22 425 66/69/73; m 032 02 088 16. Modern facilities & equipment, ambulance service & 24hr emergency clinic.

➕ **Jean-Marc Chapuis (dentist)** 13 Av de l'Indépendance; 📞22 208 88

➕ **Leontine Ramambazafy Ralainony (dentist)** 6 Rue de Russie; 📞22 263 32

➕ **Monica Hajay (dentist)** 9 Rue la Réunion; 📞22 358 70

➕ **Pharmacie de la Croix du Sud** [158 D2] 9 Av de l'Indépendance; 📞22 220 59

+ Pharmacie Isoraka [158 C6] Av Ramanantsoa; ☎ 22 285 04
+ Pharmacie Métropole [159 F6] 7 Rue Ratsimilaho; ☎ 22 200 25; e metropole@metropole.mg; www.pharmacie-metropole.com

+ Pharmacie Principale Ankorondrano (opposite Digital Bldg); ☎ 22 533 93

EMBASSIES For guidance on circumstances under which your embassy can and cannot assist you, see the box on page 126.

● Canada (Honorary Consul) Fitaratra Bldg, Ankorondrano; ☎ 22 397 37/35 (or +27 12 422 3000 for out-of-hours emergencies); e consulatcanada.madagascar@gmail.com
● EU (Delegation) Tour Zital (9th floor), Ankorondrano; ☎ 22 242 16; e delegation-madagascar@eeas.europa.eu
● France [158 D4] 3 Rue Jaures; ☎ 22 398 98 (or 22 399 16 for out-of-hours emergencies); e ambatana@moov.mg; www.ambafrance-mada.org
● Germany [156 D3] 101 Rue Rabeony; ☎ 22 238 02/03 (or +255 786 971 692 for out-of-hours emergencies); e info@antananarivo.diplo.de; www.antananarivo.diplo.de

● South Africa Rue Ravoninahitriniarivo, Ankorondrano; ☎ 22 433 50/494 82; e antananarivo.admin@foreign.gov.za
● Switzerland [158 C4] Aro Bldg, Rue des 77 Parlementaires Français; ☎ 22 629 97/98 (or +41 800 24 7 365 for out-of-hours emergencies); e ant.vertretung@eda.admin.ch; www.eda.admin.ch/antananarivo
● UK Tour Zital (9th floor), Ankorondrano; ☎ 22 330 53/356 27; e BEAntananarivo@moov.mg; www.gov.uk/government/world/madagascar. See also page 126.
● USA [150 C5] Pt PACOM; ☎ 23 480 00; m 034 49 328 54 (emergencies); e antwarden@state.gov; www.antananarivo.usembassy.gov

TOURIST INFORMATION The regional tourist office, **Ortana**, sometimes runs weekend walks and excursions. Check with them for details; they have a smart new office in Jardin Antaninarenina where you can find leaflets about many places to visit [159 E5] (☎ 22 270 51; m 032 02 270 51/032 20 270 51/034 20 270 51; e info@ortana.mg; www.tourisme-antananarivo.com; ⊕ daily 09.00–17.00).

A second Ortana information centre is at Jardin d'Andohalo [156 D5] south of the city centre, where you will also find the office of **EcoTanana**, a collective of guides, guesthouses and craftsmen supporting ecotourism in Tana (m 034 01 085 59/032 71 472 65; e ecotanana@ecotanana.net; www.ecotanana.net).

For information on trips further afield visit **ONTM**, the national tourist office, which has an information kiosk at the airport [150 C1] and an office in Antsahavola (☎ 22 661 15; e ontm@ontm.mg; www.madagascar-tourisme.com; ⊕ Mon–Fri 9.30–16.30, Sat 09.10–19.00).

In addition to the places listed below, see pages 153–4 for things to do in the Ivato airport area.

WHAT TO SEE AND DO
Rova Manjakamiadana [156 D6] (⊕ Tue–Sun 09.00–17.00, Mon closed; entry 10,000Ar) The queen's palace, or *rova*, the spiritual centre of the Merina people, dominates the skyline of Antananarivo. It was destroyed by fire in 1995, leaving only the partially collapsed stone shell – an act of arson unprecedented in Madagascar's history.

From 2005, the palace was closed for seven years for a massive US$20 million renovation project, mainly funded by UNESCO who hoped to declare it a World Heritage Site upon completion. The 70,000 granite stones (of which 20,000 were cracked by the heat of the fire) were removed one by one, numbered and catalogued.

FATHER PEDRO: MADAGASCAR'S ANSWER TO MOTHER THERESA

Marko Petrovic

Mompera ('Father') Pedro Opeka is perhaps Tana's most famous foreign resident. A charismatic, Moses-like figure, complete with bushy white beard, he is a Vincentian missionary priest, born in Argentina to Slovenian parents. In the past 20 years, he and his helpers have led over 25,000 people – many of whom used to scavenge for a living on a landfill site – to newly built estates with schools, health care and employment. A further quarter of a million of the city's poorest residents have received medical and other help from his association, Akamasoa ('good friends'). The Malagasy, especially in Tana, have taken Father Pedro for their own; some have even suggested he should be president!

If you find yourself in Tana on a Sunday, no matter if you are a believer or not, it is well worth attending morning Mass at 08.00 in the Akamasoa sports hall. The vibrant and very musical congregation numbers several thousand. Most taxi drivers know the place: at the village of Manantenasoa on the eastern outskirts of the city. It is an interesting experience to take a walk through the very orderly Akamasoa villages with their typical red-brick houses. On the ridge above, which has good views over Tana, you can visit the quarry and watch the people working. A couple of kilometres further along the RN2 is the equally orderly village of Andralanitra, where Father Pedro lives, alongside the landfill site on which hundreds once scavenged.

Find out more at www.perepedro.com.

Modern foundations were constructed from some two dozen cement piles driven 23m into the ground. The stones were then painstakingly reassembled, with expert stonemasons creating replicas of those that had been damaged, and a new slate roof constructed to the original design.

The next stage was to rebuild the wooden interior and fit it out as a museum. Unfortunately, following the 2009 coup, the project ran into funding difficulties and work stalled. The grounds of the rova were eventually reopened to the public in 2012, once it became clear that renovations would not resume anytime soon, but it is not possible to go inside the palace. Nevertheless, owing to the open nature of the external structure much of the interior can be seen from outside – and you can go into the royal chapel and reconstructed king's house, as well as see the royal tombs and royal bath. In any case, a visit is worthwhile for the near-360° views across Tana alone. Allow at least an hour for a guided tour of the compound.

Prime Minister's Palace (Palais d'Andafiavaratra) [156 D6] This former residence of Rainilaiarivony (he who married three queens; see page 7) houses a museum of the few hundred precious items that were saved from the rova fire – mostly gifts from foreign dignitaries (including Queen Victoria). It was built in 1872 by the British architect William Pool. After independence it became in turn an army barracks, law courts, a school of fine arts, the presidential palace and (again) the prime minister's palace. It was damaged by fire in 1975, then restored, but has since fallen into disrepair once more; the badly leaking roof is currently causing untold damage to the wood-panelled interior.

Owing to its decaying condition, and the theft of a royal crown, the palace was closed to the public in 2012. But that doesn't stop rova guides sometimes offering to take visitors inside anyway, as the guards will open it up for a small fee if their boss isn't around. (It's not difficult to see how the crown might have gone missing!)

Tsarasaotra Park (Lake Alarobia) (e *tsarasaotra@boogiepilgrim-madagascar. com; entry Mon–Fri 10,000Ar, Sat/Sun 12,000Ar*) This tranquil paradise of trees and birds is just 4km north of the city centre. Dominated by its lake, the 66ha park is a classified Ramsar site in recognition of its importance as a wetland habitat. A total of 27 waterbird species and 36 other birds have been recorded there, including several herons, egrets and teals. Early-morning visits are best for birdwatching. A variety of chameleons are found here too. Near the main lake an information centre has field guides for visitors' use. And tree climbing can be arranged too. The park is run by tour operator Boogie Pilgrim (see page 88) from whose office tickets must be obtained in advance, as the park is not generally open for unannounced arrivals.

Tsimbazaza Zoo [156 C7] (⏱ *daily 09.00–17.00; entry 10,000Ar*) This once-impressive botanical garden, zoo and museum has sadly deteriorated significantly. The museum and most of the lemur houses are permanently closed, including the day-to-night aye-aye enclosure that was once a big attraction. The botanical garden is spacious and well laid out but the cages of miserable animals are inadequately labelled and poorly maintained, and we have had reports from several readers of shocking behaviour by the guides. It is still very popular with local school trips and picnicking families who come chiefly to marvel at the ostriches and camels – two of the only non-native species in captivity here.

Akany Avoko Faravohitra [156 D4] (e *contact.avoko@gmail.com; www. avokofaravohitra.com*) A visit to this care home for vulnerable girls – not to be confused with the similarly named Akany Avoko in Ambohidratrimo – is invariably inspiring. Contact them in advance to arrange a tour. They would be grateful for your donations of money, medicines, clothing or other supplies. For more details, see page 137.

Centre Fihavanana [156 C5] (✆ *22 271 59/22 299 81;* m *034 13 459 91;* e *bpfihavanana@blueline.mg*) Run by the Sisters of the Good Shepherd, Centre Fihavanana (meaning 'solidarity') helps the most disadvantaged in society, including undernourished babies, destitute mothers, children from poor families, and women and youngsters in prison (see page 138 for more on the work they do). A visit to this heart-warming centre is highly recommended but do notify them in advance to arrange a convenient time for a tour. Sited near Mahamasina Stadium, it is set back from the road, just to the right of St Joseph's church. The women here work to a very high standard, producing beautiful embroidery and greeting cards. Judith Cadigan writes: 'We are so glad you suggested visiting the Sœurs du Bon Pasteur. We bought lots of embroidered linens and were shown around the school, shook hands with what felt like most of the 300 children, were serenaded by one of the classes, and were altogether greatly impressed by what the nuns are doing. We took along unused antibiotics and they were glad to have them.'

Tana Kitchen (*Alarobia-Amboniloha;* m *032 05 145 00;* e *mp@michaela-pawliczek.de*) Tana Kitchen offers a hands-on cultural cooking experience. Guests are welcomed into a beautiful Malagasy townhouse, where they spend 2–3 hours cooking a typical three-course Malagasy meal under the guidance of an experienced local chef. Only fresh food and traditional utensils are used, and there

is the option of going along to the nearby market beforehand to help choose the ingredients. Malagasy drinks and an aperitif are included, and participants each receive a souvenir recipe booklet. There is a minimum booking of two people and much larger groups can be accommodated, but you should book at least two days in advance.

Museums The **Museum of Art and Archaeology** [158 C6] (*17 Rue Dr Villette;* ☎ *24 221 65;* e *musedar@gmail.com;* ⊕ *Tue–Sat 09.30–17.00, Mon/Sun closed*) was established in 1970 by the city's university and houses some 7,000 artefacts of artistic, archaeological and ethnographic interest from across the island. All regions and ethnic groups are represented among the objects, which include items once used by sorcerers, old musical instruments and *aloalo* funerary sculptures.

A little **Pirate Museum** [158 A4] (*103 Rue de Liège;* ☎ *22 625 27;* e *piratenmuseum. madagaskar@gmail.com; www.piratenmuseum.ch;* ⊕ *Mon–Fri 08.00–17.00, Sat/ Sun by appointment*) run by Swiss tour operator PRIORI (see page 90) tells the fascinating stories of the ancient pirates of Madagascar, including William Kidd and Blackbeard, the legendary Libertalia republic, and pirate activity on Ile Sainte Marie. There is an accompanying guide booklet (in German but an English version is in the pipeline).

A charming city museum called **Antananarivo Fahiny** or **Tana d'Autrefois** ('Tana of yesteryear') opened in 2011 in the Ambohipo district (☎ *22 334 71;* e *tranovola@ moov.mg*). The historical artefacts on display are accompanied by explanatory panels charting the city's history through the 11 sovereigns who ruled the sacred hills of Imerina from 1610. Exhibits include engravings, vintage photographs, period paintings, newspapers and books, musical instruments, jewellery and models.

At Tana Water Front [156 D1] is **Le Petit** – and *petit* it certainly is – **Musée de Pierre** ('little museum of stones'), located in a hut on stilts in the lake (m *033 11 037 11/032 04 600 34/032 46 411 85;* ⊕ *Wed–Sat 10.00–16.30*). Despite its small size, some 500 Malagasy rocks, minerals and fossils are on show.

DAY EXCURSIONS FROM TANA

LEMURS PARK (m *033 11 252 59;* e *lemurspark@moov.mg; www.lemurspark.com;* ⊕ *09.00–17.00; entry 30,000Ar, or 25,000Ar for groups of 3 or more*) This free-range 'zoo' makes a good day trip, particularly for those on a quick visit who are not able to see lemurs in the wild. Bordered by the dramatic River Katsaoka, the 5ha park is divided into areas planted with endemic flora of Madagascar's different climate zones. Nine species of lemur live free; many are confiscated pets, and this is the first step towards rehabilitation. Feeding times are 10.00, noon, 14.00 and 16.00. A few nocturnal species are kept in rather small cages. The park is 22km west of Tana on RN1, clearly signposted on the right-hand side.

THE TWELVE SACRED HILLS OF IMERINA In the 1620s King Andrianjaka, so it is said, declared 12 hills around Tana to be sacred because of their historical, political or spiritual significance. Nearly two centuries later, King Andrianampoinimerina also designated 12 sacred hills, albeit a somewhat different list from his predecessor. So nowadays the 'twelve' hills in fact number more than 12 but the label persists, probably because of the significance of the number in Malagasy cosmology. Many of the hills are touristic sites, including Ambohidratrimo – covered on page 154 – and the four described below. The easiest way to visit them is to enlist the help of an independent local guide (see page 173 or visit the Ortana tourist office).

Ambohimanga (⊕ *daily 09.00–16.30;* m *034 71 109 67; www.ambohimanga-rova. com; entry 10,000Ar*) This is by far the most famous of the sacred hills, declared a UNESCO World Heritage Site in 2001. Lying 23km north of Tana, Ambohimanga ('blue hill') was long forbidden to Europeans. From here began the line of kings and queens who were to unite Madagascar into one country, and it was here that they returned for rest and relaxation among the forested slopes of this hilltop village.

Ambohimanga has 16 gates, though most are all but lost among the thick vegetation. By the main entrance is an enormous stone disc which was formerly rolled in front of the gateway each night. Inside the compound, the centrepiece is the wooden house of the great king Andrianampoinimerina, who reigned from 1787 to 1810. It is surrounded by a series of elegant royal summer houses, which have been renovated and provide a fascinating glimpse of the strong British influence during those times, with very European décor and several gifts sent to the monarchs by Queen Victoria. French influence is evident too: there are two cannons forged in Jean Laborde's Mantasoa iron foundry.

Nearby is a mundane-looking concrete pool (the concrete is a recent addition) which was used by the queens for ritual bathing and had to be filled, so they say, by 70 virgins. From a high point above the bath you can get a superb view of the hauts plateaux and Tana in the distance, and on an adjacent hill the white mausoleum of the king's *ombiasy* (witch doctor).

Ambohimanga makes an easy day trip from Tana; in light traffic the journey takes about 30 minutes by taxi or 50 minutes by taxi-brousse. Food and accommodation can be found in the area at **Relais du Rova** (*www.relaisdurova.com;* €€€), **Banana Rova** which serves organic food and has a small botanical garden (m *032 56 442 90/033 14 882 72;* e *bananarova@hotmail.fr;* €€€), **Chez Haga** (e *michele.rakotoson@ voila.fr;* €€€) and **Vohitra Paradisa** (m *034 01 807 78/034 02 155 62;* €€€).

Ilafy (⊕ *Tue–Sun 09.00–noon & 14.00–17.00, Mon closed; entry 3,000Ar*) Some 8km north of the city is the hilltop rova of Ilafy. This modest two-storey wooden vacation palace, built for King Radama II, now houses a museum of historical artefacts and Malagasy ethnography. There is an array of wooden carvings from traditional Zafimaniry windows to erotic sculptures, model houses showing the different building techniques in use across the island, and an unusual display of tribal hairstyles. Radama II's tomb is located on the hill, although his body was disinterred and moved to the rova in central Tana in 1897. Ilafy is also the site where Madagascar's first arms were manufactured by Jean Laborde in 1833. The site is on the way to Ambohimanga, so the two can easily be combined into a single day trip. The area is a good starting point for hikes through the Avaradrano region.

Ambohidrabiby This sacred hill was the capital of King Ralambo, who ruled the area from 1575 for 35 years. Both he and Rabidy, his astrologer father-in-law for whom the hill is named, are buried here. The rova itself has not been well maintained but there is a simple museum room with paintings depicting scenes from history; you can also see the large iron cauldron originally used by Jean Laborde to make gunpowder at Ilafy, and which was brought here in 1857.

Situated some 22km northeast of Tana, this is a rural area well known for **silk production**. Other nearby attractions include the **cave of Ambodifahitra** and many good paths for hiking.

Antsahadinta Once a local seat of power, this sacred hill 17km south of Tana is considered particularly significant. Here you will find another small historical and ethnological museum as well as several well-preserved wooden houses, one of the schools built by the missionary James Cameron, and a number of important royal tombs that date back more than 700 years. From the picnic area you can enjoy panoramic views and observe rural daily life.

OVERNIGHT EXCURSIONS

For wildlife lovers, the most popular overnight excursion from Tana is to Andasibe-Mantadia National Park, which is covered in *Chapter 10*, pages 273–80. Some other options are listed below.

ANJOZOROBE (*Entry 10,000Ar plus 10,000–20,000Ar per circuit*) This fantastic reserve managed by the NGO FANAMBY is some 90km northeast of Tana, reached via RN3 in 3 hours or so. The Anjozorobe–Angavo Forest Corridor, one of the last vestiges of dense forest in the central plateau of Madagascar, was established as a protected area in 2005. It covers an area of 52,200ha and stretches for over 80km. A total of 11 species of lemur are found here including indri and diademed sifaka. It is also rich in birdlife with more than 80 species observed, a similar number of amphibians and reptiles, more than 25 small mammals, and 550 types of plants including 75 orchids. The reserve itself has half a dozen hiking trails ranging in length from 1 hour to a full day. Nocturnal lemurs and chameleons can be seen on a night walk. On a community-focused circuit you can meet local villagers and participate in tree planting as part of a local sustainable development project.

There is good accommodation here at **Saha Forest Camp** (m *032 07 843 44/033 37 395 02/034 02 351 66;* e *resa@sahaforestcamp.mg; www.sahaforestcamp.mg;* €€€€– €€€€€), which has ten elegant bungalows nestled among the trees, each with en-suite facilities, hot water and balconies opening right on to the forest. The staff and restaurant are also regularly praised by readers.

AMBOHITANTELY SPECIAL RESERVE (m *033 01 958 04/032 45 457 10*) This reserve, 140km (*3hrs*) north of Tana, covers 5,600ha including 1,800ha of natural forest. It is of particular interest to botanists, being known especially for its palms – including the imposing *Dypsis decipiens* – but in addition three lemur species, nearly 70 birds, 17 reptiles and 17 amphibians have been recorded here. There is a choice of six circuits, for which the guiding fees are 3,000Ar for up to 2 hours or 5,000Ar for longer walks. Three campsites (*2,000Ar/night*) in the reserve each have toilet and shower facilities, and tents are available for hire. Note that it can get cold from May to October. To get there, take RN4 to PK 125 then turn right along a 15km access road to reach the park office, where permits can be bought and a guide allocated. For permit prices, see page 73.

MANTASOA (*www.mantasoa.com*) Some 65km east of Tana is Mantasoa, on the western shore of a large artificial lake, where in the 19th century Madagascar had its first taste of industrialisation. Indeed, industrial output was greater then than at any time during the colonial period. Thanks to Jean Laborde a whole range of industries were started, including an iron foundry which enabled Madagascar to become more or less self-sufficient in weaponry, thereby increasing the power of central government. Laborde was soon highly influential at court and he built a country residence for the queen at Mantasoa.

Many of the buildings remain. Laborde's house has been restored and is now a very interesting museum (⊕ *Mon–Sat 08.00–16.00*) set in a lovely garden.

Alongside the school playing field is a chimney, once part of the china factory. The cannon factory still stands and the large furnace of the foundry remains. All are signposted and fascinating to see; you can just imagine the effort that was required to build them. Laborde's tomb is in the cemetery outside the village.

Mantasoa can be reached by direct taxi-brousse from Tana in under 3 hours. With your own transport, turn off RN2 near PK 47 (or alternatively PK 59) and head south about 10km. At the northern end of the lake, you pass a caviar farm, set up in 2013 and expected to be exporting four tonnes annually by 2017. Local restaurants benefit from the by-product of male sturgeon.

Where to stay and eat The village and its attractions are quite spread out, but it is a pleasant area for walking – or taking relaxing boat trips on Lake Mantasoa. A day trip to Mantasoa is rewarding but it is better to stay a day or two; there are a few places to stay:

Albert & Lily (Refuge Suisse) (3 rooms) 42 660 69; m 034 04 846 74/034 44 077 00; e albelil@yahoo.fr; www.chez-albert-et-lily.com. Little guesthouse with its own restaurant (closed Wed) & bakery. HB/FB. €€€€

Domaine de l'Ermitage (32 rooms) 42 660 54; m 034 04 960 64; e ermitagehotel@ moov.mg; www.ermitagehotel-mg.com. Country club with old-fashioned atmosphere & recreational activities inc horse-riding, tennis, boating & forest walks. Rooms have safe, sat-TV, Wi-Fi & bathroom with bath. €€€€

Mantasoa Lodge (Riverside) (12 bungalows) m 034 10 087 23/034 89 246 68; e mantasoalodge@gmail.com; www. mantasoalodge.com. Fully renovated in 2012. Smart rooms in a resort-style hotel in a fantastic lakeside spot. Wi-Fi for a small fee. Bar & restaurant. Quads, bikes, tennis, massage, pedalos & heated pool. €€€€

Chalet (8 bungalows) 42 660 95; m 032 59 397 13/034 61 398 20; e lechaletmantasoa@ gmail.com. Swiss-owned with a lovely little restaurant & quaint chalets. Originally built in 1962 by a woman whose son & grandson now run it. €€€

Mantasoa Tour (2 bungalows) m 032 12 600 00/034 15 005 92; e contact@mantasoa-tour. com; www.mantasoa-tour.com. Towards the northern end of the lake, this leisure & boating centre also has cottages & a restaurant. Activities on offer: wakeboarding, jetboating, quad biking, kayaking, jet-skiing, paintballing, tubing, fishing, rowing; also vehicle hire. €€€

Domaine de mes As (Chez Edena) (11 rooms & 7 bungalows) m 034 66 797 65; e domainedemesas@gmail.com. Various categories of room, all en suite & mostly with sat-TV. Also a 14-bed dorm. Restaurant with Malagasy/Indian dishes & Wi-Fi. Pool & gym. €€–€€€

FMMB (Bible Study Society) (3 rooms & 3 bungalows) 24 809 92 (Tana office); e flambeaullb@gmail.com. Scripture union with private rooms & very cheap dorms that must be booked well in advance via the office in Tana. €–€€€

NOSY SOA PARK (22 318 51; m 034 15 597 21; e contact@nosy-soa-park.com; www. nosy-soa-park.com; ⊕ 09.30–17.00) On an island called Nosy Soa, this small private zoo includes free-ranging lemurs, tortoises, parrots, snakes, chameleons and frogs.

TSIAZOMPANIRY COMMUNITY ECOTOURISM SITE (m 033 13 670 44/033 71 613 39; e ass.tsarafara@yahoo.fr) If Mantasoa sounds too developed for your taste, this community ecotourism project run by Association Tsarafara might be for you. It is based at another artificial lake some 25km south of Mantasoa, and 53km southeast of Tana as the crow flies (85km/5hrs by poor road). Located between the two forest corridors of Fandriana–Vondrozo and Anjozorobe–Angavo, the aim is to promote local biodiversity. There are basic community-managed bungalows (or you can camp) and cooked meals can be arranged. Activities include walking circuits, boat trips, swimming, fishing and visiting an archaeological site.

AMPEFY AND THE LAKE ITASY AREA Within 3 hours' drive of the capital, this beautiful region offers much of interest as well as a chance to relax. Going west from Tana on RN1 you will reach **Analavory** after 124km. Turn left and 11km further on you will find the small town of **Ampefy**, where there are several hotels, including some very comfortable ones. East of the town is the 9km-wide **Lake Itasy**, offering the chance to indulge in watersports or simply stroll in the surrounding countryside and enjoy the scenery. A large waterfall, **Chute de la Lily**, is 7km north of Ampefy: turn left along the river before crossing it, then continue till you reach the falls. There is a second large waterfall about 20 minutes downstream. The landscape here is geologically interesting with hexagonal basalt columns.

Another sight not to be missed is the **Geysers of Andranomandraotra**. Head 4km west from Analavory, then at the sign turn right and continue 8km on a dirt road. Taxi-brousses go this far. You must pay a small fee to pass this point, from where it is a mere 1.2km walk. The colourful clay formations created by the geysers are most surreal.

 Where to stay and eat

Eucalyptus (26 rooms) m 033 05 960 73/034 06 718 33; e eucalyptusampefy@gmail. com; www.eucalyptus-hotel.com. Smart hotel with spacious en-suite rooms that have sat-TV, safe, lounge area & private terrace. Set in a wooded area on the shores of Lake Mahitrondro. Swimming pool, kids' play area & good food. €€€€

Ampefy Lodge (4 rooms & 2 bungalows) m 033 09 382 09/034 04 432 01/034 04 452 01/034 07 465 00; e ampefylodge@gmail.com; www. ampefy-lodge.com. En-suite rooms & homely bungalows with kitchenette, lounge & sat-TV. €€€

Belle Vue (8 bungalows) m 033 11 599 07/034 06 118 21; e contact@auberge-belle-vue.com; www.auberge-belle-vue.com. Smart, modern bungalows in an attractive garden. Wi-Fi. Restaurant with interesting menu. €€€

Chaumière (3 rooms & 8 bungalows) m 032 41 958 34/034 13 402 18; e lachaumieredeitasy@orange.mg. Malagasy-French owned. Tranquil spot with a smart row of bungalows looking out over rice paddies & lake. Great starting point for walks & they have pirogues for trips on the lake. €€€

Kavitaha (14 rooms & 7 bungalows) Ampefy; m 032 81 803 01/033 67 894 56/034 10 459 70; e kavitaha.ampefy@gmail.com; www. hotelkavitaha.net. Named after a village that, legend has it, was swallowed by the lake after a volcanic eruption. Rooms have private facilities & hot water. Good restaurant. Activities inc pedalos,

kayaks, pirogues, ping-pong & fishing. Ideal for families. €€€

Lengilo (10 rooms & 5 bungalows) Itasy; m 033 11 007 17; e simonix@moov.mg. En-suite accommodation & restaurant at PK 99 on RN1, 25km before Analavory. Swimming pool. €€€

Quatre Vents (Faka Ranch) m 032 07 039 04/033 08 765 68/034 02 039 04; e fedrova@ gmail.com; www.cheval-madagascar.com. This horse-riding centre has rooms. Also bike, scooter & pedalo hire. €€€

Relais de la Vierge (6 rooms & 9 bungalows) Ilot Boisé Antanimarina, Ampefy (on the way to Soavinandriana); m 034 09 701 80/034 12 519 82/034 36 917 12; e welmantjessica@ yahoo.fr; f relaisdelavierge. En-suite rooms with hot showers. Swimming pool, children's play area & good lakefront restaurant. €€€

Terrasse (10 bungalows) Ampefy; m 032 07 167 80/034 16 937 16; e laterrasse.ampefy@ moov.mg; www.ampefy.com. Simple en-suite bungalows in a garden & on the lake shore. Activities range from hiking & cycling to fishing, pedalos & river-rafting. €€€

Akany Sambatra (8 rooms & 3 bungalows) m 034 10 373 53/034 16 651 34. Various sizes of room, all en suite with hot water, and some with sat-TV. €€–€€€

Tango (7 rooms) Ampefy; m 034 72 371 98. Rather dingy & basic but cheap. No restaurant. €€–€€€

🏠 **Loharanosoa (Chez Jacky)** (2 rooms & 5 bungalows) Antanimarina; m 032 77 267 45/034 16 960 30; e aubergechezjacky@yahoo.fr. Simple affordable rooms with private facilities & lovely lakeside restaurant. Bikes & fishing. €€

🏠 **Petit Manoir Rouge** (5 rooms) m 032 05 260 96; www.manoirrouge.com. New in 2016, very affordable accommodation run by affable Frenchman who moved here after selling up his hotel of 17 years in Tana. Kitchen for clients' use. Electric-assist mountain bikes (*www.vtt.mg*). €€

TSIROANOMANDIDY Lying 222km to the west of Tana, on a surfaced road (4hrs), this town is a pleasant place to spend a day or two. Its main attraction is the large **cattle market** on Wednesdays and Thursdays. The Bara people of the south drive huge herds through the Bongolava Plateau to sell at the market.

There are a few hotels: **Bongolava** (m *033 23 997 10/034 51 131 93*), **Président** (m *033 02 971 76/034 13 607 77;* e *entreprisevonjy@gmail.com*), **Chez Marcelline** and **Manambolo**.

CARLTON
MADAGASCAR

PROBABLY
one of **THE MOST BEAUTIFUL STOPOVERS** in **MADAGASCAR**

pixa

171 ROOMS & SUITES, RESTAURANTS CAFÉ CHARLY, BISTROT, OASIS DE TANA, SWIMMING POOL, TENNIS COURT, BAKERY-PASTRY-ICE CREAM MAKER L'ÉCLAIR, CASINO, BEAUTY SALON, LOUNGE BAR KUDETA, BANK, ATM, SHOPPING ARCADE, RENT A CAR BUDGET, TRAVEL AGENCY, PRESSING, CONFERENCE ROOMS, EVENTS, CATERING, 205 SECURED PARKING SPACES, WI-FI

Feel like home

CARLTON
★★★★
MADAGASCAR

SUSIE'S PLACE

Villa Cigale Land
Ambodirano, Ivato

+261 34 53 106 04

@ info@susiesplacebb.com

🌐 www.susiesplacebb.com

Feel at home away from home ▪ 10 minutes from the airport

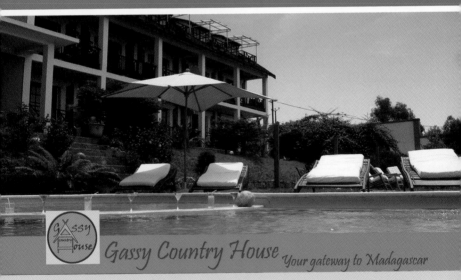

Gassy Country House *Your gateway to Madagascar*

10 junior suites with AC, free fast fiberoptic Wi-Fi, minibar, satTV
12 day rooms with ensuite bathroom

Conference room, restaurant, bar, massage, transfer, car rental, excursions
3 minutes from Ivato Antananarivo International Airport

tel: +261 (0) 20 22 489 63
mobile:+261 (0) 34 07 144 64 / +261 (0) 33 07 144 64
info@gassycountryhouse.mg / www.gassycountryhouse.mg

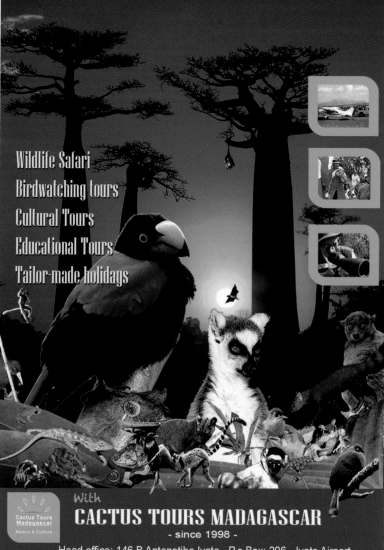

Travel
MADAGASCAR
at your own pace

- Wildlife Safari
- Birdwatching tours
- Cultural Tours
- Educational Tours
- Tailor-made holidays

With
CACTUS TOURS MADAGASCAR
- since 1998 -

Head office: 146 B Antanetibe Ivato - P.o Box: 206 - Ivato Airport
105 - Antananarivo, Madagascar
Tel: +261 20 22 018 25 / +261 34 15 057 57 Fax: +261 20 22 019 02
info@cactus-madagascar.com
www.cactus-madagascar.com

above & right Zebu cattle are near-sacred in Malagasy society; a symbol of wealth, they are generally sacrificed and eaten only on special occasions (LJ and DA) page 215

below Rice is a national obsession: the Malagasy eat more of it per capita than anyone else (DA) page 195

above   *Pachypodium*, Isalo National Park
(DA) page 37

left   The octopus tree's waving arms are
characteristic of the spiny forest
(DA) page 38

below   Despite their dramatically different
appearance, the stunted baobabs near
Andavadoaka are the same species as those
in the Avenue des Baobabs (DA) pages 42–4

above   Madagascar's thousand-plus orchid species include this epiphytic *Aerangis ellisii* (DA) pages 38–9

right   Two species of pitcher are among the insect-eating plants of Madagascar (DA) page 36

below   The Madagascar rosy periwinkle is used in the manufacture of leukaemia drugs (MS) page 44

above left   Based around a saline lake, Tsimanampetsotsa National Park protects important wetland and spiny forest habitat (DA) pages 245–6

above right   Serious hikers will find Andringitra National Park rewarding (DA) pages 213–14

left   Isalo National Park's natural swimming pool is popular with visitors hot from walking in the sun (DA) page 221

below   Red *tsingy* formations result from rain erosion on iron-rich laterite (DA) pages 66–7

above Houses alongside the Pangalanes Canal (DA)

below left A traditional highland village set amongst rice paddies (DA)

below right The *rova* palace was first built in 1839 for Queen Ranavalona I, with the stone superstructure being added by her successor 28 years later (DA) pages 174–5

bottom left The most famous of the 16 gates at Ambohimanga, a sacred site that was Madagascar's capital until 1793 (DA) page 178

above   During a *famadihana* (bone-turning) ceremony, the bodies of the ancestors are removed from the tomb and wrapped in fresh shrouds (HB) pages 15–18

left   There is a sad tale of tomb-raiding behind this carving adorning the burial place of Ranonda (HB) page 253

below   These bones at a tomb in western Madagascar are said to belong to Vazimba tribesmen (DA) page 27

above	Zebu horns and sculpted funerary poles known as *aloalo* adorn the tombs of southern Madagascar (DA) page 19
above right	*Aloalo* may be topped with all kinds of surprising carved scenes (DA)
right	Whether or not it was the cause of his demise is not clear but it appears that the occupant of this tomb had a run-in with a crocodile (DA)
below	Mahafaly tombs are typically decorated with elaborate paintings of scenes from the life of the deceased (DA) page 19

Every visitor returns home with fond memories of the welcoming people of Madagascar; interactions with the locals – especially the kids – can turn out to be the highlight of a trip (DA and PN) pages 131–44

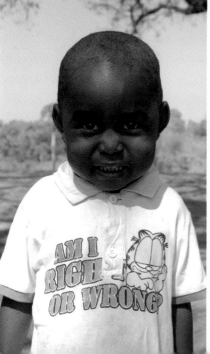

top   There are many ways to experience Madagascar, from tailor-made trips to independent backpacking. Escorted small-group tours are a great way to get the most from your visit (DA) pages 75–7

above   You can find some extraordinarily good fayre sometimes in the unlikeliest of places, such as this duck dish served at the exceptional Mad Zebu restaurant in Belo-sur-Tsiribihina (DA) page 420

left   Nowadays there is accommodation to suit every budget, including several luxurious lodges (DA) pages 102–4

8

The Highlands South of Tana

Many visitors drive the full length of Route Nationale 7 (RN7) to Toliara, either by hired car or public transport. This chapter covers the first half: from the capital through the highlands and descending to Ihosy. (The second half – the rest of the way to Toliara – is covered in the following chapter.) It is a delightful journey, providing an excellent overview of the *hauts plateaux* and Merina and Betsileo culture, as well as spectacular scenery, especially around Fianarantsoa.

The appeal of the RN7 route (apart from the fact it's mostly a good surfaced road) is the frequency and diversity of attractions and side excursions spread along its length, allowing the visitor to pack lots of different experiences into a short vacation with relatively little time spent travelling in-between. Driving nonstop in a 4x4, the 926km from Tana to Toliara takes around 17 hours, but there is enough to see and do *en route* to spend one, two or even several weeks taking it bit by bit. Beaches near to Toliara offer a relaxing conclusion to the journey.

Having reached Toliara, you need to be the adventurous type to follow a different route back to Tana so, to save doubling back, most tourists with limited time take a flight. There is some advantage to doing the trip in reverse, however: by flying to Toliara then driving back up RN7 you ensure that last-minute changes by Air Madagascar don't disrupt your onward plans (perhaps even causing you to miss your scheduled flight home).

TANA TO ANTSIRABE

It takes about 3 hours to drive to Antsirabe nonstop, but there are numerous potential pauses and diversions so most people take the best part of a day to do the 169km. The photo opportunities are terrific: all along this stretch of road you will see Merina tombs, and can watch the labour-intensive cultivation of rice paddies. About 15km from Tana look for the huge, white **replica of the *rova*** (as it was before it burned) across the paddy fields on the right. This was ex-president Didier Ratsiraka's palace, funded by North Korea.

DISTANCES IN KILOMETRES			
Ambositra–Ranomafana	138km	Antsirabe–Fianarantsoa	239km
Antananarivo–Ambatolampy	68km	Antsirabe–Miandrivazo	246km
Antananarivo–Antsirabe	169km	Antsirabe–Ihosy	442km
Antananarivo–Ambositra	259km	Fianarantsoa–Mananjary	197km
Antananarivo–Fianarantsoa	408km	Fianarantsoa–Manakara	254km
Antsirabe–Ambositra	90km	Fianarantsoa–Ihosy	210km

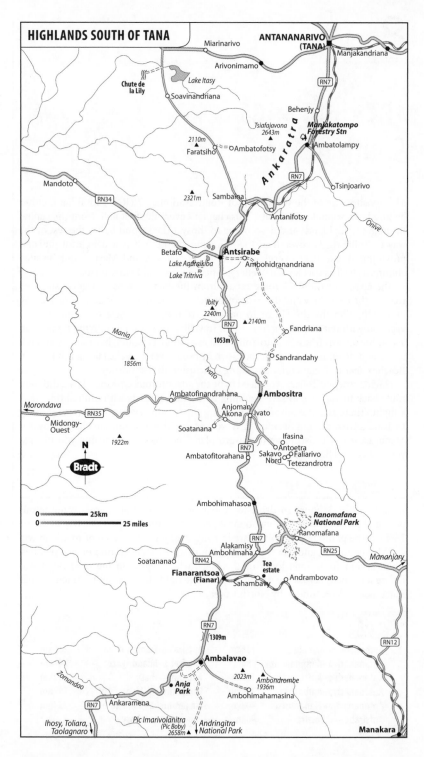

HIGHLANDS SOUTH OF TANA

ANTANANARIVO
(TANA)

Miarinarivo

Manjakandriana

Arivonimamo

RN7

Chute de
la Lily

Lake Itasy

Soavinandriana

Behenjy

Tsiafajavona
2643m

Manjakatompo
Forestry Stn

2110m
Faratsiho

Ambatofotsy

Ambatolampy

A n k a r a t r a

RN7

Tsinjoarivo

Mandoto

RN34

2321m

Sambaina

Antanifotsy

Onive

Betafo

Antsirabe

Ambohidranandriana

Lake Andraikiba

Lake Tritriva

Ibity
2240m

RN7

▲2140m

Fandriana

Mania

1053m

Sandrandahy

Nato

1856m

Morondava

RN35

Midongy-
Ouest

Ambatofinandrahana

Ambositra

1922m

Anjoman
Akona

Ivato

Ifasina

N

Soatanana

Antoetra

Bradt

Ambatofitorahana

RN7

Sakavo
Nord

Faliarivo

Tetezandrotra

Ambohimahasoa

Ranomafana
National Park

0   25km

Ranomafana

0   25 miles

RN7

Alakamisy
Ambohimaha

RN25

Mananjary

Soatanana

RN42

Tea
estate

Fianarantsoa
(Fianar)

Sahambavy

Andrambovato

RN7

1309m

RN12

Ambalavao

2023m

Ambondrombe
1936m

Anja
Park

Zomandao

Ankaramena

Ambohimahamasina

RN7

*Ihosy, Toliara,
Taolagnaro*

Pic Imarivolanitra
(Pic Boby)
2658m▲

Andringitra
National Park

Manakara

184

Roadside sellers add interest to the journey and give further cause to stop. Raffia animals and other models are found near PK 30, woven baskets just after PK 36 and garden ornaments at PK 48. Around PK 93, musical instruments are on offer, then colourfully painted toy wooden trucks from PK 102 to PK 110.

ACCUEIL VILLAGEOIS (m *033 09 895 07/034 67 147 62*; e *accueilvillageois@hotmail.fr*) A growing number of village associations in the region are joining this rural tourism collective. They can arrange short walks, longer treks and bike or car trips for cultural visits to local communities, where you can visit farms and discover rural artisans. Each participating village has set up an organisation of volunteers to facilitate local tourism, including providing simple accommodation. Booking is obligatory and in some cases at least a week's notice is required.

The current members are: Assoc Ranomiady in **Andriambilany**, 20 minutes north of Ambatolampy; Assoc Vonona in **Tsinjoarivo**, 4 hours southeast of Ambatolampy; Assoc Maingoka ('scorpion') in **Ambatofotsy**, 2 hours northwest of Sambaina (PK 133); Assoc Masoandro Miposaka ('rising sun') in **Ambohidranandriana**, an hour east of Antsirabe; Assoc Fivoarana in **Belazao**, 45 minutes (18km) west of Antsirabe; Assoc Loharanosoa in **Andranomafana**, 45 minutes (27km) west of Antsirabe; and Assoc Furcifer in **Ibity (Ihasy)**, 90 minutes south of Antsirabe.

AMBATOFOTSY (PK 21) An interesting diversion for those with their own vehicle is this lakeside resort just over 20km south of Tana. There's a small **nature park** here with around 160 plant species, a few lemurs and one or two snakes and other reptiles. There is also a museum and a couple of places to stay.

BEHENJY (PK 43) This village has been a centre for production of *foie gras* since independence. In the past couple of years, Madagascar's *foie gras* industry has really started booming. For lovers of this controversial delicacy, there is a specialist restaurant in town called **Coin de Foie Gras**.

ANDRIAMBILANY (PK 57) Two kilometres west of RN7, this little village is dominated by the view of a striking colonial **railway bridge** with ten stone arches spanning 160m across the confluence of the Andriambilany and Manjakatompo rivers. Accueil Villageois (see above) can arrange a **cottage homestay** with cultural visits to basket-weaving, metal foundry and recycling workshops.

AMBATOLAMPY (PK 68) Some 2 hours from Tana, Ambatolampy and its surrounding villages are famous for their **metalwork** – especially cooking pots, kitchen utensils and table football figures. Cast aluminium souvenirs are often for sale along the main road. The town has a colourful Thursday market (including a spectacular **cattle market** held near the river) and on Sundays there is horse racing at the nearby hippodrome. This is also the starting point for excursions to **Tsinjoarivo**, with its summer rova, and the forestry station of **Manjakatompo**. There is a branch of BOA bank in the town.

Where to stay and eat

Au Rendez-vous des Pêcheurs (7 rooms) \42 492 04; m 032 05 098 43; e socotex@moov.mg; www.madarun.com. Renowned for its restaurant. Rooms are simple but comfy, mostly with shared bathrooms (big bathtub) & a few en suite. €€–€€€

Pineta (5 rooms) next to Total fuel station; \42 493 02; e alapineta@hotmail.fr. Dbl & trpl rooms, some en suite. Italian restaurant. €€–€€€

It is a very strange, very exciting affair: a mixture of opera, dance and Speakers' Corner bound together with a sense of competition.

The performance takes place between two competing troupes of singers and musicians on a central square stage. It's an all-day event so the audience packs in early, tea and peanut vendors picking their way through the throng. Audience participation is an integral part – the best troupe is gauged by the crowd's response. Throughout the day performers come into the crowd to receive small coins offered in appreciation.

The most immediate surprise is the costumes. The men enter wearing 19th-century French, red, military frock coats and the women are clad in evening dress from the same period. Traditional *lamba* are carefully arranged around their shoulders, and the men wear straw Malagasy hats. The musicians play French military drums, fanfare trumpets, flutes, violins and clarinets. The effect is bizarre rather than beautiful.

The *hira gasy* is in four parts. First there are the introductory speeches or *kabary*. Each troupe elects a speaker who is usually a respected elder. His skill is paramount to a troupe. He begins with a long, ferociously fast, convoluted speech excusing himself and his inadequacy before the audience, ancestors, his troupe, his mother, God, his oxen, his rice fields and so on – and on! Then follows another speech glorifying God, and then a greeting largely made up of proverbs.

The hira gasy pivots around a tale of everyday life, such as the dire consequences of laziness or excessive drinking, is packed with wit, morals and proverbs and offers advice, criticism and possible solutions. The performers align themselves along two sides of the square at a time to address different parts of the audience. They sing in harsh harmony, illustrating their words with fluttering hand movements and expressive gestures, egged on by the uproarious crowd's appreciation. Then it is the dancers' turn. The tempo increases and becomes more rhythmic as two young boys take to the floor with a synchronised display of acrobatic dancing that nowadays often takes its influence from karate.

🏠 **Manja Ranch** Mandrevondry; m 033 11 993 70; e bijouxline@yahoo.fr. About 2km south of town. Owned by an American-Malagasy couple. Rooms & bungalows. B/fast inc. Camping permitted. Bike hire. €€

🏠 **Njara** The cheapest place in Ambatolampy; close to the market. €

🍴 **Evolution** m 033 01 084 27/034 04 309 00. Good food at reasonable prices.

🍴 **Iskurna** Restaurant at the south end of town; Spanish specialities.

La Ferme de Morarano d'Ambatolampy (m *032 40 978 33/032 76 450 68;* e *lafermedemorarano@yahoo.fr;* ⊕ *09.00–17.00 daily*) This farm grows medicinal plants, aromatic species and a wide range of fruits from which they make some 70 varieties of jam. Separate tours of both the **farm** and its **Madio essential oil distillery** can be arranged. They also run **Musée de la Nature de Morarano**, a botanic garden with around a hundred species on display, as well as an **insect museum** that exhibits more than 6,000 mounted specimens of butterflies and other invertebrates.

MANJAKATOMPO FORESTRY STATION 'There is very little natural forest left, but what still exists is quite unique,' reports Devin Edmonds, who visited in 2013. 'Tread lightly since it is very sensitive habitat. From the forest you can walk to a

viewpoint above camp in about 30 minutes. To hike to the summit takes at least 4 hours and you should arrange it ahead of time so you can bring a chicken as an offering to the spirits. If you plan to stay overnight, bring your tent, food and charcoal from Ambatolampy.'

Entry costs 4,000Ar, payable at the Eaux et Forêts office in Ambatolampy, from where the forest is a couple of hours' drive (25km). Guides – advisable although not obligatory – may be hired at the village halfway to the forest. It is also possible to get there by *taxi-brousse*, but they don't run every day. A handy 1995 guidebooklet includes a good map of the trails and is still available from some bookshops in Antsirabe and Tana.

TSINJOARIVO ROVA From Ambatolampy a road leads 46km southeast to Tsinjoarivo. It can be done as a day trip but you need to start early because it takes 4 hours each way. In Queen Rasoherina's time, it took three days by palanquin from Tana. A guardian can show you around the rova buildings: including the queen's, where the remains of some fine wooden carving from her bed can be seen, and others for the prime minister, chancellor and guard. The palace is situated on a promontory overlooking the spectacular **Onive Falls**. If you want to stay longer, there is a *gîte* – contact Accueil Villageois (page 185).

MERINA TOMBS Heading south, about 15 minutes beyond Ambatolampy, are some fine painted Merina tombs. These are on both sides of the road, but the most accessible are on the right.

AMBATOFOTSY HOMESTAY Two hours (75km) northwest of Sambaina (PK 133) on a good road is the isolated mountain village of Ambatofotsy, at an elevation of

ASSOCIATION MADALIEF/FITIAVANA

This inspiring Dutch-Malagasy organisation demonstrates how visitors can work with local people to make a real difference in Madagascar. Fitiavana was founded in 2000 by Malagasy women in Ambositra who used their own money to help needy children in their town. They were joined by three Dutch women who, after their visits to Madagascar, wanted to do something for the Malagasy children. They founded their organisation, Madalief, in the Netherlands to raise funds for the projects in Ambositra.

In 2003 they had raised enough funds to build an orphanage for 17 children (not all are strictly orphans; some have mothers who are unable to care for them properly). By 2006 the group had built another three houses for homeless women, which include a crèche and a sewing room. Gradually these women are rebuilding their lives, and their children (numbering now more than 40) are provided with clothes, schooling and medical care. Fitiavana has also helped families repair their houses, built two new classrooms for the local school, and runs their kindergarten, where they prepare a daily meal for the 70 children.

In 2010 they opened a guesthouse to the south of Antsirabe (see *Résidence Madalief* on page 189), providing the children with employment after they complete their education and generating funds for the organisation's social project. They also support two public schools nearby, providing materials and a daily breakfast for the 50 smallest children.

For further information or to arrange a visit contact Remi Doomernik (m *034 71 612 32*; e *remi.madagaskar@gmail.com; www.madalief.nl*).

1,700m. Visits can be arranged as part of the Accueil Villageois homestay programme (page 185). For adventurers there is the option to explore **Scorpion Mountain** and the **Ankaratra Massif**, discover basalt quarries and find a cave in the riverbed. On the cultural side, you can watch a **cart maker** at work and even get hands on, creating your own artefacts at the workshops of a **potter** and a **basket-weaver** and helping local farmers with agricultural work, including picking watercress.

ANTSIRABE (PK 169) AND AROUND

Antsirabe lies 1,500m above sea level. It was founded in 1872 by Norwegian missionaries attracted by the cool climate and the healing properties of the thermal springs. The name means 'place of much salt'. For Madagascar, this is an elegant city. A broad avenue links the handsome railway station with Hôtel des Thermes, an amazing building in both size and architectural style. At the station end is a monolith depicting Madagascar's 18 main ethnic groups.

Antsirabe is the agricultural and industrial centre of Madagascar. It is also the centre for beer: you can smell the Star Brewery as you enter the town. The cool climate allows it to produce apples, pears, plums and other temperate fruit. Indeed it can get cold enough to need a sweater in the evening between May and September.

GETTING THERE AND AWAY By taxi-brousse, Antsirabe is about 3 hours from Tana (*8,000Ar*) and a little under 6 hours from Fianarantsoa (Fianar). For a comfy option with scheduled departures, use Sonatra Plus (page 204). Onward travel costs 7,000Ar to Ambositra and 15,000Ar to Fianar. Heading west costs 15,000Ar as far as Miandrivazo or 35,000Ar all the way to Morondava.

There is currently no regular passenger service by **rail** from Tana to Antsirabe, but the Trans-Lémurie Express train runs some weekends and is also available on this route on a private-hire basis for groups (page 265).

GETTING AROUND This is the *pousse-pousse* capital of Madagascar. There are hundreds, perhaps thousands of them. The drivers are insistent that you avail yourself of a ride, and why not? But be very firm about the price (typically 1,000–2,000Ar) and be cautious if they want to take you to a different hotel from the one you request: at least one disreputable hotel in town pays pousse-pousse drivers a commission for bringing new customers, so they can be quite persistent.

 WHERE TO STAY

Top end €€€€€

🏠 **Plumeria** [191 C4] (27 rooms) 📞 44 488 91/44 488 92; m 034 44 488 91; e contact@plumeriahotelantsirabe.com; www.plumeriahotelantsirabe.com. Smart orange-&-white building near the train station, new in 2016. Modern rooms, restaurant, bar & patisserie.

Upper range €€€€

🏠 **Antsaha** [191 B1] (28 bungalows) 12km north of Antsirabe; 📞 26 343 94; m 032 29 686 33/033 16 168 50/034 04 782 31; e antsaha.hotel@yahoo.com; www.hotel-antsaha.com. Wooded area with bungalows; sat-TV. Sauna, massage, tennis, ping-pong, badminton, bikes & 2 heated pools. Restaurant, bar & pizzeria. Wi-Fi.

🏠 **Couleur Café** [191 D5] (15 rooms) 📞 44 485 26; m 032 02 200 65; e couleurcafe@moov.mg; www.couleurcafeantsirabe.com. Brick chalets in a large calm garden; very comfy & serves terrific food. Generally good but some variable reports of late. Wi-Fi.

🏠 **Flower Palace** [191 C4] (20 rooms) 50 Av Clemenceau; m 033 25 013 14/034 14 870 01; e flowerpalace@hotmail.fr. Spacious clean rooms with minimalistic smart décor, AC, TV, minibar, safe & Wi-Fi (some rooms only). Good restaurant & snack bar.

🏠 **Hôtel des Thermes** [191 B5] (30 rooms) 📞 44 487 62; **m** 032 05 262 66/033 18 961 20/034 65 487 61; **e** sht@moov.mg; www.sofitrans-sa. com. The grandest & oldest hotel in Antsirabe has been renovated. Rooms have heater, en-suite baths, minibar, sat-TV & safe. Spacious grounds offer minigolf, tennis, swimming pool, basketball, gym & massage. Wi-Fi.

🏠 **Résidence des Hauts Plateaux (Résidence Sociale)** [191 B2] (23 rooms) 📞 44 483 47; **e** mra@moov.mg; www.residence-sociale-antsirabe.com. A grand old building in a 2.5ha park, comprising not only a hotel & restaurant but also a retirement home, museum, chapel, library & clinic. Spacious rooms.

🏠 **Rivetoile** [191 B1] (26 rooms) **m** 033 74 312 74; **e** booking@rivetoile-hotel.com or rivetoilehotel@yahoo.fr; www.rivetoile-hotel.com. Bright colourful rooms with safe, TV, Wi-Fi, balcony & en-suite facilities. Good value.

🏠 **Trianon** [191 C4] (8 rooms) Rue Foch; 📞 44 051 40; **m** 032 05 051 40/034 05 051 40; **e** hotel.letrianon@gmail.com; www.hotel-letrianon-antsirabe.com. Dated but pleasant & clean. Basic en-suite rooms for 1–5 people; TV, safe & Wi-Fi. Heaters for a small fee.

🏠 **Vatolahy** [191 B3] (30 rooms) 📞 44 937 77; **m** 034 11 937 77; **e** hotelvatolahy@hotmail. fr; www.vatolahyhotel.e-monsite.com. Attractive hotel; rooms with tasteful décor, TV & Wi-Fi. Pub & tremendous restaurant. Massage & acupuncture.

Mid-range €€€

🏠 **Antsirabe Hotel** [191 B2] (9 rooms) **m** 033 03 026 94/034 07 762 02; **e** antsirabehotel@gmail.com or salama_deo@ yahoo.fr. North of the centre, a 2-floor hotel with big en-suite dbl, trpl & family rooms with sat-TV & Wi-Fi. Friendly owner & staff.

🏠 **Blue Sky** [191 D5] (10 rooms) **m** 034 61 212 16; **e** bluesky.antsirabe@gmail.com; www. mada-bluesky-tours.com/antsirabe-hotel. Under same ownership as Mada Bluesky Tours (page 193). En-suite dbl, trpl & family rooms with Wi-Fi.

🏠 **Camélia** [191 C4] (12 rooms) north of Grande Av; 📞 44 488 44; **e** laresidencecamelia@ gmail.com. A converted villa set in lovely gardens. Rooms are all right but becoming rather tired & some readers have reported lousy service.

🏠 **Cristal** [191 B1] (9 rooms) Vatofotsy; **m** 032 05 916 09/033 09 916 09/034 44 916 09;

e cristalhotel@ymail.com; www.cristal-hotel-madagascar.com. Large colourful rooms with kitchenette, minibar, sat-TV & Wi-Fi. New restaurant.

🏠 **Diamant** [191 B3] (53 rooms) Rte d'Andranobe; 📞 44 488 40/44 494 40; **e** diamant@ madawel.com; www.madawel.com/hd. Long-established Chinese-run hotel with many long corridors testament to its numerous extensions over the decades. Some rooms with fridge & TV. Cybercafé & nightclub.

🏠 **Green Park (Chez Jenny)** [191 C6] (2 rooms & 13 bungalows) Tsarasaotra; 📞 44 051 90; **m** 034 08 725 13; **e** cjennygreenparc@yahoo.fr (restaurant) or greenparktsara@yahoo.fr (hotel). Quaint bungalows in wonderful garden with pond & quaint bridges. Ask to see rooms first: some are excellent, others a bit run-down with thin mattresses. Camping permitted.

🏠 **H1** [191 C2] (19 rooms) 📞 44 490 77; **m** 032 83 993 41/033 21 981 23; **e** hotelh1abe@ gmail.com; www.hotelh1-madagascar.com or www.hotelh1antsirabe.e-monsite.com. Rooms with en-suite facilities, Wi-Fi & sat-TV; some with balcony & 3 with AC.

🏠 **Résidence Madalief** [191 D6] (13 rooms) 7km south of Antsirabe; **m** 034 40 578 89/034 71 612 32; **e** remi.madagaskar@gmail.com or residence@madalief.nl; www.madalief.nl. En-suite trpl rooms in highly recommended guesthouse; all profits go directly to social projects of Madalief (see box, page 187). Transfers into town arranged. Book in advance.

🏠 **Royal Palace** [191 D6] (36 rooms) 📞 44 490 40; **m** 034 49 040 40; **e** royalpalace@moov.mg; www.leroyalpalace.mg. Very modern new hotel; rooms with Wi-Fi, AC & TV. Gym & heated pool. Bar & restaurant called Spicy Grill. Also 4 apartments.

🏠 **Soa Guest House** [191 B1] (7 rooms & 1 bungalow) 📞 44 997 42; **m** 032 02 279 90/033 06 219 29 (manager)/033 12 591 21/033 15 279 90; **e** soa_guesthouse@outlook.com; www. soaguesthouse.com. Guesthouse attractively decorated with Malagasy artwork. Spacious rooms with balcony & shower or bath.

🏠 **Villa Nirina** [191 B3] (5 rooms) Rte d'Andranobe; 📞 44 485 97/44 486 69; **e** bbvillanirina@hotmail.fr. Cosy B&B with dbl & family rooms.

🏠 **Voyageur** [191 D3] (1 room & 9 bungalows) 📞 44 979 38; **m** 032 40 866 22/032 83 083 61; **e** androdenis@yahoo.fr or chambresvoyageur@

ANTSIRABE

For listings, see pages 188–92

yahoo.fr; www.chambres-voyageur.mg. Charming lodge of 1930s-inspired design & magnificent botanical garden (700 species) with water features, spaced-out bungalows & small restaurant.
Also in this category:

⌂ **Aty** [191 B2] e atyguesthouse@yahoo.fr

⌂ **Avana** [191 B1] e avanahotel@yahoo.fr

⌂ **Bouzou** [191 B1] ☎ 44 932 44

⌂ **Hasina** [191 A3] www.hotelhasina.com

⌂ **Imperial** [191 C5] e imperialhotel@moov.mg

⌂ **Lavilla** [191 C1] e hlavillapiscine@gmail.com

⌂ **Prima** [191 B2] e rest.manambina@yahoo.fr

⌂ **Retrait** [191 B4] e leretraitantsirabe@gmail.com

⌂ **Tulsi** [191 D6] e tulsiguesthouse@gmail.com

⌂ **Villa Salemako** [191 B3] e julirako@gmail.com

Budget €€

⌂ **Au Bon Coin** [191 A3] (8 rooms) Rue Stavanger; m 033 70 706 52/034 01 423 04/034 05 045 38; e abcbira@yahoo.fr. En-suite rooms & snack bar.

⌂ **Chez Billy** [191 B6] (8 rooms) ☎ 44 484 88; m 032 45 740 71; e chezbilly@moov.mg. B&B with

great backpacker hostel ambience; rooms for 2–5 people with shared facilities & hot water. Bike hire.

⌂ **Niavo** [191 B6] (8 rooms) Rue de la Myre de Villers; ☎ 44 484 67; m 033 11 155 47; e hotelniavo@gmail.com. Convenient location close to the market. Some rooms en suite with TV. Safe parking.

⌂ **Nitricia** [191 B1] (7 rooms) Miaramasoandro; ☎ 44 963 80; m 034 72 780 21; e rest.manambina@yahoo.fr. Friendly, relaxing atmosphere in a family home with terrace near taxi-brousse station. Hot water. Cooking facilities & TV for extra fee.

⌂ **Nouveau Synchro Pub** [191 A4] (10 rooms) Rue Pasteur Antsenakely; ☎ 44 962 24; e souveram@yahoo.fr. Basic dbl rooms & 2 studios with kitchenette, fridge & TV.
Also in this category:

⌂ **Avenir** [191 A3] m 032 02 482 70

⌂ **Cercle Mess Mixte** [191 B4] ☎ 44 483 66

⌂ **Geranium** [191 C3] e drlisy@yahoo.fr

⌂ **Joie** [191 C6] ☎ 44 962 47

⌂ **Manoro** [191 C7] ☎ 44 918 24

⌂ **Prestige** [191 A3] e prestigehotel.bira@gmail.com

⌂ **Ville d'Eau** [191 A3] ☎ 44 499 70

⌂ **Volavita** [191 B2] e volavita@gmail.com

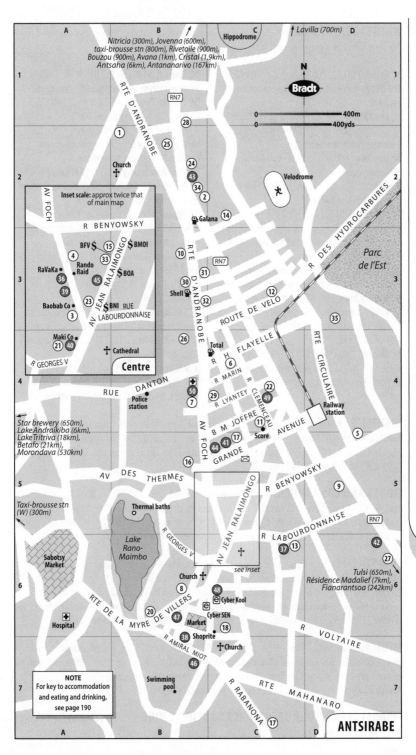

Map labels

A   B   C   D

Hippodrome

↑ Lavilla (700m)

Nitricia (300m), Jovenna (600m),
taxi-brousse stn (800m), Rivetoile (900m),
Bouzou (900m), Avana (1km), Cristal (1.9km),
Antsaha (6km), Antananarivo (167km)

N

Bradt

0 ————— 400m
0 ————— 400yds

RTE D'ANDRANOBE

RN7

① ② ⑤

Church ✝

Velodrome

② ④ ④③ ③④ ②

R DES HYDROCARBURES

AV FOCH

Inset scale: approx twice that
of main map

R BENYOWSKY

Galana ⑭

RTE D'ANDRANOBE

RN7

Parc
de l'Est

BFV $ ⑮ $ BMOI
④ ③③
RaVaKa ⑩
⑥③ Rando
Raid ④⑤ $ BOA
⑨③
Baobab Co ● ②③ RUE
③ LABOURDONNAISE

⑩

③①

Shell ⑳
③②

ROUTE DE VELO

⑫

RTE CIRCULAIRE

⑤③

Maki Co ●
②① ④⓪

✝ Cathedral

R GEORGES V   **Centre**

②⑥

Total
R H FLAYELLE
⑥

RUE   DANTON

Police
station

⑩⓪
⑦

R MARIN
②⑨ R LYANTEY
AV B M JOFFRE

②② ④⑨

Railway
station

Star brewery (650m),
Lake Andraikiba (6km),
Lake Tritriva (18km),
Betafo (21km),
Morondava (530km)

AV DES THERMES

AV FOCH

④④ ④①
GRANDE

Score ①①

⑤

⑯

R BENYOWSKY

⑨

Taxi-brousse stn
(W) (300m)

Thermal baths

Lake
Rano-
Maimbo

R GEORGES V

AV JEAN RALAIMONGO

R LABOURDONNAISE

RN7

③⑦ ①③

④②

Sabotsy
Market

Church ✝

✝
see inset

②⑦

Tulsi (650m),
Résidence Madalief (7km),
Fianarantsoa (242km)

Hospital

RTE DE LA MYRE DE VILLERS

②⓪
④⑦

⑧
Cyber Kool ④⑧
Cyber SEN

Market
⑱
Shoprite

R VOLTAIRE

③⑧
④⑥

✝ Church

NOTE
For key to accommodation
and eating and drinking,
see page 190

Swimming
pool

R AMIRAL MIOT

R RABANONA

RTE   MAHANARO

⑰

ANTSIRABE

A   B   C   D

191

✖ WHERE TO EAT AND DRINK Some of the hotel restaurants serve very good food and **Au Bon Coin** is a good snack bar.

✖ Arche [191 A3] Rue Stavanger; m 032 02 479 25. Small, French-owned place; sometimes live music.

✖ Chez Jenny [191 C6] m 032 07 751 16/033 12 127 78; ⊕ Tue–Sun. Very homely bar, crêperie & pizzeria. Much recommended.

✖ Danielle [191 B7] ⊕ Wed–Sun. Simple restaurant; good prices.

✖ Gaëlle [191 A3] ⊕ Sun–Fri. Snack bar & Chinese food. Also bike hire.

✖ Insolite [191 D6] m 032 02 158 14; ⊕ Tue–Sun. Bar & restaurant with recreation park (minigolf, bowling, badminton, etc). Malagasy & European food.

✖ Jovenna [191 B1] A surprisingly good & inexpensive eatery at the fuel station.

✖ Manambina [191 B2] Rte d'Antananarivo; ☏ 44 493 02; e rest.manambina@yahoo.fr; ⊕ Tue–Sun. Malagasy, French, Chinese & vegetarian dishes.

✖ Mihaja [191 C5] m 033 12 398 35/033 14 902 20/033 16 253 20; e akanymihaja@yahoo.fr; ⊕ Wed–Mon. Reasonable restaurant.

✖ Oasis [191 B7] m 032 07 591 56; ⊕ daily. Small restaurant with extensive Chinese menu.

✖ Pousse-Pousse [191 B6] m 032 40 275 26/032 60 569 40/033 02 555 90; e restopoussepousse@gmail.com; ⊕ Thu–Tue. Very good restaurant with an inventive menu. Cocktails & occasionally live music.

✖ Razafimamonjy [191 C6] Antsenakely; ☏ 44 483 53. Opposite the market. Good-value excellent food & cabaret Tue–Sat from 20.00.

✖ Venise [191 C4] nr railway station; ☏ 44 938 70; m 033 11 411 61; ⊕ daily. Bar & restaurant; good atmosphere; pool table.

✖ Zandina (Terrasse) [191 B4] 5 Rue Foch; m 034 17 984 22; e zandinabira@yahoo.fr; ⊕ daily. Popular restaurant, pizzeria, bar & cybercafé. Wi-Fi.

▢ Gastro Glace [191 A4] Roadside kiosk with juice & more than a dozen flavours of ice cream.

▢ Gastro Pizza [191 C5] ⊕ daily. Ice cream & pizza, inc take-away.

▢ Mirana [191 A3] Av Jean Ralaimongo; ☏ 44 491 81. Good for b/fast & take-away meals inc pizza, ice cream & pastries. Big portions.

NIGHTLIFE Antsirabe's nightlife is quite low-key. The only notable nightclub is **Tahiti** at Diamant Hotel [191 B3], which has been running for decades. It's open most nights from 21.00. Some of the hotels have bars, as do restaurants **Razafimamonjy** [191 C6] and **Tarantella** [191 C6].

MONEY AND COMMUNICATIONS Branches of the main banks – BMOI, BFV, BNI and BOA – are clustered on the main street in the centre of town. Most hotels and restaurants have free Wi-Fi. **Cyber Kool** [191 C6] and **Cyber SEN** [191 B6] are good internet cafés, as is **Multi-Service** at Zandina restaurant [191 B4].

SHOPPING For groceries and general supplies, the **Shoprite** supermarket [191 C6] near the market is the best stocked (☏ 44 497 04; ⊕ Mon–Sat 08.00–19.00, Sun 08.30–13.00). A branch of **Score** supermarket [191 C4] also has a good range of food.

Several nice **handicraft boutiques** are centrally located on the same street as Arche [191 A3], a restaurant which has **paintings** by local artists for sale.

MEDICAL The **Santé Plus** clinic (☏ 44 498 51; m 032 02 458 58; e santeplusantsirabe@gmail.com) is 'an oasis of cleanliness and professionalism in the Malagasy sea of chaos' reports Rory Graham, who had the misfortune to require their services. There is also a local branch of **Espace Medical** (☏ 032 03 155 74).

TOURIST OFFICE, TOUR OPERATORS AND VEHICLE HIRE For **bicycle hire**, try Green Park/Chez Jenny, Chez Billy or Gaëlle (all listed under hotels and restaurants).

ORTVA (regional tourist office) m 034 60 135 40/034 01 687 29; e ortvak@yahoo.fr; www.ortva. mg or www.antsirabe-tourisme.com

Mada Bluesky Tours m 033 03 026 94/034 07 762 02; e contact@mada-bluesky-tours.com or salama_deo@yahoo.fr or madablueskytour@gmail.com; www.mada-bluesky-tours.com. Vehicle rental; also guided tours in the region & beyond. See ad, page 114.

Madagascar Green Tours m 032 04 364 27/033 04 351 17; e info@madagascar-green-tours.com; www.madagascar-green-tours.com. Excursions throughout the south.

Madagaskar Touren m 033 12 048 92; e konnerth1@hotmail.com; www.urlaub-auf-madagaskar.com. All kinds of excursions & tours inc family travel & specialist trips.

Rando Raid [191 A3] m 032 04 900 21; e randoraidmadagascar@yahoo.fr; www. randoraidmadagascar.com. Bike & motorbike hire, horse-riding, microlights, trekking (guided & unguided), tent hire & multi-day tours.

RaVaKa [191 A3] Tombontsoa Bldg (next to Arche); 44 498 87; m 032 04 809 24/034 06 251 56; ⊕ Mon–Sat. Trips of 1–4 days around local village communities to see Malagasy life.

WHAT TO SEE AND DO Saturday is market day in Antsirabe, an echo of Tana before they abolished the *zoma* but with an even greater cross section of activities. It's enclosed in a walled area of the city on the hill before the road to Lake Tritriva.

Workshop tours Antsirabe has a thriving handicrafts sector and it's well worth visiting the workshops to see the skill and ingenuity of the craftsmen. Local handicrafts and products include jewellery made from zebu horn, toys crafted from old tin cans, wooden carvings, billiard tables, polished minerals, embroidered tablecloths and clothing. You can take a pousse-pousse tour round several workshops. Demonstrations are generally free but you are expected to buy something after.

Kololandy, situated 800m west of the town centre, does traditional weaving of silk, cotton, sisal and raffia (m *032 07 927 76/033 11 921 77*; e *odilerao@yahoo.fr*; *www.kololandy.com*; ⊕ *08.00–17.00*). **Mandray Galerie** (e *rhasivelo@yahoo.fr*), near the cathedral, also specialises in silk. Mme Hasivelo raises both native and exotic silkworms, from whose silk her team of weavers produces scarves and other articles. Tin-can toys are made at **Miniature Mamy** (*Parc de l'Est*; 44 961 20; m *032 42 693 00*; e *mamyminiature@moov.mg*). Nearby is the fascinating zebu horn crafts workshop **Maminirina** (m *033 80 047 10/034 31 905 81/032 63 139 56*; e *maminirinacorne@gmail.com or cornemaminirina@yahoo.fr*). It is also possible to visit local producers to see wine, beer (see *Star Brewery* below), honey, cheese (*www.lactimad.com*) and sweets (**Chez Marcel**; 44 499 71; ⊕ *05.00–13.00*) being made.

Star Brewery [191 A4] (44 481 71; e *usine.antsirabe@star.mg*) Don't miss a visit to this factory to see the famous Three Horses Beer in production. Tours are only possible Tuesday–Thursday at 09.00 and 14.00 and last a couple of hours. It is necessary to book in advance.

LAKES ANDRAIKIBA AND TRITRIVA Just 7km west of Antsirabe, **Lake Andraikiba** is a large volcanic lake often overlooked in favour of the more spectacular **Lake Tritriva**. The scenery here is picturesque and the area very peaceful. Taxi-brousses heading for Betafo pass close to the lake, or you can go by hired bicycle as a day trip – or longer if you bring a tent. Alternative accommodation is available at **Dera** (m *033 11 928 08/034 11 928 08*; e *hoteldera@yahoo.fr*; €€€) and **Laza** (44 957 99; m *033 13 103 71*; e *hotelaza@yahoo.fr*; *www.hotellaza.com*; €€€).

Lake Tritriva's name comes from *tritry* – the Malagasy word for the ridge on the back of a chameleon – and *iva*, 'deep'. And this emerald-green crater lake is indeed deep – 80m, some say. It is reached by continuing past Lake Andraikiba for 12km

8

on a rough, steep road (4x4 only) past small villages of waving kids. You will notice that these villages are relatively prosperous-looking for Madagascar; they grow the barley for the Star Brewery.

Apart from the sheer beauty of Lake Tritriva (the best light for photography is in the morning), there are all sorts of interesting features and **legends**. The water level rises in the dry season and debris thrown into the lake has reappeared down in the valley, supporting the theory of underground water channels.

Across the lake you'll see two thorn trees with intertwined branches growing on a ledge above the water. It is said that these are two lovers, forbidden to marry by their parents, who drowned themselves in Lake Tritriva. When the branches are cut, blood oozes out, so they say. You can walk right round the lake for impressive views. There is an entrance fee of 2,500Ar.

BELAZAO HOMESTAY This farming village 45 minutes west of Antsirabe on a poor road is the site of a cultural homestay in the Accueil Villageois scheme (page 185). Visitors can see rope-making, weaving and small-scale dairy farming in action, as well as discovering gemstone mines and hiking up **Mount Itavo** for panoramic views of the Antsirabe area.

BETAFO About 22km west of Antsirabe, off the tarred road to Morondava, lies Betafo, a town with typical highlands red-brick churches and houses. Dotted among the houses are *vatolahy*, standing stones erected to commemorate warrior chieftains. It is off the normal tourist circuit, and gives you an excellent insight into the Merina way of life. Monday is market day. At one end of the town is the **crater lake Tatamarina**. From there it is a walk of about 3km to the **Antafofo waterfalls** among beautiful views of rice fields and volcanic hills. 'It's very inviting for a swim,' observed reader Luc Selleslagh, 'but they told me there are ghosts in the pool under the falls which will grab your legs and pull you to the bottom.'

There are **hot springs** at Andranomafana, just beyond Betafo; for a few ariary you can have a lingering warm bath. There is an Accueil Villageois *gîte* here for those wanting to stay longer and enjoy the area, as well as rooms at **Gîte de la Cascade** (m *033 20 018 26/034 18 317 88*).

AMBOHIDRANANDRIANA HOMESTAY This village an hour east of Antsirabe is one of the most interesting participants in the Accueil Villageois programme (page 185). Apart from being a great area for hiking, you will learn about the village's rich history from a village elder, find out about **medicinal plants** used in traditional medicine and have the opportunity to see inside a huge **unfinished tomb** on which construction began in the 1970s. Local craftsmen who can demonstrate their work include a zebu horn carver, bamboo furniture-maker, carpenter, blacksmith, embroiderer and cheese-maker. Visitors can also participate in basketry, fishing and agricultural work.

MOUNT IBITY About 15km beyond Antsirabe on RN7 you pass east of the 2,250m peak of Mount Ibity, one of Madagascar's most geologically fascinating sites. There are quartzite caves and countless small quarries for semi-precious minerals such as tourmaline and rose quartz. The mountain is also home to many locally endemic plants.

The village of **Ibity** is 90 minutes by car from Antsirabe. Here is the site of the final Accueil Villageois homestay: an attractive two-storey house with four guest bedrooms. Hiking up the mountain to enjoy panoramic views to see the curiously eroded rocks near the peak is a must. One can visit local artisans to participate in

RICE   *Hilary Bradt*

The Malagasy have always had an almost mystical attachment to rice. King Andrianampoinimerina declared: 'Rice and I are one,' and loyalty to the Merina king was symbolised by industry in the rice paddies.

Today the Betsileo are masters of rice cultivation (they manage three harvests a year, rather than the normal two) and their neat terraces are a distinctive part of the scenery of the central highlands. However, rice is grown throughout the island, either in irrigated paddies or as 'hill rice' watered by the rain. Rice production is labour-intensive. First the ground must be prepared for the seeds. Often this is done by chasing zebu cattle round and round to break and soften the clods – a muddy, sticky job, but great fun for the boys who do it. Seeds are germinated in a small plot and replanted in the irrigated paddies when half grown. In October and November you will see women bent over in knee-deep water, performing this back-breaking work.

The Malagasy eat rice three times a day, the average annual consumption being 135kg per capita – the highest of any nation in the world – although this is declining because of the availability of other foods and reduced productivity. Rice marketing was nationalised in 1976, but this resulted in such a dramatic drop in the amount of rice reaching the open market that restrictions were lifted in 1984. It was too late to reverse the decline, which was mainly due to the decay of irrigation works. Despite a steady increase in acreage at the expense of the precious forest, production continues to fall.

Small farmers grow rice only for their own consumption but are forced to sell part of their crop for instant cash. Richer families in the community store this grain and sell it back at a profit later. To solve this small-scale exploitation, village co-operatives have been set up to buy rice and sell it back to the farmer at an agreed price, or at a profit to outsiders if any is left over.

pottery-making, weaving, embroidery and farming, and witness *savika omby* – a daring game where young men must hang on to a bucking zebu's hump for as long as possible.

AMBOSITRA (PK 259) AND AROUND

The next significant settlement encountered after Antsirabe follows 90km of mostly tightly winding roads: Ambositra (pronounced 'am*boo*str') is a friendly little Betsileo town. Many of the 30,000 inhabitants study here so in July and August the population drops considerably. Most visitors stop only briefly, but the surrounding countryside is very scenic, so it merits a few days' stay if you have time. Market day is Saturday (best mid-morning); raffia products are particularly plentiful.

Ambositra is the centre of Madagascar's **woodcarving** industry. Even the houses have ornately carved wooden balconies and shutters. There is an abundant choice of carved figures and marquetry (see *Shopping*, page 197).

Some readers have complained that this town has particularly persistent beggars. The problem area is mainly around Grand Hotel where the tour buses stop.

Taxi-brousses from Antsirabe take 2 hours or so (*7,000Ar*); continuing to Fianarantsoa takes 4 hours (*also 7,000Ar*).

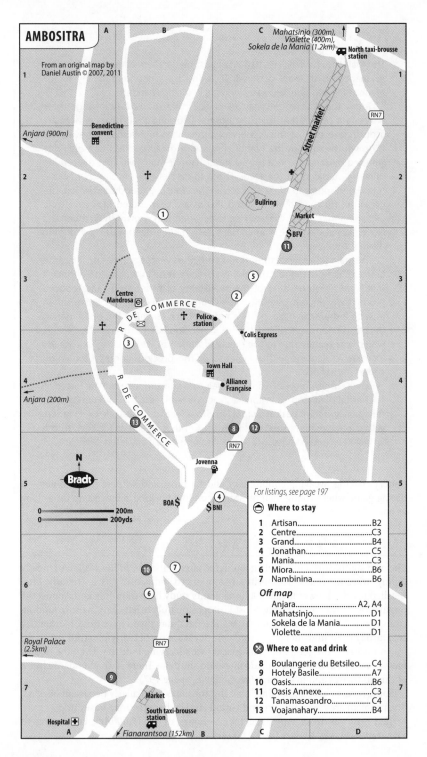

AMBOSITRA

A   B   C   D

Mahatsinjo (300m),
Violette (400m),
Sokela de la Mania (1.2km)

North taxi-brousse
station

RN7

From an original map by
Daniel Austin © 2007, 2011

Anjara (900m)

Benedictine
convent

Street market

Bullring

Market

$ BFV

11

Centre
Mandrosa

R DE COMMERCE

Police
station

Colis Express

Town Hall

Alliance
Française

R DE COMMERCE

13

8   12

RN7

N

Bradt

Jovenna

0   200m
0   200yds

BOA $

$ BNI

4

10   7

6

Royal Palace
(2.5km)

RN7

9

Market

Anjara (200m)

Hospital

South taxi-brousse
station

Fianarantsoa (152km)

For listings, see page 197

Where to stay

1	Artisan	B2
2	Centre	C3
3	Grand	B4
4	Jonathan	C5
5	Mania	C3
6	Miora	B6
7	Nambinina	B6

Off map
	Anjara	A2, A4
	Mahatsinjo	D1
	Sokela de la Mania	D1
	Violette	D1

Where to eat and drink

8	Boulangerie du Betsileo	C4
9	Hotely Basile	A7
10	Oasis	B6
11	Oasis Annexe	C3
12	Tanamasoandro	C4
13	Voajanahary	B4

WHERE TO STAY AND EAT

Artisan (Chez Victor) [196 B2] (12 rooms & 10 bungalows) m 032 51 996 09/034 04 642 53; e artisan_hotel@yahoo.fr. Nice hotel with wonderful woodwork but rooms fairly small & dark. All en suite with TV. €€€

Centre [196 C3] (14 rooms) ☎ 47 710 36; m 032 86 658 39/033 14 212 77/034 47 710 36; e hotelducentre.ambositra@yahoo. fr or hotelducentre.mada@yahoo.fr; www. hotelducentre-mada.com. Right by RN7; comfy en-suite rooms with hot water. Restaurant with Malagasy & Chinese food. €€€

Jonathan [196 C5] (13 rooms) ☎ 47 713 89; m 032 07 019 72; e contact@hoteljonathan. com or hoteljonathan77@yahoo.fr; www. hoteljonathan.com. Rooms with TV, some en suite, mostly spacious. €€€

Mania [196 C3] (16 rooms) ☎ 47 710 21; m 032 04 620 91/033 15 005 13/034 97 478 90; e toursmania@moov.mg. Clean en-suite dbl, twin & family rooms with TV. Tours organised; bikes & cars for rent. Restaurant upstairs in nearby traditional house. €€€

Sokela de la Mania [196 D1] (30 rooms) RN7; ☎ 47 711 95; m 032 02 108 12 (Tana)/034 70 756 36; e rakrapha13@yahoo.fr. Adequate but rather mediocre rooms; very helpful owner & great views over rice fields. €€€

Nambinina [196 B6] (11 rooms & 7 bungalows) m 033 13 504 73/033 16 097 80/034 13 504 73; e hotelnambinina@yahoo.com. Pleasant en-suite rooms with Wi-Fi & sat-TV. Bar & restaurant with French, Chinese & Malagasy cuisine. €€–€€€

Violette [196 D1] (6 rooms & 6 bungalows) Madiolahatra; ☎ 47 710 84; m 032 56 117 23/034 36 879 79; e motel-violette@moov.mg. North

end of town. Elegantly furnished bungalows with TV. Great views, but cheaper rooms face the road. €€–€€€

Grand Hotel [196 B4] (13 rooms) ☎ 47 712 62; m 034 02 712 62; e contact@grandhotel-ambositra.com; www.grandhotel-ambositra. com. The oldest hotel in Ambositra; a beautiful old building. Recently renovated, simple but clean & comfy rooms, some en suite. Also dormitory. €–€€€

Anjara [196 A2/A4] (10 rooms) m 032 55 931 91; e hotelanjara@outlook.fr; www. hotelanjara.blogvie.com. Beautiful traditional guesthouse on the edge of town. Simple rooms & delicious food in a friendly & welcoming home. €€

Mahatsinjo [196 D1] (12 rooms) ☎ 47 710 36; e jeannoeltours@yahoo.fr. A short walk up the hill. Very attractive, quiet & rural surroundings, but near town. €€

Miora [196 B6] (12 rooms) m 033 17 311 59/034 04 642 42; e hotelmiorambositra@yahoo. fr. Cheap rooms with shared facilities. €€

Oasis [196 B6] m 032 41 003 74/033 68 295 89/034 90 957 20; e maccorinne@yahoo.fr. Restaurant with reasonable prices, nice seating upstairs & tasty food with vegetarian options. Sometimes live music.

Oasis Annexe [196 C3] Reliable good-value snacks & meals.

Tanamasoandro [196 C4] m 034 89 694 63. A popular budget restaurant.

Voajanahary [196 B4] m 032 02 996 32 (shop)/033 12 247 52. Good simple food.

Boulangerie du Betsileo (Bon Grain) [196 C4] Bakery.

Hotely Basile [196 A7] Typical Malagasy *hotely*.

MONEY, COMMUNICATIONS AND MEDICAL Ambositra has branches of BFV, BNI and BOA banks, all with 24-hour ATMs. The BFV has a Western Union service and also opens Saturday mornings. There is a post office and branch of Colis Express (☎ 47 713 38). Internet is available at **Centre Mandrosoa** [196 B3]. For medical care, contact Espace Medical (☎ 47 712 38).

SHOPPING There are some 30 stores selling woodcarving and other **handicrafts**, almost all on the 'ring road' running round Ambositra's central hill (this circuit is an easy 1.5km walk). There are ethical problems when buying palisander and rosewood carvings – these slow-growing endemic trees are becoming very rare (page 319). That said, woodcarving is the main source of income for the town, so it's a typically Malagasy dilemma. Do try to spread your custom around; at least one outlet has a commercial arrangement with tour bus drivers to dump groups at his shop.

Visit **Angelino Tsaralaza** [196 B4] for demonstrations of different **silk production** techniques. This initiative provides an outlet for some of the silk (including wild silk) products produced by women's associations. If you want to shop ethically, this is the place to do it.

TOUR OPERATORS, VEHICLE HIRE AND GUIDES

ORTAM m 034 97 478 90/032 41 003 74; e contact.ortam@gmail.com; www.tourisme-ambositra.com. Regional tourist office.

Angelino Tsaralaza [196 B4] Excursions to silk/embroidery factory. Guides; vehicle hire.

Indigo Be [196 B3] Opposite Grand Hotel, a little further up. English-speaking guides; trekking, horse-riding & bike hire.

RSI Tours [196 A4] m 032 12 693 49. Opposite Grand Hotel. Car hire.

Tours Mania Based at Mania Hotel [196 C3]. Organises tours in & around Ambositra; also to Zafimaniry villages.

Tsangatsanga [196 B4] 47 714 48; m 032 04 621 28; e lamaisondesguides.ambositra@yahoo. fr. Tours, from walks around town up to 7-day treks with English-speaking guides. Car & tent hire.

WHAT TO SEE AND DO

Benedictine convent [196 A2] Walk 500m down the hill opposite the post office to discover this architecturally stunning 80-year-old convent and chapel. The **daily morning service** is at 06.30 (07.00 on Sunday) and there is singing each day at 11.30.

Ambositra produces more than woodcarvings: excellent quality **cheese** is made by some of the 30 cloistered nuns here. Note that access to the area where the cheese is produced is forbidden to all but the most important nuns, so you cannot watch it being made, but there is a shop where you can buy some.

Royal palace [196 A7] On a hill southwest of the town is a renovated royal palace. It is a beautiful 1½-hour walk up (there's no shortage of guides to show you the way) through rice fields with superb views across the valley. The 'palace' used to consist of two houses, but one burned down a few years ago. Two flagpoles remain, as do two tombs and a rock on which the king stood to make his speeches. There is a small **museum** which tells the history of the place.

SANDRANDAHY AND FANDRIANA A tarmac road northeast of Ambositra leads to Fandriana, well known for its raffia work. It takes about 1½ hours to cover the 45km from Ambositra. Roughly halfway is Sandrandahy, which holds a huge Wednesday market. **Hôtel Sariaka** has basic rooms for those wishing to stay. If you are in a private vehicle or on a bicycle, the dirt road from Fandriana to Antsirabe is very beautiful.

SOATANANA This village, 38km west of Ambositra, is nestled in picturesque rice paddies surrounded by granite peaks. The women produce exceptionally fine silk cloth. The region has the largest remaining area of *tapia* forest in Madagascar (*tapia* is the staple diet of the endemic silkworm, *Borocera madagascariensis*) where Feedback Madagascar/Ny Tanintsika oversees a project to reintroduce wild silkworms. A tour provides the opportunity to see all the stages in silk production, from the cocoon to weaving, including dying of the threads using natural dyes.

The trip to Soatanana can be made in an hour by private vehicle. You can organise a tour from Ambositra, hire a taxi, cycle or go most of the way by taxi-brousse. Take the paved RN35 (turn off RN7 12km south of Ambositra) for 15km west to

Anjoman' Akona, then ask for directions to Soatanana – you will need to take the dirt road that goes to Ambohimahazo.

AMBOSITRA TO FIANARANTSOA

Just south of Ambositra, near PK 266, is a turning for a **sacred cave**, signposted 'Toerana Masina', 500m west of RN7.

Continuing south, the scenery becomes increasingly spectacular. You pass dwindling remnants of the western limit of the rainforest. The road runs up and down steep hills, past neat Betsileo rice paddies interspersed with eucalyptus and pine groves. The steepest climb comes about 2 hours after Ambositra, when the vehicle labours up an endlessly curving road, through thick forests of introduced pine, and reaches the top where stalls selling fruit or baskets provide an excuse for a break. Just after **Ambatofitorahana**, for a few kilometres after PK 302, roadside sellers specialise in carved kitchenware. Half an hour further on, for a couple of kilometres either side of PK 340, the road is lined with stalls of delicious eucalyptus honey for much of the year.

Then it's down to **Ambohimahasoa** (good snacks are served at **Nirina**, which also has basic en-suite rooms). Beyond this, you pass more remnants of forests, then open country, rice paddies and houses as you begin the approach to Fianarantsoa.

ZAFIMANIRY VILLAGES This culturally fascinating region is home to the Zafimaniry, who are known for their woodcarving. Not only do they make handicrafts but their unique houses also feature ornate decoration. The Zafimaniry woodcarving culture was proclaimed a Masterpiece of the Oral and Intangible Heritage of Humanity by UNESCO in 2003.

There are 17 villages, of which most can be visited as part of an established ecotourism scheme, although it requires multi-day trekking to see more than one of them. **Antoetra** is the regional capital and the only one of the villages accessible by vehicle; however, the architecture here now uses modern materials so it is necessary to walk to one of the others to experience the original wooden Zafimaniry constructions.

The closest village is **Ifasina** ('place of dirt') which has a population of 500. It is only 5km away, but the trail is steep so it takes 2 hours. Also close enough for a day trip, so long as the weather is fine, are **Sakaivo Nord** and **Faliarivo** – each 3–4 hours' walk away. The route to the latter is the least strenuous, but the former path is more scenic and includes a viewpoint from which the whole region can be seen. Also recommended are **Fempina** and **Tetezandrotra**.

Public transport runs to Antoetra only on Wednesdays (market day) when several taxi-brousses depart local towns including Ambositra and Antsirabe around dawn, making the return journey later in the day. The turning for Antoetra is at the village of Ivato on RN7 (PK 274), from where you follow a 25km dirt track (1½hrs). The best accommodation in the area is **Sous le Soleil de Mada** (m *033 07 344 14/034 07 344 14*; e *souslesoleildemada@gmail.com; http://sousolesoleildemada.monsite-orange. fr;* **€€**) situated at the tiny village of Ambalandingana, 11km towards Antoetra from RN7 (turn down a signposted 900m track on the left). Its ten bungalows built in the traditional Zafimaniry style look out across rice paddies.

In Antoetra, there is basic dorm accommodation at **Papavelo** (m *032 02 344 99/034 20 884 46/034 85 327 02*; e *papavelo@malagasy.com or trekking@moov.mg; www.papavelotrekking.com;* **€**), where camping is permitted and tents can be hired. Visit the town hall to pay the 3,000Ar tourism fee. Guides cost from 15,000Ar per day and porters from 10,000Ar. Most of the villages have simple dormitory accommodation costing 2,000–10,000Ar per person depending on group size.

Almost all the trails are shadeless, so taking adequate sun protection is essential. Food and water also need to be organised in advance, as the villages have no shops (Sous le Soleil de Mada and Papavelo can provide picnic lunches for day trippers). Carved wooden souvenirs are on sale in each village and you are expected to purchase something to support the local craftsmen.

RANOMAFANA NATIONAL PARK

Two turnings lead from RN7 to Ranomafana: at PK 358 and PK 383. The second (30km to the national park then 6km further to Ranomafana village) is by far the better surfaced; the former is arguably more picturesque but requires a 4x4. The name 'Ranomafana' means 'hot water' and it was the waters, not the lemurs, which drew visitors in the colonial days and financed the building of the once-elegant and recently reopened Hôtel Station Thermale de Ranomafana.

These days the baths are generally ignored by visitors anxious to visit the eponymous national park. Particularly rich in wildlife, this hitherto unprotected fragment of mid-altitude rainforest first came to the world's attention with the discovery of the **golden bamboo lemur** in 1986; formal protection followed in 1991.

Among the trees are 11 further species of lemur, including red-fronted brown, red-bellied and black-and-white ruffed lemurs, as well as Milne-Edwards' sifaka, two more types of bamboo lemur and five nocturnal species. Then there are the birds: more than a hundred species with 36 endemic. And the reptiles. And the butterflies and other insects. Even if you saw no wildlife, there is enough variety in the vegetation and scenery, and enough pleasure in walking the well-constructed trails, to make a visit worthwhile. On the downside, the trails are steep and arduous, it often rains and there are leeches.

GETTING THERE AND AWAY Ranomafana is about 1½ hours from Fianar and 3½ hours from Ambositra. Plenty of taxi-brousses leave Fianar throughout the morning (6,000Ar), and there is no shortage of drivers or tour operators able to supply a private vehicle.

 WHERE TO STAY AND EAT *Map, opposite*
If you don't have a private vehicle at your disposal, take care when choosing a place to stay: most are several kilometres from the park entrance. One budget option is **camping** at the entrance, where there are sheltered tent pitches; three more campsites within the park are for those wanting to do multi-day treks.

Au Dom Nature (Domaine Nature) (20 bungalows) m 032 07 611 18; e domnatrnmf@ gmail.com; www.domainenaturemada.com. Excellent setting on a steep hillside halfway between village & park, with gorgeous river views. The quality of the service & food is only mediocre, however. €€€€

Setam Lodge (20 bungalows) \ 24 310 71 (Tana); m 032 43 607 03 (director)/033 09 872 92 (director)/034 21 470 09 (reception)/034 60 069 23 (director); e setamlodge@setam-madagascar. com; www.setam-lodge.mg. The best hotel in Ranomafana, about 1km from the park entrance. Spacious semi-detached bungalows on 3 levels

with stunning views of the forest & Namorona Valley. Good food, though limited choice. €€€€

Shanti Village (Relax) (4 bungalows) m 032 11 651 08/034 69 235 80; e shanti. ranomafana@gmail.com. Recommended with its restaurant Le Terrace. Simple rooms in lovely setting away from the bustle. B/fast inc. €€€€

Thermal (21 rooms) e thermal@lerelais. mg; www.thermal-ranomafana.mg. Once a much-loved spa retreat, this place closed in 1994 & didn't reopen until 2016, fully renovated by the owners of Karenjy cars (page 207). Bright rooms in minimalist modern style, en suite with AC. Splendid restaurant with novel menu. €€€€

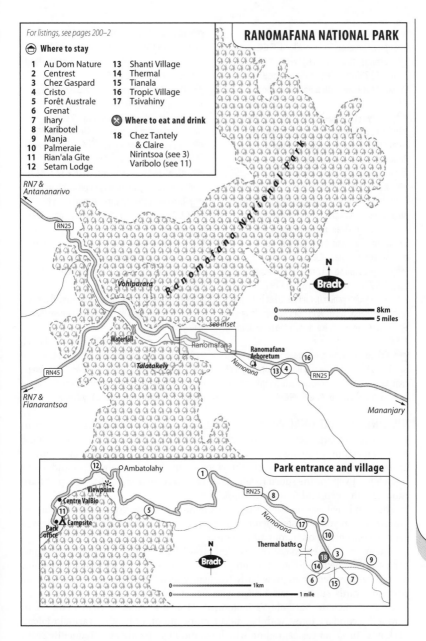

RANOMAFANA NATIONAL PARK

For listings, see pages 200–2

⬠ **Where to stay**

1 Au Dom Nature
2 Centrest
3 Chez Gaspard
4 Cristo
5 Forêt Australe
6 Grenat
7 Ihary
8 Karibotel
9 Manja
10 Palmeraie
11 Rian'ala Gîte
12 Setam Lodge
13 Shanti Village
14 Thermal
15 Tianala
16 Tropic Village
17 Tsivahiny

✕ **Where to eat and drink**

18 Chez Tantely
   & Claire
   Nirintsoa (see 3)
   Varibolo (see 11)

RN7 &
Antananarivo

RN25

Vohiparara

Ranomafana National Park

N

8km
5 miles

Waterfall

Ranomafana

Ranomafana
Arboretum
16

Talatakely

Namorona

13 4

RN25

RN45

RN7 &
Fianarantsoa

Mananjary

Park entrance and village

12   ○ Ambatolahy
Viewpoint
● Centre ValBio
11
▲ Campsite
Park
office

1

RN25   8

5

Namorona

17   2
10

Thermal baths ○

18   3
14   9
6   15   7

N

1km
1 mile

🏠 **Centrest** (18 rooms & 16 bungalows)
📱 034 16 524 33; **e** centrestsejour@gmail.com.
Very pleasant, recently refurbished & reasonably
priced accommodation, some with en-suite
facilities. **€€–€€€€**

🏠 **Chez Gaspard** (14 bungalows)
📱 032 87 115 15/033 01 155 05/034 02 115 15;

e chezgaspard.ranomafana@gmail.com. En-suite
rooms with hot water in attractive garden. **€€€**

🏠 **Forêt Australe** (18 bungalows) 📱 034 16
391 74 (reception)/034 45 479 30 (reservations);
e 01austhotel@gmail.com or contact@
groupeaustralhotel.com; www.groupeaustralhotel.
com. About 2km from the park. Quaint bungalows

with hot-water facilities. Restaurant serves Malagasy, European & Chinese food. €€€

🏠 **Grenat** (8 bungalows) m 032 74 777 37/034 12 780 84; e legrenatran@gmail.com. Elegant little hotel with simple clean rooms. Wi-Fi. €€€

🏠 **Ihary** (14 bungalows) m 032 02 526 98/033 12 857 22; e iharyhotel@gmail.com. Located just beyond the village of Ranomafana. Bungalows in a nice riverside setting; en-suite facilities. But rooms can be noisy. €€€

🏠 **Karibotel** (13 bungalows) m 033 15 629 50/033 15 629 51; e resa.karibotelranomafana@gmail.com; www.karibotel.mg. Newly built in 2014, simple clean bungalows with nice bathrooms. Swimming pool & terrace with panoramic forest view. €€€

🏠 **Tropic Village** (17 rooms) Mahatsinjorano; ✆ 22 695 76; m 034 09 435 63/034 79 878 43; e tropic.village@yahoo.fr. An upmarket hotel in Mahatsinjorano, about 9km from Ranomafana. Spacious rooms with nice view. Good restaurant. €€€

🏠 **Cristo** (6 rooms & 6 bungalows) m 033 03 878 34/034 12 353 97; e cristomadagascar@gmail.com; http://cristohotel.cabanova.fr. Simple rooms with en-suite bathrooms. €€–€€€

🏠 **Manja** (12 rooms & 20 bungalows) m 032 07 540 03/033 09 010 22/034 13 176 22; e hotelmanja@gmail.com. 5mins' walk east along river. Excellent food. €€–€€€

🏠 **Palmeraie** (9 rooms) m 033 09 637 42/034 52 251 84; e ravaoarisoaflorine@gmail.com. A good budget option with hot water & shared toilets. Restaurant on opposite side of road. €€

🏠 **Tianala** (5 rooms) m 033 41 049 44/034 15 044 04. Small guesthouse. €€

🏠 **Rian'ala Gîte** (3 rooms) m 034 12 778 62; e edm@moov.mg. Dormitory nr park entrance. €

🏠 **Tsivahiny (Ravinala)** (8 rooms) m 033 03 363 62. Basic, funky, very friendly, beautiful views & good food. €

✕ **Chez Tantely & Claire (Diavolana)** m 033 01 598 14; e diavolanaran@gmail.com. A nice welcoming little restaurant in the village. Also has rooms.

✕ **Nirintsoa** e franklin.rakotobe@gmail.com or restonirintsoa@gmail.com. Bar & restaurant with Malagasy food.

✕ **Varibolo** m 034 03 823 90/034 06 298 45/034 90 823 03; e info@varibolo.com; www.varibolo.com. Nr park entrance, with nice views overlooking forest. An ideal place to have lunch after hiking in the forest. B/fast available. Also kayak tours.

VISITING THE NATIONAL PARK (m *034 49 401 02/03*; e *ran@parcs-madagascar.com*) There is a large network of maintained trails. Most of the standard routes take a few hours, but if you are fit you could opt for the longer tours taking 6–8 hours. You will see primary forest, where the vines are thicker, the trees bigger and it will be quieter. Even for the shorter walks you need to be reasonably fit – the paths are moderate to steep, and frequently slippery.

Your guide will assume that it is mainly lemurs you have come to see; so, unless you stress that you are interested in other aspects such as botany or insects, he will tend to concentrate on mammals and birds.

You are most likely to see red-fronted brown lemurs, grey bamboo lemurs and the rarer red-bellied lemur. Star attractions such as greater bamboo lemur and golden bamboo lemur are now fairly frequently seen. There is also the spectacular Milne-Edwards' sifaka – dark brown with cream-coloured sides.

Circuits include **Varibolo-Varibolomena** (15km/4–5hrs), a challenging walk through secondary forest with bamboo lemurs and other lemurs; **Varibolo-Edena** (11km/2–3hrs), an easier trail on which bamboo lemurs are also frequently seen; **Varajatsy-Voaharanana** (8km/3–4hrs), a rather difficult trail in primary forest on which you may see black-and-white ruffed lemurs; **Varajatsy-Vohibato** (20km/2–3 days), an extension of Voaharanana to a natural pool and waterfall; **Varajatsy-Andranofady** (14km/7hrs), another fairly tough trail through a broad range of habitats including bamboo forest, swamp and past a sacred lake; and **Vohiparara-Sahamalaotra** (9km/2hrs), an easy circuit through degraded primary forest that is good for endemic birds, cultural sites, orchids and panoramic views.

In this last area, birders should be able to see brown emutail, Madagascar snipe, Meller's duck and the extremely rare slender-billed flufftail. This is also the best place for the rufous-headed ground-roller, Pollen's vanga and yellow-bellied sunbird-asity.

Permits and guides Permits (see page 73 for prices) are obtainable from the **park office** (⊕ *08.00–18.00*) where you can also easily find a guide. Guiding costs 15,000–35,000Ar (per group of up to five) depending on circuit length, or 60,000Ar for a full day. As of 2016, there is an additional community tax of 2,000Ar per person.

CENTRE VALBIO (PK 32) (m *034 13 581 71;* e *centrevalbio@gmail.com; www. centrevalbio.com*) This state-of-the-art international study centre with capacity for more than 40 researchers is the backbone of conservation work at Ranomafana. They run half-hour afternoon **tours of the centre** on which you will learn about their projects. **Evening lectures** given in English by the research scientists at 20.00 every night except Sunday are open to tourists. It is also possible to eat here. A visit is highly recommended but book ahead.

RANOMAFANA ARBORETUM (PK 40) (⊕ *daily 07.30–16.30; entry 5,000Ar*) This small community-run arboretum situated 8km past the national park entrance displays more than a hundred native trees in a 2ha plot. The trail is less than 1km but allow an hour to see everything. The specimens are labelled not just with their names, but with descriptions explaining the social roles of each species in Malagasy life, including the main purposes each type of tree is traditionally put to by the locals. You will discover why one type of wood is best for roof supports, another for door frames, and another for zebu carts; which tree is used for making rope; how the sap of another can be used for catching birds; the one considered the optimum firewood locally (despite an ability to survive forest fires); and the tree whose leaves are regarded as a better alternative to toilet paper! Most of the specimens were planted around 20 years ago but one palm is labelled as having been present on the site at the arboretum's inception and bears the following description: 'no one who has seen the tree knows its local name or knows of other palms like it'.

THERMAL BATHS (⊕ *Wed–Mon 08.00–16.30*) For a small fee you can have a wonderful warm swim in the **pool** near the village centre. Next door is a women's co-op where you can watch **silk and cotton** being woven and purchase the scarves they make.

MANIREKANA RESERVE (e *ecolodgemanirekana@gmail.com*) Some 32km beyond Ranomafana, around 7km from the village of Ifanadiana on the road that runs south towards Tolongoina, this little-known community-managed reserve offers circuits from 2 hours to multiple days. In addition to the forest flora and fauna, the set-up is geared to immersing tourists in the local culture, allowing them to experience local traditions, folk dances, regional cuisine and daily life. Accommodation is in simple Tanala huts.

FIANARANTSOA (PK 408) AND AROUND

The name means 'place of good learning'. Fianarantsoa (Fianar for short) was founded in 1830 as the administrative capital of Betsileo. The lower and upper towns are separated by a fairly steep climb ('shoulda taken a taxi' reflects reader Les Parkes, who suggests we provide a warning to 'knackered old asthmatics like me') and still further up the hill is the attractive **old town**, reachable only on foot. This delightful district was placed on the list of most threatened historical sites of World Monument Watch in 2008, but local charity **Save the Old City** is doing great work in providing grants to local residents to restore their crumbling homes and preserve their heritage.

The group also runs Imanoëla snack bar as well as Peniela guesthouse opposite **Antranobiriky church** near the hill crest. This church was rebuilt in 1889 by the English missionary Joseph Pearse, who wrote of the beams which can still be seen in the roof: 'We have had great difficulty in getting the large timbers, especially six beams 36ft long by·12in by 6in. They have to be cut in the forest very much larger than this, and then dragged here without any mechanical appliance whatever, so that it takes about 150 fellows to bring in one log and then we work them down to the required dimensions.'

GETTING THERE AND AWAY The journey by taxi-brousse takes roughly 8 hours from Tana (30,000Ar). The onward trip to Toliara takes some 11 hours (30,000Ar) or, going east, 7 hours to Manakara (13,000Ar). Between Tana and Fianar, there is now a more comfortable option offered by Cotisse Transport under their **Sonatra Plus** brand which is barely more expensive than regular taxi-brousses and has the advantages of scheduled departures and on-board Wi-Fi (m *032 12 027 02 in Fianar or 032 12 027 00 in Tana;* e *contact@cotisse-transport.com; www.cotisse-transport.com*).

Fianar is also connected to Manakara by the **FCE Railway** (page 208).

 WHERE TO STAY

Upper range €€€€

🏠 **Rizière** [205 D7] (10 rooms) Antady; 📞75 502 15; m 034 80 813 13; e direction. lariziere@gmail.com or hr.lariziere@gmail.com or info@lariziere.org; www.lariziere.org. Working hotel & restaurant of hotelier training academy opened in 2013. Over 50 trainee maids, chefs & barmen on 1–2yr courses run the operation under expert supervision. Very comfy rooms & 4ha garden. Splendid restaurant Vary Mena serves international & Malagasy cuisine. Closed Feb–Mar.

🏠 **Tsara Guest House** [205 A7] (14 rooms) Ambatolahikosoa; 📞75 502 06; m 032 05 516 12; e tsaraguest@moov.mg or tsaraguest@ tsaraguest.com; www.tsaraguest.com. Popular & universally praised by readers. An old house & garden that began life as a church; terrace has wonderful view of town. Most rooms en suite with TV & safe; also some cheaper rooms with shared facilities. Many tours offered. Wi-Fi. Cards accepted.

🏠 **Villa Sylvestre** [205 C3] (8 rooms) 📞75 511 19; m 032 11 248 07/032 49 203 33/033 78 721 74/034 21 449 97; e villasylvestre@blueline. mg; www.villasylvestre.com. Smart B&B with modern furnishings in a traditional 1920s building.

Spacious rooms with Wi-Fi, safe, coffee maker & minibar. Lounge area, terrace, courtyard, library & computers for internet. Attentive, welcoming & highly praised by all.

Mid-range €€€

🏠 **Case Madrigal** [205 D2] (4 rooms) m 032 60 316 40/034 66 011 30; e lacasemadrigal@ hotmail.fr; www.lacasemadrigal.wordpress. com. Welcoming homely B&B with cosy rooms & stunning views. Very reasonably priced sgl rooms; also an apartment. Highly recommended.

🏠 **Cotsoyannis** [205 B4] (21 rooms) 4 Rue Ramaharo; 📞75 514 72; m 032 40 209 86; e cotso@malagasy.com; www.hotel.cotsoyannis. mg. A long-established hotel; en-suite dbl rooms with good views.

🏠 **Mahamanina** [205 D1] (22 rooms) Rte d'Andriamboasary; 📞75 502 50/75 521 11; m 032 04 931 48/034 05 030 63/034 75 502 50/034 75 521 11; e hotel-mahamanina@moov.mg. Pleasant rooms; some en suite with balcony. Wi-Fi. Great restaurant. B/fast inc.

🏠 **Soafia** [205 D2] (83 rooms) Zorozoroana Ambalakisoa; 📞75 503 53; m 034 38 488 00; e soafia.hot@moov.mg. Curious rabbit warren of a hotel with cartoonesque décor. En-suite

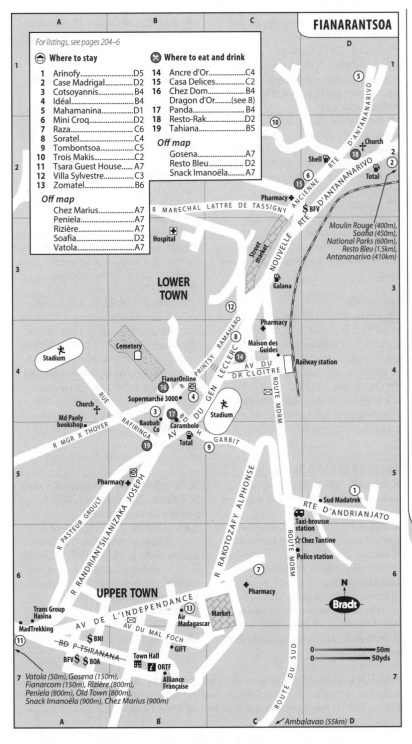

FIANARANTSOA

For listings, see pages 204–6

Where to stay

1   Arinofy..................D5
2   Case Madrigal.............D2
3   Cotsoyannis...............B4
4   Idéal.....................B4
5   Mahamanina...............D1
6   Mini Croq................D2
7   Raza.....................C6
8   Soratel..................C4
9   Tombontsoa..............C5
10 Trois Makis.............C2
11 Tsara Guest House......A7
12 Villa Sylvestre..........C3
13 Zomatel..................B6

Off map
    Chez Marius...............A7
    Peniela....................A7
    Rizière....................A7
    Soafia....................D2
    Vatola....................A7

Where to eat and drink

14 Ancre d'Or...............C4
15 Casa Delices............C2
16 Chez Dom...............B4
    Dragon d'Or........(see 8)
17 Panda...................B4
18 Resto-Rak...............D2
19 Tahiana.................B5

Off map
    Gosena..................A7
    Resto Bleu..............D2
    Snack Imanoëla.........A7

LOWER TOWN

R MARECHAL LATTRE DE TASSIGNY

Hospital

Street market

Galana

Pharmacy

Cemetery

Stadium

FianarOnline

Supermarché 3000

Maison des Guides

Railway station

Church

Md Paoly bookshop

Baobab Co

Carambole

Total

Stadium

Pharmacy

Church

Moulin Rouge (400m),
Soafia (450m),
National Parks (600m),
Resto Bleu (1.5km),
Antananarivo (410km)

Shell

Total

Sud Madatrek

Taxi-brousse station

Chez Tantine

Police station

UPPER TOWN

Trans Group Hasina

MadTrekking

Air Madagascar

Market

Pharmacy

BNI

BFV BOA

Town Hall

ORTF

Alliance Française

GIFT

N

Bradt

0   50m
0   50yds

Vatola (50m), Gosena (150m),
Fianarcom (150m), Rizière (800m),
Peniela (800m), Old Town (800m),
Snack Imanoëla (900m), Chez Marius (900m)

Ambalavao (55km)

RTE D'ANTANANARIVO
RTE ANCIENNE D'ANTANANARIVO
R PRINTSY RAMAHARO
AV DU GEN LECLERC
AV DU DR CLOITRE
ROUTE MDRM
RUE X THOYER
R RAFIRINGA
R MGR X THOYER
AV DU BD H GARBIT
R PASTEUR GROULT
R RANDRIANTSILANIZAKA JOSEPH
R RAKOTOZAFY ALPHONSE
RTE D'ANDRIANJATO
ROUTE MDRM
AV DE L'INDEPENDANCE
AV DU MAL FOCH
BD P TSIRANANA
ROUTE DU SUD

rooms with TV & minibar. Swimming pool; good restaurant; pool table in bar.

🏠 **Soratel** [205 C4] (32 rooms) Ampazambahaza; 📞75 516 66; m 033 08 988 88; e contact@soratel.com; www.soratel.com. Spacious rooms with TV, minibar, hairdryer & en-suite bath. B/fast inc.

🏠 **Tombontsoa** [205 C5] (8 rooms) Bd Hubert Garbit; 📞75 514 05; e contact@hotel-tombontsoa. com; www.hotel-tombontsoa.com. Well situated. En-suite rooms with TV, some with bath; 1 studio with kitchenette. Pool, sauna, tennis court, bar & restaurant.

🏠 **Zomatel** [205 B6] (51 rooms) Pl du Zoma; 📞75 507 97; m 034 07 255 27; e zomatel@ zomatel.com; www.zomatel-madagascar.com. Plain en-suite rooms with sat-TV, minibar & AC. Also 2 apartments with kitchenette. Spa with pool & jacuzzi.

Budget €€

🏠 **Arinofy** [205 D5] (10 rooms) 📞75 506 38; m 032 43 091 99/034 16 087 81 (manager); e arinofyhotel@gmail.com. Rooms mostly with communal facilities. Tent hire & camping (12,000Ar/tent). Organises treks & homestays.

🏠 **Chez Marius** [205 A7] (2 rooms) m 033 08 965 99/034 12 350 86; e avalisoamc@yahoo. fr. Charming guesthouse with magnificent views across Fianar to the mountains beyond.

🏠 **Idéal** [205 B4] (14 rooms) 📞75 513 67/75 901 32; m 032 43 592 63; e idealhotel.f@gmail. com. Basic hotel. Rooms mostly with shared facilities, some with TV.

🏠 **Mini Croq** [205 D2] (29 rooms) Ancienne Rte d'Antananarivo; 📞75 505 87/75 907 68; m 033 12 202 02; e mini.croq@yahoo.fr. Clean, bright rooms, mostly en suite. Good value. Popular with groups; booking advised.

🏠 **Old town homestays** (4 rooms) m 032 55 357 95/034 04 394 00; e psvv@moov.mg. Connect with the locals with a homestay in the most beautiful part of town. Booking obligatory (via charity PSVV).

🏠 **Peniela** [205 A7] (4 rooms) Rue du Rova; m 032 40 486 56; e peniela.house@yahoo.fr. Beautiful, lovingly restored presbetery building in old town. Great tranquil location; no vehicle access. Simple clean rooms with shared facilities.

🏠 **Raza** [205 C6] (4 rooms) 📞75 519 15; e kotoarivonyfils@yahoo.fr or razaotel@moov. mg. Well-furnished & spacious rooms with shared bathroom. Camping permitted (8,000Ar/person).

🏠 **Trois Makis** [205 C2] (2 rooms) 📞75 503 90; m 034 17 135 64; e troismakisfianar@gmail.com. Competitively priced & beautifully decorated small guesthouse. Private bathrooms. Food on request.

🏠 **Vatola** [205 A7] (6 rooms) 📞75 515 98. Marvellously friendly upper-town guesthouse. Rooms with communal hot showers. Excellent value inc food.

✗ WHERE TO EAT AND DRINK

✗ **Ancre d'Or** [205 C4] m 034 12 459 21. Spacious bar. Sometimes live music at w/ends. Great food & friendly staff.

✗ **Dragon d'Or** [205 C4] Downstairs at Soratel. Chinese/Malagasy restaurant; extensive menu.

✗ **Gosena** [205 A7] 📞75 516 16; ⊕ Mon–Sat. Charming old town family restaurant with soups, sandwiches & pastries.

✗ **Panda** [205 B4] Bd Garbit; 📞75 505 69; m 034 05 788 77. Chinese meals but questionable décor of crocodile skins & turtle shells.

✗ **Resto Bleu** [205 D2] Very good, inexpensive food. Friendly.

✗ **Resto-Rak** [205 D2] Malagasy food & salads.

✗ **Tahiana** [205 B5] m 032 02 786 75. A pleasant pizza & grill restaurant.

🍵 **Casa Delices** [205 C2] ⊕ Mon–Sat. Good value snacks; wonderful cakes, tarts & yoghurts.

🍵 **Chez Dom** [205 B4] m 032 02 460 78/034 01 975 78; e nono2mada@yahoo.fr. A fast-food café & bar; popular with *vazaha*. Internet access. Some local guides base themselves here.

🍵 **Snack Imanoëla** [205 A7] m 033 11 891 23/034 61 726 13; ⊕ Mon–Sat. Splendid little café in the old town.

NIGHTLIFE Fianar's nightclubs are rather simple. The best is **Soafia Dance** [205 D2] (⊕ *Tue & Thu–Sat*) at Soafia Hotel. Other options are **Moulin Rouge** [205 D2] on the outskirts of town and **Chez Tantine** [205 C6] by the taxi-brousse station.

MONEY AND COMMUNICATIONS Most of the banks/ATMs are in the upper town but there is also a BFV in the lower town (the only bank open on Saturday). There are post offices in both the upper and lower towns, with internet access at the latter. Other cybercafés are FianarOnline [205 B4] and Fianarcom [205 A7].

SHOPPING **Supermarché 3000** [205 B4] is a fairly well-stocked supermarket. For books, maps and postcards, try **Md Paoly** [205 A5]. Renowned black-and-white photographer Pierrot Men has his gallery and shop at **Labo Men** (❛ *75 500 23;* m *034 07 729 85;* e *pieromen@moov.mg; www.pierrotmen.com*) near Soafia Hotel. In addition to his books and postcards, it stocks camera cards and film. There is a good range of souvenir T-shirts and handicrafts at **Carambole** [205 B4].

TOURIST INFORMATION, TOUR OPERATORS, VEHICLE HIRE AND GUIDES

🛈 **ORTF** (regional tourist office) [205 B7] ❛75 904 67; m 032 43 231 62; e ortfianar@moov.mg or ortfianara@yahoo.fr or ortfianarantsoa@yahoo. fr. Limited information.

National Parks office [205 D2] ❛75 512 74; ⏲ Mon–Fri. The office is 250m up the dirt track opposite Jovenna fuel station on the road near the Soafia.

Fianar Touring ❛75 502 98; m 032 07 722 26/034 07 722 26; e fianartouring@moov.mg; www.fianartouring.com. Tours, trekking & car hire.

GIFT [205 B7] ❛75 514 72; m 034 08 652 17; e cotso@malagasy.com. Group of guides for town & regional tours.

MadTrekking [205 A6] ❛75 503 73; m 032 02 221 73/033 05 221 73/034 14 221 73; e mad.

trekking@moov.mg. Walks, pirogue trips, car hire & excursions inc Ranomafana, Isalo & Andringitra.

Maison des Guides [205 C4] m 034 03 123 01/032 02 728 97; e coeurmalgache@hotmail. com; ⏲ Mon–Fri. In wagon in front of railway station. Organises all types of tours & cheap accommodation.

SudMadatrek [205 D5] ❛75 932 68/506 11; e contact@sudmadatrek.mg; www.sudmadatrek. mg. Pirogue trips, car hire, trekking & excursions to Ranomafana, Isalo & Andringitra.

Trans Groupe Hasina ❛75 520 79; m 034 75 520 79/034 07 520 79; e transg.hasina@moov.mg; www.transgroupehasina-fianarantsoa.com; ⏲ Mon–Fri. Tours & car hire.

WHAT TO SEE AND DO
Exploring the town Take time to explore the old town and then visit the upper town market (best on Tuesday/Friday). On the road up to the old town is a small museum: **Musée Diocèse Fianarantsoa** [205 A7].

Karenjy factory (❛ *75 510 04;* m *034 75 510 17;* e *commercial@karenjy.mg; www. karenjy.mg*) While around town, keep your eyes peeled for slightly wacky-looking cars; you could see a Karenjy with its distinctive angular bodywork. Believe it or not, Madagascar actually has a (small) car industry, based here in Fianar. Set up in the mid-1980s, production stalled within five years after having manufactured fewer than a hundred vehicles (including a custom-designed Popemobile for John Paul II's 1989 Madagascar visit). Then in 2009 the factory was reopened. There are various models, including the **Iraka**, **Foaka** pick-up, diesel 4x4 **Mazana** sedan or convertible and, from 2014, the **Mazana II** concept car. **Factory tours** can be arranged by telephone appointment but photography is prohibited.

SAHAMBAVY This pretty valley with its lake and tea estate has its own resort-style hotel, making it well worth a stay of a day or two if you want to relax. If you don't have your own vehicle, you can get here by train or by taxi-brousse. With your own transport, take the turning at the Shell station 10km north of Fianar; Sahambavy is 13km from here by road, of which the last 4km is quite rough.

The **Sahambavy Tea Estate** (☏ *75 916 08/919 62*; e *sidexam@yahoo.fr*; ⏱ *07.30–15.30*), which employs 120 workers, has been manufacturing black tea for over 40 years and green tea since 2004. The 335ha plantation produces some 550 tonnes of tea each year, of which more than half is exported to Kenya. Guided tours of the factory take about an hour, cost 7,000Ar and end with a tasting; arrive before 14.00 to ensure you also get to see the pickers at work in the plantation.

Nearby, **Lac Hotel** (☏ *75 958 73/75 959 06*; e *lachotelsahambavy@gmail.com; www. lachotel.com*; €€€€) has 35 en-suite bungalows including a fantastic tree-house and some built out over the water. The lakeside location is a peaceful and romantic spot, safe for swimming. Other activities include horse-riding, pedalos, boat trips, cycling and hiking.

VINEYARD TOURS The famous **Lazan'i Betsileo** (☏ *75 901 27*; m *032 05 292 29/032 02 313 75*; e *lazan_i_betsileo@yahoo.fr*; ⏱ *Mon–Fri*) produces red, white, rosé and grey wines, as well as some liqueurs and aperitifs. It is located some 12km south of Fianar. It's best to book ahead for a visit.

Visitors can also witness the winemaking process at the **Cistercian-Trappist Monastery of Maromby**. You can get most of the way there by taxi-brousse (1,000Ar) or taxi (40,000Ar return).

ANDRAMBOVATO Most easily accessible by rail, Andrambovato is a great destination for those who like to get off the beaten track. It is a small rainforest village where a Malagasy NGO is working with locals to establish ecotourism. The emphasis is on hiking, with options to suit all levels of fitness. Visitors will see plenty of interest – both in the way of traditional rural life and wildlife. A local guide is obligatory and a small entrance fee is payable to the local community association. There are basic bungalows nearby owned by Lac Hotel (Sahambavy) and Tsara Guesthouse (Fianar), which can be booked via those hotels, or you can bring a tent.

FIANARANTSOA–COTE EST RAILWAY The 163km trip between Fianar and Manakara is popular with independent travellers. The train leaves for Manakara Tuesday/Saturday and takes all day, returning on Wednesday/Sunday; long delays, breakdowns, and cancellations are very common, however, so don't try to squeeze this trip into a tight inflexible itinerary. Tickets can be bought in advance from Fianar railway station (m *034 55 499 17*; e *accueil.fce@blueline.mg*) and cost 60,000Ar for the full journey or 30,000Ar as far as Manapatrana.

If travelling second class, board just before departure to get a spot by the door. This is nice and breezy, ensures you get a good view and avoids the smell of the toilet. The train stops frequently (there are 18 stations *en route*) allowing time for photography and for buying fruit and snacks from vendors.

The line, which was constructed between 1926 and 1936, passes over 67 bridges, through 48 tunnels (one is more than 1km long) and crosses the runway at Manakara airport! Many of the rails once formed part of a track in Alsace, but were seized from the Germans after World War I, and were eventually shipped to Madagascar by the French.

The lives of more than 100,000 people along the line depend on the FCE to bring supplies in and to send their produce to market. So it was a tragedy when, in 2000, cyclones caused almost 300 landslides that buried the track – and took months to clear. Locals came to understand that it was due to deforestation and poor farming methods that the mudslides had been so severe, and so new agricultural practices were quickly adopted. Now vetiver grass is planted between crops on slopes along the track to protect against washouts. A nice booklet describing the history of the FCE is available from the ticket office.

AMBALAVAO (PK 465) AND AROUND

Some 56km southwest of Fianarantsoa is a delightful highlands town: Ambalavao. The road drops steeply down to the town providing excellent views across the landscape. But RN7 does not pass through the attractive part; you should stop here at least to amble through the car-free streets which are thronged with people and take in the once-grand houses with their pillars, carved balconies and steep, red-tiled roofs. If travelling south, this is the last time you'll see typical highland architecture. The town is famous as the centre for *Antaimoro* paper-making, so a lot of tour buses stop here.

Market day is Wednesday. The Total fuel station has a small shop selling groceries and supplies including toiletries, batteries and gas canisters, and a BOA bank has opened recently.

 WHERE TO STAY AND EAT

🏠 **Tsienimparihy Lodge** (10 rooms & 8 bungalows) m 033 08 811 79. En-suite rooms & attractive thatched bungalows of various sizes; b/fast inc. €€€€

🏠 **Varangue Betsileo** (10 rooms) m 032 63 376 48; e jolymada@varangue-betsileo. com; www.varangue-betsileo.com. Located 8km south of Ambalavao, 4km before Anja Park, this beautifully planted peaceful spot enjoys incredible mountain views. Comfy en-suite rooms. Swimming pool. Local tours & circuits organised. €€€€

🏠 **Bougainvillées** (24 bungalows) ✆ 75 340 01/75 340 08; m 032 43 680 69; e auxbougainvilleesambalavao@gmail.com. Adjacent to the Antaimoro paper shop. Bungalows with en-suite bathrooms & solar-heated water. Restaurant popular with tour groups. €€€–€€€€

🏠 **Soalandy** (5 rooms) m 032 43 799 63/033 14 987 45; e soalandyambalavao@yahoo.fr. Simple rooms at a silk-producing centre. €€€

🏠 **Zongo** (10 rooms & 15 bungalows) m 033 83 724 59/034 93 742 59; e espacezongo@gmail. com. Malagasy-owned rooms (mostly en suite) at the north end of town, inc attractive tiled bungalows. Restaurant with large shady terrace & Wi-Fi. €€€

🏠 **Résidence du Betsileo** (11 rooms) m 033 83 725 54/034 10 665 45; e residencedubetsileo@ gmail.com. Centrally located & recommended. En-suite rooms with nice décor. Good restaurant. €€–€€€

🏠 **Tropik** (30 rooms) ✆ 75 340 55/75 341 82; m 033 02 012 91/034 50 481 33; e letropikhotel@ moov.mg or letropikhotel@yahoo.fr; www. letropikhotel.com. Clean & spacious en-suite sgl to family rooms with TV. Recently renovated & good value. €€–€€€

🏠 **Samoina** (4 rooms & 4 bungalows) RN7; m 033 05 029 61/033 11 444 89; e razafindrabepatrick@yahoo.fr. Northeast outskirts of town. Bungalows have en-suite bathrooms; rooms share facilities. Restaurant recommended. Good value. €€

🏠 **Tsienimparihy Hotel** (20 rooms) m 033 02 607 22/034 08 158 62; e hoteltsienimparihy@ yahoo.fr. En-suite rooms. Very good restaurant & patisserie. Car hire & tours organised. €€

🏠 **Notre** (8 rooms) Cheap but rather scruffy rooms with shared facilities. €

✖ **Fraîche Heure** ⊕ Mon–Sat. Good value Malagasy food & pizza.

🍷 **Ah-Tsin-Tsen** ✆ 75 341 97; ⊕ Tue–Sun. Snack bar owned by the Chan Foui family who have a local winery. You can buy their wine here.

WHAT TO SEE AND DO IN AMBALAVAO There are no taxis here, but most hotels can help with organising transport or tours to places nearby. **JB Trekking** (m *033 11 774 30/032 46 596 36*; e *jbtrekking@gmail.com*) near the north taxi-brousse station rents out bicycles and motorbikes, as well as camping equipment and arranging tours and treks. **Tsara Aventure** is another operator organising treks and mountain-biking tours, based next to Résidence du Betsileo. The **National Parks office** (⏱ *Mon–Fri 08.00–noon & 14.00–18.00*) is about 1km northeast of town on the main road.

Antaimoro paper factory (⏱ *Mon–Sat 07.30–11.30 & 13.00–17.00*) Ambalavao

is the home of the famous Malagasy *Antaimoro* paper. This papyrus-type paper impregnated with dried flowers is sold throughout the island made into such items as wall-hangings and lampshades. The people in this area are Betsileo, but paper-making in the area copies the coastal Antaimoro tradition which goes back to the Muslim immigrants who wrote verses from the Koran on this paper.

Antaimoro paper is traditionally made from the bark of the *avoha* tree from the eastern forests, but sisal paste is now sometimes used. After the bark is pounded and softened in water it is smoothed on to linen trays to dry in the sun. While still tacky, dried flowers are pressed into it and brushed over with a thin solution of the liquid bark to hold them in place. The open-air factory where all this happens is to the east of the town in the same compound as the Hôtel Bougainvillées. It is fascinating to see the step-by-step process, and you get a good tour. A shop sells the finished product in dozens of forms: from bookmarks and greeting cards to photo albums and picture frames.

Silk production (m *033 14 987 45/032 43 799 63;* ⏱ *07.30–17.00*) Witness the

process of silk production, from silkworm to silk scarf, at **Soalandy**. The workshop is opposite the Tropik Hotel, 100m beyond the National Parks office at the northeast end of town, and you can buy silk products here too.

If you have time to spare, combine this with a visit to **Nathocéane** (⏱ *Mon–Sat 08.00–noon & 14.00–17.00*), 250m back towards town, where you can buy T-shirts, bags and scarves and watch these items being embroidered.

Cattle market Held on Wednesday and Thursday on the outskirts of town, it gets

going as early as 03.00 – so best rise early! To get there take RN7 south and after about 1km you'll see the zebu on a hill to the left. After the market, the herdsmen take a month to walk the zebu to Tana, and you'll see these large herds on the road.

SOAVITA WINERY (⏱ *Mon–Sat 07.00–11.00 & 13.00–17.00; tours 3,000Ar*) This

place offers tours where you will be shown the various stages of winemaking by one of the workers, followed by a tasting. The turning for the winery is 3.5km from Ambalavao towards Fianar, from which point it is 1km down a track. You are advised to go to the Ah-Tsin-Tsen snack bar in town first to make an appointment to visit.

ANJA (ANJAHA) PARK (PK 477) About 13km south from Ambalavao on RN7 is

a community-run park which offers superb scenery, intriguing plants adapted to the dry southern climate, some interesting Betsileo history and several troops of cheeky **ring-tailed lemurs**.

The local people have long recognised the tourist potential here and so a few years ago they organised themselves to gain some income from it. The region is sacred to the Betsileo; their ancestors are buried here and it has always been *fady* to hunt the lemurs. The caves have provided a useful sanctuary in times of trouble and were inhabited up to a century or so ago.

The reserve covers 8ha and is home to about 300 ring-tails. Given some of the lemurs of Berenty go quite bald in the dry season because of feeding on an introduced toxic tree, this park provides a worthwhile alternative for tourists wanting a lemur fix and to benefit the local people. It costs 7,000Ar to visit the park, where you are provided with a guide (8,000Ar for 2 people). The well-maintained short trail winds past some impressive rocks, topped by waiting lemurs, to a sacred cliff where there is an apparently inaccessible tomb high in the rock face. The tour takes 1–2 hours. A longer circuit incorporating several stunning viewpoints can take up to 6 hours. There is a simple campsite at the trail head.

Most hotels and tour operators in Ambalavao and Fianar can help organise a visit. The park has mid-range accommodation: four bungalows and eight rooms.

AMBOHIMAHAMASINA Some 40km southeast of Ambalavao, Ambohimahamasina is home to a deeply sacred mountain: Ambondrombe. A community ecotourism project, FIZAM, has set up a network of trails and homestays in the area, giving travellers an opportunity to experience how rural folk live. Bordering the rainforest corridor that runs from Ranomafana to Andringitra, the beautiful Betsileo villages around Ambohimahamasina are surrounded by spectacular scenery.

The **Angavoa** trail (3hrs) is the shortest, passing wonderful scenery and interesting tombs. Of the three one-day trails, **Ambohitrampanefy** and **Ambohitravo** show you the traditional livelihoods of the region and allow you to try your hand at blacksmithing and basket-weaving, while **Itaolana** incorporates more flora and fauna and shows you the cultural value of the sacred mountain. The two-day **Ambondrombe** trail climbs to the 1,936m summit of Ambondrombe. And the three-day **Andriapiaka and Tsipoapoaka** trail passes through the rainforest to Vohipeno on the east coast. The trails are all interconnected so can be combined to make longer treks, with several homestays and campsites providing accommodation *en route*.

Guides can be found at the FIZAM office in Ambohimahamasina. There are fixed rates for guides, accommodation and meals, and the profits are used to benefit local communities.

Daily taxi-brousses come from Ambalavao (very early on market days – Monday and Thursday). By private vehicle it takes about an hour. Try to arrive in Ambohimahamasina in the morning, in good time to make arrangements for your first night's homestay. Alternatively, there are operators in Ambalavao and Fianarantsoa who can organise your trip.

ANDRINGITRA MASSIF

There are a few lodges and camps nestled among these spectacular granite peaks and domes, perfect bases for treks in and around the wonderful Andringitra National Park. With elevations varying massively – between 650m and 2,658m – it is one of the most biologically diverse sites in Madagascar. Access is very difficult in the rainy season and the park is closed from January to March.

GETTING THERE AND AWAY Travelling here by public transport is problematic: you may find a taxi-brousse to take you at least part of the way, but be prepared for a lot of walking. Most hire a car and driver in Fianar or leave it to a local tour operator (see pages 207 and 209–10) to arrange an all-inclusive visit.

Many visitors don't enter within the official boundary of the national park at all, for there are plenty of trekking paths in the surrounding mountains, but if you plan to then you need to start by visiting the office for a permit. The usual entry

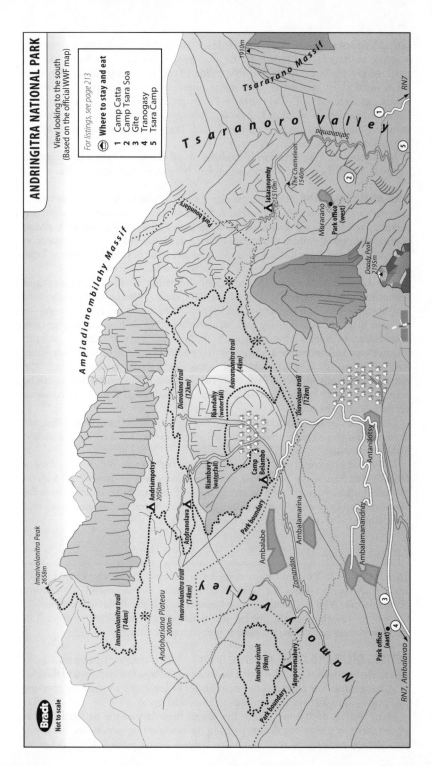

ANDRINGITRA NATIONAL PARK

View looking to the south
(Based on the official WWF map)

For listings, see page 213

Where to stay and eat
1 Camp Catta
2 Camp Tsara Soa
3 Gite
4 Tranogasy
5 Tsara Camp

Bradt
Not to scale

point for the protected area is Namoly in the east, but it can also be reached from the west via Morarano in Tsaranoro Valley. The main park office is at Namoly and a smaller one at Morarano can also issue permits but is not always manned; both are around 3 hours' drive from Ambalavao.

 WHERE TO STAY AND EAT *Map, opposite*

There are five **campsites** within the park, each with a cooking hut, running water and either a long-drop or flush toilet; a couple also have showers. Pitches cost 6,000Ar per night and camping gear can be rented. There is also a handful of more civilised lodges.

Camp Catta (12 bungalows) Tsaranoro Valley; m 034 96 957 04 (reception); e helgamada@gmail.com. West of the park, 2hrs from PK 497 on RN7, this excellent place is a centre for hiking, biking & climbing. There are lovely brick huts & lots of ring-tailed lemurs, as the name implies. Good food. Camping permitted. €€€€

Tsara Camp (15 bungalows) Tsaranoro Valley; \ 22 248 47 (reservations)/22 258 68 (Tana); m 033 12 441 27 (reservations)/033 15 530 73/034 12 657 99; e tsaracamp@ boogiepilgrim-madagascar.com; www. boogiepilgrim-madagascar.com. This tented camp is owned by Boogie Pilgrim (page 88). Large en-suite tents are pitched on wooden floors under thatched shelters, set on a spectacular plain at the foot of the massif. Treks of up to 5 days can be arranged, mostly outside the park perimeter. Closed Dec–Mar. €€€€

Camp Tsara Soa (11 bungalows) Tsaranoro Valley; \ 22 351 01; m 034 60 193 26/039 14 505 62; e fianamax@gmail.com or madamax@ madamax.com; www.madamax.com; see ad, page 215. Ecolodge geared to adventurous souls such as climbers & keen hikers. Simple bungalows & thatched round huts; excellent food. Camping permitted. €€€

Tranogasy Namoly Valley; m 033 11 264 27/033 14 306 78; e contact@tranogasy.com or tranogasy@yahoo.fr; www.tranogasy.com. Well-sited chalets (some en suite), but pricey considering it's becoming run-down. Can arrange complete package for trekkers, inc transfer from Ambalavao, guides & porters. €€€

Gîte Namoly Valley; \ 75 340 81; e arg. andringitra@gmail.com or arg@parcs-madagascar. com. This simple charming hut is comfy, but it's a 1hr drive from the trail heads. Shared cold-water facilities. You need to bring your own food, but there is a cook to prepare it for you. €€

ANDRINGITRA NATIONAL PARK (\ *75 340 81;* e *arg@parcs-madagascar.com*) Created in 1999, this 31,160ha park protects the area around Madagascar's second-highest peak: Pic d'Imarivolanitra (2,658m), meaning 'close to the sky' (formerly known as Pic Boby). Andringitra has some wildlife, but landscape, vegetation and trekking are the chief attractions. And what attractions! This is truly one of Madagascar's best-kept secrets, with barely a thousand visitors a year. The

8

THE RING-TAILED LEMURS OF ANDRINGITRA   *Hilary Bradt*

When researchers first started investigating the fauna of Andringitra, in the early 1990s, they thought they'd found a subspecies of *Lemur catta*. The lemurs here look different from those in the southern spiny desert and gallery forest of Berenty. They appear slightly larger, their fur is thicker, and the colours seem more dramatic: a chestnut back, rather than grey-brown, with whiter whites and blacker blacks. And their behaviour is different. In the absence of trees these lemurs leap from rock to rock with great agility, often on their back legs like sifakas. It is now known that this variation is simply an adaptation to their cold, treeless environment – so the lemurs of Andringitra are an ecotype, not a subspecies.

combination of granite peaks and gneiss formations, endemic succulent plants and ring-tailed lemurs (albeit at a distance) makes this an utterly different – and utterly marvellous – walking experience.

Each circuit covers different terrain, from forest and waterfalls to the frosty peak of Imarivolanitra. In the warmer, wet season the meadows are carpeted with flowers, including 30 species of orchid. Great care has been taken in creating the trails which are beautifully engineered through difficult terrain to make them as safe and easy as possible. Although the trail system covers a variety of ecosystems, the park also protects an area of montane rainforest in the east which is closed to visitors, providing sanctuary for such rare species as golden and greater bamboo lemurs.

There are five circuits: **Asaramanitra** (6km/4hrs) begins at the Belambo campsite and climbs up to two sacred waterfalls, Riambavy and Riandahy ('queen and king'), which plunge 250m off the edge of an escarpment; **Imaitso** (14km/8hrs) in the extreme east of the park takes you through a remnant of primary forest clinging to the side of a mountain with the possibility of seeing five lemur species; **Diavolana** (13km/10hrs) is the *real* Andringitra, a tough walk with an altitude gain of 500m, affording a close-up experience of the granite peaks and escarpments, with stunning views; **Isahavato** (15km/12hrs) is of botanical interest, passing some rare palms; and finally the big one, **Imarivolanitra** (28km/2–3 days), the trek to the highest peak – which needs advance planning to organise porters – offers incredible views and high-altitude flora.

There is no point in going to Andringitra unless you are equipped for walking. This means boots or tough trainers, hiking poles, daysack, good rain gear and a water bottle. Remember also that at this altitude the nights can be *very* cold, so bring appropriate clothing and camping gear. Days are pleasantly warm, but it can rain – hard – at any time. It's worth bringing a swimsuit for a freezing (but refreshing) dip in the pool on the Diavolana circuit.

The area is popular with **rock climbers** and is also a base for **paragliding** – contact Hery (**m** *034 68 381 13*).

Permits and guides The guides are well trained and knowledgeable, particularly on the medicinal use of plants, and one or two speak English. Permit prices are on page 73.

AMBALAVAO TO IHOSY

The scenery beyond Ambalavao is marvellous. Huge domes of granite dominate the grassy plains. The most striking one, with twin rock towers, is called **Varavarana Ny Atsimo** ('the door to the south'). It's visible from a long stretch of the road but the best views are around PK 493. A little further on is the **Bonnet de l'Evêque** ('bishop's cap') – a 4km-long lump of granite shaped like an upturned boat rising 600m out of the surrounding plain. Optimum viewing points are around PK 529 and PK 538.

You will notice that not only the scenery but the villages are different. Bara houses are solidly constructed from red earth (no elegant Merina pillars here) with small windows. Shortly after Ambalavao you start to see tombs – some painted with scenes from the life of the deceased.

The road passes through lots of villages along this stretch, including **Ankaramena** (PK 519), where a cattle market takes place on Fridays and there is simple accommodation, **Voatavo** (PK 547) whose name means 'pumpkin', and **Zazafotsy** (PK 566), meaning 'white child', where there is a basic hotel called Tongasoa. The turning for the very bad road to Ivohibe is at PK 598, after which the next town of importance is Ihosy (PK 611), covered in *Chapter 9* along with the rest of the journey to Toliara.

Hilary Bradt

The humpbacked cattle, zebu, which number more than half the country's human population, produce a relatively low yield in milk and meat. These animals are near-sacred and are generally not eaten by the Malagasy outside of important social or religious ceremonies. Zebu are said to have originated from northeast India, eventually spreading as far as Egypt and then down to Ethiopia and other parts of East Africa. It is not known how they were introduced to Madagascar but they are a symbol of wealth and status as well as being used for burden. An adult is worth around 650,000Ar.

Zebu come in a variety of colours, the most sought after being the *omby volavita*, which is chestnut with a white spot on the head. There are some 80 words in the Malagasy language to describe the physical attributes of zebu, in particular the colour, horns and hump.

In the south, zebu meat is always served at funerals, and among certain southern tribes the cattle are used as marriage settlements, as in mainland Africa. Whenever there is a traditional ritual or ceremony zebu are sacrificed, the heads being given to the highest-ranking members of the community. Blood is smeared on participants as it is believed to have purification properties, and the fat from the hump of the cattle is used as an ingredient for incense. I have seen a Vezo village elder wearing a domed hat apparently made from a zebu hump. Zebu milk is an important part of the diet among the Antandroy; it is *fady* for women to milk the cows but it is they who sell the curdled milk in the market.

Tourists in the south will see large herds of zebu being driven to market, a journey that may take several days. All cattle crossing regional borders must wear 'zebu passports' in the form of yellow ear tags, bearing the names of the owner and animal, along with its ID number. Cattle rustling is now a major problem. Whereas before it was mainly confined to the Bara, as an initiation into manhood, it is now organised by large, Mafia-like gangs. In former times the punishment matched the crime: a fine of ten zebu would have to be paid by the thief, five for the family from whom the cattle were stolen and five more for the king.

To the rural Malagasy a herd of zebu is as symbolic of prosperity as a new car or a large house in Western culture. Government aid programmes must take this into account; for instance, improved rice yields will indirectly lead to more environmental degradation by providing more money to buy more zebu. The French colonial government thought they had an answer: they introduced a tax on each animal. However, local politicians were quick to point out that since Malagasy women had always been exempt from taxation, the same rule should apply to cows!

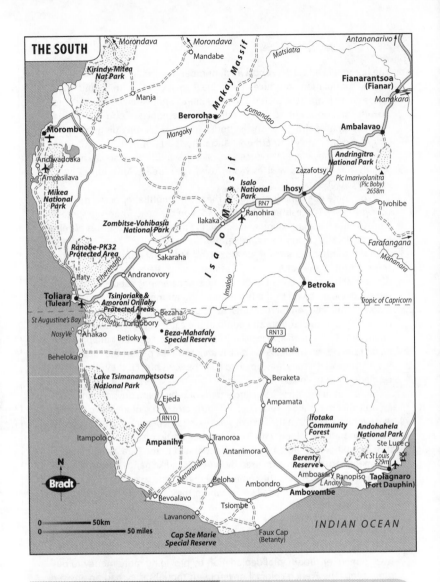

THE SOUTH

Morondava
Mandabe
Morondava
Matsiatra
Antananarivo
Kirindy-Mitea Nat Park
Makay Massif
Fianarantsoa (Fianar)
Manja
Zomandao
Manakara
Beroroha
Mangoky
Ambalavao
Morombe
Andavadoaka
Andringitra National Park
Ampasilava
Zazafotsy
Pic Imarivolanitra (Pic Boby) 2658m
Mikea National Park
Isalo National Park
Ihosy
Ivohibe
Zombitse-Vohibasia National Park
Ilakaka
RN7
Ranohira
Isalo Massif
Ranobe-PK32 Protected Area
Sakaraha
Farafangana
Mananara
Ifaty
Andranovory
Imalolo
Betroka
Fiherenano
Toliara (Tulear)
Tsinjoriake & Amoroni Onilahy Protected Areas
Bezaha
Tropic of Capricorn
St Augustine's Bay
Onilahy
Tongobory
Beza-Mahafaly Special Reserve
RN13
Nosy Ve
Anakao
Betioky
Isoanala
Beheloka
Beraketa
Lake Tsimanampetsotsa National Park
Ampamata
Linta
Ejeda
RN10
Ifotaka Community Forest
Andohahela National Park
Itampolo
Tranoroa
Ampanihy
Berenty Reserve
Ste Luce
Pic St Louis 529m
Antanimora
Amboasary
Ranopiso
Taolagnaro (Fort Dauphin)
N
Bradt
Menarandra
Beloha
L Anony
Ambondro
Ambovombe
Bevoalavo
Tsiombe
Lavanono
INDIAN OCEAN
0   50km
0   50 miles
Cap Ste Marie Special Reserve
Faux Cap (Betanty)

DISTANCES IN KILOMETRES

Ihosy–Taolagnaro	506km	Toliara–Morombe	290km
Ihosy–Betroka	132km	Bezaha–Ampanihy	199km
Ihosy–Ranohira	89km	Tsiombe–Faux Cap	30km
Ranohira–Sakaraha	122km	Tsiombe–Lavanono	94km
Sakaraha–Toliara	133km	Itampolo–Anakao	134km
Toliara–Anakao	286km	Ampanihy–Taolagnaro	334km
Toliara–Ifaty	27km	Taolagnaro–Betroka	374km
Toliara–Andavadoaka	338km	Taolagnaro–Amboasary	75km
Toliara–Bezaha	129km	Taolagnaro–Berenty	89km

9

The South

This is the most exotic and the most famous part of Madagascar, the region of spiny desert where weird cactus-like trees wave their thorny fingers in the sky, where fragments of elephant bird eggshells may still be found, and where the Mahafaly tribe erect their intriguing and often entertaining *aloalo* stelae above the graves. Here also are some of the country's most popular national parks and reserves, as well as its best beaches and coral reefs. No wonder the south features on almost all tour itineraries.

Road travel in the south can be a challenging affair, but RN7 to Toliara (Tulear) is a good paved road. Only rough tracks connect Taolagnaro to the rest of the country, though, so many visitors prefer to fly to the southeast.

HISTORY

Europeans have been coming to this area since at least 1527 when a group of 600 Portuguese sailors was shipwrecked. Later, when sailors were deliberately landing in Madagascar during the days of the spice trade in the 16th and 17th centuries, St Augustine's Bay, south of modern-day Toliara, became a favoured destination. Dutch and British came for reprovisioning – trading silver and beads for meat and fruit. One Englishman, Walter Hamond, was so overcome with the delights of Madagascar and the Malagasy ('the happiest people in the world') that fired by his enthusiasm the British attempted to establish a colony at St Augustine's Bay. It was not a success. The original 140 settlers were soon whittled down to 60 through disease and murder by the local tribesmen who became less happy when they found their favourite beads were not available for trade and that these *vazaha* showed no sign of going away. The colonists left in 1646. Fifty years later the bay was a haven for pirates.

THE PEOPLE TODAY Several ethnic groups live in the south: the Vezo (fishermen), Mikea and Masikoro (pastoralists) are subclans of the Sakalava; the Mahafaly, Antanosy, Antandroy and Bara all have their homes in the interior. These southern Malagasy are tough, dark-skinned people with African features, accustomed to the hardship of living in a region where rain seldom falls and finding water and grazing for their large herds of zebu is a constant challenge. The Bara, known for their association with cattle, are a warlike tribe who resisted Merina rule and were never really subdued until French colonial times. Cattle rustling is a time-honoured custom – traditionally a Bara does not achieve manhood until he has stolen a few of his neighbours' cows.

In contrast to the highland people, ancestors are often commemorated as individuals by many southern tribes: a rich Mahafaly or Masikoro man will have the highlights of his life perpetuated in the form of wooden carvings (aloalo) and colourful paintings adorning his tomb.

Antandroy tombs may be equally colourful. They are large and rectangular and, like those of the Mahafaly, topped with zebu skulls left over from the funeral feast; a very rich man may have over a hundred. They usually have 'male and female' standing stones (or more recently cement towers) at each side. Modern tombs can be brightly painted, though not necessarily with scenes from the life of the deceased.

In Antandroy country, burial sometimes takes place months after the day of death, which will be commemorated by the sacrifice of cattle and ritual mourning or wailing. A few days later the body is placed in the coffin – and more zebu are sacrificed. Meanwhile finishing touches will be made to the tomb, before the interment ceremony, which takes place over two days or more. The tomb is finally filled in with stones and topped with the horns of the sacrificed zebu. Then the house of the deceased is burnt to the ground. The burial ceremonies over, the family will not go near the tomb again.

The Antanosy have upright stones, cement obelisks or beautifully carved wooden memorials. These, however, are not over the graves themselves but in a sacred and secret place elsewhere.

IHOSY TO RANOHIRA

This section of RN7 crosses the Horombe Plateau – monotonous grasslands that look rather dull from a distance, but up close you can find all kinds of wonderful plants and fungi. As you approach Ranohira, *Medemia* palms enliven the scenery. 'They are properly called *Bismarckia*,' explains Kew's Henk Beentje, 'but the French didn't like the most common palm in one of their colonies being called after a German so changed the name, quite illegally according to the Code of Botanical Nomenclature!'

IHOSY (PK 602) Pronounced 'ee*oosh*', this small town is the capital of the Bara tribe. It is about 5 hours from Fianar by *taxi-brousse* and lies 15km before RN7's junction with RN13, a rocky road to the south coast (but see the warning on page 219). An almost impassable road also runs to Farafangana on the east coast (page 293).

Ihosy is a medium-sized transit town with a post office, small hospital and BOA bank (but no ATM). Try opposite Manambitsoa for internet. In town there is a square with quaint open-sided *hotely* eateries.

 Where to stay and eat

Relais Bara (16 rooms) 75 800 17. Opposite post office. Rooms mostly en suite but run-down. €€–€€€

Tamana (21 rooms) m 033 14 509 09/034 14 509 09; e fanemada@gmail.com or longobrice@gmail.com or tamanahotel.mg@gmail.com. 800m from centre towards Toliara. En-suite rooms with hot water & TV. €€–€€€

Nirina (3 rooms) m 032 02 585 93/032 07 521 95/033 81 766 97. Opposite Total fuel station. Shared facilities with hot water. Good food. €€

Ravaka (18 rooms) m 033 12 444 06/033 72 511 71/034 92 437 07. Basic dbl & family rooms, a few en suite (cold water). €€

Fenoarivo m 034 93 351 12. €

Galaxie (5 rooms) m 032 48 729 82/033 11 597 26. €

Magneva m 033 01 542 74. €

Manambitsoa (Chez Evah) m 033 73 384 54. €

ANDRANOMILITSY CAVES Located 10km beyond Ihosy and just 15 minutes on foot from RN7, this site was opened for tourism in 2013 by the regional tourist office, ORTII (m *033 17 147 75/032 72 817 04*; e *ortisalo.ihorombe@gmail.com*). The steeply inclined caves penetrate 120m deep into the Ikalamainty cliff face, which separates the crystalline northern bedrock from the southern sedimentary basin, fascinating for its decorative stalactites and stalagmites as well as its resident bats. The surrounding area is ideal for a picnic stop, with a natural swimming pool, waterfall and panoramic views.

SOUTH TO AMBOVOMBE (AND ON TO TAOLAGNARO) The RN13 running southward from Ihosy via Betroka is not recommended owing to the security situation: it is perhaps the most lawless area of Madagascar nowadays. One local contact told us in 2016 that 'murders have become so common in Betroka that the hospital staff have fled'. Most travellers going overland to Taolagnaro (Fort Dauphin) take RN10 from Andranovory and a few take the east coast road (page 295), which is being improved in an EU-funded project at the time of writing.

RANOHIRA (PK 690) In the 89km beyond Ihosy, you cross the Horombe Plateau – a good place for spotting marsh owls and harrier-hawks (especially around PK 623) – before eventually reaching Ranohira, the gateway town for the popular Isalo National Park. Getting there is no problem – if coming from Toliara (23,000Ar) note that the taxi-brousses and buses depart early, so try to book the day before – but getting away can be difficult since there is no taxi-brousse station, and southbound services are usually full by the time they reach Ranohira. You may have to find a local vehicle to take you to Ilakaka or Ihosy, where there are more taxi-brousse options.

There is also no bank, but if you get stuck some of the hotels will change cash. Accommodation listings for Ranohira are included under *Isalo National Park* below.

Located opposite Orchidée, **Joyeux Lémuriens** is well stocked with drinks, biscuits and a few tinned goods. Much bigger is **Supermarché de l'Isalo** (⊕ *Mon–Sat 08.00–noon & 14.30–18.00, Sun 14.30–18.00*), 850m from Ranohira centre towards Tana. It sells food and a surprisingly good range of camping equipment as well as clothing.

ISALO NATIONAL PARK

The combination of sandstone rocks cut by deep canyons and eroded into weird shapes, rare endemic plants and dry weather for most of the year makes this Madagascar's most popular national park. For botanists there are *Pachypodium* plants and a locally endemic *Aloe*; and for lemur lovers there are sifakas, brown lemurs and ring-tails. Isalo is also sacred to the Bara tribe; for hundreds of years they have used caves in the canyon walls as burial sites.

 WHERE TO STAY AND EAT *Map, page 220*
Affordable accommodation can be found in Ranohira while the higher-end hotels are mostly strung out along RN7 towards Ilakaka. **Camping** is possible with Momo Trek at the ITC Lodge site, as well as at nine campsites within the park.

Top end €€€€€
⌂ **Isalo Rock Lodge** (60 rooms) ☏ 22 328 60 (Tana); m 034 02 034 00/034 16 064 59; e resirl@ hms1.mg; www.isalorocklodge.com. Blending in with its rocky surroundings, this lodge sits high amid the sandstone with breathtaking views. Luxurious rooms in 10 pavilions. Spa & pool.
⌂ **Jardin du Roy** (40 rooms) ☏ 22 336 23 (Tana)/22 351 65 (Tana); m 032 07 843 44

(reservations)/033 07 123 07/034 02 123 08/034 02 351 66 (reservations); e htl@madagascar-discovery.com; www.lejardinduroy.com. Luxurious hotel built in grey stone, echoing the landscape of rocky outcrops among which it is nestled. The beautifully designed bungalows are attractively furnished, with AC, spacious bathrooms & broad verandas. Excellent restaurant, bar, big pool, spa & airstrip.

ISALO NATIONAL PARK

For listings, see pages 219–21

⊖ **Where to stay**

1 Chez Alice
2 H1
3 Isalo Ranch
4 Isalo Rock Lodge
5 Jardin du Roy
6 Joyau de l'Isalo
7 Motel d'Isalo
8 Relais de la Reine
9 Satrana Lodge
10 Toiles de l'Isalo
11 *Ranohira:*
   Berny
   ITC Lodge
   Leader Lodge
   Orchidée d'Isalo

🏠 **Relais de la Reine** (30 rooms) 📞22 351 65 (Tana); **m** 034 02 123 29; **e** resa@ lerelaisdelareine.com; www.lerelaisdelareine. com. Same ownership as neighbouring Jardin du Roy. Blocks of 6 rooms grouped around a courtyard blend into the 40ha gardens. Water is drawn from a stream & is solar heated for en-suite showers. 2 de luxe rooms have AC & bath. Pool, tennis court, basketball & horse-riding.

🏠 **Satrana Lodge** (40 bungalows) **m** 032 07 760 59 (Tana)/034 14 260 87/034 14 279 76; **e** satranalodge@cortezexpeditions.mg or satranalodgeisalo@yahoo.fr; www.satranalodge-madagascar.com. Tented bungalows with en-suite facilities & wooden deck overlooking Isalo.

Upper range €€€€

🏠 **H1** (9 bungalows) **m** 032 84 680 84/033 05 539 48; **e** hotelh1isalo@gmail.com; www.hotelh1-madagascar.com. Fairly smart new place: nothing grand but clean & efficient.

🏠 **Isalo Ranch** (20 bungalows) 📞24 319 02; **m** 033 05 510 25/033 15 510 25/034 02 510 25/034 05 510 25/034 20 319 02; **e** info@isalo-ranch.com;

www.isalo-ranch.com. Branding itself as an ecolodge, this recommended hotel has comfy bungalows, mostly en suite with solar-heated water. Public swimming pool & restaurant. Car hire. Camping permitted (8,000Ar/person).

Mid-range €€€

🏠 **Berny** (14 rooms) **m** 032 05 257 69/032 05 257 75/032 40 227 43; **e** hotelbernyisalo@orange. mg. Central dbl & trpl rooms, mostly en suite.

🏠 **Chez Alice** (15 bungalows) **m** 032 02 055 68/033 07 134 44/033 20 522 50 (owner); **e** chezalice@yahoo.fr. Bungalows & Bara-style huts on meadow 500m from town, overlooking Isalo. The gregarious proprietor speaks some English. Excellent food. Camping 3,000Ar/person; tent hire 6,000Ar.

🏠 **ITC Lodge** (21 bungalows) **m** 032 45 703 36; **e** itc.madagascar@yahoo.com; www.itclodge-isalo.com. Nr park office. Bara-style huts with shared cold-water facilities & trpl rooms with en-suite hot water. Bar & restaurant. Large camping area: 3,000Ar/person with own tent or 10,000Ar/ tent inc 2-man tent hire.

Leader Lodge (5 rooms) m 033 03 955 76/034 25 489 53; e leaderlodge@hotmail.fr or libisoa@hotmail.fr; www.leader-lodge.e-monsite. com. Malagasy family-run rooms with sat-TV & Wi-Fi in 2 villas on the east side of town near the post office. Kitchen for guests' use.

Motel d'Isalo (62 bungalows) \22 315 04 (Tana); m 032 02 621 23/032 40 837 95 (reception)/032 40 892 59; e motelisalo@moov. mg; www.motelisalo.com. The 1st hotel, coming from the north. Nice bungalows with en-suite rooms, solar heating & swimming pool. Much praised, but away from the centre of town.

Orchidée d'Isalo (45 rooms) m 032 44 676 89/033 06 918 75/034 76 942 01; e hotel@ orchidee-isalo.com; www.orchidee-isalo.com. At the centre of the village, attractive en-suite dbl & twin rooms, mostly with hot water. Reception is at Zebu Grillé, their spacious & smart restaurant.

Toiles de l'Isalo (10 bungalows) \22 245 34 (Tana); m 032 05 398 00/032 05 399 00/033 11 025 25; e toilesdisalo@moov.mg; www.hotel-toiles-isalo.mg. Dbl, twin & trpl rooms with hot water facilities. Pool & recommended restaurant.

PERMITS, GUIDES AND VEHICLES You will need to buy a permit (prices on page 73) from the **park office** in Ranohira (m *033 13 172 58/034 49 400 98*; e *isl@parcs-madagascar.com*; ☉ *07.00–17.00*). Try to make your arrangements at the office the day before so you can make an early start and avoid the heat of the day (many of the trails offer little shade). Around half of the 70 **guides** speak English; check the noticeboard for information on the specialities of each one.

For most excursions you will need a **vehicle** to get to the appropriate start point to avoid the rather dull 1–2-hour walk from Ranohira to the park boundary. Guides can organise a car and driver for you but note that they will take a commission; so if you're on a tight budget it may be cheaper to find a driver yourself.

HIKING AND TREKKING There are several established circuits providing all the Isalo specials of lemurs, cool leafy canyons and hot, dry plains with extraordinary rock formations and accompanying succulent plants. Most incorporate campsites so, if possible, arrange to camp overnight in the park; that way you can hike in the cooler parts of the day.

Momo Trek (see *Where to stay and eat*) organises **trekking** packages with guide, porters, meals and camping equipment included for 90,000–165,000Ar per person (price depends on group size) for two days, and longer treks up to 305,000–490,000Ar for six days.

The *piscine naturelle* is justifiably the most popular destination for hikers in Isalo, so can get crowded. This palm-fringed pool is a 3km hike from the car park, starting with a fairly steep elevation gain of 80m but is fairly easy and flat (albeit largely unshaded) thereafter. Constantly filled with warm water from a waterfall, the pool lies in a stunningly beautiful sunken oasis with an open-sided shelter where Benson's rock thrushes flirt with bathers.

The **Namaza** trail has you following a stream (some scrambling) up a leafy canyon to the Cascade des Nymphes. The walk takes 30–45 minutes and you are rewarded at the end with a refreshing swim in surprisingly cold and deep water. The campsite here is regularly visited by ring-tails, brown lemurs and hoopoes.

Canyon des Makis is 18km by 4x4 from Ranohira or 9km on foot. At the canyon a path goes over rocks and along the edge of the tumbling river; there are pools into which you can fling yourself at intervals and, at the top, a small waterfall under which to have a shower. The sheer rocks hung with luxuriant ferns broaden out to provide views of the bare mountain behind, and trees and palms provide shade for a picnic. A visit may be combined with the neighbouring **Canyon des Rats** for a full-day trip.

A self-guided circuit has been set up with German funding. Starting a 37km drive northwest of Ranohira, **Antsifotse** is a 3-hour circuit of moderate difficulty, including a natural pool, tombs and the possibility of seeing ring-tails and sifakas.

LA FENETRE This is a popular site – perhaps too popular at times. A natural rock formation provides a window to the setting sun. It is just off RN7 so no hiking is necessary, nor do you need a permit or guide. A taxi from Ranohira should cost about 30,000Ar for the round trip. There have been muggings here so avoid taking valuables or hanging around after dark.

ISALO INTERPRETATION CENTRE (MAISON DE L'ISALO) (⏰ *07.00–18.00; entry free*) This is a tremendous museum in a beautiful building, well worth a visit to learn more about the wildlife of the park and the people who live locally. The well-designed exhibits have multilingual explanations. Sited almost 10km south of Ranohira, a visit may most conveniently be combined with La Fenêtre.

GROTTE DES PORTUGAIS Some 45km from Ranohira at the northern extremity of the national park, this 32m-long cave is reachable by 4x4 or 4–6 days' trekking. This picturesque area is the place to head to get away from other tourists.

OTHER ACTIVITIES A **via ferrata** has been created near to the Hôtel Relais de la Reine by professional French climbers. This 500m steel cable bolted to the cliff face gives you the chance to go rock climbing in absolute safety. Suitable even for beginners, the route takes about 90 minutes and the panoramic views are particularly stunning around sunset. Harnesses, safety helmets and gloves are provided and trained guides accompany all groups.

Horse-riding is also available; enquire at Relais de la Reine.

THE MAKAY MASSIF

Stretching for more than a hundred kilometres north of the Isalo Massif, this little-known and sparsely populated mountain range remains relatively undocumented. The maze of canyons across this vast area is doubtless home to countless species still unknown to science, yet only in the last few years have expeditions begun to penetrate the area. At the forefront of these is French film-maker and explorer Evrard Wendenbaum, whose conservation organisation Naturevolution (*www.naturevolution.org*) has mounted a series of scientific surveys of the Makay over the past five years. The wheels are now being set in motion for the massif to receive formal protected status. Evrard has also made a documentary about this stunning forgotten landscape (*www.evrardwendenbaum.com*).

Adventurous travellers with at least a week to spare could visit this remarkable area. It is truly one of our planet's final frontiers – you are likely to go days without setting eyes on another soul.

GETTING THERE AND GETTING ORGANISED Isalo trekking specialists Momo Trek, based at ITC Lodge in Ranohira, have begun organising all-inclusive 1- to 2-week treks in the Makay, so this is the most hassle-free option. Otherwise you can organise transport, camping gear, porters and guides yourself – and you certainly will need a local guide, as Al Harris explains: 'it is very easy to get lost in the sinuous canyons, and many of the faces are crumbly and precipitous; absolutely no hope of getting out if you get stuck or lost'.

Southern access is best from the village of **Beronono**, which is now reachable from Ranohira in around 5 hours by good 4x4. Halfway, you need to cross the Mangoky River at **Beroroha**, so it would be wise to bring some diesel in case the ferry has none. You could also make the journey on foot or by mountain bike and send your provisions more slowly by zebu cart.

Porters and guides can be found in Beronono, where limited fresh produce is also available, but needless to say you must bring all your other provisions and camping gear with you. That said, tents are not essential: 'it is fine to sleep out in the open in the dry season,' says Al, 'just watch out for crocs by the bigger lakes'.

For those with restricted time (and a less restricted budget) there is a small airstrip at Beroroha where private plane operators can drop you – but they won't be able to land unless they call ahead to get locals to clear the termite mounds from the runway.

It is possible to conclude your visit with a descent of the **Mangoky River** (page 434), which reaches the sea north of Morombe.

RANOHIRA TO TOLIARA

The drive from Isalo to Toliara (236km) takes a minimum of 4 hours, passing through sapphire country. The sapphire rush is moving south and you will pass the temporary grass huts and piles of earth dug by fortune seekers for many kilometres. After Ilakaka the rugged mountains give way to grasslands again; following the rains there are many flowers but in the dry season it's quite monotonous.

After Sakaraha you will start to see painted tombs (some with aloalo) near the road, then you'll spot your first baobabs and pass through a cotton-growing region. Also keep an eye out for the enormous nests of hamerkop birds in roadside trees. An hour or so beyond Sakaraha is the small village of Andranovory, which has a colourful Sunday market, and some while later Toliara's table mountain comes into view on the right.

ILAKAKA (PK 729) It has been extraordinary watching the evolution of this settlement over the past decade or two. Ilakaka was just a tiny collection of a few houses that didn't even warrant a mention until the sixth edition of this guide, in which the place was described as a 'vibrant town' that had suddenly 'sprung up'. The reason: the discovery of sapphires. By the seventh edition, it had become 'like an American gold rush town' – a rapidly spreading expanse of hurriedly erected grass huts. Trouble was inevitably looming and in the eighth edition we described Ilakaka's Wild West atmosphere as 'humming with life and full of swaggering men with guns on their hips'. In the ninth edition we reported that 'tour buses now drive straight through with the windows up for fear of bandits'.

Now the excitement is largely over and it has become in many ways a normal town, the grass huts replaced by more permanent brick and concrete structures. There are plenty of showrooms where you can purchase gemstones and no shortage of hotels if you choose to stay longer, including **Friends** (m *033 63 445 22/033 80 870 74;* e *friendshotelilakaka@gmail.com*), **Val Motel** and **Vatosoa**.

Sapphire mine tours (m *033 17 720 17/033 20 123 08;* e *guillaumesoubiraa@ gmail.com*) These are run by a number of sapphire companies, including **Colorline**. Their guide takes you to the open mines allowing you to see at first hand the massive effort (and danger) involved in finding these tiny gems. A visit costs 12,000Ar per person, takes about an hour and is best on a weekday. The company also does cutting and polishing demonstrations in their showroom. Enquire at the bar called **Al_2O_3**.

ZOMBITSE-VOHIBASIA NATIONAL PARK (PK 795) (e *angaptle@gmail.com;* ⏲ *07.00–16.00*) Zombitse is a stark example of the effects of deforestation. Years of continuous felling have turned the surrounding areas into an arid moonscape and what remains is an isolated pocket of forest, thankfully now protected. The park covers 36,300ha, straddling RN7. It is an important example of a boundary zone between the western and southern domains of vegetation and so has a high level of biodiversity. Zombitse is of major significance to birdwatchers as it offers the

---

GEMSTONES   *Tim Ireland*

The crystalline rocks and gravels available to today's miners, sifters and washers of gravel were once 10–30km deep within the earth – not necessarily underground but perhaps at the heart of ancient mountains now eroded away. Millions of years ago, the land flexed upwards so the rocks now on the surface were in fact formed under tens of kilometres of other rock in conditions of great pressure and great heat – ideal for the formation of crystalline gems. Gemstones are, by their nature, dense and durable, so they survive the ravages of time. Mountains and rocks were gradually ground down and washed away towards the sea and in some areas of the west coast gem-hunters have to trace and chase the old river channels in search of deposits of the hard, bright and valuable survivors of barely imaginable eruptions and upheavals.

Elsewhere, traditional mining is necessary. To retrieve gemstones at Ilakaka, for example, an exploratory shaft is sunk until miners recognise a likely combination of rock types. Then a few bags of local gravel are washed; if the results are good, a pit is sunk and more work begins. One miner said that half a dozen bags of gravel from an exploratory hole might yield four million ariary's worth of sapphires. The catch is that the payload layer is often around 15m deep in the earth, yet only about 1m thick – a big, deep hole for what might prove to be a small yield.

When a find is made, the Malagasy miners will often arrive in great numbers from far away, willing to break their backs shifting dirt with shovels for the duration of the rush – two years? ten years? a hundred years? Curiously, the government has precluded the use of heavy machinery by the Malagasy people while outsiders are free to mine in whatever fashion they wish. Thai and Sri Lankan miners use earth-moving equipment to dig the efficient way. Strange enough, but add to this the shady nature of the gem industry: riches and smuggling. Instead of Madagascar getting rich now that its treasures are reaching the marketplace, money floods out of the country at a rate beyond anyone's wildest dreams. The richest Malagasies in the business seem not to be digging but instead are the ones providing security for the foreign buyers. The jewellery industry worldwide is trying to rebalance the distribution of money so that countries with a natural abundance of gemstones, and the indigenous miners of those riches, will get a better deal. The Kimberly Process is working well for the diamond industry and something might emerge from that for the coloured stone trade. In the meantime, if you are thinking of buying loose gemstones, remember that specialists and big business will have creamed the top off the supply. Buy something you fall in love with – there's plenty to choose from – but don't expect to get rich quick by selling it when you get home.

chance to glimpse one of Madagascar's rarest endemics, Appert's greenbul, which is confined to this forest. In addition to birds you have a good chance of seeing sifakas, red-fronted brown lemurs, and the nocturnal sportive lemur peering out of its tree hole. The locally endemic Standing's day gecko is also easily found.

The **park office** is on the southern side of RN7. There are four easy circuits (1.5–5km/1–2½hrs each) costing 3,000Ar for the guide per circuit. An early-morning visit is best for birds. It takes just over an hour to reach the park from Isalo and nearly 3 hours from Toliara, so serious birdwatchers should leave as early as possible or, better still, stay nearby. At the time of writing, camping is not permitted at the park owing to security concerns, but there are hotels at Sakaraha (17km west) and **Zombitse Ecolodge** (m *033 12 325 64;* e *ecolodge@zombitse.de or zombitse.ecolodge@gmail.com; www.zombitse.de;* €€€–€€€€) has ten bungalows located 7km beyond the park entrance. It's rather basic for the price but it is the closest place to stay and those on a tight budget can pitch their tent for 20,000Ar.

SAKARAHA (PK 812) Ilakaka's sapphire rush is spreading southward, with several gemstone stores now open along RN7 in Sakaraha. It's a town with some sinister recent history: Osama bin Laden's brother-in-law Muhammad Jamal Khalifa owned a mine in Sakaraha and was shot dead there in 2007 under mysterious circumstances (it later transpired that the US Secret Service was monitoring him at the time).

This small town offers convenient budget accommodation for visitors to Zombitse National Park and the reserve's welcome centre is also here. The best hotels are **Relais de Sakaraha** (€€) and **Palace Club** (m *032 75 709 50;* €€) but both are noisy on disco nights. **Venus** (€) offers cheap bungalows a short walk out of town.

ANDOHAROTSY (PK 839) Look out for the large distillation troughs under thatched shelters surrounded by rusting steel drums right by the roadside as you pass through this village. This strange scene is the illicit yet blatent manufacture of rum from sugarcane. But we wouldn't recommend sampling this potent moonshine as it can contain toxic methanol.

TOLIARA (PK 926)

The pronunciation of the French (Tulear) and the Malagasy names is the same: 'tool*ear*'. Toliara's history is centred on St Augustine's Bay, described at the beginning of this chapter, although the name of the town is said to derive from an encounter with one of those early sailors who asked a local inhabitant where he might moor his boat. The Malagasy replied: '*toly eroa*' ('mooring down there'). The town itself is relatively modern – 1895 – and was designed by an uninspired French architect. His tree planting was more successfully aesthetic, and the shady tamarind trees (*kily*) give welcome respite from the blazing sun.

Toliara marks the end of the popular RN7 route from the capital, an itinerary travellers typically like to round off with a few days of relaxation. The town itself has no beach – just mangroves and mudflats – so most tourists head north to Ifaty or south to Anakao in search of sun, sea and sand.

GETTING THERE AND AWAY Taxi-brousses run regularly on RN7, and cost 45,000Ar to Tana (20hrs), 30,000Ar to Fianar (10hrs), 20,000Ar to Ranohira/Isalo (5hrs) and 7,000Ar to Sakaraha/Zombitse (2hrs). **TransMadagascar** (e *info@transmadagascar. com*) runs scheduled door-to-door services along the length of RN7 in comfortable air-conditioned vehicles with a stopover in Fianarantsoa. It costs 150,000Ar for

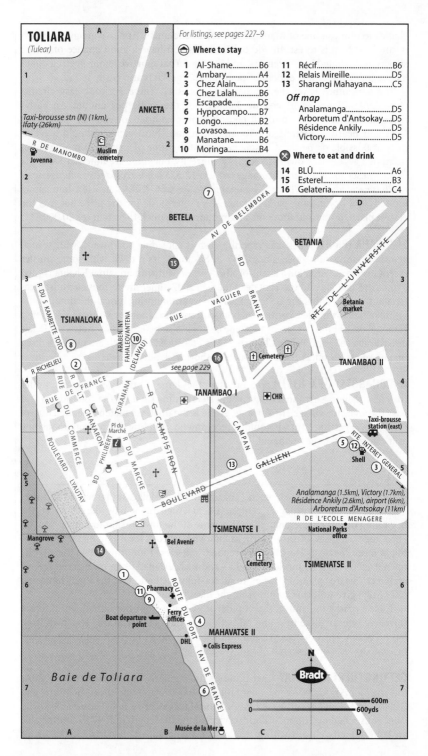

TOLIARA
(Tulear)

ANKETA

Taxi-brousse stn (N) (1km),
Ifaty (26km)

R DE MANOMBO
Jovenna
Muslim
cemetery

BETELA

BETANIA

AV DE BELEMBOKA

BD BRANLEY

TSIANALOKA

RUE VAGUIER

Betania
market

RUE DU S KAMBETTE TOTO

R RICHELIEU

ARABEN NY FAHALEOVANTENA (DELAVAU)

TANAMBAO II

see page 229

RUE DE FRANCE

R DU LT CHANARON

R DU COMMERCE

BD PHILIBERT

TSIRANANA

R DU MARCHE

R G CAMPISTRON

Pl du
Marché

TANAMBAO I

CHR

Cemetery

BD CAMPAN

Taxi-brousse
station (east)

RTE INTERET GENERAL

BOULEVARD LYAUTEY

Shell

BOULEVARD GALLIENI

Analamanga (1.5km), Victory (1.7km),
Résidence Ankily (2.6km), airport (6km),
Arboretum d'Antsokay (11km)

Mangrove

TSIMENATSE I

R DE L'ECOLE MENAGERE
National Parks
office

Bel Avenir

Cemetery

TSIMENATSE II

Pharmacy

ROUTE DU PORT (AV DE FRANCE)

Boat departure
point

Ferry
offices

DHL

MAHAVATSE II

Colis Express

N

Baie de Toliara

Bradt

0 ————— 600m
0 ————— 600yds

Musée de la Mer

For listings, see pages 227–9

Where to stay

1	Al-Shame	B6
2	Ambary	A4
3	Chez Alain	D5
4	Chez Lalah	B6
5	Escapade	D5
6	Hyppocampo	B7
7	Longo	B2
8	Lovasoa	A4
9	Manatane	B6
10	Moringa	B4
11	Récif	B6
12	Relais Mireille	D5
13	Sharangi Mahayana	C5

Off map

Analamanga	D5
Arboretum d'Antsokay	D5
Résidence Ankily	D5
Victory	D5

Where to eat and drink

14	BLÛ	A6
15	Esterel	B3
16	Gelateria	C4

the two-day journey, not including meals or accommodation. Most days *camion-brousse* services depart on the more adventurous route to Taolagnaro, which costs about 35,000Ar and takes two to three days. For the even more challenging road trip north to Morondava, see page 427.

Those heading south to Anakao usually go by **boat**; ferry operators are listed on pages 231–2.

There are **flights** most days from Tana, Morondava and Taolagnaro, but in the high season these tend to be fully booked. However, it's always worth going to the airport, whatever they say at the office.

GETTING AROUND Distances can be far but *pousse-pousses* are plentiful. A typical trip at the *vazaha* price should cost about 2,000Ar. For taxis, the going rate is 4,000Ar for any trip in town. There have been occasional muggings after dark so it is best to take a taxi if going out late. See also *Tour operators, vehicle hire and flights* on page 231.

 ## WHERE TO STAY

Top end €€€€€

🏠 **Hyppocampo** [226 B7] (10 rooms) \94 410 21; m 032 42 866 83; e hyppocampo.tulear@ gmail.com. Beautifully designed, this hotel at the south of town offers spacious rooms with AC, sat-TV/DVD, minibar & Wi-Fi. Suites also have hydro massage shower & bath. Massage, gym, jacuzzi, pool, sea-view bar & attractive garden (but pet lemurs). Visa accepted.

Upper range €€€€

🏠 **Amazone** [229 B3] (40 rooms) Bd Lyautey; \94 448 43; m 032 26 177 00/033 79 219 65/034 79 409 86; e hotelamazone.tulear@gmail.com. Under the same ownership as Victory, this 4-floor hotel opened in 2011 & has a rooftop swimming pool & gym (guests only), bar, restaurant & jacuzzi. Rooms are en suite with AC, safe, minibar, Wi-Fi, sat-TV, hairdryer & balcony. Vehicle hire. Visa accepted.

🏠 **Moringa** [226 B4] (27 rooms) Tsianaloka; \94 441 55; m 034 07 255 77/034 75 512 01; e moringa@lerelais.mg; www.moringa-tulear.mg. A well-located, reliable & efficient hotel. Rooms are en suite with sat-TV, AC, Wi-Fi, balcony & safe.

🏠 **Palétuvier** [229 A4] (55 rooms) Bd Lyautey; \94 440 39; m 032 02 542 83/032 04 804 37; e hotelpaletuviertul@gmail.com or hotelpaletuviertul@yahoo.fr. En-suite rooms with Wi-Fi, safe & minibar; many with AC. Gym & swimming pool. B/fast inc. Car hire.

🏠 **Saïfee** [229 B1] (21 rooms) Rue de l'Eglise; \94 410 82; m 032 05 410 82/034 05 410 82; e saifee_hotel@yahoo.fr; www.saifee-hoteltulear. com. Dbl, twin & trpl en-suite rooms with AC, TV & balcony; Wi-Fi. B/fast inc.

🏠 **Serena** [229 B2] (19 rooms) \94 411 73; m 032 45 377 55; e serenatulear@gmail.com; www.serenatulear.com. Attractive modern AC rooms with minibar, safe, TV & Wi-Fi. Nice b/fast terrace overlooking market. Praised by several readers. Airport transfers inc.

🏠 **Victory** [226 D5] (43 rooms) Rte de l'Aéroport; \94 410 96/94 904 72; m 032 48 411 62/033 09 438 99/034 14 904 72; e hotel.victory@ blueline.mg or hotelvictory.tulear@gmail.com; www.hoteltulear-victory.com. Away from town, a very good hotel with clean, airy en-suite rooms that have AC, hairdryer, TV, minibar, safe & Wi-Fi. Good restaurant & large pool (free for guests).

Mid-range €€€

🏠 **Chez Alain** [226 D5] (5 rooms & 15 bungalows) \94 415 27; e c.alain@moov.mg; www.hotelchezalain-tulear.com. Regularly praised & deservedly popular with rooms to suit a range of budgets: from simple bungalow to suite with AC & hot water, set in lovely garden. Bike & 4x4 hire. ReefDoctor has an information point here.

🏠 **Escapade** [226 D5] (10 bungalows) Bd Gallieni; \94 411 82; m 032 02 202 05/034 94 411 82; e escapade@moov.mg; www. escapadetulear.com. En-suite dbl & twin bungalows in peaceful garden. Restaurant with seafood specialities. Visa accepted.

🏠 **Longo** [226 B2] (12 bungalows) \94 410 11; m 032 82 614 75; e longo.hotel@yahoo. it or info@longohotelarcobaleno.com; www. longohotelarcobaleno.com. Bungalows in a pleasant garden compound; all en suite with sat-TV and a few with AC.

🏠 **Manatane** [226 B6] (25 rooms & 2 bungalows) Bd Lyautey; 📞94 412 17; m 034 02 309 09; e hotel.allshame@yahoo.fr or hotel.manatane@yahoo.fr; www.hoteltulear-manatane.com. Seafront rooms with balcony, TV & en-suite hot-water facilities. Also cheap 6-bed dorm. Wi-Fi, cybercafé, massage & bike hire. Nice restaurant.

🏠 **Récif** [226 B6] (16 rooms) Bd Lyautey; 📞94 446 88; m 032 40 755 39; e hotelrecif@yahoo.fr. En-suite rooms with Wi-Fi; some with AC & ocean view. Nice swimming pool (*5,000Ar for non-guests*), gym & restaurant.

🏠 **Sud Plazza** [229 B4] (32 rooms) 📞94 448 72/94 903 02; m 032 46 761 89; e sud_plaz@yahoo.fr. En-suite rooms in spacious gardens facing the sea, some with AC. Casino Le Joker on site. Cards accepted. Airport transfer inc.

Also in this category:

🏠 **Albatros** [229 C4] e hotelalbatros@moov.mg
🏠 **Résidence Ankily** [226 D5] e laresidenceankily@yahoo.fr
🏠 **Sharangi Mahayana** [226 C5] www.ikoabidaly.wix.com/hotel-mahayana

Budget €€

🏠 **Al-Shame** [226 B6] (30 rooms) Bd Lyautey; 📞94 447 28; m 032 05 267 24/034 02 267 24; e hotel.allshame@yahoo.fr or hotel.manatane@yahoo.fr. Simple hotel in seafront location. En-suite rooms (cold water) with Wi-Fi.

🏠 **Analamanga** [226 D5] (13 rooms) RN7; m 032 43 233 34. Bungalows on stilts in quiet setting. Basic dbl rooms & a few more expensive en-suite ones.

🏠 **Central** [229 C2] (8 rooms) Bd Tsiranana; 📞94 428 84; m 032 02 553 25/034 01 410 80. Aptly named, bang in the centre of town. Large dbl & twin rooms with en-suite hot shower, balcony, TV & optional AC.

🏠 **Chez Lalah** [226 B6] (11 rooms) Av de France; 📞94 434 17. Some rooms en suite, a couple with AC, in a garden compound. Quad & 4x4 hire.

Also in this category:

🏠 **Ambary** [226 A4] e roscarb.mg@gmail.com
🏠 **Forban** [229 B1] m 034 41 790 65
🏠 **Lovasoa** [226 A4] m 032 64 858 61
🏠 **Relais Mireille** [226 D5] e rmludi@gmail.com

❌ **WHERE TO EAT AND DRINK** Among the hotel restaurants, **Chez Alain** is especially notable for its reliable French cuisine. **Victory** and **Manatane** also serve good food.

❌ **Bar Le Bœuf** [229 A2] m 034 95 690 42; ⏰ daily 07.00–midnight. A pleasant grill bar/restaurant. Great steak; also pizza. Wi-Fi.

❌ **Bernique** [229 B4] Bd Gallieni; 📞94 449 87; e restaurantlabernique@hotmail.fr. Under new ownership. French restaurant with interesting menu; highly recommended both for meals & b/fast. Wi-Fi.

❌ **BLÛ (Bo Beach)** [226 B6] 📞94 444 05; m 032 04 009 13/032 22 915 59 (manager)/032 47 861 07/032 50 383 08/032 97 644 77; e contact@blutulear.com; www.blutulear.com; ⏰ daily 07.30–late. Breezy seafront restaurant & bar with pool table, darts & Wi-Fi.

❌ **Colombe** [229 D4] m 032 47 260 38. A simple restaurant with bar & karaoke. Good-priced food.

❌ **Corto Maltese** [229 D1] m 032 02 643 23/032 04 657 42; e corto@moov.mg; ⏰ closed Sat/Sun. One of Toliara's best restaurants, serving really delicious mainly Italian food. Menu varies day to day.

❌ **Esterel** [226 B3] Bd Tsiranana; m 032 40 618 66; e esereltulear@yahoo.it. Rich menu of predominantly Italian cuisine. Service can be a bit sluggish but nevertheless highly recommended.

❌ **Etoile de Mer** [229 B3] Bd Lyautey; m 032 02 605 65/034 07 605 65; ⏰ daily 06.00–15.00 & 18.00–23.00. Large shady outdoor eating area. Excellent pizza (inc vegetarian), great seafood; also good Afghan & Indian dishes. Bar with pool table. Wi-Fi.

❌ **Gelateria** [226 C4] 📞94 439 08; ⏰ Tue–Sun 09.30–12.30 & 16.00–22.30, Mon closed. Much-recommended ice creams; also cakes & snacks. Pizza each eve. Wi-Fi.

❌ **Jardin de Giancarlo** [229 D1] 📞94 428 18; ⏰ Tue–Sun 09.30–12.30 & 16.00–22.30, Mon closed. For years one of the best eateries in town, this exceptional Italian restaurant decorated in a pub style serves tremendous lasagne, pizza, burgers, seafood & more; also ice cream, pastries & cakes. Wi-Fi.

❌ **Maison** [229 C4] Bd Gallieni; 📞94 447 61/94 919 62; m 032 07 727 47. An airy restaurant with thatched roof & attractive dining area. Comfy bar with pool table. Wi-Fi.

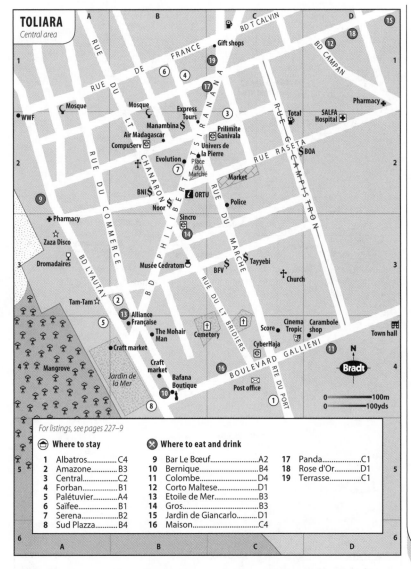

TOLIARA
Central area

BD T CALVIN
Gift shops
BD CAMPAN
RUE DE FRANCE
RUE DU
Mosque
Mosque
WWF
Express Tours
Manambina
Air Madagascar
CompuServ
Prilimite
Ganivala
Univers de la Pierre
Evolution
Place du Marché
Market
Total
SALFA Hospital
Pharmacy
RUE RASETA
BOA
RUE DU LT SIRANANA
RUE DU LT CHANARON
BNI
Noor
ORTU
Police
RUE DU MARCHE
Sincro
Pharmacy
Zaza Disco
Dromadaires
Musée Cedratom
BFV
Tayyebi
Church
RUE DU LT BRIDIERS
BD LYAUTEY
BD PHILIBERT
BD GAMPISTRON
Tam-Tam
Alliance Française
The Mohair Man
Craft market
Craft market
Bafana Boutique
Jardin de la Mer
Cemetery
Score
CyberHaja
Cinema Tropic
Carambole shop
Town hall
BOULEVARD GALLIENI
RTE DU PORT
Post office
Bradt
N
Mangrove

0 —— 100m
0 —— 100yds

For listings, see pages 227–9

⌂ Where to stay

1	Albatros	C4
2	Amazone	B3
3	Central	C2
4	Forban	B1
5	Palétuvier	A4
6	Saïfee	B1
7	Serena	B2
8	Sud Plazza	B4

✕ Where to eat and drink

9	Bar Le Bœuf	A2
10	Bernique	B4
11	Colombe	D4
12	Corto Maltese	D1
13	Etoile de Mer	B3
14	Gros	B3
15	Jardin de Giancarlo	D1
16	Maison	C4

17	Panda	C1
18	Rose d'Or	D1
19	Terrasse	C1

✕ **Panda** [229 C1] Bd Tsiranana; m 034 18 023 54; e semstul.dir@moov.mg; ⊕ Mon–Sat, Sun closed. Chinese cuisine at good prices.

✕ **Terrasse** [229 C1] m 032 02 650 60; e jeff14r@gmail.com. Very popular restaurant with a broad menu. Opens early for b/fast. Also ice cream & take-away pizza. Nice shady outdoor eating area. Wi-Fi.

▱ **Gros** [229 B3] ⊕ daily 07.00–noon & 15.30–19.30. Salon de thé.

▱ **Rose d'Or** [229 D1] m 032 54 355 29; e etvtul@moov.mg; ⊕ Wed–Mon except Sun afternoon, Tue closed. Boulangerie & patisserie. Good for coffee & b/fast.

NIGHTLIFE

♀ **Dromadaires** [229 A3] Bd Lyautey; m 032 04 009 13; e lesdromadaires@yahoo.fr. Central bar, sometimes with live music or big-screen sports showings.

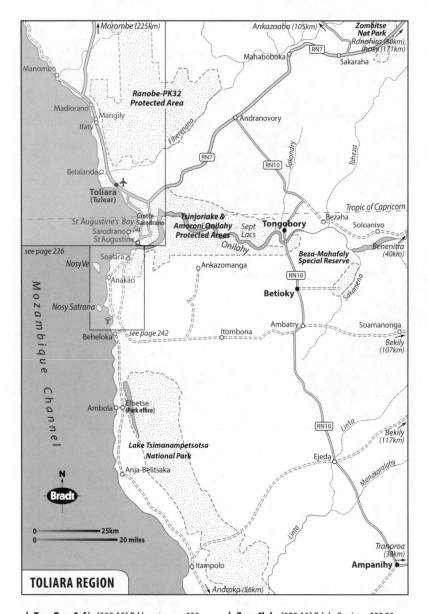

TOLIARA REGION

☆ **Tam-Tam Café** [229 A3] Bd Lyautey; m 032 02 524 48/032 04 035 12; e originaltamtam@ yahoo.com or tamtamcafe@moov.mg; ⨍ tamtam.tulear. This discotheque is very popular & less seedy than Zaza. Mostly international music. Pool table.

☆ **Zaza Club** [229 A3] Bd du Quai; m 033 23 343 01/034 02 343 01; e soleiltulear@gmail.com. This nightclub is more popular with locals. Hassling from prostitutes & local girls looking for a *vazaha* boyfriend is worse than at Tam-Tam. Music mainly Malagasy.

MONEY AND COMMUNICATIONS There are branches of **banks** BFV [229 C3], BNI [229 B2] and BOA [229 C2], all with ATMs, and Western Union services available at the first two. Bureaux de change include **Noor** [229 B2] (m *032 85 123 61/62*), **Manambina** [229 B2] (✆ *94 416 98*) and **Tayyebi** [229 C3] (✆ *94 442 51*).

On the main boulevard, the **post office** [229 C4] has a *cyberpaositra* internet room. There are also a number of other **cybercafés**, including Prilimite Ganivala [229 C2], CyberHaja [229 C4], CompuServ [229 B2] and several branches of Sincro [229 B3].

Courier companies DHL [226 B6] and Colis Express [226 B7] (m *032 03 800 83*) have offices on the road to the port.

SHOPPING There is a branch of **Score** supermarket [229 C4] (m *034 07 122 91*; ⊕ *Mon–Fri 08.30–13.00 & 14.30–19.30, Sat 08.30–19.30, Sun 08.00–12.30*) that stocks a range of fresh and tinned food, toiletries – including suncream and after-sun – stationery and other supplies, as well as having a small patisserie counter. A smaller supermarket called **Evolution** [229 B2] is next to Serena Hotel.

The **craft markets** [229 B4] are towards the end of Boulevard Gallieni near the monument and round the corner in Jardin du Mer. (Tourists should resist buying seashells here as, to ensure an intact shell, many endangered species are harvested alive.) Nearby **Bafana Boutique** [229 B4] also sells quality local crafts and the **Carambole Shop** [229 D4] stocks a good variety of souvenirs too.

For minerals and precious stones, including sapphires, rubies and emeralds, head to **Univers de la Pierre** [229 B2] (*www.universdelapierre.com*). Also worth a visit is the showroom of **The Mohair Man** [229 B4] (*www.letapismalgache.com*) to see handmade carpets from Ampanihy. Thick and hardwearing, these goat-hair mats and rugs are produced in both Malagasy and contemporary designs using natural dyes.

MEDICAL The **Centre Hôpital Régional** [226 C4] (✆ *94 418 55/59*) is the main hospital for the southwest and can handle serious emergencies. **Clinique St Luc** at Andabizy (✆ *94 422 47*; m *032 02 294 51/032 40 759 61*) is a private clinic, on the road to the airport, that can deal with most medical problems.

TOUR OPERATORS, VEHICLE HIRE AND FLIGHTS

✈ **Air Madagascar** [229 B2] Rue Henri-Martin; ✆ 94 415 85/422 33; m 032 05 222 40/033 11 222 40/034 11 222 01; e tlessmd@madagascar. com; ⊕ Mon–Fri 08.00–11.30 & 15.00–17.00, Sat 08.00–10.00, Sun closed

Budget ✆ 94 434 94; m 032 05 403 01; www. budget.mg. Car & 4x4 hire (with driver) by the day, week or month.

Dallas Club m 033 01 944 65/034 06 806 57; e madallas@gmx.fr or madallas@moov.mg. Jeep & 4x4 hire.

Express Tours & Voyages [229 B2] Bd Philibert Tsiranana; ✆ 94 419 04; m 032 07 235 25;

e etvtul@moov.mg; ⊕ Mon–Fri 08.00–noon & 15.00–18.00. Travel agency inc flights.

Quad du Capricorne ✆ 94 437 17; m 032 02 680 89/032 40 463 40; e quadtulear@gmail.com; www.le-quad-du-capricorne.com. Quad hire & guided quad tours of 4–10 days.

Quad Madagascar ✆ 24 120 50; m 033 14 873 33/034 08 373 13; e contact@quadmadagascar. com; www.quadmadagascar.com. Quad & 4x4 hire.

Touramada m 032 52 262 18; e info@ touramada.com; www.touramada.com. 4x4 hire; trekking (Isalo, Andringitra & Makay); descents of Mangoky & Onilahy rivers.

FERRY OPERATORS AND BOAT HIRE All of the boat operators have offices down by the boat departure point [226 B6].

🚢 **Anakao Express** ✆ 94 924 16; m 034 60 072 61/034 60 072 62; e transfert@anakaoexpress.

com or anakaoexpress@moov.mg; www. anakaoexpress.com. Boats to Anakao every morning.

Anakao Transfert \ 94 922 20/21;
m 034 91 468 36; e thbournonville@gmail.com
or reservations@transfert-anakao.com; www.
transfert-anakao.com. Anakao transfers for
50,000Ar one way (under-12s ½ price).
Atlantis \ 94 700 42; m 034 10 000
72; e atlantismadagascar@gmail.com; www.

atlantismadagascar.com. This dive centre also does
transfers to Anakao.
Safari Vezo \ 94 413 81/919 30;
m 034 94 413 81; e safarivezo@moov.mg; www.
safarivezo.com. An Anakao hotel that also runs
boat transfers.

WHAT TO SEE AND DO The regional tourist office, **ORTU**, is located near the market
in an office raised on stilts [229 B2] (\ *94 446 05;* m *034 20 083 82/033 73 589
86;* e *ortu601@hotmail.com or ortu.tul27@yahoo.com; www.tulear-tourisme.com;*
⊕ *Mon–Fri 08.30–noon & 15.00–18.00*). The **National Parks office** [226 D5] is on
Rue de l'Ecole Ménagère (\ *94 435 70;* m *032 07 606 77;* e *tle.parks@gmail.com;*
⊕ *Mon–Fri 07.30–noon & 14.30–18.00*).

Museums A small museum, **Musée Cedratom** [229 B3] (⊕ *Mon–Sat 07.30–11.30 &
14.30–17.30 except Sat afternoon; entry 4,000Ar*) on Boulevard Philibert Tsiranana
is run by the University of Toliara. There are some remarkable exhibits, including
a Mikea mask (genuine Malagasy masks are rare) with real human teeth. These are
well displayed and labelled, and include some Sakalava erotic tomb sculptures.

Marine enthusiasts should visit the **Musée de la Mer** [226 C7] (m *032 40 956
64/034 01 972 44/033 21 209 71;* ⊕ *Mon–Fri 08.00–11.30 & 14.30–17.30, Sat 08.00–
11.30, Sun closed; entry 10,000Ar*), also run by the university, on Route de la Porte.
The main attraction is the preserved coelacanths; seven have been caught around
Toliara of which three are on display here. The fascinating collection also includes
shells, coral, whale teeth and bones, crustaceans and lots of other marine curiosities
– as well as a somewhat out-of-place ostrich skeleton!

Orphanage Nathanael (\ *94 449 76;* e *associationedtmada@gmail.com or
centrenathanael@gmail.com; www.orphelinat-nathanael.org*) This orphanage in the
Besasavy area of Toliara welcomes visits from tourists to see the work they do. A
donation is expected.

Arboretum d'Antsokay (PK 915) (*11km from Toliara on RN7;* m *032 25 600
15/034 07 600 15;* e *info@antsokayarboretum.org; www.antsokayarboretum.org;*
⊕ *Mar–Jan 07.30–17.30, Feb closed*) This impressive botanical garden should not
be missed by anyone with an interest in the flora – and accompanying fauna – of
the southwest. Around a thousand plant species are showcased, mostly endemic to
the region, and many with medicinal qualities.

Allow an hour at the very least for the excellent English-speaking guides to
take you on a tour of the 7ha planted area of the 50ha arboretum where you will
see around 100 species of *Euphorbia* and 60 species of *Kalanchoe*, as well as an
abundance of reptiles and birds – indeed, this is one of the best places in the region
for birders. A museum, interpretation centre and gift shop complete the visit.

Try to arrive as early as possible to avoid the heat of the day as the trails are fairly
shadeless. Better still, stay overnight at **Auberge de la Table** (*www.aubergedelatable.
com; €€€*). The six comfy en-suite bungalows have hot water and there is access to
Wi-Fi and a swimming pool (free for guests). Camping is possible and excellent
meals are served at their restaurant **The Dry Forest**. For those staying overnight, a
night walk can be arranged. You are likely to see roosting birds, dozing chameleons,
scampering mouse lemurs and various nocturnal reptiles and creepy crawlies.

St Augustine's Bay and surrounds This 14km-long bay stretches from near Toliara airport southward to the Onilahy river mouth. It is an area of history and natural wonders, including dramatic sand dunes, mangroves and caves. The bay, which was mentioned by Daniel Defoe in *The King of Pirates*, was the site of an ill-fated British colony, abandoned in 1646, and later frequented by pirates.

Near the southern end of the bay is **Sarodrano Cave** – a rocky overhang beneath which lies a deep pool of clear blue water, home to a famous giant potato grouper. Swimmers will find the top layer of warm water only mildly salty, while the cooler lower layer is saline. Fresh water flows from the mountain into the pool, on top of the heavier layer of saltwater from the sea.

After a 2km stretch of mangroves you reach the Onilahy River, where a sandy spit juts 3.5km out to sea, the village of **Sarodrano** dramatically located near its tip. There is a track to this village but you can also cross directly by pirogue from Grotte Sarodrano. Upriver about 3km from the base of the spit is the riverside village of **St Augustine**. To get to St Augustine's Bay, take the turning off RN7 about 700m before the arboretum. 'It's a nice drive from Toliara through limestone spiny thicket, and birders can try to spot red-shouldered vangas on the way,' suggests local resident Louise Jasper. If you don't have a vehicle at your disposal then local tour operators and hotels can help arrange transport or you can take the daily Toliara–Sarodrano taxi-brousse (6,000Ar).

Two protected areas have recently been established locally. **Tsinjoriake Protected Area** stretches along the bay from RN7 down to the Onilahy River and includes the Sarodrano Peninsula, the caves of Binabe and Sarodrano, and Toliara's Table Mountain. **Amoron'i Onilahy** is a larger zone protecting a broad band either side of the river from Tsinjoriake to Tongobory, about 65km inland. Various ecotourism circuits are being established. You can get the latest information from the tourist office in Toliara or from Arboretum d'Antsokay (see opposite).

 Where to stay and eat

Bakuba (5 rooms) m 032 48 540 50/032 51 528 97/034 64 927 82; e bakuba@ bakubaconcept.com or bakubaconcept@gmail. com or info@bakuba-lodge.com; www.bakuba-lodge.com. This extraordinary guesthouse is highly praised by all who've stayed. Impeccably designed with exotic African-inspired décor. At the northern end of the bay (3.5km from RN7) so also ideal for the airport. Designed with exceptional attention to detail, the en-suite rooms are cosy with big beds. Infinite horizon pool, spa, hammam & massage room. Solar power. B/fast inc. €€€€€–👑

Caliente Beach (Melody Beach) (14 bungalows) ☎ 94 924 18; m 032 05 925 43; e calientebeach@gmail.com. Comfy en-suite bungalows 5km from RN7 on a good stretch of beach. Swimming pool, tennis & minigolf. €€€€

Résidence Eden (3 rooms & 4 bungalows) m 032 84 525 93/034 97 638 00; e residence. eden@orange.mg; www.hoteltularanakao.com. Beautiful little ecolodge with solar/wind power 16km from RN7, near Sarodrano. En-suite rooms;

bar & restaurant. Activities inc canoeing, pirogue trips, fishing & sailing. €€€–€€€€

Chez Andréa (10 rooms) m 032 02 258 43. Italian-owned beach bungalows on the sandy spit 800m before Sarodrano village. Thoughtfully designed, very friendly, excellent food & service. €€€

Famata Lodge (8 bungalows) ☎ 94 937 83; m 032 02 108 48/032 05 937 83; e famatalodge@ gmail.com; www.famatalodge-tulear.com. Overlooking the lagoon from atop the sand dunes about 6km from RN7. Dbl & family bungalows, some en suite; 3 are tented. Wi-Fi & solar power. Boat trips, fishing & diving. Camping permitted. €€–€€€

Au Paradis de l'Espérance (8 bungalows) m 032 40 787 53; e beauparadisesperance@ yahoo.fr. Simple clean rooms at the beach. €€

Corsaire (Chez Glover) (10 rooms) Simple rooms with shared cold-water facilities in St Augustine. €€

Longo Mamy ☎ 94 914 29; m 032 04 344 64. Nice but basic bungalows in St Augustine village. €€

🏠 **Auberge du Pêcheur** (10 rooms) m 032 42 903 90. Simple huts in Sarodrano village. €

✖ **Marmite** Ankilibe; m 032 54 416 69; e vizaburu@gmail.com

Tropic of Capricorn

There is a recently built monument marking the tropic on the road to St Augustine's Bay, about 4.5km from the RN7 turn-off. The Tropic of Capricorn marks the southernmost limit of the tropical zone (where the sun may pass overhead) beyond which is the temperate zone (where the sun is never directly above).

The problem with erecting fixed markers on the tropics – or the Equator – is that these lines are not static; they drift because the earth 'wobbles' on its axis. Consequently the tropic is moving northward at a rate of about 1cm every 6 hours (and will continue for about the next ten millennia, before drifting back again). This adds up to about 15m per year so, if you want to be really accurate about locating the tropic, first find this monument then walk northward 20 paces for every year that has passed since 2014, when it was built!

Watersports

For many, the main reason to visit the Toliara region is for the coral reefs. Most of the dive centres are located in Ifaty and there are a couple more in Anakao; these are listed in their respective sections. Dead or dying coral is disturbingly evident but some diving and snorkelling sites can still be rewarding.

Sailing and pirogue trips, typically lasting all day with a picnic lunch on a beach or small island, offer an alternative and relaxing way to enjoy the sea. Fishermen with sailboats who are willing to take tourists out for around 15,000Ar per person are easily found in Anakao and Ifaty.

Tombs

The most spectacular tombs within easy reach of the town are those of the Masikoro, a subgroup of the Sakalava. This small tribe is probably of African origin, and there is speculation that the name comes from *mashokora*, a Tanzanian word for 'scrub forest'. There are also Mahafaly and Bara tombs here.

The tombs are off RN7, a little over an hour from Toliara, and are clearly visible on the right. There are several large, rectangular tombs, flamboyantly painted with scenes from the distinguished military life of the deceased, with a few mermaids and Rambos thrown in for good measure. Oh, and a scene from the film *Titanic*. These are known as the **Tombs of Andranovory**.

Another, on the outskirts of town beyond the university, is **King Baba's Tomb**. This is set in a grove of *Didierea* trees and is interesting more for the bizarre funerary objects (an urn and a huge, cracked bell) displayed there and its spiritual significance to the local people (you may only approach barefoot) than for aesthetic value. This King Baba, who seems to have died a century or so ago, was presumably a descendant of one of the Masikoro kings of Baba mentioned in British naval accounts of the 18th century. These kings used to trade with English ships calling at St Augustine's Bay and gave their family and courtiers English names such as the Prince of Wales and the Duke of Cumberland. On the way to King Baba's Tomb you may visit the 'sacred grove', a little fenced-off park of banyan trees, all descending from one 'parent'.

Sept Lacs

Some 40km inland, on the banks of Onilahy River, is a fascinating area known as Sept Lacs. There is an environmentally important wetland and (at least) seven pools of clear, turquoise water up a fairly steep limestone valley, connected by waterfalls and surrounded by beautiful gallery forest. It takes about 4 hours to reach the area in a 4x4 from Toliara so a day trip would be pushing it; it would be better to camp overnight. It is also a good starting point from which to begin a three-day descent of the Onilahy if the water is deep enough (roughly January to June). Contact the tourist office or a local tour operator to organise a trip.

IFATY AND MANGILY

Technically speaking, Ifaty is a small fishing village 24km north of Toliara and Mangily is a separate village 4km further on. However, the former name has now come to refer to the whole area even though the latter is very much the centre of activity. Indeed, Mangily has grown into a bustling tourist resort – the beach is busy with children selling shells or asking for *cadeaux* and young women offering massages, and in the village lively merrymaking goes on well into the night – so those seeking tranquillity should opt for accommodation further up or down the coast.

The area offers not only sea, sun and sand but also snorkelling, scuba-diving and spiny forest. What it doesn't offer is banks, so make sure you bring enough cash from Toliara.

GETTING THERE AND AWAY It takes about 30 minutes to reach Mangily by car or taxi-brousse from Toliara. Taxis will do the trip for around 60,000Ar.

WHERE TO STAY *Map, page 236*

Top end €€€€€

Dunes (22 rooms & 19 bungalows) ☎22 376 69; m 032 07 109 16/034 07 109 11/034 07 109 16/034 07 109 71; e dunesifaty@shgi.mg; www. lesdunesdifaty.com. Swish en-suite accommodation with TV & 24hr electricity; sea-view villas for up to 4 people. Splendid pool, beachfront bar, excellent food & internet. Credit cards accepted.

Nautilus (40 rooms) m 032 04 848 81/032 07 418 74; e contact@nautilusmada.mg; www. nautilusmada.mg. AC bungalows for up to 6 people on a nice beach. Excellent restaurant, especially for seafood. Swimming pool. Diving, whale-watching & glass-bottom boat. Visa accepted.

Paradisier (21 bungalows) m 032 07 660 09/032 07 843 44 (Tana)/034 02 351 66; e htl@madagascar-discovery.com or paradisier@ paradisier.net; www.paradisier.net. Comfy en-suite bungalows with fan; also a luxury suite. Infinity-edge pool & good food. Wi-Fi. B/fast inc. Nature walks great for birds & reptiles.

Upper range €€€€

Ifaty Beach Club (15 bungalows) ☎94 914 27; m 034 29 709 99/034 31 463 84; e ifatybeachclub@moov.mg; www.ifaty.com. En-suite bungalows for up to 4 people. Beachfront restaurant with good meals. Pool, massage & quad tours.

Lagon (5 rooms) ☎94 902 13; m 034 66 552 31; e bambooclubifaty@gmail.com. Self-catering apartments rentable by the day, week or month.

Princesse du Lagon (7 rooms) m 034 98 887 49; e info@princessedulagon.com; www. princessedulagon.com. This boutique spa hotel aims for a Zen atmosphere. A Persepolis-inspired spa offers a full range of relaxation treatments inc massage, body scrub, face mask & aromatherapy; yoga pavilion, gym & infinite horizon pool. The en-suite rooms have AC, sat-TV/DVD, Wi-Fi & balcony. Whale-watching & diving.

Solidaire (10 bungalows) m 034 02 666 60; e info@hotelsolidairemangily.com; www. hotelsolidaire.org or www.hotelsolidairemangily. com. Run by local NGO Bel Avenir, the hotel aims to promote sustainable community development. En-suite rooms with safe & solar power. Restaurant, bar & swimming pool.

Mid-range €€€

Bamboo Club (24 bungalows) ☎94 902 13; m 034 66 552 31; e bambooclubifaty@ gmail.com; www.bamboo-club.com. Good-value Belgian-owned bungalows, en suite with solar power, in nicely planted 14ha beachfront garden with small pool. Snorkelling, windsurfing, pirogue trips, fishing, village visits, volleyball, zebu cart outings.

Chez Daniel (5 bungalows) ☎94 930 39; m 032 04 678 53; e daniel.mangily@gmail. com. Comfy traditional seafront bungalows, en suite with solar power. Owned by a welcoming Malagasy-French couple.

Coq du Village (Chez Alex)
(13 bungalows) m 032 04 658 73/034 08 266 64.
Basic en-suite dbl bungalows with hot water &
cheaper tpl ones with communal cold showers.

Ikotel (12 bungalows) \ 94 901 14/94
901 42; m 032 04 702 48; e iko.abidaly@moov.
mg or mahayanahotels@yahoo.fr; www.ikotel-
tulear.com. Solid spacious en-suite bungalows
at the beach, though only the restaurant has a
sea view.

Maroloko (8 rooms) m 034 20 034 43;
e villamaroloko@yahoo.com; www.maroloko.
com. Renovated in 2012 under new Réunionais
ownership. Great location with charming décor in
rooms for 2–4 people, all en suite with hot water.
Beachfront restaurant.

Also in this category:

Casa Nostra e hotelvovotelo@gmail.com
Jardin de Béravy www.hotel-
jardindeberavy-tulear.com
Mangily www.mangilyhotel.com

Budget €€
Auberg'inn (Chez Bodo & Jean-Yves)
(11 bungalows) e lauberginn@gmail.com; http://
laubergine.free.fr. Splendid budget option 5mins
from the beach. Beautiful garden with a small bar
& quaint bungalows for 2–8 people with cold-
water facilities; the largest has a kitchenette.

Chez Freddy Village (4 bungalows)
m 034 19 842 76; e freddymada@yahoo.fr.
Well-run rooms with communal cold-water
showers. Excellent restaurant.

Chez Susie (18 bungalows) m 034 31 577
80. Swiss-owned rooms in a central but calm spot,
en suite with cold water facilities.

Sur la Plage (Chez Cécile)
(12 bungalows) \ 94 907 00; m 032 89 100
84/034 19 844 91/034 94 907 00;
e surlaplagechezcecile@yahoo.fr; www.
surlaplagechezcecile.com. As its name suggests,
this laid-back bar & restaurant (with bungalows
in a garden behind) is right on the beach. Indeed,
Cécile is a lady who likes to say things how they
are: she has just opened another hotel a bit
further north, called Un Peu Plus au Nord
(page 240).

✖ WHERE TO EAT, DRINK AND DANCE
Almost all of the hotels listed above
have restaurants. Also worth checking

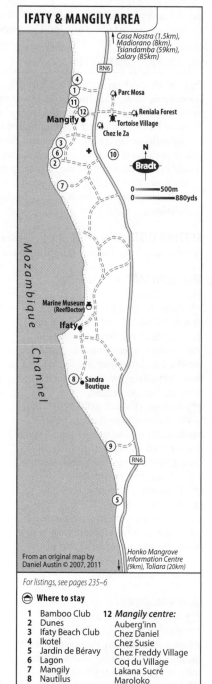

IFATY & MANGILY AREA

*Casa Nostra (1.5km),
Madiorano (8km),
Tsiandamba (59km),
Salary (85km)*

RN6

Parc Mosa

Reniala Forest

Mangily

Tortoise Village

Chez le Za

N

Bradt

0 ————— 500m
0 ————————— 880yds

Mozambique Channel

Marine Museum
(ReefDoctor)

Ifaty

Sandra
Boutique

RN6

*From an original map by
Daniel Austin © 2007, 2011*

*Honko Mangrove
Information Centre
(9km), Toliara (20km)*

For listings, see pages 235–6

🛏 **Where to stay**

1	Bamboo Club	12	*Mangily centre:*
2	Dunes		Auberg'inn
3	Ifaty Beach Club		Chez Daniel
4	Ikotel		Chez Susie
5	Jardin de Béravy		Chez Freddy Village
6	Lagon		Coq du Village
7	Mangily		Lakana Sucré
8	Nautilus		Maroloko
9	Paradisier		Princesse du Lagon
10	Solidaire		
11	Sur la Plage		*Off map*
			Casa Nostra

out is **Lakana Sucré** at Mangily Scuba dive centre (e *mangilyscuba@gmail. com; www.ifatyscuba.com*). On the main road in the centre of the village is discotheque **M Sébastien**.

WHAT TO SEE AND DO Diving is one of the main attractions but there are some super inland reserves that even non-naturalists will enjoy. Louise Jasper offers some sound advice: 'all land-based activities are best done very early in the day, especially in summer months, as the heat coming off the red sand is a killer'.

Reniala Forest (✆ *94 417 56/906 76*; m *032 02 513 49/034 03 720 40*; e *info@ reniala-madagascar.com or reniala-mada@blueline.mg; www.reniala-ecotourisme. jimdo.com;* ⊕ *summer 08.00–18.00, winter 07.30–17.30; circuits 18,000–20,000Ar pp*) This outstanding reserve protects 45ha of spiny forest, especially recommended for those interested in birds and flora. An early-morning visit more or less guarantees long-tailed ground-roller and sub-desert mesite. Guides, who live at the reserve and can be arranged on arrival, are excellent at locating these two species and are also knowledgeable about the area's unique plant life. Serious birders will want to start before sunrise; this should be arranged the day before and costs extra. In addition to birds there are around a thousand *Adansonia rubrostipa* baobabs (including one 13m in circumference) as well as *Didierea* and *Euphorbia*. Circuits take 45 minutes to 2 hours and night walks are also possible.

Parc Mosa (m *032 43 259 90/032 61 129 09; entry 10,000Ar*) This is another private reserve with excellent birding prospects. Sadly, several readers have complained of unethical practices and overcharging here, and Mosa's staff are known to ambush tourists *en route* to Reniala Forest to persuade them to visit here instead.

Chez le Za (m *032 02 514 36; entry 7,000Ar for 1hr guided walk or 9,000Ar for 1½hrs*) Near to Reniala Forest and Parc Mosa, this small reserve also offers guided tours of ornithological and botanical interest. You will learn about traditional medicinal plants in the botanical garden area.

Tortoise Village (m *032 02 072 75/032 40 307 50/034 19 841 55;* ⊕ *daily 09.00– 17.00*) Tortoise Village was set up by a group of conservation organisations for the protection of the two southwestern species: spider and radiated tortoises. Both are seriously threatened by illegal trade (for pets abroad) and hunting (by locals for food). Around 1,200 are resident including some confiscated by customs.

Set in 7ha of spiny forest with small baobabs, with a further 7ha of fenced areas, the guided tour will show you the tortoises and explain the efforts to conserve them. Allow an hour for a visit; you may see other reptiles, birds and brown lemurs.

Ranobe-PK 32 Reserve (m *033 21 457 42; e valoherysedera@yahoo.fr*) This newly created protected area has been set up with assistance from WWF. Tourist infrastructure is still in its early stages but visits can be arranged, including a 2-hour pirogue trip on Ranobe Lake, a half-hour walking circuit in which three different baobab species can be seen and a Masikoro village visit to see local agricultural techniques.

Establishment of the reserve has been complicated by the presence of Toliara Sands, a new mining project in the area that is expected to produce half a million tonnes of ilmenite (titanium ore) and zircon-rich concentrate annually for at least the next two decades.

Most injuries from sea creatures are due to inexperience, unfamiliarity with the local environment, or self defence by the animal. Below are some of the marine nasties you may encounter and the first-aid measures should you be hurt.

SEA URCHINS The most common injury to swimmers and snorkellers is from sea urchins, often from stepping on one. It is painful but not dangerous. Wash the wound and remove the spines with tweezers or, if you have nothing else, use a toothpick or similar; the wound will not heal until all the bits are out.

BITES The majority of bites are in self defence. Sharks and moray eels are the two animals that could attack swimmers or divers on the reef, as well as titan triggerfish during the nesting season. The primary concern is to control bleeding and minimise the risk of infection, so apply firm bandages or strips of cloth then clean the wound with lots of water and seek medical advice.

RAY, SCORPIONFISH, LIONFISH AND STONEFISH STINGS Symptoms include immediate pain, laceration, nausea, vomiting, shock, swelling and occasionally collapse. Good first aid will help more than anything doctors can offer. Immerse the wound in hot water for 30–90 minutes and repeat if pain recurs. Remove any visible pieces of the stinger and irrigate vigorously with fresh water. Once the worst of the pain has subsided, clean and dress the wound. Over the next few days look out for spreading redness, throbbing or fever; these symptoms imply infection which will need antibiotic treatment.

FIRE CORAL, ANEMONE, HYDROID OR JELLYFISH STINGS Anemones are beautiful creatures that live among the coral and have stinging tentacles. Brushing against any coral will give a nasty abrasion which is inflamed and slow to heal. Fire coral looks like coral, but on closer examination there are fine stinging cells. Hydroids are small marine creatures that look like plants, also with stinging cells. Jellyfish are commonly encountered in tropical waters.

If stung by any of these rinse with seawater (not fresh water). If the stinger was a box jellyfish there will be characteristic cross-hatched tentacle-prints on the skin surface and irrigation with vinegar will inactivate the stingers. (Vinegar actually makes things worse if the jellyfish is a Portuguese man-of-war.) Shave off the area with a credit card to remove stinging cells, being very careful not to sting yourself, then apply hydrocortisone cream. If collapse occurs, give cardio-pulmonary resuscitation and get medical help.

CONE SHELLS Cone shells contain a dartlike projection at the front, which can deliver a potentially deadly sting. If stung, apply a pressure bandage, immobilise the limb and seek medical attention.

SEA SNAKES Sea snake venom is some of the most potent known to man. Fortunately they are usually timid and sluggish so you are unlikely to be bitten unless you tease or handle one, or disturb a mating bundle. Symptoms of a bite may include stiffness and aching, respiratory distress, difficulty swallowing or speaking, or weakness. Treat by applying a pressure bandage and immobilising the limb, then seek medical attention. Do not use the suction technique.

Marine Museum (m *032 78 647 35*) This small information centre was created by ReefDoctor (page 144) for tourists, locals and schoolchildren. Information posters accompanied by exhibits such as shells educate visitors about local marine environments.

Mangrove Information Centre (m *032 54 042 76/032 70 465 04*; e *honkomad@ yahoo.com; www.honko.org*) At Ambondrolava, midway between Toliara and Ifaty, is this wetland centre created by the Belgian NGO Honko. The organisation works to restore nearby mangroves and teach locals to use them sustainably. For tourists, the centrepiece is an elevated boardwalk through the mangrove along which guides lead visitors while explaining about the habitat. This is also one of the best wetland sites for birding in the area, with a hide that enables close viewing. You can also explore the site by kayak. Mangrove visits take 1–3 hours, depending on the circuit selected, and cost 10,000–20,000Ar per person. Additionally there are guided tours of Ambondrolava village that offer cultural insight and give visitors the opportunity to buy locally produced honey and woven baskets.

Ho Avy (e *mad.hoavy@gmail.com; www.hoavy.org*) This non-profit Czech-US-Malagasy collaboration is dedicated to conservation and sustainable development in the local area. It has done a lot of reforestation work and is also focusing on environmental education, training and promotion of sustainable livelihoods. Ho Avy is now in the early stages of developing ecotourism projects, so contact the organisation if you are interested to see its work.

Diving and other watersports An offshore patch reef called **Massif des Roses** (located opposite Mangily Hotel) is protected by Ranobe Marine Reserve and offers excellent **snorkelling**. Entry permits cost 5,000Ar and can be bought from any of the dive centres. There is a kitesurfing centre based at Mangily Hotel called **Kitesurf Découverte** (m *032 22 140 09/034 85 552 77*; e *loic.guiriec@gmail.com*). **Whale-watching** safaris are offered by many boat operators in Ifaty during the July to October season. **Dive centres** include:

🤿 **Albatros** e lalbatros_8@yahoo.fr. Based at Princesse du Lagon. CMAS & PADI.
🤿 **Atimoo Plongée** ☎94 937 01; m 032 04 529 17; e club@atimoo.com; www.atimoo.com. PADI.
🤿 **Ifaty Plongée** Based at Ifaty Beach Club (see the hotel for contact details). Fishing & diving.
🤿 **Madagascar Sport Concept** m 032 04 362 76/032 04 346 63; e info@madagascar-sport-

concept.com; www.kitesurfamadagascar.com. Based at Hôtel de la Plage (see below). Diving, fishing, kitesurfing & whale-watching. PADI.
🤿 **Mangily Scuba** m 034 64 781 76; e mangilyscuba@gmail.com; www.ifatyscuba. com. Based at Coq du Village. Diving, snorkelling, whale-watching, surfing & boat trips to the Mangrove Information Centre. PADI.

NORTH OF IFATY

Beyond Ifaty, the coastal road sees far fewer travellers. The scenery becomes more rural and hotels more isolated. See the map on page 428 for this section.

MADIORANO This village a few kilometres north of Ifaty (38km from Toliara) offers a more peaceful setting, with a few **places to stay:**

🏠 **Hôtel de la Plage** (15 bungalows)
☎94 906 92; m 032 04 362 76/033 37 362 76;
e hotelplagetulear@blueline.mg; www.hotelplage-tulear.com. Well-run hotel with

attractive en-suite bungalows. Activities inc diving, fishing, kayaking & kitesurfing. €€€€€

🏠 **Mira** (21 bungalows) 📞94 912 71; m 032 02 621 44; e lamira.hotel@moov.mg. Highly rated, spacious & very comfortable with wonderful food. Fishing, windsurfing, boat trips & 4x4/quad hire. €€€€€

🏠 **Belle Vue** (18 rooms & 12 bungalows) m 032 04 647 22/034 11 112 11;

e jimmyhotelbellevue@yahoo.com. Good rooms with hot water. Tremendous ocean views from the restaurant. €€€€

🏠 **Poseidon (Soleil Couchant)** (10 bungalows) m 034 29 100 38 (dive club)/034 47 360 15; e hotel_poseidon@yahoo.fr; www. hotelposeidon-padiresort.com. Diving & whale-watching resort with comfy rooms. €€€

TSIANDAMBA AND AMBATOVAKY Continuing up the coast from Madiorano, you pass through the large villages of **Manombo** and **Tsifota**, both with well-stocked markets and very basic accommodation, before reaching **Tsiandamba** after around 52km (1¾hrs by 4x4).

Some 7km before Tsiandamba on a broad sandy beach is an isolated and very exclusive hotel, 3 hours (80km) from Toliara.

The rather plush **Ankasy Lodge** has five gigantic, solar-powered bungalows of stone construction, stylishly furnished with huge beds (📞26 409 08; m 032 05 255 53/034 85 020 10; e resa@ankasy.com; www.ankasy.com). The reef sits 2km offshore, protecting a vast turquoise lagoon where guests can snorkel, waterski, kitesurf or windsurf. Tsiandamba village itself has simple beachfront accommodation at **Hotel Tealongo**, also known as **Chez Odilon** (m 032 04 105 45/032 69 126 18; €€). Some 4km up the beach is **Un Peu Plus au Nord** (m 032 89 100 84/034 19 844 91; www.unpeuplusaunordcecile. com; €€€€). And at Ambatovaky is **Forest Deco** or **Chez Guillaume** (m 032 52 262 18/033 12 753 96; e guillaumedebejarry@yahoo.fr or info@touramada.com; €€€€).

SALARY This is in fact a *pair* of small villages 2km apart. They are sometimes distinguished as 'Salary Sud' and 'Salary Nord' but rather confusingly their official designations are **Salary Nord I** and **Salary Nord II** respectively, apparently in recognition of a similarly named village some 125km further south.

The coastline here is very beautiful; diving and snorkelling are rewarding. Cellphones typically don't work here but under certain weather conditions a weak Orange signal can be obtained in the evenings.

 Where to stay and eat There are places to stay in both villages:

🏠 **Salary Bay** (11 bungalows) Salary Nord II; 📞75 514 86/+881631513480 (satellite); m 032 49 120 16; e salarybay@malagasy. com; www.salarybay.com. An upmarket set of comfortable, thatched en-suite bungalows in a good beach location. Diving (e fredlucasdiving@ gmail.com), snorkelling, fishing, massage, pirogue/ boat/quad/4x4 trips & walks. Private airstrip. €€€€€

🏠 **Sirena del Mare (Chez Francesco & Claire)** (6 bungalows) Salary Nord II; e salaryfrancesco@yahoo.it. We found the Italian proprietor ebullient, enterprising & very welcoming, but more than one female reader has complained of misogynistic treatment here. The

food is also an enigma with travellers variously describing it as 'heavenly' & 'bland'! The sparsely furnished bungalows with their outside bucket showers seem rather overpriced but snorkelling in the area is 2nd to none. €€€

🏠 **Espadon (Chez Anselme)** (4 bungalows) Salary Nord I; m 032 40 438 12/034 64 781 01. Basic bungalows with squat toilets & bucket showers; owned by village président. €€

🏠 **Takaliko (Chez Jean-Louis)** (12 bungalows) Salary Nord I; m 032 61 271 08. Reasonably priced simple rooms inc colourful double-decker huts with bucket showers. €–€€

BEKODOY At Bekodoy, about 8km further on than Salary Nord II, is upper-range accommodation with five stone bungalows situated on a broad beach of white sand and a turquoise lagoon that extends 4km out to sea. **Smeralda Bay Guest House** (m *032 04 700 07;* e *smeraldabay@yahoo.it;* €€€€) offers spacious and comfortable accommodation with hot water and electricity. Cuisine is mainly Italian, using fresh seafood and served with homemade bread.

ANDRAVONA Another couple of kilometres further on, near the tiny village of Andravona, is a swanky new lodge built by the family that owns Chocolaterie Robert. **Mikea Lodge** (m *032 11 100 32/032 50 100 31;* e *contact@mikealodge. com; www.mikealodge.com;* €€€€€; *see ad, 4th colour section*) has splendid tented bungalows and offers a plethora of activities from diving, kayaking and kitesurfing to quad biking, catamaran trips and visits to the Mikea Forest.

AMBATOMILO This is a small fishing village with a population of about 500, located some 125km from Toliara – almost a third of the way to Morondava. By 4x4, it takes around 1½ hours to get here from Salary or 4 hours from Ifaty. There is no cellphone signal and one very much has the feeling of being in the middle of nowhere.

The six bungalows of **Shangri-La Lodge** are sited 3km north of the village and boast spectacular views over the lagoon and a splendid beach (m *032 40 333 61;* e *info@ambatomilo.com; www.ambatomilo.com;* €€€€). Travellers on a budget will find lodging in the village at **Floma** (m *032 40 785 08/034 87 232 51;* €€), which has eight rooms.

CONTINUING TO MORONDAVA Heading north becomes progressively difficult. It is possible to reach Andavadoaka, Morombe, Belo-sur-Mer and eventually Morondava, but for much of the year some sections of the road are impassable and it is necessary to take to the sea. The journey along this section of coast is described on pages 427–33.

ANAKAO

South of Toliara, Anakao is a pretty little Vezo fishing village with colourful boats drawn up on the sands. Hotels catering for all budgets have opened in recent years so it now competes with Ifaty for beaches and opportunities for snorkelling, diving, birdwatching and mangrove trips.

If seafood is not your thing, your dining options in Anakao will be very limited; consider bringing some supplementary tinned food from Toliara. And note that obtaining fresh water is a problem in this arid area, so most hotels do not have running water. Since 2013, Anakao has a good cellphone signal (Telma).

GETTING THERE AND AWAY Anakao is accessible most easily by 35km boat transfer from Toliara (1hr), but costs at least 50,000Ar per person or 80,000Ar return; operators are listed on pages 86–90.

By dirt road via St Augustine's Bay it is 46km, but it is necessary to cross the Onilahy River. There is a car ferry – Bac Fiavota – connecting Sarodrano to Soalara, but it runs a very limited schedule and is fairly expensive to get them to lay on a special crossing just for you. Call ahead to find out its timetable (m *034 03 265 50/032 43 260 00*). Alternatively, you can avoid the river crossing by taking the RN7 inland to the RN10 turning, but it's a circuitous route of 286km taking at least 6½ hours.

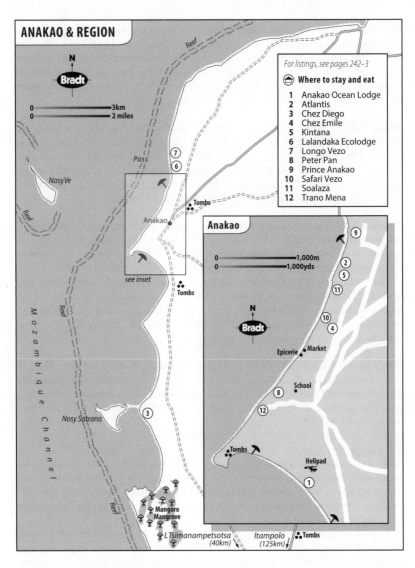

ANAKAO & REGION

N

Bradt

0 _____ 3km
0 _____ 2 miles

For listings, see pages 242–3

Where to stay and eat

1 Anakao Ocean Lodge
2 Atlantis
3 Chez Diego
4 Chez Emile
5 Kintana
6 Lalandaka Ecolodge
7 Longo Vezo
8 Peter Pan
9 Prince Anakao
10 Safari Vezo
11 Soalaza
12 Trano Mena

Reef

NosyVe

Pass

Reef

Anakao

see inset

Tombs

Tombs

M o z a m b i q u e   C h a n n e l

Reef

Nosy Satrana

Reef

Mangoro
Mangrove

L Tsimanampetsotsa
(40km)

Itampolo
(125km)

Tombs

Anakao

0 _____ 1,000m
0 _____ 1,000yds

N

Bradt

Epicerie Market

School

Tombs

Helipad

If you are not travelling with a vehicle then the secret to getting to Anakao on a budget is to take a taxi-brousse to Sarodrano for 6,000Ar (page 233) then find a sail pirogue to take you across the river mouth and round the headland to Anakao for around 20,000Ar (this takes less than an hour if the wind is in your favour), or alternatively get a boatman to take you across the river to Soalara, where you can catch the nightly Beheloka taxi-brousse to Anakao.

 WHERE TO STAY AND EAT *Map, above*

Anakao Ocean Lodge (25 bungalows) Andovoke Bay; ☎ 94 919 57/94 921 76/94 922 43; m 032 05 306 92; e anakaooceanlodge@gmail. com; www.anakao-madagascar.com. Top-notch

boutique hotel with beautiful bungalows (built between 1999 & 2007 with stone mined 6km away at Antsirafaly) with AC, safe, minibar, veranda & hot showers. On-site desalination plant produces fresh water. Diving, kayaking, sailing, surfing, kitesurfing, fishing, massage/reflexology spa, quads, excursions & splendid restaurant. Helipad. €€€€€–👑

🏠 **Chez Diego (Altra Faccia della Luna)**
(3 bungalows) ☎ 94 903 70; m 034 68 514 43; e laltraluna@hotmail.it; www.laltraluna.it. Guesthouse ambience; magically lit by dozens of candles at night. 7km south of village. Stunning dbl rooms with bucket showers. Beautiful stone pier. Kayaks, whale-watching & mangrove visits. €€€€

🏠 **Prince Anakao** (17 bungalows) ☎ 94 901 99/94 923 45; m 034 45 468 25/034 64 866 33; e prince.anakao@gmail.com; www. hotelprinceanakao.com. Sturdy bungalows, en suite with hot showers. New bar & restaurant; pool table, kayaking, snorkelling & pirogue trips. Sauna, jacuzzi, swimming pool & boutique just added. €€€–€€€€

🏠 **Safari Vezo** (2 rooms & 17 bungalows) ☎ 94 413 81 (reservations)/94 919 30 (hotel); m 034 94 413 81 (reservations)/034 94 919 30 (hotel); e safarivezo@moov.mg; www.safarivezo. com. Stylish seafront rooms, most with safe, minibar & veranda; smart clean bathrooms with tiled sit-down bucket showers (hot water in winter). Surfing, whale-watching, pirogue trips & massage. €€€–€€€€

🏠 **Kintana** (3 bungalows) m 032 02 245 50/034 52 606 52; e nieljm@gmail.com. Guesthouse run by English-speaking French former ski instructor & his Malagasy wife & 2 boys, who eat together with guests. Nice bungalows with hot bucket showers & great sea views. Fishing & pirogue trips. €€€

🏠 **Lalandaka Ecolodge** (13 bungalows) ☎ 94 922 21; m 032 05 622 80; e reservation@ lalandaka.com; www.lalandaka.com. Bungalows with bucket showers (hot water on request). Kitesurfing & quad hire. €€€

🏠 **Longo Vezo (Chez Eric & Carole)**
(8 bungalows) m 032 02 631 23/032 02 695 12/034 96 577 69; e longo.vezo@yahoo.fr; www. longovezo.com. Comfy bungalows with en-suite bucket showers & hammocks; quiet location. 3 boats for whale-watching, diving (www.plongee-madagascar.com) & excursions; also surfing & kayaking. €€€

🏠 **Peter Pan** (11 bungalows) ☎ 94 921 40; m 032 82 614 54; e chezpeter.pan@gmail.com; www.peterpanhotel.com. Lively backpacker ambience with lots of hammocks but rooms to suit a wide range of budgets: from bungalows with communal facilities to comfy apartments with Wi-Fi. Restaurant with Italian-influenced daily menu; cocktails & sometimes live local music. Boat trips inc fishing. €€–€€€€

🏠 **Atlantis** (4 bungalows) ☎ 94 700 42; m 034 10 000 72 (owner); e atlantismadagascar@ gmail.com; www.atlantismadagascar.com. En-suite rooms with hot water. Owned by Australian & French PADI dive instructors; better known as a dive centre & bar-restaurant. Also surfing, kitesurfing, whale-watching & 4x4 trips. €€–€€€

🏠 **Soalaza (Chez Solange)** (5 bungalows) ☎ 94 920 63; m 032 04 180 93; e soalazy@yahoo. fr. Rooms with en-suite cold showers or cheaper with bucket showers. No restaurant. €€–€€€

🏠 **Trano Mena (Chez Stoick)** (12 bungalows) m 032 83 923 34. Simple wooden & brick bungalows with bucket showers & en-suite toilets. €€–€€€

🏠 **Chez Emile** (9 bungalows) ☎ 94 922 45; m 032 04 023 76; e chezemile.anakao@yahoo.fr. Bucket showers & shared squat toilet. Rooms are in dunes 200m behind beach; restaurant/bar/shop is on the beach. €€

WHAT TO SEE AND DO The beach around the village itself is very busy – what with local life revolving around fishing – and not particularly clean, so for **swimming and sunbathing** head further along the shore.

Lake Tsimanampetsotsa National Park (covered on page 245) is a highly recommended excursion from Anakao; any hotel can help you arrange a trip.

Exploring A day spent investigating the area on foot is rewarding. Take the track behind the village heading south. On the outskirts of Anakao you will find some interesting **tombs** (one has a satellite dish on the roof to provide eternal entertainment for the ancestors) and will then come to a small peninsula with a couple more tombs. It is still possible to find fragments of subfossil eggshell from the long-extinct elephant bird here, but please keep your collecting instincts under control so that others can enjoy this extraordinary glimpse of the past. It is illegal to take these eggshells out of the country.

Birders would be well advised to take an early-morning walk on one of the tracks through the spiny forest, setting off shortly before sunrise.

There is an old **colonial mining railway** from Soalara (north of Anakao) to Sakoa, about 50km away. It no longer functions but you can do an excursion there by quad. **Anakao Quad** (e *pascalcocquerel@yahoo.fr or cardonajacques@live.fr; www. anakaoquad-madagascar.com*) hires out quads; they are based at Lalandaka Ecolodge.

Mangoro mangrove is about an hour's walk down the beach from Chez Diego, but it is more rewarding to explore this place by boat. The birdlife is good with bee-eaters, vasa parrots, flamingos, harrier-hawks and plovers among species seen.

Watersports Most of the hotels have snorkelling gear for their guests. Nosy Ve (see *Nearby islands* below) is a more rewarding site than Anakao's lagoon. The best months for diving are between April and December when the water is clear of sediment from Onilahy River. Italian-run PADI dive centre **Il Camaleonte** based just outside Peter Pan Hotel offers scuba-diving at more than 20 sites, as well as kitesurfing, stand-up paddle boarding and kayaking (m *032 63 672 34;* e *camaleonteanakao@gmail.com; www.ilcamaleonteanakao.wordpress.com*). Further up the beach is a second PADI dive outfit called **Atlantis**, operated by a French-Swiss team (☏ *94 700 42;* m *034 10 000 72;* e *atlantismadagascar@gmail.com; www.atlantismadagascar.com*). The surf experts are **Nono Surf**, based at Safari Vezo.

Nearby islands Lying 4km west of Anakao is **Nosy Ve**, a sacred site. It has a long history of European domination since a Dutchman landed there in 1595; it was officially taken over by the French in 1888 before their conquest of the mainland, although it is hard to see why: it is a flat, scrub-covered little island.

What makes Nosy Ve special to modern-day invaders is the tranquillity of its white beaches, the snorkelling on its fringing reef, and the world's southernmost breeding colony of red-tailed tropic-birds. They breed year-round at nest sites under bushes at the southern end of the island.

A 5,000Ar fee must be paid to visit the island. Camping is not allowed and there are no buildings. Visits are dependent for their success on wind and tide (strong wind makes snorkelling difficult; high tide is equally unrewarding for snorkellers and beachcombers). For this reason visits with fishermen using pirogues, which can land at low tide, are more successful than by large motorboats. With little natural shade on the island, make sure your boatman erects a sail on the beach to provide respite from the burning sun. There are *fady* prohibiting harming the tropic-birds and defecating on the beach, and tourists should also respect the ancestors by keeping away from the tombs.

Further south, **Nosy Satrana** is a small peaceful island closer to the shore (in fact you can walk out to it on a sandbar at low tide). It offers excellent diving and good snorkelling, but no tropic-birds.

SOUTH OF ANAKAO

You can drive on a sandy coast road until you reach Madagascar's southern tip, whereafter you can join RN10 to continue to Taolagnaro. However, the road is slow going in parts and, once the Linta and Menarandra rivers swell after November, you won't get much further than Itampolo. Note that Ambola, Efoetse and Itampolo have no reliable cellphone signal.

BEHELOKA AND AMBOLA These two fishing villages offer the nearest accommodation to Lake Tsimanampetsotsa National Park. Beheloka is 20km north of the lake and Ambola is 6km to its west. The **park office** at Efoetse, just 2km inland from Ambola, can be reached in 1½ hours from Anakao by 4x4. From Toliara there are weekly taxi-brousses to Beheloka, or you can arrange a direct boat transfer to Ambola. **Places to stay** include bungalows built by Madagascar National Parks as well as a few hotels:

🏠 **Domaine d'Ambola** (7 rooms) m 034 66 413 47; e contact@ambola-madagascar. com; www.ambola-madagascar.com. A simple attractive beachfront hotel. Rooms mostly en suite but a couple of cheaper ones have private bathrooms which are separated. **€€€€–€€€€€**

🏠 **Canne à Sucre** (4 rooms & 4 bungalows) Beheloka; m 034 74 860 44; e mjbbmada@ hotmail.fr. Rooms with communal facilities & bungalows with en-suite bathrooms, on a gorgeous bay of turquoise water. Camping for 8,000Ar. **€€€**

🏠 **Vahombe** (13 bungalows) Ambola; m 034 84 152 42/034 99 383 42. Simple dbl rooms, mostly with en-suite bucket showers. **€€€**

LAKE TSIMANAMPETSOTSA NATIONAL PARK (m *033 03 866 51*; e *tsp@parcs-madagascar.com*) Renowned for its waterfowl, the shallow **soda lake** – 15km long by 2km at its widest point – is the focus for this terrific national park. The large limestone plateau here has some of the most striking spiny forest vegetation in Madagascar, with countless locally endemic species. There are several extraordinary baobabs, pachypodiums and also a magnificent banyan tree with its aerial roots hugging the side of a cliff face to find purchase in the soil some 20m below.

'There are so many reasons to visit this magical place,' enthuses Toliara resident Louise Jasper, who has been several times: 'the crazy stunted baobab forest, caves and sinkholes, giant fig trees full of green pigeons and parrots (when in fruit), the colour-changing lake with flamingos, endemic mongooses, lemurs sunbathing at dawn, a variety of walks, tortoises in the rainy season (till at least March), lovely views over the lake and bat caves too.'

Lying about 50km south of Anakao, a visit is manageable as a day trip but an overnight stay is recommended. From the park office at Efoetse to the **main campsite** takes about 25 minutes by 4x4 (45mins in the rainy season). There are sheltered tent pitches, a squat toilet and bucket shower facilities, a cooking place and picnic tables.

Two **viewpoints** offer spectacular panoramas over the lake. The first is a 10-minute drive south of the campsite, and the second about an hour beyond that. From the track, which runs along the lake's eastern shore, it takes about 20 minutes to climb up to each viewpoint. There are a couple of excellent circuits starting at the campsite – on which baobabs, large pachypodiums, tortoises, numerous lizards and many birds may be seen – and night walks are possible from here too. Broad-striped mongooses regularly visit the campsite at night. In fact, they can be a nuisance as they will snatch unattended food and even enter unsecured tents or vehicles if something inside smells good.

There is a cave nearby where each evening ring-tailed lemurs climb across a vertical rock face to sleep on a high ledge where they are safe from fossas. Also close to the campsite is the sacred **Mitoho Cave** with a pool harbouring blind fish.

The usual park entry fee must be paid (page 73) at the office. You pick up your guide here as well. Most circuits in the park cost 15,000Ar but this only applies for day trips as there is a fixed guiding fee of 30,000Ar per day for multi-day visits. A cook can be hired to prepare meals and tents are also available from the office.

If you are here between August and October you stand a good chance of witnessing a passing funeral ceremony, for in this region burials may officially take place only during this period.

Cave diving The park has a network of flooded caves, including **Aven Cave** where remarkably well-preserved bones of extinct species such as giant lemurs and elephant birds have been found in impressive numbers. An 'underwater museum' has recently been set up and Madagascar National Parks are collaborating with the Madagascar Cave Diving Association to open the site to dive tourists. It is also possible to dive in Malaza Manga and Mitoho caves.

ITAMPOLO Ambola to Itampolo takes 2 hours in a good 4x4 (5–6hrs by taxi-brousse). There are many Mahafaly tombs along the first three-quarters of this section, some with aloalo, some sporting zebu horns, some concrete ones painted with colourful scenes and a few extravagantly tiled. The road passes through spiny forest, but with very few baobabs or octopus trees, except for the last 10km into Itampolo where octopus trees and prickly pear are in abundance. Also keep your eyes peeled for tortoises along the road from here southward. Itampolo has a few **places to stay:**

🏠 **Gîte d'Etape Sud Sud** (3 rooms & 4 bungalows) 📞 94 415 27; e c.alain@moov.mg; www.hotelchezalain-tulear.com. Under same ownership as Chez Alain in Toliara. A choice of simple, comfortable bungalows & rooms above a restaurant-bar. Camping for 10,000Ar. €€€

🏠 **Royale (Chez Nany)** (6 bungalows) Located 1.5km northwest of the village behind the dunes. Outdoor latrine & bucket shower. Camping for 10,000Ar. €€

🏠 **Vahombe (Chez Jean-Robert)** (6 bungalows) m 033 08 296 57. Simple rooms & bucket showers. €€

ANDROKA AND BEYOND This village an hour from Itampolo (2–3hrs by taxi-brousse) is on the south side of the Linta river mouth. There is cellphone reception here (Orange) and seven cheap basic bungalows at **Namako**, also known as **Chez Jean-Jacques** (m *032 66 274 59*; €) If you are continuing on the coast road, turn to page 249.

TOLIARA TO TAOLAGNARO (FORT DAUPHIN)

Camion-brousses from Toliara to Taolagnaro go via the inland route (RN10) and take two to three days. It's a shame to pass through such an exciting area without stopping, however. Much more interesting is to rent a vehicle and driver, or to do the trip in stages, staying at some or all of Betioky, Ampanihy, Beloha, Tsiombe and Ambovombe (of which only the last has a bank). Except for the long-distance camion-brousse no regular taxi-brousse services operate on the stretch from Betioky to Ambondro, though, so you would be reliant on hitchhiking or finding local private vehicles *en route*.

TOLIARA TO BETIOKY The turning for RN10 is at **Andranovory** (70km/1hr from Toliara). It takes about 4 hours to get to **Betioky** by 4x4 (8hrs/10,000Ar by taxi-brousse). The town has full cellphone coverage, a hospital, several eateries and market day is Tuesday. The cheapest rooms are at **Mahasoa** (m *033 09 148 97/033*

12 160 37; €–€€) and the best are the four en-suite bungalows of **Odette** (m *033 05 223 81;* €€). A third option is **Tsaramandroso** (m *033 09 414 79;* €€) where the bungalows and rooms are mainly en suite but with cold water only.

BEZA-MAHAFALY SPECIAL RESERVE (m *034 49 401 95/033 04 139 48/032 60 044 79;* e *bzm@parcs-madagascar.com or andriswilliam@yahoo.fr)*The reserve protects two distinct types of forest – spiny forest and gallery (riverine) forest – with habituated lemurs much in evidence. There are also four species of tenrec including the rare large-eared one, *Geogale aurita*, three carnivores including the fossa, countless reptiles and over 100 bird species. Beza-Mahafaly primarily exists for researchers but a small trickle of tourists also find their way here.

There are four circuits: a **gallery forest** walk takes around 2 hours; the **spiny forest** trail takes about 4 hours if you start and finish at the office, or half that if you have a 4x4 to drive you to the trail head; visits to **Ihazoara Canyon** takes less than an hour, as do walks to **Lake Andriakera** (particularly good for birds and incorporating some Mahafaly tombs). Ring-tailed lemurs and Verreaux's sifakas are easy to see around the camping area in the daytime and sportive lemurs and mouse lemurs can be seen on a **night walk** in the gallery forest.

The reserve is 1½ hours east of Betioky by 4x4 on a poor road, which may take considerably longer in the rainy season. Alternatively you could get there by motorbike or zebu cart. Guides and permits (prices on page 73) may be obtained on arrival, but it is best to call ahead to check the guides are on-site and not in Betioky. Since mid-2012 there is cellphone reception (Orange) at the park.

Each circuit costs 15,000Ar per group of up to five people, or 20,000Ar for night walks. Tent pitches are 10,000Ar per night and there are also a couple of rooms for the same price which, if not in use by researchers or staff, may be used by tourists. A cook can be hired for 5,000Ar per day but you need to provide the food.

BETIOKY TO AMPANIHY There are many Mahafaly tombs along this stretch, which takes at least 4 hours by 4x4 (8hrs by camion-brousse) because the road is in poor condition. Some 20km south of Betioky is the small village of **Ambatry**, 8km beyond which is the turning on the right for Beheloka and Anakao. Some 56km beyond the turn is **Ejeda** (from where a bad 77km track runs to Itampolo on the coast) and 50km after that comes **Ampanihy**. The name means 'place of bats' but it is now the place of goats: mohair carpet-weaving has long been a local industry. Carpets made here can be purchased from **The Mohair Man** showroom in Toliara (page 231). There are seven spacious basic rooms with en-suite bucket showers at **Angora** (m *033 12 232 82;* e *josangora@gmail.com;* €€) and camping is allowed in the garden. Cheaper but run-down rooms can be found at a guesthouse called **Filaos** (€).

AMPANIHY TO TSIOMBE After Ampanihy you enter Antandroy country and will understand why their name means 'people of the thorns'. The road deteriorates further, being little more than a pile of rocks for much of the 41km to **Tranoroa** (literally 'two houses'), a major weaving town. The road improves slightly over the 61km to **Beloha** but it is still painfully slow going – giving you plenty of time to spot tortoises and tombs. From Ampanihy it takes at least 4½ hours by 4x4 (about 10hrs by camion-brousse). A 39km road runs south from Beloha to Lavanono (page 249).

The next 55km to **Tsiombe** is the most interesting stretch of the entire journey, with baobabs, tortoises and tombs. The town has a Friday market and full cellphone coverage, but no bank or fuel station. Weary travellers in search of a night's rest will find 15 rooms, mostly en suite, at **Paradis du Sud** (m *033 23 151 39/033 82 892 24;* **€€–€€€**) and in the centre with nine rooms is **Sirène** (m *033 01 559 09;* **€–€€**) with communal toilets and en-suite bucket showers. Two roads lead from this village to **Faux Cap** and **Cap Sainte Marie**. If you are in the area in August, ask around about the **Rebeke music festival**, an event hosted annually in Tsiombe.

TSIOMBE TO AMBOVOMBE About 16km beyond Tsiombe look out for a huge tomb that is a replica *rova* palace. The next place you come to is **Ambondro**, the main centre for weaving in the region. Though much of the cloth is made in surrounding villages and brought into the town to sell, you can purchase direct from the makers. There is an impressive zebu market held on Saturdays. From there it is 30km to **Ambovombe** (meaning 'place of many wells'), a bustling town that holds a colourful Monday market. In the centre of town is a cybercafé and a BOA bank (⊕ *Mon–Fri 08.00–11.30 & 14.00–16.30*). **Places to stay** include:

🏠 **Lazan'androy** (11 rooms) m 032 44 609 83/033 24 923 10. En-suite bathrooms with hot water. No food but Oasis is right in front. **€€–€€€**
🏠 **Ezaka Magnevarova** (12 rooms) m 032 02 042 52/033 76 741 42; e ferdinand.mbinina@ yahoo.fr. Rooms with communal toilets & bucket showers. **€€**
🏠 **Ikonda** (10 rooms) m 032 04 210 89/033 07 980 68; e bedeisa_ma@yahoo.fr. Just out of

town towards Taolagnaro with en-suite cold-water facilities. **€€**
🏠 **Oasis** (4 rooms) m 033 18 723 18/033 24 651 13; e oasisandroy@gmail.com. Rooms with bucket showers. Good restaurant. Noisy karaoke on Fri/Sat. **€€**
🏠 **Source** (5 bungalows) m 033 40 673 88. Simple bungalows with bucket showers. **€€**

AMBOVOMBE TO TAOLAGNARO Some 35km beyond Ambovombe is **Amboasary**, the lively town that marks the turn-off to Ifotaka and Berenty (page 250). It has a busy market, a post office and full cellphone coverage. But there is no fuel station, bank or decent hotel (in any case, locals say the town is not safe after dark and it would be best not to stay overnight). From here you are 3–4 hours (75km) away from Taolagnaro on a paved-but-pot-holed road that mostly passes through cultivated land.

About 12km southeast of Amboasary is **Lake Anony**, a brackish lagoon of particular interest to birders. Continuing 8km to its southern end, you will find flamingos and dramatic 20m-high sand dunes. The lake has a white beach of broken seashells, which are gathered and taken by truck to Tana where they are ground and added as a calcium supplement to poultry feed.

Just north of Lake Anony are two small salt lakes that become bright pink in December after the rains. **Pink lakes** occur in just a few places around the world where there is the right combination of conditions – high salinity, high temperature and intense light – to promote growth of an algae that accumulates beta-carotene at concentrations up to 50 times that found in carrots; also contributing to the colour, a pink-hued halobacterium grows within the salt crust on the bottom of the lake.

The nearby mountain of **Ankodida** is a remnant of transition forest, home to ring-tailed lemurs. It is a new 10,744ha community-managed protected area being developed for ecotourism with WWF assistance, along with a 1,053ha reserve called **Ambatotsirongorongo**. The latter is a transition forest fragment aiming to restore 310ha of forest south of Ranopiso, a small town 38km from Amboasary towards Taolagnaro. From Ranopiso, a track leads 19km to the coastal village of Analapatsa, where a luxury hotel is being built on a tiny islet just offshore.

LAVANONO Dramatically situated on a beach below the 150m-high Karimbola cliffs, Lavanono is a surfers' paradise and a great end-of-the-earth spot for a chilled beach retreat – although it was brought slightly closer to the outside world with the arrival of cellphone coverage (Orange) in 2012. It is accessible by a rocky, tortoise-strewn road from Beloha (39km/1½hrs) – keep your eyes open for at least two tombs topped by large models of aircraft on the way! There are three **places to stay** in the village:

🏠 **Lavanono Lodge (Chez Gigi)**
(8 bungalows) m 032 22 187 37; e gigi@
lavanono.com; www.lavanono.com. Quirky surfing
lodge explicitly selective about class of guest:
passing trade & backpacker types not welcome.
Rooms among attractively planted grounds with
communal squat toilet & bucket showers. Wi-Fi.
Min stay 2 nights. Food quite pricey. €€€€

🏠 **Tea-Longo (Chez Evelyne)** (7 bungalows)
m 032 66 285 81; e tea.longo100@yahoo.fr.
Beachfront bungalows with verandas; communal
squat toilet & bucket showers. Electricity in eve.
€€–€€€

🏠 **Bel Avenir (Chez Georgette)**
(6 bungalows) m 032 27 106 68. Basic huts.
Electricity in eve. €€

CAP SAINTE MARIE (m *034 49 401 85;* e *csm@parcs-madagascar.com*) The special reserve of Cap Sainte Marie is the southernmost tip of Madagascar and home to thousands of radiated tortoises. The **park office** is 4.5km north of the reserve limit, from where it is a further 9km drive to the **lighthouse**. This exposed headland is covered in extraordinary dwarf vegetation, the result of the constant wind roaring across. As you stand and gaze out to sea, with nothing but 4,600km of ocean separating you from Antarctica, it is extraordinary to realise that you are even further south – by about 30km – than Uluru (Ayer's Rock) in Australia.

Permits are obtained from the park office (prices on page 73); guiding costs 5,000Ar for the botanically fascinating cape walk and 7,000Ar for a trail to see a 'window' rock formation, seafront caves and elephant bird eggshell fragments. There is a 5km drive between the two circuits and it takes around 3 hours to complete both.

You can get here via sandy roads from Tsiombe (49km/1½hrs) or Faux Cap (50km/1½hrs), but the latter route is a maze of tracks so you will need to ask locals for directions at regular intervals to avoid getting lost. You can also come directly from Lavanono without retracing your steps to RN10: after climbing the cliff road behind Lavanono take the right turn after 200m (signposted 'Fort Dauphin') then after 18km there is a right-hand fork with a sign indicating 9km to Cap Sainte Marie.

FAUX CAP The village here is called **Betanty**, a quintessential Antandroy coastal settlement. This dramatic, lonely place is isolated from the outside world not only by the poor roads, but by wild seas and a treacherous coral reef. The huge, shifting sand dunes are littered with fragments of *Aepyornis* shell. It is an extraordinary place worth making the effort to visit and there's a lagoon where you can swim safely. Market day is Monday and this is the only day of the week when Betanty is served by public transport: the taxi-brousse leaves Tsiombe around 04.00 and takes 3½ hours to do the 30km.

Behind a nice stretch of beach are seven comfy thatched stone bungalows at **Libertalia Beach Club** (m *032 07 560 41;* e *madalibertalia@yahoo.fr; www. madalibertalia.com;* €€€€). The cheaper option in town is **Cactus** (m *032 68 373 41/033 07 998 12;* €€€) where there are eight bungalows with en-suite bucket showers.

The South   **THE FAR SOUTH**

9

For the final 50km of its journey to the coast, Mandrare River's western bank is dominated by vast sisal plantations dotted with the occasional baobab. The area marks a transitional zone between the rainforests east of the Anosyenne Mountains and spiny forest to the west, and the remaining forests have exceptionally high species endemism. The valley is also home to one of Madagascar's longest-established ecotourism destinations and some spectacular protected forests offering wildlife-viewing opportunities that are second to none.

SISAL This crop was introduced to Madagascar in the interwar years, with the first exports taking place in 1922 when 42 tonnes were sent to France. There was a 60-fold increase in output by 1938 and sisal plantations in the Toliara and Taolagnaro regions had expanded to cover 3,500ha. Uses of the product include the manufacture of rope, twine, carpets and dartboards. The market continued to grow until, in 1952, a synthetic substitute was developed in the USA and demand fell. The French government stepped in with subsidies and bought 10,000 tonnes.

The Toliara plantations were closed in 1958 leaving only those in the Mandrare Valley. By the 1990s, 30,000ha of endemic spiny forest (over 100 square miles!) had been cleared to make way for the crop. Now there are five sisal companies here: four French – including the owners of Berenty Reserve – and one Swedish. Together they employ several thousand people in the tough and low-paid jobs of harvesting and processing the leaves. Until recently, tourists could take factory tours to see the process, but this was attracting increasingly regular complaints about working conditions so it is no longer allowed and the plantation owners have even become nervous about tourists taking photos of workers in the fields.

Sisal plants reproduce by creating fully formed plantlets on a tall flower spike. These are gathered and planted out when they reach about 20cm tall. After four years they can start to be harvested. This involves cutting the bottom 10–12 leaves each year for the next three or four years, by which time the plants have reached the end of their useful life, so then the field is burned and left fallow for a year before starting the process over. The cycle thus takes about eight years, and along the sisal belt fields can be seen at all stages of the process.

The harvested leaves are crushed on a machine then hung on wires to dry in the sun for two days before being packed into 150kg bales for export. In 2007, the Mandrare Valley was responsible for 4% of global sisal production. And here's something to think about: since the 1990s, resurgence in demand has put more native forests at risk. Why? Because we 'green' consumers in the West are insisting on biodegradable packaging!

BERENTY (m *033 23 210 06 for reception or 033 23 210 08/033 23 210 12 for bookings;* e *berenty@madagascar-resorts.com or fortdauphin@madagascar-resorts. com; www.madagascar-resorts.com*) This small private reserve some 3 hours' drive west of Taolagnaro is one of the most famous in Madagascar, not least for being the site where renowned primatologist Alison Jolly studied lemurs for five decades. It's pricey but most visitors love it for the combination of tame lemurs, reasonably comfy accommodation, knowledgeable guides and easy forest trails.

There are some 30 bungalows and rooms as well as a restaurant within the reserve complex. Don't try turning up unannounced – they generally insist you use their transfers from Taolagnaro. Most visitors to Berenty are on package tours but independent travellers can organise a trip here through the Dauphin Hotel in Taolagnaro (page 257).

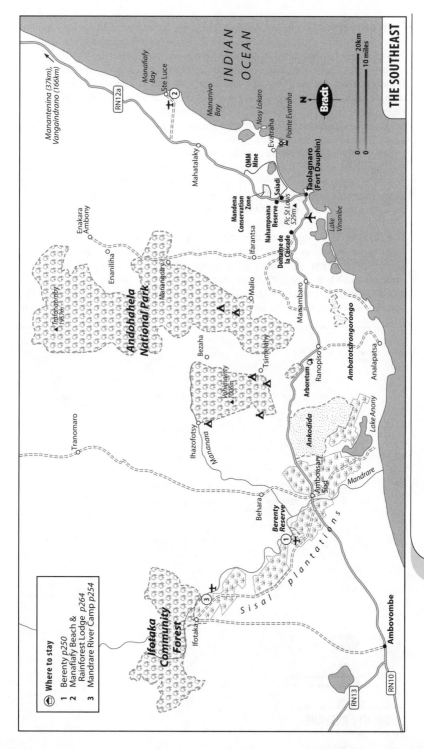

THE SOUTHEAST

INDIAN OCEAN

Manantenina (37km),
Vangaindrano (166km)

RN12a

Manafiafy
Bay

Ste Luce

②

Mananivo Bay

Nosy Lokaro

Evatraha

Pointe Evatraha

Mahatalaky

QMM Mine

Saïadi

Taolagnaro (Fort Dauphin)

Lake Vinanibe

Enakara Ambony

Enaniliha

Mandena Conservation Zone

Ifarantsa

Nahampoana Reserve

Pic St Louis 529m

Domaine de la Cascade

Manangotry

△Trafotaomby 1957m

Andohahela National Park

Malio

Mananibaro

Ambatotsirongorongo

Ranopiso

Analapatsa

Bezaha

Vohindava 1000m

Arboretum

Tsimelahy

Ankodida

Lake Anony

Ihazofotsy

Mananara

Tranomaro

Behara

Berenty Reserve

Ambatosary Sud

Mandrare

①

③

Ifotaka

Ifotaka Community Forest

S i s a l   P l a n t a t i o n s

Amboombe

RN13

RN10

N

Bradt

0   20km

0   10 miles

Where to stay

1 Berenty *p250*
2 Manafiafy Beach &
   Rainforest Lodge *p264*
3 Mandrare River Camp *p254*

251

The road to Berenty The reserve lies 87km (3hrs) to the west of Taolagnaro and the drive there is part of the experience. Indeed, the obligatory transfer in the reserve's own minibus is accompanied by a guide who will point out interesting sights *en route*.

For the first half of the journey the skyline comprises rugged green mountains. **Travellers' trees** dot the landscape and near Ranopiso is a grove of the very rare **triangle palm**. You may pause to see some endemic carnivorous **pitcher plants** too. Keep an eye out for what look like clusters of missiles lurking in the forest. These **Antanosy cenotaphs** commemorate those buried in a communal tomb or instances where the body could not be recovered.

Beyond Ranopiso the landscape flattens out and the bizarre fingers of *Didierea* and *Alluaudia* appear, interspersed with the bulky trunks of baobabs – the unique flora of the **spiny forest**. You will stop for some souvenir shopping at an enterprising local community that sells **woodcarvings**, and probably at a village market too, before turning off the main road for the final 8km through sisal fields.

The reserve Although located in the arid south, Berenty's position on the River Mandrare ensures a good water supply for the habitat of gallery (riverine) forest. To the south is a small area of spiny forest with some mature *Alluaudia* trees, some of which tower over 15m – an extraordinary sight. The joy of Berenty is its broad forest trails that allow safe wandering on your own; get up at dawn for the best birdwatching, to see the lemurs opening their arms to the sun, and to enjoy

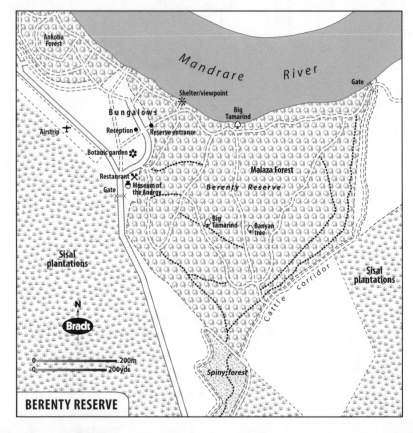

BERENTY RESERVE

THE TOMB OF RANONDA   *Hilary Bradt*

When I first started leading trips to Madagascar in the 1980s we always visited Berenty. It was one reliable success in an island of mishaps. So once a year I would make the drive from Taolagnaro and stop at a tiny settlement beside the road to see the Tomb of Ranonda. The village had a collection of wooden carvings commemorating the dead. Unlike the Mahafaly, the Antanosy people rarely use figurative carvings, preferring to mark burial places with concrete cenotaphs. So this was a rarity, but what set it apart from any other tomb I've seen was the exquisite craftsmanship. We even know the sculptor's name: Fiasia. Ranonda herself was evidently a religious young woman – she holds a Bible and a cross – but much livelier is the man losing a leg to a crocodile and an expertly carved boatload of people, their expressions tranquil except for the helmsman who poles his overloaded canoe to its end: the vessel sank and all on board were drowned. His face shows some anxiety as he looks round, perhaps at the oncoming waves.

The boat-people were the most famous but my favourite was a group of three zebu. These animals, destined to be sacrificed to the ancestors, are usually portrayed in a stylised form with an exaggeratedly large hump. So it was with the two bulls but among them was a cow and her calf. Here the sculptor has moved away from symbolism and used his chisels with real affection for his subject. Like all southerners, he would have lived with cattle all his life, and his knowledge is revealed in the way the cow's head is turned as she licks her suckling calf. The youngster responds by flicking its tail across her muzzle. Towering above them was their protector – a wooden herdsman.

For seven years I stopped my busload of tourists and showed them the carvings. The first year the children were too shy to approach us but peeped, bright-eyed, from the dark doorways of their huts. As years passed they became bolder. Tourists didn't linger, and no-one thought of giving anything back to the village whose beautiful memorial provided so much pleasure. And these children were starving. Literally. I'm haunted by a photo I took of a little boy whose distended stomach and stick-like limbs show the classic signs of malnutrition. I used to fantasise about somehow persuading an NGO to set up a health clinic here, funded from income generated by tourists visiting the tomb. But I did nothing.

In 1989 I stopped as usual and led my group to the tomb. Only the herdsman remained where the carved cattle used to stand under his watchful eye. The cow and her calf, and the two bulls, had been ripped away leaving only the jagged remains of their wooded plinth. In their place was a row of fresh zebu skulls, 'A tourist stole it', explained our driver. The skulls were from the cattle slaughtered by this impoverished village to calm the ancestors' rage at this desecration.

Buses no longer stop at the village. There's no point. The tomb is surrounded by a high fence of sharpened stakes. To take a photograph, tourists must pay €5. 'Not worth it', they mutter after peering through the fence with binoculars. I agree. The carvings have deteriorated, the wood has darkened and split, and lichen blotches the features of the boat-people. Somewhere, in a private collection of 'primitive art', the cow still licks her calf. Their wood retains its original grey smoothness, denied its destiny to grow old and return to the earth. And I ache for that village and its loss. Which is worse: its loss of trust or the loss of something that was not art but the tangible soul of an ancestor?

the coolness of the forest before breakfast. And a guided night walk in the spiny forest is not to be missed.

Berenty is most famous for its lemurs; if you have ever seen these in a TV documentary, chances are they were filmed here. Brown lemurs, ring-tails and sifakas are all guaranteed sightings. There are approximately 500 **ring-tailed lemurs** in Berenty, and the population has stayed remarkably stable considering only a quarter of babies survive to adulthood. The females are dominant over the males and receptive to mating for only a week or so in April or May, so there is much competition among males for this once-a-year treat. The young are born in September. Attractive though they are, no ring-tail can compete with the **Verreaux's sifaka** for soft-toy cuddliness, with its creamy white fur, brown cap, and black face. There are about 300 of them in the reserve. Unlike ring-tails, they only rarely come down to the ground but, when they do, the length of their legs in comparison with their short arms necessitates a comical form of locomotion: jumping with feet together like competitors in a sack race. The **red-fronted brown lemurs** were introduced from the west and are now well established and almost as tame as the ring-tails.

There are other lemurs which, being nocturnal, are harder to spot. The **white-footed sportive lemur** can be seen peering out of its tree hole during the day and **grey mouse lemurs** may be glimpsed in the beam of a flashlight on a night walk.

Among other wildlife, **fruit bats** congregate in noisy groups in one part of the forest. **Birdwatching** is rewarding, with nearly a hundred species recorded. You are likely to see the hook-billed vanga, crested coua, giant coua, coucal, grey-headed lovebirds and the beautiful Madagascar paradise flycatcher. If you visit from mid-October to May you will see a variety of migrant birds: broad-billed roller, Malagasy lesser cuckoo and lots of waders (sanderlings, greenshank, sandpiper, white-throated plover). **Reptiles** include two chameleon species and the huge but placid Dumeril's boa.

Museum of the Androy
Also within the Berenty complex, this is undoubtedly the best ethnological museum in Madagascar. If your interest in the region extends beyond the wildlife, you should allow at least an hour here. Several of the rooms are given over to an explanation (in English and French) of the traditional practices of the Antandroy people and even a full-size replica house.

IFOTAKA Over 22,000ha of spiny and gallery forest have been protected in a sustainable management programme here since 2006. Wildlife includes Verreaux's sifakas and ring-tailed lemurs. But word is the area has become rather lawless in the last couple of years, so we suggest you take local advice on the banditry situation before arranging a visit to the community forest.

A few kilometres away, however, in a small stand of forest on the banks of the river, it is safe to stay at the wonderful **Mandrare River Camp** (\ *22 022 26;* m *032 05 619 00/032 05 619 99/033 11 262 25/034 11 262 25;* e *erika@madaclassic.com; www.madaclassic.com;* ⊕ *closed Jan–Feb;* ☕; *see ad, 4th colour section; map, page 251*). British-owned and with a predominantly anglophone clientele, this exclusive lodge comprises seven spacious furnished safari tents, with solar power, private wooden verandas, thatched shelters and smart en-suite bathrooms built from stone; there is also a riverfront swimming pool and a private airstrip nearby that offers an alternative to coming overland. Activities include spiny forest and gallery forest walks, visits to local villages, markets and a school built by the hotel, as well as traditional Antandroy dance performances and trips to Lac Anony for flamingos and other wetland birds.

HISTORY The remains of two forts can still be seen: Fort Flacourt built in 1643; and another that dates from 1504 – thus making it the oldest building in the country – erected by shipwrecked Portuguese sailors. This ill-fated group of 80 accidental colonists stayed about 15 years before falling foul of the local tribes. The survivors fled to the countryside where disease and hostile natives finished them off.

A 1642 French expedition by the Société Française de l'Orient had instructions to 'found colonies and commerce in Madagascar and to take possession of it in the name of His Most Christian Majesty'. An early settlement at Sainte Luce was soon abandoned in favour of a healthier peninsula to the south, and a fort was built and named after the dauphin (later Louis XIV). At first the Antanosy were quite keen on the trading opportunity but were less enthusiastic about losing their land. The heavily defended fort survived only by use of force and with many casualties on both sides. The French finally abandoned it in 1674, but their 30-year occupation formed one of the foundations of their later claim to the island as a colony.

TAOLAGNARO TODAY This laid-back town is beautifully located on a peninsula, bordered on three sides by beaches and breakers and backed by high green mountains which dwindle into spiny forest to the west. People generally still use the French name, Fort Dauphin, but to be consistent with the rest of the book we stick to 'Taolagnaro'. You'll also find the Malagasy name used on Air Mad schedules and many maps. The face of the town has changed greatly in the last few years with the construction of a controversial ilmenite mine (page 261).

GETTING THERE AND AWAY All roads connecting Taolagnaro to the rest of the country are in poor condition at the time of writing. There are direct taxi-brousses to Tana via RN13 (80,000Ar/2 days) – but see the warning on page 219 about this route. It would be far safer to go to Tana via Toliara (4 days nonstop; see page 246) or Vangaindrano (3 days; page 295). Considering the time and discomfort in reaching this region overland, most tourists fly. **Flights** run daily but are sometimes routed via Toliara.

GETTING AROUND Taxis cost 1,000Ar per person for short trips in town (2,000Ar at night), 6,000Ar to the airport, or 15,000Ar to Ehoala Port. The official rate for longer private hire is 20,000Ar per hour. For car hire, see page 260.

WHERE TO STAY
Top end €€€€€

🏠 **Kaleta** [258 E3] (37 rooms) m 034 08 621 28 (manager)/034 92 212 87/034 92 212 88; e kaletaresa@moov.mg. Classy business-style hotel under same ownership as Colbert in Tana. En-suite rooms with safe, minibar, AC, hairdryer, Wi-Fi & sat-TV; some with bath. Massage, public pool & spa. Restaurant Dauphinois is excellent; also divine patisserie. Visa accepted.

🏠 **Talinjoo** [256 D7] (8 rooms) m 034 05 212 35; e contact@talinjoo.com or talinjoo@yahoo.com; www.talinjoo.com. Built by Air Fort Services in 2009.

Stylish rooms with AC, balcony & stunning sea view. Massage. Wi-Fi in communal areas. Visa accepted.

Upper range €€€€

🏠 **Azura** [256 C6] (19 rooms) 📞 92 211 17; m 033 15 755 01/034 02 410 19; e azura.hotel@moov.mg. Smart contemporary rooms with TV, AC, minibar, Wi-Fi & en-suite bathroom. Spa, pool & tour operator.

🏠 **Croix du Sud** [258 B4] (32 rooms) m 032 05 416 84/032 05 416 98/033 23 210 08; e croixsud@madagascar-resorts.com or

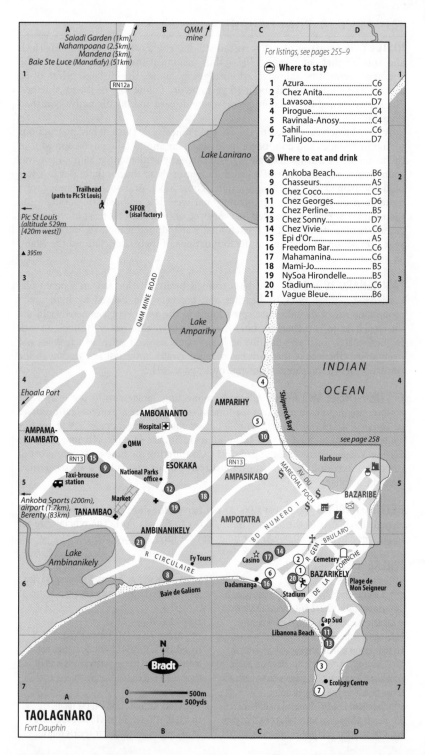

fortdauphin@madagascar-resorts.com; www.madagascar-resorts.com. Under same ownership as Berenty Reserve. You're expected to stay here or at nearby Dauphin if you plan to visit Berenty.

🏠 **Dauphin** [258 B4] (20 rooms) 📞92 211 56; m 032 05 416 83/033 23 210 07; e fortdauphin@ madagascar-resorts.com; www.madagascar-resorts. com. Lovely garden. Expensive airport transfers.

🏠 **Lavasoa** [256 D7] (2 rooms & 4 bungalows) m 033 12 517 03; e info@lavasoa.mg; www. lavasoa.com. Bungalows have en-suite bathroom, safe, minibar & balcony overlooking Libanona Beach; some with Wi-Fi. B/fast but no restaurant (works on HB with Tanlinjoo). Excursions to Lokaro, Vinanibe & Faux Cap; 4x4 rental.

🏠 **Marina** [258 C2] (24 rooms) m 032 05 231 47 (owner)/034 81 881 65 (reception); e hotelpanorama_lamarina@yahoo.fr or reception@hotel-lamarina.com; www.hotel-lamarina.com. Dbl rooms & 6-person suites, all with en-suite hot water, safe, minibar, AC & sat-TV.

🏠 **Phare** [258 C1] (14 rooms) m 033 11 254 89/034 55 517 54. Dbl rooms with TV, AC, minibar & hot showers. Wi-Fi. B/fast inc. Visa accepted.

Mid-range €€€

🏠 **Chez Anita** [256 C6] (8 rooms & 6 bungalows) 📞92 904 22; m 032 49 579 51/033 03 049 52/033 12 679 83; e anitahotel.restaurant@ gmail.com. Bungalows nestled in a quiet garden tucked away from the main road. Dbl & trpl with hot water & TV.

🏠 **Népènthes** [258 B2] (13 bungalows) Ampasikabo; 📞92 211 43; m 032 04 455 54/034 60 832 54; e hotel@lenepenthes.mg or lenepenthes@lenepenthes.mg. Dbl bungalows & restaurant in quiet, spacious grounds. Boat trips to Lokaro/Evatraha.

🏠 **Port** [258 C1] (17 rooms) m 032 11 001 88/033 11 001 88/034 11 001 88/034 14 001 88; e leporthotel@gmail.com; www.leport-hotel. com. Opened in 2012; en-suite rooms with Wi-Fi; some with AC & balcony. Suites have kitchenette. 4x4 hire. The hotel owns Andranara Park, a 4ha site

west of town with medicinal & essential oil plants. It's a nice picnic spot with snacks available, but they have recently added a zoo with lemurs & tortoises.

🏠 **Ravinala-Anosy** [256 C4] (5 bungalows) m 032 57 088 18/033 12 197 65; e fravinaclaris@ yahoo.fr; www.leravinala-madagascar.com. Well-organised clean accommodation. Spacious rooms & friendly owner.

🏠 **Soavy** [258 B2] (15 rooms & 6 bungalows) m 034 13 212 16/034 85 152 82/032 27 576 23; e deriazi@yahoo.fr or robert.deriazy@moov.mg. Spacious rooms in a tranquil spot; en suite with TV & minibar facilities.

🏠 **Tournesol** [258 A1] (4 rooms & 8 bungalows) m 032 22 508 08 (reception)/032 42 613 77 (manager)/033 12 513 16 (manager); e vaohitarl@yahoo.fr. On outskirts of town. Rooms with TV in nice communal garden; stunning views of Pic St Louis. Resident guide Narcisse organises excursions.

Budget €€

🏠 **Mahavoky** [258 E3] (12 rooms) Bazaribe; 📞92 902 32/92 914 15; m 033 12 513 36/034 19 456 89; e hotel.mahavoky@yahoo.fr. Inexpensive, large dbl & twin rooms with communal outside hot showers & toilet. Games room & good restaurant.

🏠 **Mahavoky Annexe** [258 D1] (9 rooms) m 032 07 990 70/034 21 493 80; e hotel. mahavoky@yahoo.fr. Centrally located. Most rooms have a balcony with dramatic views of the shipwrecks in the bay. Cheaper rooms face road. Great food.

🏠 **Pirogue** [256 C4] (5 bungalows) m 033 11 111 08/033 64 830 13. Simple but adequate rooms.

🏠 **Sahil** [256 C6] (7 rooms) Bazarikely; 📞92 912 39; m 032 40 461 69/033 12 784 49/034 95 126 88 (manager). Modest clean hotel; 2nd-floor panoramic view of Baie de Galions. Dbl en-suite rooms.

🏠 **Tsara Fandray** [258 C4] (7 rooms) Ambinanikely; m 032 43 267 94/032 57 633 97/033 12 428 56/034 67 208 91; e rasoablandine@hotmail.fr. Simple rooms in a quiet area some 2km from the centre.

✖ WHERE TO EAT AND DRINK

✖ **Ankoba Beach (Chez Marceline)** [256 B6] m 032 40 287 15/033 17 306 28; ⏱ Tue–Sun, Mon closed. Nice restaurant in top location but doesn't open late.

✖ **Chasseurs** [256 A5] m 032 94 033 34/034 20 123 17; e lechasseur11@hotmail.fr; ⏱ 07.30–late. Quick service, late opening & reliable Malagasy food.

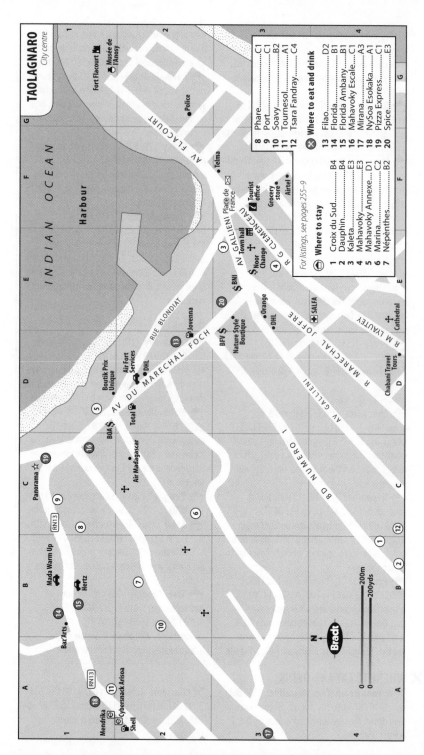

TAOLAGNARO
City centre

INDIAN OCEAN

Harbour

Fort Flacourt

Musée de l'Anosy

Police

Telma

Place de France

Tourist office

Grocery store

Airtel

Noor Change

Town Hall

BNI

AV GALLIENI

R G CLEMENCEAU

Orange

DHL

SALFA

Nature Style Boutique

BFV

Jovenna

Air Fort Services

DHL

Boutik Prix Unique

Total

BOA

Air Madagascar

AV DU MARECHAL FOCH

RUE BLONDIAT

R MARECHAL JOFFRE

R M LYAUTEY

Cathedral

Chabani Travel Tours

AV GALLIENI

BD NUMERO 1

Panorama

Mada Warm Up

Hertz

Baz'Arts

Mendrika

Cybersnack Arisoa

Shell

RN13

RN13

200m
200yds

N

Bradt

For listings, see pages 255–9

Where to stay
1 Croix du Sud............B4
2 Dauphin...................B4
3 Kaleta......................E3
4 Mahavoky.................E3
5 Mahavoky Annexe.....D1
6 Marina.....................C2
7 Népenthes................B2
8 Phare......................C1
9 Port.........................C1
10 Soavy......................B2
11 Tournesol................A1
12 Tsara Fandray..........C4

Where to eat and drink
13 Filao........................D2
14 Florida.....................B1
15 Florida Ambany........B1
16 Mahavoky Escale......C1
17 Mirana.....................A3
18 NySoa Esokaka.........A1
19 Pizza Express...........C1
20 Spice.......................E3

✖ **Chez Coco** [256 C5] m 032 47 804 38. Cheap Chinese & Malagasy food. A good place to eat if staying at Ravinala hotel opposite, which has no restaurant.

✖ **Chez Georges (Local)** [256 D6] Libanona Beach; m 032 48 097 38; e georgesliban@yahoo. fr; ⏰ 07.30–20.30. Lovely pub-restaurant with stunning sunset views over Libanona Bay. Fantastic seafood.

✖ **Chez Perline** [256 B5] m 032 04 929 51/033 11 433 06; e zaiforona.perline@orange.mg. Specialises in seafood dishes such as lobster & crab.

✖ **Chez Vivie** [256 D6] m 032 40 394 72/033 12 515 80; e vivieresto@yahoo.fr. Family-run restaurant serving Malagasy dishes at bargain prices. Portions not large, but food is tasty & service amenable.

✖ **Filao** [258 D2] m 032 43 288 58/032 89 018 95; e lauretforest@gmail.com; ⏰ Mon–Sat 11.30–22.00, Sun closed. Lunch sandwiches & European cuisine.

✖ **Florida (Las Vegas)** [258 B1] m 034 45 081 71; ⏰ 06.00–late. Pizza, seafood & many Malagasy dishes. Good terrace for relaxing.

✖ **Mahamanina** [256 C6] m 034 16 862 76. Meals & snacks as well as a small supermarket that imported products inc cheese & wine.

✖ **Mirana (Chez Bernard)** [258 A3] m 034 01 637 04/034 04 409 25; e baugere@yahoo.fr; ⏰ Mon–Sat, Sun closed. Much-recommended restaurant.

✖ **Pizza Express** [258 C1] m 033 64 654 10. Pizza restaurant next to Panorama Club overlooking Shipwreck Bay; delivery available.

✖ **Spice (La Recrea)** [258 E3] m 033 64 654 11; ⏰ Tue–Sun 08.15–14.30 & 18.00–22.00, Mon closed. Asian food inc delivery & take-away.

✖ **Stadium** [256 C6] m 033 20 826 96/034 15 308 33. Popular with locals, serving grills, pizza & more. Karaoke.

✖ **Vague Bleue** [256 B6] m 034 15 546 26; ⏰ 07.00–22.00. Typical Malagasy cuisine.

☕ **Chez Sonny** [256 D7] m 033 21 342 54. A simple but very trendy beach shack on Libanona Beach run by a Malagasy-French couple; awesome atmosphere & deservedly popular especially with surfers.

☕ **Epi d'Or** [256 A5] m 034 05 210 81. A bakery-cum-café with a wide selection of cakes, pastries, desserts & ice cream.

☕ **Florida Ambany (Surf's Up)** [258 B1] m 034 45 081 71. A laid-back place for a snack opposite Florida bar, under the same ownership.

☕ **Freedom Bar** [256 C6] Faux Cap; m 032 22 436 15. With ice-cold drinks, great snacks & beautiful views from a vantage point perched above the ocean this is *the* place to be for a sundowner. Occasional cabarets.

☕ **Mahavoky Escale** [258 C1] m 032 89 736 64/034 12 266 25. This family-run *hotely* is a lively local place for drinks & brochettes.

☕ **Mami-Jo** [256 B5] m 033 12 716 77/033 18 551 36/034 85 158 58; e mamijo_fortdauphin@ yahoo.com. A small but popular Malagasy & Chinese cuisine *hotely*; great for a quick, cheap meal; patisserie too.

☕ **NySoa Esokaka** [258 A1] m 033 04 778 88/034 18 254 11. Patisserie with fresh juice & sandwiches.

☕ **NySoa Hirondelle** [256 B5] m 033 04 778 88/034 18 254 11. Pastries, snacks, sandwiches & drinks to take away.

NIGHTLIFE A good place to chill with a drink is **Chez Sonny** [256 D7]. In the next bay, **Freedom Bar** [256 C6] has loud music and is popular from sunset through to the early hours. **Panorama Club** is a better spot for dancing, but seems to go through a regular cycle of prolonged closures. More popular with locals – and thus with a more packed and lively atmosphere – is **Florida** [258 B1] (formerly **Las Vegas**), which also offers a separate space for karaoke.

MONEY, COMMUNICATIONS AND MEDICAL The **post office** [258 F3] has Western Union services (⏰ *Mon–Fri 08.30–noon & 13.30–17.00, Sat 08.30–11.00*), as do the BFV [258 E3], BOA [258 D1] and BNI [258 E3] **banks**, which close at weekends but have 24-hour ATMs. Near BNI is a bureau de change called **Noor Change** [258 E3] (m *032 85 123 62*). There is a **DHL office** [258 D2] at the tour operator Air Fort Services (page 260).

Many **cybercafés** are dotted around, including at the town hall [258 E3] and chamber of commerce, both of which are near to the tourist office [258 F3].

Centre Médical de Taolagnaro [258 B4] is a well-equipped 24-hour clinic operated by the much recommended Dr Jane Olivier from South Africa (m *034 20 009 11 in emergencies or 032 20 009 12 for appointments;* e *gestionnaire.cmdt@gmail.com*).

SHOPPING Taolagnaro has some distinctive local crafts. Most typical are the heavy (and expensive) silver bracelets worn traditionally by men. Also on offer are handmade shoes and raffia handbags. The souvenir shops are mostly along the main road, but the **craft market** (just north of Panorama) and the boutiques inside Kaleta Hotel are also worth a browse.

For general supplies, try the mini-market called **Boutik Prix Unique** (opposite BOA) or the grocery store on the road running southeast from the tourist office.

TOUR OPERATORS, VEHICLE HIRE AND FLIGHTS

✈ **Air Madagascar** [258 C2] Av du Maréchal Foch; ✆ 92 211 22; m 032 05 222 80/034 11 222 24; e ftussmd@airmadagascar.com; ⊕ Mon–Fri 07.30–noon & 14.00–17.30, Sat 08.00–10.00

Air Fort Services [258 D2] ✆ 92 212 24; m 032 05 212 34; e air.fort@moov.mg or contact@airfortservices.com; www.airfortservices. com; ⊕ Mon–Fri 08.00–noon & 14.00–17.00, Sat 08.00–noon. Car, bus & 4x4 hire inc driver/guide. Tours, excursions & flight reservations.

Anosy Discovery m 034 11 001 88; e dewa_v88@yahoo.com. Minibus & 4x4 rental.

Atallah m 032 04 647 74/033 11 254 89; e atallah.touroperator@yahoo.fr. Tours & 4x4 hire.

Chabani Travel Tours [258 D4] m 033 12 415 00/02; e chabani.travel@moov.mg or chabanitravel@gmail.com; ⊕ Mon–Fri 08.00–

noon & 14.00–18.00, Sat 08.00–noon. Vehicle hire & tours/excursions throughout the south.

Hertz [258 B1] SICAM Bldg; ✆ 92 210 76; m 032 05 221 53; e jrakotonarivo@sicam.mg. Car, 4x4 & minibus hire.

Dadamanga Travel Services [256 C6] m 034 20 990 99/034 93 175 88; e reservations@dadamanga. com; www.dadamanga.com or www.sainte-luce-reserve.org. Reliable local & national tour operator run by friendly Aussie Brett Massoud, who has lived in the area since forever. All English-speaking guides. See ad, 2nd colour section.

Korobo Tours m 032 63 522 20/34 40 049 99; e info@korobotours.com; www.korobotours. com. Tours of Taolagnaro & excursions throughout the region, combining activity, wildlife & cultural experiences; run by passionate local guides.

WHAT TO SEE AND DO *For an overview of the southeast region, see map, page 251.* Taolagnaro offers a choice of beach or mountain. The best easy-to-reach beach is **Libanona** [256 D6], with excellent swimming (beware the strong current), snorkelling and tide pools. But be cautious about visiting remote beaches (or even those near the town around dawn or dusk) as there have been some muggings and assaults.

Note that Ifotaka and Berenty are covered under *Mandrare Valley* (page 250).

In Taolagnaro centre, there is a fairly helpful regional tourist office, **ORTFD** [258 F3] (*Rue Realy Abel;* ✆ *92 904 12;* m *032 11 006 23/28;* e *contact@fort-dauphin.org; www.fort-dauphin.org;* ⊕ *Mon–Fri 08.30–noon & 14.30–17.00*). The **National Parks office** [256 B5] (✆ *92 904 85*) is behind Chez Perline.

Fort Flacourt [258 G1] (m *034 17 346 92/033 02 176 05/032 04 702 53;* e *museeflacourt@gmail.com;* ⊕ *Mon–Sat 08.30–11.30 & 14.30–17.00*) This fort is now a working military compound so a guide is obligatory for a tour. A small museum here, **Musée de l'Anosy**, exhibits old maps, photographs, uniforms and other cultural artefacts.

Watersports With some of the most superb coastline of the Indian Ocean, the south of Madagascar offers fantastic **surfing** opportunities. Good spots are Ankoba Beach (best for beginners); Monseigneur Bay (intermediate, best May/June/December); Baie des Galions (at the south end, if the wind is right); and

Vinanibe Beach (pronounced 'Venom Bay' by some in the surfing fraternity – with the strongest beachbreak and a fast tube that can exceed 300m, best April–June). Evatraha and Lokaro (page 263) are also popular surf spots.

With bases at both Monseigneur Bay and Ankoba Beach, the **Monseigneur Bay Surf Club** (m *032 53 098 75;* e *tsilavo@yahoo.fr*) can provide an instructor and surfing gear.

Domaine de la Cascade (m *032 07 678 23/032 11 414 00;* e *domainedelacascade@ gmail.com; entry 15,000Ar*) At Manantantely, meaning 'place of honey', this tranquil park contains tree nurseries, fruit plantations, an apiary and a natural waterfall. There are rooms (40,000Ar) if you want to stay and campsites too (8,000Ar per night plus 18,000Ar if you need to hire a tent). Located about 8km west of Taolagnaro, on the way to Amboasary, this is a great place to take a picnic, hike, or swim in the waterfall pools.

Nahampoana Reserve (m *032 05 212 35/032 11 212 34;* e *contact@airfortservices. com; entry 16,000Ar pp inc guided tour, min 2 people*) This is an easily accessible zoo-cum-reserve and botanical garden owned by Air Fort Services [258 D2] (page 260) who can provide transport to get there. The 50ha park is just 7.5km (15mins) north of Taolagnaro. Although some species are from other parts of Madagascar, it provides the usual tame lemurs, reptiles and regional vegetation. Allow a full day for a visit or stay in one of the en-suite rooms (70,000Ar including breakfast).

Saiadi Garden (m *033 12 176 09/032 05 416 83*) This botanical garden 6km north of Taolagnaro has been set up by the owners of Berenty as a competitor to the nearby Nahampoana Reserve. A half-day visit is recommended to take in the palms, ferns, bamboos, orchids, *Pachypodium* plants, elephant ears and travellers' trees. There are also tortoises, crocodiles and tame lemurs on show. A visit can be organised via the Dauphin Hotel, but if you want to combine the trip to see both Saiadi and Nahampoana (they're less than 2km apart) then you had best find independent transport because apparently each place's owner forbids their vehicles to go to the other's sites.

Mandena Conservation Zone (m *032 03 044 23/033 12 815 04/034 65 047 92;* e *yvette.rabeninary@riotinto.com; entry 15,000Ar inc guided walk & boat trip*) This protected reserve was established by QMM, a billion-dollar mining project operated by Rio Tinto, with a 20% stake from the Malagasy government. The mine, which is initially projected to run for 40 years, extracts ilmenite (titanium ore) which is then exported to Canada to be processed into chemicals used for whitening (in paint, toothpaste, paper, etc). The Mandena mining zone has been operating since 2008 and they plan to expand imminently to Sainte Luce further north and eventually to a third site west of Taolagnaro.

The reserve is 10km north of town and protects 230ha of rare littoral forest in the region that is the centre of the controversial project. The conservation area includes 160ha of the least degraded fragments of forest and 60ha of wetlands. Twenty-two species of flora are endemic to this region, with about 200 species of large trees. The experience has been thoughtfully conceived to give tourists as much variety as possible, and the local Antanosy community is involved. It is primarily a botanical experience, but you'll also see plenty of birds, reptiles and perhaps some of the six lemur species too. There is an easy circuit which takes 3–4 hours and a wonderful boat trip along a *Pandanus*-fringed waterway.

For those wishing to stay overnight, there is a campsite (5,000Ar) with toilet and shower facilities, a simple restaurant and a newly built bungalow.

Andrew Cooke

Extractive industries include mining, oil and gas exploration/production, processing and transportation. They impact ecosystems and species biodiversity directly through their physical footprint on the land or seabed, water use and pollution, and indirectly through new infrastructure, human settlements and secondary industrial development. But, despite their destructive image, extractive industries account for only a small fraction of threats to biodiversity worldwide: logging, hunting, fishing, crops, livestock, urban development, invasive species, pollution, fire, climate change, human recreation and transport *each* have greater impacts.

Extractive industries in Madagascar include large-scale mining and small-scale or 'artisanal' mining, onshore and offshore petroleum exploration and petroleum production (currently limited to just one small oilfield in the west). Some mines are in areas of biodiversity importance but most are in areas already degraded by agriculture and bush-fires. Even those in biodiversity-rich regions account for a small percentage of biodiversity losses. Sherritt International's Ambatovy nickel mine, for example, will clear 1,500ha of remaining eastern forest and scrub over the mine's 30-year life, while about 30 times as much of the same forest type is lost *annually* due to clearance for agriculture.

The more responsible of the extractive companies address biodiversity comprehensively in their environmental management plans. Two leading mining investments have sought to achieve a net positive impact on biodiversity in Madagascar. QMM/Rio Tinto in the southeast placed initial emphasis on set-asides, tree plantations and continuous restoration, but more recently complemented its programme with conservation action to enhance the quality of coastal forest set-asides and by supporting the conservation of nearby upland forests. Ambatovy seeks net biodiversity gain through set-asides, impact minimisation, restoration and conservation of about 20,000ha of forest offset sites.

These projects have already yielded useful lessons and shown that, although mining will inevitably cause localised loss of biodiversity, investment projects can

Portuguese Fort The tour to the old fort involves a pirogue ride up Vinanibe River, about 6km from Taolagnaro, and then a short walk to the sturdy-looking stone fortress (the walls are 1m thick) set in zebu-grazed parkland. This is the oldest surviving building in Madagascar, and worth a visit for the beautiful surroundings. Despite its name, it pre-dates the Portuguese visitors and is thought originally to have been a 14th-century Swahili site. The fort is built on an islet in Lake Vinanibe (if you want to stay in the area, see the next section for nearby accommodation).

Lake Vinanibe Less than 10km west of Taolagnaro is this large lake, famous for its prawns. The lake is perfect for sailing and the whole area of hills and dunes is great for strolling. **Vinanibe Lodge** (✆ 92 910 56; m *032 05 416 98/033 12 176 09/033 23 210 12*; e *fortdauphin@madagascar-resorts.com; www.madagascar-resorts.com*; €€€) has 15 charming en-suite rooms in eight bungalows at a tranquil spot on the lakeshore. **Chez Anita** in Taolagnaro (page 257) also has four bungalows and a restaurant at Vinanibe.

Ranopiso Arboretum (✆ 92 213 25; m *032 05 588 66*; e *contact@sear.mg*) About an hour (40km) west of Taolagnaro lies this 2ha botanical garden, founded in

provide alternative livelihoods and support conservation efforts to achieve net gain over the baseline trend. Doing so requires the constructive engagement of key stakeholders including the local population who need to share in the benefits if they are to be able to support conservation efforts.

The experience is different for artisanal and small-scale mining (ASM), which targets mainly gold and gemstones. Given the absence of investment or effective regulation, and frequent 'rushes' and incursions into protected areas, artisanal mining has little chance of generating positive conservation outcomes, although it can improve livelihoods. Efforts are under way to formalise and regulate the ASM sector, which could provide the basis for environmentally responsible operations, site restoration and ultimately contributions to local wildlife conservation.

Madagascar has benefited from pro-biodiversity policies and several of these should contribute to positive conservation outcomes from the extractive industries. The Environmental Impact Assessment process requires projects to avoid or minimise impacts and restore affected habitats as far as possible. Responsible international investors such as the International Finance Corporation and 'Equator' banks require their clients to generate a neutral or net positive impact on biodiversity through applying the 'mitigation hierarchy' (avoid, minimise, restore, offset). In order to reinforce this approach and embed it within national environmental policy, the COMBO project (COnservation, impact Mitigation and Biodiversity Offsets in Africa), led by Wildlife Conservation Society, Biotope and Forest Trends, is promoting application of these measures for investments in Madagascar – a country with considerable extractive industry potential. With appropriate policy-making, the extractive industries can help achieve positive conservation outcomes.

Andrew Cooke is a UK-based extractive industries sustainability specialist, with 25 years' experience working on environmental conservation in Madagascar and Africa.

1980 by the Société d'Exploration Agricole de Ranopiso (SEAR). The arboretum harbours 160 species, including more than 60 endemic to the south of Madagascar. Nearby is a factory where SEAR produces leukaemia drugs from the endemic Madagascar periwinkle (see box, page 44).

Evatraha and Lokaro Evatraha is a very attractive coastal village at the opposite end of the sweeping bay north of Taolagnaro, situated at a river mouth just south of Lokaro. Day trips by boat can be organised through Taolagnaro tour operators. There are two cheaply priced en-suite double bungalows if you decide to stay.

There is no public transport, but Evatraha can be reached from Taolagnaro either by pirogue (a peaceful sail via inland waterways), 4x4 (2 hours), mountain bike (but the last 15km is tough due to deep sand) or on foot (a 3-hour/10km walk along the beach). From Evatraha, it is an hour's walk through hills and forest to the beach at Lokaro.

The isolated Bay of Lokaro is arguably the most beautiful spot on the southeast coast. Given the beauty of the area there is a strong case for staying longer than a day trip. There are some beautiful spots to camp and four bungalows with an open-air restaurant can be found at **Camp Pirate**, under the same ownership as Taolagnaro's Lavasoa Hotel. Alternative places to stay are **Exotica** and **Lacan'olo-Bée**, both owned by Ravinala-Anosy Hotel in town. See page 257 for contact details of these places.

Baie Sainte Luce and Manafiafy About 65km (2hrs by 4x4) up the coast from Taolagnaro is this beautiful and historically interesting bay, with a superb beach, where the 17th-century French colonists first landed.

Australian Brett Massoud, original founder of the NGO Azafady (now called SEED Madagascar) and now owner of the tour operator Dadamanga (page 260; see also ad, 2nd colour section), has set up **Sainte Luce Reserve**, which protects 26ha of primary forest and five lemur species. Hikes, pirogue trips, night walks and camping are all possible but get in touch ahead of time to arrange a visit (e *admin@ sainte-luce-reserve.org; www.sainte-luce-reserve.org*).

The area has cellphone signal (Orange and Telma). It is possible to reach Manafiafy by taxi-brousse but most people come with a hired 4x4 or tour operator. The transfer will be provided if you are staying at the area's top-notch ecolodge, **Manafiafy Beach & Rainforest Lodge** (❦ *22 022 26;* m *032 05 619 00/032 05 619 99/033 11 262 25/034 11 262 25;* e *erika@madaclassic.com; www.manafiafy.com;* ☕; *see ad, 4th colour section; map, page 251).* Under the same ownership as Mandrare River Camp (page 254), this exclusive beachfront property is hard to fault. A literal stone's throw from the water's edge, each spacious en-suite thatched bungalow has been designed with the utmost attention to detail, each discreetly nestled among the forest and sufficiently spaced from its neighbours so as to be truly private. Activities include forest walks, boat trips, canoeing in the mangroves, guided tours of Manafiafy village and the option of sleeping under the stars in a tree tent on a deserted paradise island. The lodge has a minimum stay of two nights – not that anybody would want to leave sooner than that!

Andohahela National Park (m *034 49 401 86;* e *ahl@parcs-madagascar.com*) With three distinct zones, the reserve spans rainforest, spiny forest and transition forest, and thus is of major importance and interest. (It should be noted that since 2012 there has been a British FCO warning in place about banditry in and around this park. You should ask around to establish the latest situation; at the time of writing day visits are possible with caution but camping may be risky.)

The **rainforest area (Malio)** has a trail system and campsites, plus all the rainforest requisites: waterfalls, orchids and lemurs, as well as birds including the rare red-tailed newtonia. Visiting the **spiny forest zones (Ihazofotsy and Mangatsiaka)** can be quite arduous because of the lack of shade, but these areas are wonderful for wildlife, birding and botany. If you're lucky you should see sifakas, small mammals such as tenrecs, reptiles, and plenty of birds endemic to the south, such as running coua and sickle-billed vanga. The **transition forest (Tsimelahy)** is scenically and botanically outstanding, and is the only part of Madagascar where the rare triangle palm grows.

A visit to most areas of the national park requires a 4x4 and much of it is out of range of a day trip, so camping is necessary to see the best Andohahela has to offer. Local tour operators can arrange all-inclusive trips from Taolagnaro. Guide fees are around 10,000Ar per circuit per group of up to six, camping costs 3,000–10,000Ar per tent depending on which campsite you use, and porters are available; for permit prices see page 73.

10

East of Tana

Since the early days of the Merina Kingdom, there has been a link from the capital to the country's main port, Toamasina. The route between the two cities would have been established during the expansionist days of King Radama I, when dignitaries were carried by palanquin and goods transported on the heads of porters. It gained greater importance during missionary times but, despite the track up the escarpment being narrow, difficult and slippery for much of the year, a proper road was not built for fear this would facilitate an outside invasion. In the event, the French invaded via Mahajanga – and they soon set about constructing this road to the east.

Nowadays RN2, as it is called, is largely in reasonable condition, having been resurfaced and the bridges repaired in 2006 with EU funding. Many visitors take this route from the capital; most are heading for Andasibe but some continue to the coast. Travelling the road's full length takes you the 358km to Toamasina, although many tourists opt to travel the final third by boat along the Pangalanes Canal.

Connecting port to capital, RN2 is the artery to Madagascar's heart, and as such it is continually busy with container trucks, fuel tankers and fleets of newly imported 4x4s. Many of them take the frequent tight blind bends far too fast with inevitable results; it is no coincidence that RN2 was featured in a 2012 episode of the BBC television series *World's Most Dangerous Roads*. So keep alert, especially if on a bicycle and, even if you don't usually suffer from motion sickness, you would be well advised to take precautions on this trip.

ANTANANARIVO–COTE EST RAILWAY

Constructed between 1901 and 1922, this railway was heavily used during colonial times but trains stopped running in the 1980s. For years the line lay disused, until it was privatised in 2002 and a massive track replacement programme was undertaken to bring most of it back into usable condition. Passenger trains have now been reinstated on the Tana to Toamasina line (although scheduled services currently only run beyond Moramanga) so this offers an alternative to RN2, and the side-branch up to Lake Alaotra has also reopened.

The passenger service, called **Dia Soa**, comprises a train with three 72-seat carriages. It runs from Moramanga to Toamasina (10hrs) on Monday and back on Tuesday; from Moramanga to Ambatondrazaka near Lake Alaotra (6hrs) on Wednesday and back on Thursday morning; from Moramanga to Brickaville (8hrs) on Thursday evening and back on Friday; and Moramanga to Ambatondrazaka again on Saturday then back on Sunday. Prices range from 2,000Ar to 20,000Ar depending how far you go and which class you opt for (first class has comfy wicker chairs, generous legroom and openable windows with blinds). Contact MadaRail

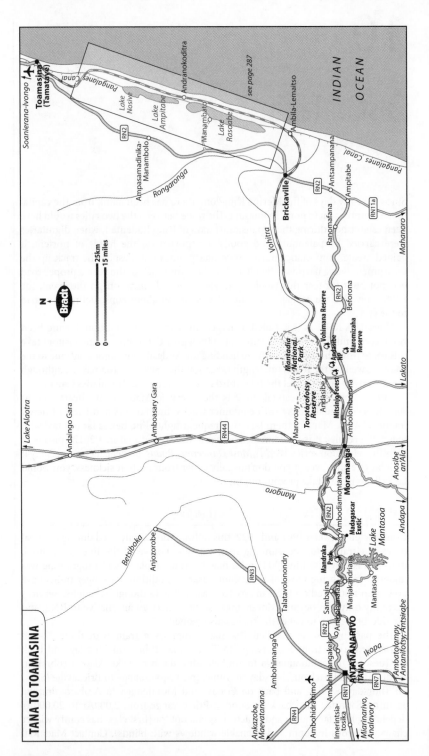

TANA TO TOAMASINA

for the latest schedule (✆ 22 345 99 in Tana, 56 824 71 in Moramanga, 53 339 91 in Toamasina; e tourisme@madarail.mg or zaka.com@jovenna.mg; www.madarail.mg).

TANA TO MORAMANGA

After the hectic atmosphere of Tana, the journey to Moramanga introduces first-time visitors to Madagascar to traditional rural life. Rice fields, *hotely* eateries and roadside stalls selling seasonal fruits line the route, and it is a fine opportunity to observe activities that make up the daily routine of the vast majority of Malagasy people living outside the major cities.

The 10km of road to **Ambohimangakely** is surrounded by rice fields which, in the early morning, are filled with local people pursuing the all-important business of supplying their families with rice: digging, sowing, transplanting, weeding and harvesting. The following 20km takes you through the town of **Ambohimalaza**, steeped in history and tradition. Shortly after passing through the little village of **Nandihizania** (PK 28) and the curiously named town of **Carion**, you can relax in the knowledge that it's downhill the rest of the way, for the PK 36 milestone marks RN2's highest point at an elevation of 1,570m.

The following pages describe the journey as you descend from the *hauts plateaux*. The flat, straight stretches of road give way to a long series of steep, winding sections and hairpin bends as you head towards the plain below, admiring the fine views of the forest clinging to the precipitous slopes of the mountains to your left; it's a good vantage point from which to survey the next phase of your journey across the flat plains towards Moramanga. If you can take your eyes off the scenery and your face out of your paper bag (you really *should* have taken our advice about those travel sickness tablets), look out for enterprising locals transporting goods in oil drums balanced on tiny carts down the hair-raisingly steep stretches of road. As the mountains of the hauts plateaux recede into the distance behind you, the road to Moramanga takes you through numerous small villages and stretches of thinly populated countryside, with occasional charcoal sellers along the way.

SAMBAINA (PK 42) In 2005, Sambaina was chosen by the United Nations as a **Millennium Village**, one of 14 across Africa to be developed as a leading international project in the field of poverty eradication through the application of information and communication technologies. Among its achievements are the inauguration of a 'digital classroom' for 600 teenage students, a community cyber-centre at the town hall, computer facilities and 'telemedicine' for the health centre, and developments in local e-governance. UN investment came to an end in 2013, with the hope that Sambaina's residents have reached the stage where they can stand on their own feet and maintain their infrastructure.

MANJAKANDRIANA (PK 48) This sprawling town has a good choice of hotely eateries, so is an alternative breakfast stop if you have made a predawn start from Tana. There is a BOA bank, hospital, pharmacy, fuel station and post office, and **Manja Motel** on the left has basic rooms. This is also where you should turn if you are heading south to Lake Mantasoa (see pages 179–80).

MANDRAKA PARK (PK 60) AND AROUND After the small town of **Ambatolaona** (PK 58), the landscape rapidly becomes more forested. There is also an alternative route to Mantasoa starting from here. A little further on is **Mandraka Park** (m *033 14 709 42/034 89 403 27*; e *mandrakapark@wanadoo.fr; www.mandrakapark.com*), where

10

activities include hiking, boating and tree climbing. There is a restaurant that serves pizzas, as well as bungalows and a dorm if you want to stay.

Next comes the little village of Andasibe (PK 61) – but alas you have not arrived at the national park sooner than expected; this is a *different* Andasibe – and just beyond the PK 63 milestone you will come to a botanical site called **Park of Orchids**, where there are also waterfalls. From here, the road follows the Manambolo River for 15km or so.

MADAGASCAR EXOTIC (PK 72) (✆ 22 321 01; ⏰ 08.00–17.00; entry 15,000Ar) Also

known as Réserve Peyrieras and Mandraka Reptile Farm, this is a small farm-cum-zoo at Marozevo. The facility provides the opportunity for close viewing of some of the island's most extraordinary reptiles and invertebrates: chameleons, leaf-tailed geckos, butterflies, crocodiles and a few mammals. An adjacent patch of forest is home to relocated Verreaux's sifakas and common brown lemurs that are habituated.

Readers both rant and rave about this place: 'depressing cramped cages and so-called guides that treat the animal inmates with sickening disrespect' complains one, 'a nasty rip-off' summarises another curtly, but 'wow! what fantastic photo opportunities for rarely seen reptiles' enthuses a third. It is argued that these endangered species are being protected by being captive-bred, but the purpose is for export into the pet trade and in the past the guides have openly admitted some are collected illegally from the wild.

ANDRIAMAMOVOKA (PK 78) AND AROUND Just beyond the small village of

Ambodiamontana (PK 73) – where rabbit is a menu speciality – is **Andriamamovoka**, from where it is a few minutes' walk to a spectacular **waterfall** that flows into the forest. Local village association Kanto has collaborated with the regional tourist board to open this site up to visitors (m 034 08 806 24).

Just before PK 89 is **Plantation Bemasoandro**, which develops responsible solutions to a number of environmental problems, especially that of erosion by the planting of vetiver grass (m 034 02 282 31/034 02 282 25; e *plantation. bemasoandro@yahoo.fr; www.vetiver-madagascar.org;* ⏰ 08.00–18.00).

MORAMANGA (PK 109–12) Moramanga means, prosaically, 'cheap mangoes' – but,

although there is a large market here, it seems the prices are no more of a bargain than elsewhere. As one of only two significant towns along RN2, this is the stopping point of choice for public transport and trucks; there is heavy traffic day and night so hotel rooms facing the street can be noisy. On the plus side you can always find an open restaurant. And there are BFV, BNI and BOA banks. The regional tourist office, ORTALMA, also has an office here (✆ 56 908 13; m 034 64 939 60/034 10 018 58; e *ortalma01@gmail.com; www.ortalma.org;* ⏰ *Mon–Fri 08.00–12.30 & 14.30–17.30, Sat 08.00–13.30*).

Getting there and away Taxi-brousses from Tana cost 7,000Ar and take less than 3 hours; to Toamasina is around 6 hours (15,000Ar). **Trains** connect Moramanga with Ambatondrazaka and Toamasina, with stops at a couple of dozen villages in-between (see page 265).

 Where to stay and eat

🏠 **Bezanozano** (13 rooms & 15 bungalows) ✆ 56 825 98; m 032 69 769 03/033 28 761 66/034 15 045 82; e bezanozanohotel@yahoo.fr. Smart en-suite rooms set well back from the main road; AC, Wi-Fi & some with bath. Swimming pool & volleyball court. Regional tourist office is here. **€€€–€€€€**

🏠 **Hazavana** (18 rooms) 📞 56 825 08; m 033 12 539 00/034 74 367 72; e rasamy@moov.mg. Rooms with toilet, hot shower, fan & balcony. No food. Wi-Fi in reception. €€€

🏠 **Ravaka** (9 rooms) 📞 56 907 16; m 033 70 705 60/034 72 607 04; e ravakahotel@yahoo.fr. New hotel nr Jovenna. Stylish rooms with Wi-Fi & en-suite facilities. €€€

🏠 **Diamant** (13 rooms) 📞 56 823 76; m 033 37 672 12; e espacediamant@hotmail.fr. Opposite the church. Comfortable clean rooms with small veranda, some en suite. €€–€€€

🏠 **Emeraude** (20 rooms) 📞 56 821 57; m 033 07 293 53; e emeraudehotel@gmail.com. Centrally located en-suite rooms; a little dingy. B/fast but no restaurant. €€–€€€

🏠 **Motel Mialy** (7 rooms) m 034 36 379 34/034 49 204 34/034 49 204 35; e ss_mialy@ fastservice.com. At the Jovenna station. Dbl, twin & family rooms with hot shower & toilet. €€

🏠 **Nadia** (11 rooms) 📞 56 822 43; m 033 13 848 98; e hotelnadiamoramanga@gmail.com. Sgl & dbl rooms with facilities; some with TV. €€

🏠 **Fihavanana** (11 rooms & 6 bungalows) 📞 56 820 63. Basic rooms with shared facilities & en-suite bungalows. €–€€

🏠 **Mada** (21 rooms) m 033 23 717 01. Low-price en-suite rooms right opposite the train station. €–€€

🏠 **Maitso an'Ala** (5 rooms) 📞 56 820 94; m 032 02 922 02. Very simple dbl & twin rooms. €

✖ **Au Coq d'Or** 📞 56 820 45; m 033 12 905 38. Nr Emeraude. Chinese, Malagasy & European menu & good pastries.

✖ **Flore Orientale** 📞 56 820 20. A deservedly popular Chinese restaurant nr the market.

✖ **Ravaka** Recommended restaurant & bar, with Malagasy, Indian & seafood specialities.

✖ **Sirène Dorée** 📞 56 820 35; m 033 11 754 75. On RN2 at the west of town. Good restaurant with Chinese & European menu & pizzas.

☆ **Cool Cocktail Club** m 034 08 694 24; e santatrah@yahoo.fr; 📘 Coolcocktail Moramanga. Located between Galana & Total. Dance floor, pool table, karaoke & Wi-Fi.

What to see and do Turn left on entering the town and drive 800m to have a look at the **mausoleum** for the people who died during the uprising in 1947, and then the **Police Museum** (m *033 20 974 50/034 90 225 61;* ⊕ *Mon–Fri 08.00–11.30 & 13.00–17.00, Sat/Sun 09.00–10.00 & 14.00–16.00; entry 5,000Ar*), which was set up in 1963 and not long ago renovated with Dutch funding following partial destruction by a 2012 cyclone. The curator speaks English and will show you around this comprehensive collection, mainly of police history, but also local cultural exhibits. There are displays of transport, guns, cannons (one a gift from George IV to Radama I in 1817), police uniforms and even an intriguing array of genuine murder weapons.

HEADING NORTH OR SOUTH Moramanga lies at a crossroads. To the north is RN44 which leads to Lake Alaotra, described below. To the south is a rough but interesting road to Anosibe an'Ala and the Chutes de Mort, a large waterfall 53km from Moramanga. If you are continuing east along RN2, skip to page 273.

LAKE ALAOTRA

More than half a million people now live around the lake, and deforestation has silted it up so that its maximum dry-season depth is only 60cm. Introduction of exotic fish has done further damage. However, all is not lost; an environmental campaign led by Durrell Wildlife Conservation Trust has led to fishing restrictions and bans on marsh burning and lemur-hunting. Local people now recognise the role the marshes play in providing water, a spawning ground for fish and weaving materials for basketry – an important source of income here.

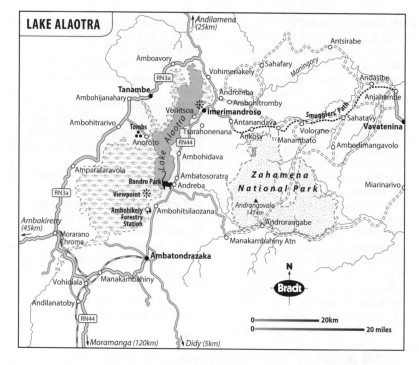

In 2006 the area was given protected status, and an ecotourism project developed to give tourists a chance to see one of Madagascar's most endangered species: the Lac Alaotra gentle lemur. Annual monitoring has shown that lemur populations have stabilised and that fish catches are on the increase.

A tour of the lake by road needs at least a full day and takes you through village after village where rice, cattle, fishing and geese – along with tomatoes and onions – are the mainstays of rural life.

AMBATONDRAZAKA On the southeast side of the lake, this is the main town of the area, with branches of the main banks, and is a good centre for excursions. Its name means 'the place of Razaka's stone'; legend has it that Razaka was one of three children of a local elder called Randriambololona. Razaka grew up to be childless and so took on responsibility for her sisters' children, marking the adoption agreement with a sacrifice at a small oblong stone. The actual stone is long lost but a replica was installed in 1976 on the original site and can be seen today on the southwest corner of the rather grand Sacré Cœur church. Razaka's two sisters, Rasaheno and Ramiangaly, were memorialised in the names of a pair of nearby hills: Ambohitseheno and Ambohimiangaly.

Market day is Saturday.

Getting there and away A **taxi-brousse** from Tana to Ambatondrazaka takes around 6 hours, or a little over half that to travel the 157km from Moramanga (15,000Ar). The **train** from Moramanga offers a slower but more comfortable option (see page 265). This stops at Amboasary, Bembary, Andaingo, Ambohimena, Anosiroa, Andilanatoby, Vohidala and Manakamahiny *en route*, passing mostly rice paddies and the logging of eucalyptus.

⌂ Where to stay and eat

⌂ **Irinah** (5 rooms) ☏ 54 815 23; m 033 20 938 19/034 04 853 88/034 47 183 30; e nainarjm@yahoo.fr. Dbl & twin en-suite rooms with Wi-Fi. Cybercafé. €€€

⌂ **Les 3 Cocotiers** (12 rooms) m 034 11 100 32; e les3cocotiers503@gmail.com. On the north side of town at the turning to Andreba. Dbl, twin & family rooms with bathroom, sat-TV, Wi-Fi & AC. €€€

⌂ **Zama Meva** (7 rooms) ☏ 54 812 10; m 034 09 598 18; e zamameva@gmail.com. At south end of town. Recently renovated dbl rooms with private bathrooms. Restaurant for guests only. €€€

⌂ **Ifarihy** (3 rooms); m 034 37 317 08; e ifarihy.maisondhotes@yahoo.fr. Small guesthouse. €€–€€€

⌂ **Max-Irène** (23 rooms) ☏ 54 813 86; m 033 14 644 88. e maxirene52@yahoo.fr. Budget rooms with en-suite shower, some also with toilet & hot water. B/fast but no restaurant. €€

⌂ **Nab** (14 rooms) ☏ 54 812 13. Rooms in 2 locations; some with private facilities. Hot water. €€

✗ **Irinah** ⊕ closed Mon. Malagasy & European food inc pizza, with vegetarian options; good prices.

AMBOHITSILAOZANA At this village some 15km north of Ambatondrazaka is a long-established forestry station called **Ambohikely**, an isolated 17ha patch of forest that is home to a large flying fox colony. Next door, a collaborative project between Madagascar and France is experimenting with raising dairy cattle for milk and cheese. You can follow a track 2km northwest to a viewpoint looking out across the lake.

Also of interest here is the **Centre Agronomique du Lac Alaotra** (CALA) – a Swiss co-operation for botanical research, with a meteorological station that has gathered almost a century of data. Ask nicely and they'll show you the library with over 200m of sagging shelves laden with dusty tomes dating back more than 130 years. The room also houses a taxonomic museum of local species with around a hundred stuffed specimens (mostly birds). The extensive former grounds – sadly no longer actively maintained – include a long avenue of eucalyptus, another showcasing several species of bamboo, and a third with numerous lychee species.

ANDREBA TO IMERIMANDROSO Another 9km further on is the village of Andreba. Be sure to stop here for a visit to **Bandro Park**. *Bandro* is the Malagasy name for the rare and locally endemic Lac Alaotra gentle lemur. In order to see them you will need to book a pirogue trip, for this is the only lemur to inhabit an aquatic habitat of reed beds. A 2-hour guided boat tour on the lake and into the park costs 20,000Ar per two-person pirogue (plus park entry fee of 10,000Ar/person). The best time to visit is from March to June when the water level is highest. You need to start before dawn so stay overnight at the nearby Camp Bandro (details on page 272).

Just after Andreba comes the village of **Ambatosoratra** – short for the original name of Ambatosorapanorompondradama, which means 'the place of the stone of the *fanorona* game of Radama', for it is said the king once paused here to play this Malagasy game (see box, page 169).

Continuing 9km northward brings you to **Ambohidava**, which was once the end of the railway line. There are no plans to reopen the Ambatondrazaka–Ambohidava section though, which is just as well because the train station has been taken over by a primary school, dozens of locals have built their houses directly on the tracks, and most of the rails have gradually been stolen and sold to Chinese scrap metal merchants!

You come to a right-hand junction after the next 13km, from which a 2km track brings you to the charming little village of Tsarahonenana with its old FJKM church that dates back to 1869. Hidden away 500m north of the village is an early 19th-century walled site called **Anatalonty** – but you should ask permission before visiting as it is now a private family home. King Radama I's military chief, Ralakomanana, resided here; you can still see his tomb and those of his two wives, the impressive surrounding double wall, and a sacrificial stone.

Back at the main road, a left turn takes you 2km to the tranquil lakeside village of **Vohitsoa**, where the women are famous for their basketry. From here it is just 4km to **Imerimandroso** (market day Monday), which has some panoramic lake views and you can see the island of Nosy Ambatonakatrana, where the people of Imerimandroso fled when Radama I invaded their town. It is *fady* for people to live there, but there are several tombs including one over 20m long.

Where to stay and eat

🏠 **Fara** (7 rooms) Vohitsoa; m 033 76 707 46/034 40 477 07/033 74 707 46. House with gorgeous antique furnishings & pretty garden. Communal bucket showers. Camping permitted. Pirogue trips on the lake. €€

🏠 **Tongarivo** (3 rooms) Vohitsoa; m 033 07 077 95/034 46 616 38/034 61 316 14; e cheztongarivo@gmail.com; www.tongarivo. jimdo.com. Rooms with communal cold-water facilities in a peaceful house owned by the vice president of the regional tourist office. Generator

power. Also sells woven handicrafts from local women's co-operative. €€

🏠 **Camp Bandro** (4 bungalows) PK 179, RN44; m 032 57 005 30/034 10 147 60; e karinahcarno@ gmail.com or rmialisoalucile@yahoo.fr; www. madagascar-wildlife-conservation.org/ ecotourism/eco-tourism-camp-bandro. The place to stay for Parc Bandro visits, in a lakeside spot just south of Andreba. Simple huts with communal squat toilet & bucket shower. Meals available with advance notice. €

ZAHAMENA NATIONAL PARK Zahamena is a wonderful, but little-visited, national park (✆ 57 300 24; m 033 07 666 12/034 49 401 54; e zahamena.park@yahoo.fr). Its 66,000ha protects 13 lemur species (including indri), more than a hundred varieties of reptile and amphibian, 112 birds and a diverse range of flora – including two locally endemic ferns.

Access is usually from Imerimandroso via the park office at **Antanandava** (although one can in theory also access it from the west), typically as a three-day camping package which can be organised in Ambatondrazaka, including guides, porters and supplies. The park has five campsites and you will need to bring your own tent. See page 73 for permit prices.

Sadly sapphires and rubies have recently been discovered in the park and the resulting influx of prospectors has caused a lot of damage.

THE SMUGGLERS' PATH Occasional adventurers hike the Smugglers' Path from here to the east coast. It's very tough, very steep and very deforested, so don't expect forest or wildlife except for the short stretch passing through Zahamena. The route takes four to five days, beginning in Imerimandroso and passing through Antanandava, Ankosy, Antenina, Manambato and Sahatavy before ending in Ambohibe, from where you can catch a taxi-brousse to Vavatenina and thence to the east coast.

WESTERN SIDE OF LAKE ALAOTRA Following RN44 road further north, it eventually meets RN3a, which brings you back round the opposite side of the lake in a loop. You pass **Tanambe**, which is becoming a sapphire town and developing a certain feeling of lawlessness; other villages in this area are beginning to follow suit.

Some 36km beyond Tanambe, at Antsapanana, it is worth making a detour: turn towards the lake on to a dead straight 9km road that leads to the lakeside village of Anororo. About 2km before the village are two dozen gigantic **tombs** that look just like two-storey houses. In among these you will also notice some older grassy burial mounds.

MORAMANGA TO ANDASIBE

Continuing east on RN2, the turning for Andasibe is at PK 136, just 23km beyond Moramanga. Along this stretch it is interesting to stop at **Ambolomborona** (PK 124) to visit **Hôtel Juema**, a traditional hotely. For a small fee, you can take a tour of the family business to watch the fascinating process of **bamboo furniture** being made.

ANDASIBE AREA

Since the late 1990s the long-established reserve of Analamazaotra Forest, sometimes known by its colonial name of Périnet, has been co-managed with Mantadia (20km to the north) as **Andasibe-Mantadia National Park**. Because of its proximity to Tana and its exceptional fauna, this is now one of Madagascar's most popular reserves. The moist montane forests are home to a wide variety of lemurs, birds, reptiles and invertebrates. Also in the area are several independently managed protected areas, most notably **Mitsinjo Forest**.

Although the vast majority of visitors spend one or two nights here it is just possible to visit Andasibe as a long day trip from Tana. You will need to leave before dawn to have much chance of seeing and hearing the indri.

Be aware that in the winter months (May–August) it can feel very cold in Andasibe, and indeed it can get chilly at any time of year so bring warm clothing as well as waterproofs.

Andasibe village is really just a simple Malagasy village – no bank, no taxis… although there is a good cybercafé: **Indritech/Vohikala**. The village is 3.5km from RN2 and 2km beyond the park office. At the post office, you can watch bats emerging at dusk (see box, pages 60–1).

GETTING THERE AND AWAY Plenty of **taxi-brousses** ply RN2 from Tana, but taking one direct to the junction for Andasibe is expensive (20,000Ar). Far cheaper and not much slower is to get one to Moramanga (5,000Ar), then find local transport for the last few kilometres (2,000Ar by taxi-brousse or 4,000Ar by train). For a more comfortable option, take a **Cotisse** taxi-brousse for 24,000Ar (m *032 11 027 33;* e *cotissetana@alpa.mg or cotissetransport@yahoo.fr; www.cotisse-transport.com*).

The **train** journey from Moramanga takes 45 minutes, and from Toamasina it's 9 hours or so.

 WHERE TO STAY AND EAT There are now hotels to suit every budget as well as the possibility of **camping**. There are tent shelters (10,000–40,000Ar/tent depending on size) at Mitsinjo Forest with access to hot showers. Camping is also permitted at the entrance to the national park and on the lawn at Feon'ny Ala.

Andasibe Hotel [274 A4] (20 bungalows)
m 034 14 126 27 (reception)/034 14 326 27
(reservations); e infos@andasibehotel-resto.com;
www.andasibehotel-resto.com. Excellent hotel
surrounded by greenery. Spacious en-suite rooms
with beautiful décor, heater, minibar, safe & terrace.
Small swimming pool; massage available; bike hire.
Visa accepted. €€€€–

Vakôna [274 B3] (28 bungalows) m 033 02
010 01/033 02 016 36 (Tana)/034 15 705 80;
e vakona@moov.mg; www.hotelvakona.com.
The name is Malagasy for the Pandanus plant.
Thoughtfully designed with bar, lounge-dining room
with central log fire & attractive grounds. Much-
praised food. Bungalows are quiet & comfortable.
The lodge owns a little island, which is a sanctuary
for ex-pet lemurs, & a small zoo. €€€€€

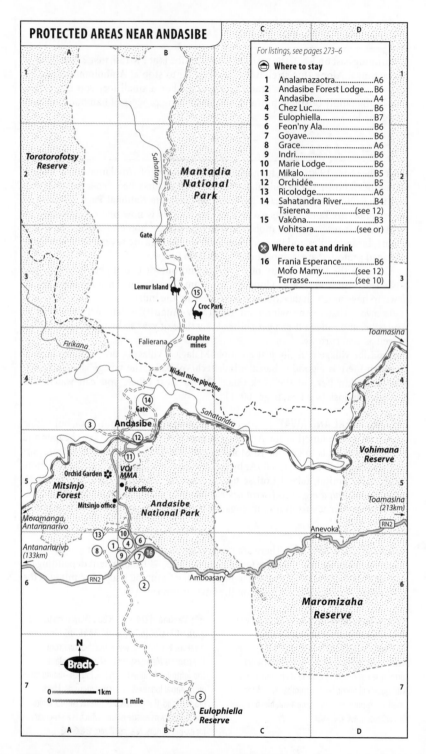

PROTECTED AREAS NEAR ANDASIBE

For listings, see pages 273–6

Where to stay

1	Analamazaotra	A6
2	Andasibe Forest Lodge	B6
3	Andasibe	A4
4	Chez Luc	B6
5	Eulophiella	B7
6	Feon'ny Ala	B6
7	Goyave	B6
8	Grace	A6
9	Indri	B6
10	Marie Lodge	B6
11	Mikalo	B5
12	Orchidée	B5
13	Ricolodge	A6
14	Sahatandra River	B4
	Tsierena	(see 12)
15	Vakôna	B3
	Vohitsara	(see or)

Where to eat and drink

16	Frania Esperance	B6
	Mofo Mamy	(see 12)
	Terrasse	(see 10)

Torotorofotsy Reserve

Mantadia National Park

Sahatany

Gate

Lemur Island

(15)

Croc Park

Firikana

Falierana

Graphite mines

Toamasina

Nickel mine pipeline

(14)

Gate

Sahatandra

(3)

Andasibe

(12)

(11)

Vohimana Reserve

Orchid Garden

VOI MMA

Park office

Mitsinjo Forest

Mitsinjo office

Andasibe National Park

Moramanga, Antananarivo

Toamasina (213km)

RN2

(13)

(10)

Anevoka

Antananarivo (133km)

(8) (1) (4) (6)

(9) (7) (16)

RN2

(2)

Amboasary

Maromizaha Reserve

N

Bradt

0 ———— 1km
0 ———— 1 mile

(5)

Eulophiella Reserve

🏠 **Sahatandra River** [274 B4] (10 rooms & 21 bungalows) m 032 05 019 29/033 80 019 29/034 14 019 29/034 87 297 80 (manager); e sahatandra.river.hotel@gmail.com; www. sahatandra-river-hotel.mg. Brand new in 2016; on the banks of the river from which it takes its name. Attractively landscaped gardens with pool & helipad! Classy rooms with Wi-Fi & sat-TV, some with kitchenette. Tennis court, jet-skis, canoes & bikes. €€€€–€€€€€

🏠 **Analamazaotra Hotel** [274 A6] (10 bungalows) m 032 71 795 97/034 02 795 97, or in Tana 034 02 796 82/034 71 796 82; e analamazaotra.hotel@gmail.com or contact@ analamazaotra-hotel.com; www.analamazaotra-hotel.com. New in 2016. A row of fairy-tale pink little cottages (we can't say for sure if they have gingerbread roofs) around a swimming pool. €€€€

🏠 **Eulophiella** [274 B7] (17 bungalows) ☎ 22 242 30; m 032 07 567 82; e eulophiellandasib@ eulophiella.com; www.eulophiella.com. Down a 5km track off RN2 this hotel, named after an endemic orchid, offers well-spaced en-suite bungalows in 2 sizes. Recommended restaurant. There's a small private reserve where night walks are possible. €€€€

🏠 **Goyave** [274 B6] (6 bungalows) m 032 74 910 90/034 08 885 99. Set back opposite RN2 junction for Andasibe. New en-suite bungalows with Wi-Fi. They also run a roadside eatery & snack shop. €€€€

🏠 **Indri** [274 B6] (21 bungalows) m 034 06 340 89; e indrilodge@yahoo.fr; www. indrilodgeandasibe.com. En-suite bungalows in a garden next to RN2. Restaurant & swimming pool. €€€€

🏠 **Grace** [274 A6] (9 bungalows) ☎ 22 240 64; m 033 03 308 66 (Tana)/034 16 310 92/034 45 222 05 (Tana); e gracelodge.andasibe@yahoo. fr. Run by a friendly English-speaking Malagasy woman. Lovely bungalows in meticulously maintained grounds with small swimming pool & on-site chapel! Car & bike hire. 'The best place I stayed in Madagascar' says reader Les Parkes. €€€–€€€€

🏠 **Andasibe Forest Lodge** [274 B6] (10 bungalows) ☎ 22 261 14; m 033 03 150 25; e mea@moov.mg. Built by the owners of Feon'ny Ala, but separately managed. En-suite bungalows set around a small lake facing a forest. €€€

🏠 **Mikalo** [274 B5] (15 bungalows) m 033 11 696 92/034 11 696 92. We have received very variable reports from readers about the bungalows but the restaurant is good if a touch on the pricey side. €€€

🏠 **Orchidée** [274 B5] (16 rooms) ☎ 56 832 05; m 034 36 024 49; e hotelorchideeandasibe@ yahoo.fr. Recently moved to a new building. En-suite rooms with hot water. €€€

🏠 **Ricolodge** [274 A6] (5 bungalows) m 032 11 882 98/034 11 882 98/034 20 882 98; e ricolodge.andasibe@gmail.com or ricomadagascar@yahoo.fr; www.ricolodge.weebly. com. Run by Rico Rakotovazaha, president of the National Guide Federation. Set in the forest (mostly eucalyptus) 1km up a dirt track. Wi-Fi in the dining area. Tent hire; camping permitted. €€€

🏠 **Chez Luc** [274 B6] (7 rooms & 4 bungalows) m 034 10 948 82/034 46 045 07; e rajerisoaluc@ yahoo.fr. Guesthouse owned by expert birding guide. Simple rooms with shared facilities & en-suite rustic bungalows. Meals next door at La Terrasse. €€–€€€

🏠 **Feon'ny Ala** [274 B6] (44 bungalows) ☎ 56 832 02; m 032 05 832 02/034 05 832 02. It is a popular place in a prime location facing the national park – close enough to hear the indri call, hence the name which means 'voice of the forest'. Most bungalows en suite but a small number of budget ones with shared facilities. Restaurant with Wi-Fi. Camping possible. €€–€€€

🏠 **Marie Lodge** [274 B6] (13 rooms & 1 bungalow) m 032 64 962 02/034 18 094 19; e razafindrasolomarie@yahoo.fr; www. guesthousemarieandasibe.com. Elegant guesthouse next to Chez Luc (Marie & Luc are siblings). En-suite rooms with hot water & Wi-Fi (for a small fee). Large handicraft shop. €€–€€€

🏠 **Tsierena** [274 B5] (5 rooms) m 033 01 603 20/034 96 876 74; e tsierena@gmail.com. New guesthouse in the village; 4 dbl rooms with shared facilities & an en-suite family room. Wi-Fi. €€

🏠 **Vohitsara** [274 B5] (10 rooms) m 033 14 899 63/034 15 854 24/034 60 899 69; e vohitsara@gmail.com. Excellent budget B&B run by the affable Mama Bozy & family. Clean comfy rooms; shared facilities with hot water. €€

✖ **Frania Espérance** [274 B6] m 034 45 753 46. A simple Malagasy eatery on RN2 opposite Andasibe turning.

✕ Terrasse [274 B6] At Marie Lodge, this is a reliable restaurant serving Malagasy, Chinese & European cuisine inc pizza.

🖵 Mofo Mamy [274 B5] **m** 034 15 854 24. Tremendous little patisserie & pizzeria opposite the post office in the village.

ANDASIBE NATIONAL PARK (✆ *53 327 07;* **e** *andasibe.parks@gmail.com*) This 810ha reserve protects the largest of the lemurs, the **indri**. Standing about a metre high, with a barely visible tail, black-and-white markings and a surprised teddy-bear face, the indri looks more like a gone-wrong panda than a lemur. The long back legs are immensely powerful, and an indri can propel itself 10m, executing a turn in mid-air, to hug a new tree and gaze down benevolently at its observers. And you *will* be an observer; everyone now sees indris here, and most also hear them. For it is the voice that makes this lemur extra-special: while other lemurs grunt or swear, the indri sings. It is an eerie, wailing sound – a cross between whale song and a siren – and it carries for up to 3km as troops call to each other across the forest. They generally call at dawn, mid-morning, and sometimes shortly before dusk. During the middle of the day they take a long siesta in the canopy.

There are 11 species of lemur altogether in Andasibe, although you will not see them all. You may find grey bamboo lemurs, common brown lemurs and perhaps a sleeping avahi (woolly lemur) curled up in the fork of a tree. Diademed sifakas and black-and-white ruffed lemurs have been translocated here from Mantadia and from forest cleared to make way for the Ambatovy nickel and cobalt mine.

In addition to lemurs there are tenrecs, beautiful and varied insects, spiders and reptiles – especially chameleons and boas. Birdwatchers will want to look out for the velvet asity, blue coua and nuthatch vanga.

Leeches can be an unpleasant aspect of the reserve when pushing through vegetation if it's been raining recently. Tuck your trousers into your socks and apply insect repellent, which will help keep them at bay.

The trails in Andasibe have been carefully constructed, but there is quite a steep ascent (up steps) to the plateau where the indri are found, and to follow these animals you may have to scramble a bit.

Night walks are not allowed in the national park itself (but are in neighbouring Mitsinjo Forest and VOI MMA), though it's worth going on a guided nocturnal stroll along the road for the frogs and chameleons which are easier to see at night.

Permits and guides The **park office** (🕐 *06.00–16.00*) and visitor centre are midway between RN2 and Andasibe village. Here you can buy your tickets (prices on page 73) and arrange a guide. The Andasibe guides are among the best in Madagascar and an example to the rest of the country for knowledge, enthusiasm and an awareness of what tourists want. All the guides know where to find indri and other lemurs, but if you have very particular interests – birds, amphibians or plants, say – let them know at the desk and they may be able to allocate you a specialist.

Circuits range from 2 hours (40,000Ar for the guide per group of up to four) to 4 hours (60,000Ar).

MITSINJO FOREST (**m** *033 16 170 89/034 96 876 74;* **e** *mitsinjo@hotmail.com;* 🕐 *07.00–17.00 & 18.30–21.00; www.associationmitsinjo.wordpress.com*) While offering broadly the same attractions as the national park, this fabulous local NGO is promoting reforestation and other conservation measures. It also operates the reserve of **Torotorofotsy** (see page 279) and has an excellent handicrafts shop at the park entrance.

MITSINJO AND THE ANDASIBE FOREST CORRIDOR PROJECT

Rainer Dolch, Association Mitsinjo

Over the last hundred years or so, population growth and poverty have taken their toll on Madagascar's eastern rainforest belt. The increasing need for timber, charcoal and new agricultural land has led to extensive deforestation. This loss of trees contributes to greenhouse gas emissions and climate change (both local and global), which further exacerbates poverty and environmental degradation in a downward spiral.

One of the larger remaining forests is Ankeniheny-Zahamena, but even this has become severely fragmented. Forest fragmentation spells disaster because numerous isolated patches of forest cannot support the same diversity of species as a single larger one. When an area of forest gets cut off, the wildlife it contains risks becoming inbred and these small populations are less able to recover from problems such as outbreaks of disease and cyclones. Extinctions are inevitable.

Association Mitsinjo has been a driving force to halt deforestation in the region by reconnecting fragments with forest 'corridors' and improving livelihoods for local people. Reforestation activities were kick-started by the innovative Andasibe Forest Restoration Project (known by its Malagasy acronym TAMS). In partnership with international and national NGOs, as well as government agencies, more than 25 nurseries grew some 500,000 seedlings of 150 mostly endemic trees each year. More than a million trees were planted and local farmers voluntarily made parts of their fallow land available for reforestation, benefiting both in terms of security of land tenure, as well as other forms of sustainable and more productive agriculture provided by the project.

TAMS unfortunately terminated prematurely, before carbon credits could be traded via the World Bank, but it is envisaged to trade them on the voluntary market so farmers can benefit in terms of direct payments. Tourists can already offset their carbon emissions by donating directly to the project or by actively planting rainforest tree seedlings. Continuity of the forest restoration project is ensured by a new partnership with the Finnish Association for Nature Conservation. Benefits to both biodiversity and local communities will soon be studied by the Ecological Services for Poverty Alleviation, a collaboration of British and Malagasy universities and scientific institutions.

The project fits into Mitsinjo's philosophy of conservation work going hand in hand with rural development. Working closely with local communities on agricultural and health issues is the key to success. Several conservation and research projects are carried out together with local communities, the most significant success being protection of the greater bamboo lemur, one of the world's rarest primates, rediscovered in the area by Mitsinjo in 2007.

Situated just over the road from Andasibe National Park, this 700ha tract of Analamazaotra Forest is home to seven groups of indri, a couple of which are habituated. Walks here are thrilling, not only for the ease with which a wide variety of wildlife can be seen, but also the professionalism and enthusiasm of the guides and the work that the association is doing. Chris Howles agrees: 'We look back at the 4½-hour trek we did as one of the highlights of the holiday. Our guide spoke good English and had a very good knowledge of all the local

East of Tana   ANDASIBE AREA

10

flora and fauna. He worked hard to find everything for us, including of course a family of indri. They came really close to us and we stayed with them for about 45 minutes, stopping when our necks started to ache from all that looking up in the trees!'

One circuit, the **Reforestation Trail**, offers visitors the chance to plant an endemic tree. Mitsinjo has six tree nurseries, some of which you can visit. Thousands of seedlings of 151 endemic species are being raised to help re-establish corridors between blocks of isolated forest (see box, page 277).

One of the big highlights here is the **night walks** – highly recommended (especially since the national park forbids after-dark visits). Derek Schuurman reports that 'Goodman's mouse lemur is readily seen; your chances of seeing reptiles such as Parson's chameleons and *Uroplatus* geckos are better here and you are bound to see a lot of frogs and other nocturnal creatures'.

In addition to reforestation work, Mitsinjo has set up Madagascar's first amphibian captive-breeding facility (see box, page 50), operates an environmental education campaign at six local schools, and has ongoing community projects in family planning and providing local villages with wells to access clean water.

Permits, guides and transport Here your guide and permit are included in a per-person ticket price for each circuit. For this reason, Mitsinjo generally works out more economical than the national park, especially for solo travellers and couples. Trails range from 1 to 5 hours and cost 30,000–65,000Ar per head; night walks cost 20,000Ar (1½hrs). For those interested in culture, they also offer village tours and visits to a sacred tree. The **park office** is 250m from that of the national park, towards RN2 on the opposite side of the road. Forest guides are freelance so many of those who work in the national park are also accredited to work in this forest too.

Mitsinjo has a **4x4 vehicle** which may be hired (with driver) for transfers: 50,000Ar to Vakôna Forest Lodge, Moramanga or Vohimana Reserve; 100,000Ar (day return) to Mantadia National Park or Torotorofotsy; 320,000Ar to Tana; and 420,000Ar to Toamasina.

Tree climbing (f *GasyClimb*) Eddy Manatijara, based at the Mitsinjo office, runs **GasiClimb**. Activities include zip-line, rope ladder, tree climbing, canopy nets and hammocks. You can get right up into the canopy. Whether you are interested in enjoying the climbing as an adventure sport or simply using it as a means to get up into the rainforest canopy to see the wildlife there, the experience can be tailored to your needs and level of fitness. Prices range from 30,000Ar to 100,000Ar. Try to book at least a day in advance.

ORCHID GARDEN Next to the road, between the park offices and Andasibe village, this small lake is a particularly attractive spot in October and November. Being a joint project between the national park and Mitsinjo, visitors who have purchased a permit from either may visit it.

VOI MMA (e *voimmandasibe@gmail.com*) This small 28ha portion of forest is managed by a newly formed group of local guides. Furry-eared dwarf lemurs, Goodman's mouse lemurs, snakes, frogs and chameleons may be seen here. Walks cost 20,000–30,000Ar and short night walks are also possible (12,000Ar). A larger proportion of the ticket price goes to the guides than at the other parks, where more of the funds are used for conservation activities.

MANTADIA NATIONAL PARK While Andasibe is for almost everyone, Mantadia (several times larger and 20km to the north) is for the enthusiast. The trails are rugged but the rewards are exceptional. Mantadia varies more in altitude (800–1,260m) than the more popular section and consequently harbours different species. What makes it so special is that, in contrast to Andasibe, it comprises virtually untouched primary forest. There are 12,000ha with just a few constructed trails – visitors must be prepared to work for their wildlife – but this is a naturalist's gold mine with many seldom-seen species of mammals, reptiles and birds.

You may see the beautiful golden-coloured diademed sifaka and some indri (curiously much darker in colour than in Andasibe). Some of the trails are steep in parts, but the effort is rewarded with gorgeous views across the forest and super birdwatching possibilities, including specials such as the scaly ground-roller, pitta-like ground-roller and red-breasted coua.

To do justice to Mantadia you should spend the whole day there, leaving at dawn and taking a picnic. Guides (40,000–70,000Ar/circuit, up to four people) and permits are arranged at the Andasibe park office and you will need your own transport; guides can help you find a vehicle or you can enquire at Mitsinjo's office.

TOROTOROFOTSY RESERVE This marsh 11km west of Andasibe – an important part of any birding trip – was declared a Ramsar Site in 2005. Including forest as well as wetlands, the 9,800ha reserve is also famous for its rare golden mantella frogs and a population of even rarer greater bamboo lemurs.

It's an excellent area for trekking and camping (or you can arrange a homestay). Enquire at Mitsinjo to organise a visit; see page 276 if you need transport. One day costs 60,000Ar, but night walks are rewarding so it is worth going for longer.

MAROMIZAHA RESERVE (✆ 22 660 48; m 034 87 015 44; e gerp@moov.mg; entry 15,000Ar) Located 5km from the Andasibe turning on RN2, Maromizaha (meaning 'much to see') is being rehabilitated as a 1,850ha area of protected forest with EU funding under the co-management of GERP, the Malagasy primate study group. There are some beautiful trails and the opportunity to see similar wildlife to that found at Mantadia. There is a cave full of fruit bats and botanists will be interested to see the locally endemic *marola* palm. Ask the guides at Andasibe to help organise a visit; camping is possible.

On the southeast side of Maromizaha, about 3 hours' hike south of RN2, is **Vohidrazana**, a virtually unexplored rainforest with no trails. Extremely adventurous travellers could hook up with some guides to mount an expedition here.

VOHIMANA RESERVE (PK 149) (✆ 22 674 90; m 033 02 287 08; e vohimana@mate. mg; www.madagascar-environnement.org) This forest reserve east of Andasibe is protected through a partnership between local villagers and the NGO Man And The Environment (MATE). They are working towards reducing the local community's dependence on slash-and-burn farming.

The rainforest here has a great range of elevations (700–1,080m) and consequently species diversity is correspondingly high, especially in reptiles and amphibians. In fact, this 1,600ha site is thought to have the richest diversity of endemic frogs of any area its size *worldwide*; Vohimana is home to more than 80 amphibian species. Reptiles are similarly plentiful, star among them being the Pinocchio chameleon – an extraordinarily prolific fibber if his impressive nasal dimensions are any indication! This is just one of several species found here that do not occur at Andasibe. Lemurs number 11 varieties, including indri and red-bellied lemurs.

You can divide your time between seeing what MATE is doing to help Madagascar's environmental crisis – such as visiting the **tree nursery** (these saplings are used to establish forest corridors linking isolated areas of forest), the **essential oil distillery** which demonstrates that revenue can be earned from the leaves of trees without having to cut them down (*www.huiles-essentielles-madagascar.com*), the **model farm** running trials with new agricultural methods – and searching for wildlife.

There are half a dozen **walking circuits** varying from 2 to 12km (1–3hrs), passing through beautiful rainforest, cultivated fields and spectacular viewpoints. Some of the trails follow the railway line and a century-old disused tunnel is now adopted by four bat species as their home.

The reserve has some simple accommodation with shared facilities and a nice communal dining area. Accommodation and meals should be pre-booked.

Vohimana is on the north side of RN2 about 15km past the turn-off to Andasibe, near the village of Ambavaniasy. The trail head is just before PK 149. Walking to the reserve takes about 45 minutes from RN2, but with a private vehicle you can take a new mine road part of the way, cutting the walk to 20 minutes.

ANDASIBE TO BRICKAVILLE

The start of the journey from Andasibe down to Toamasina is lovely, taking you through lush, mist-enshrouded rainforest. This eventually gives way to eucalyptus woods, and those in turn to *savoka* (secondary vegetation) dotted with travellers' palms, and then finally *bozaka* – the stubbly grassland that results from continual slash-and-burn.

After passing through **Ampasimbe** (PK 178), which has a large market, and **Antongombato** (PK 191), you reach **Ranomafana** (PK 205) – this is a name encountered often in Madagascar since it simply means 'hot water'. Here it refers to a natural hot spring that is considered sacred by locals, who use it to ask for blessings from the ancestors. The path is just beyond the village before the bridge; ask for directions to '*la source sacrée*'.

ANTSAMPANANA (PK 218) Some 1½ hours' drive beyond Andasibe is this small town at the junction of RN2 with the road to Vatomandry (page 288). This is where to look for a taxi-brousse going south.

The town is brimming with stalls offering a huge variety of fruit and vegetables: good for reprovisioning and photography. If you want to dally longer, **Espérance** offers basic accommodation and **Fantasia** is a recommended restaurant.

BRICKAVILLE (AMPASIMANOLOTRA) (PK 247–50) Fields of maize and other crops indicate that you are entering the second significant town on this national road. Everyone knows this place as Brickaville, but its official Malagasy name is often used on maps. After the relatively smooth RN2 passing through wide open spaces, the noise and industry of Brickaville can come as a bit of a shock. It is the centre of sugarcane and citrus production and has a BOA bank and a few hotels, but few people would stay intentionally. **Capricorne** (m *033 11 764 60*) is fairly respectable if you find yourself in need of a bed for the night. Fruit, vegetables and friendly hotely can be found in abundance, allowing ample opportunity for refreshment before embarking on the final 110km. Immediately after the town centre, you cross the longest bridge on RN2, spanning 260m across the Rianala River.

BRICKAVILLE TO TOAMASINA

After Brickaville, RN2 turns north and the elevation drops below 50m as you start to glimpse the ocean and Pangalanes lakes. The remaining journey to Toamasina is fairly uneventful, passing through degraded forest and palm plantations, so many travellers prefer to float serenely (or speedboat energetically, if time is short) up the Pangalanes Canal. If this is you, turn to page 283 for the rest of the journey.

Remaining on RN2 for this final stretch, you will pass many roadside stalls selling seasonal fruit such as pineapples, bananas and jackfruit. Boys may also be seen at the roadside selling eels and sometimes the odd bushmeat tenrec too. Around PK 291 you will find honey sellers.

HOPE IN A PLASTIC BOTTLE   *Theresa Haine*

In Toamasina, I found myself enthralled by a story of rubbish! While visiting SAF – a Malagasy development organisation – I talked with my friend Charnette about her project to tackle the mountains of rubbish polluting the town.

She started at grass-roots level by setting up training courses in recycling and vegetable growing. For pots, they use plastic bags and soft drinks bottles from the rubbish heaps. These are cleaned and the people taught how to make compost from scraps. The first seeds are given free of charge.

I visited several households and was impressed to see a wonderfully healthy assortment of salad vegetables, and even strawberries, growing on every available ledge, step and windowsill. Many even have a surplus to sell at market. The enthusiasm of all involved was infectious.

One memorable visit was to a disabled man of 29 who lives in a two-room shack with his 11-year-old son. He'd lost his wife nine months before and sent his younger son to live with his grandmother in the forest. The older boy chose to remain with his father, but the loss of his mother affected him very badly. The father has great difficulty walking but can ride a bicycle. After the death of his mother the boy became very withdrawn. His school grades plummeted and he spent every spare moment riding obsessively up and down their lane on his father's bike.

The father signed up for one of Charnette's courses and his son was intrigued to see him collecting discarded plastic bags and planting seeds in them. A little while later the boy came home with some drink bottles which he cut in half then asked his father for help sowing seeds.

They planted some aubergines, but had to take them to Grandma's once they were growing well as they have so little space in their tiny house. From the moment he started growing his aubergines the boy's school grades started to improve, and he finished that academic year third in his class – to the great delight of his father.

I visited them towards the end of the school holidays, but the boy was not home. 'He's gone to his grandmother's because he was so desperate to see how his aubergines are doing,' his father commented with a proud smile.

Theresa Haine, MBE, was for many years co-ordinator of Money for Madagascar, a charity that has been funding development work in Madagascar for well over three decades; see page 143 for details.

From **Ambodibonara** (PK 319) the road follows the Fanandrana River for 18km to a town of the same name at its confluence with the Ivondro River – which the road crosses via a 210m bridge. **Antanambo** (PK 333) marks the start of a few-kilometre stretch along which women sell colourful woven chairs and stools, before you finally enter the outskirts of Toamasina – which is covered in *Chapter 12*.

11

South of Toamasina

This chapter covers the section of east coast from Toamasina southward. Visitors often take boat trips on the sleepy Pangalanes Canal – an inland waterway that runs parallel to the shoreline and boasts some beautiful lake resorts.

Further down the coast are the two seaside towns of Mananjary and Manakara, the latter being a popular tourist destination as it is the terminus of the railway journey from Fianarantsoa. Most then head back to Fianarantsoa (via Ranomafana National Park) by road, but a trickle of visitors continue south to Farafangana. Beyond this small town, the road condition worsens significantly and there are many rivers to cross, but a few of the most intrepid travellers make it all the way to Taolagnaro (Fort Dauphin).

PANGALANES CANAL

This series of lakes was linked by artificial canals in early French colonial times for commercial use, a quiet inland waterway being preferable to an often stormy sea. The original canal ran 665km from Toamasina to Vangaindrano (see box, page 285), which would make it the world's fifth-longest canal today but for the fact that only around two-thirds of it remain navigable. The quiet waters of the canal and lakes are now much used by locals for transporting their goods in pirogues and for fishing.

The 1- to 4-day trips offered by tour operators are focused primarily on the northernmost section of the canal, which has been developed for tourism with lakeside bungalows and private nature reserves competing with the traditional ocean resorts. The main centre is **Lake Ampitabe**, 60km south of Toamasina.

GETTING THERE AND AWAY The main access points to the canal are Toamasina (at its northern extremity) and **Manambato** (about 20mins' drive from RN2). It is also possible to drive from RN2 to the southern shore of Lake Ampitabe in around 2 hours by 4x4. For some 65m a railway runs parallel, between canal and ocean, on a strip of land that is as narrow as 100m in places. The station for Lake Ampitabe is

DISTANCES IN KILOMETRES			
Toamasina–Vatomandry	189km	Mananjary–Fianarantsoa	197km
Vatomandry–Mahanoro	70km	Manakara–Farafangana	109km
Mahanoro–Nosy Varika	91km	Manakara–Ranomafana	191km
Mananjary–Manakara	179km	Manakara–Fianarantsoa	254km
Mananjary–Ranomafana	107km	Farafangana–Vangaindrano	75km

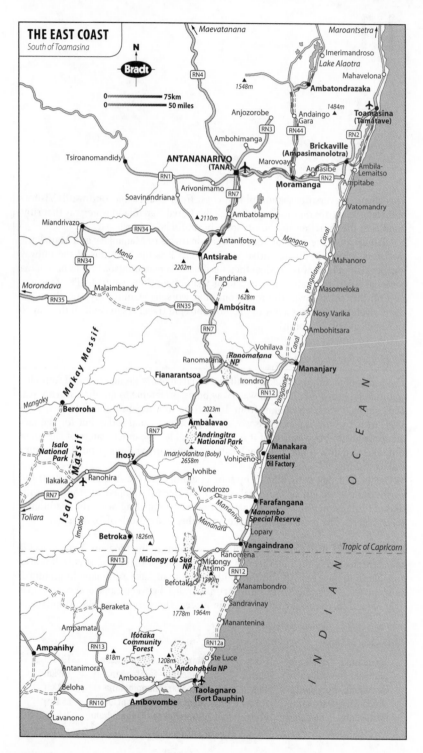

THE EAST COAST
South of Toamasina

N

Bradt

0 ———— 75km
0 ———— 50 miles

Maevatanana
Maroantsetra

Imerimandroso
Lake Alaotra
Mahavelona

RN4

▲ *1548m*

Ambatondrazaka

Anjozorobe

Andaingo ▲ *1484m*
Gara

Toamasina
(Tamatave)

Ambohimanga

RN3

RN44

RN2

Tsiroanomandidy

ANTANANARIVO
(TANA)

Marovoay

Brickaville
(Ampasimanolotra)

Andasibe

Ambila-
Lemaitso

RN1

Arivonimamo

RN7

Moramanga

RN2

Ampitabe

Soavinandriana

Vatomandry

Miandrivazo

▲ *2110m*

Ambatolampy

RN34

Antanifotsy

Mangoro

Canal

Mahanoro

RN34

Antsirabe

Mania

▲ *2202m*

Fandriana

Masomeloka

Morondava

Malaimbandy

▲ *1628m*

RN35

Ambositra

Nosy Varika

RN35

RN7

Ambohitsara

Vohilava

Ranomafana
NP

Pangalanes

Ranomatana

Mananjary

Fianarantsoa

Irondro

RN12

Pangalanes

Canal

Mangoky

Makay Massif

Beroroha

▲ *2023m*

Ambalavao

Andringitra
National Park

Manakara

Isalo
National
Park

Imarivolanitra (Boby)
2658m

Vohipeno

Essential
Oil Factory

Ihosy

Ivohibe

Ilakaka

Ranohira

Vondrozo

Isalo Massif

RN7

Imaloto

Ivohibe

Mananivo

Farafangana

Manombo
Special Reserve

Toliara

Betroka

▲ *1826m*

Mananara

Lopary

Vangaindrano

Tropic of Capricorn

RN13

Midongy du Sud
NP

Ranomena

Midongy
Atsimo

▲ *1399m*

RN12

Befotaka

Manambondro

Beraketa

▲ *1778m* ▲ *1964m*

Sandravinay

Ampamata

Manantenina

Ifotaka
Community
Forest

RN12a

Ampanihy

RN13

▲ *818m*

▲ *1208m*

Ste Luce

Antanimora

Andohahela NP

Amboasary

Taolagnaro
(Fort Dauphin)

Beloha

RN10

Ambovombe

Lavanono

INDIAN

OCEAN

The Canal des Pangalanes was created in colonial times to provide a safe means of transport along the east coast. The shore is surf-beaten and the few harbours are shallow and dangerous. The inland water passage provided a safe alternative and around the turn of the century regular ferry services were in operation. The canal interconnected the natural rivers and lagoons, where necessary cutting through the low-lying coastal plain. At intervals it crosses rivers which flow to the sea, providing access for fishermen and ensuring that the level is stable.

The waterways fell into disuse, but in the 1980s a grand project to rehabilitate them was carried out. Silted canals were dredged, new warehouses built and a fleet of modern tug barge units purchased to operate a cargo service. That may once have worked, but now the warehouses and quaysides are empty and the tug barge units lie in a jumble in the harbour at Toamasina.

Meanwhile, local people make good use of the waterways. Mechanised ferries run from Toamasina and every house along the way seems to have a wooden pirogue. The communities face the water and for many people it is the only reliable means of transport, especially in the wet season. It is also a vital source of livelihood and the stakes of fish traps almost fill the channels, while fields of cassava line the banks. Piles of dried fish, wood and charcoal stand in heaps awaiting collection by the returning ferries. Coming from the town, they are overflowing with people competing for space with beer crates, bicycles, sacks of food and all the other paraphernalia of life.

To travel on the Pangalanes is a joy – well, mostly. Start at Toamasina and you get the worst bit over and done with quickly. Boats leave from the bleak Port Fluvial, with its empty warehouses and discarded tugs. The first, manmade, cut of the canal runs south from the town, past the oil refinery. The air is thick with the smell of hydrocarbons and greasy black outfalls show all too clearly the source of the grey slime that coats the water hyacinth – seemingly the only thing capable of growing. But persevere and soon you start to pass family canoes tied to the bank and the slender, deeply loaded ferry boats pushed by struggling outboard motors. As the water starts to clear, the vegetation recolonises the riverbank and the pervasive odour of industrialisation slips away.

The artificial straightness of the first sections gives way to twisting channels and the wider expanses of lagoons and lakes – a world where communities of thatched wooden houses cluster around small landing places, grey rectangles in a canvas of green and blue, delineated here and there by the stark white of sandy beaches.

Andranokoditra, for Lake Rasoamasay disembark at **Ampanotoamaizina,** and there is also a stop at **Ambila-Lemaitso.** Trains run from Toamasina and Moramanga (page 265).

Most of the hotels can provide boat transfers from the various access points as part of the package. By motor launch it takes about 45 minutes to reach Lake Ampitabe from Manambato or just under 2 hours from Toamasina.

LAKE NOSIVE This is the first lake encountered, coming from Toamasina. At its north end, in the village of Amboditandroroho, good food and lodging can be found at **Runtamtam** (m *034 37 310 43*; e *runtamtam@pangalanes.net*; *www.pangalanes. net*; €€€; *see map, page 287*). They also have boats for canal cruises and transfers.

LAKES AMPITABE AND RASOAMASAY Also known as Akanin'ny Nofy ('nest of dreams'), Lake Ampitabe has broad white beaches, clean water for swimming, a private nature reserve with several introduced species of lemur and the Lac aux Népènthes, where there are literally thousands of insect-eating pitcher plants. Lake Rasoamasay is some 10km further south.

🏠 **Where to stay and eat** *Map, opposite*

There are several places to stay spanning a broad spectrum of budgets.

🏠 **Bush House** (11 bungalows) Lake Ampitabe; ☎22 248 47; m 033 05 530 71/033 12 441 27; e bushhouse@boogiepilgrim-madagascar. com; www.boogiepilgrim-madagascar.com. Simple bungalows constructed from local materials with simple handcrafted furnishings, en-suite facilities & lake-view terrace. €€€€

🏠 **Fantasia Village** (7 bungalows) Lake Ampitabe; ☎57 909 72; m 032 04 795 79/034 46 177 97; e fraste@fantasiavillage.com; www. fantasiavillage.com. Run by a welcoming Italian-Malagasy couple. Attractive stone & bamboo bungalows. Excellent restaurant with BBQ specialities. €€€€

🏠 **Palmarium** (15 bungalows) Lake Ampitabe; ☎57 908 83; m 032 41 330 39/033 14 847 34/034 17 729 77; e hotelpalmarium@ yahoo.fr; www.palmarium.biz. Spacious en-suite bungalows with hot water & electric sockets. Nice restaurant & private reserve. €€€€

🏠 **Pangalanes Jungle Nofy** (12 bungalows) Lake Ampitabe; m 032 05 931 58/034 47

931 58 (owner)/034 72 343 77 (reception); e pangalanesjunglenofy@gmail.com; www. hotelpangalanes-junglenofy.com. Unsophisticated but highly praised with some bungalows on stilts over the water; good service & food. €€€€

🏠 **Ony** (20 bungalows) Lake Rasoamasay; ☎53 918 40; m 033 11 587 25/033 14 732 21; e onyhotel.pangalanes@gmail.com; http:// onyhotel.free.fr. Malagasy-owned hotel in marvellous setting between 2 lakes, affording guests the double pleasure of watching the sun both rise & set across the water. Beachfront en-suite bungalows. Camping permitted. €€€

🏠 **Orchidées** (5 bungalows) Andranokoditra; m 034 27 059 93 (manager)/034 76 399 53 (chef). En-suite solar-powered rustic bungalows next to the village. €€–€€€

🏠 **Habitant** (6 bungalows) Andranokoditra; ☎22 674 90 (Tana); m 034 05 737 29 (manager)/034 79 000 17. Run by MATE, the NGO responsible for Vohibola Reserve. Traditional huts. Meals available. €

Palmarium Reserve (*Entry 13,000Ar or free for guests*) Alongside the Palmarium Hotel this 50ha reserve of littoral forest protects a wide variety of palms, hence its name. It has broad, well-maintained trails on flat terrain and some ten different species of very tame (and mostly transplanted) lemurs, including ruffed lemurs, sifakas, indri and crowned lemurs. There are also orchids, carnivorous pitcher plants and mini-fauna such as chameleons, frogs and eye-catching insects as well as many birds. Allow 2 hours for a guided walk.

Vohibola Community Reserve This is a project run by MATE (Man And The Environment) protecting 2,200ha of the last remaining eastern littoral forest. The reserve, which stretches 9.5km northward from Lake Ampitabe, is degraded but there is a major reforestation programme in operation, and tourists have the hands-on opportunity to contribute by planting an indigenous tree. Among the species protected are four endangered tree species. One in particular, *Humbertiodendron saboureaui*, had not been seen for more than half a century and was presumed extinct until 33 specimens were discovered clinging on in this forest. There are two interesting and contrasting circuits: the **Discovery Trail** (4hrs) and the **Wetlands Trail** (2½hrs). Visits range from 2 hours to a full day with food included.

MANAMBATO AND LAKE RASOABE

Manambato is a picturesque resort on the white sandy shores of Lake Rasoabe, popular with Tana families for weekend getaways (the bathing is much safer than in the ocean). Turn off 11km beyond Brickaville and take the 7km track – it gets muddy after rain but is usually passable in a taxi; there is no public transport.

 Where to stay and eat *Map, opposite*

 Acacias (15 bungalows) Lac Rasoabe; 📞 22 404 29; m 032 04 811 97/032 12 338 35/032 43 129 93/033 05 875 01/033 12 338 35/034 04 244 97; e info@acaciasbungalows.com or socyin@moov.mg; www.acaciasbungalows.com. Quaint en-suite bungalows for 2–5 people. €€€

 Chez Luigi (4 rooms & 3 bungalows) Manambato; 📞 56 720 20; m 033 02 720 20/033 20 552 55/033 29 365 50/034 20 345 80/034 80 325 80; e chezluigi.irma@yahoo.fr. En-suite facilities with hot water. Boat trips. €€€

 Espace Vacance (21 rooms & 4 bungalows); m 033 11 991 28/034 20 991 28/033 24 991 28; e rafidisonlalao@hotmail.fr; www.manambato.com. Pleasant, clean hotel opened in 2015. En-suite rooms, some with kitchenette. €€€

 Orania Lodge (Au Bon Coin Zanatany) (8 bungalows & 4 rooms) Manambato; m 032 84 607 41/032 85 715 46/034 18 130 51/034 18 148 84; e oranialodge@gmail.com. Smart blue-and-white bungalows with en-suite facilities; opened in 2015. Boat trips & transfers. €€–€€€

 Mantalys (Chez Rene) (8 rooms) m 032 82 464 19/033 14 037 58/033 18 695 17/034 66 399 49. Natural bungalows nestled among vegetation. €€

 Epibar Manambato. Basic rooms with shared facilities & cold water. €

 Hibiscus (4 bungalows) Manambato. Simple bungalows with shared facilities & bucket showers. €

For listings, see pages 286–7

Where to stay and eat

1 Acacias	Mantalys (see 3)
2 Bush House	6 Ony
3 Chez Luigi	Orania Lodge (see 3)
Epibar (see 3)	Orchidées (see 5)
Espace Vacance (see 1)	7 Palmarium
4 Fantasia Village	8 Pangalanes Jungle
5 Habitant	Nofy
Hibiscus (see 3)	9 Runtamtam

AMBILA-LEMAITSO This quiet town, where you could happily get stuck for a couple of days, is stretched along a narrow strip of land between the sea and the Pangalanes Canal. Little more than a sandbar, the canal and beach are so close here that you would struggle to fit a football pitch between them. It is easiest to get here by train or boat.

By vehicle, it is necessary to take a 17km road from Brickaville to a ferry point to cross the canal, from where the town is a 4km walk north.

Where to stay and eat

Green Club (5 bungalows) 22 269 34 (Tana); m 034 49 150 00/034 49 151 74; e greenclub_ambila@yahoo.fr; www.greenclub-madagascar.com. Comfy en-suite accommodation. Wellness centre with massage & fitness facilities. €€€

Nirvana (10 bungalows) m 033 11 427 80/033 15 017 78/033 91 423 06; e nirvanabckvll@gmail.com. Situated in a breathtaking spot opposite the ferry point 4km south of the village, this is a charming French-run guesthouse. Comfy en-suite bungalows with hot water & a tremendous restaurant. €€–€€€

Relais Malaky (17 rooms) 56 260 13; m 033 64 064 97/034 07 680 00 (Tana); e relais.malaky@moov.mg; f relais.malaky. Close to the station. A range of bungalows & rooms, some en suite; solar electricity. Pleasant restaurant. €€–€€€

River Garden (8 rooms) m 033 37 102 22; e nirina.rabarison@yahoo.fr. Simple bungalows at good rates. €€

Tropicana Basic wooden dbl & family bungalows near the station. €€

VATOMANDRY The name of this town means 'sleeping rocks' – named for two flat, black boulders close to the shore. It was an important town in its time, growing from a small settlement on the bank of the River Sandramanongy to the administrative centre of the Hova government in the pre-colonial 19th century. At this time, Vatomandry was a prosperous port and merchandise was carried by porters to the capital along the paths of the eastern forest. It is also the birthplace of former President Ratsiraka.

The town lies some 150km south of Toamasina on the Pangalanes Canal and marks the end of this navigable section (the waterway becomes passable again beyond Mahanoro).

Where to stay and eat

Casadoro (16 bungalows) m 033 11 411 22/033 12 026 29. Basic en-suite bungalows. €€€

Espace Constellation (20 rooms) m 033 07 328 15; e miharyfifi@yahoo.fr. Rooms with minibar & AC. €€€

Grand Hotel (15 rooms) 53 821 77; m 033 38 416 07/033 79 760 94/034 38 416 07; e grandhotelvatomandry@yahoo.fr. Rooms with AC. €€€

Espace Zazah Robert (30 rooms & 15 bungalows) m 033 04 609 25/034 39 260 71; e espa.zaro@yahoo.fr. Traditional riverside bungalows & en-suite rooms with TV & AC. €€–€€€

Toky Horizon (12 rooms) m 033 11 151 38/033 14 094 83; e horizon_tina6@yahoo.fr. Simple rooms with TV & AC. €€–€€€

THE EAST COAST FROM VATOMANDRY TO MANANJARY

MAHANORO The name means 'happy-making', but whether Mahanoro will have this effect on all visitors is debatable. With the Mangoro River to its south, canal to its west and sea to the east, it is unsurprising that most of the places of interest are watery (although there is said to be a Merina fortress here). The town has a BOA bank and the impressive **Chutes de la Sahatsio** are 18km to the north.

Where to stay and eat

🏠 **Prestige** 📞 53 901 21/53 901 29. Simple traditional 2–4-person huts with en-suite facilities. €€–€€€

🏠 **Tropicana** (12 bungalows) 📞 53 901 33; m 033 02 075 75/033 02 791 08. Restaurant on the main street; bungalows on the seafront. €€–€€€

🏠 **Ansafa** m 033 02 376 37/034 71 153 37; e ninisyansafa@gmail.com. Simple bungalows & restaurant nr taxi-brousse station. €€

🏠 **Canella** m 033 07 433 54/034 20 590 06; e njavaline@yahoo.fr. Colourful simple huts. €€

🏠 **Mahamanina** m 032 07 352 08/033 07 877 19/034 20 877 19. Simple bungalows. €–€€

NOSY VARIKA It means 'lemur island' although you'd be lucky to see any *varika* (brown lemurs) here now. The most interesting excursion in the area is to the **Chutes de la Sakaleona**, a waterfall which plunges 200m, but this requires an expedition of two or three days. Nosy Varika has one hotel, with bungalows: **Volazara** (m *033 04 152 04;* e *volazara.hotel@yahoo.fr;* €€). From here to Mananjary the road condition becomes truly terrible.

AMBOHITSARA This isolated village 60km north of Mananjary is only accessible by boat. Apart from the opportunity to relax on and around the Pangalanes, one of Madagascar's most enigmatic sights is here: a stone elephant. Depending on whose version of the story you believe, the carving is said to have been brought here from Mecca or Yemen by the ancestors, perhaps 800 years ago.

THE EAST COAST FROM MANANJARY TO TAOLAGNARO

MANANJARY Reachable in 5 hours from Fianarantsoa by good road (RN45 via Ranomafana), this sleepy little town has a good choice of places to stay and a couple of banks (BFV and BOA).

The beach is rather dirty here but the lively weekend fish market held at the river mouth is worth a visit. Every seven years, mass circumcision ceremonies known as *sambatra* are performed in the area (next one in 2021).

Where to stay and eat

🏠 **Vahiny Lodge** (12 bungalows) m 032 02 468 22/033 04 630 87/034 20 468 22; e vahinylodge@yahoo.fr. A resort hotel on the edge of town near the airport. Classy restaurant, swimming pool & spacious bungalows with bathroom, terrace, safe, TV/DVD & minibar. €€€€€

🏠 **Idéal** (16 rooms & 10 bungalows) m 032 40 815 43. Spacious but reportedly becoming a bit run-down. Pirogue hire. €€€

🏠 **Jardin de la Mer** (7 bungalows) m 032 04 896 39/034 07 896 39; e jardindelamer@free.fr; www.jardindelamer.net. Comfy en-suite sgl & twin beach bungalows, swimming pool & restaurant. Camping permitted. €€€

🏠 **Picadow** (1 room & 10 bungalows) www.hotel-lepicadow-mananjary.com. En-suite trpl rooms with hot water. €€€

🏠 **Sorafa** (10 rooms & 5 bungalows) Bd Maritime; m 032 68 558 92/034 14 268 95;

e sorafahotel.mnj@gmail.com. Pleasant beach bungalows, some with verandas. Sgl & dbl rooms, pool & top restaurant with great pizza. €€€

🏠 **Patio** (9 rooms) m 034 98 283 66; e pierrejean.bastin@hotmail.com. Centrally located en-suite rooms with hot water. Tapas restaurant. €€–€€€

🏠 **Chez Stenny** (3 rooms & 3 bungalows) m 032 41 973 34. Small, friendly guesthouse. Cold water only. €€

🏠 **Ivonna** (12 bungalows) m 032 02 049 93/034 19 857 46. Good-value simple dbl & family bungalows. €€

🏠 **Bons Amis** (6 rooms) Cold water only. €–€€

✗ **Grillion** Nr cathedral. Good-value food.

✗ **Route des Epices** Best restaurant in town. Nr cathedral. Also runs birding tours.

11

Whenever I visit far-flung corners of Madagascar, I find myself regularly astounded at the local people's resourcefulness. Romain, an ingenious eastern farmer, is a prime example of the ability of the Malagasy to make something out of almost nothing. On his plot of land he grows a variety of crops but the jewel in his crown is a homemade hydro-electric power system! He and his son have constructed an impressive dam across a nearby stream. They built a water-powered generator and used wires extracted from discarded lorry tyres to rig up a supply to the house, successfully running electric lights and even a small television.

Recently disaster struck: the whole installation was buried in a landslip following a major cyclone. But Romain is not just entrepreneurial, he is tenacious with it, so he set about digging out literally tons of soil by hand. Having retrieved and cleaned his machinery, he restored it to working order – then hopefully rewarded himself with a well-deserved snooze in front of his resurrected TV.

MANAKARA 'Manakara is a former fishing village that gained importance as the terminus of the Fianarantsoa–Côte Est railway, despite a mediocre road,' declares a motorists' handbook published in 1971 by the Automobile-Club de Madagascar. It continues: 'The newer part of town is beautiful, with its parallel boulevards planted with lawns and palm trees. The municipal officials are to be praised for Manakara is certainly one of Madagascar's cleanest cities.'

It seems little has changed in the intervening half-century, although the road (RN45) has since been improved. Attractive ex-colonial buildings are set back from a seafront shaded by filao trees – an area described as a 'popular picnic spot' in the 1971 handbook – bringing a certain charm to this rather sleepy seaside town.

There are several banks and a post office. Plentiful *pousse-pousses* provide the best means of getting around (typical fare 1,500Ar), especially to the *taxi-brousse* station which is 2km north of the centre [291 B1].

Guides are easily found and a number of places near the canal run boat trips or hire out kayaks.

Swimming after eating pork is *fady* here, and in any case even vegetarian swimming is inadvisable owing to dangerous currents and sharks. But the sea is rewarding anyway: from the broad beach you can watch the captivating waves breaking on the reef 450m offshore. Note that the bridge connecting the two halves of town partially collapsed in 2012; pedestrians can still cross with care but a pontoon bridge has now been set up for traffic.

Getting there and away Manakara is the end of the **railway** journey from Fianarantsoa. At the time of writing trains depart for Fianar on Wednesday, Friday and Sunday mornings (theoretically at 06.45 but it usually runs late and cancellations are common), returning on Tuesdays, Thursdays and Saturdays (page 265).

By **taxi-brousse**, Mananjary and Fianarantsoa are respectively about 5 and 7 hours away and cost around 14,000Ar. It takes 3 hours to Farafangana (7,000Ar) or 4½ to Vangaindrano (11,000Ar). A direct taxi-brousse to Tana should cost 30,000Ar.

Madagascar Sensations (m *034 10 157 07*; e *chris.manary@yahoo.fr*) organises transfers and boat trips in the area.

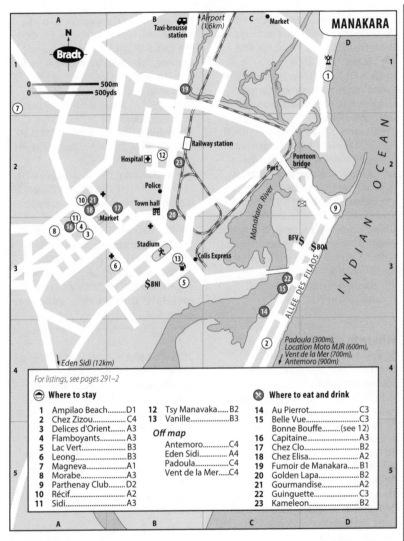

MANAKARA

For listings, see pages 291–2

🛏 **Where to stay**

1 Ampilao Beach..........D1
2 Chez Zizou.................C4
3 Delices d'Orient..........A3
4 Flamboyants...............A3
5 Lac Vert......................B3
6 Leong..........................B3
7 Magneva.....................A1
8 Morabe........................A3
9 Parthenay Club............D2
10 Récif...........................A2
11 Sidi.............................A3
12 Tsy Manavaka.......B2
13 Vanille....................B3

Off map
    Antemoro................C4
    Eden Sidi................A4
    Padoula...................C4
    Vent de la Mer.......C4

😋 **Where to eat and drink**

14 Au Pierrot...........................C3
15 Belle Vue...........................C3
    Bonne Bouffe..........(see 12)
16 Capitaine...........................A3
17 Chez Clo............................B2
18 Chez Elisa..........................A2
19 Fumoir de Manakara.......B1
20 Golden Lapa......................B2
21 Gourmandise.....................A2
22 Guinguette.........................C3
23 Kameleon...........................B2

🏠 Where to stay

🏠 **Parthenay Club** [291 D2]
(15 bungalows) 📞72 216 63; m 034 29 803 14;
e hotelparthenay@yahoo.fr. En-suite rooms &
a 4-bed dorm. Prime seafront spot with sandy
beach. Recommended comfy but dingy bungalows
with AC. Food very good. Bike & 4x4 hire. €€€€

🏠 **Vanille** [291 B3] (9 rooms & 8 bungalows) 📞72
210 23; m 034 17 209 68; e hotellavanillemanakara@
yahoo.fr. Five en-suite rooms with TV in town; other
rooms & lovely bungalows sited 8km away. €€€€

🏠 **Sidi** [291 A3] (56 rooms) m 033 02 803
90/034 09 227 98 (manager)/034 09 277 98/034

85 559 16 (reception); e sidihotel@moov.mg.
En-suite rooms with TV; some with AC. Nightclub
Fri–Sun from 21.00. €€€–€€€€

🏠 **Ampilao Beach** [291 D1] (8 bungalows)
m 034 03 746 33. Seafront location 3km from town;
run by Alain & Dora. Restaurant recommended. €€€

🏠 **Antemoro** [291 C4] (5 bungalows) m 032
63 125 00/033 05 009 18; e hotelantemoro@
gmail.com; www.hotel-antemoro.blogspot.com.
Quiet en-suite bungalows near beach. €€€

🏠 **Chez Zizou** [291 C4] (8 bungalows) m 032
04 913 54/033 32 913 54/034 05 913 54;

e zizoumanakara@gmail.com; www. chezzizoumanakara.jimdo.com. Seafront spot with TV & hot water. B/fast inc. Scooter hire. €€€

🏠 **Lac Vert** [291 B3] (6 bungalows) m 034 19 918 75; e rajeanmi@hotmail.com or reservationlacvert@yahoo.fr; www.lacvert.e-monsite.com. Lovely cosy bungalows just 10mins' walk from town. €€€

🏠 **Magneva** [291 A1] (18 rooms) m 034 17 166 35/034 40 767 08; e magnevahotel@yahoo. fr; www.magnevahotel.com. Comfy rooms set amid pleasantly landscaped gardens with large swimming pool; b/fast inc. €€€

🏠 **Delices d'Orient** [291 A3] (15 rooms & 9 bungalows) ☎ 72 217 34; m 032 41 747 95; e delicehotel@orange.mg. Good centrally located en-suite rooms with splendid restaurant (great seafood) & an excellent annexe of bungalows at the river mouth. €€–€€€

🏠 **Flamboyants** [291 A3] (6 rooms & 5 bungalows) m 032 52 459 51;

e leflamboyantmanakara@yahoo.fr. Great value hotel owned by helpful French consul. €€–€€€

🏠 **Eden Sidi** [291 A4] (8 rooms & 10 bungalows) ☎ 72 212 85. Nice bungalows 13km south of town. €€

🏠 **Leong** [291 B3] (25 rooms) ☎ 72 216 88; m 033 02 633 33. Budget rooms with TV; 2 with AC; 3 cheap sgl rooms. €€

🏠 **Padoula** [291 C4] (9 rooms) m 033 11 441 73/033 14 085 28. Basic with cold water. Camping permitted. €€

🏠 **Tsy Manavaka** [291 B2] (6 rooms) m 034 13 904 77/034 80 510 73; e parany_71@yahoo.fr. Opposite the train station, above restaurant Bonne Bouffe. €€

🏠 **Vent de la Mer** [291 C4] (6 rooms) m 034 12 221 59. Dbl en suite with hot water. €€

🏠 **Récif** [291 A4] (8 rooms) m 032 42 331 96. Centrally located rooms with fan; some en suite. €–€€

🏠 **Morabe** [291 A3] (10 rooms & 5 bungalows) m 032 45 859 92. Dbl with shared facilities in nice garden. €

✖ Where to eat and drink

✖ **Belle Vue** [291 C3] m 032 46 828 50/033 06 072 87/034 41 125 09; e hotel. labellevuedemanakara@live.fr; ⏲ daily 07.00–midnight. Waterfront bar with meals & snacks; *poisson au coco* especially recommended.

✖ **Bonne Bouffe** [291 B2] ⏲ daily 06.00–21.30. Restaurant & patisserie; can also provide picnics.

✖ **Capitaine** [291 A3] ⏲ daily noon–late. Popular with *vazaha*.

✖ **Chez Clo** [291 B2] ⏲ Fri–Wed 08.00–21.00, Thu closed. Restaurant & *salon de thé*.

✖ **Fumoir de Manakara** [291 B1] ⏲ daily except Wed lunch. Nice French-owned restaurant with reasonable prices.

✖ **Gourmandise** [291 A2] ⏲ daily 09.00–late. Highly recommended Chinese food.

✖ **Guinguette** [291 C3] m 032 02 683 35; ⏲ Wed–Mon 08.00–23.00, Tue noon–23.00. Restaurant in splendid riverfront spot. Canoe hire.

✖ **Kameleon** [291 B2] e laetitia.zinsou@gmail. com. Restaurant, pizzeria & bar.

🍺 **Au Pierrot** [291 C3] Waterfront snack bar.

🍺 **Chez Elisa** [291 A2] ⏲ daily 09.00–late. Snack bar. Also runs boat trips.

🍺 **Golden Lapa** [291 B2] Little café & karaoke joint.

ESSENTIAL OIL FACTORY (m *032 44 653 25; entry 10,000Ar*) Midway between Manakara and Vohipeno, this research operation has started running tours. You can see the 30ha plantation of vanilla, ylang-ylang and other aromatic flora, as well as visiting the distillery and learning about the whole production process.

VOHIPENO Situated some 45km south of Manakara, this is the end of the good road. Vohipeno is the centre of the Antaimoro tribe who reportedly came from Arabia six centuries ago, bringing the first script to Madagascar. They are the inheritors of the 'great writings', *sorabe*, written in Malagasy using Arabic script. The sacred sorabe continues to be written, still in Arabic, still on Antaimoro paper. The scribes who practise this art are known as *katibo* and the writing and their knowledge of it gives them a special power. The writing itself ranges from accounts of historical events to astrology.

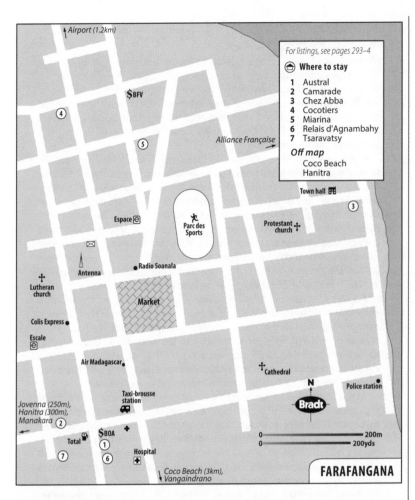

For listings, see pages 293–4

Where to stay
1 Austral
2 Camarade
3 Chez Abba
4 Cocotiers
5 Miarina
6 Relais d'Agnambahy
7 Tsaravatsy

Off map
    Coco Beach
    Hanitra

Airport (1.2km)

$ BFV

Alliance Française

Town hall

Espace ℮

Parc des Sports

Protestant church ✝

Radio Soanala

Antenna

✝ Lutheran church

Market

Colis Express ●

Escale ℮

Air Madagascar ●

✝ Cathedral

N

Police station

Bradt

Taxi-brousse station

Jovenna (250m), Hanitra (300m), Manakara ②

Total

$ BOA

Hospital

0   200m
0   200yds

Coco Beach (3km), Vangaindrano

FARAFANGANA

FARAFANGANA On the map this appears to be a seaside resort, but its position near the mouth of a river means that the beach and ocean are not easily accessible. There is a busy market (Tuesday), a few banks (the BFV has an ATM) and a Jovenna shop stocked with tinned and packet foods. A taxi-brousse from Tana to Farafangana takes about 17 hours (33,000Ar), but most people will come here via Ranomafana (15,000Ar) or Manakara (7,000Ar). Continuing to Vangaindrano costs 4,000Ar and takes an hour.

Where to stay and eat *Map, above*

Coco Beach (10 bungalows) ☏ 73 911 87/73 911 88. Beachside bungalows 3km south of the centre. En suite with hot water. **€€€**

Cocotiers (15 rooms) ☏ 73 911 87/73 911 88. Dbl, twin & trpl en-suite rooms, some with AC. **€€€**

Austral (24 rooms) m 034 16 391 75/034 45 479 30; e 01austhotel@gmail.com or contact@groupeaustralhotel.com; www.groupeaustralhotel.

com. Spacious rooms with Wi-Fi, TV & private bathrooms; some with AC. Well sited for taxi-brousse station. Restaurant with Malagasy, Chinese & European menu. **€€–€€€**

Chez Abba (15 bungalows) m 032 41 033 89/032 44 369 84/033 12 639 01/034 19 985 66. Seafront bungalows with simple bucket showers. **€€**

Miarina (7 rooms) m 032 07 586 70. Dbl rooms, some en suite. **€€**

My alarm clock went off at a quarter to four in the morning. I quickly got up and cycled the half mile or so to the Antaimoro fishermen's village at the northern end of Farafangana, with a half-moon lighting the way. The village was fast asleep but soon one of the fishermen, with whom I had arranged to go sea fishing, appeared. He quietly took my bicycle and pulled it into his little wooden house. The other members of the family were still sleeping but a cock was already beginning to crow.

With an oar each in hand, we set off to the nearby river where the pirogues lie on the sandy beach. We waded through the warm water to reach the long sandy bank that separates river from ocean. There we were joined by another two fishermen and we all clambered into a larger, wider pirogue shaped more like a banana in order to better tackle the waves. I thought we would have more difficulty getting over the violent breakers, but our departure was timed perfectly and we were past them in no time. We paddled away from the coast, where lone fishermen in small boats were casting their nets. Every so often we saw a fish coming to the surface and the fishermen, instead of exclaiming 'trondro!' ('fish'), said 'laoka!' which means 'food to accompany rice'!

About half a mile out to sea we came across our first float. It was pulled aboard followed by the net. The net had been left for two days, as the fishermen normally go out on alternate days – weather permitting, of course. The net was 50m long, with a heavy stone to anchor it to the seabed. We checked five or six nets that morning. One contained a kind of flat fish, whose wings were cut off and tied to the net as bait before it was put back in the water. Another contained three small, toothless sharks, brown and white in colour.

At first I didn't feel seasick, but by the end the smell of the sea, the fish and the constant rise and fall of our small vessel on the large waves combined to make me ill. The fishermen said they were not sick – even on their first ever outing – saying they were 'already used to it'. They meant they already had the sea in their blood, since their forefathers were all fishermen. They had no idea where Europe, America, Japan and so on lie, and they were fascinated when I pointed out the general direction of these places.

Our arrival on the beach was as perfect as the departure: beautifully executed despite the large waves. We all happily jumped out of the narrow boat in which we had been sitting or crouching for almost 4 hours.

Camarade Simple rooms west of the taxi-brousse station. €

Hanitra Cheap rooms close to Jovenna. €

Relais d'Agnambahy Central basic rooms nr BOA bank. €

Tsaravatsy ☏ 73 910 36. Very basic central accommodation. €

WEST TO IHOSY For the seriously adventurous, the road to Ihosy is just about passable in the dry season by 4x4 or motorbike. Taxi-brousses run as far as **Vondrozo**. You can continue by car to the **Vevembe** region, at which point the passable road ends and jungle takes over. You will probably need a guide to help you reach the next stretch of passable road at **Ivohibe** because of the numerous trails that have been created by the locals. If you make it to Ivohibe you're home and dry; there are taxi-brousses to Ihosy. But beware: the area is said to be infested with bandits.

MANOMBO SPECIAL RESERVE This reserve 25km south of Farafangana protects around 5,000ha of littoral forest. It is home to eight species of lemur including the southernmost population of black-and-white ruffed lemurs and the extremely rare grey-headed lemur which is among the world's 25 most endangered primates. Manombo also has the highest diversity of land snails of any rainforest in the world. There is no accommodation but visitors can camp at the park office on the main road, 4km from the forest.

LOPARY AND MAHABO-MANANIVO These villages are 2km apart, near the Mananivo river mouth, around 22km before Vangaindrano. The Mahabo-Mananivo market (Sunday morning) is good for high-quality basket-weaving. Lopary has a much bigger market (also Sunday), known for its fish and woven mats.

VANGAINDRANO This has the atmosphere of a frontier town, and indeed heading south the road gets *really* bad. Few tourists come here. There is a BOA bank (they can change euros but not travellers' cheques and there's no ATM). Market day is Monday. There is not much by way of attractions but you could take an excursion to a regional museum, **Papan'ny Do Mahasianaka** (30km south of town), or go and see the **clove plantations** at Matanga (head 20km south then turn east for 9km).

 Where to stay and eat

🏠 **Tropic** (12 rooms) Reasonable rooms just past the stadium 1km southwest of the market; some en suite. Restaurant Mandarine has grill & seafood specialities. The owner very active in the region's tourist scene. €€–€€€

🏠 **Shell Motel** (11 bungalows) m 032 45 500 12. So named for its proximity to the fuel station at the north of town. Hot water. €–€€

🏠 **Antsika** Very basic with bucket showers. €

🏠 **Guerit** Simple accommodation. €

🏠 **Hunotel** Basic with cold bucket showers. €

🏠 **Jupiter** Simple rooms; 4x4 hire. €

MIDONGY DU SUD NATIONAL PARK Well off the beaten track, this park is challenging to reach (impossible in the rainy season) and has little tourist infrastructure. It comprises 192,000ha of mountainous and often rainy terrain.

From Vangaindrano head east. You can cover the 94km to Ranomena in 2 hours but the remaining 42km to Midongy Atsimo, where there is basic accommodation, is much slower going. One reader took 6 hours but it's highly weather-dependent. Visit the park office (the yellow building on the hill as you enter town) to arrange permits and a guide (see page 73 for permit prices).

CONTINUING TO TAOLAGNARO (FORT DAUPHIN) The road to Taolagnaro is terrible and most of the 230km requires a 4x4. The trip involves no fewer than ten river crossings, which are the most interesting aspect of the journey; the scenery in-between is rather dull. If you're lucky and none of the ferries stationed at the crossing points is broken down, then in a good vehicle and good weather the trip can be achieved in one *very* long day. However, most vehicles make the journey over two days, typically overnighting in simple bungalows at **Manantenina** just after the fifth river crossing.

The first of the river crossings is 32km south of Vangaindrano. It is fady to wear red or gold (including jewellery) on this crossing. All the ferries are free and operate 06.00–18.00. A tip of 2,000Ar or so per vehicle is usual, but you'll have to pay more if you want to be taken across after hours.

A two-day *camion-brousse* departs Vangaindrano once a week (m *032 62 811 63*). Delays are common and it's not unknown for travellers to take four or five days to reach Taolagnaro.

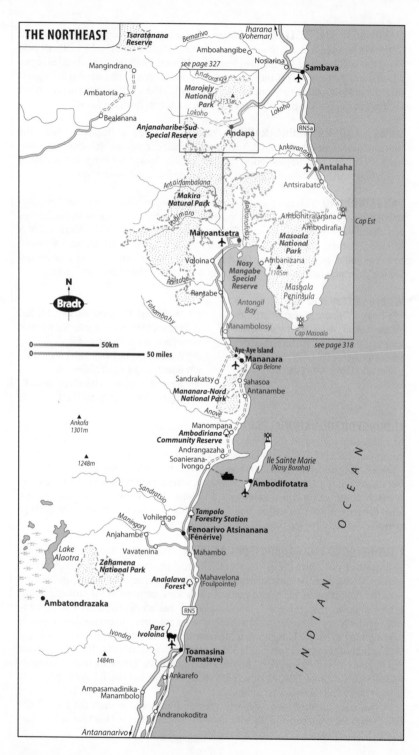

THE NORTHEAST

Tsaratanana Reserve

Bemarivo

Mangindrano

Iharana (Vohemar)

Amboahangibe

Nosiarina

Sambava

Ambatoria

see page 327

Andraranga

Marojejy National Park

▲ 2133m

Lokoho

Bealanana

Lokoho

Anjanaharibe-Sud Special Reserve

Andapa

RN5a

Ankavanana

Antsahabo

✈ **Antalaha**

Antsirabato

Antainambalana

Makira Natural Park

Ambohitralanana

Ambodirafia

Cap Est

Vohimaro

Maroantsetra ✈

Andranofotsy

Masoala National Park

Voloina

Ambanizana

▲ 1105m

Antabe

N

Rantabe

Bradt

Rantabe

Nosy Mangabe Special Reserve

Masoala Peninsula

Antongil Bay

Fahambahy

Manambolosy

Cap Masoala ☂

0 ———— 50km

0 ———— 50 miles

see page 318

Aye-Aye Island

Mananara

Cap Belone

Sandrakatsy

Sahasoa

Antanambe

Mananara-Nord National Park

Anove

▲ Ankofa 1301m

Manompana

Ambodiriana Community Reserve

Andrangazaha

▲ 1248m

Soanierana-Ivongo

Ile Sainte Marie (Nosy Boraha)

Sandratsio

Ambodifotatra ✈

Maningory

Vohilengo

Tampolo Forestry Station

Anjahambe

Fenoarivo Atsinanana (Fénérive)

Vavatenina

Mahambo

Lake Alaotra

Zahamena National Park

Mahavelona (Foulpointe)

Analalava Forest

Ambatondrazaka

RN5

Ivondro

Parc Ivoloina

▲ 1484m

Toamasina (Tamatave)

Ankarefo

I N D I A N   O C E A N

Ampasamadinika-Manambolo

Andranokoditra

Antananarivo →

296

12

Toamasina and the Northeast

Punished by rain and occasional cyclones, eastern Madagascar has a reputation for being challenging to travellers. In July 1817 James Hastie wrote in his diary: 'If this is the good season for travelling this country, I assert it is impossible to proceed in the bad.' With this in mind, those who are not up for an adventure might be better avoiding the wettest months of January to March and remembering that June to August can be very damp as well. The optimum period to visit is September to December. The east coast is also notorious for sharks and dangerous currents so, although there are beautiful beaches, swimming is safe only in protected zones.

Despite – or perhaps because of – these drawbacks, the northeast is arguably the most rewarding region for independent travellers, and has an increasing number of beautifully situated upmarket hotels for that once-in-a-lifetime holiday. Much of Madagascar's unique flora and fauna is concentrated in the eastern rainforests and any serious naturalist will want to pay a visit. Other attractions are the rugged mountain scenery with rivers tumbling down to the Indian Ocean; abundant fruit and seafood; plantations of everything from coffee, vanilla and cloves to bananas, coconuts and lychees; and access to the lovely island of Ile Sainte Marie (covered in *Chapter 13*, page 333).

HISTORY

This region has an interesting history dominated by European pirates and slave traders. While powerful kingdoms were being forged in other parts of the country, the east coast remained divided among numerous small clans. It was not until the 18th century that the region was unified by Ratsimilaho, a ruler who had briefly been educated in Britain as he was the son of English pirate Thomas White and a native queen. The success of his unification, prompted by an attempt by Chief Ramanano to take over all the east coast ports, was furthered by his judiciously marrying an important princess. By his death in 1754 he ruled an area stretching from the Masoala Peninsula to Mananjary.

The result of this liaison of various tribes was the Betsimisaraka, now the second-largest ethnic group in Madagascar. Some (in the area of Maroantsetra) practise second burial, although with less ritual than the Merina and Betsileo.

DISTANCES IN KILOMETRES			
Toamasina–Foulpointe	60km	Iharana–Sambava	153km
Toamasina–Mahambo	85km	Sambava–Antalaha	89km
Toamasina–Soanierana-Ivongo	163km	Sambava–Andapa	119km

The capital of the region is **Toamasina** which, like all the east coast ports, began as a pirate community. In the late 18th century its harbour attracted the French, who already had a foothold in Ile Sainte Marie, and Napoleon I sent his agent Sylvain Roux to establish a trading post there. In 1811, Sir Robert Farquhar, governor of the newly British island of Mauritius, sent a small naval squadron to take the port of Toamasina. This was not simply an extension of the usual British–French antagonism, but an effort to stamp out slavery at its source. Madagascar was the main supplier to the Indian Ocean and the slave trade had been abolished by the British parliament in 1807. The attack was successful and Sylvain Roux was exiled. During subsequent years, trade between Mauritius and Madagascar built Toamasina into a major port. In 1845, after a royal edict subjecting European traders to the harsh Malagasy laws, French and British warships bombarded the town, but a landing was repelled leaving 20 dead. During the 1883–85 war the French occupied Toamasina but Malagasy troops successfully defended the nearby fort of Farafaty.

Legend has it that the name comes from Radama I who is said to have tasted the seawater here and remarked, for he was clearly a perspicacious king, '*Toa masina*' – 'It's salty'.

TOAMASINA (TAMATAVE)

Still widely known as Tamatave, Toamasina has always had an air of shabby elegance with some fine palm-lined boulevards and once-impressive colonial houses. Every few years it's hit by a cyclone, and spends some time in a new state of shabbiness before rebuilding. As you'd expect, it's a spirited, bustling city with a good variety of bars, snack bars and restaurants.

GETTING THERE AND AWAY RN2 is one of the country's best-maintained roads and is the fastest and cheapest way of reaching Toamasina from Tana; this route is covered in *Chapter 10*. *Taxi-brousses* run every day and take around 7 hours (20,000Ar). A premium option with six scheduled departures per day and more comfortable vehicles with on-board Wi-Fi for 24,000–30,000Ar is run by **Cotisse** (m *032 11 027 33/35*; e *cotissetana@alpa.mg in Tana or cotissetransport@yahoo.fr in Toamasina; www.cotisse-transport.com*).

A **railway** line follows roughly the same route as RN2. There are no scheduled passenger services on the line from Tana to Moramanga, but from there you can come by train via Andasibe and the Pangalanes Canal (more details on page 265).

There are daily **flights** between Tana and Toamasina, as well as less frequent connections by air to Ile Sainte Marie, Maroantsetra, Antalaha and Sambava.

Boats leave from Port Fluvial at the southwest edge of the town for trips down the Pangalanes Canal.

Heading north, the road is good as far as Soanierana-Ivongo, beyond which it is terrible, but passable with persistence in the dry season as far as Maroantsetra. From Soanierana are **ferries** across to Ile Sainte Marie (page 334) and a three-times-a-week boat service to Mananara (120,000Ar/5–10hrs) and Maroantsetra (170,000Ar/8–12hrs), weather permitting, run by Melissa Express, whose office is at Toamasina's taxi-brousse station (m *032 447 43 03/032 02 073 64*; e *melissaexpress1@gmail.com*). The ticket prices include a shuttle bus from Toamasina to Soanierana, where you may have to stay overnight as boat departure times depend on the tides.

If you ask at the port, you may also find **cargo boats** heading up the coast. These will take passengers and are significantly cheaper than Melissa Express but also a lot slower, much less safe and do not run to a regular schedule.

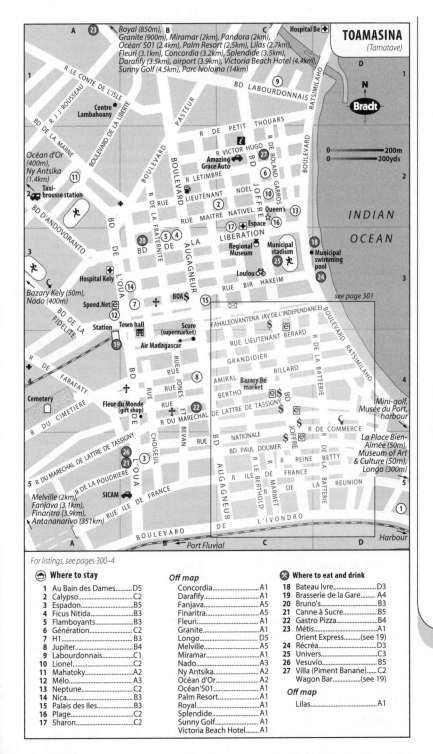

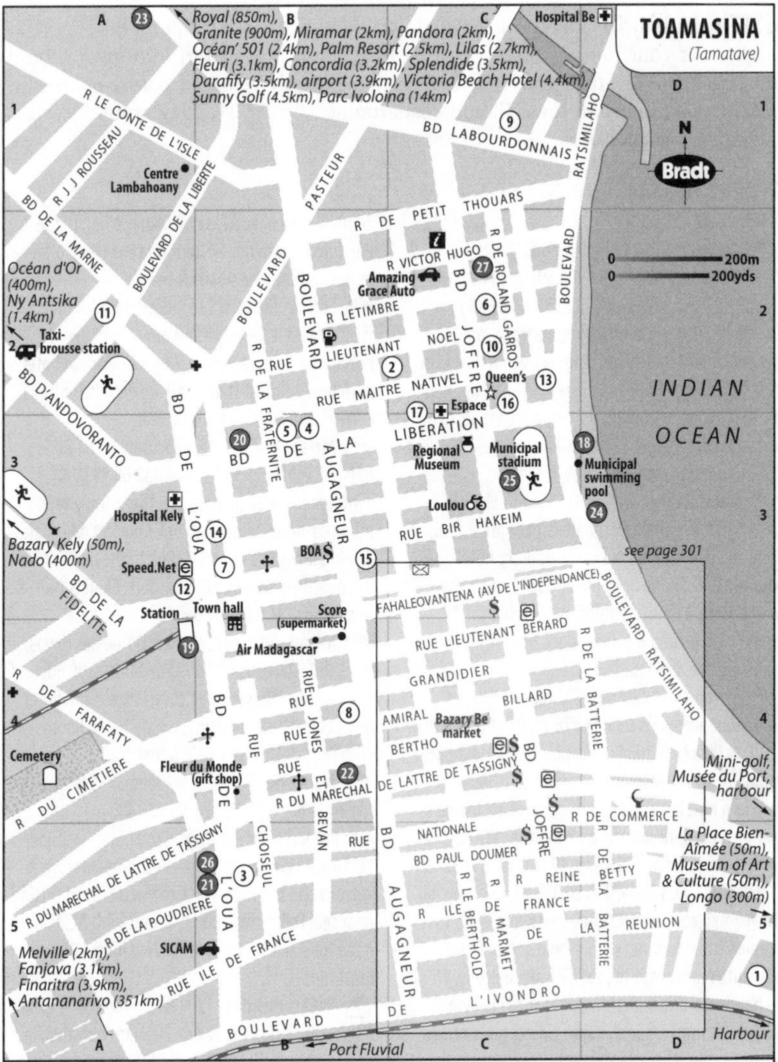
TOAMASINA
(Tamatave)
Royal (850m), Granite (900m), Miramar (2km), Pandora (2km), Océan' 501 (2.4km), Palm Resort (2.5km), Lilas (2.7km), Fleuri (3.1km), Concordia (3.2km), Splendide (3.5km), Darafify (3.5km), airport (3.9km), Victoria Beach Hotel (4.4km), Sunny Golf (4.5km), Parc Ivoloina (14km)
Hospital Be
R LE CONTE DE L'ISLE
R J J ROUSSEAU
Centre Lambahoany
BD LABOURDONNAIS
RATSIMILAHO
BD DE LA MARNE
BOULEVARD DE LA LIBERTE
PASTEUR
R DE PETIT THOUARS
Océan d'Or (400m), Ny Antsika (1.4km)
Taxi-brousse station
R VICTOR HUGO
Amazing Grace Auto
R DE ROLAND GARROS
BOULEVARD
R LETIMBRE
RUE LIEUTENANT NOEL
BD JOFFRE
BD D'ANDOVORANTO
R DE LA FRATERNITE
RUE MAITRE NATIVEL
Queen's
Espace
LIBERATION
BD DE LA AUGAGNEUR
Regional Museum
Municipal stadium
Municipal swimming pool
INDIAN OCEAN
Hospital Kely
BD DE L'OUA
Loulou
RUE BIR HAKEIM
Bazary Kely (50m), Nado (400m)
Speed.Net
BOA
see page 301
BD DE LA FIDELITE
FAHALEOVANTENA (AV DE L'INDEPENDANCE)
BOULEVARD RATSIMILAHO
Station
Town hall
Score (supermarket)
Air Madagascar
RUE LIEUTENANT BERARD
R DE LA BATTERIE
R DE FARAFATY
GRANDIDIER
RUE JONES
BILLARD
AMIRAL
Bazary Be market
BERTHO
Cemetery
Fleur du Monde (gift shop)
BD DE LATTRE DE TASSIGNY
Mini-golf, Musée du Port, harbour
R DU CIMETIERE
RUE ET BEVAN
R DU MARECHAL
R DE COMMERCE
NATIONALE
La Place Bien-Aîmée (50m), Museum of Art & Culture (50m), Longo (300m)
BD PAUL DOUMER
R REINE BETTY
R DU MARECHAL DE LATTRE DE TASSIGNY
CHOISEUL
R LE BERTHOLD
R DE MARMET
R ILE DE FRANCE
R DE LA POUDRIERE
REUNION
SICAM
Melville (2km), Fanjava (3.1km), Finaritra (3.9km), Antananarivo (351km)
RUE ILE DE FRANCE
BOULEVARD DE L'IVONDRO
Port Fluvial
Harbour
0 200m
0 200yds
Bradt

For listings, see pages 300–4

Where to stay

1 Au Bain des Dames..........D5
2 Calypso..........C2
3 Espadon..........B5
4 Ficus Nitida..........B3
5 Flamboyants..........B3
6 Génération..........C2
7 H1..........B3
8 Jupiter..........B4
9 Labourdonnais..........C1
10 Lionel..........C2
11 Mahatoky..........A2
12 Mélo..........A3
13 Neptune..........C2
14 Nica..........B3
15 Palais des Iles..........B3
16 Plage..........C2
17 Sharon..........C2

Off map

Concordia..........A1
Darafify..........A1
Fanjava..........A5
Finaritra..........A5
Fleuri..........A1
Granite..........A1
Longo..........D5
Melville..........A5
Miramar..........A1
Nado..........A3
Ny Antsika..........A2
Océan d'Or..........A2
Océan'501..........A1
Palm Resort..........A1
Royal..........A1
Splendide..........A1
Sunny Golf..........A1
Victoria Beach Hotel..........A1

Where to eat and drink

18 Bateau Ivre..........D3
19 Brasserie de la Gare..........A4
20 Bruno's..........B3
21 Canne à Sucre..........B5
22 Gastro Pizza..........B4
23 Métis..........A1
Orient Express..........(see 19)
24 Récréa..........D3
25 Univers..........C3
26 Vesuvio..........B5
27 Villa (Piment Banane)..........C2
Wagon Bar..........(see 19)

Off map

Lilas..........A1

GETTING AROUND A **taxi** ride in the town should cost 3,000Ar, or a little more at night or if your journey involves a dirt road. From the airport into town should be 10,000Ar. **Tuk-tuks** and *cyclo-pousses* have largely replaced *pousse-pousses* in recent years; a trip in town should cost around 2,000Ar. Walking around town is not advisable after dark.

WHERE TO STAY
Top end €€€€€

Calypso [299 C2] (48 rooms) Rue Noël; 53 304 57/53 304 58/53 304 59/53 304 91; m 032 07 131 33/033 37 131 33/034 07 131 32/034 07 131 33; e info@hotelcalypso.mg or reservation@hotelcalypso.mg; www.hotelcalypso.mg. Splendid 5-floor business-style hotel opened in 2010, with swimming pool, spa, massage, gym & hammam. Attractive rooms have AC, sat-TV, Wi-Fi, minibar, safe & balcony. B/fast inc.

Palm Resort [299 A1] (21 rooms) m 033 37 170 07; e palmresort.toamasina@gmail.com. New in 2012, a colourful contemporary hotel near the beach & 5mins from the airport. 7 villas each comprising 3 rooms with AC, Wi-Fi & big sat-TV; some with jacuzzi & private pool. Spa with beauty salon, sauna & massage.

Splendide [299 A1] (22 rooms) Ambalamanasy; m 033 47 778 28/034 06 737 29/034 06 870 64/034 09 601 69; e splendide.h@gmail.com; www.splendide-hotel.com. Very modern hotel nr airport with good-value rooms in various categories, some with balcony. Wi-Fi.

Sunny Golf [299 A1] (49 rooms) m 032 05 336 08/033 11 313 64/034 20 336 11; e sunnygolf.tm@gmail.com; www.sunnymada.com. Next to airport (transfers inc) with 4-hole golf practice. En-suite rooms with AC, sat-TV, safe, balcony, Wi-Fi & hairdryer. B/fast inc. Massage. Price inc gym, tennis, swimming pool, horse-riding, table tennis & pool table. Also 1 apartment.

Victoria Beach Hotel [299 A1] (48 rooms) m 032 03 286 28/033 01 286 28/034 05 286 28; e vichotelm@163.com; www.vicbeach.com. We've had mixed reports about this new Chinese-owned hotel. Rooms have faux antique furnishing & offer TV, AC, Wi-Fi & balcony. Pool, gym, spa & wellness centre.

Upper range €€€€

Java [301 B2] (40 rooms) 34 Bd Joffre; 53 316 26; m 034 12 252 53; e java_hotel_madagascar@moov.mg or javahotelmg@gmail.com; www.java-hotel-tamatave.com. Opened in 2010. Rooms have AC, sat-TV, safe, Wi-Fi, fridge & en-suite bathrooms. Restaurant Le Verseau offers a range of dishes inc salads & snacks.

Joffre [301 C3] (32 rooms) 18 Bd Joffre; 53 323 90; e hotel.joffre@moov.mg; www.hoteljoffre-tamatave.com. Atmospheric old hotel with new 'colonial' rooms. All are en suite with AC & Wi-Fi. Uninspiring buffet b/fast.

Miramar [299 A1] (20 bungalows) Bd Ratsimilaho; 53 332 15; m 032 65 993 74; e miramar-hotel-tmv@netcourrier.com; www.miramar-hotel-tamatave.com. Comfortable chalets & bungalows in a good location to the north, near the beach & convenient for airport. Chalets (fan) & bungalows (AC). Deep pool.

Miray [301 A3] (26 rooms) Rue des Hovas; 53 350 82; m 034 07 609 79/034 10 500 60; e reception.miray@gmail.com; www.mirayhotel.mg. Central 2-floor business-style hotel. Rooms with AC, sat-TV, Wi-Fi, safe & minibar.

Neptune [299 C2] (47 rooms) 35 Bd Ratsimilaho; 53 322 26/53 326 40; e neptuneresa@moov.mg; www.hotel-neptune-tamatave.com. Once the poshest hotel in town & still not bad but rooms lack character. Good setting near sea. Dbl, twin & family rooms with AC. Pool, good food & nice bar. Free Wi-Fi in lobby. Disco most nights.

Palais des Iles [299 B3] (3 rooms) 53 314 33; e tsarisland@moov.mg. Intimate guesthouse in a 1930s colonial mansion. En-suite rooms. Excellent restaurant.

Sharon [299 C2] (44 rooms) Bd de la Libération; 53 304 20; m 032 05 304 20; e sharonhotel@moov.mg; www.sharonhotel.mg. Modern rooms with AC, minibar, safe, sat-TV & Wi-Fi. Gym, pool, beauty salon, massage & sauna. Good restaurant Rose des Vents & excellent pizzeria.

Veranda [301 C1] (16 rooms) 5 Rue Berard; 53 340 86; m 032 45 832 86; e laveranda@moov.mg; www.veranda-hotel-restaurant-tamatave.com. En-suite rooms with Wi-Fi, AC, TV & some with balcony. Popular restaurant.

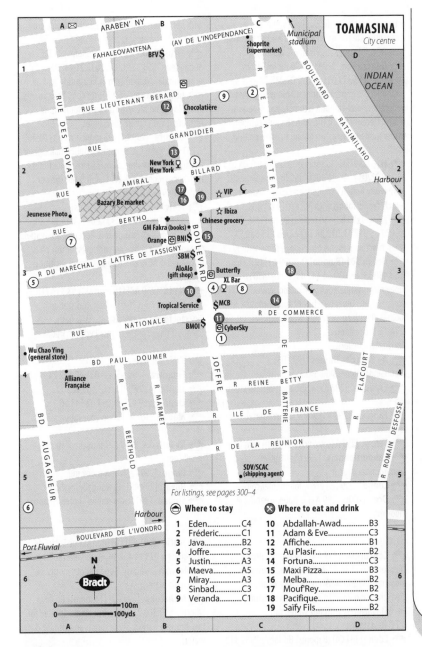

For listings, see pages 300–4

🛏 Where to stay

1	Eden................C4
2	Fréderic..........C1
3	Java................B2
4	Joffre.............C3
5	Justin.............A3
6	Maeva............A5
7	Miray.............A3
8	Sinbad...........C3
9	Veranda.........C1

🍴 Where to eat and drink

10	Abdallah-Awad............B3
11	Adam & Eve................C3
12	Affiche.......................B1
13	Au Plasir....................B2
14	Fortuna......................C3
15	Maxi Pizza.................B3
16	Melba........................B2
17	Mouf'Rey...................B2
18	Pacifique...................C3
19	Saïfy Fils...................B2

Mid-range €€€

Darafify [299 A1] (20 bungalows) Ampanalana; m 034 60 468 82; e contact. darafify@gmail.com. Seafront location not far from airport. En-suite bungalows of various types. Kids' playground. Restaurant is much praised.

Flamboyants [299 B3] (36 rooms) Bd de la Libération; ☎ 53 323 50; m 032 71 093 51. Recommended hotel with decent-sized rooms that are en suite with TV; some with AC. Bar & restaurant.

Fréderic [301 C1] (21 rooms) 33 Rue de la Batterie; m 032 74 883 36/034 47 245 16;

e frederichotel@live.fr. Excellent value. Large, clean, en-suite rooms on a central backstreet. Most have AC & TV; some with fridge & balcony.

🏠 **Génération** [299 C2] (30 rooms) 129 Bd Joffre; ☎ 53 321 05; m 032 02 238 22 (manager); e generationhotel@moov.mg; www.generationhotel-tamatave.com. Large, pleasant rooms. Decent restaurant 'with the only competent waiter in Madagascar' according to one exacting reader!

🏠 **H1** [299 B3] (12 rooms) ☎ 53 316 03; m 033 28 358 33/034 98 226 10; e hotelh1tmm@gmail.com; www.hotelh1-madagascar.com. Clean dbl, twin & family rooms with AC, sat-TV & Wi-Fi.

🏠 **Nica** [299 B3] (30 rooms) Bd de l'OUA; m 032 25 912 43/032 28 142 62/033 11 869 51. Clean functional rooms on 4 floors, some with AC.

🏠 **Océan'501 (Ravinala)** [299 A1] (9 rooms) ☎ 53 450 35; m 032 64 147 43; e ocean501@moov.mg or waibelerick@moov.mg; www.ocean501.biz. Quiet beachfront spot; various rooms, all with en-suite hot-water facilities, sat-TV & Wi-Fi. Top restaurant.

Also in this category:

🏠 **Au Bain des Dames** [299 D5] e aubaindesdames@moov.mg

🏠 **Espadon** [299 B5] e espadon-hotel@moov.mg

🏠 **Fanjava** [299 A5] www.fanjava-hotel-tamatave.com

🏠 **Fleuri** [299 A1] www.hotel-fleuri.com

🏠 **Labourdonnais** [299 C1] http://labourdonnais.free.fr

🏠 **Longo** [299 D5] www.longohotel.com

🏠 **Océan d'Or** [299 A2] e hotel.oceandor@moov.mg

Budget €€

🏠 **Concordia** [299 A1] (14 rooms) Rte de l'Aéroport; m 034 52 293 00; e chanpowoo@moov.mg. Within walking distance of airport. Pleasant bungalows in an attractive setting; en-suite facilities with hot water, fan & TV. Restaurant.

🏠 **Eden** [301 C4] (8 rooms) Bd Joffre; ☎ 53 312 90; m 032 04 628 82/032 40 247 78/034 45 017 08; e calypstour793@gmail.com. Appropriately situated near Adam & Eve snack bar. Basic rooms

with hot water; some en suite with balcony, but some quite run-down.

🏠 **Ficus Nitida** [299 B3] (7 rooms) 31 Bd Augagneur; ☎ 53 323 08; m 032 21 447 38; e ficusnitida8@gmail.com or ficusnitida@gmail.com; http://ficus-nitida.lyl-resto.com. Basic rooms in a colonial building. Best known for its large restaurant with Creole specialities.

🏠 **Granite** [299 A1] (38 rooms) m 033 01 199 37/033 14 954 67; e legranitehotel@gmail.com or legranitehotel@yahoo.com; 🄵 Le Granite Hotel. Functional rooms with Wi-Fi, fan & hot shower. Malagasy & Asian food.

🏠 **Melville** [299 A5] (60 rooms) ☎ 53 331 80; m 032 07 331 80/033 07 331 80; e hotelmelville@orange.mg. Recently renovated. Cheapest rooms have no windows; better ones have sat-TV, AC & en-suite hot-water facilities. Cybercafé.

🏠 **Nado** [299 A3] (15 rooms) ☎ 53 333 11; e sedo@moov.mg. Not far from bus station. Pleasant rooms, some with AC, TV & bath. Cheapest rooms are very small with shared facilities.

Also in this category:

🏠 **Finaritra** [299 A5] m 032 40 122 74

🏠 **Jupiter** [299 B4] m 032 02 062 27

🏠 **Lionel** [299 C2] m 032 02 543 56

🏠 **Maeva** [301 A5] www.maevabungalows.net

🏠 **Ny Antsika** [299 A2] e nyantsikahotel@gmail.com

🏠 **Plage** [299 C2] e fg@moov.mg

🏠 **Royal** [299 A1] e kwangaby@yahoo.fr

🏠 **Sinbad** [301 C3] e sinbad_hotel@yahoo.fr

Penny-pincher €

🏠 **Justin** [301 A3] (16 rooms) Rue Lattre de Tassigny; m 033 14 458 54. Humble establishment popular with Malagasy. Good budget rooms; en suite (cold water).

🏠 **Mahatoky** [299 A2] (14 rooms) Bd de la Liberté; ☎ 53 300 21. Basic, but ideally located for taxi-brousse station. Some rooms en suite (cold water).

🏠 **Mélo** [299 A3] (11 rooms) Bd de l'OUA. No fan/AC but clean & extremely cheap dbl rooms with en-suite cold shower.

✖ **WHERE TO EAT AND DRINK** There is no shortage of places to eat out, especially if you like Chinese cuisine. Several hotels have excellent restaurants worth trying, most notably **Veranda**, **Calypso** and **Palais des Iles** in town and, towards the airport, **Océan'501** (which often has live music) and **Darafify**.

✕ **Affiche** [301 B1] Bd Joffre; ☏ 53 305 45/53 315 45; m 032 04 618 44/032 56 443 28; ⏰ Sat–Thu 07.30–23.00, Fri closed. Tasty menu inc pizza; fast service.

✕ **Bateau Ivre** [299 D3] Bd Ratsimilaho; ☏ 53 350 51; e batoivre@moov.mg; ⏰ 09.00–23.30. Characterful beachfront bar & restaurant. Moderately priced European food; seafood a speciality. Live music & swimming pool. Wi-Fi.

✕ **Brasserie de la Gare** [299 A4] Gare des Manguiers; m 032 27 647 32/034 05 420 67; www. garedesmanguiers.mg; ⏰ Mon–Sat 11.30–14.00 & 18.00–late, Sun closed. Smart restaurant with many Italian specialities inc homemade ice cream; menu frequently updated. Sometimes live music.

✕ **Fortuna** [301 C3] 11 Rue de la Batterie; ☏ 53 338 23/53 338 28; m 032 07 085 80/032 40 002 42; e masyjeanguy@gmail.com; ⏰ 11.00–13.30 & 18.00–21.30 (restaurant); 07.15–11.00 & 17.00–20.30 (*soupe chinoise*); both closed Mon. Chinese restaurant & adjacent *soupe chinoise* serving soup & noodle specialities.

✕ **Métis (Mora Mora)** [299 A1] Bd Labourdonnais; m 032 86 379 55. Good food with a diverse menu featuring French & Malagasy dishes. Nice décor with TV & bar.

✕ **Orient Express** [299 A4] Gare des Manguiers; m 032 27 647 32/034 05 420 67; www. garedesmanguiers.mg; ⏰ Mon–Sat 11.30–14.00 & 18.00–late, Sun closed. Stylish new place with innovative gourmet menu based on fresh seasonal produce.

✕ **Pacifique** [301 C3] 22 Rue Clemenceau; ☏ 53 322 23; m 034 64 780 53 (manager); ⏰ 11.00–14.00 & 18.00–22.00 (restaurant); 09.00–13.30 & 18.00–21.30 (*soupe chinoise*); both closed Mon. Chinese restaurant serving very good meals at reasonable prices.

✕ **Récréa** [299 D3] Bd Ratsimilaho; m 032 04 610 71/034 95 042 58; ⏰ 11.00–23.00. Pleasant setting on the beach. Good food & nice place for a drink. Live music some w/ends. Bar, billiards & boutique.

✕ **Univers** [299 C3] Bd Joffre; ⏰ 24hrs. Rather gritty outfit in the west side of the stadium. Serves grills & simple dishes.

✕ **Vesuvio** [299 B5] Bd de l'OUA; ☏ 53 935 19; ⏰ 11.30–14.00 & 17.30–21.30, except Wed

lunch. Very good pizza. Also Creole food. Eat in, take-away & delivery.

✕ **Villa (Piment Banane)** [299 C2] Rue Victor Hugo; ☏ 53 312 64; m 034 08 043 09; ⏰ 10.00–15.00 & 18.00–22.30 or later. Long praised as one of the best places to eat out in town. Recently changed hands but still seems popular. Inside & outside dining.

🍽 **Abdallah-Awad** [301 B3] off Bd Joffre; ⏰ Mon–Sat 08.00–noon & 14.30–18.30, Sun closed. Coconut & coffee ice creams highly recommended by local expats.

🍽 **Adam & Eve** [301 C3] 13 Rue Nationale; m 032 11 579 61/034 11 579 61; e adameve33456@yahoo.fr; ⏰ Mon–Sat 08.00–20.30, Sun closed. A long-time *vazaha* favourite with good prices. Particularly good value for b/fast. Delectable milkshakes. Always busy.

🍽 **Au Plaisir** [301 B2] 10 Bd Joffre. Centrally located *salon de thé*.

🍽 **Bruno's** [299 B3] Bd de la Libération; ☏ 53 333 78; ⏰ 08.00–noon & 15.00–19.00. Best pastries & cakes in town, but get there early. Great coffee & ice cream; good for b/fast.

🍽 **Canne à Sucre** [299 B5] Bd de l'OUA; ⏰ Mon–Sat 07.00–midnight, Sun closed. Karaoke bar with Malagasy & Creole specialities.

🍽 **Gastro Pizza** [299 B4] Good pizzas & ice cream from this popular chain, with branches in the town centre, at Bazary Kely & next to Bateau Ivre.

🍽 **Lilas** [299 A1] Rte d'Ivoloina; m 033 07 462 63; ⏰ Tue–Sun 07.30–13.00 & 15.30–19.30, Mon closed. Small but clean & pleasant family-run Chinese restaurant. Tasty meals & soups at good prices.

🍽 **Maxi Pizza** [301 B3] Bd Joffre. Hole-in-the-wall pizza kiosk with a few pavement tables.

🍽 **Melba** [301 B2] Bd Joffre; ⏰ Mon–Sat 07.00–noon & 15.30–18.30, Sun 07.00–noon. Pleasant little café with pastries, ice creams & good b/fast.

🍽 **Mouf'Rey** [301 B2] Reliable bakery with good bread & a range of pastries.

🍽 **Saïfy Fils** [301 B2] 30 Bd Joffre; ☏ 53 928 80; ⏰ 06.30–noon & 15.30–18.30, except Sun afternoon. Avg pastries, but decent coffee & fruit juices in season. B/fast & other savouries available.

12

🖥 **Wagon Bar** [299 A4] Gare des Manguiers; m 032 27 647 32/034 05 420 67; www. garedesmanguiers.mg; ⏱ Thu–Sat 19.00– midnight. Burgers, draught beer & cocktails with a relaxed ambience.

NIGHTLIFE

🍸 **New York New York** [301 B2] 5th floor, Azura Trade Center, Bd Joffre; m 032 05 400 05/032 96 350 86/034 92 543 29; e newyorkbar501@ outlook.fr; 🇫 New York New York Bar; ⏱ Mon– Sat 17.00–03.00, Sun closed. Tapas & shisha lounge with modern style; indoor & outdoor areas.
🍸 **XL Bar** [301 C3] Lively bar with loud music & plenty of dancing.
☆ **Ibiza** [301 C2] Rue Bertho; ⏱ Mon–Sat. Regular discotheque.
☆ **Neptune** [299 C2] At the hotel of the same name, this is a disco with an easy-going ambience.

☆ **Pandora** [299 A1] m 032 46 087 36/032 88 759 27; ⏱ Fri/Sat 22.00–late. Near the Miramar. An interesting & imaginatively decorated nightclub. Simple snacks served inc pizza.
☆ **Queen's Club** [299 C2] m 033 18 376 42. Small discotheque in the centre.
☆ **Stone Club** [299 B4] At Jupiter, this is a simple nightclub frequented mainly by locals.
☆ **VIP** [301 C2] 9 Rue Bertho; m 032 29 599 78/034 07 131 32; e leviptamatave@gmail.com; ⏱ Thu–Sat 22.00–06.00. Fancy new nightclub with big dance floor, big TVs, AC & modern sound/ lighting equipment. Many themed nights.

MONEY AND COMMUNICATIONS Toamasina has branches of all the major **banks**, all with ATMs and Western Union services. There are also many money changers around town; **NCH-Change** is recommended (*23 Bd Joffre*; m *032 07 158 58*; e *nch@ moov.mg*; ⏱ *Mon–Fri 08.00–17.00*).

There are several cybercafés, especially around Boulevard Joffre and Bazary Be, including **Orange Cyber** [301 B3], **CyberSky** [301 C4] (e *cyberskytmm@yahoo.fr*), **Speed.Net** [299 A3] (e *speedcomputertamatave@yahoo.fr*), **Butterfly** [301 C3] (e *butterfly.network.computer@gmail.com*) and at hotel **Melville** [299 A5].

Courier company **TNT** has a local branch (*16 Bd Joffre*; m *032 61 924 43*; e *commercial3@tnt.mg*).

SHOPPING There are two well-stocked supermarkets on Avenue de l'Indépendance: **Shoprite** [301 C1] (🕿 *53 316 88*; ⏱ *Mon–Thu 08.30–13.00 & 14.30–19.00, Fri/ Sat 08.30–19.00, Sun 09.00–13.00*) and **Score** [299 B4] (⏱ *Mon–Sat 08.30–13.00 & 14.30–19.00, Sun 08.30–12.30*). A second branch of Score is near Bazary Kely. Another supermarket is **Wu Chao Ying** [301 A4] (🕿 *53 923 08*), which also sells a good range of camping and outdoor gear.

In typical Malagasy logic, **Bazary Be** ('big market') [301 B2] in Toamasina is actually much smaller than **Bazary Kely** ('small market') [299 A3]. There is also a **floating market** on the Pangalanes Canal.

Toamasina is known for its tablecloths and woven baskets, and Bazary Be is a great place to find such goods. Many new tourist shops have opened in the area and along Boulevard Joffre, selling handicrafts, T-shirts and other souvenirs. **GM Fakra** is a mainly French bookshop with a decent selection of postcards, books and CDs of Malagasy music [301 B3] (🕿 *53 321 30*; ⏱ *Mon–Fri 08.00–noon & 14.30–18.00, Sat 08.00–noon*).

MEDICAL The clinic **Espace Medical** has a base in Toamasina [299 C2] (🕿 *53 315 66*; m *034 07 088 23*; *www.espacemedical.mg*). In an emergency call their central hotline (m *034 02 009 11*).

TOUR OPERATORS, VEHICLE HIRE AND FLIGHTS

✈ **Air Madagascar** [299 B4] 53 323 56/327 38; m 032 07 222 02/034 11 222 25; e tmmssmd@airmadagascar.com; ⊕ Mon–Fri 08.00–11.30 & 14.00–17.30, Sat 08.00–11.30

✈ **Madagasikara Airways** m 032 05 970 09/034 05 970 09/034 05 970 08

Ariane Tourism 53 307 35; m 033 09 70 53/034 03 035 05/032 07 729 51; e arianetour@yahoo.fr or arianetour@moov.mg; www.arianetourism-madagascar.com. Vehicle hire & tour operator attached to a tourism school.

Balladeuses m 034 67 017 92/032 41 405 13; e balladeuseiv@gmail.com. Fleet of 5 boats for Pangalanes trips.

Calypso Tours [301 C4] 53 304 57/58; m 032 04 628 82/032 40 247 78; e calypstour793@gmail.com. Based at Eden Hotel. Organiser of excursions, camping & especially Pangalanes Canal trips.

Diahnay Tours m 032 50 713 13/033 25 583 94/034 69 714 84; e diahnaytours@gmail.com or contact@diahnaytours.com; www.diahnaytours.com. Regional specialist for adventure, wildlife, history, culture & discovery. Based at the airport. See ad, page 282.

ElidolysMada 53 329 75; m 033 15 327 21/032 11 650 06; e elidolysmada@yahoo.fr or elidolysmada@orange.mg; www.elidolysmada.com. Tours inc Pangalanes & Ile Sainte Marie.

Mada Tour Antoka m 034 16 491 34/033 08 654 55/032 40 474 10; e mada.tour.antoka@gmail.com; www.mada-tour-antoka.com. East coast specialist with 4x4 rental.

Reis Travel 53 308 59; m 032 05 308 59; e reistravelmm@gmail.com. Launched in 2014. Local visits, excursions & vehicles.

Tamatave Fishing Club m 033 11 940 55/034 11 940 55; e tamatave.fishing@moov.mg. Offers fishing & diving trips.

Tropical Service [301 B3] 23 Bd Joffre; 53 336 79/89; m 032 02 173 12y; e tropicalservice@moov.mg; www.croisiere-madagascar.com. Travel agent inc car hire & ferry bookings.

🚗 **Amazing Grace** [299 C2] Rue Victor Hugo; 53 301 52; m 032 02 456 89/034 29 606 05. Vehicle hire.

🚗 **Mbola Tsara Voyage** [299 A2] 32 Bd Andovoranto m 032 02 162 76/033 75 629 35; e contact@mbolatsaravoyage.com; www.mbolatsaravoyage.com. 4x4 rental with driver.

🚗 **Rent 501** m 032 07 030 60/032 11 110 86/032 05 110 69; e contact@rent501.mg; www.rent501-madagascar.com. Quad, car & 4x4 hire.

TOURIST INFORMATION
The regional tourist information office is called **ORTT** [299 C2] (*83 Bd Joffre;* 53 912 14; m *034 45 450 85/032 41 581 16;* e *accueil.ortt@moov.mg or officetouristmv@yahoo.fr; www.tamatave501.com;* ⊕ *Mon–Fri 08.00–11.30 & 14.30–17.00, Sat 08.00–noon*). There is a regional guide federation, **FRGT**, with around 80 members (m *034 96 945 58*).

The **Alliance Française** [301 A4] often holds concerts, exhibitions, lectures and classes and can give information on other local festivals and events (53 334 94; m *033 15 325 86;* e *aftamve@moov.mg*).

WHAT TO SEE AND DO

City tour An organisation called the Friends of Toamasina, known by its French acronym ATOA, aims to raise awareness and encourage protection of the city's old buildings, many dating from the early colonial era. ATOA runs guided historical tours of the old part of the city; contact them to arrange one (53 315 79; m *032 07 437 21/032 11 566 31;* e *fortin.chan@moov.mg*). Alternatively, if you prefer to explore at your own pace, a pamphlet on sale at the tourist information office and GM Fakra bookshop details a self-guided city tour.

Museums There are three museums. The **Musée du Port** [299 D4] at the entrance of the harbour area details the history of Toamasina, both city and port, with a small section devoted to local culture. It has a particularly impressive collection of old photographs. The **Regional Museum** [299 C3] (⊕ *Tue–Sun 09.00–16.00*) is run by the university and brands itself a 'museum of ethnology, history and archaeology'.

There are exhibits from around the island relating to traditional village life, religious beliefs, musical instruments and so on. Signboards include text in English. The third is the **Museum of Art and Culture**, located next to Place Bien-Aimée [299 D5], a tranquil garden with magnificent banyan trees near the port.

Minigolf [299 D4] (⊕ *Mon–Sat 08.00–21.00*) This 18-hole course is at the end of Rue de Commerce. 'Sounds corny but it is nicely laid out and kept up with a bar and grill restaurant,' says Charlie Welch.

Horse-riding [299 A1] (℄ *53 342 93*) For those who have ever harboured romantic notions of riding a horse down a tropical beach, here's your chance. The equestrian centre is located off the main road to the airport, just south of the turning to Miramar Hotel.

Centre Lambahoany [299 A1] (*Bd de la Liberté;* m *034 01 149 10/032 71 938 69;* e *info@lambahoany.org; www.lambahoany.org*) This cultural and ecotourism centre run by a multilingual Dutch couple in the heart of the city runs art, language and cultural classes for locals, as well as hosting occasional music and dance events. There are seven mid-range bungalows for tourists who wish to stay.

The main goal of Project Lambahoany is to develop ecotourism in Fetraomby, northwest of Brickaville, giving the villagers supplementary income and a good reason to protect the forest. They can arrange treks of three to five days in this area, well off the beaten track, staying in simple accommodation and with the opportunity to see plenty of wildlife including indri.

Ile aux Prunes (Nosy Alanana) Located 12km north of Toamasina port and about 4.5km offshore, this 28ha beach-fringed island is covered in forest and topped by Africa's tallest lighthouse. Activities include swimming, snorkelling, walking around the island's coastline (2km), observing the resident flying fox colony and – from July to September – whale-watching either from a boat or the top of the lighthouse. Taller than the Statue of Liberty, Nelson's Column or the Leaning Tower of Pisa, this octagonal construction measures 60m high, making it the fourth-biggest lighthouse in the southern hemisphere.

The island can be reached in 40 minutes or so by boat. To arrange a visit, contact Maitsomanga (m *034 66 328 69;* e *maitsomanga@gmail.com; www.sites.google.com/ site/maitsomanga*). Other islands south of Toamasina can also be visited: Ile aux Sables (1hr) and Nosy Dombala (1½hrs).

The road north from Toamasina is tarred and in reasonable condition for the 163km to Soanierana-Ivongo.

PARC IVOLOINA (\ 53 308 42 *office*/53 996 54 *park;* m *032 05 103 07;* e *tim@ savethelemur.org or mfgmad@moov.mg; www.parcivoloina.org;* ⊕ *09.00–17.00; entry 20,000Ar, guide 10,000Ar)* This exceptional conservation centre and zoo with a 280ha reserve is run by the Madagascar Fauna & Flora Group, a consortium of some 30 zoos worldwide, and is well worth a visit.

You can explore the park on a network of forest and lakeside trails of varying levels of difficulty, which include wildlife interpretation boards, two waterfalls, a small pool and a viewpoint. Guides are not obligatory except for big groups. An abundance of birds, reptiles and lemurs can be seen from the trails. Free-ranging lemurs include black-and-white ruffed, white-fronted brown, red-bellied and crowned lemurs. There are other lemurs kept in captivity, including five aye-ayes (after-hours visits to see these nocturnal creatures active can be arranged with advance notice), as well as reptiles (tortoises, chameleons and boas), tenrecs, vasa parrots and tomato frogs. A snack bar which also sells souvenirs is located near the entrance and you can take a leisurely pirogue trip on the lake.

Do visit the education centre, where children from local primary schools come to learn about the importance of conservation in the area. The centre runs a teacher-training project, as well as courses in forest management, nursery management, reforestation, composting, intensive rice culture and more. The agro-forestry model station, which you see near the entrance, helps teach sustainable agriculture techniques to Malagasy cultivators.

Ivoloina is 12km north of Toamasina. It is possible to get there by taxi-brousse (1,500Ar), although only as far as the village, from where there is a 4km track to the park (but those on foot can take the 2km shortcut: turn left off the track 60m past the small bridge and welcome arch). The easiest way is to take a taxi from town directly to the park (about 70,000Ar for the round trip); tuk-tuk and pousse-pousse are more budget-friendly alternatives. If camping, you'll need to provide your own tent and food.

CONTINUING NORTH Some 16km from Toamasina at Antetezambaro, and about 7km further on at Ambodiatafana, there are some out-of-the-way **places to stay**:

🏠 **Chez Paul** (6 rooms) Ambodiatafana; m 032 44 203 76/033 19 258 49/033 71 932 67; e chezpaul@hotmail.fr; www.chezpaul-madagascar.com. Quiet & relaxing seaside spot offering en-suite rooms with sat-TV & simple but tasty local cuisine. **€€€**

🏠 **Taratra Village** (10 bungalows) Antetezambaro; \ 53 305 88; m 034 63 204 80; e taratravillage@ymail.com. A countryside leisure area with large swimming pools, artificial lake & sports facilities. An assortment of chalets, some en suite. Solar power. A delightful spot for strolls & picnics. **€€€**

FOULPOINTE (MAHAVELONA) The town of Foulpointe is experiencing a surge in popularity as a beach destination but it otherwise is unremarkable, except for nearby **Fort Manda**, with mighty walls faced with an iron-hard mixture of sand, shells and eggs. Some old British cannons marked with the royal initials 'GR' can be seen at this circular fortress, which was built in the early 19th century by local Merina governor Rafaralahy shortly after the Merina conquest of the east coast. The entry fee is 3,000Ar and guided tours are available.

12

There is also a **golf course**, created in 1967 and recently expanded to a full 18 holes. Much of the course is on undulating ground so several of the holes have to be played blind.

Foulpointe is 60km from Toamasina (5,000Ar/1½hrs by taxi-brousse). It is a beach resort with calm waters (safe for swimming), popular with Malagasy and *vazaha* alike.

Where to stay and eat

Azura (36 rooms) PK 60, RN5; m 032 03 420 66/033 37 420 66/034 05 420 66/034 11 007 64; e azuraresort@gmail.com or azuraresort@ moov.mg or info@azuragolf.mg; www.azuragolf. mg. New in 2015, this 37ha luxury hotel has its own 18-hole golf course, as well as tennis courts, pool, kayaks & spa. Spacious rooms with contemporary furnishings equipped with king-size bed, private terrace, TV, Wi-Fi & minibar. Restaraunt Corail serves gourmet delights. Golf buggies for the 600m beach transfer. ☸

Cigale (8 rooms) m 032 07 907 79/034 07 907 79; e contact@hotel-lacigale.com; www. hotel-lacigale.com. French-run beachfront hotel. Clean en-suite rooms with Wi-Fi, balcony & safe; some also with AC, minibar & sea view. €€€€

Zina (23 rooms) m 034 66 714 66. Brand-new hotel offering en-suite rooms on 3 floors around a central courtyard with swimming pool; AC, sat-TV, Wi-Fi, minibar & safe. Terrace with sea view. B/fast inc. €€€€

Lagon (10 bungalows) m 033 03 361 80/033 09 106 32; e hotelagon1@yahoo. fr or lagonfoulpointe@gmail.com; www. lagonfoulpointe.com. Bungalows all of unique designs & different sizes, a hop, skip & jump from the beach. €€€–€€€€

Au Beau Séjour (4 rooms) \ 53 952 33; m 032 40 561 56/033 14 457 35/033 14 657 54/034 74 953 19; e aubeausejour501@gmail. com; www.aubeausejour.com. Studios & villas ideal for medium & long stays. €€€

Génération (14 rooms & 7 bungalows) \ 57 220 22; m 032 11 238 22; e generationhotel@ moov.mg; www.generationhotel-tamatave.com/ foulpointe. Set back from the beach, en-suite rooms with safe & hot water; some with TV. Wi-Fi. Under same ownership as hotel with same name in Toamasina. €€€

Grand Bleu (3 rooms & 7 bungalows) m 032 02 311 61 (reception)/034 07 220 06; e hotel.joffre@moov.mg; www.grandbleu-tamatave.com. En-suite beachfront accommodation. Rooms have AC. Also a 6-bed villa. €€€

Les 3 Cocotiers (20 rooms) m 034 11 100 05 (Tana)/034 11 100 06; e les3cocotiers@ymail. com. Clean functional rooms with TV & en-suite bathroom. €€€

Lovencie Lodge (10 rooms & 8 bungalows) m 032 04 142 14/034 07 142 14; e contact@ lovencielodge.com. 1km from town with trpl bungalows & dbl/trpl rooms, all en suite with AC, sat-TV & Wi-Fi. Swimming pool. €€€

Manda Beach (24 rooms & 18 bungalows) m 032 03 220 00/033 15 220 00/034 11 220 00; e mandabeach@moov.mg; www.mandabeach-hotel.com. Bright rooms & excellent bungalows set in a garden around a pool. Credit cards accepted. €€€

Raozy (9 bungalows) m 032 51 584 92; f Bungalow Raozy. A row of small dbl bungalows with bathrooms 125m from the beach. Wi-Fi. 4x4 hire. €€€

Au Gentil Pêcheur (5 rooms & 20 bungalows) m 034 16 581 16; e augentilpecheur@yahoo.fr. Beachfront, next to Manda Beach. Bungalows & good food. Credit cards accepted. €€

ANALALAVA COMMUNITY RESERVE (m *033 15 324 83/032 02 773 94*) This is a 204ha fragment of low-elevation humid forest 7km southwest of Foulpointe (4x4 required in the rainy season). Although small and degraded, it is of high conservation importance, being the only forest remaining in the area and supporting a rich biodiversity including 26 palms, 20 orchids, five lemurs (including the rare Simmons' mouse lemur, a species discovered in 2006), 52 birds, and flying foxes.

Managed by the local community with assistance from Missouri Botanical Gardens, it has recently been opened up to ecotourism with an easy 1-hour circuit, a moderate 3-hour circuit and a night walk circuit. Permits can be bought on arrival and guides are obligatory. There are two rooms, two bungalows and a campsite with toilet and shower facilities. A local women's association prepares authentic Betsimisaraka meals.

MAHAMBO This is a lovely beach resort with safe swimming, offering a more tranquil alternative to Foulpointe with excellent beaches and four great and consistent **surfing** spots (a couple of surf schools rent out boards and gear). You can also take a **pirogue trip** up a nearby river.

Mahambo is 85km from Toamasina (6,000Ar/2hrs by taxi-brousse). From Soanierana-Ivongo or Ile Sainte Marie, you can also get here by ferry (page 298).

⌂ Where to stay and eat

⌂ **Pirogue** (6 rooms & 10 bungalows) m 032 03 768 10/032 03 768 18 (restaurant)/033 05 971 17/033 08 768 10/033 08 768 18 (manager); e info@lapirogue-hotel.com or la.pirogue@gmail.com; www.pirogue-hotel.com. Wonderful bungalows, very tastefully decorated with artisanal products. Fishing & boat trips. Good restaurant. Wi-Fi. €€€€–€€€€€

⌂ **Hibiscus** (6 bungalows) m 032 77 098 59/034 17 821 11; e hibiscus.mahambo@gmail. com. Set among 3ha of lush gardens a few steps from the sea, the bungalows each have a private terrace & en-suite facilities. €€€

⌂ **Mamaki Onja (Pil Pil Manga)** (2 bungalows) m 032 60 906 05/033 01 181 92; www.mamakionja.wordpress.com. Set in a lush garden near the sea, this place styles itself as a surf camp; gear available for hire. Camping permitted. €€€

⌂ **Chez Sandrina** m 033 08 593 84/033 11 941 44. Bungalows with shared cold-water facilities. €€

⌂ **Orchidées** (6 bungalows) m 032 57 188 81/032 79 001 31/032 85 334 61. Good-value dbl & family rooms set in garden in a perfect location near beach. €€

⌂ **Urich** m 033 07 171 69. Well-kept cosy en-suite bungalows (cold water). €€

⌂ **Vanilla Café** m 032 49 529 97. Simple clean bungalows run by a group of friendly ex-rappers from Fianarantsoa. Splendid restaurant. €€

⌂ **Ylang-Ylang** (10 bungalows) m 033 08 268 22/033 14 041 86/033 76 659 96; e petalepirogue@yahoo.fr. A nice bungalow complex set in a quiet garden. Bungalows for up to 6 people; all with hot water. Good restaurant. €€

⌂ **Zanatany** (7 bungalows) m 032 05 324 73/033 15 324 73/034 45 756 66. En-suite wooden bungalows (cold water). €€

VAVATENINA AND THE SMUGGLERS' PATH Between Mahambo and Fenoarivo is a road leading inland to Vavatenina (where there are basic bungalows) and on to Anjahambe. This town marks the end of the Smugglers' Path from Lake Alaotra (see page 272), though only a masochist would attempt it in the uphill direction starting from this end.

FENOARIVO ATSINANANA (FÉNÉRIVE EST) Some 15km beyond Mahambo is the former capital of the Betsimisaraka Empire. There is a factory in town which distils the essence of cloves, cinnamon and green peppers for the perfume industry. They are not geared up for tourist visits but will show you round if you ask. There are branches of BOA and BNI – the last banks on the route north until Mananara.

⌂ Where to stay and eat

⌂ **Sahorana Lodge** (3 bungalows) m 033 82 926 67/034 17 074 47; e sahoranalodge@ hotmail.fr; www.sahoranalodge.com. The young couple running this lodge, John & Sandra, take responsible tourism seriously, with solar power & spacious bungalows made from

sustainable natural materials. 5min from the beach. €€€

⌂ **Ruschia Village** (6 rooms & 18 bungalows) ☎ 53 314 64. Bright bungalows in secluded beachfront setting. Hot water & electricity eves only. €€–€€€

TAMPOLO FOREST (m *034 05 742 49*; e *mia.razafimahefa@gmail.com*) About 10km north of Fenoarivo is this 675ha forestry station. It is managed by the agricultural branch of Tana's university (*www.essa-forets.org*) and partly supported by the Lemur Conservation Foundation (*www.lemurreserve.org*).

There is an interpretive museum and paths into the coastal forest that can be taken with guides, offering a good opportunity to see some of Madagascar's most endangered flora: the littoral forest. Wildlife includes seven lemur species, 19 lizards, 12 snakes, 16 frogs and 52 birds.

Visitors can be accommodated in a six-bed guesthouse (Trano Soa), a 20-bed dorm hut and campsites for those with their own tents.

SOANIERANA-IVONGO At the end of the tarred road, this little town is the embarkation point for the ferry crossing to Ile Sainte Marie. The boat transfers of Melissa Express to Mananara and Maroantsetra also start here (page 298). Soanierana (or 'S-Ivongo' as it is often abbreviated) has only the most basic accommodation.

AMBATOVAKY SPECIAL RESERVE (m *032 04 923 05*; e *tmv.parks@gmail.com*) This very isolated special reserve between the Marimbona and Simianona rivers has protected 60,050ha of low-altitude primary rainforest west of Soanierana since 1958. Ranging between 400m and 1,185m elevation, this remote forest is home to 11 species of lemur (including aye-aye, indri, diademed sifaka and black-and-white ruffed lemur), 110 birds (including the rare Madagascar serpent eagle) and 113 frogs and reptiles. The eating of pork, goat, frogs and lemurs is *fady* in the area.

The park office is in Soanierana, where you can get information about visiting the reserve. Infrastructure in the forest is minimal; as yet no circuits have been officially established. Access is by boat (3–7hrs) upriver followed by a hike of a day or so.

SOANIERANA-IVONGO TO MAROANTSETRA

The road is in a terrible condition – including countless rivers with dodgy bridges or ferry crossings – for almost all of this 239km stretch, but nowadays taxi-brousses do make it through, except in the rainy season (January–March). Co-operatives KoFiMan and KoFiFen both operate a Toamasina–Maroantsetra service (160,000Ar) on roughly alternate days and the latter also offers private 4x4 transfers (1,500,000Ar).

The taxi-brousse takes at least 2½ days, typically 3½, and sometimes up to a week to get through! 'The journey on this spectacularly difficult trail may well be the most uncomfortable taxi-brousse trip in Madagascar,' notes Chris Inman, 'but it's probably the safest, as it's impossible to get up excessive speed.' James Wright's party of three rented out a taxi-brousse all to themselves: 'We had a fantastic time. The road was rough, always uncomfortable and often slow. The ferries in particular were frustrating. I didn't, however, feel unsafe at any point.'

Be aware that, heading north from Toamasina, taxi-brousses rarely have empty places until well beyond Soanierana; finding onward transport will be challenging if you want to break the Toamasina–Maroantsetra route into stages, so we recommend hiring a 4x4 and driver if you want to see the sights *en route*. Those whose objective is simply to reach Mananara or Maroantsetra, rather than to have an adventure along the way, should opt for the Melissa Express boat transfer (page 298).

MANOMPANA This charming and characterful village, some 40km from Soanierana, is a peaceful destination in itself. There is good surfing and swimming in the area and an attractive lagoon at Pointe Titingue. A French volunteer-run cultural centre for local children, **La Marmaille à La Case**, makes for an inspiring visit (m *033 73 802 94*; e *marmaillemada@aol.com; http://marmaillealacase.free.fr*).

Where to stay and eat

Au Bout du Monde Sahabevava; www. ivoyage.fr/auboutdumonde. 4km south of Manompana. Bungalows in a shady 3ha garden; owned by a globetrotting Frenchman. Bike hire. **€–€€**

Bon Ancrage (Chez Wen-Ki) (9 bungalows) 53 957 72; m 033 19 746 41. Secluded spacious beachfront bungalows with bucket showers, but becoming run-down say recent guests. Charming owner. Bike hire. **€–€€**

Zaetoune (4 bungalows) 57 911 82. Near the taxi-brousse station. Shared facilities. **€**

AMBODIRIANA FOREST (m *033 13 846 97; entry 5,000Ar, guide 5,000Ar*) About 6km northwest of Manompana, this small reserve protects 65ha of lowland rainforest and is home to eight lemur species. There are three dramatic waterfalls connected by well-marked paths including a botanical trail. A day visit is quite possible but there are basic camping facilities and a cheap bungalow for those wishing to stay a night.

They also run fascinating tours of Manompana village during which you will learn about shipbuilding, clove distillation and local customs. You will see the baker's oven, coffee being dried on mats, vanilla pods drying in glass Coca-Cola bottles and sea cucumbers drying on mats before being shipped to Japan for sushi, and witness production of *betsabetsa*, a bitter local alcoholic drink made in a week using sugarcane juice. Visit ADEFA's office in the village for more information.

ANTANAMBE Around 37km north of Manompana, on the southern edge of the Mananara-Nord National Park, is this pretty village with a couple of places to stay.

Where to stay and eat

Tany Marina (Chez Grondin) (6 bungalows) m 033 01 100 59. This lodge is deservedly popular. Considering its remote location it is rather comfy, with gas cooking, filtered running water, pressure showers, flush toilets & comfortable beds, not to mention a great restaurant with Creole & French cooking & fresh fish. Diving/fishing excursions & tours to Mananara-Nord. **€€–€€€**

Vahibe Budget accommodation next to the ferry some 2km north of town. **€**

SAHASOA The 15km or so from Antanambe to Sahasoa, the gateway village to Mananara-Nord National Park, is in a particularly dreadful state and it may take several hours. But the views from this coast-hugging road are spectacular. The **park office** is at the southern end of the village. Three spacious seafront bungalows are run by the local women's association (m *033 19 671 81*; **€€**) and very basic huts can be found at **Hôtel du Centre** (**€**).

MANANARA-NORD NATIONAL PARK (*22 596 28*; m *034 49 401 56*; e *mananara_ nationalpark@yahoo.fr*) This park is part of a UNESCO Biosphere Reserve covering an area of 144,000ha, with a variety of ecosystems including tropical humid forest, sandy coastal plains with littoral vegetation, river vegetation, mangrove formations, marshlands and coral reefs. Despite its name and apparent proximity to Mananara, the state of the road means that the entry (at Sahasoa) is half a day's journey away by 4x4.

A handful of adventurous tourists visit the park's marine reserve that protects, among other things, dugongs. At its centre is the small island of **Nosy Atafana**, where Madagascar flying foxes can be seen in great numbers. You can arrange a boat via the park office; the trip takes 2 hours each way. There is a campsite on the island.

Very few people visit the forest, which from Sahasoa is a 2-hour hike inland across degraded habitat. Camping is possible at the edge of the park. The terrain is moderately tough going, with three trails of 16–20km and many impressive views.

Guides for both the terrestrial and marine areas cost 12,000Ar per day, porters 8,000Ar and camping 5,000Ar per tent. The park has welcome centres in both Antanambe and Mananara, which you would be well advised to visit before proceeding to Sahasoa since the park cannot always cater for unexpected visitors.

SERANAMBE Ongoing transport becomes increasingly scarce and the condition of the road doesn't get any better. Midway along the 32km stretch from Sahasoa to Mananara is this small village with very basic accommodation at **Capital** (**€**).

MANANARA Near this small friendly town 127km north of Soanierana is one of the only places in Madagascar where visitors stand a good chance of seeing a free-ranging aye-aye. Mananara has a lively market, BOA bank and cellphone coverage. About 3km south of the village is a secluded bay, protected by a reef, with safe swimming.

There is a small airport for charter planes but no scheduled flights at the time of writing; otherwise you can come by taxi-brousse (page 310) or Melissa Express, the twice-weekly boat service connecting Mananara with Maroantsetra and Toamasina (see page 298).

Where to stay and eat

Aye-Aye (6 bungalows) m 032 95 883 96. On the beachfront opposite the airport with pleasant en-suite bungalows. Can arrange Aye-Aye Island visits. **€€**

Chez Roger (6 bungalows) m 032 52 329 87. Run by Roger, owner of Aye-Aye Island. Good en-suite bungalows with hot water & reliable restaurant. **€–€€**

AYE-AYE ISLAND This is *the* reason most people come to Mananara. The privately owned river island of about 6ha has a few resident aye-ayes, transplanted here some decades ago for their protection, as well as white-fronted brown lemurs. Normally aye-ayes live high in the rainforest canopy and have large territories. On Aye-Aye Island, however, their range is restricted by the island's small size and the trees are much lower and less dense, so they are comparatively easy to see. They are partial to coconuts and coconut palms are found in abundance here.

A sighting is by no means guaranteed, but at least half of the tourists who make an evening visit to the island are lucky. Chances are increased for those staying overnight (you can camp or there's a small hut) but not everyone is successful. Wybe Rood wonders if the elusive animal even exists: 'Didn't see any! After having spent almost two years in Madagascar, and having been to Nosy Mangabe and Aye-Aye Island, I am now convinced this creature is a fabrication!'

Botanically the island is interesting; not only are there coconuts, but bananas, pineapples, jackfruits, papayas, vanilla, coffee, cloves and maize are all cultivated.

Visits can be arranged at the hotels in Mananara. The cost is 20,000Ar per person, including the pirogue crossing.

ANTONGIL BAY Mananara is situated at the mouth of Antongil Bay, a large inlet some 80km long and 30km wide. In 2015 the whole bay was designated as

Madagascar's first shark sanctuary. The new marine protections include restrictions on international fishing boats in the bay, the establishment of locally managed marine areas, and the granting of exclusive use and management rights to local communities. The measures are hoped to help protect Antongil Bay's 19 species of shark and marine ecosystems while supporting local livelihoods.

From Mananara, the road runs 112km up the western side of the bay, past villages Manambolosy, Rantabe, and Voloina, to Maroantsetra – shortly beyond which the road terminates (continuing overland to Antalaha means a trek across Masoala Peninsula).

Reader Jeremy Sabel reports that Mananara to Maroantsetra 'took 14 hours in a 4x4 taxi-brousse. The road was terrible and the passengers were packed in like sardines, and two suffered from motion sickness.' Dylan Lossie did it in the opposite direction: 'We went by taxi-brousse but the vehicle completely collapsed after 20km and we had to leave the poor driver and his destroyed vehicle behind. We walked 2km to Voloina. Then another 12km to Rantabe, where we camped on a beach. The roads are in a terrible state. Nevertheless, the area is beautiful and I would not have missed it!'

MAROANTSETRA Nestled at the back of Antongil Bay, Maroantsetra is Madagascar at its most authentic. Well away from the usual tourist circuits, it is a prosperous, friendly little town, and the gateway to a number of Madagascar's most impressive rainforest protected areas.

One can arrange a local tour to see nearby village life, vanilla and cinnamon plantations and the huge locally endemic tomato frogs that live in people's backyards.

Getting there and away Flights are often booked up well in advance. Currently at least two flights a week connect Maroantsetra with Tana, sometimes via Toamasina. The airport is 8km from town (15,000Ar by taxi).

You can come **by road** from the south if you have several days to spare and an adventurous spirit (page 310) or otherwise by **boat** from Soanierana with Melissa Express (page 298) whose Maroantsetra office is opposite Pagode Inn.

From Antalaha and Cap Est to the east, there is no road, but you can hike over several days (page 321).

 Where to stay and eat

🏠 **Relais du Masoala** [314 A7] (15 bungalows) m 034 14 003 16/033 12 447 48/034 14 279 76; e relaisdumasoala@cortezexpeditions. mg. Spacious bungalows with swimming pool set in 7ha of gardens & coconut groves overlooking Antongil Bay. Very comfortable; good food. €€€€–€€€€€

🏠 **Hippocampe** [314 A7] (3 bungalows & 6 rooms) m 032 64 418 99; e madahippocampe@ live.fr; www.madahippocampe.com. Seafront B&B 1km past Relais du Masoala. Swimming pool. 4x4s, fishing gear & boats (can do transfers from Ile Sainte Marie). €€€€

🏠 **Masoala Resort** [314 A7] (13 bungalows) m 032 11 075 51/033 11 051 52/033 14 075 51; e info@masoalaresort.com or masoala.resort@ yahoo.fr; www.masoalaresort.com. Indian-owned beachfront hotel; beautiful

en-suite bungalows with TV, minibar & balcony with hammock & great view; most with AC & sat-TV. Swimming pool. Camping possible. Visa accepted. €€€€

🏠 **Manga Beach** [314 C6] (17 rooms) m 032 40 676 88/032 54 795 04/034 07 019 77; e mangabeach.hotel@yahoo.com; www. mangabeach-madagascar.com. Riverside location with views across the bay to Nosy Mangabe. Comfy en-suite rooms with AC, minibar, TV & Wi-Fi. €€€–€€€€

🏠 **Coco Beach** [314 A7] (10 bungalows) m 032 04 807 58/032 47 025 91; e cocobeachhotelmaroantsetra@yahoo.fr. Good-value riverside en-suite dbl bungalows, some with hot water. Meals of variable quality; service always slow. Striped tenrecs may be seen in the garden at night. €€–€€€

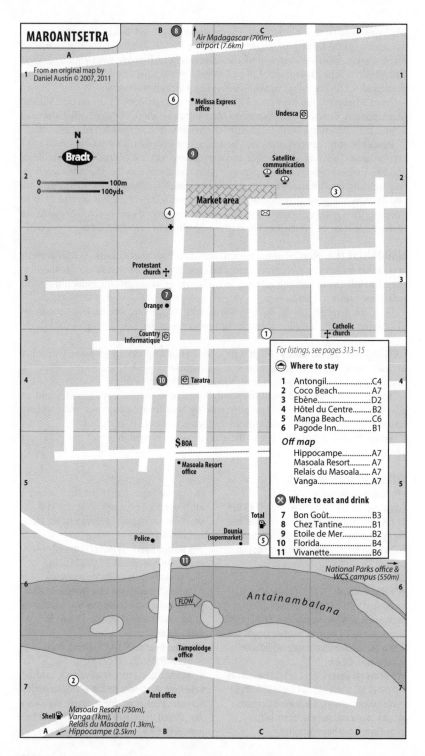

MAROANTSETRA

From an original map by
Daniel Austin © 2007, 2011

Air Madagascar (700m),
airport (7.6km)

N

Bradt

0 ____ 100m
0 ____ 100yds

Melissa Express
office

Undesca

Satellite
communication
dishes

Market area

Protestant
church

Orange

Country
Informatique

Taratra

Catholic
church

$ BOA

Masoala Resort
office

Total

Dounia
(supermarket)

Police

Antainambalana

FLOW

National Parks office &
WCS campus (550m)

Tampolodge
office

Arol office

Shell
Masoala Resort (750m),
Vanga (1km),
Relais du Masoala (1.3km),
Hippocampe (2.5km)

For listings, see pages 313–15

Where to stay

1 Antongil.......................C4
2 Coco Beach.................A7
3 Ebène...........................D2
4 Hôtel du Centre.........B2
5 Manga Beach.............C6
6 Pagode Inn.................B1

Off map

Hippocampe................A7
Masoala Resort...........A7
Relais du Masoala.......A7
Vanga............................A7

Where to eat and drink

7 Bon Goût.....................B3
8 Chez Tantine..............B1
9 Etoile de Mer.............B2
10 Florida..........................B4
11 Vivanette.....................B6

🏠 **Ebène** [314 D2] (16 bungalows) m 032 49 971 16/033 14 908 73; e mahafenokathy@yahoo. fr. Basic en-suite rooms at 2 locations: in town & nr the river. €€

🏠 **Pagode Inn** [314 B1] (16 bungalows) m 032 75 373 03/032 78 398 02/033 05 198 99. Dbl bungalows with hot or (much cheaper) cold water. Good restaurant. €€

🏠 **Vanga** [314 A7] m 032 43 877 43/032 88 391 59; e hotelevanga@yahoo.fr. Spacious beachfront bungalows looking out to Nosy Mangabe. En-suite but cold water only. €€

🏠 **Antongil** [314 C4] (8 rooms) ✆57 720 17. Rooms have fans, wide communal balconies, showers & shared toilets. €

🏠 **Hôtel du Centre** [314 B2] ✆57 721 31. Across from the market; inexpensive rooms & bungalows. €

✕ **Chez Tantine** [314 B1] Recommended Malagasy eatery near the north market.

✕ **Etoile de Mer** [314 B2] A simple Chinese restaurant behind the central market.

✕ **Florida** [314 B4] A popular Chinese restaurant recommended by reader Steve C.

✕ **Vivanette** [314 B6] Open-air restaurant & bar built out over the river. To the right as you come into town from the Coco Beach. Good food.

☕ **Bon Goût** [314 B3] A *salon de thé*; good for b/fast. Nice bread, croissants, *pains au chocolat* & cakes.

Money and communications Maroantsetra has just one bank, a branch of BOA [314 B5] with an ATM. There is a Western Union service both here and at the post office [314 C2]. Internet is available at a number of cybercafés around town [314 B4/C1].

Tour operators and park offices The regional tourist office is ORTANALA (m *032 52 357 90*; e *ortanala@gmail.com*). The Wildlife Conservation Society, which administers Makira Natural Park, opened a riverside Environmental Campus at the southeast of town in 2013 [314 D6]. The site includes a welcome centre, the Masoala Interpretation Centre, an ecoshop and a viewpoint tower for seeing Antongil Bay. Madagascar National Parks (m *032 41 944 46*), responsible for Masoala National Park and Nosy Mangabe Special Reserve, has also constructed an office at this site – entirely from endangered rosewood!

In addition to the park offices, most of the hotels run excursions or can hook you up with someone who does, and here are some local tour operators:

Mada Expeditions m 032 11 882 68/032 40 377 77; e contact@mada-expeditions.com; www. mada-expeditions.com. Tana-based but specialises particularly in trips up RN5 & kayaking around Masoala.

Nico Tours m 034 21 685 85/032 86 953 64; e masoalasafary@gmail.com; www. nicotoursmasoala.wordpress.com. Run by the young & Affable guide Nico, offering tours & treks in the area inc Makira.

CPALI (m *032 04 452 46*; e *mamycpali@gmail.com*) Short for 'Conservation through Poverty Alleviation, International', this is a sustainable livelihoods project focused primarily on wild silk production with a local partner called SEPALI. Farmers plant native host trees on their land and rear species of silk that are very different from those on the plateau.

Guided by a member of the team, you can tour an active farm with a butterfly garden and silk-processing centre – but check ahead as these are seasonal. Visitors are expected to make a donation. For more on CPALI, see page 138.

FARANKARAINA TROPICAL PARK Situated 9km east of Maroantsetra, this 1,650ha reserve is managed by Antongil Conservation (a collaboration of British and French zoos) and was opened to ecotourism in 2008. Red-fronted brown lemurs and black-and-white ruffed lemurs live here and aye-ayes are sometimes seen, as

Journey up the coffee-coloured river that opens into the sea at Maroantsetra and you will discover Madagascar's last large tract of intact rainforest. While the Masoala Peninsula has long been frequented by birders and hikers, Makira remains almost entirely uncharted terrain. Though remote and difficult to access, discovering its pristine heart is worth every effort.

We set up a research camp deep inside Makira and established camera trap grids in the surrounding forest to survey the resident carnivore species.

The forest is stunningly beautiful and astonishingly diverse. The giant trees rise up to form one of the world's highest rainforest canopies. Small puddles immediately fill with tadpoles. Technicolor mantella frogs flit around the forest floor. Pygmy chameleons stalk their tiny prey in the leaf litter.

Daytime walks into the forest rewarded me with regular lemur sightings, including that of white-fronted, brown and occasionally red-bellied lemurs. The raucous calls of the black-and-white ruffed lemurs were heard on a daily basis, but the beautiful striped animals were rarely seen. At night in the lower canopy I would find brown mouse, eastern woolly, greater dwarf, and a pair of eastern fork-marked lemurs that barked loudly from the giant *Canarium* tree in our camp.

Each morning I would open my tent and wake to the wail of Madagascar's largest lemur species, the ape-like indri. Their sound is a sonorous and mournful warble that reverberates throughout the entire forest, more reminiscent of whale song than of any primate. These are perhaps the last forests where the indri remains totally wild and largely naïve to humans.

One night in camp I was woken by a sudden squawking of our three 'camp chickens' (the unfortunate birds had been lugged in on foot for miles by the Malagasy crew). I threw open my tent and just caught green eyeshine in the light of my head torch before the creature slunk into the forest. The chickens were quivering in a corner, feathers everywhere – a fossa had just paid us a visit! This predator is Madagascar's answer to wolves and leopards: an overgrown tree-climbing mongoose with a taste for lemur. I must have scared it off as I emerged from my tent. The following night the same avian racket jerked me from my slumber; the chickens had been attacked again, but this time I found a 4m tree boa with bronze chicken feathers still dangling from its lower jaw.

The great green forests of Makira and their many residents are, however, far from safe. I witnessed many signs of illegal rosewood logging, agricultural encroachment and lemur poaching (lemurs and fossa are trapped and killed for meat or brought out of the forest alive in cages to be sold as pets).

As part of Madagascar's – and possibly the world's – most unique and wildest rainforest wilderness, Makira is worth every ounce of the effort it requires to get there. Unlike adjacent Masoala, much of Makira is still unexplored. While checking the camera traps one morning I encountered a bird I didn't recognise and couldn't identify. Puzzled by the sighting I shrugged it off until encountering the same species several more times. Upon returning to the UK I consulted the country's leading ornithologists, sending them my notes and photos. The bird doesn't even closely resemble any known bird in the country. Though it is yet to be confirmed, all evidence suggests the species is completely new to science.

Toby Nowlan is an expedition leader and researcher for the BBC Natural History Unit.

are leaf-tailed geckos. There are four circuits (1–4km each) on which to explore the park. Nearby villages are being increasingly involved in forest management and an annual Lemurs Festival – with dancing and drawing contests and traditional music – attracts hundreds of locals.

Entrance to the park costs 10,000Ar per person and guides 25,000Ar per day per group. You can camp for 5,000Ar or stay in a simple bungalow for 50,000Ar. Antongil Conservation has an office in Maroantsetra where you can arrange your visit. Access is by pirogue (3,000Ar/1½hrs) to the village of Andranofotsy, from where the park is an hour's walk along the beach or a further half-hour pirogue ride (5,000Ar). Alternatively motorboat transfers can be arranged from Maroantsetra for 150,000Ar.

MAKIRA NATURAL PARK (✆ 22 597 89; e *wcsmad@moov.mg*) This protected area between Masoala and Marojejy national parks was established in 2012 and covers a massive 372,470ha – almost twice the size of Mauritius. See the box opposite for a recent visitor's description of this enchanting forest.

At the time of writing, infrastructure for ecotourism is still in the early stages of development, but there is already a community-run site called Sahavilory Camp. Access is by boat upriver and Makira's nearest fringes can even be visited as a day trip from Maroantsetra. Visit the WCS Environmental Campus in town to organise a trip there.

MASOALA PENINSULA

Masoala (pronounced 'mash*wahl*') is one of the largest and most diverse areas of virgin rainforest in Madagascar. The peninsula's importance was recognised by the French back in 1927 when they created a small reserve there, but independent Madagascar was swift to remove the protection in 1964. However, in 1997 most of the peninsula (240,000ha) was declared a national park, and later three marine sections were added.

Despite difficulty of access and dodgy weather, this area is perhaps the leading destination for ecotourists who want to see the country's most important natural habitat in terms of biodiversity – the eastern rainforest, exemplified by Nosy Mangabe and the Masoala-Makira rainforest belt. These places require fitness and fortitude but the rewards for nature lovers are great. Fitness is needed for the hills and mud which are an aspect of all the reserves, and fortitude because this is the wettest place in Madagascar, with annual rainfall exceeding 500cm. The driest months tend to be November and December.

Switzerland's Zoo Zürich has established a link with Masoala and finances development projects to encourage conservation. Their Masoala Kely exhibit – an 11,000m² indoor replica rainforest at their Zürich zoo – is well worth visiting.

MASOALA NATIONAL PARK (✆ 88 812 89; m 033 49 402 74/033 49 402 75/032 02 675 72; e *masoala.park@yahoo.fr* or *msl@parcs-madagascar.com*) Visitors should be warned that logging and clearance for agriculture still persist (see box, page 319) and maps of the peninsula tend to look deceptively green. That said, there are still large expanses of virgin forest along with stunning beaches of golden sand dotted with eroded rocks. Some parts of the peninsula, seen on a sunny day, can arguably be described as the most beautiful in Madagascar.

The wildlife is equally stunning. You will need to work for it, but nevertheless the opportunity to see the red ruffed lemur in its only habitat, helmet and Bernier's

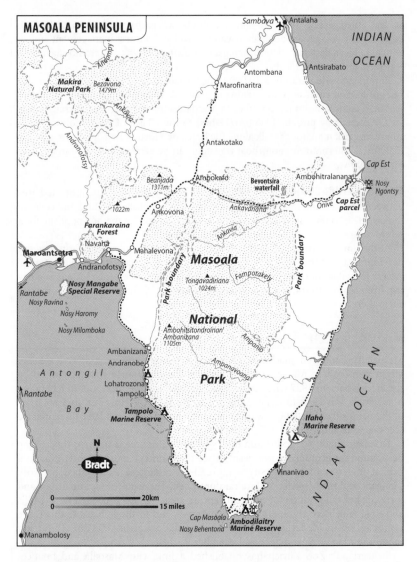

MASOALA PENINSULA

Sambava • Antalaha

INDIAN

OCEAN

Antombana
Marofinaritra

Antsirabato

Makira Natural Park
Bezavona 1479m

Antakotako

Cap Est

Beanjada 1311m
Ampokafo
Bevontsira waterfall
Ambohitralanana
Nosy Ngontsy

1022m
Ankovona
Ankavanaha
Onive
Cap Est parcel

Farankaraina Forest
Navaha
Mahalevona

Ankavia

Maroantsetra
Andranofotsy

Masoala

Park boundary

Park boundary

Tongavadiriana 1024m
Fampotakely

Rantabe
Nosy Ravina
Nosy Haromy
Nosy Milomboka

Nosy Mangabe Special Reserve

National

Ambohitsitondroinan' Ambanizana 1105m

Ampanio

Ambanizana
Andranobe

Ampanavoana

A n t o n g i l

Lohatrozona
Tampolo

Park

Rantabe

B a y

Tampolo Marine Reserve

Ifaho Marine Reserve

N

Bradt

0   20km
0   15 miles

Vinanivao

INDIAN   OCEAN

• Manambolosy

Cap Masoala
Nosy Behentona
Ambodilaitry Marine Reserve

vangas, scaly ground-roller and other rare endemic birds plus a host of reptiles and invertebrates is not to be missed.

Unless you're up for some serious trekking, Masoala can be reached from Maroantsetra only by boat (1½–2hrs). Boat transfers do not come cheap but sharing with others will reduce the expense. To keep costs down, avoid going through a tour operator or hotel and negotiate a package combining Masoala and Nosy Mangabe directly with a boat operator (your park guide can help with bargaining). Crossings of the bay should be made as early in the morning as possible to avoid rough seas. By asking around, those on a tight budget may be able to find a local cargo boat willing to drop them on the peninsula.

Park permits should be purchased at the office in Maroantsetra; prices are on page 73. Guides cost 100,000Ar for a full day or 150,000Ar for an expert birding guide.

Derek Schuurman

The 2009 coup left a political vacuum which was swiftly exploited by loggers who began plundering protected areas for precious wood. Most of this illegal activity took place in the rainforests of the Atsinanana, collectively recognised as a World Heritage Site. In just a few months, at least 100,000 rosewood and ebony trees worth hundreds of millions of dollars were felled. The logs, the vast majority of which were shipped to China, begin their journey to the ports by being floated down rivers, but the density of the wood is such that every tree needs to be strapped to half a dozen lighter-weight species to prevent it from sinking. Further trees are cut so the loggers can get access to the precious timber. Consequently total losses to the forests over that year alone must be well over a million trees.

Driven by demand in China, where the burgeoning middle class has developed a penchant for Ming-style rosewood furniture, a number of locals (including some hoteliers) snatched the opportunity to make a quick buck. The Chinese mafia became involved, considerably increasing criminal activity and silencing those who spoke out. Conservative estimates put the number of rosewood-laden shipping containers to flood out of Madagascar's east-coast ports over the first year at around 1,500, but the reality may be many more.

Corrupt officials at all levels were implicated in the trade: export was legalised, several timber harvesters were given official licences and most who had been brought to justice mysteriously walked free. This political involvement is nothing new; in recent decades, illegal logging activity has peaked prior to elections, indicating this form of revenue is used to fund political campaigns.

International pressure, orchestrated by a global underground network of conservationists and others, focused on the shipping companies transporting the cargo. Faced with publicity of the controversial nature of their activities, some relented but many continued covertly. Delmas was one of the last to stop, but was forced to resume when the corrupt government threatened to cancel their contracts to transport other goods.

Shipments carried on into 2010, but were halted temporarily when a decree was finally signed by the deputy prime minister declaring that those cutting and exporting rosewood and ebony would be prosecuted. But alas the decree was not worth the paper it was written on, for barely a month after the moratorium came into force the prime minister authorised a new export of 79 containers of rosewood. This shipment left Madagascar with a Singapore-registered shipping company after the French embassy advised Delmas against accepting the contract.

Since then, there has been a protracted debate over what to do with the vast number of unexported logs. In October 2013 the Environmental Investigation Agency, supported by many conservationists, sent an open letter to the Malagasy government asking them not to sign a decree that would permit a one-off sale of these stocks to China. Amazingly this was successful and the decree was not signed, but the stocks continued to be smuggled out. In 2016, displeased with the lack of positive action from the Malagasy government, the CITES secretariat recommended sanctions be placed on the island until it proves that concrete actions are being taken to curb illegal logging and trade in precious woods, including investigations and prosecutions.

Where to stay

Camping is possible at half a dozen sites around the peninsula, costing 5,000–7,000Ar per night. There are also several lodges near Tampolo on the peninsula's west coast.

Dounia Forest Lodge (Petit Relais) (7 bungalows) Lohatrozona; m 032 40 213 81/034 05 500 28; e dounia.lodge@douniagroup.com or orhanrado@gmail.com; www.douniagroup. com. New spacious beachfront bungalows, but constructed predominantly from palisander. More basic than you would expect for the price but with 24hr electricity & Wi-Fi it offers more creature comforts than any other accommodation in this remote area. FB.

Masoala Forest Lodge (6 bungalows) +27790432072 (South Africa); e info@ masoalaforestlodge.com or masoalaforestlodge@ gmail.com; www.masoalaforestlodge.com. Highly praised by all. Amazing serene location with palm-thatched tree-houses elevated on stilted wooden platforms providing uninterrupted canopy views. Activities inc kayaking, rainforest walks, village visits & forest yoga retreats. Package inc charter flight from Tana.

Hippocampe Tampolo (10 bungalows) m 032 64 418 99; e madahippocampe@live.fr; www.madahippocampe.com. The forest annexe of Hippocampe in Maroantsetra (see page 313). En-suite bungalows; boat hire, diving & fishing. €€€€

Tampolodge (11 bungalows) m 032 42 713 37/034 31 747 97; e tampolodge@yahoo. fr; www.tampolodge.com. Ecolodge with fairly simple but comfy wooden huts nestled among cloves, lychee & vanilla plants in a seafront spot at the edge of the rainforest. Excellent food. €€€€

Chez Arol Ecolodge (Arollodge) (8 bungalows) m 032 40 889 02/033 12 902 77; e ecolodgechezarol@gmail.com or masoala@ free.fr; http://arollodge.free.fr. Comfy rustic palm-thatched huts, mostly en suite, set back from the beach. Now with 24hr electricity. Welcoming & well run. Camping permitted. Excursions & diving organised. €€€

NOSY MANGABE In fine weather the island of Nosy Mangabe is superb. This 520ha special reserve has beautiful sandy coves, marvellous trees with huge buttress roots and also strangler figs. And it's bursting with wildlife including, of course, its famous aye-ayes which were released here in the 1960s to prevent what was then thought to be their imminent extinction. There is plenty of other wildlife to see so, while a day visit is quite possible, a couple of nights' stay is recommended. Inhabiting the island are weird-and-wonderful leaf-tailed geckos, green-backed mantella frogs, stump-tailed chameleons, white-fronted brown lemurs and black-and-white ruffed lemurs. The bay offers excellent swimming and you may see dolphins and turtles enjoying it too. Aye-aye sightings are rare and in any case night walks are forbidden nowadays.

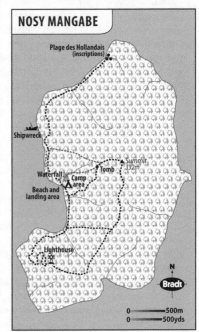

The circuits are well maintained and range in difficulty from easy to moderate. In rain – and it rains often – the paths can get slippery. Trails lead variously to the 332m summit, a rather rusty old lighthouse, and the Plage des Hollandais with its fascinating 17th-century Dutch inscriptions carved on the rocks (if you don't get time to do this last trail, ask your boatman to stop by there when you leave).

As the whole island is a protected area, there are no hotels on Nosy Mangabe, but the reserve runs a campsite with sheltered pitches (5,000Ar), showers, flush toilets, and a couple of newly constructed huts for those without tents. Permits (prices on page 73) are available from the park office on the island itself. The same guides cover both Masoala and Nosy Mangabe, at the same prices. If staying overnight, you are expected to provide or pay for your guide's food (2,000Ar daily). For your own meals, you can bring a camp stove or employ the services of a cook (some guides will double as cooks if you pay them a little extra). Boat crossings from Maroantsetra take about 30 minutes and cost 100,000Ar return (per boat) with an additional nightly fee for waiting if you are staying for multiple days.

TREKKING TO THE EAST COAST There are no roads crossing Masoala Peninsula, but you can organise a guided trek from Maroantsetra to Cap Est (6 days across the neck of the peninsula or about 11 days following its coastline), Antalaha (4 days, with the last 30km from Marofinaritra possible by taxi-brousse), or northward to Andapa (8 days). As most of these routes pass through parts of the national park, you are obliged to take a guide and buy a park permit. Wildlife is not a major feature of these treks but you will meet plenty of friendly locals.

Much of the walking is quite strenuous with little shade, especially on the trail to Antalaha, with countless rivers to ford by a combination of log bridges, pirogues or wading. Reader Jeremy Sabel crossed to Cap Est 'in the dry season but it was raining constantly. If you don't mind leeches, slipping, falling, getting muddy and crossing rivers up to your chest, then this is the hike for you. It's definitely not the option for those who just want a stroll; and I recommend taking porters. You must have camping equipment, bring food and be prepared to hike for up to 8 hours per day. I really enjoyed the experience.'

CAP EST The most easterly point of Madagascar, Cap Est can be accessed via boat, on foot from Maroantsetra or by taxi-brousse from Antalaha (3hrs). Some 2.5km southeast of the headland is a white 19m-tall iron lighthouse built in 1906. The littoral forest inland from Cap Est is part of Masoala National Park and an excellent place to see the insectivorous Masoala pitcher plant. This is also the closest access from the coast to the impressive Bevontsira Waterfall, 2–3 days' walk inland towards Maroantsetra.

Just 600m up the beach from the point is **Résidence du Cap** (m *032 48 920 56/032 43 195 78*; e *ibrahimdasy@yahoo.fr*; €€). Once a rather upmarket hotel, it was all but flattened by cyclones in 2004, 2007 and 2011, but reopened in 2015 at a more modest level. Its five bungalows are mostly en suite.

ANTALAHA TO IHARANA (VOHEMAR)

This lush region is usually known as SAVA, an acronym standing for its key towns: Sambava, Antalaha, Vohemar and Andapa. The first three lie along a 175km stretch of coastline connected by a good road, while the last is a 105km drive inland and acts as the gateway town to the stunning mountainous national park of Marojejy. The SAVA region produces about half of the world's vanilla, as well as many spices and other crops.

ANTALAHA This prosperous, vanilla-financed town suffers direct hits from occasional major cyclones, but always bounces back in true Malagasy fashion.

Antalaha has a couple of cybercafés, a post office and branches of the main banks (BFV, BNI and BOA) with ATMs.

Getting there and away The road connecting Iharana to RN6 and the rest of Madagascar is horrendous. (Seasoned adventure traveller Carol Snyder, who did less than half of it by good 4x4 in perfect weather, likened sections to a dry riverbed and summarised: 'what a gruelling road!') There are rumours that improvements are in the pipeline, but until then the only easy way to get to Antalaha is to fly; there is a local Air Madagascar office (m *032 07 222 13*; e *anmssmd@airmadagascar.com*). The alternatives are to trek across the Masoala Peninsula from Maroantsetra, or come by sea on a cargo boat from Maroantsetra or Toamasina.

Where to stay and eat

Ankavanana Lodge (3 bungalows) Sarahandrano; m 032 05 618 74. Experience authentic Madagascar at this family-run rural ecolodge 4km from town. Bungalows have private facilities & solar power. You can witness vanilla processing in season (Jul–Nov). €€€€

Océan Momo (20 bungalows) m 032 02 164 23/032 02 340 69/034 05 340 69/034 29 505 92; e oceanmomo@blueline.mg; www.ocean-momo.com. AC bungalows. Wi-Fi. Boycotted by some tour operators as a result of the owner's alleged involvement with illegal rosewood logging. Readers have recently complained that they serve crayfish out of the legal season. €€€€

Hazovôla (22 rooms) m 032 05 000 65/032 41 287 11; e h.hazovolaantalaha@yahoo.fr; www.hotelantalaha.com. Rooms with minibar, safe, Wi-Fi & TV. The owner of this hotel has also been implicated in logging. €€€–€€€€

Atlantis (2 rooms & 8 bungalows) m 032 02 071 34/032 02 397 29; e stesoazara@yahoo.fr. Nice location in an attractive & peaceful garden. €€–€€€

Nanie (4 rooms & 4 bungalows) m 032 45 760 92; e anissaberiziky@gmail.com. Basic bungalows, right next to the sea opposite the pier; some with AC. Sea-view restaurant. €€–€€€

Florida (12 rooms) 88 951 25. A choice of rooms, some with AC & hot water. €€

Liane (4 rooms) m 032 45 771 54; e rajaonal@yahoo.fr. Welcoming & clean; rooms with shared facilities. €€

Riviera (11 rooms) m 032 04 654 38/032 07 536 04/032 41 801 72. Simple rooms with shared facilities. €€

Villa Malaza (5 rooms) m 032 61 823 09/034 84 571 11; e villa.malaza@yahoo.fr; www.villa-malaza.com. Guesthouse run by Malagasy-French couple Gisèle & Alain. Comfy rooms & relaxed atmosphere. €€

Vitasoa (12 rooms & 3 bungalows) Rue du Havre; 88 956 67; m 032 07 520 90/034 01 950 20; e hotelvitasoa@yahoo.fr. Good-value central hotel with hot water & good restaurant. €€

Cocotier (22 rooms) m 032 04 297 30/032 07 161 10. Spacious rooms, some with bathroom; Asian cuisine. €–€€

Cap Est m 032 55 913 80. Opened in 2015 by Malagasy-French couple Blondine & Roland, serving excellent food in modest 1st-floor surroundings.

Chez Joice Rue Rangaika; m 032 02 375 72/032 07 765 14; e jpcjeanpierrechan@gmail.com. Restaurant & *salon de thé*.

Fleur de Lotus m 032 02 200 68. Good-value Chinese restaurant.

Jeannick Gargote m 032 05 591 48. A much-loved fairy-tale Swiss-run eatery offering raclette but also Malagasy cuisine & pizza.

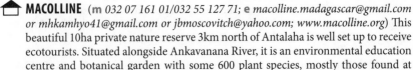

MACOLLINE (m *032 07 161 01/032 55 127 71*; e *macolline.madagascar@gmail.com or mhkamhyo41@gmail.com or jbmoscovitch@yahoo.com*; *www.macolline.org*) This beautiful 10ha private nature reserve 3km north of Antalaha is well set up to receive ecotourists. Situated alongside Ankavanana River, it is an environmental education centre and botanical garden with some 600 plant species, mostly those found at Masoala and Marojejy.

Activities include easy and moderate hiking trails, taking in the coastline and scenery from a viewpoint, tasting a selection of wild fruits, a canoe trip, visiting a local brick factory, a cultural village tour and planting an endemic tree as part of Macolline's reforestation programme. A guided visit costs 15,000–65,000Ar (taking 1½–6 hours), depending on which package of activities you opt for. Picnic lunches can be provided for 10,000Ar. Stop by at Kam Hyo pharmacy (under the same ownership) in town for more information.

SAMBAVA The capital of SAVA and centre of the vanilla- and coconut-growing region, Sambava is also an important area for clove and coffee production. It hosts the annual **Festivanille** vanilla festival for a few days each October, a cultural event aimed at increasing knowledge and understanding about the vanilla industry.

The town essentially comprises two very long streets running parallel to the beach. At the western end is a good market known as *bazary kely*, not because it's particularly *kely* or 'small' (it isn't – and certainly not on Tuesday, market day), but because there used to be two markets and no-one felt inclined to change the name when they were amalgamated. BIC is the best of the cybercafés and in town you are spoilt for choice with banks: there are five in the centre.

Getting there and away Sambava has **flight** connections with Tana, Toamasina, Antsiranana and Maroantsetra. The airport is not far from town – you can even walk it.

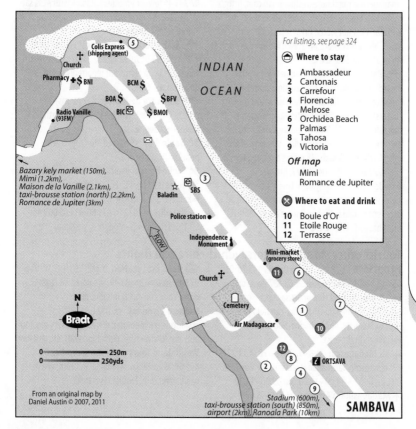

Regular **taxi-brousses** serve the good roads north to Iharana (153km/4hrs/8,000Ar) and south to Antalaha (89km/2hrs/7,000Ar) – or faster by 4x4 (around 2hrs and 1¼hrs respectively). Sambava has separate north and south taxi-brousse stations. In the dry season, reaching Antsiranana takes about 15 hours by taxi-brousse (50,000Ar) or 10 hours by 4x4.

Where to stay and eat *Map, page 323*

Carrefour (25 rooms) ☎ 88 920 60 (reception); m 032 11 340 01/032 44 340 08 (manager); e hotelcarrefour@yahoo.fr; www. hotelcarrefoursambava.com. Nr the beach, with en-suite bathrooms, some with hot water & some with AC, TV & minibar. Wi-Fi on terrace. €€€–€€€€

Melrose (17 rooms) m 032 04 572 14/032 83 046 74/034 03 884 19; e hotel@melrose-sambava.mg or melrosehotel@yahoo.fr; www. melrose-sambava.mg. Wide range of room grades all with fan & TV, some with AC, minibar, balcony & safe. Wi-Fi. Cards accepted. €€–€€€€

Mimi (12 rooms & 4 bungalows) m 032 04 636 29 (manager)/032 07 610 28/032 40 288 55 (manager); e mimi.hotel.resto@gmail.com; http:// mimi-hotel.marojejy.com. Smart en-suite rooms with sat-TV & hot water. Great restaurant with Wi-Fi. Many excursions organised inc Marojejy & Anjanaharibe-Sud. €€€

Palmas (2 rooms & 6 bungalows) m 032 05 145 76/032 40 073 72; e laspalmas.hotel@ gmail.com; www.laspalmas-hotelsambava.com. Nicely situated beachfront hotel. Rooms & some bungalows have AC. Wi-Fi & massage. They organise excursions inc to a nearby vanilla plantation. €€€

Orchidea Beach (8 rooms & 2 bungalows) ☎ 88 923 24; m 032 04 383 77; http:// orchideabeach.marojejy.com. Lovely beachfront hotel set in a beautifully planted garden, with an excellent restaurant & bar. Rooms are en suite & most have AC. €€–€€€

Victoria (19 rooms) Rue du Commerce; ☎ 88 809 26; m 032 21 906 19/033 02 420 07/033 71 336 64/034 02 420 07; e victoriahotelsava@ gmail.com. En-suite rooms with sat-TV & Wi-Fi; some with AC. Cybercafé downstairs. Also 4x4 hire. €€–€€€

Cantonais (8 rooms) m 032 02 125 86/032 46 426 71. A range of rooms, some with hot water. Becoming run-down. €€

Florencia (20 rooms & 2 bungalows) m 032 02 466 21/032 05 765 91. Clean rooms with TV & en-suite hot-water facilities in a garden. Also an annexe nearby. €€

Tahosa (Tantsinanana) (10 rooms) m 032 07 741 46 (owner's mother). Rooms with AC & sat-TV, but seem a little worn. Recommended Creole & European restaurant. €€

Ambassadeur (Chez Zoe) m 032 02 113 47/032 02 927 45/032 79 837 74; e razafizoe@ yahoo.fr. Cheap rooms but reportedly going downhill. €–€€

Romance de Jupiter (12 rooms) m 032 04 633 89. Very basic. Beyond north taxi-brousse station. €

✗ **Boule d'Or** ⊙ closed Mon. Deservedly popular pizza place.

✗ **Etoile Rouge** Typical Chinese restaurant.

✗ **Terrasse** m 032 26 206 51. Lively restaurant & karaoke bar. Also 4x4 hire.

☆ **Baladin** m 032 05 671 60/034 05 009 45; ⊙ Thu/Fri/Sat eves. Modern-style disco.

Tourist office, tour operators, vehicle hire and flights

🄩 **ORTSAVA** ☎ 88 920 87; m 032 05 145 76/032 05 618 74/032 04 636 29/032 67 487 76; e ort. sava.bureau@gmail.com or ort.sava.pca@gmail. com. This regional tourism office can help with trips to Marojejy, Anjanaharibe-Sud & other excursions in the area.

✈ **Air Madagascar** ☎ 88 920 37; m 034 11 222 12; e svbssmd@airmadagascar.com; ⊙ Mon–Fri 09.00–11.00 & 14.00–18.00, Sat 09.00–11.30

✈ **Madagasikara Airways** m 032 05 970 15/034 05 970 24

🚗 **Nord-Est Location** m 032 07 145 36/034 07 145 36/034 20 483 49; e voromailala208@ gmail.com. Car, 4x4 & minibus hire.

Soaland Discovery m 032 07 411 07; e sldiscovery@moov.mg; www.sldiscovery.mg. Tour operator for river trips, plantation visits, etc; 4x4 hire.

Vanillaland Tours ☎ 88 906 87; m 032 02 495 69; e vanillaland@vanillaland.com; www. vanillaland.com. Excursions & treks.

What to see and do Visits to **plantations**, factories and packaging workshops are central to local tourism. A tour of the Lopat vanilla factory will open your eyes to the laborious process of preparing one of the country's main exports. Cocoa and coconut plantation tours are also possible (contact the tourist office).

For relaxation seekers, Sambava has no shortage of **beach**, but the dramatic seafront often has huge – and dangerous – waves. At the airport end of town, however, is the beautiful Ampandrozonana Bay where the ocean is calm and safe for **swimming** (just follow the beach until you arrive at some tennis and basketball courts).

A visit to the rainforest reserves near Andapa is not to be missed – see page 328.

Maison de la Vanille (✆ 88 923 42; m 032 07 145 30) If you are looking for vanilla, be sure to visit this specialist shop in the town centre. It's not the cheapest option but quality is guaranteed. They sell not only pods of different grades, but also extract, powder, vanilla-infused sugar, and various presentation boxes for souvenirs and gifts.

Soavoanio coconut plantation Stretching both north and south from Sambava, this 5,000ha grove of coconut trees is planted with a mixture of a dwarf Malaysian species and a larger African variety, which are crossed to yield well over 10 million of the familiar hairy fruits (botanically speaking they are 'drupes', not nuts) each year. Visitors can stroll between endless avenues of palms and even assist workers with the labour-intensive procedure of removing male flowers and artificially pollinating female ones, as is necessary in the production of hybrid coconuts. This visit can be combined with Ranoala Park (see below), which is at the plantation's southern end.

Ranoala Park (m 032 81 600 36/034 02 600 36; e *jaosoajp@ymail.com*) This 4ha botanical garden, with tree nursery and zoo, is situated 15 minutes south of Sambava. Visitors can see 45 species of medicinal plants and two large tree nurseries, one growing fruit trees and the other some 30 forest species. A number of lemurs have been entrusted to the park and live in partial freedom. Musical campfire evenings can be organised for groups who contact them in advance. Allow an hour or so for a visit.

Ambariomiambana This village some 7km from Sambava in the direction of Andapa is the starting point for a 1½-hour hike to a waterfall, accompanied by the guardian of the falls who will tell the strange story that brought him here. From the village, you will pass mango trees, rice paddies, plantations of bananas, cloves, coffee and sugarcane, lychee trees and orange groves before arriving at a sacred forest. At its heart is a waterfall where locals come to make wishes and leave offerings to the ancestors. Contact the tourist office to arrange this excursion.

Vola Maitso and Bemarivo River Some 20 minutes north of Sambava is the Vola Maitso plantation, where you will find vanilla, cocoa, pepper, coconuts, and numerous fruits under cultivation. The landscape here is beautiful, with a good viewpoint and some interesting tombs. You can take a pirogue down Bemarivo River, floating 13.5km to the sea and enjoying the scenery before returning to Sambava through the northern parts of Soavoanio coconut plantation.

CONTINUING TO IHARANA Heading north on the good road, the next town of importance is Iharana (Vohemar). If that's where you're going, turn to *Chapter 14*, page 343.

Vanilla is a major foreign currency earner for Madagascar, which together with Réunion and the Comoros grows over half of the world's crop. Its cultivation is centred on the eastern coastal region around Andapa, Antalaha and Sambava.

The climbing plants are grown supported on 1½m-high moisture-retaining trunks and under ideal conditions take three years to mature. When they bloom the vines are checked on alternate days for open flowers to hand-pollinate. The pod then takes nine months to develop. Each 15–20cm pod will contain tens of thousands of tiny seeds.

They go to a processing plant to be prepared for the commercial market. First they are plunged into a cauldron of hot water (70°C) for 2 minutes and are kept hot for two days. During this time the pods change colour from green to chestnut brown. Next they are laid out in the sun each morning for three to four weeks.

After maturing, the pods are sorted by size, bundled and tied with raffia. They are checked for quality by sniffing and bending before being packed into wooden crates, with most of the product going to the USA for use in ice cream.

The vanilla used in cultivation in Madagascar is *Vanilla planifolia* which originates from Mexico. It was brought to Madagascar by the French once the secret of hand-pollination had been discovered (the flower has no natural pollinator in its foreign home). The culinary and pharmaceutical use of vanilla dates back to pre-Aztec times when it was used as a drink or as an ingredient of a lotion against fatigue for those holding public office. Similarly a native Malagasy vanilla stem can be found for sale on Tana markets as a male invigorator.

Four different species of vanilla orchid occur naturally in Madagascar, most of them totally leafless. One can be seen on the roadside between Sambava and Antalaha resembling lengths of red-green tubing festooned over the scrub. Another is found in the spiny forest near Berenty. Most of the native species contain sap that burns the skin and their fruits contain too little vanillin to make cultivation economic.

Although conventionally used for cooking, vanilla is also an insect repellent, and the wonderful-smelling pods can be put in drawers to scent clothing or linen.

When cooking you can re-use the pods for as long as you remember to retrieve them – wash and dry them after each use. Vanilla does wonders for tea or coffee (just add a pod to the teapot or coffee filter, or grind a dried pod with the coffee beans) and can be boiled with milk to make a yummy hot drink (add a dash of brandy) or custard. Put some beans in your sugar tin and the flavour will be absorbed. Vanilla adds a subtle flavour to chicken or duck, rice or… whatever you fancy!

ANDAPA AREA

Andapa lies in a fertile and beautiful region, a 105km drive southwest of Sambava. It is where much of north Madagascar's rice is grown and is also a major coffee-producing area. To help facilitate export, the EEC provided funding to build an all-weather road in the 1960s. It has been resurfaced subsequently and remains in good condition. The journey to Andapa is really beautiful, with the jagged peaks

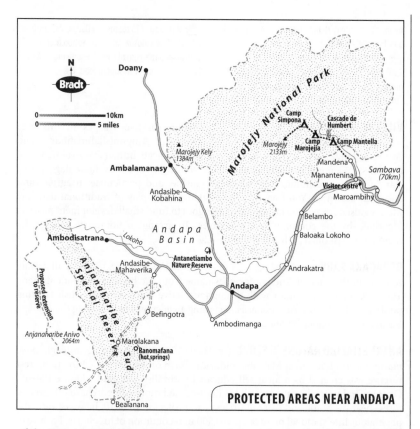

PROTECTED AREAS NEAR ANDAPA

of the Marojejy Massif to the right, and bamboo- and palm-thatch villages by the roadside. The journey takes 3 hours by taxi-brousse (7,000Ar).

The area is best known for Marojejy National Park and Anjanaharibe-Sud Special Reserve, two of Madagascar's most exciting wilderness areas, in some of the most remote pristine rainforests remaining.

ANDAPA Andapa is an attractive and welcoming little town, perhaps because it sees relatively few tourists. BOA and BNI have bank branches there.

Peace Corps volunteer Arianna Pattek has recently helped set up an **English-language library** and cultural centre for the Andapa community (*CISCO, Beanana;* m *034 85 442 40/034 84 902 67/032 40 187 06;* ⊕ *Mon–Fri 08.00–11.30 & 14.00–18.00*). Tourists are very welcome to visit; the students and teachers love to practise their English with native speakers, and any donations of English books will be very gratefully received.

🏠 Where to stay and eat

🏠 **Soaland Chalet** (6 rooms) Rue Ramandraibe; m 032 07 411 07; e flavienne@marojejy.com. Guesthouse with nice rooms for up to 4 people. €€€

🏠 **Beanana** (10 rooms) m 032 40 226 10; e hsbeanana@yahoo.fr; http://beanana.marojejy.

com. En-suite rooms grouped round a courtyard & overlooking a beautiful garden. Excellent service & value for money. €€–€€€

🏠 **Riziky** (6 bungalows) m 032 40 214 22; e riziky.bungalows@gmail.com; http://riziky. marojejy.com. Quiet bungalows on east side of town, all en suite with hot water. Car, motorbike & bike hire. €€–€€€

🏠 **Amis Annexe** (14 rooms) m 032 81 204 25/034 45 922 88; e clubdesamisannexandapa@ gmail.com. En-suite rooms & restaurant with Chinese specialities. €€

🏠 **Vatosoa** (15 rooms) m 032 40 235 28/034 04 720 90; e vatosoa_andapa@yahoo.fr or vatosoaandapa@gmail.com. En-suite rooms & large restaurant with superb food. €€

VILLAGE HOMESTAYS The women's associations of five villages in this area – Ambodimanga, Andapahely, Ambalavoanio, Ampontsilahinafindra and Ampontsilahy – are collaborating to offer visitors an immersive experience of Betsimisaraka and Tsimihety culture. You will be welcomed in the Malagasy way, stay in a genuine home, taste the local cuisine, and participate in agricultural and craft activities. You may even be treated to a display of traditional dancing. Money raised from these hosting activities goes to fund small development projects identified by the communities themselves. To arrange a homestay, contact the regional tourist office, ORTSAVA (page 324).

BERADAKA PARK (m *034 25 836 94;* e *parcberadaka@yahoo.fr*) This small private reserve on the edge of Andapa takes its name from the huge frogs resident there. The park offers a 2–3-hour walk through attractive landscapes, past fish-farming pools, crop fields and fruit orchards, including a viewpoint overlooking the Andapa Basin and Anjanaharibe-Sud.

ANTANETIAMBO NATURE RESERVE (m *034 93 557 40/034 48 372 52; antanetiambo. marojejy.com*) Located at Matsobe-Sud, 7km north of Andapa, this 14ha rainforest reserve was created by a local self-educated naturalist and guide, Désiré Rabary. Over several years, he saved up all his hard-earned money to purchase this area of forest near his home and worked tirelessly to protect it. In 2010, he was awarded a prestigious international prize of US$10,000 in recognition of his efforts. Each year, the Seacology Prize goes to an 'indigenous islander for exceptional achievement in preserving the environment and culture of his or her home island'. At the award ceremony in California, Désiré announced: 'I plan to use these funds for such projects as reforestation, developing tourist infrastructure and purchasing the land around Antanetiambo to increase the size of the reserve.'

During a 2-hour guided walk (conducted in English, French or Malagasy), visitors can see frogs, chameleons, reptiles, birds and lemurs, and learn not only about the wildlife but also the cultural values and practices of the Tsimihety people. You can visit a large *Paratilapia* fish farm and discover traditional farming practices. Visitors are also encouraged to stay and share a traditional meal at the family home.

MAROJEJY NATIONAL PARK (✆ *88 070 27;* m *034 49 400 86;* e *mrj@parcs-madagascar.com* or *mrj.parks@gmail.com; www.marojejy.com*) This stunningly beautiful national park was established in 1998 (having been a closed reserve since 1952) and designated a UNESCO World Heritage Site in 2007. Covering 55,500ha, the park is permeated by eight rivers and rises to 2,132m at its peak. You need to be reasonably fit and able to tolerate the heat to enjoy it fully, but there are few other areas in Madagascar to compare for awesome splendour and the feeling of ultimate wilderness. Imposing mountains and craggy cliffs are surrounded by lush rainforests full of wildlife.

The big stars here are the all-white silky sifakas. Of some 500 primate species worldwide, this one has the unfortunate distinction of being among the five

Erik Patel, Charles Welch, Lanto Andrianandrasana & Anne Yoder

The Duke Lemur Center (DLC), based at North Carolina's Duke University, initiated a community-based initiative called the SAVA Conservation Project in 2012. DLC has led the world in lemur research for over 40 years and is a founding member of the Madagascar Fauna & Flora Group.

The SAVA region was chosen for this initiative because of its tremendous biodiversity and unique mountain ranges. The project was further motivated by increases in habitat disturbance such as illegal logging, bushmeat hunting and slash-and-burn agriculture since the 2009 political crisis began, as well as the limited presence of environmental NGOs in the region.

Some of the last remaining large tracts of undisturbed low-elevation rainforest are found here as well as rare high-elevation habitats. Due to the large number of elevational zones, biodiversity is magnificently high. Indeed, eminent botanist Henri Humbert's classic 1955 book about Marojejy is entitled *A Marvel of Nature*. He felt the massif was the most impressive range in Madagascar due to its floral diversity, size and pristine natural state – more than 2,000 species of flowering plants are found here. This region may contain more ferns, reptiles and amphibians, and forest-dwelling birds than any other protected area in the country. Insect diversity (dung beetles and ants have been studied most) is also remarkably high, as is that of primates, with 11 species of lemur. The silky sifaka, one of the rarest mammals in the world with fewer than 2,000 individuals remaining, is a key flagship species.

Saving these species can only be accomplished by engaging local communities as partners and supporting Madagascar National Parks. Based out of its Sambava office, the project follows a multifaceted community-based approach to biodiversity conservation. The extensive environmental education programme includes structured educational visits to Marojejy National Park with local student groups as well as a teacher-training programme, introducing environmental education into the primary school curriculum at dozens of schools. To diminish bushmeat hunting, fish-farming of a locally endemic *Paratilapia* species is being introduced as an alternative protein and income source. Restocking of local rivers with this endangered species is also helping to re-establish wild populations. Reforestation campaigns in collaboration with the Belgian NGO Graine de Vie have been established, with approximately 10,000 seedlings of fast-growing endemics and fruit trees being planted annually in each of several villages locally. Forest monitoring and boundary demarcation of Marojejy is being improved in collaboration with Madagascar National Parks, and lemur research and conservation projects have been undertaken with Duke University students.

Dr Erik Patel (e patel.erik@gmail.com) is SAVA Conservation's Post-Doctoral Project Director; Lanto Andrianandrasana (e alantoharivelo@yahoo.fr) is Project Manager. See http://lemur.duke.edu to learn more.

rarest. But there's plenty else besides: helmet vangas, panther chameleons, leaf-tailed geckos, frogs galore, huge millipedes, wonderful spiders... and lots of leeches.

LEECHES   *Hilary Bradt*

Few classes of invertebrates elicit more disgust than leeches. Perhaps some facts about these extraordinarily well-adapted animals will give them more appeal.

Terrestrial leeches such as those found in Madagascar are small (1–2cm long) and find their warm-blooded prey by vibrations and odour. Suckers at each end enable the leech to move around in a series of loops and to attach itself to a leaf by its posterior while seeking its meal with the front end. It has sharp jaws and can quickly – and painlessly – bite through the skin and start feeding. When it has filled its digestive tract with blood the leech drops off and digests its meal. This process can take several months since leeches have pouches all along their gut to hold as much blood as possible – up to ten times their own weight. The salivary glands manufacture an anti-coagulant which prevents the blood clotting during feeding and digestion. This is why leech wounds bleed so spectacularly. Leeches also inject an anaesthetic so you don't feel them biting.

Leeches are hermaphrodites but still have pretty exciting sex lives. To consummate their union they need to exchange packets of sperm. This is done either the conventional way via a leechy penis or by injection, allowing the sperm to make its way through the body tissues to find and fertilise the eggs.

Readers who are disappointed with the small size of Malagasy leeches will be interested to hear that an expedition to French Guiana in the 1970s discovered the world's largest leech: at full stretch 45cm long!

Wherever there are blood vessels there are leeches, and travellers compete for the worst leech story. Here's one from researcher Frankie Kerridge: 'A highlight was my guide getting a leech on his eyeball. Mega shouting and screaming. Got it off by killing it (slowly) with a tobacco leaf.'

Reader T T Terpening had an equally gruesome experience: a leech in his nose. This he dealt with thus: 'I pushed on my left nostril with my finger and blew hard. Some blood, a little snot, and a big glossy leech flew out into the rainforest litter.' But then: 'My guide said a dab of tobacco will keep my respiratory system leech-free for the remainder of the hike. I take a scoop and plug both nostrils. Immediately I feel dizzy and sick and my nose burns. I brace myself against a tree and my head clears. My nose definitely still feels weird. Over the next minute I come to the realisation that another leech is travelling the length of my sinus. "Probably running away from the tobacco," says my guide helpfully. Within 12 hours the leech has run its course, journeying the length of my nose, then sinus to my throat where I eventually swallow it.'

See page 122 for advice on dealing with latched-on leeches.

The park office and **visitor centre** is at the village of Manantenina (PK 66), a little over halfway from Sambava to Andapa (coming from the former it's 5,000Ar by taxi-brousse, or 3,000Ar from the latter). There are three camps at different altitudes, each of which has some four-person chalets with bunk-beds and space for tents. There are basic communal shower and toilet blocks and separate cooking and eating areas.

Situated 5 hours' walk from the park entrance (the first half of which can be done by 4x4, if you prefer) is **Camp Mantella** (*425m elevation; 6 bungalows;* €€) in the heart of superb lowland rainforest, with many chameleons, leaf-tailed geckos and frogs. An hour or two further on is **Camp Marojejia** (*750m; 4 bungalows;* €€), at the transition between lowland and mid-altitude rainforest opposite an amazing outcrop of forest-cloaked rock. Beyond this point, the trail gets very tough, the compensation for which is that this area offers the best chance of seeing a silky sifaka. **Camp Simpona** (*1,250m; 2 bungalows;* €€) is a welcome sight. The forest is more stunted because of the altitude, but there are still silky sifakas and birds such as rufous-headed ground-roller and yellow-bellied sunbird-asity. A viewing platform offers a breathtaking vista. It is a further 4–5-hour climb to the peak at 2,133m, but you need good weather and that's far from guaranteed. If you're in luck then the view from the top is awesome and the feeling of space and wilderness unmatched.

You will need proper hiking boots and a hiking pole would be useful. Pack warm clothing for the nights and a bandana to mop your streaming face during the very hot days. The best times to visit are April to May and September to December when there's less rain. Booking ahead is recommended for September to November.

Guides and trackers cost 45,000–70,000Ar per day, porters 5,000–10,000Ar per camp transit and cooks 30,000Ar a day. Camping costs 10,000–15,000Ar, plus 10,000Ar (per group of up to six) for use of the kitchen facilities. For permit prices, see page 73.

ANJANAHARIBE-SUD SPECIAL RESERVE (✆ 88 070 27; *http://anjanaharibe. marojejy.com*) This comprises 28,624ha of mountainous rainforest. The name means 'place of the great God' and, although only 20km southwest of Andapa, it is appropriately difficult to reach. The wildlife is not easy to see since it was hunted until recently, but repays the effort. This is the most northerly range of the indri, which here occurs in a very dark form – almost black. The silky sifaka is also found here, but you are more likely to see the troops of white-fronted brown lemurs. Birders will be on the lookout for four species of ground-roller.

Even without seeing any mammals it is a most rewarding visit, with an easy-to-follow (though rugged) trail through primary forest to some hot springs. The reserve is also a vital element in the prosperity of the area: the Lokoho River, which rises in Anjanaharibe-Sud, is the only source of water for the largest irrigated rice producer in the country.

The normal access route is from the east, via Andasibe-Mahaverika and Befingotra, along a very poor road. It takes about an hour to reach the campsite and a further hour to the hot springs. There are three springs: one is too hot to keep your feet in but the others – one shallow and one deep – merge with cool stream water and make the temperature much more pleasant.

Prices for permits, guides and camping are as for Marojejy, above.

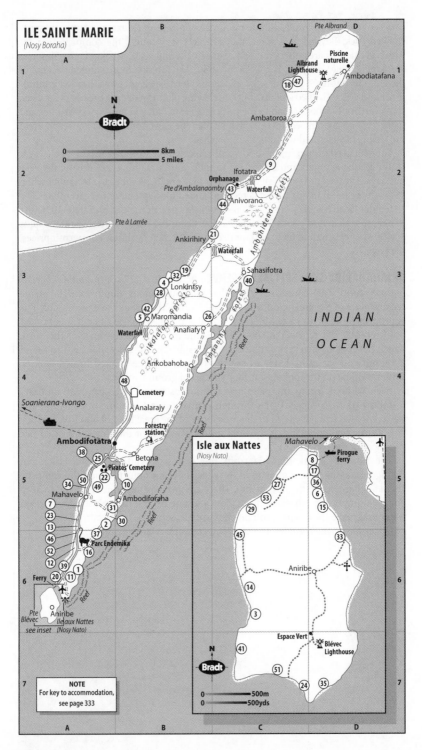

ILE SAINTE MARIE
(Nosy Boraha)

A   B   C   D

Pte Albrand

Piscine naturelle

Albrand Lighthouse

18 47

Ambodiatafana

1

N

Bradt

0   8km
0   5 miles

Ambatoroa

9

2

Ifotatra
Orphanage
Pte d'Ambalanaomby 43 **Waterfall**
Anivorano
44

Pte à Larrée

21

Ankirihiry

Waterfall

32 19
4
28   **Lonkintsy**

Sahasifotra
40

42
5   **Maromandia**
Waterfall   26
Anafiafy

Ambohidena Forest

Ikalalao Forest
Ampanihy Forest

Reef

INDIAN OCEAN

Ankobahoba

48
Cemetery

Analarajy

Forestry station

Ambodifotatra
38
25
22   **Pirates' Cemetery**
10
Betona

34 50
49
Mahavelo
7
23   31   **Ambodiforaha**
13   2   30
46   37
52   16   **Parc Endemika**
12 39
1
Ferry 20 11
Pte
Blévec Aniribe
see inset **Ile aux Nattes**
(Nosy Nato)

Reef

Isle aux Nattes
(Nosy Nato)

Mahavelo

Pirogue ferry
8
17
27   36
53   6
29   15

45   33

Aniribe

14

3

41   **Espace Vert** **Blévec Lighthouse**

51
24   35

N

Bradt

0   500m
0   500yds

A   B   C   D

NOTE
For key to accommodation, see page 333

Ile Sainte Marie (Nosy Boraha)

Here is a cliché of a tropical island with endless deserted beaches overhung by coconut palms, bays protected from sharks by coral reefs, hills covered with luxuriant vegetation and fantastic whale-watching in season. Although developed for tourism, it has been done in a tasteful, low-key way and the island maintains a traditional ambience: most of the hotels are small-scale with rustic bungalows.

Travellers love it: 'As soon as we saw the island from the air, we were ready to ditch our travel plans and spend the rest of our trip nestled in paradise. Everything about the island is intoxicating: the smell of cloves drying in the sun, the taste of *coco* rum and the warmth of the sea.' In addition to this heady, holiday atmosphere, Ile Sainte Marie is the best place in Madagascar for whale-watching.

The island, due east of Soanierana-Ivongo, is 50km long and 7km at its widest point, with the tiny but delightful Ile aux Nattes just off its southern tip. The only significant town is **Ambodifotatra**; other small villages comprise mainly bamboo and palm huts. The island is almost universally known as Sainte Marie – few use its Malagasy name: Nosy Boraha.

Sainte Marie unfortunately – or perhaps fortunately, given the dangers of overdevelopment – has a far less settled weather pattern than its island rival, Nosy Be. Cyclones cause damage every few years. At any time of year expect several days of rain and wind, but interspersed with calm sunny weather. The best months for a visit tend to be June and mid-August to December, but good weather is possible anytime.

Note that on Sainte Marie, in addition to the daily *vignette touristique*, there is a one-off tax of 10,000Ar per person (payable at your first hotel).

The airport is sited at the southern tip of the main island, beyond which is the smaller island of Ile aux Nattes – covered at the end of this chapter (pages 341–2).

HISTORY The origin of the island's Malagasy name 'Nosy Boraha' is obscure. It means either 'island of Abraham' or 'island of Ibrahim', with probable reference to an early Semitic culture. It was named Ile Sainte Marie by European sailors when the island became the major hideout of pirates in the Indian Ocean. From the 1680s to around 1720 these pirates dominated the seas around Africa. Among a Madagascar pirate population which, in its heyday, numbered nearly a thousand were Englishmen (including William Kidd, Thomas White, Henry Every, Christopher Condent, Robert Culliford and Adam Baldridge), Welshmen (David Williams), Irishmen (Edward England), Frenchmen (Olivier Levasseur), Americans (Thomas Tew) and Jamaicans (James Plaintain).

Later another Frenchman, Jean-Onésime 'La Bigorne' Filet, was shipwrecked on Sainte Marie while escaping the wrath of a jealous husband in Réunion. La Bigorne turned his amorous attentions with remarkable success to Princess Bety, daughter of King Ratsimilaho. Upon their marriage the happy couple received Nosy Boraha as a gift from the king, and the island was in turn presented to the mother country by La Bigorne – or rather, put under the protection of France by Queen Bety – thus France gained its first piece of Madagascar in 1750.

GETTING THERE AND AWAY

By air Flights go most days from Tana or Toamasina to Sainte Marie, but they can be heavily booked (especially in July and August) so try to make your reservations well in advance. There are also now direct flights from Réunion. The Air Mad local office is in the north of Ambodifotatra (*Rue Dadare Dominique;* ✆ *57 400 46;* m *032 07 222 08/034 11 222 13;* e *smsssmd@airmadagascar.com;* ⊕ *Mon–Fri 07.30–noon & 14.30–18.00, Sat 08.00–10.00*), down the side street opposite Hortensia Hotel. Madagasikara Airways (m *032 05 970 10/034 05 970 16*) has their base in the airport.

By sea A few companies run ferry services between Soanierana-Ivongo and Ambodifotatra every morning. You can take a *taxi-brousse* north from Toamasina to Soanierana and buy your ferry ticket there but it is safer to buy a combination bus and ferry ticket in Toamasina. This way you don't risk missing the crossing if the vehicle gets delayed, or turning up to find the ferry fully booked. The crossing can be quite hairy (there have been a number of accidents including one in 2011 that claimed 11 lives) so it's worth picking a reliable operator.

The new **Blue Marine** (m *032 25 792 66/034 70 433 01 in Toamasina/034 70 433 02 in Ambodifotatra/034 70 433 03 in Soanierana/034 70 433 06 in Tana;* e *contact@bluemarine-madagascar.com or feno@bluemarine-madagascar.com; www.bluemarine-madagascar.com*) operates a passenger ferry called *El Condor*; it's a 27m catamaran with twin 500hp engines and a seating capacity of 104. It generally leaves Ambodifotatra at 06.00 daily for the 2½-hour crossing to Soanierana, returning at 09.30, but times are somewhat tide-dependent. The price is 100,000Ar one way plus 10,000Ar for the land transfer from Toamasina.

Then there is **Sainte-Marie Tours** (*40 Bd Joffre, Toamasina;* ✆ *53 987 49;* m *032 62 870 99;* e *sms.tours.net@gmail.com or sms.tours.net@ymail.com; www.sainte-marie-tours.mg*) running a 15m 58-passenger boat called *Gasikara Be* with twin 260hp engines (duration 1hr or so). Their daily crossings cost 120,000Ar each way including the optional bus connection (3hrs).

Cap Sainte-Marie (✆ 57 404 06 in Ambodifotatra/53 351 48 in Toamasina; m 032 05 118 08 in Ambodifotatra/032 05 218 08 in Toamasina; e contact@cap-sainte-marie.com; www.cap-sainte-marie.com) charge similar rates for the 2-hour trip in their 12m 40-seat ferry.

Melissa Express (m 032 44 743 03/032 02 073 64; e melissaexpress1@gmail.com) offers a competitive price and 2-hour crossing time. However, as this boat also serves Mananara and Maroantsetra (page 298) it only does the Sainte Marie crossing on certain mornings (Tue/Thu/Sat at the time of writing).

GETTING AROUND THE ISLAND
A paved road runs for 50km or so up the length of the west coast, a drive of around 2 hours. A limited taxi-brousse service exists, but it's worth flagging down any vehicle for a lift. Taxis and tuk-tuks are easily found in the centre of Ambodifotatra and at the airport, or can be summoned by any hotel reception.

There are also many dirt tracks for which you need a 4x4 or motorbike. Most hotels have bikes for rent and many also rent scooters, motorbikes and quads, though sometimes for guests only. For guided quad and buggy tours, contact **Quad Sainte Marie** (m 032 40 745 39; e quadsaintemarie@sfr.fr; www.quadsaintemarie.com). **Loc' Clair** (m 034 18 793 36; e pelagie.saintemarie@gmail.com; www.loc-clair.com) in Ambodifotatra hires out 4x4s with AC.

AMBODIFOTATRA
This town is growing; it has several boutiques, two banks with ATMs (BFV and BOA), several restaurants and a patisserie. Market days are Tuesday and Thursday, and there's a small supermarket, **Super-Mahafapou** (⊕ Mon–Sat 07.30–noon & 14.30–19.00, Sun 07.30–noon), on the north side of the harbour. There is also a police post (m 034 71 171 07), pharmacy (m 032 72 982 52) and small hospital (✆ 57 400 08).

The **tourist information office** is alongside the harbour (✆ 57 901 47; m 034 57 901 47; ⊕ Mon–Sat 08.00–noon & 14.00–18.00).

🏠 Where to stay and eat

🏠 **Bigorne** (5 bungalows) ✆ 57 401 23. About 400m north of the harbour. A good bar & restaurant with en-suite bungalows crowded in the back garden. €€€

🏠 **Case à Paulo** (3 bungalows) m 032 04 242 97/032 69 036 42; e lacaseapaulo@yahoo.fr. Rooms with kitchenette, fridge & TV/DVD; excellent option for longer stays. €€€

🏠 **Polina** (6 bungalows) Av Bigorne; m 032 96 156 67/034 45 123 92; e lapolina@gmail.com or marcelnadia44@gmail.com. En-suite seaside bungalows with TV, fan & hot water. Large restaurant. Bike hire. €€€

🏠 **Vieux Fort** (7 rooms) 11 Rue Verges; m 034 67 456 79; e levieuxfort@gmail.com; www.levieuxfort.com. Near the old church on the south side of town, with great sea views. Smart en-suite rooms in 4 villas inc a studio with kitchenette. Wi-Fi in reception. Bar & restaurant. €€€

🏠 **Freddy** (4 rooms) m 032 83 079 50. Big bright rooms with AC in this centrally located hotel; some en suite. Freddy & Lala are very hospitable. €€–€€€

🏠 **Hortensia** (12 rooms) ✆ 57 400 09/57 403 69; e lamerveille_hortensia@yahoo.fr. Just 250m north of the harbour. Clean, spacious rooms with hot water. Family rooms have sea views; dbl rooms have balconies facing the road. Good, reasonably priced restaurant. €€–€€€

🏠 **Paillote** (7 rooms) Facing the harbour. Popular restaurant with good pizzas. Also driverless 4x4 hire. €€–€€€

🏠 **Palmiers** (7 bungalows) m 032 04 960 94/034 27 351 67; e hotel.palmiers@yahoo.fr. Some 200m up a track from Drakkar. Simple bungalows, some with kitchenette. €€–€€€

🏠 **Zinnia** (5 rooms & 6 bungalows) ✆ 57 400 09. Right by the harbour wall. Dbl bungalows with cold showers, fans & outside flush toilet. Rooms

13

with shared facilities. Pleasant restaurant. Same ownership as Hortensia. €€

✗ Banane m 032 42 424 53; e michellabanane@yahoo.fr. 200m north of the harbour. A *vazaha* hang-out with sea-view terrace, bar, pool table & good food. Also has rooms & dorm.

✗ Barachois Across from the harbour. Outside tables good for people-watching. Very comprehensive menu.

✗ Cambusa m 034 73 442 40; e lacambusasm@yahoo.fr; ⊕ Wed–Mon 11.00–14.30 & 18.00–22.30; Tue closed. Regularly praised Italian food inc pizza & homemade ice cream; amiable owner.

✗ Gargote à Bord 'Eaux Small cosy restaurant-bar on the path to the pirate cemetery.

✗ Idylle Beach m 032 48 684 81; e info@idyllebeach.com; www.idyllebeach.com. At the north end of town, this stylish restaurant & bar has a relaxed ambience & sumptuous menu, inc their specialities zebu lasagne & a seafood medley called Royal Idylle Beach. Wi-Fi. They also recently added two upper-range guest rooms & have Hobie-Cat 14/16 sports catamarans for hire.

✗ Mama Santa Opposite Hortensia. Opened by Rasoa Fanga in 2009, it has built up a reputation as a tremendous pizzeria.

✗ Restaurant du Quai m 032 40 428 83/032 43 163 47; e alexischanyuking@yahoo.fr. Harbourside Chinese restaurant.

⌨ Choco Pain m 032 81 959 93; e ma_diane@hotmail.fr. Patisserie & café opposite the landing jetty.

Nightlife The best discotheque here is **First One Club** (m *033 02 366 77/032 40 022 99*). Alternatively there's **Case à Nono** (m *034 09 537 42/032 02 316 54; e djbob515@yahoo.fr; ⊕ Thu/Sat 21.00–04.00*) but you will need to take a taxi as it is a few kilometres south of town.

What to see and do in Ambodifotatra

There are some interesting sights around the town which are an easy cycle ride from most of the hotels. There is a **Catholic church** built in 1837, which serves as a reminder that Sainte Marie was owned by France from 1750. As a further reminder of French domination there is a **war monument** to a French–British skirmish in 1845.

The **pirates' cemetery** is just after the bay bridge south of town. A signposted track leads to the cemetery. It's impassable at high tide but you can cross by pirogue (agree the price in advance). This is quite an impressive place, with gravestones dating from the 1830s, including one carved with a classic skull and crossbones. There is a 2,000Ar charge to visit the cemetery or 10,000Ar with a guide.

Halfway across the bay bridge, the road passes over the tiny (4.5ha) Ilot Madame, where the **Palace of Queen Bety** (also known as the governor's residence) has recently been renovated as part of a cultural heritage project that ultimately aims to turn it into a museum.

 BEACH HOTELS Most of the beach hotels are ranged along the west coast, with a handful in the east. Several more are on Ile aux Nattes to the south (see page 341).

Bear in mind that airport transfers to the more isolated hotels north of Ambodifotatra are most expensive and there are fewer alternatives to eating (perhaps expensive) meals at your hotel. Those on a tight budget would do best to stay in Ambodifotatra where there is a choice of eateries and other facilities within walking distance.

Prices for high season (Sep to mid-Nov, Christmas and school holidays) tend to be substantially higher than for low season and be aware that – unusually for Madagascar – prices are sometimes quoted per person, not per room.

Luxury 👑

🏠 Adonys Eden Lodge [332 A6] (6 bungalows) ☎ 57 906 49; m 032 52 721 60/032 64 019 46; e adonysedenlodge@yahoo.fr; www.adonysedenlodge.com. Surrounded by palms, this is the only hotel on a broad 2.5km beach of dazzling white sand. The design is a seamless synthesis of traditional & contemporary materials, with all the trappings. Hosts Adonys & Manfred will make you feel very welcome. Highly praised by all.

🏠 **Princesse Bora** [332 A6] (20 bungalows) ✆ 57 040 03; m 032 07 090 48; e info@ princessebora.com or resa@princessebora.com; www.princesse-bora.com; see ad, 4th colour section. Within walking distance of the airport, but transfers are usually by zebu cart. Owned by François-Xavier Mayer, whose family has been on Ste Marie for over 200 years, & his partner (architect of the hotel) Sophie de Michelis. Beautifully designed, this hotel is excellent in every respect. The Jungle Spa offers relaxation & pampering. In whale-watching season (Jul–Sep) it becomes a centre of scientific study, with guests going out with research teams to help collect data.

🏠 **Riake Resort** [332 C3] (11 bungalows) ✆ 57 907 11/57 912 86; m 032 40 377 95; e info@ riakeresort.com; www.riakeresort.com. Opened in 2011 by an Italian who fell in love with Ile Sainte Marie on a 2005 holiday. Charming en-suite wooden bungalows with 4-poster beds set in front of a natural forest, along a huge remote beach. Wi-Fi. Beautiful restaurant serves European & local dishes in seafood & pizzas. Very hospitable staff & attentive service.

🏠 **Soanambo** [332 A6] (48 rooms) ✆ 23 640 53 (Tana); m 034 20 150 58/034 44 416 17 (manager)/034 44 416 20; e info@hsm.mg or resa@hsm.mg; www.soanambo.mg. Relatively large 4-star hotel of contemporary design with orchid garden & terrace bar/restaurant from which you can watch whales. Private beach, swimming pool & beauty salon with massage parlour. Guests are treated like royalty.

Top end €€€€€

🏠 **Boraha Village** [332 B5] (15 bungalows) ✆ 57 912 18; m 032 54 547 68; e contact@ borahavillage.com or info@borahavillage.com; www.boraha.com. This welcoming hotel has seafront bungalows with hammocks; no beach as such but there's a lovely jetty for relaxing. Activities inc fishing, waterskiing, canoeing, biking & pirogue trips. Min stay 2 nights.

🏠 **Club Paradise** [332 A6] (9 bungalows) m 032 82 223 58; e hotelclubparadise9@gmail. com; www.hotel-clubparadise.com. Take the

turning at Parc Endemika. Bungalows right on the beach in a tranquil bay; each with private veranda, safe & en-suite facilities.

🏠 **EcoLodge Ravoraha** [332 A6] (3 rooms & 13 bungalows) m 032 40 513 90; e info@ravoraha. com; www.ravoraha.com. Responsible travel is the number 1 priority at this charming boutique hotel. They make every effort to reduce their impact on the environment & have forged strong community links with the bustling village immediately next door. Traditional bungalows inc a new tree-house. Wi-Fi in restaurant. They also have an annexe, **Las Palapas**, with a fine holiday villa for up to 10 people.

🏠 **Hibiscus** [332 C3] (2 bungalows) m 034 20 515 15; e marc.blondel@moov.mg. Holiday villas (max 6 people) 21km north of Ambodifotatra, complete with kitchenette; housekeeper & optional cook. Ideal for longer stays.

🏠 **Masoandro** [332 B3] (18 bungalows) ✆ 23 640 53 (Tana)/57 910 43; m 034 20 150 58 (Tana)/034 44 416 14 (management); e info@ hsm.mg or masoandro@hsm.mg or resa@hsm.mg; www.masoandro.mg. Bungalows in 2 categories: 'luxe' (with TV, minibar, safe, Wi-Fi, lounge & huge terrace) are significantly better than 'superior'. All en suite with AC. Infinity-edge pool, lovely location & beautiful views.

🏠 **Natiora Green Lodge** [332 B3] (7 bungalows) ✆ 57 906 56; m 032 71 964 56/034 54 423 51/034 60 323 74 (manager); e lodge@ natiora.com or residences@natiora.com; www. natiora.com. Nestled between sea & forest in an intimate cove with a 700m stony beach, this lush 6ha plot is a little paradise for nature lovers; strong ethical & sustainability theme. The thatched villas are fully equipped, even inc kitchenette.

🏠 **Piment Vanille** [332 A6] (3 bungalows) m 034 12 314 83; e pimentvanille515@gmail. com; www.location-ile-sainte-marie.net. On the eastern beach opposite Vohilava; attractively furnished with wind & solar power. Motorbike, quad & bike hire.

🏠 **Sainte Marie Lodge (Eden Bé)** [332 C2] (10 rooms) m 034 19 059 52; e info@ saintemarielodge.com; www.hotel-saintemarielodge-madagascar.com. It is clear that a lot of effort has gone into designing this guesthouse, in a relaxing spot in the peaceful north of the island. Rooms have safe, desk, minibar, AC, TV, Wi-Fi, private terrace & en-suite facilities; most are suites with a sea view.

13

⌂ **Tonga Soa Beach** [332 B4] (3 bungalows) m 032 94 962 46; e tongasoabeach@yahoo.com; www.tongasoabeach.com. Waterfront villas for 2–8 people; comfy & simply furnished with shady private terraces. Inc housekeeper & guardian.

⌂ **Vohilava** [332 A6] (6 rooms & 1 bungalow) ☎57 900 16; m 032 04 757 84/034 17 668 63; e vohilava@gmail.com; www.vohilava.com. Various spacious holiday villas for rent for 2–10 people; all beautifully furnished inc terrace complete with hammocks. HB & FB options; a housekeeper takes care of cooking & cleaning. Visa & MasterCard accepted.

Upper range €€€€

⌂ **Crique** [332 B3] (12 bungalows) m 032 03 117 25/034 03 117 25; e lacrique@moov.mg; www.lacrique-saintemarie.com. One of Ste Marie's longest-established hotels; deservedly popular so book ahead. Extremely pretty location, right on the beach. Mostly en suite with hot water but also a couple of cheaper basic bungalows. Good beach for snorkelling. Wonderful ambience & delicious, good-value meals.

⌂ **Lakana** [332 A5] (15 bungalows) ☎57 910 42; m 032 02 132 84/032 07 090 22/034 01 060 10; e hotellakana@gmail.com or lakana@moov. mg; www.sainte-marie-hotel.com. Simple but comfortable wooden bungalows, inc some perched magnificently on stilts above the sea. Wi-Fi. Excellent location. Visa accepted.

⌂ **Libertalia** [332 A5] (13 bungalows) m 032 02 923 03/034 18 997 27; e libertalia@ moov.mg; www.lelibertalia.com. Popular, friendly hotel in a very nice setting; often fully booked. There's a jetty out to a small private islet. Excellent food in stunning restaurant, with an ambience that belies its reasonable prices. Regularly praised by readers.

⌂ **Mirana Plage** [332 A5] (5 bungalows) m 032 51 896 66; e arminjoneric@yahoo.fr or miranaplage@hotmail.com; www.miranaplage. com. Describing themselves as 'not a hotel on a beach but a beach in a hotel', this place has a pretty laid-back vibe. Kitesurfing outfit Kitpitaine Flame is based here.

⌂ **Mora Mora** [332 A5] (11 bungalows) ☎57 040 80/57 906 82/57 913 78; m 032 07 090 98/033 07 709 69/034 10 385 30; e moramoravillage@gmail.com; www.moramora. info. En-suite dbl & family bungalows. Italian-

owned place specialising in boat trips to watch whales & watersports inc diving. No beach.

⌂ **Pirate** [332 A5] (4 bungalows) Opposite Libertalia; m 032 02 030 18/032 02 672 44/034 13 935 14. Bungalows with hot shower & sea-view balcony; 2 with kitchenette.

⌂ **Samaria Cosy Lodge** [332 C2] (5 bungalows) ☎57 907 18; m 034 20 515 15; e contact@samaria-hotel.com or marc.blondel@ moov.mg; www.samaria-hotel.com. Chic new wood & granite sea-view bungalows on a small private inlet near Anivorano village. Excursions inc whale-watching, bikes, quads, pirogues & diving.

⌂ **Tipaniers Lodge** [332 C1] (7 bungalows) ☎57 907 07/57 907 16; m 033 25 172 14; e info@ tipaniers.com; www.tipaniers.com. Solar-powered ecolodge with pretty thatched bungalows. Restaurant serves mainly fresh seafood. Fishing, whale-watching & other boat trips.

⌂ **Vanilla Café** [332 A5] (5 bungalows) just north of Palourde; m 032 40 239 43/032 40 698 38. Simple en-suite bungalows; great food.

⌂ **Vanivola** [332 A5] (10 rooms & 9 bungalows) m 032 05 720 19 (Tana)/032 42 357 67; e infos@hotel-vanivola-madagascar.com; www.hotel-vanivola-madagascar.com. French-run hotel with pool, TV lounge, atmospheric bar & funky restaurant. Seafront bungalows with AC, TV & Wi-Fi; also some cheaper rooms.

Mid-range €€€

⌂ **Air Bleu** [332 A5] (4 rooms & 2 bungalows) m 032 24 307 63/034 31 027 86; www. hotelrestoairbleu.sitew.com. Intimate & welcoming French-owned east-coast hotel with very good French & Malagasy food. Bike, motorbike & quad hire; 4x4 & boat trips. There is also a villa for 6–8 people.

⌂ **Antafondro** [332 B3] (10 bungalows) m 032 70 060 73/033 37 156 88/034 60 420 69; e antafondrolodge@yahoo.fr; www.antafondrolodge-madagascar.com. Wooden bungalows of traditional local design, 7 right on the seafront; all have en-suite bathrooms & 3 have kitchenette.

⌂ **Atafana** [332 B3] (9 bungalows) m 032 04 637 81/032 43 620 55/032 70 252 50/034 60 420 13; e hotel_atafana@yahoo.fr; www.atafana.net. In a beautiful bay 18km north of the main town, this resort offers good value for a great location. En-suite bungalows, good snorkelling & tasty food. Highly recommended for relaxation. Bike, motorbike & 4x4 hire.

🏠 **Baleine** [332 A5] (10 bungalows) m 032 40 257 18/032 64 945 07/034 04 719 62; e lantoualbert@moov.mg or lantouedibert@ yahoo.fr; www.hotel-la-baleine.com. Rustic bungalows, mostly en suite with hot water, but also some budget ones. Owner Albert Lantou sponsors local projects inc a youth football club.

🏠 **Bon Endroit** [332 C2] (5 bungalows) 📞57 906 62; m 033 09 624 38/034 16 438 49; e lebonendroit.sm@gmail.com; www. lebonendroit.net. In a wonderfully tranquil corner of northwest Ile Sainte Marie, Arnaud & Nouba's guesthouse has simple comfy bungalows with en-suite bathrooms at very reasonable prices. Activities inc kayaking, biking, fishing & snorkelling.

🏠 **Chez Mireille** [332 A6] (5 bungalows) Vohilava; m 032 04 864 95/034 13 652 49; e mireille.vohilava@hotmail.fr; www.mireille-sainte-marie.com. No-nonsense traditional bungalows on a palm-shaded beach. Bike hire.

🏠 **Chez Pierrot** [332 A5] (8 bungalows) m 032 02 040 55/034 01 060 91/034 02 040 55; e chezpierrot@moov.mg. Clean, functional bungalows, some en suite with hot water.

🏠 **Cocoteraie Robert** [332 C1] (13 bungalows) 📞57 901 76 (evening); m 034 29 666 98/034 45 300 47; e cocoteraierobert@gmail.com. Dating to 1972, this is Ile Sainte Marie's oldest hotel. In an isolated spot; a good choice if you want a quiet beach.

🏠 **Jardins d'Eden** [332 A5] (4 bungalows) m 034 09 265 76; e lesjardinsdeden. saintemarie515@gmail.com or lesjardinsdeden@ moov.mg; www.jardinsdeden-saintemarie-madagascar.com. This guesthouse near the pirate cemetery occupies a lushly planted spot in an elevated position with tremendous views. The rooms are simple but clean & comfy, with balconies. Marvellous Malagasy & Creole food & some Indian specialities.

🏠 **Rocher (Chez Emilienne)** [332 B3] (7 bungalows) 📞57 040 16/57 912 98; m 032 57 568 42; http://lerocher.emilienne.free.fr. Emilienne's charming & cheerful character (& splendid cooking) makes this an unforgettable place to stay. Bungalows en suite with hot water.

Budget €€

🏠 **Chez Didier** [332 A6] (4 bungalows) m 032 40 843 87. Noisy & basic with shared facilities & cold water.

🏠 **Mangrove Gourmande** [332 B3] 📞57 901 98. Just north of Anafiafy. Low-price bungalows & good-value food.

🏠 **Palourde** [332 A5] (3 rooms & 6 bungalows) m 032 02 157 80/034 06 092 25; e lapalourdeclementine@yahoo.fr. Clean en-suite bungalows on a mediocre beach. The friendly Malagasy-Mauritian owner is a great cook.

WHAT TO SEE AND DO

Whale-watching July to September is the best time to see humpback whales but you could be lucky in June or October. You can watch them from any of the beachfront hotels or take a boat excursion (offered by most hotels and dive centres). For a really hands-on experience, stay at Princesse Bora where you'll get the chance to assist whale researchers. Take plenty of water, suncream and a waterproof jacket.

The very active **Association CETAMADA** (m *032 05 090 05/032 81 973 00*; e *president@cetamada.org*; *www.cetamada.org*) oversees whale and dolphin research and awareness-raising in the area, and ensures operators adhere to a whale-watching code of conduct: welfare guidelines on viewing distance, boat speed, maximum observation period, approach angle, and so on. Check their website to see which boat operators are signed up the charter.

Each July, Sainte Marie hosts an impressive nine-day **Festival des Baleines** (*www. festivaldesbaleines.com*) to mark the start of the season. It includes a carnival, concerts with famous singers, dancing and games, sports competitions including trail running and mountain biking, exhibitions, school events and film screenings.

Snorkelling and diving The shallows around Sainte Marie are ideal for snorkelling and diving, despite the inshore waters being overfished. Most of the coral reefs are in good condition and the water is usually clear, although some of the huge table corals have been broken off by fish traps. The best snorkelling sites are near Atafana and La Crique, and also the west side of Ile aux Nattes; most hotels have masks and fins for guests.

Dive operators include **Lémurien Palmé** (*Ambodifotatra;* \ *57 040 15;* m *032 04 816 56;* e *info@lemurien-palme.com or lemurienpalme@moov.mg; www. lemurien-palme.com*), **Il Balenottero** (*Ambodifotatra;* \ *57 400 36;* m *032 05 501 25;* e *contact@il-balenottero.com; www.il-balenottero.com*) and based at Princesse Bora Hotel is **Bora Dive & Research** (m *032 07 090 90;* e *info@boraresearch.com; www. boraresearch.com*).

Exploring the island You can discover Sainte Marie on foot or by bike, motorbike or quad (page 335). In the low season, if you are fit and energetic, you could walk or cycle around most of the island and take your chance on places to stay, but during peak seasons most of the hotels may be full. Adventure Tours can arrange all kinds of guided visits either walking or by vehicle (m *034 31 028 70/034 09 265 76;* e *adventuretours@moov.mg*).

At the southern tip of Sainte Marie there is a **viewpoint** [332 A6] from which you can see Ile aux Nattes and watch the sunset. Head 1km or so past the airport and follow the signs for 'Panorama'.

At the far northeast, beyond the end of the road, is an impressive *piscine naturelle* with a waterfall, a big pool and enormous basalt rocks [332 D1]. The beach here is beautiful. Also in the area is **Albrand Lighthouse** [332 D1], built in 1931 to replace an earlier iron tower constructed in 1906. If you can find the keeper, do ask to go inside and take in the magnificent panorama from the top, 16 metres up.

It is well worth taking a **pirogue trip** (or sea kayaks) to explore the coast, especially around **Forêt d'Ampanihy** on the eastern side.

Parc Endemika [332 A6] (☉ *Mon–Sat 08.00–noon & 14.00–17.00; entry 15,000Ar, under-10s 5,000Ar*) is small park-cum-zoo at Vohilava where a guided tour takes around an hour.

ILE AUX NATTES (NOSY NATO)

To many people this little island off the south coast of Sainte Marie is even better than the main island. Being roadless and car-free it is much more peaceful. Debbie Fellner reflects: 'If I were to do the trip again, I'd split my time equally between both islands. Ile aux Nattes is about as fantasy-islandesque as it gets. Pristine beaches, quiet village, hidden bungalows, excellent restaurants.'

A pirogue transfer here from near the airport on Sainte Marie costs 2,000Ar, or more to be taken directly to your chosen hotel.

WHERE TO STAY AND EAT

Orchidée Napoleon [332 D6] (3 bungalows) Solar-powered seaside bungalows reserved for guests of Soanambo Hotel (on the main island, see page 337) wishing to make an overnight visit to Ile aux Nattes. 👑

Analatsara [332 C6] (5 bungalows) m 032 02 127 70; e lebaronjpbriois@gmail.com; www. analatsara.net. Run by a Frenchman who calls himself 'The Baron', this guesthouse is pleasant but very pricey, especially considering the bathrooms are communal with hot water only at certain hours. The food, however, is exquisite – so do at least pass by for a meal. One of the bungalows is large enough for 6 people & another is built as a tree-house entered via a trapdoor! €€€€€

Baboo Village [332 D5] (15 bungalows) 📞57 905 63/57 914 48; e infos@baboo-village. com; www.baboo-village.com. En-suite bungalows, large & airy with hot water on request; 4 are right on the water. Wonderful dining area on a jetty. Boutique, massage, netball, bikes & boats for excursions. €€€€€

Coco Lodge [332 D5] (3 bungalows) 📞22 755 01; m 032 21 616 40; www.cocolodge. com. Self-catering accommodation for up to 8 people. €€€€

Lémuriens [332 C7] (9 bungalows) m 032 41 973 03; e info@les-lemuriens.com; www.les-lemuriens.com. After destruction by a 2008 cyclone, this place reinvented itself as an ecolodge. Most of the bungalows have en-suite bathrooms with hot water. The hotel commands a

spectacular position so it's worth the walk down here for a drink or seafood meal in the lagoon-front restaurant even if you stay elsewhere. €€€€

Maningory [332 C5] (13 bungalows) 📞57 902 58; m 032 07 090 05; e maningory.hotel@ gmail.com; www.maningoryhotel.com. Stylishly rebuilt in wood & stone in 2014; idyllic location. Wi-Fi. Boats for whale-watching & fishing. €€€€

Meva Paradis [332 C5] (8 bungalows) m 032 46 802 81/034 11 825 99 (manager); e hotelmevaparadis@yahoo.com; www. mevaparadis.com. Run by a Malagasy-American couple; pleasant palm-thatched bungalows by a white-sand beach that is close to perfection. Restaurant-bar with homely atmosphere. Wi-Fi. €€€€

Paradisa [332 D7] (8 bungalows) 📞57 905 84; m 034 20 554 11; e contact@paradisahotel-camping.com; www.paradisahotel-camping. com. En-suite bungalows; some along the beach. Massage, windsurfing, kayaking, fishing & boat trips. Camping for around 30,000Ar/tent. €€€€

Petite Traversée [332 D5] (8 bungalows) 📞57 905 62; m 032 42 360 52; e lapetitetraversee@gmail.com. South African owner Ockie goes out of his way to make sure nobody leaves this place disappointed. Highly recommended; described by one reader as 'heaven on earth'. €€€€

Sambatra [332 C6] (5 bungalows) m 033 76 834 99; e sambatrabeachlodge@gmail. com; www.sambatrabeachlodge.com. Completely rebuilt in 2013, with fantastic thatched stone bungalows & smart new restaurant. €€€€

🏠 **Villa Ravinala** [332 C7] (1 bungalow) e 2bcorse@gmail.com; www. villaravinalamadagascar.com. Beautiful house for a group of up to 8 people. €€€€

🏠 **Ylang Village** [332 C5] (7 bungalows) m 032 40 698 38/032 43 821 67/034 71 208 30; e ylang2@wanadoo.fr. Simple local-style bungalows nr the beach. €€€€

🏠 **Bar de la Marine** [332 C5] (4 bungalows) m 032 41 041 02/032 46 233 18; e contact@ bardelamarine.com; www.bardelamarine.com. Basic accommodation with shared cold showers. Restaurant & boutique right at the pirogue crossing point. €€€

🏠 **Chez Sica** [332 C6] (9 bungalows) m 032 04 607 74/032 41 656 98/032 42 478 86; www.chezsica.com. Very good value dbl & family

bungalows in a beautiful palm-shaded seafront garden with hammocks to relax in. No restaurant, but there are many eateries nearby & a communal kitchen for guests' use. €€€

🏠 **Robinsonnade** [332 C7] (7 bungalows) ☎ 57 911 70; m 032 40 445 99; e contact@ larobinsonnade.com or larobinsonnade@moov. mg; www.larobinsonnade.com. Simple thatched bungalows, some en suite. Also 2 magnificent tree-house bungalows at a more upper-range price. Massage & 10-person boat for excursions. €€€

🏠 **Chez Tity** [332 D5] (5 bungalows) m 034 04 362 03; e cheztity@gmail.com. Simple but nice huts (named after famous philosophers), some en suite. Cold showers but they'll prepare you some hot water for washing if you ask nicely. Fantastic fresh food; the owner is a former chef, musician & children's author. €–€€

WHAT TO SEE AND DO The circumference of the island is 8km, and it takes at least 3 hours to walk round it, but some parts are impassable at high tide.

There is much to see during a short walking tour, including the island's unique and amazing orchid, *Eulophiella roempleriana*, known popularly as *l'orchidée rose*. It is 2m high with deep pink flowers.

The best **beaches** are in the north of the island: calm, shallow, crystal-clear water, with soft white sand overhung by picture-postcard palms.

A small trip to the interior of the island is also recommended. **Aniribe** village at the centre is pure unspoiled Madagascar. Head south from there up to the old **lighthouse** [332 D7], a rather squat (7m tall) masonry construction from 1914.

above	Its kangaroo-like locomotion gives the Madagascar giant jumping rat its name (DA) pages 420–1
right	Despite its feline appearance, the fossa is an overgrown relative of the mongoose (DA) page 64
below left	A flying fox, one of Madagascar's 43 bat species, in flight (DA) pages 60–1
below right	Some 34 tenrec species inhabit Madagascar; many resemble hedgehogs, like this lesser hedgehog tenrec (LJ) page 62
bottom	Between July and September, humpback whales visit Madagascar waters to calve (NG) page 64

above   Black-and-white ruffed lemurs feed on fruit, nectar and flowers (DA) page 56

left   The mouse lemur group comprises 21 species — including the world's smallest primate, weighing just 30g (DA) page 58

below left   The crowned sifaka comes from remote regions in the west of the island (DA) page 57

below   The largest living lemur is the indri. It cannot survive in captivity so conservation of wild populations is critical (DA) page 57

above left Like all sportive lemurs, Hubbard's sportive lemur is nocturnal but may be seen peering out of a tree hole during the day (DA) page 59

above right The aye-aye occupies the evolutionary niche normally filled by woodpeckers elsewhere in the world and was once believed to be a type of squirrel (DA) page 59

right A female white-fronted brown lemur from Nosy Mangabe Special Reserve (DA) page 56

below Coquerel's sifaka can leap spectacular distances between trees (DA) page 57

Almost all of the several hundred Malagasy frog species are endemic: *Aglyptodactylus madagascariensis* (*above left*) turns yellow only during mating time; *Boophis sandrae* (*above*) is a recently described species; and *Boophis Pyrrhus* (*left*) is easily seen around Andasibe (all DA) pages 48–9

With a little luck, in the southwest you could see a spider tortoise (*left*), one of the five tortoise species that occurs on the island — four of which are endemic (DA) page 52

From the impressively well camouflaged to the outrageously flamboyant: leaf-tailed geckos (*bottom left*) are masters of disguise, while day geckos (*bottom right*) can be spectacularly bright (both DA) page 49

The panther chameleon (*above*) is one of the most variable and vibrantly coloured species (LJ); stump-tailed/leaf chameleons (*above right*) are much smaller and more drab in hue (DA) page 51

Madagascar has no dangerous snakes, despite the appearance of some like this *Phisalixella arctifasciata* (*below right*) (DA). Twig-mimic snakes (*below*) have extraordinary 'noses' (HB) page 50

above   Verreaux's coua is one of nine coua species, all endemic (LJ)

left   Like all couas, the giant coua exhibits conspicuous blue skin around its eye (DA)

below left   The endemic vanga family contains well over a dozen remarkably different species with a glorious diversity of beak designs, each adapted to their preferred diet. Most striking of all is the helmet vanga's monstrous blue bill (NG)

below right   The owl visitors are most likely to see is the Madagascar scops owl (DA)

above left	The crested drongo occurs island-wide (DA)
above right	Madagascar malachite kingfishers are typically found near water (DA)
right	Madagascar paradise flycatchers often nest near forest trails (DA)
below left	Madagascar bee-eaters are frequently seen in pairs (LJ)
below right	Red-tailed tropicbirds nest on offshore islets (LJ)

above left   The comet moth is one of the world's largest moths (NG)

above right   It is easy to see how giraffe-necked weevils got their name (EH)

left   Caterpillars come in all shapes and sizes (DA)

below left   Giant millipedes may exceed 15cm (DA)

below right   The bright colours of rainbow milkweed locusts warn of their toxicity (DA)

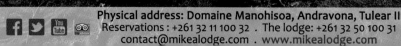

one of the most beautiful jewels of the southwest

truly mystical encounters

MIKEA
lodge

10 fully
equipped luxury tents

Mikea National Park

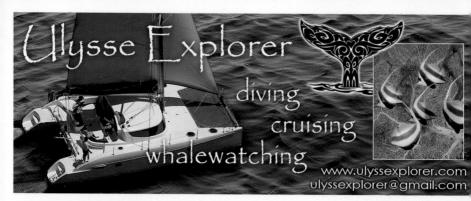

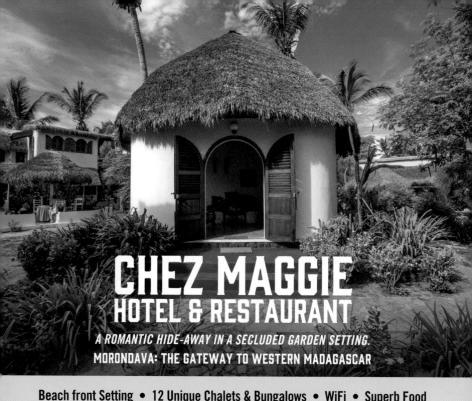

CHEZ MAGGIE
HOTEL & RESTAURANT

A ROMANTIC HIDE-AWAY IN A SECLUDED GARDEN SETTING.
MORONDAVA: THE GATEWAY TO WESTERN MADAGASCAR

Beach front Setting • 12 Unique Chalets & Bungalows • WiFi • Superb Food
Wondrous Sunsets • Vehicle Rental & Multi-Lingual Guide Service

Excursions : Tsingy de Bemaraha, Kirindy Forest, Ave of the Baobabs, Belo sur Mer
Quality custom tours throughout Madagascar with Remote River Expeditions

www.chezmaggie.com   info@chezmaggie.com
phone : + (261) 20 95 523 47   mobile : + (261) 324 732 670

4 Years ~ Tripadvisor Certificate of Excellence Winner

Gondwana park

*A private TSINGY park
just beside Ankarana Lodge*

www.ankarana-parc.com

RELAX TO THE RHYTHM OF PARADISE

NOSY
SABA
MADAGASCAR

+261 (0)20 22 434 00 • +261 (0)32 03 333 02
contact@nosysaba.mg • www.nosysaba.mg
The most authentic private island resort!

14

The North

The north of Madagascar is characterised by its variety. With the Tsaratanana Massif (including Maromokotro, Madagascar's highest peak) bringing more rain to the Nosy Be area than is normal for the west coast, and the pocket of dry climate around Antsiranana (Diego Suarez), the weather can alter dramatically within short distances. The Antsiranana area has seven months of dry weather, with almost all of its 95cm annual rainfall concentrated between December and April. With changes of weather come changes of vegetation and its accompanying fauna, making this region particularly interesting to botanists and other naturalists.

This is the domain of the Antankarana people. Cut off by rugged mountains, the Antankarana were left to their own devices until the mid-1700s when they were conquered by the Sakalava; they in turn submitted to the Merina king Radama I, aided by his military advisor James Hastie, in 1823.

The road between Antsiranana and Tana is around 1,200km, with several severely degraded sections, so many prefer to fly.

ANTSIRANANA (DIEGO SUAREZ)

HISTORY Forgivingly named after a 16th-century Portuguese explorer who arrived and proceeded to murder and rape the inhabitants or sell them into slavery, this large town has had an eventful history with truth blending into fiction. An often-told tale is that pirates founded a utopian anarchist colony known as Libertalia or Libertatia here. The story started in a 1724 book called *A General History of the Robberies and Murders of the Most Notorious Pyrates and also Their Policies, Discipline and Government*, widely suspected to have been penned by Daniel Defoe under a pseudonym. Many modern historians consider it a fiction.

Most people still call the town Diego. The Malagasy name simply means 'port' and its strategic importance as a deep-water harbour has long been recognised. The French installed a military base here in 1885, and the town played an important role in World War II when Madagascar was under the control of the Vichy French (see box, pages 352–3). To prevent Japanese warships and submarines making use of the magnificent harbour, and thus threatening vital sea routes, Britain and the Allies captured and occupied Diego Suarez in 1942. There are British and French cemeteries honouring those killed.

A tremendously detailed 280-page historical guidebook, *Les Fortifications de la Baie de Diego Suarez* – available locally for 95,000Ar – will delight military history buffs (*www.fortifications-de-diego-suarez.info*). It is a collaboration between journalists from *La Tribune de Diego* and Association Ambre (*http://ambre.cyber-diego.com*), an organisation that preserves local heritage.

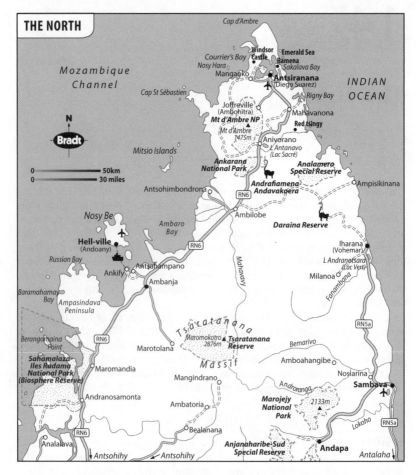

THE NORTH

Cap d'Ambre

Windsor Castle
Emerald Sea
Courrier's Bay
Ramena
Nosy Hara
Sakalava Bay
Mangaoko
Antsiranana
(Diego Suarez)

Mozambique Channel

Cap St Sébastien

Rigny Bay

INDIAN OCEAN

Joffreville
(Ambohitra)
Mt d'Ambre NP
Mahavanona
Red tsingy
Mt d'Ambre
1475m

N

Bradt

Anivorano
L'Antanavo
(Lac Sacré)

Mitsio Islands

Ankarana
National Park
*Analamera
Special Reserve*

0 ————— 50km
0 ————— 30 miles

*Andrafiamena
Andavakoera*
Ampisikinana

Antsohimbondrona

RN6

Nosy Be

Ambilobe

Daraina Reserve

Hell-ville
(Andoany)

Ambaro
Bay

RN6

Iharana
(Vohemar)

Russian Bay

Antsahampano

L Andranotsara
(Lac Vert)

Ankify

Ambanja

Milanoa

*Baramahamay
Bay*
*Ampasindava
Peninsula*

Tsaratanana

Mahavavy

Fanambana

RN5a

*Berangomaina
Point*

RN6

Marotolana

Maromokotro
2876m
Tsaratanana
Reserve

Bemarivo

*Sahamalaza-
Iles Radama
National Park
(Biosphere Reserve)*

Maromandia

Massif

Amboahangibe

Noslarina

Mangindrano

Androranga

Sambava

Andranosamonta

Ambatoria

*Marojejy
National
Park*
2133m

Lokoho

RN5a

RN6

Bealanana

Analalava

Antsohihy
Antsohihy

*Anjanaharibe-Sud
Special Reserve*

Andapa

Antalaha

ANTSIRANANA TODAY This is Madagascar's fifth-largest town and is of interest to visitors for its diverse attractions and superb location. The harbour is encircled by hills and to the east is a large bay with a 'sugarloaf', Nosy Lonja (literally 'conical island'), in the middle. The port's isolation behind its mountain barrier and its long association with non-Malagasy races have given it an unusually cosmopolitan population and lots of colour: there are Arabs, Creoles (descendants of Europeans), Indians, Chinese and Comorans.

Almost everyone enjoys Antsiranana. Lee Miller writes: 'The area north of Place Foch is the old colonial sector, with an atmosphere of faded French occupation. Big brick colonial buildings, with street arcades topped by upper-storey verandas,

DISTANCES IN KILOMETRES			
Ambondromamy–Antsiranana	756km	Antsiranana–Ambanja	240km
Antsohihy–Ambanja	217km	Antsiranana–Anivorano	75km
Antsiranana–Ambilobe	138km	Antsiranana–Daraina	245km
Antsiranana–Ankarana	108km	Antsiranana–Iharana (Vohemar)	301km

crumbling in disuse, abandon and neglect. Here is where you find most of the tourist activity: hotels, restaurants and handicraft shops. It has a languid, empty feel. But walk south down Rue Lafayette, then Rue du Suffren, and the activity increases exponentially as you find yourself in the bustle of the Malagasy centre.'

A set of pamphlets giving historical background to a series of self-guided walking tours of the town is available from the tourist office [346 C1].

If you want to relax on a beach for a few days, stay at **Ramena** (page 351) or, if kitesurfing and windsurfing are your thing, don't miss the east coast bays (page 353).

GETTING THERE AND AWAY There are **flights** to and from Tana every day, weekly services to Nosy Be and Sambava, and also internationally to the Comoros. Taxis are easily found at the airport for the 8km trip into town (12,000Ar), but a considerably cheaper alternative is to walk 250m to the main road and wait for a *taxi-brousse*.

The **overland** route between Ambanja (nearest town to Nosy Be) and Antsiranana is scenically beautiful but the road is degraded. Tougher still, but possible in good weather, is the road to Iharana (Vohemar). Both routes are described later in this chapter (see pages 365–6 and 363).

From Antsiranana, direct taxi-brousses to Tana cost 80,000Ar and take nearly 24 hours. Mahajanga is about 18 hours away (60,000Ar).

GETTING AROUND Within the town, taxis should cost a flat rate per person of 1,000Ar (1,500Ar at night) – or more on a private-hire basis. Tuk-tuks are now quite common and cost a bit less than taxis.

WHERE TO STAY
In Antsiranana

Luxury ♛

Grand Hotel [346 C4] (66 rooms) 46 Rue Colbert; 82 230 63; m 032 40 881 43; e grandhotel_diego@yahoo.fr; www.grand-hotel-diego.com. Centrally located high-standard rooms with TV, AC, minibar & Wi-Fi. Large public pool, patisserie, 2 restaurants, bar & boutique.

Top end €€€€€

Allamanda [346 B1](24 rooms) Rue Richelieu; 82 210 33/82 231 47; m 032 07 666 15; e hotelallamanda@gmail.com; www.hotels-diego.com. Upmarket hotel at the north end of town. En-suite rooms with AC, minibar & TV. Cards accepted. Restaurant Le Melville arguably the best eatery in town; prices not excessive.

Upper range €€€€

Colbert [346 C3] (34 rooms) 51 Rue Colbert; 82 232 89; m 034 07 666 13; e hlcdiego@moov.mg; www.hlcdiego.com. En-suite rooms with AC, safe & TV in 4 standards. Good restaurant, but expensive.

De la Poste [346 C1] (80 rooms) Bd Bazeilles; m 032 04 785 75; e contact@diego-hoteldelaposte.com; www.diego-hoteldelaposte.

com. Dbl en-suite rooms with Wi-Fi, AC & TV. Reportedly increasingly attracting an unsavoury clientele. Airport transfers inc.

Firdoss [346 B4] (34 rooms) 11 Rue Lavigerie; 82 240 22; m 032 57 746 01/033 13 983 53/034 03 341 28; e reservation@hotelfirdoss.com; www.hotelfirdoss.com. Smart interior: TV, Wi-Fi, AC & minibar in rooms; some with small balcony; 2 suites with kitchenette.

Imperial [346 C3] (40 rooms) 65 Rue Colbert; m 032 05 233 29; e accueil@hotelimperial-diego.com; www.hotelimperial-diego.com. Dbl rooms with AC, TV, minibar & balcony. Visa accepted.

Terrasse du Voyageur [346 C7] (26 rooms) Rue du Mozambique; 82 240 63; m 034 20 061 04/034 20 061 06; e reception@terrasseduvoyageur-hotel.com; www.terrasseduvoyageur-hotel.com. Sgl, dbl & twin rooms with safe, sat-TV & Wi-Fi; some with AC. The hotel is connected to a cultural centre which hosts music, films & shows.

Victoria (Emeraude) [346 C5] (19 rooms) Rue Rigault; 82 225 44; m 034 11 225 44; e levictoria@moov.mg; www.hotelvictoriadiego.com. Very smart en-suite rooms & suites with Wi-Fi, AC, sat-TV, minibar, writing desk & safe;

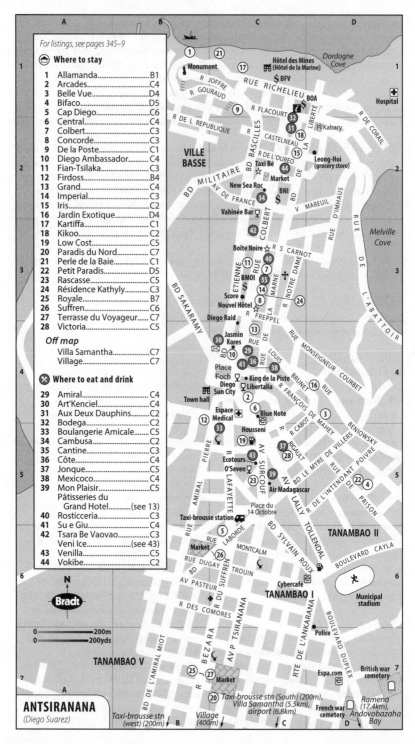

For listings, see pages 345–9

🛏 Where to stay

1	Allamanda	B1
2	Arcades	C4
3	Belle Vue	D4
4	Bifaco	D5
5	Cap Diego	C6
6	Central	C4
7	Colbert	C3
8	Concorde	C3
9	De la Poste	C1
10	Diego Ambassador	C4
11	Fian-Tsilaka	C3
12	Firdoss	B4
13	Grand	C4
14	Imperial	C3
15	Iris	C2
16	Jardin Exotique	D4
17	Kartiffa	C1
18	Kikoo	C2
19	Low Cost	C5
20	Paradis du Nord	C7
21	Perle de la Baie	C1
22	Petit Paradis	D5
23	Rascasse	C5
24	Résidence Kathyly	C3
25	Royale	B7
26	Suffren	C6
27	Terrasse du Voyageur	C7
28	Victoria	C5

Off map
	Villa Samantha	C7
	Village	C7

✖ Where to eat and drink

29	Amiral	C4
30	Art'Kenciel	C4
31	Aux Deux Dauphins	C2
32	Bodega	C2
33	Boulangerie Amicale	C5
34	Cambusa	C3
35	Cantine	C3
36	Côte	C4
37	Jonque	C5
38	Mexicoco	C4
39	Mon Plaisir	C5
	Pâtisseries du Grand Hotel	(see 13)
40	Rosticceria	C3
41	Su e Giu	C4
42	Tsara Be Vaovao	C3
	Veni Ice	(see 43)
43	Venilla	C5
44	Vokibe	C2

ANTSIRANANA
(Diego Suarez)

some with ceiling mirror over the bed! A spa offers professional massages.

🏠 **Villa Samantha** [346 C7] (5 rooms) PK 7, Rte d'Ambilobe; **m** 032 55 501 93; **e** villasamantha.diego@gmail.com; www. villasamantha-diegosuarez.com. En-suite rooms with sat-TV/DVD, safe, Wi-Fi & minibar, set around a swimming pool. Also an apartment with kitchenette.

🏠 **Village** [346 C7] (14 bungalows) Av Tsiranana; **m** 032 02 306 78/032 07 910 70; **e** levillagediego@yahoo.fr; www.levillage-diego. com. Spacious bungalows with lounge area & kitchenette. Bar, restaurant, swimming pool & Wi-Fi; 4x4 excursions.

Mid-range €€€

🏠 **Arcades** [346 C4] (8 rooms) 3 Av Tollendal; ☎82 231 04; **m** 032 02 617 95; **e** arcades@ blueline.mg or arcadesdiego@gmail.com. Quaint colonial building with courtyard, restaurant & bar. Simple rooms, mostly en suite; some with AC & Wi-Fi. Popular restaurant.

🏠 **Bifaco** [346 D5] (5 rooms) 8b Rue Chanzy; **m** 032 25 156 76; **e** bifaco.mada@gmail.com; www.bifacomada.wix.com/diego-suarez-dormir. Great value en-suite dbl & trpl rooms with Wi-Fi, sat-TV, fridge & safe. Airport transfer inc.

🏠 **Central** [346 C4] (10 rooms) 5 Av Tollendal; ☎82 240 25; **m** 032 51 746 82; **e** chdiego@moov. mg; www.centralhotel-diegosuarez.com. Reliable outfit in a good location; clean rooms with Wi-Fi & some with balcony. Visa accepted.

🏠 **Fian-Tsilaka** [346 C3] (20 rooms) 13 Bd Etienne; **m** 032 04 067 95; **e** dom.bigot@wanadoo. fr. En-suite dbl rooms, some with hot water & AC.

🏠 **Low Cost (Bougainvilliers)** [346 C5] (4 rooms) Rue Duchesne; ☎82 232 93; **m** 032 02 445 20/032 02 445 22; **e** cyber.delta@yahoo. fr. Central rooms with hot-water facilities, AC & Wi-Fi. Also a shared kitchen for guests' use & 2 apartments.

🏠 **Perle de la Baie (Baie de Diego Suarez)** [346 C1] (5 rooms) 5 Rue Richelieu; ☎82 233 04; **m** 032 04 434 50/033 18 826 73; **e** perledelabaie@gmail.com; www.perledelabaie. blogspot.com. B&B on 2 floors at the far north of town with stunning bay view, run by friendly

Malagasy-French couple Claire & Juvet since 2013. Simple comfy rooms, mostly with shared facilities. 'Newly renovated & very clean' reports Farnoush Farahji.

🏠 **Petit Paradis** [346 D5] (7 rooms) Rue de la Prison; **m** 032 02 212 77/032 47 891 13; **e** petit. paradis.diego@gmail.com; www.petitparadis-hotel-diegosuarez.com. Beautiful hotel with good prices & service. En-suite rooms with AC, Wi-Fi & safe. Also an apartment with kitchenette.

🏠 **Rascasse** [346 C5] (22 rooms) Rue Surcouf; ☎82 223 64/82 229 25; **e** sglveni@moov.mg or sglveni@yahoo.fr; www.venillarascasse-diego. com. A range of good-value rooms in a convenient location. All rooms en suite; some with fans, others with AC & TV.

🏠 **Résidence Kathyly** [346 C3] (6 rooms) 19 Rue de la Marne; ☎82 226 89; **m** 032 40 071 17 (manager)/032 41 738 70; **e** residence.kathyly@ gmail.com; www.kathyly-residence.com. A well-located small guesthouse with rooms named after different animals. Private bathrooms, sat-TV, Wi-Fi & AC. Shared kitchen at guests' disposal.

Also in this category:

🏠 **Belle Vue** [346 D4] **e** hbellevueds@gmail. com

🏠 **Cap Diego** [346 C6] **m** 032 29 885 50

🏠 **Concorde** [346 C3] **e** hotel_concorde@ yahoo.fr

🏠 **Diego Ambassador** [346 C4] **e** hoteldiegoambassador@yahoo.fr

🏠 **Iris** [346 C2] ☎82 900 79

🏠 **Jardin Exotique** [346 D4] jardinexotique. hotel-diegosuarez.com

🏠 **Kartiffa** [346 C1] www.kartiffa.com

🏠 **Kikoo** [346 C2] www.kikoohotel.com

🏠 **Paradis du Nord** [346 C7] www. leparadisdunord-diego.com

Budget €€

🏠 **Royale** [346 B7] (16 rooms) 10 Rue Justin Bezara; ☎82 228 15; **m** 032 04 590 39. Cell-like rooms but clean, with fan & safe; cold water.

🏠 **Suffren** [346 C6] (12 rooms) 6 Rue Suffren; **m** 032 59 209 67/034 89 657 44. Range of en-suite rooms, some with AC & hot water.

On Andovobazaha Bay (road to Ramena) On the sweeping bay just east of town you will find some of the nicest hotels in the area, on the road to Ramena, offering a quieter and more scenic location than Antsiranana itself.

🏠 **Note Bleue Park** (20 rooms) PK 3, Rte de Ramena; m 032 07 125 48; e bleudiego@gmail.com; www.diego-hotel.com. Luxury boutique hotel with spectacular view overlooking sugarloaf island. Watersports, gym & huge swimming pool. Big bright en-suite rooms with Wi-Fi, AC, sat-TV, minibar & balcony. Suites also have jacuzzi & large lounge. Small botanic garden & excellent restaurant Route des Epices. Credit cards accepted. 👑

🏠 **Meva Plage** (8 bungalows) m 032 07 935 94/032 43 817 70; e mevaplage@gmail.com; www.mevaplagehotel.com. Pleasant beach hotel 3km before Ramena (although the beach is more mangrove mud than sand); en-suite waterfront bungalows with AC & Wi-Fi. Visa accepted. €€€€€

🏠 **Suarez Hotel** (12 bungalows) m 032 07 416 17/032 07 416 18; e info@kingdelapiste.com or infos@suarez-hotel.com; www.suarez-hotel.com. Well-spaced classy bungalows opposite the Nosy Lonja in the bay. Excellent restaurant La Fleur de Sel. €€€€€

🏠 **Jungle Park** (14 rooms) nr Andavakoera, Vallée des Perroquets; 📞 82 218 54; m 032 04 724 46; e newsearoc@gmail.com or newsearoc@newsearoc.com; www.jungle-park-nature.com. In a valley behind the bay, a unique hotel constructed in the tree canopy comprising a series of tree-houses, platforms, hammocks & restaurant interconnected by steps, rope bridges & aerial runways, built around a central ground-level kitchen. There

are also some adobe ecodomes. Environmental interpretation centre engaged in community projects. Activities inc caving, rock climbing, tree climbing, birdwatching & mountain biking. FB; reservation obligatory; 45min transfer from Antsiranana inc; closed Jan/Feb. €€€€–€€€€€

🏠 **Ankarea** (6 bungalows) m 032 40 119 52/032 67 848 09; e info@ankarea.com; www.ankarea.com. Comfy & stylish bungalows set among mango trees & orchids; an intimate & welcoming atmosphere with top-notch food. Good views of Nosy Lonja. Airport transfers (*gratis*) & excursions. €€€€

🏠 **Villa Diego** (5 bungalows) m 032 68 509 37; e villadiegohotel@gmail.com; www.villadiego-hotel-diegosuarez.com. Charming bungalows with spectacular bay view from large terrace; en suite with hot water. Wi-Fi & AC option. Large swimming pool. B/fast inc. €€€–€€€€

🏠 **Careva** (5 bungalows) 📞 82 226 84; m 032 07 719 74/032 40 302 28; e carevahotel@gmail.com; www.careva.hotelsmada.com. Bungalows just on east side of town overlooking the bay with AC, hot water & fridge. 4x4 hire & excursions. €€€

🏠 **Hôtel de la Baie** (15 bungalows) PK 2, Rte de Ramena; m 032 50 777 36/032 64 457 82 (manager); e hoteldelabaiediego@yahoo.fr; www.hoteldelabaiediego.com. Bungalows in a garden setting, all with sat-TV/DVD, AC & Wi-Fi; most with kitchenette. 'Beautiful swimming pool,' says Remi Doomernik. €€€

✖ **WHERE TO EAT AND DRINK** Among the hotel restaurants, two stand out in particular. Terrasse du Voyageur serves a mainly Malagasy menu of excellent quality and generous portions. Allamanda's seafront restaurant Melville has a refined ambience and one of the tastiest menus in town. Advance booking for both places is advised.

✖ **Amiral** [346 C4] 79 Rue Colbert; m 032 61 591 09/032 63 464 37; e amiral.roger@gmail.com; ⏲ Thu–Tue 09.00–late, Wed closed. New relaxed little restaurant run by a Malagasy-French couple; some exquisite dishes at reasonable prices.

✖ **Art'Kenciel** [346 C4] m 032 88 605 54; e nicolaschauvin51@yahoo.fr. New French-run eatery in attractive colonial building with pleasant breezy terrace. Wi-Fi. Sometimes live music.

✖ **Aux Deux Dauphins (Chez Marcel et Lydie)** [346 C4] Rue Colbert; m 032 02 504 37/032 04 123 18; e baret.dolys@yahoo.fr or barretmarcel@ymail.com. Malagasy and Réunionais specialities. Karaoke w/day eves & live music Fri/Sat.

✖ **Bodega** [346 C2] 5 Rue Colbert; m 032 04 734 43; e bodegadiegosuarez@gmail.com or cyrilmz@yahoo.fr; ⏲ Mon 17.00–late, Tue–Sat 09.00–14.00 & 17.00–late, Sun closed. Lively Spanish-owned restaurant with fantastic atmosphere & very personal service. Restaurant menu changes daily. Wi-Fi.

✖ **Cambusa** [346 C2] 28 Rue Colbert; m 032 54 672 16; ⏲ Mon–Sat 10.00–22.30, Sun closed. Unpretentious Italian-owned eatery reportedly with fast service.

✖ **Cantine** [346 C3] 61 Rue Colbert; m 032 05 259 79/032 81 745 41; e s.razafitiana@yahoo.fr. Not quite as utilitarian as the name might imply. Big menu of straightforward filling food at reasonable prices.

✗ **Côte** [346 C4] 51 Rue de la Marne; m 032 07 730 34/032 11 109 89/032 78 318 61; ⊕ Mon–Sat 06.30–14.00 & 16.00–22.00, Sun closed. New in 2015, an attractively decorated meat & seafood grill restaurant offering Malagasy, European & Chinese cuisine.

✗ **Jonque** [346 C5] 7 Rue Rigault; m 032 07 076 54; e lajonquediegosuarez@gmail.com. Vietnamese cuisine.

✗ **Mexicoco** [346 C4] 1 Rue François de Mahy; ☎ 82 218 51; m 032 45 558 82; e bjas@hotmail.fr; ⊕ closed Tue. Despite the name & Mexican-themed décor, the cuisine in this French-run establishment is European. Nevertheless the quality is reliable.

✗ **Mon Plaisir** [346 C5] Av Surcouf; m 032 26 394 61/032 26 394 62; e ash.amiin@yahoo.com. Halal restaurant & snack bar.

✗ **Rosticceria** [346 C3] 47 Rue Colbert; m 032 67 637 03. Intimate little Italian restaurant with veranda, now under Swiss ownership. Highly recommended for its excellent food & great atmosphere.

✗ **Su e Giu** [346 C4] 85 Rue Colbert; m 032 27 427 93; e suegiudiego@gmail.com; ⊕ eves only.

Widely praised homely Italian restaurant serving world-class pizzas at good prices; several vegetarian options. On the corner of the main square, with open-air seating upstairs & often live music.

✗ **Tsara Be Vaovao** [346 C3] 36 Rue Colbert; m 032 04 940 97; http://tsarabe.normada.com; ⊕ Mon–Sat 09.00–23.00, Sun 17.00–23.00. Nice restaurant with excellent food, but pricey.

✗ **Venilla** [346 C5] Rue Surcouf; ☎ 82 229 25; e sglveni@moov.mg or sglveni@yahoo.fr; www. venillarascasse-diego.com; ⊕ 11.00–14.00 & 19.00–22.30. Open since 1989 & among the best restaurants in town, yet keeps its prices reasonable.

◻ **Boulangerie Amicale** [346 C5] Rue Lafayette. Excellent hot rolls & *pains au chocolat*.

◻ **Pâtisseries du Grand Hotel** [346 C4] Good range of quality pastries & cakes.

◻ **Veni Ice** [346 C5] m 032 07 912 88; e sglveni.ice@gmail.com; ⊕ Tue–Sun 15.30–22.00, Mon closed. Pastries, cakes, smoothies, crêpes & more, located at the front of Venilla restaurant.

◻ **Vokibe** [346 C2] Rue Colbert; m 032 04 012 01. Snack bar with a name that means 'full up'; pizzas, burgers & salads. Pool table. Also scooter hire.

NIGHTLIFE

♀ **Diego Sun City** [346 C4] Av Tollendal; m 032 44 155 72/032 62 492 71; ⊕ daily 17.00–late. This place tries to be everything at once: bar, restaurant, pizzeria, snack bar & nightclub. Fri karaoke; Sat dancing.

♀ **Libertalia** [346 C4] 1 Rue Colbert; m 032 69 804 00; ⊕ Mon–Thu 08.00–02.00, Fri/Sat 08.00–06.00, Sun closed. Snack bar & bar popular with late-night revellers.

♀ **O'Seven** [346 C5] 8 Rue Surcouf; m 032 42 104 49; ⊕ Mon–Sat 10.00–late. Cocktail bar with dance floor; DJ at w/ends. Snacks.

♀ **Vahinée Bar** [346 C2] 32 Rue Colbert; ☎ 82 226 53; m 032 46 272 17; e sylro@orange.mg;

⊕ 24hrs. Recommended for its wonderful atmosphere, staff & live music events. Pool table, snacks & Wi-Fi.

☆ **Boîte Noir** [346 C3] Rue Colbert; ⊕ Thu–Sun 22.00–late. Entry 5,000Ar. A stylish nightclub with small dance floor. Pizzas.

☆ **Nouvel Hôtel** [346 C3] Rue Freppel; ⊕ daily until 05.00. A popular disco with the locals; opened in the 1980s by a Breton maths teacher.

☆ **Taxi Bé** [346 C2] Bd Bazeilles; m 032 81 782 57. Disco & concert bar with 'deejay night' every Wed & live *salegy* music Thu from 21.00.

SHOPPING Antsiranana has some high-quality souvenir shops, mostly along Rue Colbert and Rue Lafayette. There is a **Score** supermarket [346 C3] (⊕ *Mon–Sat 08.30–13.00 & 15.00–19.30, Sun 08.30–11.30*) and a handful of grocery stores scattered around. For a treat, visit **La Chocolatière** [346 C4] on Place Foch (m *032 03 311 73/032 50 804 07*; e *choconos@yahoo.fr*; ⊕ *Mon–Sat 10.00–13.00 & 15.00–17.00*).

MONEY There are branches of all the major banks: BFV [346 C1], BNI [346 C2], BOA [346 C1] and BMOI [346 C3], mostly now with ATMs and Western Union. The Grand Hotel [346 C4] also has a small branch of BFV on-site.

MEDICAL Antsiranana has plenty of pharmacies. There is also a hospital [346 D1] (📞 82 218 61) and the services of Espace Medical [346 C4] are recommended for emergencies (📞 82 216 56; m 034 05 096 96; www.espace-medical.mg). Also recommended is Dr Anante Govindjee (📞 82 213 53; m 032 07 098 05).

TOUR OPERATORS, VEHICLE HIRE AND FLIGHTS

✈ **Air Madagascar** [346 C5] 5 Av Surcouf; 📞82 214 75; m 032 05 222 04/034 11 222 04; e diessmd@airmadagascar.com; ⊕ Mon–Fri 07.30–11.00 & 14.30–17.00, Sat 08.00–10.00

✈ **Madagasikara Airways** m 032 05 970 04/034 05 970 23

Cap Nord Voyages [346 C3] 51 Rue Colbert; 📞82 235 06/82 233 87; m 032 07 188 74; e cap.nord. voyages@moov.mg; www.cap-nord-voyages.com. At Colbert Hotel. Specialists in multi-day tours of the north but also do day trips. Minibus & 4x4 hire.

Diego Raid [346 C4] 72 Rue Colbert; m 032 58 890 77/032 40 001 75; e contact@diegoraid. com; www.diegoraid.com. Quad hire & guided excursions; also 4x4s.

Ecotours [346 C5] 14 Av Surcouf; m 032 02 568 36/032 02 305 62; e madagascarecotours@yahoo. fr. Good prices & English-speaking guides.

Evasion Sans Frontière [346 C4] 62 Rue Colbert; 📞82 217 23; m 032 11 003 96/032 05 365 31; e esfdiego2@moov.mg; www. evasionsansfrontiere.com. Tour agency working throughout the north & especially around Nosy Be.

Extra Voyage m 032 02 431 34; e madadiego201@yahoo.fr; www.extravoyagemada. com. Regional tour specialist & vehicle rental.

Jasmin Kores Tours [346 C4] 86 Rue Colbert; m 032 04 056 62/032 86 356 96/034 36 363 62; e jasminkores@yahoo.fr. Set up in 2012 by a well-known local guide. Offers tours to all the main sites.

King de la Piste [346 C4] Bd Bazeilles; m 032 04 908 10; e info@kingdelapiste.com; www. kingdelapiste.de. Organises trips to most of

the region, inc hard-to-reach places: Windsor Castle, Cap d'Ambre, Analamera & Sakalava Bay. Excursions by 4x4, motorbike & bike. Personal & efficient service.

Loc 4L PK 2, Rte de Ramena; 📞82 901 71; m 032 52 200 25; e loc4ldiego@gmail.com. Renault 4s (some convertible) with & without driver.

Locaquad [346 C2] Kikoo Hotel; m 032 87 161 41/032 05 035 10; e fabrypie@yahoo.fr; www. location-quad-diego-suarez.e-monsite.com. Quad hire & guided quad excursions to all the area's popular spots.

Madaway Tours [346 C4] 32 Rue Colbert; m 032 40 649 07/032 40 888 14; e madaway. tours@gmail.com; www.madawaytours.com. Tour operator for all standard excursions.

Mistral [346 C2] 37 Bd de la Liberté; m 032 05 234 72/033 15 234 72/034 05 234 72; e mistral. mada@gmail.com. Tours & 4x4 hire.

Nazia Location m 032 05 230 27; e nazialoca@ yahoo.fr. Many different models of 4x4 with drivers.

New Sea Roc [346 C2] 26 Rue Colbert; 📞82 218 54; m 032 04 724 46; e newsearoc@moov. mg; www.newsearoc.com. Adventure sporting excursions inc climbing, caving, kayaking, paintballing & mountainboarding.

Paradis du Nord [346 C7] Av Villaret Joyeuse; 📞82 214 05/82 229 01; m 032 04 859 64/033 02 004 11/032 07 075 86; e paradisdunord@moov. mg; www.leparadisdunord-diego.com. At the hotel of the same name. A reliable operator with a fleet of 4x4s & minibuses with good drivers.

WHAT TO SEE AND DO The well-organised regional tourist office **ORTDS** [346 C1] is located at the intersection of Rue Colbert and Rue Flacourt (m 032 96 420 93/032 43 231 62/032 07 125 48/032 07 711 11; e tourismediego@gmail.com; www.office-tourisme-diego-suarez.com; ⊕ Mon–Fri 08.00–noon & 15.00–18.00, Sat 08.30–11.30).

If you are in need of a guide, contact the local guides association (m 032 04 790 76/032 04 637 44) or check the ORTDS website for a list of names with contact details.

British war cemetery [346 D7] (⊕ 06.00–18.00) On the outskirts of town on the road that leads to the airport, the British Commonwealth Cemetery is well signposted on a side road opposite the main Malagasy cemetery. Impeccably maintained by the Commonwealth War Graves Commission, this is a peaceful and moving place. Here is a sad insight into Anglo-Malagasy history: rows of graves of the British and Commonwealth troops killed in Madagascar between 1942 and 1944, half of them no older than 25. Among the 315 graves, 53 soldiers belonged to the King's African Rifles, 29 from the East African Army Service Corps, 16 East African Artillery, and 17 Northern Rhodesia Regiment, as well as 36 Royal Scots Fusiliers, 12 Royal Welch Fusiliers, 13 Seaforth Highlanders, 37 from the South and East Lancashire regiments, 12 Royal Artillery, and 11 Royal Air Force. There are also 10 soldiers from South African regiments and one from the Belgian Army.

The **French war cemetery** [346 D7] is nearby, alongside the local cemetery.

Montagne des Français (French Mountain)
Officially a protected area since 2013, this 340m mountain gets its name from the memorial to the French and Malagasy killed during the Allied invasion in 1942.

There is a well-maintained walking trail – a hot but rewarding climb (2–4hrs) with splendid views and some caves to visit. Go early in the morning for the best birdwatching and to avoid the heat of the day. A guide is obligatory. At the foot of the mountain, close to the road, are some specimens of the critically endangered locally endemic baobab species, *Adansonia suarezensis* (they are the ones with smooth reddish bark; the grey-barked ones are *A. madagascariensis*). The reserve is also home to five lemur species (the crowned lemur is the only diurnal one), 50 birds, 40 reptiles, 19 frogs, and over 240 plants including at least nine that are locally endemic. Since 2000, these cliffs and the interior of the cave have become a Mecca for rock climbers and there are now many bolted routes.

For those seeking accommodation with a difference, why not try living like lemurs in the forest canopy? You can stay in a tree-house at **Jungle Park** (page 348).

Zegny'Zo arts festival
(m *032 04 931 81/032 02 358 15; www.zolobe.com*) If you are around in May, don't miss the free week-long carnival-like Zegny'Zo festival. Launched in 2007, this lively annual celebration includes parades, puppetry, musical events, circus acts, dancing, film shows, plays and street painting.

RAMENA AND THE EAST COAST

The beach resort of Ramena provides a pleasant alternative to staying in Antsiranana. It is about 18km from the town centre, 45 minutes from the airport. Get there by taxi-brousse (2,500Ar each way) or by private taxi (about 65,000Ar round trip). It's a beautiful drive around the curve of the bay, with some fine baobabs *en route*. Alternatively you can arrange a boat to take you there across the bay.

 WHERE TO STAY AND EAT

5 Trop Près (3 rooms) m 032 07 724 63/032 07 740 60; e le5troppres@gmail. com; www.normada.com/5trop. The name is pronounced 'Saint-Tropez'. Right on the beach. Good restaurant. €€€

Casa en Falafy (Chez Bruno) (20 bungalows) 82 907 54; m 032 02 674 33; www. case-en-falafy.com. En-suite thatched bungalows for 3–7 people; quiet location 70m from beach. €€€

Lakana (10 bungalows) m 032 04 969 98/032 56 214 47; e lakana.ramena@gmail.com;

www.lakana-hotel-ramena.com. Bungalows with AC, safe, Wi-Fi & en-suite bathrooms. This is also a kitesurfing & windsurfing centre. Visa accepted. €€€

Manguier (4 rooms) PK 17, Rte de Ramena; 82 929 58; m 032 27 428 31/033 11 943 24; e lemanguier@yahoo.fr. By the road just before Ramena, 500m from the beach; cosy rooms in a quiet spot shaded by large mango trees. €€€

Palm Beach (6 bungalows) m 032 02 409 04; e palmbeach@gmail.com. En-suite bungalows with fans. €€€

14

In the days before mass air transportation, Madagascar's geographical location gave the island immense strategic importance. In World War II, British convoys to the Middle East and India sailed round the north of Madagascar, passing the great French naval base of Antsirane (now Antsiranana) at Diego Suarez. Antsirane, its harbour facilities completed in 1935, was France's most modern colonial port with a dry dock that could accommodate 28,000-ton battleships and an arsenal capable of repairing the largest of guns.

It was evident to both the Allied and Axis powers that whoever held Diego Suarez controlled the western Indian Ocean. As the French authorities in Madagascar were firm supporters of the German-influenced Vichy Government, Britain believed that it had to occupy the island before it was handed over to her enemies. So, in the spring of 1942, Britain mounted Operation Ironclad, its first ever large-scale combined land, sea and air operation, to capture Diego Suarez as the initial step in occupying the whole island.

A force of some 13,000 troops with tanks and artillery, supported by 46 warships and transport vessels and 101 aircraft of the Fleet Air Arm, assembled to the north of Cap d'Ambre before dawn on 5 May 1942. The narrow entrance to Diego Suarez Bay was known to be powerfully defended by large-calibre artillery so the British decided to land in Courrier's Bay and march across country to take Antsirane from the landward side.

The first troops to land were commandos, who captured the small battery that overlooked Courrier's Bay. The French and Senegalese defenders were still asleep and the position was taken with little loss of life. However, a small French force ensconced in an observation post on the summit of Windsor Castle could not be dislodged. For two days the French clung to their eyrie, despite repeated bombardments from the Royal Navy and attacks by the Fleet Air Arm and the commandos.

With the beaches secured, the main British force landed and began its march upon Antsirane. Meanwhile, the Fleet Air Arm depth-charged and torpedoed the French warships and submarines at anchor in Diego Suarez Bay and bombed Arrachart airfield. But the defenders were now at their posts and an intense battle for possession of Diego Suarez began.

Some three miles to the south of Antsirane the French had built a strong defensive line across the isthmus of the Antsirane Peninsula. Devised by General Joffre in 1909, it comprised a trench network and an anti-tank ditch strengthened

🏠 **Badamera Park** (4 rooms & 3 bungalows) 📞 82 910 56; m 032 07 733 50; e badamera@ hotmail.com; www.badamera.com. German-run attractive garden in breezy location. Buffet with live performance every Sun. €€–€€€

🏠 **Chez Grandmère Jeanette** Very simple cheap accommodation. Food on request. €€

🏠 **Oasis** (4 rooms & 1 bungalow) 📞 82 925 08; m 034 08 261 70. Basic dbl rooms with AC & en-suite facilities (cold water). €€

🍴 **Emeraude** m 032 50 583 80; e lillijb@ hotmail.fr. Restaurant & bar right on the beach with tremendous seafood. Disco every Sat night.

🍴 **Gargote Chez Marie** Small place with cheap but excellent food.

🍴 **Sabri Beach** m 034 97 733 73; ⊕ daily. Beachfront restaurant & bar often hosting concerts & events.

DIVING Based in Ramena, MadaScaph (m *032 48 012 52*; e *info@madascaph.com*; *www.madascaph.com*) offers PADI-accredited scuba-diving in the bays of the region.

by forts and pillboxes housing artillery and machine guns. For two days the British forces assaulted the French line without success and with mounting losses.

The breakthrough came on the evening of 6 May when a British destroyer charged through the entrance of Diego Suarez Bay under the guns of the French batteries. The destroyer successfully landed a body of 50 Marines on to the quay. This tiny force stormed through the town, capturing the main barracks and the artillery headquarters. This disruption in their rear finally broke the defenders' resolve and when the main frontal attack was renewed the French line was overrun.

The fighting resulted in more than a thousand casualties. The British commander submitted recommendations for more than 250 decorations, including three posthumous Victoria Crosses.

Britain's vital route to the east had been secured – but only in the nick of time. Barely three weeks after the capture of Antsirane, a Japanese submarine flotilla arrived off the coast of Madagascar. In a daring night raid the Japanese attacked the ships in Diego Suarez Bay, sinking one supply ship and severely damaging the flagship of the British expedition, the battleship *Ramillies*.

With the island's main naval base in British hands, it was expected that the French governor general, Armand Annet, would bow to the inevitable and relinquish control of the whole island. However, despite months of negotiations, Annet refused to surrender and Britain was forced to mount further military operations.

In September 1942, British and Commonwealth troops landed at Majunga and Tamatave. Brushing aside all attempts to stop and delay them, the Allies captured Tananarive only to find that Annet had retreated to the south of the island. But when a South African force landed at Tulear, Annet realised that he was trapped.

The French strung out surrender negotiations until one minute after midnight on 6 November – exactly six months and one day after the start of the British attack upon Diego Suarez. The significance of this was that French troops involved in a campaign lasting longer than six months were entitled to a medal and an increased state pension!

After a brief period of British Military Administration, the island was handed over to General de Gaulle's Free French movement. The key naval base of Antsirane, however, remained under British control until 1944.

John Grehan is the author of The Forgotten Invasion; *see page 443.*

MINIGOLF (m *032 02 010 66*) About 1km from the centre of the village, on the road to Antsiranana, is a French-owned 14-hole minigolf course called Chez Lali et Lys; it costs 10,000Ar per person. There is also a grill restaurant and swimming pool at the site.

EAST COAST BAYS AND KITESURFING SPOTS Rounding the headland beyond Ramena – Cap Miné – you reach two small beaches known as **Dunes Bay** and **Pigeons Bay**. A walk here has good birdwatching and wildlife prospects, but part of the route passes through the Orangea military zone so you will need to buy a 5,000Ar permit from one of the sentries. Along the way, you can see two lighthouses (the keeper will gladly give visitors a tour) and various ruins including some canons and a 1939 French gun emplacement.

Continuing southward down the coastline, you reach the beautiful 2km-long **Sakalava Bay**. It takes about 3 hours to walk here from Ramena, but coming from

Antsiranana it can be accessed more directly by turning right 6km before Ramena and following a 4.5km dirt track. A day trip here from Antsiranana should cost around 100,000Ar return by taxi. About 1km further south is an 800m-long beach called **Andovokonko Bay**. Both places are world-class spots for kitesurfing and windsurfing, and a number of surf lodges have sprung up over the past decade to take advantage of the reliable wind of 20–40 knots that blows every day throughout the April to November season. All of the lodges listed below have their own kitesurfing schools, or alternatively you can contact Kite Alizé (m *032 58 216 99*; e *kitealize@gmail.com; www.kitealize.com*) or Mada-Océan Kite (m *032 56 214 47/32 04 969 98*; e *lakana. ramena@gmail.com; www.kite-ocean-madagascar.sitew.com*).

Opposite the Ramena headland, on the northern side of the mouth to Antsiranana's great natural harbour, is the Babaomby Peninsula, alongside which lies a 10km lagoon of such a stunning turquoise hue that it is known as the **Emerald Sea**. Accessible by 8km boat trip from Ramena (or 15km from Antsiranana), this is another perfect kitesurfing spot. The shallow water is also excellent for swimming, snorkelling and windsurfing.

Where to stay and eat

Mantasaly (32 rooms & 16 bungalows) Andovokonko Bay; +35722376342 (reservations, Cyprus); m 032 03 166 01; e contact@mantasaly.com or oceandunesmada1@gmail.com or reservations@ mantasaly.com; www.mantasaly.com. New in 2016 & describing itself as an 'eco-resort & kitesurfer's paradise'. Restaurant, bar, nightclub & kite shop with all the gear.

Océan Paradise Lodge (8 bungalows) Emerald Sea; m 032 45 248 01/032 73 852 21/032 83 339 94/034 70 083 87; e info@oceanparadiselodge.com; www. oceanparadiselodge.com. Dutch-run kitesurfing lodge also offering fishing, snorkelling & excursions by boat/4x4. Airport transfers inc.

Paillottes de Babaomby (2 rooms & 6 bungalows) Emerald Sea; 82 928 09/82 942 74; m 032 62 402 63/032 67 381 81; e les.paillottes. de.babaomby@gmail.com or robert.saez@skynet. be; www.kitesurfmadagascar.com or www.mer-emeraude-hotel.com. Like other lodges in this area, the focus is on kitesurfing. Describing itself

as an ecolodge, it has Wi-Fi, swimming pool & gourmet cuisine. Airport transfers inc.

Babaomby Island Lodge (10 bungalows) Emerald Sea; m 032 55 009 39/032 67 381 81/033 15 199 70; e babaomby@hotmail.com; www. babaomby.com. Established in 2007, this much-respected kitesurfing & windsurfing centre offers water's edge tented bungalows on stilts. Closed Dec–Mar. €€€€€

Royal Sakalava (15 bungalows) Sakalava Bay; 82 926 36; m 032 05 777 05/032 05 777 99/032 05 888 99; e royalsakalava@gmail.com; www.royalsakalava.com. En-suite dbl & family bungalows facing the sea. Solar power. IKO-qualified kitesurfing instructor. Also windsurfing & quad biking. Wi-Fi. €€€€

Sakalava Lodge (15 bungalows) Sakalava Bay; 82 927 73; m 032 67 385 95; e sakalava1@ gmail.com; www.sakalava.com. Ecolodge run by passionate kitesurfer & windsurfer Gregory. The 3ha plot has a restaurant, bar & pool, with lemurs & birds in the surrounding forest. Comfy rustic bungalows: some seafront, with cheaper ones behind. Closed Dec–Mar. €€€€

EXCURSIONS WEST FROM ANTSIRANANA

WINDSOR CASTLE A few hours' drive due west from Antsiranana, this 391m-high monolith is steep-sided and flat-topped, so made a perfect lookout point during times of war. The views from here are superb. It was fortified by the French, occupied by the Vichy forces, and liberated by the British. A ruined staircase still runs to the top (if you can find it – best to take a guide) but it is a hot, shadeless climb so make sure you have plenty of water and sun protection. There are many endemic succulents including a local species of pachypodium, *P. windsorii*.

To get there, take the road that runs west across the salt pans to Antsahampano, then turn north for 12km before making a left turn and heading a further 5km.

COURRIER'S BAY Courrier's Bay, half an hour beyond Windsor Castle, is an exceptionally fine beach. This west-coast area of rugged beauty is the starting point for a number of hiking, fishing, climbing and diving activities, as well as visits to Nosy Hara.

NOSY HARA MARINE NATIONAL PARK (m *033 49 400 85;* e *nsh-parc@gmail.com*) Situated in Courrier's Bay, this newly protected reserve covers 125,000ha and comprises a 3.5km-long island surrounded by a scattering of more than a dozen much smaller islets, mostly formed from jagged *tsingy* limestone. The wildlife is abundant: whales, dolphins, five species of turtle, and even dugongs inhabit these waters, as well as 108 types of coral – and fish eagles and egrets in the sky above. Endemic to the island is the world's smallest chameleon, *Brookesia micra*. It was described in 2012, knocking the former record-holder, *B. minima* of Montagne d'Ambre, off top spot. The area is great for exploring, snorkelling and rock climbing.

From Antsiranana, it is a 90-minute drive through salt pans and mango plantations to the village of Ampasindava, from where a tour of the islands can be made by pirogue. The main island is 6.5km offshore. A camping trip of at least three days is recommended; you have the option of sleeping in tents, huts or caves. Contact New Sea Roc (see page 350) for details of camping, climbing and kayaking.

CAP D'AMBRE Remote and rarely visited, Cap d'Ambre – the northernmost part of Madagascar – is reached via the route to Windsor Castle. Driving from Antsiranana to the disused lighthouse at the point of the cape takes about 7 hours in a 4x4, the best route being via Bedarabe and Ambatonjanohavy.

The area has fantastic views, with both the Indian Ocean and the Mozambique Channel visible at once. There are good opportunities for hiking or mountain biking and areas of tsingy to explore.

MONTAGNE D'AMBRE (AMBER MOUNTAIN) NATIONAL PARK

This 18,500ha national park was created in 1958, the French colonial government recognising the unique nature of the volcanic massif and its forest. The park is part of the Montagne d'Ambre Reserves Complex which also includes Ankarana (page 360), Analamera (page 358) and Forêt d'Ambre. The project was the first to involve local people in all stages of planning and management. The aims of conservation, rural development and education have largely been achieved. Ecotourism has been encouraged successfully with good information and facilities now available.

Montagne d'Ambre National Park is a splendid example of montane rainforest: the massif ranges in altitude from 850m to 1,475m and has its own microclimate with rainfall similar to the eastern region. It is one of the most visitor-friendly of Madagascar's protected areas, with broad trails, fascinating flora and fauna, a comfortable climate and readily available information. In the dry season vehicles can drive right up to the main picnic area, giving a unique opportunity (in Madagascar) for elderly or disabled visitors to see the rainforest and its inhabitants.

The most rewarding time to visit is during the warm season (September to November); there will be some rain, but most animals are active and the lemurs have babies. It is usually relatively dry from May to August, and wettest from December to April. Temperatures on the mountain are much cooler than down in

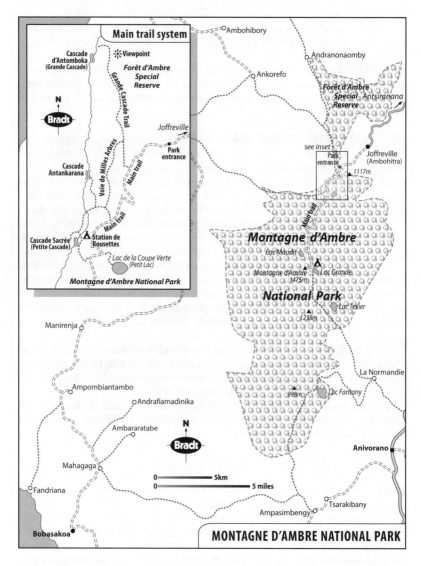

Main trail system

Cascade
d'Antomboka
(Grande Cascade)

☀ Viewpoint

*Forêt d'Ambre
Special
Reserve*

Grande Cascade Trail

N

Bradt

Joffreville

Cascade
Antankarana

Voie de Milles Arbres

Main trail

Park
entrance

Cascade Sacrée
(Petite Cascade)

Main trail

△ Station de
Rousettes

Lac de la Coupe Verte
(Petit Lac)

Montagne d'Ambre National Park

Ambohibory

Andranonaomby

Ankorefo

*Forêt d'Ambre
Special Antsiranana
Reserve*

see inset

Park
entrance

Joffreville
(Ambohitra)

▲ 1117m

Main Trail

Montagne d'Ambre

Lac Maudit

△

Montagne d'Ambre ▲ Lac Grande
1475m

National Park

Lac Texier

▲
1238m

La Normandie

Manirenja

▲
998m

Lac Fantany

Ampombiantambo

Andrafiamadinika

Ambararatabe

Anivorano

N

Bradt

0 _____ 5km
0 _____ 5 miles

Mahagaga

Fandriana

Ampasimbengy

Tsarakibany

Bobasakoa

MONTAGNE D'AMBRE NATIONAL PARK

Antsiranana and there is a strong wind – *varatraza* – most days so it can feel quite cold. It is often wet and muddy (and there may be leeches) so be wary of wearing shorts and sandals, however hot and dry you feel at sea level. Bring waterproofs, insect repellent and even a light sweater.

You should also be aware that, as Antsiranana is on the itinerary of some cruise ships, for three or four days each year the park is inundated with hundreds of day trippers.

PERMITS AND GUIDES (e *mda@parcs-madagascar.com*) Permits are available from the park office at the entrance or the National Parks office on the outskirts of Antsiranana towards the airport (see page 73 for prices). Guides can be found at the park office. Circuits cost 25,000–50,000Ar per group of up to five. All tour operators and most hotels can assist in planning a visit here.

GETTING THERE AND AWAY The entrance to the park is 33km south of Antsiranana, 4km beyond the town of Joffreville (Ambohitra). Taxi-brousses go as far as Joffreville (1–2½hrs; 5,000Ar). A taxi costs 80,000Ar or so to the park entrance (4km further up the hill) or 130,000Ar for a return day trip.

WHERE TO STAY AND EAT There are tent shelters and a hut with bunks in the park for visitors equipped with sleeping bags. From the wildlife point of view, staying in or near the park is far preferable to making a day trip from Antsiranana.

A campsite at the picnic area, known as Station des Rousettes, has running water, shower, toilet and barbecue facilities. Firewood is available from the warden, but bring your own food.

More comfortable accommodation is to be found around Joffreville:

Domaine de Fontenay (9 rooms) 82 908 71/82 927 67; m 032 11 345 81/033 11 345 81; e contact@lefontenay-madagascar.com; www. lefontenay-madagascar.com. A delightfully quirky hotel in a beautifully furnished & renovated manor house. Warm hospitality, spacious chic rooms & delightful cooking. The gardens are home to Galileo the giant tortoise. A 300ha private nature park is particularly good for reptiles & has a reforestation programme. Night walks are permitted and aye-ayes have been spotted on occasion. 🌿

Litchi Tree (6 rooms) m 033 03 422 72; e thelitchitree@hotmail.com; www.thelitchitree. com. Set in a grove of lychees & mangoes, this charming guesthouse is a meticulously restored villa dating to 1902. Spacious rooms with solar-heated water in en-suite facilities. Lounge bar with impressive collection of whiskies & gins. €€€€€

Nature Lodge (12 bungalows) m 034 20 123 06; e resa@naturelodge-ambre.com; www. naturelodge-ambre.com; see ad, 4th colour section. Very comfortable dbl & trpl bungalows with Wi-Fi & en-suite hot showers; solar power. Tastefully designed bar & restaurant with excellent food. Leaf-tailed geckos are often found on the mango trees here. €€€€€

Hôtellerie du Monastère (8 rooms) m 032 04 795 24/032 42 024 91/034 99 349 49; e benedictines@moov.mg or contact@ gitesaintbenoit.com; www.gitesaintbenoit.com. Benedictine convent with good-value en-suite rooms & dorms with 5–7 beds. Communal meals. €€€

Relais de la Montagne d'Ambre (3 rooms & 4 bungalows) m 032 88 475 06; e montagnedambre@gmail.com. Very friendly guesthouse with excellent food; basic rooms inc some suspended in the trees. €€€

FLORA AND FAUNA Montagne d'Ambre is as exciting for its plants as for its animals. All visitors are impressed by the tree ferns and the huge, epiphytic bird's nest ferns growing on big trees. The distinctive *Pandanus* is also common and you can see Madagascar's endemic cycad. Huge strangler figs add to the spectacle.

Most visitors want to see lemurs and two diurnal species have become habituated: Sanford's brown lemur and crowned lemur. Male Sanford's lemurs have white/beige ear-tufts and side whiskers surrounding black faces, while the females are more uniform in colour with no whiskers and a grey face. Crowned lemurs get their names from the triangular head markings, most distinctive in the male. Young are born from September to November. There are also five species of nocturnal lemur. Another mammal often seen is the ring-tailed mongoose, and if you are really lucky you could see a fossa or its relative the falanouc.

At eye level you may spot some large chameleons, also often seen crossing the road during the drive up from Antsiranana. A good guide should be able to find some of the tiny *Brookesia* chameleons that David Attenborough came here to film for his *Life in Cold Blood* series in 2007 (at the time thought to be the world's smallest chameleon, but see page 355), and also the most amazingly camouflaged of all lizards, the mossy leaf-tailed gecko. Plus there are many frogs, pill millipedes rolling into perfect balls, butterflies and other invertebrates.

Even non-birders will be fascinated by the numerous species here: the Madagascar crested ibis is striking enough to impress anybody, as is the Madagascar paradise flycatcher with its long, trailing tail feathers. The locally endemic Amber Mountain rock thrush is tame and ubiquitous, and the black-and-white magpie robin is often seen. The jackpot, perhaps, is one of Madagascar's most beautiful birds: the pitta-like ground-roller.

TRAILS, WATERFALLS AND LAKES The park has more than 30km of paths, many of which are quite flat and easy. Three waterfalls provide the focal points for day visitors. If time is short and you want to watch wildlife rather than walk far, go to the **Cascade Sacrée**, an idyllic fern-fringed grotto with waterfalls splashing into a pool. This is only about 100m along the track beyond the picnic area (Station des Rousettes) and on the way you should see lemurs, chameleons, orchids and birds galore. Take a small path on your left to the river for a possible glimpse of the white-throated rail and the Madagascar malachite kingfisher.

The **Sentier Touristique** is also easy and starts near the Station des Rousettes. The path terminates at a viewpoint above **Cascade Antankarana**: a highly photogenic spot.

The walk to the **Cascade d'Antomboka** is tougher, with some up-and-down stretches, and a steep descent to the waterfall. There is excellent birdwatching here, some lovely tree ferns and a good chance of seeing lemurs.

On your way back you'll pass a path marked 'Voie des Mille Arbres'. It's a roller coaster of a walk, but very rewarding, and eventually joins the main track. Ring-tailed mongooses are often seen along this stretch.

Sadly wildlife is reportedly becoming harder to see near the busier main trail system, so if you're visiting for more than a day trip then one of the longer hikes is recommended.

Beyond the Cascade d'Antomboka, the trail eventually reaches a river and the rarest of all baobab species: *Adansonia perrieri*. There are two or three in the area, and the largest stands at a truly impressive 25m or so tall with a massive girth. This is a tough walk; allow 3–4 hours for the round trip.

Other walks from Station des Rousettes include the easy climb to the viewpoint above the crater lake, **Lac de la Coupe Verte**. A full day's walk takes you to a crater lake known as **Lac Maudit**, or Matsabory Fantany, then on for another hour to **Lac Grand**. Beyond that is the highest point in the park, the peak of **Montagne d'Ambre** itself (1,475m). Unless you are a fit, fast walker it would be best to take two days on this trek and camp by Lac Grand. That way you can wait for weather conditions to allow the spectacular view.

EXCURSIONS SOUTH FROM ANTSIRANANA

RED TSINGY About an hour south of Antsiranana are these spectacular geological features. Like the spiky grey tsingy of Ankarana and Bemaraha, the red tsingy are erosion phenomena, but these colourful cousins are more delicate as they are formed from laterite rather than limestone, giving them a striking orange-red hue and a rather more rounded Daliesque appearance.

Three main patches of red tsingy are accessible on a 17km track that begins 46km south of Antsiranana. An entry fee of 2,000Ar is charged per vehicle. You will need a 4x4 to get there and it's not accessible at all during the wet season (roughly Dec–Mar).

ANALAMERA (ANALAMERANA) SPECIAL RESERVE (m *032 04 751 27*; e *analamerana.parks@gmail.com* or *mahefa.christian@yahoo.fr*) This 34,700ha reserve is in remote and virtually unexplored deciduous forest southeast of

Montagne d'Ambre – the last refuge of the very rare Perrier's sifaka. You may also see crowned lemurs, Sanford's brown lemurs and endangered birds such as the white-breasted mesite and Van Dam's vanga. The park merits a couple of nights' camping, but there are no facilities, so visitors must be totally self-sufficient.

To reach the reserve from Antsiranana drive 60km south on the main road, and then a further 25km on a dreadful stretch which is impassable in the rainy season. An alternative route in starts 45km south of Antsiranana. Guides and porters can be organised in the nearby village of Menagisy, but it is more sensible to arrange the visit through a tour operator in Antsiranana (essential if you need an English-speaking guide). Visit the park office in Anivorano (PK 75) first to get permits.

ANDRAFIAMENA-ANDAVAKOERA With broadly similar wildlife to Analamera, including Perrier's sifakas, this 30,000ha forest 6 hours' trek east of Ankarana has a varied landscape ranging from sandstone and limestone outcrops to dry transitional forest. In 2013, the conservation NGO FANAMBY opened accommodation here: **Black Lemur Camp** has four rooms and two bungalows (**** *22 636 61;* **m** *032 42 768 57;* **e** *friendlycamp@madagascar-discovery.com; www.association-fanamby.org;* **€€€€**). Five hiking circuits have been set up starting from the camp.

LAKE ANTANAVO (LAC SACRÉ) The turning is 75km south of Antsiranana at Anivorano, where you must buy a permit (4,000Ar/person) before proceeding to the sacred lake along a 4km track that is impassable in the rainy season. It attracts visitors more for its legends than for the reality of a not particularly scenic lake, and the possibility of seeing a crocodile. Locals feed them occasionally, so ask a tour operator in Antsiranana when the next croc-feeding day is.

The story is that once upon a time Anivorano was situated amid semi-desert and a thirsty traveller arrived at the village asking for a drink. When his request was refused he warned the villagers that they would soon have more water than they could cope with. No sooner had he left than the earth opened, water gushed out, and the mean locals and their houses were inundated. The crocodiles which now inhabit the lake are considered to be ancestors and to wear jewellery belonging to their previous selves. The most important crocodile was said to wear a bracelet. In 1990, so they say, a big croc came up into the rice fields and was killed by a mob of young locals. But when they saw that it was the famous bracelet-wearing one, the worried villagers gave him a proper burial in the cemetery. Then one by one all those involved in the killing mysteriously died.

NOSY ANKAO In a difficult-to-access spot just off the east coast, some 75km southeast of Antsiranana, lies Nosy Ankao, the largest (348ha) of a five-island archipelago. At its northwestern end is an ultra-luxury island resort built by African safari group Time+Tide in 2016 and accessible only by private helicopter transfer from Antsiranana or Nosy Be. **Miavana** (*www.timeandtideafrica.com*) has 14 exceptional villas with up to three bedrooms. They are extremely spacious and fully equipped with all creature comforts, even down to a Madagascar-themed mini-library in each one. Naturally, such exclusivity doesn't come cheap (around €2,200 per person per night full-board) but the area offers remarkably pristine marine diversity, which Miavana is at pains to protect. Guests explore the bays and lagoons with a 'Blue Safari' guide. Activities include fishing, whale-watching, kitesurfing, snorkelling, diving, birdwatching, viewing nesting turtles and trips by boat/helicopter.

Two to three hours south of Antsiranana is the limestone massif of Ankarana. An 'island' of tsingy (limestone karst pinnacles) and forest, the massif is penetrated by numerous caves and canyons. Some of the largest caves have collapsed, forming isolated pockets of river-fed forest with their own perfectly protected flora and fauna. Dry deciduous forest grows around the periphery and into the wider canyons. The caves and their rivers are also home to crocodiles, some reportedly 6m long. Their presence is an enigma – this underworld of darkness would not seem to be a suitable habitat for large cold-blooded reptiles at all – and they are thought to be the only Nile crocodiles in the world leading a troglodytic existence. The reserve is also known for its many lemur species, including crowned and Sanford's brown lemurs, and the inquisitive ring-tailed mongoose, but it is marvellous for birds, reptiles and insects as well.

It is not difficult to do Ankarana independently, provided you have your own tent or settle for a day visit only, but most visitors prefer to let a local tour operator take care of the logistics. Levels of organisation and comfort vary considerably, so your choice will depend on your budget. Any Antsiranana-based tour operator can arrange an all-inclusive camping visit.

GETTING THERE AND AWAY The main entrance to this reserve is on the east side at Mahamasina on RN6, 108km south of Antsiranana. By taxi-brousse it is about 5½ hours from Ambanja or 4½ hours from Antsiranana (7,000Ar). There is a **park office** (⊕ *daily 07.30–16.00*) near the trail head, from where it is a couple of hours' walk into the reserve.

There are two other gateways, but a 4x4 is required to access them: the southwest entry point is near Amboandriky, and the northwest one (not reachable in the rainy season) is at Matsaborimanga.

PERMITS AND GUIDES (e *ank@parcs-madagascar.com*) A permit for Ankarana may be purchased at the entrance or alternatively from the National Parks office in Antsiranana. See page 73 for permit prices. Guides are compulsory and can be found at the park office in Mahamasina. Guide fees range from 25,000Ar to 50,000Ar per circuit.

 WHERE TO STAY AND EAT *Map, opposite*
Within the park itself are several campsites. The main one, formerly known as Camp des Anglais (following a British expedition in the 1980s), has been renamed **Campement Anilotra**. It is equipped with long-drop toilets and picnic tables, and offers plenty of shade and a chance to bathe in the river running through the cave. The water supply is a 10-minute walk down a slippery slope.

The usual alternative campsite is **Campement d'Andrafiabe** (Camp des Américains), which is handy for the Andrafiabe Cave. It has a water supply and toilets, but can get crowded and has little shade.

An increasingly popular camp is **Camp des Princes**, which has long-drop toilets and picnic tables. Water is a problem: it's hard to get in the dry season so you need to bring your own. There is a bat cave nearby and some small tsingy about half an hour's walk away, but to reach the main tsingy you must walk a 32km round trip.

Camp Amposatelo is about 2 hours from Campement Anilotra and is a good base for visiting Lac Vert and some of the best tsingy.

Outside the park, there are several accommodation options.

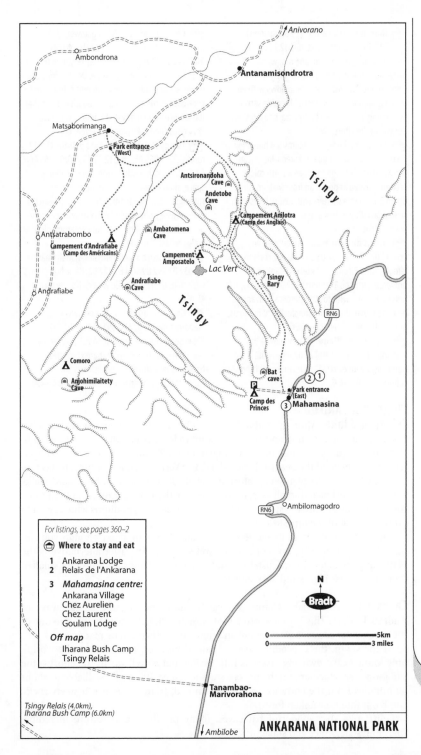

Anivorano

Ambondrona

Antanamisondrotra

Matsaborimanga

Park entrance (West)

Antsironandoha Cave

Andetobe Cave

Tsingy

Antsatrabombo

Campement d'Andrafiabe (Camp des Américains)

Ambatomena Cave

Campement Anilotra (Camp des Anglais)

Campement Amposatelo

Lac Vert

Tsingy Rary

Andrafiabe

Andrafiabe Cave

Tsingy

RN6

Comoro

Anjohimilaitety Cave

Bat cave

Park entrance (East)

Camp des Princes

Mahamasina

RN6

Ambilomagodro

For listings, see pages 360–2

⌂ **Where to stay and eat**

1 Ankarana Lodge
2 Relais de l'Ankarana

3 *Mahamasina centre:*
Ankarana Village
Chez Aurelien
Chez Laurent
Goulam Lodge

Off map
Iharana Bush Camp
Tsingy Relais

N

Bradt

0 — 5km
0 — 3 miles

Tsingy Relais (4.0km),
Iharana Bush Camp (6.0km)

Tanambao-Marivorahona

Ambilobe

ANKARANA NATIONAL PARK

Iharana Bush Camp (16 bungalows)
\22 312 10; m 032 11 003 96/032 11 062
96; e iharana_lodge@blueline.mg; www.
iharanabushcamp.com. Quite simple yet very
comfortable & stylish rustic bungalows with en-
suite bathrooms in a wonderful lakeside setting.
Swimming pool. Quite a bumpy track to get there
but worth the effort. 🏠

Ankarana Lodge (7 rooms & 3 bungalows)
m 032 04 908 10; e info@ankarana-lodge.com;
www.ankarana-lodge.com; see ad, 4th colour
section. Located approx 1km from Mahamasina,
dbl rooms & large shelters with luxury tents with
shared facilities as well as en-suite bungalows
with AC. €€€€€

Relais de l'Ankarana (6 bungalows)
m 032 02 222 94/032 05 057 24; e ankarana.
lerelais@gmail.com; www.relaisdelankarana.
unblog.fr. Situated 1km north of Mahamasina, this
hotel is popular with tour operators so advance
booking is essential. Quite simple dbl/twin rooms,
but comfortable & reliable. €€€€

Ankarana Village (6 bungalows)
Mahamasina; m 032 40 722 02. Pretty dbl & trpl
bungalows with electricity & en-suite cold shower;
communal toilet. €€

Chez Aurelien (18 bungalows)
Mahamasina; m 032 02 786 00/032 40 630
14/034 68 589 71; e aurelien_ank@yahoo.fr.
Basic bungalows, some en suite. One reader was
delighted to 'photograph 4 different species of
cockroach in the bathroom' but another notes that
it has since 'been renovated & is now very nice'.
Very good food. Camping permitted. €€

Tsingy Relais (Chez Tonton Robert) (17
rooms) \82 065 65; m 032 02 759 30/032 65 666
57. Palm-thatch pavilion with dining & lounge
space, simple rooms & shared toilets but no
running water. Independent travellers can catch a
taxi-brousse from Ambilobe to Antsaravibe (only
dependable May–Nov); get out at Maromena &
walk the last 2km. €€

Chez Laurent (8 bungalows) Mahamasina;
m 032 07 992 89/034 87 427 62. Basic bungalows
with shared facilities (cold water). No electricity.
€–€€

Goulam Lodge (12 bungalows)
Mahamasina; m 032 02 691 06/032 52 682
82; e goulamguide_ds@yahoo.fr. Dbl & family
bungalows with electricity; shared facilities.
Goulam speaks excellent English & is an
experienced guide specialised in reptiles. €–€€

WHAT TO SEE AND DO

Tsingy and lake Although found in a few other countries, tsingy is very much a
Madagascar phenomenon and you won't want to leave Ankarana without seeing it.
If staying at Anilotra Camp, the best tsingy is about 2 hours away, over very rugged
terrain, just beyond the beautiful crater lake, **Lac Vert**. This is a very hot, all-day trip
(start early and take plenty of water) and is absolutely magnificent. Board walks
have been constructed to allow safe passage over the tsingy, protecting the fragile
rock while you admire the strange succulents such as pachypodiums which seem to
grow right out of the limestone.

Lac Vert is as green as its name suggests, and if you are crazy enough you can
hike down a steep, slippery slope to the water's edge. An easier alternative is the
Petit Tsingy which is found just 15 minutes from the campsite. Although smaller,
there are similar plants and also lemurs.

Caves From Andrafiabe Camp you can explore the gigantic passageways of
Andrafiabe Cave. This is well worth a visit with an exit halfway through into one of
the spectacular canyons from where an interesting return can be made.

At the south, the **Crocodile Cave**, so named because it is home to the world's
only known cave-dwelling crocs, is little visited but is well worth the effort – the
situation is spectacular and the passageways are huge. It is easily walkable in about
30 minutes from the entrance to the eastern end, from where it is a steep, rocky
climb out into the sunken forest.

Don't miss the wonderful bat caves, many of which also feature incredible
sparkling stalagmites and stalactites.

Shrimp and sugar factories There is an aquaculture centre, **Gambas de l'Ankarana**, 12km from Campement d'Andrafiabe. You can visit to learn the ins and outs of shrimp breeding, and witness the manufacture and packaging of shrimp products.

Not far away, it is also possible to visit the **Sirama** sugar factory and stroll through the fields of sugarcane.

Gondwana Park (*www.ankarana-parc.com; entry 25,000Ar or free for guests of Ankarana Lodge*) This newly opened private reserve near Mahamasina was set up by Ankarana Lodge and offers the possibility to experience the wonders of this tsingy landscape even for those passing by in a rush. And, unlike in the national park, night walks are permitted – and highly recommended. See ad, 4th colour section.

FROM ANTSIRANANA TO IHARANA (VOHEMAR) BY ROAD

From Antsiranana as far as Ambilobe, RN6 is a tarred but degraded road; by taxi-brousse it takes about 5½ hours to cover the 138km. The next 163km to Iharana on RN5a, however, is in abysmal condition, taking 12 hours at best – much longer after rain.

If you can possibly afford it, hire a private car. This is not just because it cuts the trip down to a manageable 9 hours or so, but it also gives you the chance to visit the reserve of Daraina *en route*.

AMBILOBE This is a very gritty transit town, busy at all hours with traffic. It lies at an important junction linking Antsiranana in the north with Iharana on the east coast, so you may need to stop here. There are branches of BNI and BOA banks.

On the road towards Iharana, 25 minutes out of Ambilobe, **Dadilahy Waterfall** offers a picnic shelter and the possibility of swimming. For details of this and other nearby attractions, contact the local tourist office, GOTDA (m *032 58 078 17*; e *gotda_ambilobe@yahoo.fr*). If you're passing through in late July or early August, you may catch the annual **Kabiry** regional cultural festival, which combines traditional oratory, music and dance (*kabiry* is the name of a traditional trumpet-like musical instrument).

Getting there and away There are frequent taxi-brousses to Ambanja (up to 3hrs; 6,000Ar) and Antsiranana (4hrs; 15,000Ar). They cruise around town from early in the morning collecting customers, so pick an almost-full one if you want a reasonably quick getaway. There are also *bachés* (canvas-covered pick-up trucks) for the very rough journey to Iharana via Daraina.

Where to stay and eat

Floridas Eden (21 bungalows) m 032 05 033 83/032 25 033 83/034 98 684 54; e floridasseden@gmail.com; www.floridas-eden-ambilobe.com. En-suite rooms with TV/DVD, some with AC. Restaurant serves French & Malagasy food on a large terrace. €€€

Noor (14 rooms) m 032 42 509 00. Behind the Jovenna fuel station at the north of town. It's an old-fashioned place built around a courtyard with rather grubby en-suite bathrooms & some AC rooms; a few have hot water & TV. €€€

Diana (10 rooms & 10 bungalows) ☏ 82 065 39; m 032 43 055 33. Dbl rooms with en-suite cold showers; some with AC & TV. Situated 2.5km from centre (towards Ambanja) so more peaceful. Restaurant opens early & closes late. €€–€€€

Kilimanjaro Amoronala; m 032 27 803 44/032 44 447 30. New hotel on the north side of town offering rooms with fan & sat-TV; some with AC & fridge. €€–€€€

National (10 rooms) ☏ 82 065 41. Good en-suite dbl rooms, some with AC & TV. €€–€€€

🏠 **Rayan** (6 rooms) 📱 033 04 710 28. En-suite rooms: dbl with fan or family with AC & kitchenette. €€

🏠 **Jiraninakahy** (14 rooms) Antafiankasike; 📱 032 27 804 59/032 58 228 64. Low-price rooms & some with AC, sat-TV & fridge. €–€€

🏠 **Golden (Amicale)** (9 rooms) 📱 032 02 902 61. Very noisy with cold water only & poor security – but cheap. €

✖ **Coco Pizza** By far the best eatery; opposite Jovenna. Range of delicious thin-crust pizzas cooked in a wood-fired oven.

✖ **Escargot** An acceptable restaurant down a side street in the centre.

DARAINA This is a small town 56km northwest of Iharana (3hrs), or 114km (7hrs) from Ambilobe. These are typical dry-season travel times by 4x4; taxi-brousses can take twice as long (price 50,000Ar all the way from Iharana to Ambilobe) and the road is impassable in the rainy season (Dec–Apr). If you are taking that road anyway, a stop at Daraina makes the whole journey worthwhile; if you're in Iharana it's worth making it an excursion.

The reason to go here is to visit Loky-Manambato protected area to see the beautiful **golden-crowned sifaka**, one of the rarest of all lemurs and listed among the 25 most threatened primates in the world. Rare though it may be, you *will* see the sifaka, and close-up too (see box below). The sifaka tend to sleep in the scorching heat of midday, so if coming for a day trip make a really early start. But, if you can, it is worth staying overnight because in recent years **aye-ayes** have been seen here with increasing regularity. For the best chance of a sighting, stake out a nest (the guides know where several are located) from well before dusk.

The Malagasy NGO FANAMBY is working with the local communities to preserve the forests and the lemurs. The region has deposits of gold and is rich in

---

SOME OF THE WORLD'S RAREST PRIMATES   *Lee Miller*

On arriving in Daraina, we find a guide and head to the forest. The forest floor is pockmarked with holes in the ground, 1½m across and equally deep. We realise that these are dug by gold miners; and indeed we come upon a group of people panning for gold.

After hiking in the heat for another half-hour, our guide points to the top of a tree where we see a sifaka! Soon enough, he motions us along further, and there is a group of eight more, all far up in the trees. As we watch them, they begin to come down to us, scrambling down the trunks, and leaping from tree to tree. Their leaping is one of the most amazing things I've ever seen. They are spring-loaded. With barely a sign that it is about to leap, a sifaka will suddenly thrust with its back legs and shoot 6–10m horizontally to another tree, grabbing effortlessly to cling to that trunk; beautiful and thrilling.

They keep coming down, peering around the trees at us, until some are just 2m away, watching us with their curious brown eyes. A little baby clings to his mother's back as she approaches. As she settles in to watch us, he asserts his independence and climbs on to a nearby branch, only to leap again onto her back at the slightest sound. Later we watch as she walks on her hind legs across the forest floor, walking in a kind of dance with her baby riding along. It is *fady* to kill them and so they have no fear of humans. These are among the rarest primates in the world; yet here, in their home, they are so easily viewed. It is a remarkable and delightful opportunity, well worth the discomforts of the journey.

semi-precious stones, one of the factors causing conflict with conservation efforts; visitors will witness the huge scale of the illegal mining problem.

Guides charge 25,000Ar. Allow about 3 hours for a visit to the sifakas. There are two options of **places to stay**:

🏠 **Camp Tattersalli** (4 bungalows) ☎ 22 636 61; m 032 26 219 27; e friendlycamp@ madagascar-discovery.com; www.association-fanamby.org. Simple bungalows with basic private bathrooms & a central dining area. €€€€

🏠 **Lémurien Blanc** (5 rooms & 10 bungalows) m 032 51 078 93/032 81 947 60/034 04 111 64; e lemurien.blanc@gmail.com; www. lemurienblanc.com. En-suite rooms with 24hr solar power. Reasonable restaurant, bar & bakery. 4x4, quad & buggy hire €€€

IHARANA (VOHEMAR) This seafront town, known almost universally as Vohemar, marks the end of the good road north from Sambava and Andapa, and the start of the rather bad road connecting the east coast with RN6.

Part of its charm is a near absence of tourists, but there are a couple of beachfront hotels. And in contrast to the roaring ocean further down the coast, Iharana's bay is sheltered and protected by a reef. If you potter along the low-tide pools you can find a wealth of sea creatures. Keep walking and you'll pass a sacred tree, hung with white cloth and zebu skulls. It's a reminder that the local culture is still very much intact in this isolated place.

The town itself is nothing special. There are BFV and BOA banks, an internet café, a pharmacy, a lively nightclub (Zanzibar), a few restaurants and some surprisingly good gift shops.

Getting there and away The easiest way to get here is to fly to Sambava then take a taxi-brousse for the 3-hour road journey (10,000Ar). The route from Antsiranana is described earlier in this chapter.

🏠 **Where to stay and eat**

🏠 **Baie d'Iharana** (16 rooms) m 032 05 221 68/032 07 131 46/032 43 805 31/032 43 805 35; e baiediharana@gmail.com; www. normada.com/iharana. Upmarket hotel set in a beautiful garden with super views of the bay from comfortable AC rooms with balconies. The spacious dining room has ocean views. Easy beach access. Excursions organised, inc to Daraina; 4x4 & bike hire. €€€€

🏠 **Vohémar Beach Bungalows** (5 bungalows) m 032 02 687 41/032 07 774 42.

New hotel among coconut trees on the edge of the bay. Bungalows with private bathrooms & Chinese-Malagasy restaurant. €€€

🏠 **Galaxy** (4 rooms & 8 bungalows) m 032 02 507 10/034 02 507 10; e hotelgalaxyvohemar@ yahoo.fr. Located 200m behind BOA. Simple bungalows, some en suite. €€–€€€

🏠 **Lagon Bleu** (3 rooms & 2 bungalows) Rue des Dames de France; m 032 04 396 46/032 48 501 27; e lagon_bleu@yahoo.fr. En-suite rooms set in a garden. €€

AMBILOBE TO AMBANJA (AND ON TO NOSY BE)

The pot-holed RN6 is popular with travellers heading for Nosy Be – but there is plenty to see in the area so it is a shame to rush. The 102km Ambilobe to Ambanja section is in particularly terrible condition.

AMBANJA This is a pleasant little town set amid lush scenery. It has BFV, BNI and BOA banks, a post office, several pharmacies, some cybercafés and a tourist office opposite the town hall. The area is beautiful, with the country's second-largest mangrove nearby and hills filled with plantations of cocoa, ylang-ylang, pepper and spices.

If you are passing through in August/September, you may see the four-day **Sorogno** festival (*www.festival-sorogno.com*) with a carnival atmosphere of traditional singing, dancing and sports events, or the **Vagnono** festival held shortly afterwards at nearby Anivorano. The local tourist office, GOTS, can give more information on what's on locally (**m** *032 50 584 33/033 05 306 32/032 46 477 47*; **e** *gotsambanja@yahoo.fr*).

Getting there and away Ankify (the **ferry** departure point for Nosy Be) is 22km away and takes 30 minutes by taxi (20,000Ar) or 45 minutes by taxi-brousse (4,000Ar).

Taxi-brousses run north and south: Antsiranana (7hrs; 17,000Ar), Antsohihy (4hrs; 24,000Ar), Mahajanga (14hrs; 50,000Ar) and Tana (16hrs; 65,000Ar). Malagasycar Transport Première Classe provides a comfortable, air-conditioned minibus option from Tana at scheduled departure times and with meals included (**m** *032 40 134 76/033 15 488 88/034 22 588 88*; **e** *malagasycar@gmail.com*; *www. malagasycar.com*). It costs around 170,000Ar and takes approximately 16 hours. Bookings can be made at the Maki boutique or Palma Nova Hotel in Ambanja or Oasis restaurant in Hell-Ville.

 Where to stay and eat

🏠 **Diamant 10** (7 rooms) ✆86 502 59; **m** 032 73 058 98. En-suite rooms with AC & fridge. **€€€**

🏠 **Meridien** (10 rooms) **m** 032 47 782 29/034 37 852 04; **e** houshm@yahoo.fr. Nice place; en-suite (cold water) rooms with TV, some with AC. **€€€**

🏠 **Patricia** (8 rooms) ✆86 500 22; **m** 032 58 973 11; **e** restaurantpatricia@gmail.com. Rooms with fan or for a slightly higher price with AC. **€€€**

🏠 **Timonière** ✆86 935 32; **m** 032 59 215 03/032 69 240 83; **e** latimoniereambanja@yahoo. fr. Guesthouse offering rooms with fan, sat-TV, minibar & private facilities. **€€€**

🏠 **Cocotiers** (13 rooms & 1 bungalow) **m** 032 50 966 97. Dbl rooms with en-suite cold showers, a few with AC. Also 8-person villa with hot water. Good restaurant. **€€–€€€**

🏠 **Nord Inn** (10 rooms) **m** 032 07 763 12/032 66 514 04. Attractive building with clean rooms, some with AC. No food. **€€–€€€**

🏠 **Palma Nova** (10 rooms) **m** 032 04 611 21/032 88 930 88; **e** contact@palmanova-ambanja.com or palma_nova@yahoo.fr; www.palmanova-ambanja.com. Peaceful setting 1km from centre. Dbl, twin & trpl en-suite rooms, some with AC. Bike hire & ecotours of the area. **€€–€€€**

🏠 **Ylang-Ylang** (12 rooms) **m** 032 05 502 40. Range of rooms with TV, some en suite & with fridge. Rather run-down: Wi-Fi, AC & hot water often broken but 'they have a good shop downstairs' reports Ariel Jacobs. **€€–€€€**

🏠 **Hermes** (5 bungalows) **m** 032 04 243 48/032 54 221 84/034 64 185 52. En-suite dbl bungalows & large restaurant. **€€**

🏠 **Nosy Koumba** (15 rooms) **m** 032 04 912 01/032 56 308 36/032 69 514 59/032 79 903 56. Simple budget rooms. **€€**

🏠 **Salama Rose** **m** 032 45 243 27. Basic cheap rooms. **€–€€**

Cocoa plantation Near to the village of Andzavibe a few kilometres north of Ambanja is **Plantation Millot**, where you can get a half-day tour of the 1,350ha cocoa bean plantation and essential oil distillery for 30,000Ar. They also have a restaurant serving European and Malagasy food and three en-suite rooms at **Chez Mado** (**m** *032 04 631 24/032 04 666 10*; *www.cananga.fr*; **€€€**).

ANKIFY AREA This beautiful area of coast has some good hotels. But don't expect a proper village here – there are no shops or other ways of whiling away the time

Nigel Vardy, mountaineer

Wandering into the Tsaratanana Massif to ascend Maromokotro – Madagascar's highest peak at 2,876m – is a task rarely undertaken by any climber. Its remoteness requires a 14-day round trip on foot, crossing waist-deep rivers, bashing through dense jungle and summiting on a peak reminiscent of the Pennines. The peak is held sacred by the locals so we took a plentiful supply of white chickens with us to appease the ancestors. The climate varies incredibly from burning grassland to freezing moorland in only a few days, and requires stamina for the 30-plus kilometres you have to cover each day. A local guide with porters led the way for me through the maze of hills and valleys, walking barefoot as I followed on in walking boots. Theirs was the last laugh, however, as my boots fell apart from the combination of dry, wet, dust and mud. I finished in sports sandals.

Initially we followed the river out of Ambanja before breaking off into the hills and leaving the last villages behind. Suddenly we were in a world of tall grass, then thick forest, before the moorland opened up. Being a Derbyshire lad it almost felt like home as we approached the summit and soon I overlooked most of northern Madagascar. It was here we left a white chicken along with money, tobacco and alcohol as a blessing. Quite what a chicken does left to its own devices at almost 3,000m I'm not sure! Heading home was an epic in itself as the jungle paths were almost non-existent and dawn-till-dark days were spent cutting through the dense undergrowth hoping we were going in the right direction. Soon the first villages appeared and once again the savannah opened up before us on the long walk home.

This climb marked the end of a four-year challenge in which Nigel scaled the highest peaks of the world's seven largest islands (www.mrfrostbite.com).

as you are waiting for the ferry. Hotel transfers to the ferry port typically cost 15,000Ar, but you should be able to find a local vehicle for 5,000Ar – or walk.

Where to stay and eat

Antoremba Lodge (7 bungalows) m 032 56 627 72; e info@antoremba-lodge.com; www.antoremba-lodge.com. Accessible only by boat, located 2km around the headland west of Ankify on its own secluded beach facing Nosy Komba. Nestled among luxuriant vegetation are a handful of very spacious, luxurious beachfront villas, constructed mainly from local materials. Universally highly praised. Fantastic food. Wi-Fi.

Ankify Lodge (8 bungalows) m 032 42 287 36 (excursions)/032 45 334 61; e contact@ankifylodge.com; www.ankifylodge.com. Stone bungalows, en-suite cold water for 2–4 people, 4km from ferry. Private beach; snorkelling possible. €€€€

Balafomanga (3 rooms) m 032 07 185 63; e maisonsurlaplage.balafomanga@gmail.com;

L'Ange Bleu. A traditional house with a patio overlooking the sea towards Nosy Komba. Simple clean rooms. They also operate 12m 8-berth catamaran *L'Ange Bleu* (e ange.bleu.croisiere@gmail.com). €€€€

Baobab (20 bungalows) m 033 07 208 87/033 07 208 88/033 62 954 55; e baobab.ankify@gmail.com. Nestled between rocky cliffs & a beach that overlooks Nosy Komba, 1.5km from ferry. Rather run-down bungalows with separate bathrooms (cold water) in garden area. Electricity in evenings. €€€€

Panoramique (Chez Nono) (4 rooms & 2 bungalows) m 032 04 664 22/032 07 927 97/034 17 505 77. En-suite rooms (cold water), 1 with kitchenette; 4.5km from ferry. €€€€

14

Chocolate from Madagascar has been making waves in recent years. Largest and most famous of the local makers is Chocolaterie Robert, which has won several international awards. Originally established in 1940 in Brickaville, the company was sold to the present owners in 1977 and the factory moved to the capital.

The cocoa beans come from around Ambanja, grown by a co-operative of 125 farmers and harvested twice a year (May and October/November). They are checked in an on-site laboratory and sorted into three quality levels. At the factory any foreign matter such as stones is first removed and the beans are processed in batches of 100kg in a roaster to develop flavour and aroma – a process that takes 45 minutes at a temperature which fluctuates according to a secret formula. Next they go through a cooler and into a winnowing machine to crush the beans and remove the shells. The result, known as 'nibs', goes to a three-level grinder to produce cocoa mass – a thick liquid (because the bean is 45% fat) that has to be stored at 65–75°C.

Next they are squeezed on a press to extract the cocoa butter; the remains are called 'cocoa cake', which is used to manufacture cocoa powder. A conching machine then mixes the ingredients (cocoa powder, milk powder from New Zealand, sugar from India, and cocoa mass) in varying proportions depending on the product being made that day. They also make an organic chocolate using Malagasy sugar instead.

The mixture proceeds to a tempering machine. Depending on the temperature and time settings, there is a degree of butter pre-crystallisation, to control the gloss and give the finished chocolate a good 'break'. The chocolate now goes into a conveyor moulding line, then through a tapping machine at 7°C to remove all the air bubbles. After this comes the de-moulding machine – essentially a big hammer to knock the chocolate out of the mould – and a sorting stage where the product gets a visual check and a metal detector scan to catch any metallic impurities, before finally going on to the packaging stage.

Nine types of chocolate are produced for the export market, as well as commercial products including couverture chocolate, raw nibs, and cocoa butter. The UK is their main export market at present but they also export to Japan, France and Denmark. In 2014, Chocolaterie Robert processed 300 tonnes of beans for the domestic market and 60 tonnes of finished product for foreign buyers, with plans to increase exports to the same level as domestic sales within a few years, having just won four medals in the International Chocolate Awards in New York (gold for 50% milk chocolate, silver for 85% dark chocolate, silver for white chocolate with vanilla, and bronze for 65% dark chocolate) then several more awards at the 2014 world finals held in London.

The factory has a core staff of around 125, which swells with temporary workers to about 200 during the peak seasons of Easter and Christmas. They also make candies and complex-shaped chocolates such as hollow Santas, but these are too fragile for export. Also for the local market, they produce desserts and a range of chocolate box assortments. These can be purchased at their various outlets, including four around Tana (at the factory in Soanierana, in the duty-free lounge of Ivato airport, in Antaninarenina and in Antanimena), as well as in Toamasina, Antsiranana and Antsirabe.

In the UK, single-origin Malagasy chocolate of various brands is available in Sainsbury's, Waitrose and Tesco.

Ankify-Marina (Chez Dudu) (7 rooms & 3 bungalows) 📞 86 920 80; m 032 74 900 30/033 17 846 03. Dbl Rooms, 3km from ferry. Electricity in evenings. Nice local food. Car & boat hire. €€€

Mangroves Basic rooms at the port. €
Porte Rouge Basic rooms at the port. €

BAOBAB BEACH On the opposite side of Ampasindava Bay from Ankify is a multi-award-winning luxury ecolodge only really accessible by boat. **Eden Lodge** (m *032 02 203 61/032 55 044 68/034 86 931 19*; e *resa@edenlodge.net; www.edenlodge.net;* 🌊) has good food and facilities, including Wi-Fi, in a tremendous location with a marvellous beach and lush forest. Its eight chic tented bungalows with stylish private bathrooms are entirely solar powered.

CONTINUING SOUTH FROM AMBANJA TO MAHAJANGA For a description of this journey see *Chapter 16*, page 410.

BAYS AND INLETS ACCESSIBLE TO YACHTS

The bays below could be reached by adventurous hikers or cyclists (many are near villages) but are visited mainly by yachties. Catamaran charters in the area are listed in *Chapter 15*, page 373.

RUSSIAN BAY This is a beautiful and remote place opposite the Nosy Be archipelago. It provides excellent anchorages, all-round shelter and is a traditional 'hurricane hole'. The marine life in the bay itself is terrific, offering wonderful snorkelling and diving, especially on the reefs outside the entrance. There is excellent fishing too and in the right season (Oct–Dec) whales are commonly sighted. This is also one of the best spots in which to seek the very rare whale shark. The beaches are known turtle-nesting sites. The moist tropical deciduous woods harbour abundant birdlife, reptiles and lemurs, and there is a choice of trails for day hikes.

The bay's name dates back to the 1904–05 Russo–Japanese War when a Russian fleet spent nine weeks harboured here. On their departure, they left behind a leaky transport ship to sink at anchor in the bay.

BARAMAHAMAY BAY (MAROAKA) The Baramahamay River is navigable for about 3km inland and provides a beautiful, well-sheltered anchorage with verdant hills behind sunny, white beaches. The wide bay is conspicuous as a large gap in the coastline. Yachties should approach on the north side of the bay and anchor near the villages in 8m over sand and mud. These villages are known also for their blacksmiths, who make large knives and *pangas*, and another is famous for its wild honey. Your chances of seeing rare Madagascar fish eagles here are good.

BERANGOMAINA POINT The bay inside this headland opposite the Radama Islands is an attractive, well-sheltered anchorage. Good visibility is needed to access the bay, however, as there are many scattered reef patches. The channel is at its deepest on the north side, where the depth exceeds 15m right up to the reef. Anchor off the beach before the village, in 10m over a mud bottom. This place is for self-sufficient travellers only; no provisions are available.

The North BAYS AND INLETS ACCESSIBLE TO YACHTS

14

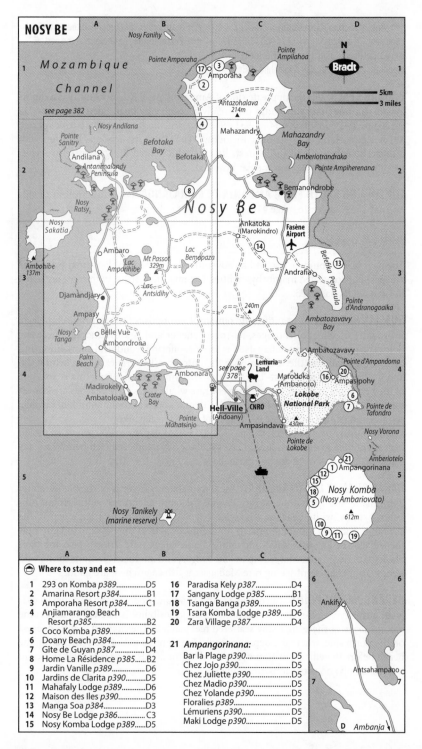

NOSY BE

A B C D

Nosy Fanihy

Pointe Amporaha

Pointe Ampilahoa

(17) (3)
(2) Amporaha

Mozambique

Channel

Antazohalava 214m

see page 382

(4) Mahazandry

Befotaka Bay

Mahazandry Bay

Befotaka

Amberiotrandraka

Pointe Sanitry

Nosy Andilana

Pointe Ampiherenana

Andilana

Antanimalandy Peninsula

Bemanondrobe

(8)

Nosy Be

Nosy Ratsy

Nosy Sakatia

Ankatoka (Marokindro)

Fasène Airport

Ambaro

Mt Passot 329m

Lac Amparihibe

Lac Bemapaza

(14)

Andrafia

(13)

Befeñka Peninsula

Ambohibe 137m

Lac Antsidihy

Pointe d'Andranogoaika

Djamandjary

240m

Ambatozavavy Bay

Ampasy

Nosy Tanga

Belle Vue

Ambondrona

Ambatozavavy

Pointe d'Ampandoma

Palm Beach

Ambonara

see page 378

Lemuria Land

(20)
(16) Ampasipohy

(6)
(7)

Madirokely

Crater Bay

CNRO

Maroñoka (Ambanoro)

Lokobe National Park

Pointe de Tafondro

Ambatoloaka

Hell-Ville (Andoany)

Ampasindava

Nosy Vorona

Pointe Mahatsinjo

430m

Pointe de Lokobe

Amberiotelo

(21)
(1) Ampangorinana

Nosy Tanikely (marine reserve)

(15) (12)
(18)
(5)

Nosy Komba (Nosy Ambariovato)

612m

(10)
(9) (11) (19)

Ankify

Antsahampano

Ambanja

🛏 **Where to stay and eat**

1	293 on Komba *p389*	D5
2	Amarina Resort *p384*	B1
3	Amporaha Resort *p384*	C1
4	Anjiamarango Beach Resort *p385*	B2
5	Coco Komba *p389*	D5
6	Doany Beach *p384*	D4
7	Gîte de Guyan *p387*	D4
8	Home La Résidence *p385*	B2
9	Jardin Vanille *p389*	D6
10	Jardins de Clarita *p390*	D5
11	Mahafaly Lodge *p389*	D6
12	Maison des Iles *p390*	D5
13	Manga Soa *p384*	D3
14	Nosy Be Lodge *p386*	C3
15	Nosy Komba Lodge *p389*	D5

16	Paradisa Kely *p387*	D4
17	Sangany Lodge *p385*	B1
18	Tsanga Banga *p389*	D5
19	Tsara Komba Lodge *p389*	D6
20	Zara Village *p387*	D4

21	*Ampangorinana:*	
	Bar la Plage *p390*	D5
	Chez Jojo *p390*	D5
	Chez Juliette *p390*	D5
	Chez Madio *p390*	D5
	Chez Yolande *p390*	D5
	Floralies *p389*	D5
	Lémuriens *p390*	D5
	Maki Lodge *p390*	D5

15

Nosy Be and Nearby Islands

The name means 'big island' and is pronounced *'nossy bay'* by the local Sakalava people, although *'nooss bay'* is nearer the highland pronunciation. It is blessed with an almost perfect climate for much of the year. Fertile and prosperous, with the heady scent of ylang-ylang blossoms giving it the tourist-brochure name of 'Perfumed Isle', this is the place to come for a rest – providing you can afford it. Compared with the rest of Madagascar, Nosy Be is expensive.

Tourism developed here long before the mainland, so inevitably the island seems touristy to adventurous travellers. Since the demise of the sugar industry, all available land is being bought up for hotel development, pushing prices ever higher. That said, Nosy Be has much to offer – from good seafood and beaches to scuba-diving and boat trips. It also has many more luxury hotel options than in the rest of Madagascar, and a significantly higher proportion of Italian-owned ones (French and Italian tourists now visit Nosy Be in equal numbers, together comprising 86% of the island's visitors).

The only significant town is **Hell-Ville**, which is where the ferry port is as well as such services as banks and airline offices. It has some basic accommodation but no beach; most tourists will want to stay at the better hotels stretching along the west coast. The beachfront village of **Ambatoloaka** in the southwest comprises a couple of dozen hotels and restaurants, so this is the place to stay if you want to be within walking distance of eateries and nightlife. Heading north, the hotels become progressively more isolated and the beaches better. For an even more exclusive experience, consider staying on one of the islets surrounding Nosy Be.

Thanks are especially due to Harriet Joao of MadagasCaT for feedback on this chapter.

HISTORY

Nosy Be's charms were recognised as long ago as 1649 when the English colonel Robert Hunt wrote: 'I do believe, by God's blessing, that not any part of the world is more advantageous for a plantation, being every way as well for pleasure as well as profit, in my estimation.' Hunt was attempting to set up an English colony on the island, known then as Assada, but failed because of hostile natives and disease.

Future immigrants, both accidental and intentional, contributed to Nosy Be's racial variety. Shipwrecked Indians built a magnificent settlement several centuries ago in the southeast of the island, where the ruins can still be seen. The crew of a Russian ship that arrived during the Russo–Japanese War of 1904–05 are buried in the Hell-Ville cemetery. Other arrivals were Arabs, Comorans and – more recently – Europeans flocking to Madagascar's foremost holiday resort.

When King Radama I was completing his wars of conquest, the Boina kings took refuge in Nosy Be. First they sought protection from the Sultan of Zanzibar, who sent a warship in 1838 then, two years later, they requested help from Commander Passot who had docked his ship at Nosy Be. The Frenchman was only too happy to oblige and asked Admiral de Hell, the governor of Bourbon Island (now Réunion), to place Nosy Be under the protection of France. The island was formally annexed in 1841.

TRANSPORT

GETTING THERE AND AWAY Nearly 85% of visitors to Nosy Be arrive by air, two-thirds of those directly from abroad. There are several **international flights**: Air Mad runs services from Paris; Airlink connects Nosy Be with Johannesburg; Air Austral flies from Paris, Mauritius, and Mayotte via Réunion; and Air Italy connects with Milan. Air Mad and Madagasikara Airways runs **domestic flights** from Tana, Antsiranana and Mahajanga. Be warned that there have been problems with passengers being asked for money at passport control and customs in the airport; such requests should be ignored.

Speedboat ferries serve the crossing from Ankify (page 366) to Hell-Ville, leaving as and when they fill up (roughly hourly) and taking 30 minutes. It should cost 10,000–20,000Ar but operators have a habit of overcharging *vazaha* or trying to impose a fee for luggage. Transfers can be pre-booked for specific times but this costs more.

GETTING AROUND There is one good road running in a loop around the island from the airport past Hell-Ville, Ambatoloaka, most of the west-coast hotels, and back to the airport. Many of the others are tracks, often completely impassable in a normal vehicle. Occasional *taxi-brousse* services run on the main road. There are also plenty of **taxis**, operating on either a private hire or a (much cheaper) shared basis. A private taxi from Hell-Ville to the airport or Ambatoloaka takes 25 minutes and costs 35,000Ar.

Bikes, scooters, motorbikes, quads and cars are hired out by several **vehicle-rental agencies** (see under *Hell-Ville* and *Ambatoloaka*) and also many hotels.

Boat transfers to accommodation on nearby islands are usually provided by those hotels, and numerous boat operators run trips from half-day excursions to multi-day liveaboard cruises. **Helicopter** transfers are also possible.

ACTIVITIES AND EXCURSIONS

The **tourist office** [378 C3] in Hell-Ville is very helpful (\ *86 920 62;* m *032 05 546 52/032 05 837 00/032 05 837 04/034 05 119 95;* e *info@nosybe-tourisme.com or ortnb@moov.mg; www.nosybe-tourisme.com*).

TOUR OPERATORS The following companies offer **hiking** or **cycling** tours of Nosy Be. Most also do **4x4 excursions** and **boat trips** to the nearby islands; for visits to islands further afield, see *Yacht charters* opposite.

Escapades \86 927 66; m 033 12 126 24; e commercial@escapades.mg; www.escapades. mg. All kinds of excursions & activities.
Evasion Sans Frontière Hell-Ville (nr BFV [378 C3]); \86 062 44; m 032 11 005 96; e info@

mada-evasion.mg or esf.nosybe@blueline.mg; www.mada-evasion.com. General travel agency.
Kokoa Travel Hell-Ville; \86 921 22; m 033 11 241 22/032 11 425 29; e kokoa@moov.mg or kokoa.direction@gmail.com; www.kokoa-nosybe. com. Excursions by boat & 4x4.

Libertalia Aventure Delastelle Bldg, Hell-Ville; ☎ 86 925 41; m 032 04 611 21/032 02 079 54/032 69 783 91; e contact@libertalia-aventure.com or libertaliaventure@yahoo.fr; www.libertalia-aventure.com. Island trips of 1–13 days; trekking; biking; 4x4 circuits.

Mada In Travel Ambonara; ☎ 86 923 31; m 032 02 394 99/034 02 394 99; e paolo.madain@moov.mg; www.mada-in-nosybe.com. Italian-run; fishing, quad tours & excursions.

Mirenda Tours Ambatoloaka; m 034 40 123 93; e mirendratours@yahoo.fr; www.mada-mirendra-tours.com. Treks & boat trips. 4x4 rental.

Nosy Be Original m 032 40 524 88/032 05 524 90; e info@nosybe-original.com; www.nosybe-original.com. Island hopping, whale-watching, fishing, diving & excursions with their own boats, 4x4s & minibuses.

Nosy-Be Paradise Tours Ambatoloaka; m 034 44 272 35/032 04 272 35; e contact@nosybeparadisetours.com; www.nosybeparadisetours.com. Beach, nature & culture tours.

YACHT CHARTERS

Chartering a liveaboard yacht gives you the chance to spend several days exploring the far reaches of the region's islands and reefs. They are typically catamarans with a chef among the crew for the exclusive service of your group (charters are not shared with strangers).

⚠ **Ange Bleu** m 032 07 185 63; e ange.bleu.croisiere@gmail.com. Catamaran with 4 dbl cabins.

⚠ **Blue Maki** m 032 26 855 31; e info@madagascart-and-dreams.com; www.madagascart-and-dreams.com/en/blue-maki. Well-equipped catamaran.

⚠ **Bossi** ☎ +27 82 579 5249 (South Africa); e bookings@bossiadventures.com; www.bossiadventures.com. Trips of 3+ days on catamarans *Bossi* & larger *Adiva*; also specialised sport fishing boat *Joz-Joz*.

⚠ **Djebel Amour** ☎ +262 692 65 23 46 (Réunion); e contact@djebelamour.com; www.djebelamour.com. Charters on spacious 10-bed 17m trimaran *Djebel Amour II*.

⚠ **Fifi Cata** m 032 60 897 14; e fifidiving@gmail.com; www.fificata-nosybe.com. 13m cat for charters.

⚠ **MadagasCaT** Nosy Sakatia; ☎ +27 21 200 0173/+27 79 149 6438 (South Africa); e info@madagascat.co.za; www.madagascat.co.za. Popular & highly recommended charters in yachts *Gecko* (sail) & *Maki-Cat* (motor) for cruising, diving, fishing or even a dedicated kayaking itinerary. Excellent personal service; they can also organise the rest of your holiday throughout Madagascar.

⚠ **Madavoile** Ambatoloaka; ☎ 86 065 55; m 032 04 223 55/032 22 266 27; e info@madavoile.com; www.madavoile.com. Cruises for relaxation, fishing & diving on catamarans *Aquatic 2, Kalife, Lady Corsica, Shadok* & monohull *Anushka*.

⚠ **Ulysse Explorer** m 032 04 802 80; e ulyssexplorer@gmail.com; www.ulyssexplorer.com. Charters of 8-berth catamarans *Ulysse Explorer* & *Calypso*; diving & fishing. See ad, 4th colour section.

OTHER BOAT OPERATORS

These are smaller boats offering day trips to nearby islands and camping tours – an economical alternative to yacht charters, but less luxurious and lacking the range to reach the most impressive islands (Radamas and Mitsios).

⚠ **Alefa** Madirokely; ☎ 86 060 70; m 032 07 934 78; e alefamada@gmail.com; www.pirogue-madagascar.com. Round-island sailing pirogue trips typically 4–11 days, camping with cooks, tents, etc, provided.

⚠ **Madagascar Island Safaris** ☎ +27 21 783 0400/+27 76 644 9158 (South Africa); e info@madagascarislandsafaris.co.za;

www.madagascarislandsafaris.co.za. Adventurous dhow tours, staying at permanent camps in Lokobe, Russian Bay & Mahalina. Also kayaking. See ad, page 394.

⚠ **Nosy Trans** m 032 55 909 13; e nosy.trans@gmail.com. A shaded 22-seat 200hp vessel available for transfers or day charters.

DIVING

Although much of the coral close to Nosy Be is degraded, there are still some stunning sites, especially around the pristine little islands of the region.

15

Indeed, the Radama and Mitsio archipelagos have some world-class dive sites. Some of the companies listed under *Yacht charters* have diving equipment and MadagasCaT offer liveaboard dive charters.

Plongeurs de l'Archipel de Nosy Be (e *divingnosybe@gmail.com*), a local association of dive clubs, was set up in 2012 to guarantee a certain level of safety and environmental good practice; all the operators listed below are members. The optimum time for diving is May to October.

🤿 **Aqua** Ambaro; m 033 02 020 40/032 05 020 39; e gianluca@aquamadagascar.com or info@aquamadagascar.com; www.aquamadagascar.com. PADI.

🤿 **Blue Vision** Andilana; m 034 254 87 17/032 607 46 16; e info@divebluevision.com; www.divebluevision.com. PADI.

🤿 **Forever Dive** Madirokely; m 032 07 125 65/032 84 913 81; e info@foreverdive.com; www.foreverdive.com. PADI & NAUI.

🤿 **Love Bubble** m 032 42 509 98; e bibi@lovebubblediving.com; www.lovebubble.it. Offers nitrox & night dives. CMAS & PADI.

🤿 **Madablu** m 032 40 542 92/034 60 168 53; e madablu@gmail.com; www.madablu.com. PADI.

🤿 **Madaplouf** (nr Vanila Hotel [314 B3]); 📞86 938 65; m 033 14 248 33/033 02 096 13; e madaplouf@gmail.com; www.madaplouf.com. Offers night dives. PADI, CMAS & NASE.

🤿 **Manta** Ambondrona; m 032 07 207 10; e info@mantadiveclub.it; www.mantadiveclub.it. PADI, CEDIP & NAUI.

🤿 **Océane's Dream** Ambatoloaka; m 032 07 127 82/032 52 346 01; e resa@oceanesdream.com; www.oceanesdream.com. PADI, CMAS & FFESSM.

🤿 **Sakalav'** (nr Vanila Hotel [314 A3]); m 032 05 437 21/032 07 437 21; e sakalav.diving@yahoo.fr; www.sakalav-diving.com. Free souvenir video of your dive. Also night dives. CMAS & PADI.

🤿 **Sakatia Lodge** Nosy Sakatia; m 032 02 770 99/032 41 165 16; e sakatialodge@sakatia.co.za; www.sakatia.co.za. Underwater photography specialists; offers nitrox & night (inc UV-fluo) dives. NAUI.

🤿 **Tropical** Ambatoloaka (at Coco Plage); m 032 49 462 51/032 02 493 16; e tropical.diving@gmail.com or tropical.diving@moov.mg; www.tropical-diving.com. PADI, CMAS.

SNORKELLING The prospects for snorkelling around the coastline of Nosy Be itself are not great, although the **Andilana** area is reasonable. Significantly better are the surrounding islets: the protected **Nosy Tanikely** has wonderful snorkelling, as does the tiny **Nosy Fanihy**, 3km offshore from Amarina Ora Resort. **Nosy Sakatia** and **Nosy Komba** are also recommended.

But serious enthusiasts should consider heading to islands further afield. **Nosy Tsarabanjina** is excellent and the **Radama** and **Mitsio** archipelagos are truly exceptional spots both for snorkelling and diving. Snorkelling trips are offered by most of the operators of boat excursions, dive outfits and yacht charters.

WATERSPORTS

Kayak Madagascar Nosy Komba; m 032 40 142 13; e kayakmadagascar@moov.mg. 5–7-day kayak tours of the area staying in a different place each night. Run by South African Bert Spalding, who is based in Ampangorina.

Nosy Be Kite Surf Ambondrona (nr Domaine Manga Be [314 B6]); m 032 02 316 87; e info@nosybekitesurf.com; www.nosybekitesurf.com. Kitesurfing for beginners to experienced. Season: Jul–Nov.

WHALE-WATCHING (AND OTHER SEA LIFE) **Humpback whales** (see box, pages 340–1) tend to be around from mid-August until the end of October. During this period, most of the boat and dive operators offer whale-watching trips. **Turtles** and **dolphins** may be seen year-round. You might just see a **whale shark** if you are around between mid-July and late November and, if you are *very* lucky, a **manta ray**.

DEEP-SEA FISHING The area offers rewarding fishing year-round. Serious fishermen can expect to catch giant trevally (kingfish), sailfish, wahoo, king mackerel and yellow fin tuna. Dog fish tuna are rare but can be caught with the right guide. Capture and release is encouraged. Many companies offer day trips and longer packages, and most of the operators listed under *Yacht charters* also offer fishing.

Barracuda Ambatoloaka. Hotel (page 381) specialising in fishing; ½–7-day packages.

Fishing World m 032 07 125 13; e fishingworld@moov.mg or lefrereloic@gmail. com; www.fishingworld-nosybe.net. Fishing trips of 1–8 days.

Madagascar Fishing Adventures Sakatia Lodge, Nosy Sakatia; +27 82 379 0349/+27 21 783 3561 (South Africa); e info@ madagascarfishingadventures.co.za; www. madagascarfishingadventures.co.za. Experts in land-based & liveaboard fishing holidays.

Manou Madirokely; 86 062 12; m 032 04 444 84; e amatmc@moov.mg; www. nosybefishingmanou.com. Fishing trips of 1–12 days.

Nosy Be Fishing Ambatoloaka; 86 933 61; m 032 40 142 43; e gianni@nosybefishing. com; www.nosybefishing.com. Experienced Italian fishing operator.

Stela Fishing Club Ankibanivato; m 032 74 535 11/032 68 156 60; e stelafishingclub@ orange.fr or Kam83@orange.fr; www. stelafishingclub.com. Hotel (8 bungalows) specialised in fishing holidays; 2 boats.

QUAD BIKING

Black and White Ambatoloaka; m 034 61 183 07. Quads & motorbikes.

Mada-Services Dar-es-Salam 86 921 46; m 032 07 761 24/032 02 590 38; e vdm@mada-services.com; www.mada-services.com. Quads, motorbikes & mountain bikes.

Quad Run Andilana; 86 921 51; m 032 40 169 99/033 14 146 31. Hire of dbl quads.

Tsanga Tsanga Tour Ambaro; m 033 14 334 20; e isoal@moov.mg

HORSE-RIDING Located near Vanila Hotel, **Ambaro Ranch** [382 A3] (m *032 43 691 78; e l2d2@hotmail.fr; www.ambaroranchnosybe.blogspot.com*) offers horse-riding from 30 minutes along the beach to a half-day exploring the island's interior. Group rides for up to five people are possible as well as lessons for children.

PLEASURE FLIGHTS Based at Pearls International golf course [382 A3], **Insolite Travel Fly** (m *032 11 427 15/032 07 427 50; e itf@itf.mg; www.insolite-travel-fly.com*) has choppers and fixed-wing light aircraft for hotel transfers and pleasure flights over Mont Passot, islands, Ankarana tsingy, etc.

MUSIC FESTIVAL (*www.festival-donia.com*) The week-long **Donia** festival is held each Pentecost (May/June) in the Hell-Ville football ground [378 C2] with groups coming from across the Indian Ocean. Besides the concerts, there are satellite events such as a carnival, dance performances, a beauty pageant, sports events and children's entertainment.

OCEANOGRAPHIC MUSEUM (m *032 40 728 14/032 42 029 08/032 56 308 96; e cnro_ nosybe@yahoo.fr; http://cnro.recherches.gov.mg;* ⊕ *Mon–Fri 08.00–18.00, w/end by prior arrangement; entry 5,000Ar pp*) Marine research centre **CNRO** [370 C4], up on the hill east of Hell-Ville, has run this interesting museum since 1950. It displays some 600 preserved species and aims to raise awareness of marine conservation.

ESPACE ZENY (m *034 19 419 45/034 36 649 45; e espace_zeny@moov.mg*) This park and cultural museum site at Mahatsinjo, a couple of kilometres southwest of Hell-

15

Ville, is most famous for its sacred tree. Covering several thousand square metres, you might easily think this is a forest, but all the 'trunks' in fact belong to a single gigantic banyan fig thought to be over two centuries old. For the local Sakalava, it is a place of prayer and sacrifice, as evidenced by the many offerings including pieces of red-and-white cloth, zebu skulls, rum and honey.

The tree is dedicated to Tsiomeko, who in 1836 became monarch of the Boina kingdom of northwest Madagascar at the tender age of eight, only to lose it four years later when Merina invaders annexed it to their growing empire. Queen Tsiomeko fled to Nosy Be, and died in childbirth not long after, aged just 15.

LOKOBE NATIONAL PARK For decades a closed 'strict reserve', Lokobe has finally been opened to the public. Covering some 740ha (not counting 122ha of marine park), the reserve is home to 42 species of birds, 50 reptiles, 14 amphibians, and three lemurs, including black lemurs and the locally endemic Hawks' sportive lemur. Botanists may be interested to see the *Dypsis ampasindavae* palm which is found only here. There are three hiking trails (1–2½km/2–3hrs) of varying levels of difficulty and pirogue trips are also an option. For permit prices, see page 73.

If you want to come to the area for more than a day trip, there are a few options to suit a range of budgets: see **Paradisa Kely**, **Lokobe Lodge**, **Gîte de Guyan**, **Domaine de Lokobe**, **Doany Beach** and **Zara Village** in the *Beach hotels and other accommodation* section, page 383.

MARODOKA (m *032 41 327 97*; e *ravinala.marodoka@yahoo.fr or contact@ravinala-marodoka.com; www.ravinala-marodoka.com*) Near to Lokobe, a proactive local women's association runs an excellent cultural heritage experience, through which you can discover the early history of Nosy Be as well as local traditions, song, dance and cuisine.

GOLF The million-dollar **Pearls International** golf course [382 A3] took almost five years to build and was opened in 2014. With 18 holes spread over 25ha, it also boasts a driving range, clubhouse restaurant, gym, tennis court, swimming pool and helipad. Nearby hotel **Résidence du Golf** has a practice putting green.

TSARA TANETY (*www.nosybeprojects.com*) This project is under development. At its core is a 100ha forest reserve 5km from Hell-Ville on the road to the airport. Some parts of the forest are in good condition, with 116 types to tree identified and animals that include 30 bird species, 16 reptiles, seven mammals and two frogs.

In time the developers hope the eco-site will include a tree nursery, restaurant, museum, handicrafts village, children's play area, tennis court, swimming pool, minigolf, health centre, and around 80 villas – all supported by solar power.

LEMURIA LAND [370 C4] (m *032 11 040 70/72/75*; e *direction@lemurialand.com; www.lemurialand.com*; ⊕ *Mon–Sat 08.30–17.00; entry 35,000Ar*) Marketing itself as a zoological and botanical park, Lemuria Land seems firmly aimed at French and Italian tourists, who generally speaking appear to delight in lemur-on-your-shoulder interactions. Anglophone travellers in our experience have more mixed views, with many feeling that exploitation of animals purely for entertainment is a Victorian concept with little place in the modern world.

Either way, this place is well organised (although a number of species are misidentified). Visitors will see ring-tailed lemurs and three species of sifaka, as well as black, common brown, crowned, black-and-white ruffed, red-fronted brown and red-bellied lemurs. In addition, there are endemic ducks, wild boars, crocodiles, tomato frogs, radiated tortoises, snakes, chameleons, leaf-tailed geckos, iguanas, plated lizards, day geckos – and even giant tortoises from the Seychelles.

Bizarrely, the Nosy Be tourist office suggests the perfect way to visit this zoo is on horseback, noting that 'you'll have the pleasure to meet nature whilst seated grandly upon nature'!

MONT PASSOT (m *032 02 930 68;* e *montpassot@gmail.com*) A popular excursion is the trip to to one of the island's highest points, Mont Passot (326m). The access road and viewpoint have been much improved in recent years, with a new observation platform, welcome centre and souvenir shops. *En route* there are good views of a series of deep-blue crater lakes, which are said to contain crocodiles, as well as being the home of the spirits of the Sakalava and Antakarana princes. Supposedly it is *fady* to fish there, or to smoke, wear trousers or any garment put on over the feet, or a hat, while on the lakes' shores. It is a beautiful spot, and there are three new hiking circuits (2–5hrs/4–6km) allowing you to explore the 300ha of dense forest here.

HELL-VILLE (ANDOANY)

The name comes from Admiral de Hell rather than an evocation of the state of the town. Hell-Ville is actually quite a smart little place (at least by Malagasy standards), its main street lined with boutiques and tourist shops. There is a market selling fresh produce and an interesting cemetery.

 WHERE TO STAY There are plenty of hotels in Hell-Ville, but all quite basic. For budget travellers a night here while you investigate the cheaper beach hotels is almost essential.

Upper range €€€€

Ambonara [378 A1] (8 bungalows) \86 613 67; m 032 02 611 12; e ambonara@moov. mg; www.nosy-be-holidays.com. Built on an old coffee plantation about 1km north of the town centre, these en-suite bungalows are constructed from natural local materials & set in a garden filled with heavenly scents. The bar has 20 sorts of *rhum arrangé* & the restaurant is tremendous.

Mid-range €€€

Abud [378 B2] (30 rooms) Rte Principal; m 032 45 885 23. A central 5-storey hotel with

comfortable small rooms, some en suite (cold water).

Bel Hôtel's [378 B1] (28 rooms) \86 613 25; m 032 05 025 23/032 80 951 25/033 41 916 25; e belhotels@yahoo.fr; www.belhotels-nosybe. com. New 3-floor hotel with some of the best & cleanest rooms in town, each with en-suite facilities, hot water, safe, minibar, sat-TV & Wi-Fi; some with AC.

Belle Vue [378 C2] (19 rooms) Rue Tsiomeko; \86 613 84/86 931 34; m 032 04 798 94/032 78 408 62; e bellevuehotel_nosybe@yahoo.fr. Dbl & trpl rooms, some with AC & some en suite.

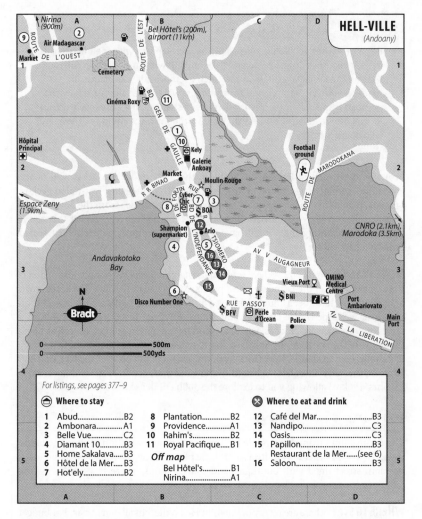

For listings, see pages 377–9

Where to stay

1	Abud	B2
2	Ambonara	A1
3	Belle Vue	C2
4	Diamant 10	B3
5	Home Sakalava	B3
6	Hôtel de la Mer	B3
7	Hot'ely	B2
8	Plantation	B2
9	Providence	A1
10	Rahim's	B2
11	Royal Pacifique	B1

Off map

	Bel Hôtel's	B1
	Nirina	A1

Where to eat and drink

12	Café del Mar	B3
13	Nandipo	C3
14	Oasis	C3
15	Papillon	B3
	Restaurant de la Mer	(see 6)
16	Saloon	B3

🛏 **Diamant 10** [378 B3] (14 rooms) Bd Dr Manceau; ☎ 86 614 48; m 032 07 739 14. Comfortable en-suite rooms with AC.

🛏 **Home Sakalava** [378 B3] (5 rooms) Rue Tsiomeko; m 032 21 709 93; e homesakalava@gmail.com; www.home-sakalava-nosybe.com. Comfy guesthouse in a beautiful old colonial building, run by a very amicable young Malagasy couple. Bright & nicely decorated rooms with en-suite bathrooms, Wi-Fi & sat-TV. Small restaurant.

🛏 **Hôtel de la Mer** [378 B3] (16 rooms) Bd Dr Manceau; ☎ 86 610 32; m 032 40 877 37; e hdlm@moov.mg or omada@moov.mg. Basic rooms, some en suite with sea view.

🛏 **Nirina** [378 A1] (5 bungalows) m 032 56 301 00; e info@chez-nirina.com; www.chez-nirina.com. Quaintly attractive hotel on outskirts of town. Very clean rooms with Wi-Fi & en-suite facilities. Bike hire.

🛏 **Plantation** [378 B2] (6 rooms) m 032 07 934 45; e plantation_b@yahoo.fr. Small & intimate; better known as a restaurant.

🛏 **Providence** [378 A1] (11 rooms) ☎ 86 614 22; m 032 40 178 49/032 44 227 17/034 14 227 17; e laprovidencehotel@yahoo.fr; www.hotel-laprovidence.com. En-suite rooms with TV & hot water (some with AC) on road out of town.

Penny-pincher and budget €–€€

🏠 **Rahim's** [378 B2] (23 rooms) Rue Poincaré; 📞 86 611 16; m 032 40 249 75 (manager)/032 58 070 90. Simple cheap dbl & family rooms. €€

🏠 **Royal Pacifique** [378 B1] (9 rooms) m 032 04 028 30. Clean rooms with hot water & some with AC. Also a self-catering apartment. €€

🏠 **Hot'ely** [378 B2] (30 rooms) Bd de l'Indépendance; 🔲 hot.ely.3. New in 2013, this 3-storey hotel opposite Cyberchic has basic clean dbl rooms with squat toilets & bucket showers. €

🍴 **WHERE TO EAT AND DRINK** Of the hotel restaurants, **Plantation** is especially recommended for its pricey but delicious French cuisine and **Ambonara** for its seafood and zebu steaks.

🍴 **Café del Mar** [378 B3] Opposite BOA. New & already popular; mainly Chinese, Thai & Malagasy cuisine.

🍴 **Nandipo** [378 C3] Rue Albert I; m 032 04 482 32; e nandipomadagascar@yahoo.com; ⏱ 07.00–midnight. Great ambience in this popular bar & restaurant. Serves pizzas, snacks & ice cream. Pool table & darts. Wi-Fi.

🍴 **Papillon** [378 B3] 📞 86 615 82. Popular Italian restaurant.

🍴 **Restaurant de la Mer** [378 B3] e restaurantdelamer@moov.mg; ⏱ Mon–Fri 06.00–23.00. Good food & great pizzas on a breezy sea-view terrace.

🍴 **Saloon (Chez Jeanne)** [378 B3] 📞 86 921 77. Bar & restaurant with pool table. They also have rooms.

🍺 **Oasis** [378 C3] m 034 75 119 95; e oasis. nosy-be@croustipain.mg. Snack bar & café with fresh croissants & *pains au chocolat* daily. Also cakes & ice cream. Terrace good for people-watching.

NIGHTLIFE

🍷 **Vieux Port** [378 D3] A popular place at the old port. Wild nights. Usually gets going around 22.00, with live music. Great salegy & reggae music.

☆ **Disco Number One** [378 B3] 📞 86 610 32; e omada@moov.mg; ⏱ Fri–Sun 21.00–late. In a basement beneath Hôtel de la Mer.

☆ **Moulin Rouge** [378 B2] 📞 86 610 36; ⏱ Fri–Mon & Wed 22.00–dawn. Discotheque near the market. Serves pizzas during the day.

SHOPPING The large number of tourists visiting Nosy Be has made it a centre for souvenir production, giving you the opportunity to buy direct from the makers and benefit local people. Mind you, much of the stuff comes from Tana. Unique to Nosy Be are the carved pirogues, clay animals and Richelieu-embroidered curtains and tablecloths. Handicraft sellers frequent the road to the port and a developing **tourist market** on the road out of town, and there are some high-quality goods in Hell-Ville's boutiques.

The **indoor market** [378 B2] is well worth a visit and is the best place for vanilla and spices, both for quality and price. A short distance to the north is a small mall, **Galerie Ankoay** [378 B2], with its restaurant and two floors of shops built around a central bar shaped like a ship. There is also a supermarket called **Shampion** [378 B3] (⏱ *Mon–Sat 07.00–13.00 & 15.00–19.00, Sun 07.30–12.30*).

INTERNET Of Hell-Ville's cybercafés, **Cyberchic** [378 B2] (e *andosoa@moov.mg*; ⏱ *08.00–22.00*) opposite the BOA bank is one of the most reliable. **Ylang. Net** in Galerie Ankoay (see above) is cheaper and also open every day. And near the tourist office is **Perle d'Océan** [378 C3] (⏱ *Mon–Sat 08.00–noon & 14.00–19.00*).

VEHICLE HIRE

🚗 **Location Bienvenue** m 032 02 088 46/032 04 756 06. Low-price vehicle rentals.

🚗 **Nosy Be Immo** ☎ 86 610 36; m 034 68 692 14; e info@immo-nosybe.com; www.immo-nosybe.com. All kinds of vehicles & transfers arranged.

🚗 **Nosy Easy Rent** ☎ 86 063 08; m 033 11 611 00/032 04 399 59; e nosyeasy.rent@live.fr; www.nosyeasyrent.com. Motorbikes, cars & 4x4s.

🚗 **ZigZag** ☎ 86 921 81; m 032 04 159 84; e bienvenue@zigzag-madagascar.com; www.zigzag-madagascar.com. Self-drive 2CVs; also bikes, mopeds & bus trips.

MEDICAL Based midway between Hell-Ville and Ambatoloaka, **Espace Médical** (☎ 86 620 57; m 034 05 431 15; www.espacemedical.mg) provides excellent 24-hour medical services. In Hell-Ville itself are **OMINO** medical centre [378 D3] (☎ 86 611 91/93) and the **Hôpital Principal** [378 A2] (☎ 86 613 95).

Pharmacies **Tsarajoro** [378 B2] (*Bd Gen de Gaulle;* ☎ 86 613 82) and **Nouroudine** [378 B2] (*Rue Binao;* ☎ 86 610 38) are well stocked.

MONEY

$ BNI [378 C3] Rue Passot; ☉ Mon–Fri 08.00–15.30. Visa; MasterCard; Western Union; 24hr ATM.

$ BFV [378 C3] Rue Gouhot; ☉ Mon–Fri 07.30–11.30 & 14.00–16.00. Visa; Western Union; 24hr ATM.

$ BOA [378 B2] Rue Gallieni; ☉ Mon–Fri 07.30–11.30 & 14.30–16.30. MasterCard; Western Union.

$ Western Union Service at Abud Hotel [378 B2]; ☉ Mon–Fri 08.00–11.30 & 14.00–17.00, Sat 09.00–13.00

AIRLINE OFFICES

✈ **Air Madagascar** [378 A1] North Hell-Ville; ☎ 86 612 18/86 613 57; m 032 05 222 51/034 11 222 00; e nosssmd@airmadagascar.com; www.airmadagascar.com; ☉ Mon–Fri 08.00–11.00 & 14.30–17.00, Sat 08.00–09.30

✈ **Air Austral** [378 C3] Rue Gallieni; ☎ 86 612 32; e nosybe@air-austral.com; www.air-austral.com; ☉ Mon–Fri 08.00–noon & 14.00–17.30, Sat 09.00–noon. Near BFV bank.

AMBATOLOAKA

Once a charming fishing village, Ambatoloaka has long since filled with bars and good-time girls. In an effort to clamp down on sex tourism, some of the hotels are wary about taking single men.

That said, there are signs Ambatoloaka has turned a corner and is beginning to shed its shabbiness. For now, this lively spot offers the best options for inexpensive places to stay in Nosy Be and is the place to be if you're looking for nightlife rather than tranquillity. Most of the hotels are positioned along the beach, which is the most popular in Nosy Be despite being inferior to those further north.

🏠 WHERE TO STAY

Top end €€€€€

 Sarimanok (15 rooms) m 032 05 909 09/034 02 909 11/034 49 909 09 (reception) or 032 05 909 10/034 02 909 10 (manager); e contact@sarimanok.mg or hotelsarimanok@gmail.com; www.hotel-sarimanok-nosy-be.com. This contemporary hotel offers spacious dbl & family rooms in 3 standards with king-size beds, Wi-Fi, AC, minibar, sat-TV, safe & most with ocean/pool view from large bay windows of mirrored one-way glass. Superior rooms also have a balcony. Beachfront lounge area & stylish restaurant-bar intriguingly named Ba Tu Mo Ch.

🏠 **Transat** (3 bungalows) m 032 07 126 65; e mada.letransat@gmail.com; www.hotel-transat-nosy-be.com. Very stylishly designed spacious bungalows on the beach.

Upper range €€€€

Barracuda (8 rooms) m 034 43 662 46/034 45 534 53; e contact@barracuda-mada.com or jhmoramora@hotmail.com; www.barracuda-mada.com. Sgl to family-size rooms with AC & shared facilities (cold water).

Benjamin (7 rooms & 1 bungalow) m 032 02 408 13; e contact@hotelbenjamin-nosybe. com; www.hotelbenjamin-nosybe.com. Very comfortable bungalows with terraces set in a nice garden. Also 4-bedroom Villa Razambe for up to 8 people, with pool.

Boucaniers (17 bungalows) m 032 02 675 20; e boucaniers@moov.mg; www.hotel-lesboucaniers-nosybe.com. Tastefully furnished bungalows, some with ocean views. AC option.

Chez Gérard et Francine (9 rooms) m 032 07 127 93; e gerardetfrancine@gmail.com or gerardetfrancine@moov.mg; www.gerard-et-francine.com. Set in a beautiful peaceful garden at the south of the village, ideal for those wanting to steer clear of the local nightlife. En-suite rooms with fridge & Wi-Fi; some with balcony. B/fast inc.

Clair de Lune (7 bungalows) m 032 75 083 09; e lescheres@gmail.com; www.clair-de-lune-nosybe.com. Charming, quiet B&B on breezy hillside 500m west of village. Bungalows with lovely bathrooms set in lovely garden with swimming pool. No single men. Airport transfers inc for stays of 3+ nights. Closed Jan–Mar.

Coco Plage (13 rooms) m 032 40 401 30/032 65 008 08; e coco.plage@orange.mg; www.cocoplage-nosybe.com. Dbl & twin rooms with TV, minibar, AC & safe; some with sea view.

Koko Loko (6 rooms) m 032 05 659 84/032 70 856 58; e davidilly1@yahoo.fr or vickytana@ yahoo.fr; http://kokoloko.hotel-nosy-be.com/fr. 50m from the beach, spacious & bright rooms with AC, minibar, safe & sat-TV. Kitchen.

Résidence d'Ambatoloaka (12 rooms) m 034 03 617 30/034 05 918 25/034 39 412 84; e alexanaivo@moov.mg or didierbezana@yahoo.

ca or eganagey@gmail.com. Good beachfront restaurant but rooms are on the other side of the road. AC for extra charge. B/fast inc.

Villa Gaia (4 rooms) 86 060 91; m 032 04 772 06; e contact@villa-gaia.com; www. villa-gaia.com. B&B in a charming colonial villa 150m from beach. En-suite rooms with minibar. Swimming pool.

Ylang Ylang (8 rooms) m 032 07 126 93; www.hotel-lylangylang.com. Sgl & dbl en-suite rooms with safe. British-owned in beachfront location.

Mid-range €€€

Caravelle (5 bungalows) m 032 40 284 54; e pascal@hotel-nosybe.com; www.hotel-nosybe. com. Good-value bungalows, en suite (hot water) with small lounge & balcony, at far north of village.

Chez Pat (Soleil et Découvertes) (6 rooms) 86 614 24; m 032 04 793 15/032 40 247 86. Beachfront dbl & family en-suite rooms (cold water). Bar & restaurant on terrace; French dishes & pizza.

Coucher du Soleil (3 rooms & 10 bungalows) 86 928 42; m 032 02 087 21; e coucherdusoleil@ moov.mg; www.coucherdusoleil-nosybe.com. Hotel & restaurant; clean, comfy en-suite bungalows (cold water). Not on the beach, but sea view.

Dauphin (14 rooms) m 032 02 994 58/032 46 686 21; e hotelledauphin@yahoo.fr. Dbl en-suite rooms (cold water), some with balcony, at north of village.

Espadon (20 rooms & 4 bungalows) m 032 11 021 21/032 11 040 59/034 22 021 21; e contact@espadon-nosybe.com or contact@ hotelespadon-nosybe.com; www.espadon-nosybe. com. Beachfront hotel & restaurant with pleasant garden. Comfy rooms with TV, AC & minibar. Specialises in deep-sea fishing.

Villa Catherine (5 rooms) 86 931 10; m 034 13 204 89. Dbl rooms, inc 1 en suite. Also 14 self-catering units with sea-view balconies.

WHERE TO EAT AND DRINK The hotel restaurants **Ba Tu Mo Ch** (at Sarimanok) and **Beach Bar** (at Espadon) are particularly recommended.

Chez Angeline 86 616 21; ⏲ Tue–Sun, Mon closed. Popular long-established restaurant, famous for seafood & *poulet au coco*.

Chez Térésa (Bel Rose) m 032 04 664 75. A small pink & white restaurant that wouldn't look

out of place in Hansel & Gretel. Italian, French & Malagasy cuisine; vegetarian options.

Karibo m 032 53 678 73. Just outside the village. Refined cuisine with Mediterranean & Italian specialities. Homemade ice cream. Lively bar.

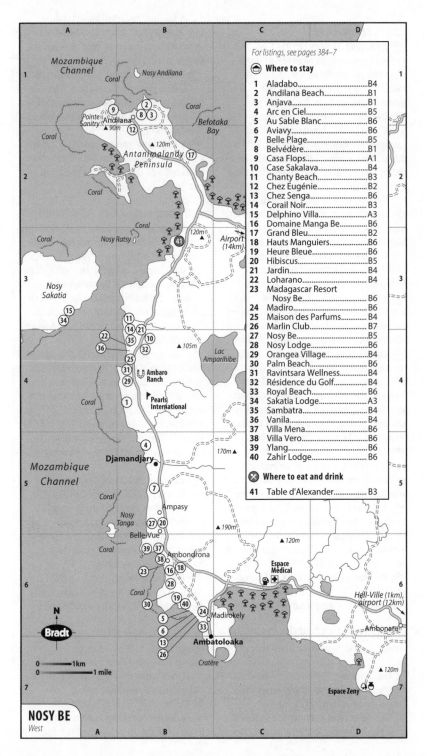

For listings, see pages 384–7

Where to stay

1	Aladabo	B4
2	Andilana Beach	B1
3	Anjava	B1
4	Arc en Ciel	B5
5	Au Sable Blanc	B6
6	Aviavy	B6
7	Belle Plage	B5
8	Belvédère	B1
9	Casa Flops	A1
10	Case Sakalava	B4
11	Chanty Beach	B3
12	Chez Eugénie	B2
13	Chez Senga	B6
14	Corail Noir	B3
15	Delphino Villa	A3
16	Domaine Manga Be	B6
17	Grand Bleu	B2
18	Hauts Manguiers	B6
19	Heure Bleue	B6
20	Hibiscus	B5
21	Jardin	B4
22	Loharano	B4
23	Madagascar Resort Nosy Be	B6
24	Madiro	B4
25	Maison des Parfums	B4
26	Marlin Club	B7
27	Nosy Be	B5
28	Nosy Lodge	B6
29	Orangea Village	B4
30	Palm Beach	B6
31	Ravintsara Wellness	B4
32	Résidence du Golf	B4
33	Royal Beach	B6
34	Sakatia Lodge	A3
35	Sambatra	B4
36	Vanila	B4
37	Villa Mena	B6
38	Villa Vero	B6
39	Ylang	B6
40	Zahir Lodge	B6

Where to eat and drink

41	Table d'Alexander	B3

NOSY BE
West

✕ Zeburger m 032 64 970 12; e zeburger. nosybe@gmail.com; www.zeburger.mg. Popular eatery with more than just burgers; generous portions.

🖵 Baobab Kafé m 032 04 676 63. Serves mainly snacks: sandwiches, crêpes, etc. Cocktail bar.

NIGHTLIFE The nightclubs are all situated along the road between hotels Espadon and Dauphin at the northern end of town.

♀ Sawadi m 032 42 413 59. In the heart of the village, a smart cocktail & tapas bar with cosy seating. Themed nights with live music & full moon parties.

☆ Djembe m 032 87 164 83; ⊕ Mon–Wed & Sat. Well-equipped nightclub with AC, high-tech lighting, special effects, mirrored walls & a waterfall behind the bar. Also pool tables & pizza. Often live gigs.

☆ Sirène 🅵 lasirenediscotheque; ⊕ Thu–Sat. Discotheque sited opposite Djembe (at least 1 of the 2 is open every night).

☆ Taxi Be m 032 59 187 86; ⊕ Wed–Mon 21.00–late, closed Tue. Lively bar & disco with funky décor & enjoyable ambience. Big screens for sports events.

SHOPPING There are a couple of small handicraft boutiques but Ambatoloaka has limited options for provisions shopping, so you may wish to stock up in Hell-Ville first. There is a small supermarket, **Big Bazar**, just out of the village towards Madirokely.

VEHICLE HIRE

🚗 Locamad m 032 42 062 42. Motorbikes.

🚗 Locascoot m 032 02 196 15. Scooter hire.

🚗 Location Jeunesse m 032 59 055 26/032 04 663 87. Bikes, scooters & motorbikes. Also hires tents & snorkelling gear.

🚗 Mada-Services ☎ 86 921 46; m 032 02 590 38/032 07 761 24; e vdm@mada-servces.com;

www.mada-services.com. Motorbike rental nr Big Bazar supermarket.

🚗 Moto Mada m 032 02 680 25/032 44 229 96. Motorbike rental.

🚗 Nosy Red Cars ☎ 86 620 35; m 032 41 547 82. Self-drive 2-seat cars & Renault 4s.

EMERGENCIES There is a **police** post at the north end of the village. Pharmacy **Toko** (☎ 86 927 82; ⊕ 24hrs) in the centre is reliable, and for medical care **Espace Médical** (page 380) is 4.5km away on the road to Hell-Ville. In 2015, thanks to Italian NGO Life for Madagascar (www.lifeformadagascar.org), the country finally got a hyperbaric recompression chamber for diving emergencies. It is located in Ambatoloaka at the clinic **Vie et Harmonie** (m 032 48 986 53/032 74 585 71/032 74 585 51).

🏠 BEACH HOTELS AND OTHER ACCOMMODATION

Hotels are dotted all over Nosy Be, most especially in beachfront locations along the sandy western coast. There are many very high-quality lodgings with standards (and prices) comparable to tropical island resorts elsewhere in the world. Prices can vary substantially between the high season (usually mid-Jul to mid-Sep, and Christmas) and low season, and are often quoted per person rather than per room by the more exclusive places.

Keep in mind that the accommodation categories in this book – luxury, top-end, etc – are based entirely on fixed price bands. As a consequence of the notably higher prices of Nosy Be's beach lodges compared with mainland Madagascar, hotels in a given category here are not likely to be of the same standing as others in that category elsewhere in the country.

A professional organisation of tourist operators on Nosy Be was set up in 2010. Some 55 members, including 35 hotels, had signed up to the **GIHTNB** charter by 2014, committing to a code of conduct to minimise their impact on the environment, improve social integration and professionalise their operation (*www.gihtnb.com*).

LUXURY ⬥

Amarina Resort [370 B1] (58 rooms) m 032 07 307 47/034 11 000 27; e booking@ voihotels.com; www.voihotels.com/hotels/voi-amarina-resort-madagascar. This hotel has all the facilities you'd expect: AC, private balconies, Wi-Fi, massage & pool. The spacious en-suite rooms have a sea view facing the sunset. Snorkelling is excellent in the lagoon & at the beautiful coral island opposite. Boats for excursions/transfers & activities range from biking, kayaking & fishing to gym & volleyball.

Amporaha Resort [370 C1] (13 rooms) m 032 67 745 77/034 10 383 32; e contact@ amporaharesort.com; www.amporaharesort. com. With beautiful décor blending traditional & modern in a pristine & quite remote natural setting on a splendid beach. Rooms with AC, sat-TV/DVD, safe & Wi-Fi. Excellent service & fantastic food.

Andilana Beach [382 B1] (208 rooms) m 033 15 250 00 (Tana)/034 65 000 05 (Tana)/034 65 000 06 (Tana)/034 65 000 07 (Tana)/034 65 000 08/034 65 000 09/034 65 000 10; e info@ andilanaresort.com; www.andilanaresort.com or www.nosybe.com. All-inc hotel using the Club Med format: meals, snacks, drinks, numerous sports & all other activities are inc in the price. Don't expect to experience the 'real' Madagascar here; with every facility imaginable within the security perimeter few venture out of the resort.

Belle Plage [382 B5] (16 bungalows) ☎86 927 34; e hotel@belleplage.com; www.belleplage. com. Swiss-owned en-suite bungalows with AC in a wonderful garden right on a private beach. Quiet location.

Corail Noir [382 B3] (31 rooms & 9 bungalows) ☎86 920 52/86 920 53; m 032 62 144 88; e booking@corailnoir-madagascar.com; www. corailnoir-madagascar.com. Ground-floor rooms with little front garden, 1st floor with balcony & bungalows with decks out front. Next to the beach opposite Nosy Sakatia. Buildings are mostly stone, bamboo & palm leaves & decorated very simply but tastefully. A couple of readers have complained of staff being aggressively reprimanded in front of guests.

Doany Beach [370 B4] (2 bungalows) m 032 02 095 15; e doanybeach@gmail.com; www.doanybeach.com. A very quiet & intimate place that can sleep max 7 people in 2 beachfront bungalows. The authentic Malagasy style, attention to detail & personal service are praised by all who stay.

Hauts Manguiers [382 B6] (10 rooms) m 032 05 621 18/032 05 621 20 (manager); e contact@nosybe-location-hauts-manguiers. com or reservations@hauts-manguiers.com; www.hauts-manguiers.com. Thatched wooden bungalows with sea view. Swimming pool. Recent visitors have sent very mixed reviews about the quality of service.

Loharano [382 B4] (24 rooms) m 033 14 334 20/034 04 182 70/034 16 436 31; e hotelloharano@ gmail.com; www.loharanohotelnosybe.com. AC rooms in 10 bungalows but has just been taken over & seems to be suffering management issues. It's an attractive little hotel set around a central garden & swimming pool so hopefully standards will recover soon.

Manga Soa [370 D3] (7 bungalows) m 034 05 839 21; e info@manga-soa-lodge.com or resamangasoalodge@gmail.com; www.manga-soa-lodge.com. Tucked on a quiet little beach far from the hustle & bustle, this ecolodge is a truly fantastic new addition to the Nosy Be hotel scene. The food is nothing short of divine & the staff could not be more helpful. Elegantly furnished rooms with minibar, TV, safe & Wi-Fi, set in a seafront tropical garden. Massage & infinity horizon pool.

Palm Beach [382 B6] (51 rooms & 12 bungalows) m 032 03 666 07/032 11 660 66/032 11 660 68/033 11 660 66/034 11 660 66/034 11 660 68; e fabio.dalessandro@palmbeach-nosybe. com or reservation@palmbeach-nosybe.com; www. palmbeach-nosybe.com. Large complex opened in 2014 catering to a predominantly Italian clientele. Elegant well-appointed rooms mostly with good views. It's not the quietest of places & service could be better, but the food is generally excellent & the facilities such as the spa are top notch.

Ravintsara Wellness Hotel [382 B4] (20 bungalows) ☎86 066 32/86 066 33; m 032 07 137

76/034 86 066 37; e resa@ravintsara.mg; www. ravintsarahotel.com. Opened in 2012, this exclusive spa resort is set in an exquisite 5ha tropical garden by the sea. Very spacious bungalows with AC, safe, minibar, sat-TV, Wi-Fi & en-suite facilities. Sumptuous food is served in 2 restaurants. The 'wellness centre' inc a hammam, jacuzzis, massage rooms, a Zen space module for rest/yoga/massage & beauty salon.

🏠 **Royal Beach** [382 B6] (66 rooms) 📞 86 930 41; m 032 05 322 44/032 05 323 44/034 07 122 44; e reservation@royalbeach.mg or royalbeach@royalbeach.mg; www.royalbeach-nosybe.com. Rooms are en suite with TV, AC & balcony (many with sea view); suites also have baths. B/fast inc. Sauna, hammam, massage, pool, gym & huge new spa. Pizzeria, swish restaurant & lounge bar; live music most eves.

🏠 **Sangany Lodge** [370 B1] (10 bungalows) m 034 08 125 61; e sanganylodge@yahoo.fr; www.sanganylodge.com. New in 2011, these large villas overlook the sea & each has a private terrace, lounge, desk, bath/jacuzzi & outside shower. Also a tree-house room.

🏠 **Vanila** [382 B4] (57 rooms) 📞 86 921 01/86 921 02/86 921 03; m 032 02 203 60 (manager)/032 03 921 01/034 21 329 93/034 86 921 01; e info@vanila-hotel.com; www.vanila-hotel.com. Comfy rooms with AC, TV & private terrace. Prestige suites also have hi-fi, DVD player & jacuzzi. Wi-Fi. Lovely garden with 2 rim-flow swimming pools; 2 restaurants.

🏠 **Zahir Lodge** [382 B6] (8 bungalows) m 032 05 938 80/032 49 494 75; e info@lezahir-lodge-nosybe.com; www.lezahir-lodge-nosybe.com. Set around a garden & swimming pool, the en-suite rooms have safe, Wi-Fi & kitchenette; unique décor of Malagasy crafts.

TOP END €€€€€

🏠 **Anjiamarango Beach Resort** [370 B2] (35 bungalows) m 032 02 655 98; e contact@anjiamarango-beach-resort.com; www.anjiamarango-beach-resort.com. Beautiful gigantic bungalows right on the beach in a quiet, idyllic setting. Each has a lounge area, desk, corner bath with shower, fridge & Wi-Fi (during limited hours of electricity).

🏠 **Arc en Ciel** [382 B5] (10 rooms) m 032 02 049 39/032 02 265 30; e info@hotelarcenciel.net; www.hotelarcenciel.net. Large tastefully furnished rooms; clean & spacious. Infinity-edge pool.

🏠 **Chanty Beach** [382 B3] (3 rooms & 2 bungalows) 📞 86 928 16; m 034 86 928 16; e chantybeach@gmail.com; www.chantybeach-hotel.com. Charming self-catering bungalows & en-suite rooms with AC on a private beach.

🏠 **Grand Bleu** [382 B2] (15 bungalows) 📞 85 920 23; m 032 02 194 84/033 14 248 16; e contact@legrandbleunosybe.com; www.legrandbleunosybe.com. Deservedly popular place with quaint bungalows, mostly with minibar & safe; some with sea view. Friendly service.

🏠 **Heure Bleue** [382 B6] (18 bungalows) Madirokely; 📞 86 060 20; m 032 02 203 61/032 65 568 05; e resa@heurebleue.com; www.heurebleue.com. Recently awarded African Hotel Award for Best Renovation & Refurbishment. It boasts a rim-flow tidal pool & a freshwater one. En-suite bungalows with fridge, balcony & Wi-Fi. The only downside is the noisy weekly disco nearby.

🏠 **Hibiscus** [382 B5] (3 bungalows) m 032 40 047 33; e leshibiscus.sp@hotmail.fr; 🇫 leshibiscusnosybe. Comfortable stylish rooms 10mins' walk from the beach. Good food.

🏠 **Home La Résidence** [370 B2] (15 bungalows) m 034 02 932 32/034 02 934 34; e reservation@home-la-residence.com; www.home-la-residence.com or www.home-madagascar.com. A 10ha site with 800m beachfront & self-contained holiday villas with TV, AC, Wi-Fi, safe, kitchen & most with jacuzzi; ideal for families or groups of 4–10 people. Communal restaurant, bar, swimming pool & kids' club.

🏠 **Jardin** [382 B4] (14 rooms) 📞 86 920 52/86 920 53; m 032 62 144 88; e booking@lejardin-madagascar.com; www.lejardin-madagascar.com. Chic ethnic design in an impeccably kept garden with 20m pool. En-suite trpl rooms with AC, minibar, TV & safe.

🏠 **Madagascar Resort Nosy Be** [382 B6] (5 rooms) m 032 05 233 30/032 07 291 78 (owner); e booking@madaresortnosybe.com; www.madaresortnosybe.com. New at the start of 2016. Despite the uninspired name, this intimate guesthouse is characterful & welcoming. En-suite rooms with Wi-Fi & sea view. Swimming pool, restaurant & bike hire. Visa & AmEx accepted.

🏠 **Madiro** [382 B6] (18 rooms) m 032 04 750 48/032 04 968 03; e madirohotel@moov.mg; www.madiro-hotel.com. Tastefully decorated en-suite rooms, some with AC & Wi-Fi, arranged around central swimming pool in a lovely garden

15

alongside a good beach. Free gym. Restaurant with Italian specialities.

🏠 **Marlin Club** [382 B7] (22 rooms) m 032 07 125 95/032 07 127 61. B&B specialised in deep-sea fishing.

🏠 **Nosy Be Hotel** [382 B5] (50 rooms) ☎86 061 51; m 032 40 011 46/034 06 771 86/034 06 771 87/034 06 771 88/034 06 771 89; e contact@ nosybehotel.com; www.nosybehotel.com. Boutique spa hotel with beautiful design. Service is so-so but there is an excellent spa with massage & reflexology treatments. Spacious rooms with AC set in a lovely garden.

🏠 **Nosy Lodge** [382 B6] (22 rooms) m 032 40 452 04; e contact@nosylodge.com; www. nosylodge.com. Surrounded by greenery, this is a heavenly boutique hotel with exceptional attention to detail, much-lauded staff & a restaurant with a tremendous reputation. Several rooms have a sea view. It is unfortunate that they have created a 'zoo' with captive lemurs, tortoises, boas & a crocodile.

🏠 **Orangea Village** [382 B4] (25 rooms) m 032 04 200 85/032 05 905 58 (reception)/032 66 537 78; e reservation@orangea.net; www. orangea.net. Owned & run by an enthusiastic French-Belgian couple, this is an exceptionally attractive & relaxing place. Bungalows & rooms (some with AC) set in beautiful garden with pool. Top food.

UPPER RANGE €€€€

🏠 **Anjava** [382 B1] (4 bungalows) e hjmickael@gmail.com or lanjavansb@gmail. com; www.anjava.com. Small homely outfit with clean en-suite bungalows, some with AC.

🏠 **Au Sable Blanc** [382 B6] (12 rooms) m 032 11 105 52; e info@au-sable-blanc. com; www.au-sable-blanc.com or ◼ au.sable. blanc. Waterfront apartments & studios run as B&B ideal for visitors wanting to stay a couple of weeks or more. All with kitchenette, TV, safe, Wi-Fi & hot water.

🏠 **Aviavy** [382 B6] (13 rooms) m 032 40 585 59/034 07 207 87; e contact.aviavy@gmail. com; www.nosy-be-hotel.com. Indian-owned beachfront hotel with sat-TV, Wi-Fi, AC, safe & minibar; no alcohol or smoking allowed. Some correspondents have complained of poor service. Fishing excursions.

🏠 **Belvédère (Chez Loulou)** [382 B1] (6 rooms) m 032 76 751 99; e aubelvederehtl@ gmail.com. Set on a hill close to the beach; lovely view over Andilana Bay. B/fast inc. Restaurant Chez Loulou does excellent meals & Sun buffet lunch.

🏠 **Casa Flops** [382 A1] (4 rooms) m 032 05 888 30; e lacasaflops@gmail.com; www.casaflops-nosybe.com. Eco-guesthouse for the responsible tourist. Rooms constructed from natural materials, with solar power.

🏠 **Case Sakalava** [382 B4] (5 rooms) m 032 05 437 21; e case.sakalava@yahoo.com; www. case-sakalava.com. Hilltop ecolodge 750m inland but with panoramic sea views; solar & wind power. En-suite rooms. Guided walks with local villagers.

🏠 **Chez Eugénie** [382 B2] (3 rooms & 2 bungalows) ☎86 923 53; m 032 40 634 48; e chezeugenie@yahoo.fr; www.chez-eugenie. com. Intimate & friendly out-of-the-way place with en-suite rooms & fantastic food. Praised by countless readers. B/fast inc.

🏠 **Domaine Manga Be** [382 B6] (60 rooms) m 032 04 688 84/032 42 092 82; e domainemangabe@moov.mg; www. domainemangabe.com. Various rooms, suites & villas for 2–6 people, some with sea view.

🏠 **Maison des Parfums** [382 B4] (11 rooms & 2 bungalows) m 032 40 483 07/032 41 384 01/034 12 883 06; e maisondesparfums@yahoo.fr; www.la-maison-des-parfums-nosybe.com. From dbl rooms to waterfront villas with kitchenette. Wi-Fi.

🏠 **Nosy Be Lodge** [370 C3] m 032 07 137 77; e nosybelodge@gmail.com; www.nosy-be-lodge. com. On an 11ha site in the interior of the island, these beautiful simple rustic bungalows have large airy verandas. Welcoming staff & excellent restaurant.

🏠 **Résidence du Golf (Jardin des Plantes)** [382 B4] (5 rooms) m 032 02 868 67; e jeanloupflandre@live.fr. Near the beach & the new golf club, this hotel offers a practice putting green. Studios with kitchenettes & bathrooms.

🏠 **Sambatra** [382 B4] (4 bungalows) ☎86 937 72; m 032 67 251 17; e isoal@moov.mg. Beachfront B&B owned by Tsanga Tsanga Tour (page 375). Simple clean bungalows with hot water.

🏠 **Villa Mena** [382 B6] (2 rooms) m 032 41 686 63; e villamenanosybe@gmail.com; www. hotel-villamena-nosybe.com or www.villamena.

mg. Guesthouse run by a French former set designer & director. Attractively decorated spacious rooms with sat-TV, minibar & safe. Kitchen area for guests' use.

🏠 **Ylang** [382 B6] (4 bungalows) m 032 78 490 46; e pascal.momboisse@yahoo.fr or ylanghotel@gmail.com; www.ylanghotel.com. Family-run hotel set amid a pretty garden with a swimming pool, gym, game room, bar, restaurant & Wi-Fi zone. Rooms are en suite with AC, fridge & safe. Car, 4x4, scooter & quad hire.

🏠 **Zara Village** [370 D4] (1 bungalow) m 032 95 998 14/033 23 222 33/034 17 471 57; e villagezara@gmail.com; www.zaravillage.e-monsite.com. A holiday villa with 4 dbl rooms, lounge, dining room, kitchen & swimming pool just 50m from the sea.

MID-RANGE €€€

🏠 **Aladabo** [382 B4] (8 bungalows) m 032 02 323 93; e aladabo@moov.mg; www.hotelaladabo.

com. Traditional en-suite bungalow guesthouse, run by affable co-managers Jimmy & Biscuit.

🏠 **Chez Senga** [382 B6] (3 rooms) ✆86 930 18; m 032 40 378 01; e hotelsenga@moov. mg. Simple en-suite bungalows with fan. Highly regarded restaurant, well known for its local specialities. Very good value.

🏠 **Gîte de Guyan** [370 B4] (4 rooms) m 032 46 383 49; e guyan.lokobe@gmail.com; www. hotelguyanlokobe-nosybe.com. A tranquil spot with welcoming hosts praised by several readers. En-suite rooms in a large rustic house at the seafront.

🏠 **Paradisa Kely** [370 D4] (6 bungalows) ✆86 922 97/86 938 68; m 032 04 944 21/032 59 700 36; e paradisakely@gmail.com or sanchalain@ free.fr. Welcoming beachfront hotel on the edge of Lokobe, accessible only by boat; en-suite bungalows for 2–6 people.

🏠 **Villa Vero** [382 B6] (9 bungalows) m 032 02 171 34/034 02 171 34/034 05 646 90/034 91 812 70; e villavero2@yahoo.fr. Bungalows with fan & en-suite cold showers.

✖ **WHERE TO EAT AND DRINK** Most of the main hotels have good restaurants: the best food is served at **Belvédère**, **Chez Eugénie**, **Chez Senga**, **Amporaha Resort**, **Manga Soa**, **Ravintsara**, **Royal Beach** and **Nosy Lodge** – although not all are easy to get to for guests staying elsewhere. The price you pay for opting for the tranquillity of a more isolated hotel is that you may have no choice but to eat all your meals there.

There are very few independent eateries outside Hell-Ville and Ambatoloaka, but notable is **Table d'Alexander** [382 B3] (m *033 14 247 22*) which serves splendid food in a beautiful setting.

ISLANDS AROUND NOSY BE

No visit to Nosy Be is complete without an excursion to **Nosy Tanikely** and **Nosy Komba**. Most Nosy Be hotels do excursions to these islands and will let you do the sensible thing of taking an overnight break on the latter.

Both Nosy Komba and **Nosy Sakatia** have decent accommodation and offer tranquil alternatives to the rather crowded main island.

NOSY KOMBA (NOSY AMBARIOVATO) (*www.nosykomba.com*) Back in the 1970s, Nosy Komba was an isolated island with an occasional boat service, a tiny village (**Ampangorinana**), and a troop of **black lemurs** ('*komba*') that were held to be sacred. Now all that has changed: tourists arrive by the boatload from Nosy Be and passing cruise ships.

It is the lemurs that bring in the visitors. During the 1980s the villagers made nothing out of these visits apart from the sale of clay animals which they glazed with the acid of spent batteries. Then they instigated a modest fee for seeing the lemurs. Now they have taken on the works: 'tribal' dancing, face decoration, a vast handicrafts market (tablecloths a speciality), escorted walks – anything that will earn a dollar or two.

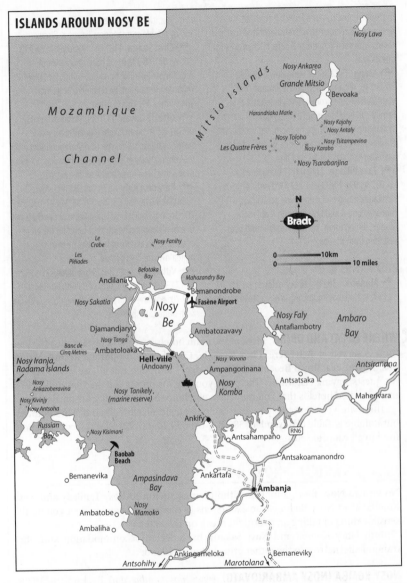

Nosy Lava

Mitsio Islands

Nosy Ankarea

Grande Mitsio

Bevoaka

Harandriaka Marie

Nosy Kajohy
Nosy Antaly

Nosy Toloho
Les Quatre Frères
Nosy Tsitampevina
Nosy Karabo

Nosy Tsarabanjina

Mozambique

Channel

N

Bradt

0 ————10km
0 ——————— 10 miles

Le Crabe
Les Pléiades

Nosy Fanihy

Andilana
Befotaka Bay
Mahazandry Bay

Nosy Sakatia
Bemanondrobe
Fasène Airport

Nosy Be

Nosy Faly
Antafiambotry

Ambaro Bay

Djamandjary
Nosy Tanga
Banc de Cinq Metres
Ambatoloaka
Ambatozavavy

Hell-ville
(Andoany)

Nosy Vorona
Ampangorinana

Nosy Komba

Antsatsaka

Antsiranana

Nosy Iranja, Radama Islands

Nosy Ankazoberavina
Nosy Kivinjy
Nosy Antsoha

Russian Bay

Nosy Kisimani

Nosy Tanikely, (marine reserve)

Ankify

Maherivara

Antsahampano

RN6

Antsakoamanondro

Baobab Beach

Bemanevika

Ampasindava Bay

Ankartafa

Ambanja

Ambatobe
Nosy Mamoko

Ambaliha

Ankingameloka

Antsohihy

Bemaneviky

Marotolana

All that said, away from the village on the **southern beaches** there is still tranquillity to be found, and some excellent hotels.

Visitors can take a hike up the hill for **spectacular views** of the whole area (the 630m peak is far higher than any point on Nosy Be) but start early before it gets too hot. A guide costs 20,000Ar and the round trip should take 4–5 hours. If you want the lemur-on-your-shoulder experience then it's just a 5-minute walk uphill from Ampangorinana to **Lemur Park** (*entry 6,000Ar*).

The cheapest way to reach Nosy Komba is by pirogue from Port Ambariovato [378 D3] (east of the main port in Hell-Ville) or Ankify. Don't be scammed into paying for an extra ticket for your bag.

Alison Jolly, primatologist

Female lemurs tend to be dominant over males, unlike in most monkeys and apes. In some lemur species, such as ring-tails and the white sifakas of Berenty, males virtually never challenge females. In others, such as brown lemurs, it is nearer 50:50, depending on the individual's character. The black lemurs of Nosy Komba are intermediate. Their females are likely to dominate males but are not certain to. If you are feeding them, the blonde females are apt to be in the forefront of the scrimmage with only a few of the black males. Watch to see who grabs food from whom and – even more telling – who does not dare grab.

Female dominance also applies to sex. An unwilling female chases off a male, or even bites him. Or she may just sit down with her tail over her genitals – a perfect chastity belt. A lemur's hands can't hold another's tail, so if she puts it down, or just sits down, he is flummoxed. And in most lemur species, he would never dream of challenging her desires.

Also note the way the males rub their wet, smelly testicles and anal region on the females. Some females do not appreciate this and tell them off with a snarl. Males may also rub their bottoms on branches to scent-mark them, then rub their heads on the branch to transfer the scent to their forehead.

You can tell a lot about a lemur's mood by where it is looking – a long hard stare is a threat; quick glances while head-flagging away is submissive. The tail, though, won't tell you much except how the animal is balanced on a branch or your shoulder. They use tails to keep track of each other, but not to signal mood.

✕ Where to stay and eat

Tsara Komba Lodge [370 D6] (8 bungalows) m 032 07 440 40; e edentkl@orange.fr or maryse.zohar@orange.fr; www.tsarakomba.com. Very exclusive, beautiful lodges with solar-heated water overlooking a tiny beach. The high price is justified by the profits they put back into the village, renovating the houses & school, building a dispensary & working to provide safe water & solar power. ♨

Jardin Vanille [370 D6] (1 room & 8 bungalows) m 032 07 127 97; e info@jardinvanille.com or jardinvanille@gmail.com; www.jardinvanille.com. Delightful mangrove-wood bungalows on stilts set into the hillside above the beach – 62 steps up! En-suite bungalows with minibar & balcony; the suite is right on the sea. Wild black lemurs nearby. €€€€€–♨

293 on Komba [370 D5] (5 rooms) m 034 09 417 01/034 47 139 75/034 85 674 68; e stay@293onkomba.com; www.293onkomba.com. Intimate & exclusive B&B lovingly run by South African Marcine. Tremendous food. No under-16s. €€€€€

Coco Komba [370 D5] (5 bungalows) m 032 88 211 37/032 88 477 13; e contact@coco-komba.com; www.coco-komba.com. A small, charming place in a creek on a quiet part of the island. Solar-powered bungalows with safe & terrace; mostly with sea view. Activities inc fishing & cooking. €€€€€

Floralies [370 D5] (8 bungalows) m 032 02 200 38; e floralieskomba@yahoo.fr. The new owners have just renovated these dbl bungalows, beautifully situated at the end of a quiet beach opposite Lokobe. Bar & restaurant. B/fast inc. €€€€€

Nosy Komba Lodge [370 D5] (3 bungalows) m 032 78 255 85; e nosykombalodge@yahoo.fr; www.nosykombalodge.com. New in 2012, these comfy & attractive lodgings have hot water, safe & internet access. €€€€€

Tsanga Banga [370 D5] (1 bungalow) m 032 41 533 49; e tsangabanga@gmail.com; www.tsangabanga.com. Smart 3-room rental home for up to 8 people in total. €€€€€

Mahafaly Lodge [370 D6] (4 rooms & 1 bungalow) m 032 07 126 57. Owned by an

15

English-speaking Malagasy prince of the region who delights in enlightening guests about local culture, tradition & history. Wonderful garden with beautiful rooms & splendid views. €€€€–€€€€€

🏠 **Jardins de Clarita** [370 D5] (3 bungalows) m 032 45 260 04; e lesjardinsdeclarita@gmail.com; www.lesjardinsdeclarita.com. Charming guesthouse in a lovely tropical garden. €€€€

🏠 **Maki Lodge** [370 D5] (5 bungalows) m 032 85 477 34/034 88 477 34; e info@lemakilodge-madagascar.com; www.lemakilodge-madagascar.com. Perched dramatically on a large rock, these rooms have great views. Attentive service & Wi-Fi zone. €€€€

🏠 **Maison des Iles** [370 D5] (1 bungalow) e mdi.nosykomba@gmail.com. Rental home for up to 5 people; min stay 1 week. €€€

🏠 **Chez Yolande** [370 D5] (8 bungalows) e casinca@hotmail.com. Seafront bungalows, some en suite but cold water. Solar electricity. €€–€€€

🏠 **Chez Jojo (Au Coucher du Soleil)** [370 D5] (10 rooms) m 032 02 215 74. Dbl bungalows with shared facilities & some with balcony. €€

🏠 **Chez Juliette** [370 D5] (5 bungalows) m 033 14 470 34. Simple bungalows with shared facilities (cold water). €–€€

🏠 **Chez Madio** [370 D5] (6 bungalows) ✆ 86 926 72; e c3chicco@hotmail.com. Mme Madio is very welcoming. Basic good-value bungalows for 2–4 people; squat toilets & bucket showers. €–€€

🏠 **Lémuriens** [370 D5] (10 bungalows) m 032 44 986 88; e hotel.lemuriens@yahoo.fr. Basic bungalows with en-suite toilet & cold shower or (cheaper) shower only. €–€€

☆ **Bar la Plage** [370 D5] m 032 41 793 11. Come to watch the ocean over a beer or wine. Internet available.

NOSY SAKATIA This 4km-long island with a population of 450 is situated just 750m off the west coast of Nosy Be and is in the process of becoming a marine reserve. Once seriously denuded, it has made a remarkable recovery under a programme encouraging locals to plant pineapples instead of rice. It is fady to take a dog to Nosy Sakatia; it is also fady to wash laundry in the river there on a Tuesday or to enter the sacred forest of Ambohibe.

Ferry crossings cost 20,000Ar, or cheaper for guests staying on Nosy Sakatia. An association called **Sakatia Tourist Guides** has been established, offering pirogue trips to the island in search of orchids and wildlife (m *032 27 483 08;* e *sakatiatg@yahoo.fr*).

🏠 **Where to stay**

🏠 **Sakatia Lodge** (11 bungalows) m 032 02 770 99/032 04 934 02; e reservations@sakatia.co.za or sakatialodge@sakatia.co.za; www.sakatia.co.za. Smart dbl/trpl bungalows & beachfront villas. Family-style dining & attentive personal service. Apart from being a very well-run & highly praised place to stay, it is the base for one of the region's best dive centres (see *Sakatia Lodge*, page 374), top-class sport fishing outfit Madagascar Fishing Adventures (page 375) & MadagasCaT's superb yacht charters (page 373). €€€€–€€€€€

🏠 **Delphino Villa (Chez Richard)** (4 bungalows) m 032 04 844 05/034 02 844 05; e delphino.villa.sakatia@gmail.com. Simple rustic bungalows at the water's edge with good snorkelling (mask & fins provided). €€€

NOSY TANIKELY (*Entry 20,000Ar*) This marine reserve lures snorkellers and bird enthusiasts. Although now much visited, indeed sometimes overcrowded, it is still a lovely little island. In clear water you can see an amazing variety of marine life: coral, starfish, anemones, every colour and shape of fish, turtles and lobsters. (With this captivating world beneath your gaze there is a real danger of forgetting the passing of time and becoming seriously sunburnt, so wear a T-shirt and shorts.)

Don't think you have finished with Nosy Tanikely when you come out of the water; at low tide it is possible to walk right round the island. During the 1.5km circumambulation you may see black and brown lemurs, flying foxes and graceful white-tailed tropic-birds. The walk involves some scrambling round rock pools but nothing too challenging. Then there is the short climb up to the **lighthouse** at the top of the island for the view.

NOSY VORONA ('BIRD ISLAND') This speck of an island northeast of Nosy Komba offers you the chance to live out your desert island fantasy. Barely covering 1ha, and complete with a hammock slung between palm trees on a sandy beach, it comes as close to the remote desert island cliché as you'll get. The single four-room bungalow (accommodating up to eight people) shares the island only with an old lighthouse and costs around €100 per person per night on a full-board basis (m *032 02 367 03;* e *nosyvorona@gmail.com;* €€€€€).

NOSY MAMOKO This little island is at the southwest end of Ampasindava Bay. Known among the yachting fraternity for its exceptional shelter in all weathers, there is good anchorage in the channel between the island and the mainland, in 15m over a sandy bottom.

OTHER NEARBY UNINHABITED ISLANDS The apple-core-shaped **Nosy Tanga**, measuring 400m across, lies opposite Nosy Be Hotel on the west coast. Less than 1km offshore it is easily reached by canoe. In the bay to the east of Nosy Sakatia is the sacred rocky island of **Nosy Ratsy** ('bad island'), just 100m across. At the northwest of Nosy Be, 700m offshore, is **Nosy Andilana** with striking white beaches of dead coral. Opposite Amarina Ora Resort the picturesque coral island of **Nosy Fanihy** ('bat island') is great for snorkelling but harder to reach without a motorboat, being 3.5km offshore. In Mahazandry Bay lies the crescent-shaped **Amberiotrandraka** ('tenrec island'). It's a tidal island (ie: connected to the shore at low tide) and, being on the east side of Nosy Be, is rarely visited by tourists. Just south of Nosy Vorona is **Amberiotelo**, a chain of three islets (which is what the name means) connected by an S-shaped sandbar. It's a nice vantage point from which to watch the sun set behind Nosy Komba.

MITSIO ISLANDS (NORTHEAST OF NOSY BE)

The Mitsio archipelago lies some 50km from Nosy Be, so is beyond the range of a day trip, but a number of yacht charters offer multi-day excursions here from Nosy Be. This is the Maldives of Madagascar, with world-class diving and perfect beaches.

GRANDE MITSIO The largest island is populated by local Malagasy – Antakarana and Sakalava – who survive on their denuded island through farming, cattle and goats. Overgrazing has devastated the island but some forest remains in the southern part. Huge basalt columns known as the **Organ Pipes** are a prominent feature on the northwest tip, used as an adventure playground by enterprising goats. There is a basic campsite on the southwest coast.

The island attracts yachts to its coral reefs and good anchorages; Maribe Bay provides good anchorage, protected between two hills.

NOSY TSARABANJINA The name means 'good-looking' and this is indeed a small but incredibly beautiful island. The red, grey and black volcanic rocks, rising quite high at its centre, have a mass of lush, green vegetation clinging to them, including baobabs and pachypodiums. But its real glory is the pure white beaches of coarse sand, along which laps crystal-clear ocean. Turtles and rays rest near the beaches.

15

Divers can be kept busy for a couple of days, and there are walking trails. Yachties can anchor off the southwest, at 6m over a sandy bottom.

The highlight is the luxury hotel **Constance Tsarabanjina** (m *034 02 152 29/034 20 152 29;* e *resa@tsarabanjina.com; www.tsarabanjina.com;* 🏨). This is a beautifully designed collection of 25 recently refurbished en-suite chalets constructed predominantly of natural materials. Despite the exclusivity there is a total lack of pretension as guests are encouraged to cast aside their footwear and go barefoot. Besides relaxing on the island's three beaches, other free activities at your disposal include snorkelling, waterskiing, tennis, volleyball, sailing and aquagym. Massage, fishing, diving and boat excursions are on offer – and there is a helipad for those who want to arrive in style.

NOSY ANKAREA This island is privately owned so get permission before visiting. There are some gorgeous, sun-drenched beaches and the low hills make for pleasant walking excursions in relatively undisturbed forest.

LES QUATRE FRERES ('THE FOUR BROTHERS') These are four imposing lumps of silver basalt (Nosy Beangovo, Nosy Betalinjona, Nosy Antsoha and Nosy Betanihazo) rising 51–88m from the sea. Two of them are home to hundreds of nesting seabirds, including brown boobies, frigate birds and white-tailed tropic-birds; and a pair of Madagascar fish eagles nests on one. The sides drop vertically to about 20–30m, and divers come here because three of the boulders can be circumnavigated during one vigorous dive. Yachties can anchor to the southeast of Nosy Beangovo, roughly 100m from the mouth of a cave, at a depth of about 10m. Currents reach up to one knot. The best marine life is in the lee. There are huge caves, spectacular overhangs and rockfalls in the area.

NOSY LAVA This elongated reef, 3.5km by 1.5km, rises to 160m at its peak and is covered in vegetation. It is the northernmost island in the archipelago and home to another pair of fish eagles. A good beach runs along the northern side. Not to be confused with the former prison island of the same name 230km further down the coast (page 410).

ISLANDS SOUTHWEST OF NOSY BE

The islands are listed below in the order they are encountered heading away from Nosy Be. It is possible to get as far as Nosy Iranja for a day trip (1½hrs each way) but visiting the Radamas requires a multi-day cruise.

NOSY ANKAZOBERAVINA True to its name (meaning 'island with big-leaved trees') this 14ha paradise, 26km from Nosy Be, has plenty of large trees. The forest is home to flying foxes, chameleons and a few lemurs, and there are mangroves and a beautiful palm-lined beach on the northern side. The area is a marine reserve and turtles come to the island to lay their eggs.

Ecolodge Nature Sauvage (Ankazoberavina Ecovillage) (m *032 04 802 80;* e *ulyssexplorer@gmail.com; www.ankazoberavina.it;* €€€€€–🏨; *see ad, 4th colour section*), which owns the whole island, has eight comfortable en-suite bungalows, each designed to take a family of four. Accommodation is on a full-board basis. Closed January–March.

NOSY KIVINJY (SUGARLOAF ROCK) This great dome-shaped basalt boulder with 'organ-pipe' formations on one side is also known as the **Fifth Brother**, banished by his siblings 85km northeast. Not recommended for diving or anchorage as there are strong northeast-flowing currents around the islet. It is strictly fady to climb or even touch this island but fishing nearby is invariably rewarding.

NOSY ANTSOHA AND ANGODROGA The little forested island of Nosy Antsoha covers just 3ha with a broad sandy beach on its eastern side, off which the snorkelling is reasonably good. Around 1.3km southeast of Nosy Kivinjy, the island lies just 600m offshore from the mainland. Nosy Be's zoo, Lemuria Land (page 376), has set up a lemur reserve here with six introduced species. A resident guardian can give you a guided tour (*entry 10,000Ar per person*).

On the summit is a single romantic cabin known as the 'Lov Room'; this is part of **Coco Beach Hotel**, which also has beach cabins, a tree-house room and a beachfront swimming pool at Angodroga on the shore opposite Nosy Antsoha (✆ *86 940 69;* m *034 05 041 20;* e *resa@cocobeachexperiences.com; www.cocobeachexperiences. com;* €€€€€–�־).

NOSY IRANJA Some 50km southwest of Nosy Be, this is actually a pair of small islands connected by a 1.25km sandbar (walkable at low tide). It has incredibly clear turquoise waters, beautiful white beaches and a charming old **lighthouse** designed by Gustave Eiffel of Eiffel Tower fame.

It was once a beautiful peaceful place inhabited by fisherfolk and an important breeding reserve for both hawksbill and green turtles, until a luxury hotel was built amid considerable controversy. For some years it suffered management issues and then eventually closed down.

It is possible to visit as a day trip or on a yacht charter – or stay overnight in one of the six bungalows at **Le Zahir at Iranja** (m *032 05 938 80/032 49 494 75;* e *info@ lezahir-lodge-nosybe.com; www.lezahir-lodge-nosybe.com;* ☖).

RADAMA ISLANDS The Radama archipelago, which lies 90km to the southwest of Nosy Be (and thus is only really accessible by yacht), is part of one of Madagascar's newest national parks (page 411). The islands compete with the Mitsios for the best diving sites in Madagascar and are set in a breathtaking coastline of bays backed by high mountains. Most of these high sandstone islands are steep-sided above and below the water and covered with scrub, grass and trees. Sharp eroded rock formations, however, render the remaining forest rather difficult to explore.

Nosy Kalakajoro The northernmost island of the group features dense, impenetrable forest on the south side. There are good beaches on the southern side and snorkelling is worthwhile off the southeast. Yachts should anchor 100m off the southeast side in 10–12m over good holding sand and mud, to get protection from the north-to-west winds.

Accommodation opened here a few years ago: **Tsara Lodge** (m *032 72 730 03/034 07 207 87; www.tsara-lodge.com;* ☖) has six wooden en-suite bungalows.

Nosy Berafia (or Nosy Ovy – 'Potato Island') This is the largest of the Radamas, but the environmental degradation is terrible. Nearly all the trees have been cut and goats have completed the destruction of its flora. Red soil weeps from gaping scars into the surrounding water. But if you want to visit, boats can anchor off the east side, near a protected rocky outcrop.

Nosy Antanimora With its broad sandy beaches and turquoise water Nosy Antanimora lives up to its name, which translates loosely as 'land of relaxation'.

15

Nosy Valiha This 800ha island with its own airstrip is privately owned, so you should not visit without permission. At the time of writing it was up for sale for €15 million.

NOSY SABA, NOSY IFAHO AND (THE OTHER) NOSY LAVA These islands some 40km further southwest are covered on pages 410–11.

16

The West

The west of Madagascar offers a mostly dry climate, deciduous forest (with a growing number of excellent reserves to protect it), tranquil rivers to float down and plenty of safe sandy beaches. It is effectively divided into two sections: the north, with its gateway town of Mahajanga, and the south with Morondava providing access. No roads directly link these two regions – the traveller is obliged to return to Tana by road or air, or otherwise face the uncomfortable but adventurous journey by *boutre* (cargo boat).

The west is the best region in which to see one of Madagascar's most extraordinary natural wonders: the *tsingy* limestone pinnacles that form dramatic, impenetrable forests of spikes and spires. The endemic succulents that struggle for a foothold in this waterless environment add to the otherworldly feeling. On a larger scale, elephantine baobab trees are dotted throughout this region.

The west is also home to the Sakalava people, once the largest and most powerful tribe. Their kingdom was founded early in the 17th century by Prince Andriamisara whose son succeeded him and, with the aid of firearms acquired from European traders, conquered the southwestern area between the Onilahy and Manambolo rivers – a region that became known as the Menabe. Later kings conquered first the Boina (the area from the Manambolo to north of present-day Mahajanga) and then the northwest coast as far as Antsiranana.

Eventually the kingdom broke up and in the 19th century came under the control of the Merina. The Sakalava did not take kindly to domination and sporadic guerrilla warfare continued in the Menabe area until colonial times. In 1883, the French bombarded two fortresses in the region and an attack on Mahajanga followed. This was the beginning of the end of Madagascar as an independent kingdom.

The modern Sakalava have relatively dark skins as a result of immigration from across the Mozambique Channel. African influence shows not only in the racial characteristics of the people, but also in their language and customs. There are a number of Bantu words in their dialect, and their belief in *tromba* (spirit possession) and *dady* (royal relics cult) is of similar origin.

The Sakalava do not practise second burial. Some of their funerary art rivals that of the Mahafaly; birds and naked figures are a feature of Sakalava tombs, the latter frequently in erotic positions. Concepts of sexuality and rebirth are implied here. The female figures are often disproportionately large, perhaps recognising

DISTANCES IN KILOMETRES

Antananarivo–Ankarafantsika	453km		Antananarivo–Morondava	701km
Ankarafantsika–Mahajanga	108km		Miandrivazo–Morondava	286km
Antananarivo–Mahajanga	561km		Morondava–Belo-sur-Tsiribihina	106km

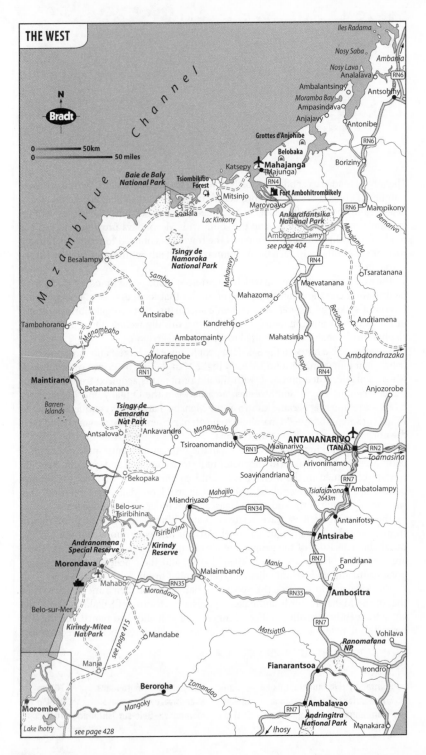

N
Bradt

0 ———— 50km
0 ———— 50 miles

Iles Radama

Nosy Saba

Ambania

RN6

Nosy Lava
Analalava

Ambalantsingy
Antsohihy

Moramba Bay
Ampasindava

Anjajavy
Antonibe

RN6

Grottes d'Anjohibe
Belobaka

Borizny

Katsepy
Mahajanga
(Majunga)

Baie de Baly
National Park
Tsiombikibo
Forest

RN4

Fort Ambohitrombikely

Mitsinjo

Marovoayo

RN6

Mampikony

Soalala

Lac Kinkony

Ankarafantsika
National Park

see page 404

Ambondromamy

Bemarivo

Mozambique Channel

Tsingy de
Namoroka
National Park

RN4

Mahajamba

Tsaratanana

Besalampy

Sambao

Mahavavy

Mahazoma

Maevatanana

Betsiboka

Andtiamena

Antsirabe

Kandreho

Mahatsinja

Ikopa

Ambatondrazaka

Tambohorano

Manambaho

Ambatomainty

RN4

Morafenobe

RN1

Maintirano

Betatanana

Anjozorobe

Barren
Islands

Tsingy de
Bemaraha
Nat Park

Manambolo

Ankavandra

ANTANANARIVO
(TANA)

RN2

Antsalova

Tsiroanomandidy

RN1

Miarinarivo

Toamasina

Analavory

Arivonimamo

Bekopaka

Soavinandriana

Belo-sur-
Tsiribihina

Tsiafajavona
2643m

RN7

Ambatolampy

Mahajilo

Miandrivazo

Andranomena
Special Reserve

Tsiribihina

Kirindy
Reserve

RN34

Antanifotsy

Antsirabe

RN7

Fandriana

Morondava

Mahabo

RN35

Malaimbandy

Mania

Belo-sur-Mer

Morondava

RN35

Ambositra

Kirindy-Mitea
Nat Park

see page 415

Mandabe

Matsiatra

RN7

Vohilava

Manja

Ranomafana
NP

Irondro

Berohoha

Zomandao

Fianarantsoa

Morombe

Lake Ihotry

see page 428

Mangoky

RN7

Ambalavao

Andringitra
National Park

Manakara

↙ *Ihosy*

the importance of women in the Sakalava culture. Sakalava royalty do not require elaborate tombs since kings are considered to continue their spiritual existence through a medium with healing powers, and in royal relics. The box on page 419 describes an encounter with the present-day royal family.

MAHAJANGA (MAJUNGA)

Mahajanga is a hot but breezy town with a large Indian population. A wide boulevard follows the sea along the western side, terminating near a lighthouse. At its elbow is the Mahajanga baobab, said to be at least 700 years old. (It has an impressive circumference of 20.7m – measured in 2011 by reader Trevor Chandler, a retired biologist – but it's not quite the largest in Madagascar; see page 430.) This area comes alive after dark: be sure to indulge in the local life by sampling the delicious zebu brochettes being barbecued along the street.

HISTORY Ideally located for trade with East Africa, Arabia and western Asia, Mahajanga has been a major commercial port since 1745, when the Boina capital was moved here from Marovoay. One ruler of the Boina was Queen Ravahiny, a very able monarch who maintained the unity of the Boina which was threatened by rebellions in both the north and the south. It was Mahajanga which provided her with her imported riches and caught the admiration of visiting foreigners. Madagascar was at that time a major supplier of slaves to Arab traders and in return received jewels and rich fabrics. Indian merchants were active then, as today, with a variety of exotic goods. Some of these traders from the east stayed on, the Indians remaining a separate community and running small businesses. More Indians arrived during colonial times.

During the 1883–85 war, Mahajanga served as the base for the military expedition to Antananarivo which consolidated the French Protectorate. Shortly thereafter the French set about enlarging Mahajanga and reclaiming swampland from the Bombetoka river delta. Much of today's extensive town is on reclaimed land.

In World War II Mahajanga was seized from the Vichy French by British forces (see boxes on pages 9 and 352–3).

GETTING THERE AND AWAY Mahajanga is 560km from Tana on a good road (RN4). Mahajanga opened a big *taxi-brousse* station in 2010; standard services take around 10 hours from Tana and cost 25,000Ar. **Cotisse Transport** (m *032 11 027 10/11;* e *cotisse.mahajanga@alpha.mg; www.cotisse-transport.com*) runs scheduled departures from Tana in comfortable vehicles, departing in both directions at 07.00 and 17.00, for 32,000Ar. **Transport Première Classe** (m *033 15 488 88/034 22 588 88/034 49 588 88/032 04 904 57;* e *malagasycar@gmail.com; www.malagasycar.com*) offers a service for 78,000Ar that includes breakfast and lunch (book at the Grand Mellis Hotel in Tana).

There are regular Air Mad **flights** between Mahajanga and Tana, and weekly flights direct to Antsiranana. Air Austral (*www.air-austral.com*) also flies here weekly from Réunion. Taxi-brousses pass close to the airport if you want to avoid getting a taxi the 6km into town.

For the truly adventurous the cargo **boats** – *boutres* – plying the west coast will take passengers but this mode of transport is not for the faint-hearted.

WHERE TO STAY Listed here is the accommodation in Mahajanga itself. For places to stay near the airport and along the beaches north of town, see *Amborovy* on page 401.

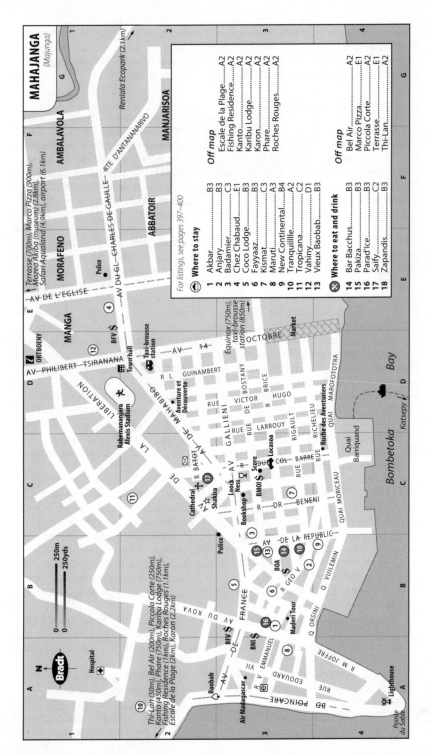

MAHAJANGA
(Majunga)

Renjala Ecopark (2.1km)

AMBALAVOLA

AMBATOVOLA

MANJARISOA

ABBATOIR

For listings, see pages 397–400

Where to stay

1 Akbar...............................B3
2 Anjary.............................B3
3 Badamier.........................C3
4 Chez Chabaud..................E1
5 Coco Lodge.....................B3
6 Fayyaaz...........................B3
7 Kismat.............................C3
8 Maruti..............................A3
9 New Continental.............A2
10 Tranquillle.......................A2
11 Tropicana........................C2
12 Vahiny.............................D1
13 Vieux Baobab..................B3

Off map

Escale de la Plage............A2
Fishing Residence............A2
Kanto................................A2
Karibu Lodge....................A2
Karon...............................A2
Phare...............................A2
Roches Rouges................A2

Where to eat and drink

14 Bar Bacchus...................B3
15 Pakiza.............................B3
16 Parad'ice........................B3
17 Saify...............................C2
18 Zapandis.........................B3

Off map

Bel Air.............................A2
Marco Pizza....................E1
Piccola Corte...................A2
Terrasse..........................E1
Thi-Lan...........................A2

AV DE L'EGLISE

MANGA

ORTBOENY

MORAFENO

Police

RTE D'ANTANANARIVO

AV DU GL-CHARLES-DE-GAULLE

Town hall

Taxi-brousse
station

AV PHILIBERT TSIRANANA

AV 14 OCTOBRE

R L GUINAMBERT

Aventure et
Découverte

RUE VICTOR HUGO

RUE DE BOSTANY

RUE GALLIENI

RUE LARROUY

R BRICE

Locosa

DU COL BARRE

AV DU COL BARRE

RUE RIGAULT

RUE RICHELIEU

QUAI MAROFOTOTRA

Market

Bay

OCTOBRE

Equinox (750m),
taxi-brousse
station (850m)

Rabemananjara
Alexis Stadium

AV DE LA LIBERATION

AV DE LA MAHABIBO

R BATOT

Cathedral

Shakita

Bookshop

Food
Ness

Score

BMOI

R DR BENENI

QUAI MORICEAU

Ruche des Aventuriers

Quai
Barriquand

Quai

Bombetoka
Bay

Katsepy

Thi-Lan (50m), Bel Air (200m), Piccola Corte (250m),
Kanto (450m), Phare (750m), Karibu Lodge (750m),
Fishing Residence (1km), Roches Rouges (1km),
Escale de la Plage (2km), Karon (2.2km)

Hospital

AV DU ROVA

AV DE FRANCE

BFV

BNI

Maderi Tour

BOA

R GEO V

AV -DE LA- REPUBLIC

Q VUILEMIN

Q ORSINI

BD POINCARE

RUE EDOUARD

R V VII

RUE EMMANUEL

R M JOFFRE

Air Madagascar

Baobab

Lighthouse

Pointe
du Sable

N

Bradt

0   250m
0   250yds

Terrasse (700m), Marco Pizza (900m),
Mozeo Akiba (museum) (2.8km),
Safari Aqualand (4.9km), airport (6.1km)

Police

Top end €€€€€

🏠 **Karibu Lodge** [398 A2] (15 rooms) Bd
Marcoz; 📞 62 247 05/62 247 10/62 247 11;
📱 033 37 247 11; 📧 karibulodge@moov.mg;
www.karibu-lodge.com or www.karibulodge.net.
Splendid & beautifully situated hotel. Spacious
rooms all with sea view, AC, minibar, sat-TV
& Wi-Fi. Restaurant, bar & small pool. Credit
cards accepted.

Upper range €€€€

🏠 **Badamier** [398 C3] (32 rooms) Av de la
République; 📞 62 240 65; 📱 032 57 435 75/033 13
122 17/034 05 240 65; 📧 hotelebadamier@moov.
mg; www.hotelmajunga-lebadamier.com. Smart
4-floor hotel; centrally located. En-suite dbl rooms
with AC, TV, Wi-Fi, safe & balcony; more expensive
suites also have minibar, lounge & sea view.

🏠 **Coco Lodge** [398 B3] (19 rooms) 49 Av
de France; 📞 62 230 23; 📱 034 07 011 11/034
07 011 34; 📧 cocolodge@moov.mg; www.
cocolodgemajunga-madagascar.com; see ad, 4th
colour section. Smart, spacious en-suite rooms
with big bed, sat-TV, AC, Wi-Fi, safe & minibar;
built around charming central courtyard with
lovely pool & excellent new restaurant. Spa &
gym opening soon. Credit cards accepted.

🏠 **Fishing Residence** [398 A2] (14 rooms
& 6 bungalows) 58 Bd Marcoz; 📞 62 220 81;
📱 032 04 682 20/032 05 160 93 (manager);
📧 franc.ky.06@hotmail.fr; www.fishingresidence.
com. Fully renovated in 2013. Family bungalows
& dbl AC rooms, all with en-suite facilities & TV.
Poolside restaurant in tranquil seafront garden.

🏠 **Roches Rouges** [398 A2] (19 rooms) 📞 62
020 01; 📱 032 05 875 80; 📧 roches-rouges@moov.
mg; www.rochesrouges.mg. Rooms with sea view,
TV, minibar, AC, safe & Wi-Fi. Swimming pool.
Good food, especially seafood.

🏠 **Tropicana** [398 C2] (16 bungalows) Rue
Lacaze, Mangarivotra; 📞 62 220 69; 📱 032 58 416
77; 📧 tropicana.mahajanga@gmail.com; www.

hotel-majunga.com. Up the hill from Don Bosco
school behind the cathedral. Pleasant en-suite
bungalows with AC & sat-TV away from the centre.

Mid-range €€€

🏠 **Maruti** [398 A3] (8 rooms) 📱 033 14 066
60/034 21 639 07. New in 2013, dbl rooms with
AC, safe, TV, Wi-Fi & en-suite bathroom.

🏠 **New Continental** [398 B4] (25 rooms)
Av de la République; 📞 62 225 70; 📱 032 69 614
06; 📧 hcontinental@moov.mg. Dbl, trpl & family
rooms with en-suite facilities, AC, TV & safe.

🏠 **Phare** [398 A2] (23 rooms) Bd Marcoz;
📞 62 235 00; 📱 032 03 383 14/033 25 206 70;
📧 hotelduphare@moov.mg. En-suite dbl & twin
rooms, some with AC & minibar.

🏠 **Tranquillle** [398 A2] (6 rooms & 3
bungalows) La Corniche; 📞 62 231 31; 📱 032 07
524 59/032 43 962 89; 📧 tranquillllle@yahoo.fr.
Yes, the name really is spelled with a quadruple-L!
Cosy, quiet place with small pool, en-suite rooms &
bungalows with shared bathrooms.
Also in this category:
🏠 **Akbar** [398 B3] 📧 hotelakbar@moov.mg
🏠 **Anjary** [398 B3] www.anjary-hotel.com
🏠 **Escale de la Plage** [398 A2] 📱 032 40
442 34
🏠 **Fayyaaz** [398 B3] 📞 62 227 40
🏠 **Karon** [398 A2] 📧 chezkaron@moov.mg
🏠 **Kismat** [398 C3] 📧 asifkismat@yahoo.fr
🏠 **Vahiny** [398 D1] 📱 032 57 612 12
🏠 **Vieux Baobab** [398 B3] 📧 hvb@moov.mg

Budget €€

🏠 **Chez Chabaud** [398 E1] (28 rooms) 📞 62
233 27; 📱 032 40 530 05. Near town hall. Some
very cheap rooms with shared facilities; also good-
value rooms with AC/TV.

🏠 **Kanto** [398 A2] (11 rooms) La Corniche;
📞 62 229 78. Overlooking the sea to the north of
town. Low-price dbl rooms with fans, some en
suite.

✗ WHERE TO EAT AND DRINK

✗ **Bar Bacchus** [398 B3] Highly praised chic
French restaurant with African décor. Wi-Fi.
✗ **Bel Air** [398 A2] La Corniche; 📱 032 02 935
49; 📧 nicksbelair@yahoo.fr; 🕓 09.00–late. French
& Malagasy dishes in ocean-view setting.
✗ **Marco Pizza** [398 E1] 53 Rte d'Amborovy;
📱 032 11 110 32/033 11 110 32. Top-quality

pizza: eat-in, take-away & delivery. Also ice cream
& cocktails.
✗ **Pakiza** [398 B3] Av de la République;
🕓 Wed–Mon, Tue closed. Pizzas & Indian food;
also ice creams, milkshakes & juices.
✗ **Piccola Corte (Petite Cour)** [398 A2] Bd
Marcoz; 📞 62 221 12; 📱 032 07 750 57/034 90 546

43; e rovaitito@gmail.com; ⏱ daily except Sun eve. Cosy atmosphere with varied menu inc Italian specialities.

✘ **Terrasse** [398 E1] Bar & restaurant with wood-oven pizza, inc take-away.

✘ **Thi-Lan** [398 A2] La Corniche; ☎ 62 229 61; e thilan@moov.mg; ⏱ Mon–Sat 10.00–14.00 & 18.00–22.00, Sun closed. Vietnamese specialities.

💻 **Parad'Ice** [398 B3] Off Bd Poincaré; ⏱ Mon–Sat 08.00–22.00, Sun closed. Splendid ice cream & good b/fast.

💻 **Saify** [398 C2] Av de Mahabibo; ☎ 62 222 33; ⏱ Mon–Sat 07.00–noon & 15.00–20.00, Sun 07.00–noon. Great for b/fast, ice cream & snacks.

💻 **Zapandis** [398 B3] ⏱ Fri–Wed, closed Thu. Café with marvellous pastries.

NIGHTLIFE

🍸 **Loock Ness** [398 C3] m 032 05 244 03; www. loockness.canalblog.com. Pub & bar with snacks inc pizza. Sometimes live music & karaoke. Wi-Fi.

☆ **Equinox** [398 E3] m 032 04 375 98/034 01 401 00; e equinox.majunga@gmail.com.

Discotheque with pool table, karaoke & big screen for sports.

☆ **Shakira** [398 C2] Italian-owned lounge bar & club; a chic venue, usually busy Thu–Sat.

MONEY, COMMUNICATIONS AND MEDICAL All the major **banks** have branches with ATMs here, including BNI, BFV, BOA and BMOI. In the centre, next to the cathedral, is the main **post office** [398 C2]. The excellent **Espace Médical** group has a clinic in Mahajanga (☎ 62 248 21; m 034 02 00 911 in emergencies/034 02 172 26 for appointments; www.espacemedical.mg).

SHOPPING There is a **Score** supermarket [398 C3] (☎ 62 248 74/75; e maj@score. mg; ⏱ Mon–Fri 08.00–13.00 & 15.00–19.00, Sat 08.00–19.00, Sun 08.00–noon) in town and a new **Shoprite** supermarket on the road to the airport.

The bookshop **Librairie de Madagascar** [398 C3] sells a few postcards and sometimes has local maps.

TOURIST INFORMATION, TOUR OPERATORS, VEHICLE HIRE AND FLIGHTS

🛈 **ORTBoeny** [398 D1] 14 Av Tsiranana; ☎ 62 931 88; m 034 08 088 80/034 40 029 89; e ortmajunga@moov.mg; www.majunga.org; ⏱ Mon–Fri 08.00–noon & 14.30–18.00, Sat 08.00–noon. The regional tourist office & local guides association; active & helpful.

✈ **Air Madagascar** [398 A3] Av Gillan; ☎ 62 224 21/61; m 032 05 222 06/034 11 222 07; e mjnssmd@airmadagascar.com; ⏱ Mon–Fri 07.30–11.30 & 14.30–17.00, Sat 08.00–10.00

✈ **Madagasikara Airways** m 032 05 970 16/034 05 970 31

Aventure et Découverte [398 D2] ☎ 62 934 75; m 034 08 521 96/032 05 521 97/033 02 069 79; e aventure.decouverte@free.fr; www.aventure-decouverte.com; ⏱ Mon–Sat 08.00–noon &

14.30–18.00. Fishing, pirogue trips & tours. Also hires quads, motorbikes & 4x4s (with/without driver).

Locasoa [398 C3] ☎ 62 931 27; m 032 40 053 70; e locasoa@yahoo.fr; ⏱ 08.00–noon & 15.00–18.30. Car & 4x4 rental.

Maderi Tour [398 B3] Rue Jules Ferry; ☎ 62 023 34; m 034 60 594 66; e contact@maderi-tour. com or maderitour@yahoo.fr; www.maderi-tour. com; ⏱ Mon–Fri 08.00–noon & 14.30–18.00, Sat 08.00–noon. Various local excursions & tours; also transfers to Tana incorporating an overnight visit to Ankarafantsika.

Piste Rouge m 032 45 902 35; e pisterouge@ gmail.com; www.pisterouge-madagascar.com. Motorbike & quad hire/excursions.

WHAT TO SEE AND DO

City tour The tourist office has installed a sequence of 18 numbered plaques at historically notable sites around Mahajanga, making an interesting self-guided walking tour that takes around 2½ hours. If you are not feeling that energetic, the tour can also be done by *pousse-pousse*. Contact the tourist office (ORTBoeny) for more details.

Mozea Akiba (Museum) [398 E1] (m *032 07 766 93/032 05 579 42;* e *heryraveloson@hotmail.com;* ☺ *Tue–Fri 08.00–noon & 15.00–17.00, Sat/Sun 15.00–17.00)* This museum is situated right near the entrance of the university at Ambondrona in Mahajanga. It has displays showing the history of the region, as well as an exhibition of palaeontology and ethnology. There are also photos and descriptions of some of Mahajanga's tourist sites such as the Cirque Rouge and Grottes d'Anjohibe. Signs are in French with some also in English.

Reniala Ecopark and SIB factory [398 G1] (☎ *62 243 31;* e *info@reniala.mg; entry 2,000Ar)* On the eastern outskirts of Mahajanga, this 25ha complex has a little of something for everyone. There are **soap and essential oil** factories (allow an hour for a tour, weekdays only); the newly opened **Musée Barday**, a museum about the history of region and the family that owns the site, and also old industrial machines; a **zoo and botanical garden** (allow 2 hours to see this); visits to a nearby **mangrove**; a family **farm**; as well as lodgings, campsite, restaurant and picnic area.

Katsepy [398 D4] Katsepy is a fishing village across the bay from Mahajanga, reached by a 45-minute ferry crossing (one or two per day). The surroundings include a vast coconut plantation and a small forest where sifakas may be seen. Visitors can find food and lodgings at the excellent **Chez Chabaud** (m *032 07 067 34)*, which featured to much acclaim in the very first edition of this guide nearly three decades ago.

Built in 1901, **Katsepy lighthouse** has recently been rehabilitated, upgraded to solar power and reopened to the public (*entry 5,000Ar)*. At 36m tall it offers splendid panoramic views of the area including Bombetoka Bay and the town of Mahajanga beyond. It is 7km north of Katsepy – about 1½ hours on foot.

Also in the area is **Antrema** (m *032 04 462 28;* e *vavindraza@live.fr)*, a reserve and biocultural project. It includes several ecosystems – from forests and lakes to dunes and mangroves – with walking trails of 1–5 hours' duration as well as a campsite with cooking facilities (book at least three days in advance via Mahajanga's tourist office). You may see up to five types of lemur and many different wetland birds. On the cultural side, there are numerous sacred Sakalava sites.

Amborovy Near to the airport, 5–7km north of town, is this area with a sandy beach known as **Petite Plage**, which is popular with locals for weekend outings. A couple of kilometres further north is another good beach, called **Grand Pavois**.

About 1km from the airport on the road into town is **Safari Aqualand** [398 E1], a growing collection of swimming pools and water slides mainly designed for children, with a restaurant, sunbeds, massage and minigolf for the adults (m *032 05 682 20;* e *fevedaniel@yahoo.fr)*.

🏠 *Where to stay and eat*

🏠 **Sunny** (22 rooms) ☎ 62 918 13; m 032 07 257 70/033 11 235 87; e sunnymajunga@gmail. com; www.sunnymada.com. Close to the airport. Rooms with AC & Wi-Fi. Swimming pool, gym, tennis, horse-riding & car rental. Credit cards accepted. €€€€–€€€€€

🏠 **Cocobeach** (8 rooms) m 034 19 445 10/034 69 771 15; e hotelcocobeach@yahoo.fr. En-suite rooms with sat-TV & AC. Large swimming pool. Restaurant with sea view. €€€€

🏠 **Terrasse** (2 bungalows) m 032 82 180 85. Rooms with kitchenettes. Great seafront bar & restaurant (*closed Mon)*; also jet-ski hire. €€€€

🏠 **Edenakely** (15 bungalows) ☎ 62 929 39; m 032 55 558 00/034 36 577 39; e edenakely@ moov.mg; www.edenakely.com. Bungalows with AC & en-suite bathrooms. Restaurant, bar & swimming pool. Visa accepted. €€€–€€€€

🏠 **Zaha Motel** (12 rooms & 22 bungalows) ☎ 62 919 28; m 034 65 262 63; e zahamotel.

majunga@gmail.com or zahamotel.mjn@sofitrans.
mg. Somewhat run-down rooms with TV, AC, Wi-Fi
& en-suite hot-water facilities. €€€–€€€€

🏠 **Apache** (3 bungalows) m 032 04 486
11/034 16 820 05; e rapache@moov.mg.
Large bungalows for 5–9 people; en suite with
kitchenettes. Friendly dog after whom the hotel is
named. €€€

🏠 **Tamarinier** (2 rooms & 3 bungalows)
m 033 75 967 05/034 45 455 06;
e letamarinier@moov.mg. Malagasy family-run
hotel opened in 2014 right at the beach; en-suite
rooms. €€€

🏠 **Campiland Grand Pavois** (6 bungalows)
m 032 11 301 63; e info@campiland.com; www.
campiland.com. This good-value 3ha camping
complex has a restaurant & places for 80 tents.
Their canvas bungalows each house 4 people.
Activities inc trampolining, swimming, ping-pong
& other games. €€

🏠 **Convent Sacré Cœur** Reader Sunniva
Gylver recommends the very simple & affordable
rooms here. €

Also in this area:

🏠 **Cayana** e cayana.reservation@yahoo.fr
🏠 **O'Relax** e aureliebe79@yahoo.fr
🏠 **Palmeraie** e lapalmeraie401@yahoo.fr

Cirque Rouge (*Entry 5,000Ar*) Not far from Grand Pavois, about 11km (30mins)
north of Mahajanga, this is a canyon ending in an amphitheatre of red-, beige-
and lilac-coloured rock eroded into strange peaks and spires. It is a beautiful and
dramatic spot that – with its stream of fresh water running to the nearby beach –
makes an idyllic camping place. For a day visit, give yourself at least an hour to look
around. Late afternoon is best, when the low sun sets the reds and mauves alight.

Fort Ambohitrombikely This impressive fort, 20km southeast of Mahajanga,
was built on the highest point in the region in 1824 by King Radama I. It is worth a
visit for the views and sense of history.

Antsanitia (📞 62 023 34/911 00; m 032 03 911 11; e contact@antsanitia.com; www.
antsanitia.com; €€€€€) This ecologically responsible beachfront hotel complex,
about an hour's drive (20km) up the coast from Mahajanga, is much praised by
readers. The hotel, restaurant and location are all excellent. There are broad beaches
of white sand and, being further from the Betsiboka's silty delta than Amborovy,
the waters are clearer. There are 12 rooms, nine bungalows, a swimming pool, sport
fishing centre, snorkelling and kayaking gear, and a 16m trimaran for multi-day
cruises up the west coast (for groups of 4–7). The hotel arranges transfers from
Mahajanga, but otherwise you will need a 4x4 as the road is bad.

    La Dune offers budget accommodation nearby (contact details as for Tranquilllle
on page 399).

Belobaka caves Although classed as a tourist site since the 1940s, these six caves
are little known. The first is a sacred place where people come to make wishes, but
the other five are more spectacular for stalactites and stalagmites. It is said a fence
and gate were once erected to manage the tourism, but the resident spirits objected
to this arrangement and sent lightning which struck and destroyed the barrier.

    Local tour operators can arrange a visit, or you can get here in 20 minutes or
so by car: take RN4 12km out of town then turn left for 2km. Caretaker Tahiana
should be on hand to show you the path.

Anjohibe caves Anjohibe means 'big cave' so this name is common in the region.
The famous **Grottes d'Anjohibe** are about 90km (3–4hrs) northeast of Mahajanga and
accessible only by 4x4, and only in the dry season (Apr–Oct). There are two places
to visit: the caves themselves and **Andranojoby Lake**, a natural swimming pool above

the 20m-high **Mahafanina waterfalls**. The caves are full of stalactites, stalagmites and bats, and have several kilometres of passages. Dan Carlsson excavated them in 1996: 'It seems as though the caves have been used for normal living but also as a place of sacrifice. We found pottery with ash, charcoal and animal bones; also several hippopotamus bones believed to be some million years old.'

ANKARAFANTSIKA NATIONAL PARK

(℡ 62 226 56/780 00; m 033 02 131 86; e akf@parcs-madagascar.com, mjg.parks@ gmail.com) This is a super national park: it's easy to get to, thrilling to visit with abundant wildlife and clear, level or stepped paths which make hiking a pleasure. Ankarafantsika straddles RN4, 108km from Mahajanga. The most visited part of the reserve is on the southwestern side of the road, with Lake Ravelobe to the north – but the park covers over 130,000ha stretching all the way up to Mahajamba River. The name Ankarafantsika comes from the word *garafantsy*, which means either 'hill of thorns' or 'nail in the skull'.

GETTING THERE AND AWAY It takes 3 hours by road from Mahajanga, and if you are in a private vehicle it is worth stopping at Lake Amboromalandy, a reservoir which is a great place to see waterfowl. Coming from Tana, it takes 7–8 hours by taxi-brousse. When leaving the park, flagging down a vehicle heading north is usually easy enough but those going to Tana are normally full so, to avoid having to return first to Mahajanga, your best bet may be to make advance arrangements with a Mahajanga–Tana bus operator to pick you up at a specified time.

WHERE TO STAY AND EAT At the entrance, in the park office compound, is a campsite and restaurant, both of which were transferred to private management in 2012 to improve the quality of service. The restaurant **Pygargue** is excellent (m 032 05 560 59; e resaankarafantsika@gmail.com; ⊕ daily 06.00–22.00). The campsite comprises 14 pitches (some sheltered), a toilet and shower block, and kitchen facilities. Some 4km southeast is a cheaper, community-run campsite where you will be well looked after by locals.

The national park has retained responsibility for operating its seven en-suite bungalows (contact details are above). Alternative lodgings are located at Andranofasika, 5km southeast of the park office, at **Blue Vanga Lodge** with six comfortable en-suite bungalows and a restaurant (m 032 43 030 20/034 08 522 22; e bluevangalodge@gmail.com, booking@bluevanga-lodge.com; www.bluevanga-lodge.com; €€€€).

VISITING THE PARK This is typical dry, deciduous forest with sparse understorey and lots of lianas. In the dry winter season many of the trees have shed their leaves, but in the wet months the forest is a sea of bright greens. Conspicuous is the tree with menacing spines, *Hura crepitans*, an introduced species from Central America. There are 130 bird species (with highlights such as the Van Dam's vanga, Madagascar fish eagle and white-breasted mesite), eight easily seen lemurs and reptiles galore.

Wildlife viewing in Ankarafantsika starts as soon as you arrive: Coquerel's sifakas are frequently seen around the car park. They are extremely handsome animals with silky white fur and chestnut-brown arms and thighs. On your walks you may also see mongoose lemurs, western woolly lemurs and sportive lemurs; and this is the only place where you might see the golden-brown mouse lemur, *Microcebus*

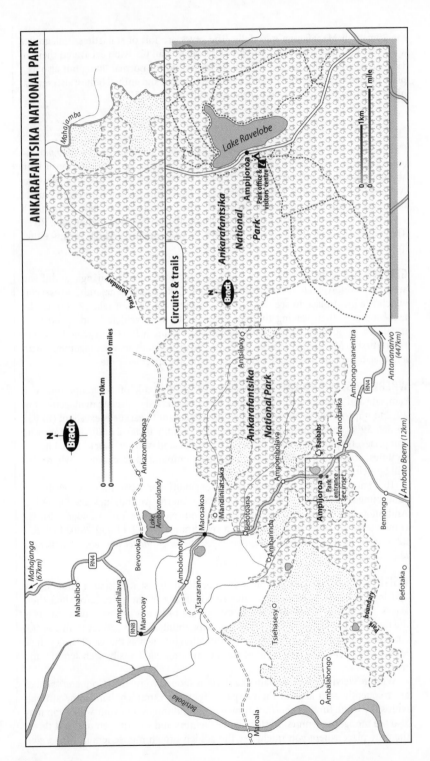

ANKARAFANTSIKA NATIONAL PARK

Circuits & trails

Lake Ravelobe

Ampijoroa

Park office &
visitors' centre

Ankarafantsika
National
Park

1km

1 mile

Mahajamba

Park boundary

Ankarafantsika
National Park

Antsiloky

Ankazomborona

Lake
Ambondromalandy

Mandinilatsaka

Marosakoa

Belotoana

Ambohimananenitra

RN4

Antananarivo
(447km)

Ampombolava

Andranofasika

Ambato Boeny (12km)

Bemongo

Baobabs

Ampijoroa

Park
entrance
see inset

Ambarinda

Bevovoka

Ambolomoty

Tsararano

RN8

Marovoay

Amparihilava

Mahabibo

Mahajanga
(67km)

Tsiehasesy

Ambalabongo

Maroala

Befotaka

Park boundary

Betsiboka

10km

10 miles

404

ravelobensis. If you're keen to see crocodiles they may be sighted year round, but the best months are July to October.

There is a very good trail system with plenty to occupy you for at least a couple of days. The shortest and easiest is **Circuit Coquereli** (1½hrs), on which you may see sifakas and brown lemurs. More botany-focused is **Circuit Retendrika** (2–3hrs), which is also good for birding. A visit to the park's famous **pachypodiums** will take about 2 hours. A similar length of time is required to go and see the tall *Adansonia madagascariensis* **baobabs**, but if you're pressed for time you can drive part of the way. On **Circuit Source de Vie** (3–4hrs) you will gain an insight into local culture and everyday rural life. **Circuit Ankarokaroka** (3hrs) offers a hike through forest and savannah to the **canyon**, an amazing multicoloured erosion feature. There's plenty of wildlife to see *en route*, or you can go to the canyon by 4x4. **Boat trips** (1–2hrs) are the best way to see **Lake Ravelobe** – particularly rewarding for birders and a good chance of sighting crocs.

It is also worth spending some time in the recently refurbished **interpretation centre** at the park office, where you can learn about local *fady*, traditional ceremonies and how the Malagasy use the forest and lake.

Permits and guides Permits are available at the park office (see page 73 for prices). Guides, most of whom speak English, can be picked up at the same place. Boat tours of Lake Ravelobe cost 15,000Ar per person (minimum two).

ANGONOKA PROJECT Ankarafantsika is also home to one of Madagascar's most successful captive-breeding programmes (see box, pages 68–9). After many years of research, ploughshares – the world's rarest tortoises – are breeding readily and being reintroduced to their original habitat. Almost as rare, the attractive little flat-tailed tortoise (*kapidolo*) is also being bred here, as is the Madagascar big-headed (side-necked) turtle.

The site is fortified as a result of 73 individuals being stolen in a raid by an animal-trafficking gang in 1996 (no surprise, perhaps, given these tortoises are thought to change hands for up to US$50,000 each on the black market) so it is possible for tourists to glimpse them only through a chain-link fence. Nowadays unique tracking numbers are engraved into their shells in a bid to reduce their value to illicit collectors.

SOUTHWEST OF MAHAJANGA

From Katsepy (page 401) a road, of sorts, provides access to the tsingy and wetlands which are of great interest to anyone who loves Madagascar's diversity of landscape, plants and wildlife. Access is exceptionally difficult, however, so even adventurous travellers may prefer an organised tour.

NOSY BOENY (NOSY ANTSOHERIBORY) This is a small island (about 60ha, of which a third is mangrove) in Boina Bay, with some fascinating Antalaotra ruins dating from the 16th century. The ruins include several cemeteries, houses and mosques. The island is sacred to the local people so camping is prohibited – but day visits are allowed. To reach the island, start from Katsepy and continue by road to the village of Boeny-Ampasy on the west side of the bay, where there are bungalows. A 1½-hour boat journey brings you to Nosy Boeny.

MAHAVAVY-KINKONY WETLAND COMPLEX With backing from the NGO BirdLife International (*www.birdlife.org*) and Asity (*www.asity-madagascar.org*) this wetland area received protected status in 2007. The two dozen interconnected lakes, river, delta, bays, marshland, mangroves, forest, savannah and caves included in the 268,236ha reserve form a haven for birders and other wildlife enthusiasts.

The wide variety of ecosystems here leads to extraordinary biodiversity, with plenty of fauna: nine species of lemur, including crowned and Decken's sifakas and the mongoose lemur, a similar number of bats, a host of reptiles and, of course, fish. But it is the birds that cause the most excitement: 143 species. And this is the only site where *all* of the Malagasy western waterfowl species may be seen. July to September is the best period for seeing breeding birds.

In the **Tsiombikibo Classified Forest**, near Mitsinjo, are several small beautiful ponds which are the refuge of white-backed ducks and African pygmy geese. Mitsinjo is the capital of the district but the gateway town is Namakia. It is a tough place to access independently. The port of Namakia may be reached in 5–6 hours by motorboat from Mahajanga but the sea is usually quite rough. Alternatively, from Katsepy it is 3–4 hours' drive, but the road beyond Mitsinjo is in poor condition and blocked during the rainy season. The towns of Mitsinjo and Namakia have very basic accommodation and camping is possible too.

SOALALA Only a handful of adventurous travellers come to Soalala, but this fascinating port is gaining importance as the gateway town to Tsingy de Namoroka and Baie de Baly national parks. John and Valerie Middleton report that 'there are several very large African baobabs and impressive pachypodiums. It was previously a French fort and at least two ancient cannons can be seen on the seafront. There are also many good eating places. Across the bay is a massive French shrimp farm.'

There is budget **accommodation** in the town and one hotel owner, Maurice Bonafous, can organise all-in tours locally, including a 4x4 with air conditioning (m *033 12 179 55*; e *bonafous@moov.mg*).

Getting there and away Taxi-brousses from Katsepy go to Soalala a few times week (12hrs/30,000Ar). By **4x4** it takes 8 hours from Mahajanga (including the 90-minute ferry crossing of Bombetoka Bay) but the road is only passable from May to November.

Alternatively, *boutres* (**cargo boats**) from Mahajanga frequently call at Soalala. It should cost around 10,000Ar for a passenger but it is not a trip for softies. Other types of boats sometimes also make the trip, taking 6–12 hours. It is fady to take peanuts on this journey or to bring pork to the area.

Soalala also has an airstrip for light **aircraft**.

BAIE DE BALY NATIONAL PARK (m *034 49 401 33;* e *bb@parcs-madagascar.com*) This 57,000ha park is across the bay from Soalala, occupying the better part of the northwest peninsula and extending east across the bay to Cap Sada. It protects a variety of terrestrial and aquatic ecosystems: mangrove forests, coastal dunes, rivers, permanent lakes and dense dry semi-deciduous forests. The idyllic coastal villages surrounding the park offer visitors a glimpse into the Sakalava way of life. **Bemosary**, **Maroalika** and **Batainomby** feature the most attractive white-sand beaches on the peninsula. Camping is permitted, but there are no facilities.

The two must-see inhabitants of the park are the locally endemic ploughshare tortoise and the very rare Madagascar fish eagle. Baie de Baly also hosts a large community of migratory birds including the greater flamingo. Dolphins have been known to trail the outgoing boat traffic.

While there is a park office in Soalala, you are best advised to visit the regional National Parks office in Mahajanga first to make arrangements.

TSINGY DE NAMOROKA NATIONAL PARK Although protected since 1966, Tsingy de Namoroka only gained national park status in 2002. It is 164km southwest of Mahajanga and 50km south of Soalala. The park offers three distinct circuits (each taking 3 hours or more) showcasing the dense sub-humid forests of the west, crocodile caves, canyons and savannah – habitats for an impressive array of wildlife. Among them are 81 species of birds, including the endangered Madagascar teal and the crested ibis. The 30 species of reptile include a black-and-yellow striped nocturnal snake endemic to Namoroka and the locally endemic side-necked (big-headed) turtle. Lemurs include Decken's sifaka, red-fronted brown lemurs and western grey bamboo lemurs, as well as nocturnal species.

Many of the cave networks in Namoroka are unexplored and unmapped and should be entered only with a guide. Access arrangements are the same as for Baie de Baly (see above).

FLY-IN BEACH RESORTS NORTHEAST OF MAHAJANGA

If you look on a map of Madagascar, you'll see a glorious expanse of nothingness along the indented coastline between Mahajanga and Nosy Be. This is where a few entrepreneurs have established some stunning, isolated fly-in resorts. Note that they generally close for January and February.

LODGE DES TERRES BLANCHES (m *034 55 070 90;* e *contact@lodgetb.com; www. lodgeterresblanches.com;*) About 105km from Mahajanga, this ecolodge really does qualify for the cliché 'best kept secret' (at least from English-speaking tourists) since it sees far fewer visitors than the other fly-in resorts and no tour groups. Access is by light aircraft, boat or possibly by 4x4 (Apr–Nov only).

Anyone who has spent time in Madagascar will realise that the Malagasy are not the most monogamous of peoples. The same is true for the island's parrots. The greater vasa parrots of Madagascar are those big black squawking things you see flying around the forest canopy. They are not particularly pretty as parrots go, having drab brownish-black plumage, long necks and even bald heads for some of each year. But vasa parrots have one of the most exhilarating sex lives of any animal on Earth. It's the females that are dominant over the males (they're 25% bigger) and they pursue the little chaps ardently all through September and October. It's the girls that do the chasing. And they seem to know what they're doing as most females end up with four to eight mates.

You can imagine what a headache this is for the males, having to compete to fertilise the eggs of the female with all your best buddies. The male parrots have risen to the challenge, however, with some utterly unbelievable evolutionary adaptations. For a start they have a penis. Birds in general don't have penises; both sexes just have cloacal openings which are pressed together to transfer the sperm. Not so for vasa parrots: the males have evolved a penis somewhat bigger than a golf ball which they erect out of their cloaca as and when they need it. Courtship before sex takes an appropriately long time – several weeks in fact – and on the big day the female might consort with a half-dozen males before settling down with one at midday. And of course this is not ordinary lovemaking.

Sex in most bird species doesn't look that fun to be honest – it's all over pretty quickly with a kiss of the cloacas lasting a couple of seconds, and both partners then wander off in different directions pretending they don't know each other. But in vasa parrots sex lasts a full 2 hours with the male and female locked together in passionate coitus. Tied together for 2 hours you can see them crooning over each other, preening their partner's plumage, squawking when things get a bit rough. So much so that it frequently attracts onlookers: a whole crowd of parrots

There is simple but comfortable accommodation in eight solar-powered double bungalows next to a gorgeous white beach fringed with forest. Compared with the luxury lodges this is a simple, do-it-yourself resort. Guests eat together in the lodge, and there is a bar with a fridge for guests to help themselves.

If you want to go on a hike or to be dropped off in a cove somewhere for the day, picnics can be arranged. This is a popular resort for sport fishermen, and the two boats are largely used for fishing trips. However, you can arrange to be taken to some beautiful coves along the coast, or to baobab-arrayed islands, or to an area of tsingy. Other activities include snorkelling, kayaking and whale-watching in season.

ANJAJAVY (☏ *23 327 59;* m *034 44 447 47;* e *bookings@anjajavy.com or bookings@ anjajavylhotel.mg; www.anjajavy.com;* ☕) Located 128km up the coast from Mahajanga, this is not just a luxury seaside hotel: in addition to its 24 villas it protects 450ha of dry deciduous forest. In some places this grows right on the tsingy limestone.

Wildlife viewing here is effortless, including Coquerel's sifakas and other lemurs. There are flocks of bright green grey-headed lovebirds, sickle-billed vangas, crested ibises, crested couas, Madagascar fish eagles and vasa parrots. You may also see beautiful butterflies, plentiful chameleons, hognose snakes and ground boas.

can turn up to watch. Sometimes things get a bit out of hand and some of her other boyfriends get a bit frisky and try jumping on top of the copulating pair, sometimes managing to disturb them and have a go themselves. However, it's all down to the female's choice as she has the beak and claws to control her diminutive boyfriends.

After such persistent promiscuity, when it comes to feed the chicks you can imagine the confusion. The males have normally found several girlfriends for themselves as well, and these avian harems often mean it's not clear which chicks belong to which dad. It's the males that do all the work bringing in the food and you can see the lads vexing over which of their girlfriends to feed next. Once again the females don't just sit back and see what happens; they sing long, complex songs to get attention. Each female has her own unique song, so November in the forests of Madagascar is rather like a huge singing contest where females with chicks compete to be the best singer. And it works; females singing longer or more complex songs attract more males and get more food. The males benefit from feeding the best-singing girlfriends because these are also the strongest birds with the most chicks in the nest.

Greater vasa parrots have the most complex sex life of any parrot so far studied. Scientists think most others are monogamous – real bastions of chastity in the avian world. So vasas have broken all the rules and are pillars of promiscuity instead. That's evolution in isolation for you. Like so much of Madagascar's wildlife, if you leave some normal, decent-living animals by themselves in the middle of the Indian Ocean for a few dozen million years they are bound to come up with something bizarre.

Jonathan Ekstrom did his PhD research on the greater vasa parrot. He now runs The Biodiversity Consultancy in the UK (www.thebiodiversityconsultancy.com).

There's a couple of caves too, spectacular enough with stalactites and stalagmites (and bats), and one with the skulls of an extinct lemur species embedded in the rocks. Perhaps most startlingly for botanists, Anjajavy and the nearby Moramba Bay hold an undescribed species of cycad tree. Then there are the coral reefs, tsingy, pristine beaches, extensive mangroves, lovely swimming pool and 'oasis' garden, not to mention total comfort, brilliant service and superb food. And even Wi-Fi for those unable to sever their electronic umbilical cord to the outside world. A range of activities is on offer, including guided forest walks, sailing, windsurfing, snorkelling, mountain biking and village visits. For an additional fee you can also indulge in deep-sea fishing, waterskiing and massages.

Three nights is the minimum stay; five allows you to appreciate all Anjajavy has to offer. To fit as much into a day as possible, the hotel operates in its own time zone bubble – an hour ahead of the rest of Madagascar!

LA MAISON DE MAROVASA-BE (m *032 07 418 14;* e *reservations@marovasabe.com; www.marovasabe.com;* 🐾) Situated 136km northeast of Mahajanga in Moramba Bay, this lodge is accessible by light aircraft from Mahajanga (45mins) or Tana (2hrs). There are three suites and six luxury rooms, all with en-suite bathrooms and balconies.

The location is, perhaps, not as attractive as that of the other two lodges, and its forest has suffered from slash-and-burn agriculture (*tavy*). However, the hotel

16

itself is delightfully thought-out, offers true luxury with a beautiful swimming pool and other amenities, and is well located for interesting boat trips. The owners are also involved with Ecole du Monde, a local NGO working to benefit local communities. The work includes reforestation projects and guests can contribute by planting a tree.

NORTHEAST OF MAHAJANGA BY ROAD

Ambondromamy is the start of RN6 (at its junction with RN4), from where it is 84km (1½–2hrs) north to Mampikony, a major centre for onion production. The best hotel is the very basic **Cocotiers**. Then it's 82km (2½–3hrs) to **Boriziny** (Port Bergé), where onions give way to tobacco and cotton, and the best place to stay is **Le Monde**. Antsohihy lies another 133km (2–3hrs) beyond.

ANTSOHIHY This uninspiring transit town makes a central base for exploration, being at the crossroads of four important destinations: southwest to Tana, north to **Ambanja** (217km/4 hours on a tarred but decaying road), northeast to **Bealanana** (difficult, and virtually impassable in the rainy season) and southeast to **Befandriana** and **Mandritsara**. It's also possible to travel west by sea or (adventurously) by land. Transport company **Besady+** (m 032 05 072 00/03/05) runs taxi-brousse connections to Tana for 50,000Ar each way.

The best place to stay in Antsohihy is **Sofia Belle Vue** (m 032 02 503 77/032 40 503 77; e sofia@bellevue.mg; €€€–€€€€) which has ten spacious rooms and three bungalows, as well as a swimming pool. More affordable but grittier places to stay include **Paradisier** (m 032 84 576 38; €€€), **Anaïs** (m 032 04 857 54/033 19 526 83; €€–€€€) and **Biaina** (📞 67 012 03; m 032 44 176 56; €€).

ANALALAVA AND NARINDA BAY Antsohihy is situated near a fjord-like arm of the sea which becomes River Loza, along which taxi boats called *teftefs* operate. There is a regular boat service to **Analalava**, an isolated village at the mouth of this inlet, accessible in the dry season by taxi-brousse (at least 4hrs) but otherwise only by boat (5hrs) or light aircraft; the best lodgings are at **Malibu** and **Varatraza**. Based in Analalava, Jean Pierre has a good boat with motor and sail and he can also supply camping gear (m 032 43 573 75).

Small islands Just offshore from Analalava are some tiny islets; the closest (7km away) are **Nosy Lango** and **Nosy Ifaho**, each no more than 20ha and home to birds, bats, boas and goats. Both are forested and the latter is sacred. Some fishermen also inhabit the island but, as it is fady to move fire or light (including torches) after dark, few people stay overnight.

Beyond these is the even smaller islet (9ha) of **Nosy Soy**, around 15km out from Analalava. Some 4km to the north and smallest of all is the 1ha **Nosy Toloho**.

Nosy Lava Situated 2km north of Nosy Toloho and around 10km offshore is the far larger (3,100ha) Nosy Lava, which means 'long island' – a slightly odd name for an island 6km by 8km.

Until 2004 it was a maximum-security prison, opened in 1911 by the French, housing up to 700 of the country's most vicious murderers and other criminals. Jolijn Geels reports that some of the former prisoners have chosen to stay and now act as guardians to the abandoned and decaying prison buildings of which they will give a guided tour on request.

Note that this place is not to be confused with the Nosy Lava in the Mitsio archipelago (page 392).

Nosy Saba This is a paradise island of coral, chameleons, coconut palms, curving bays of yellow sand and small but dense forest with clouds of fruit bats. Covering 135ha, it sits 6.5km offshore around 32km north of Analalava. It is now home to a luxury lodge, complete with private airstrip and 9-hole golf course. **Nosy Saba Island Resort** offers 27 villas right on a glorious soft-sand beach (\ *22 434 00;* m *032 03 333 02;* e *contact@nosysaba.mg; www.nosysaba.com;* 🛥; *see ad, 4th colour section).*

SAHAMALAZA-ILES RADAMA NATIONAL PARK (m *034 49 401 39/032 02 972 66/032 24 047 45/032 47 891 39/033 62 019 97;* e *sml.parks@gmail.com)*
Inaugurated in 2007, this is the country's newest national park, contained within one of Madagascar's three UNESCO Biosphere Reserves. It includes both terrestrial habitats in the Sahamalaza region north of Antsohihy and marine parcels among the Radama archipelago; see the map on page 344. (Note that the Radama Islands themselves are covered at the end of *Chapter 15* because they are generally accessed by yacht from Nosy Be.)

A great diversity of habitats and ecosystems are included in this 153,000ha biosphere reserve (of which 26,000ha is protected by national park status). There is 11,000ha of low, dry littoral forest, home to the critically endangered blue-eyed black lemur (the only blue-eyed primate besides humans) and locally endemic Sahamalaza sportive lemur. The marine ecosystem includes reefs (with at least 216 species of coral identified and 251 fish), seagrass beds, mudflats and 10,000ha of mangroves supporting all eight species of mangrove tree known in Madagascar. This habitat is ecologically important for the conservation of five threatened bird species including the Madagascar fish eagle.

The park has tremendous potential and, although it is still in the nascent stages of development for tourist infrastructure, travellers can already experience several areas. Visits may be organised from Antsohihy, Analalava or the **park office** in Maromandia (121km north of Antsohihy on RN6). You can organise mangrove boat trips, snorkelling, hiking, birdwatching and visits to sites of cultural importance including royal tombs. As well as helping to organise boats and guides, the National Parks office also hires out camping equipment.

Those wishing to see the blue-eyed black lemurs should arrange a visit to **Ankarafa Forest**. This is 47km (4hrs) by 4x4 from Andranosamonta (33km south of Maromandia) on a track that is only passable from May to November. Alternatively, it can be accessed from the sea: take a boat to Marovato (opposite Nosy Saba) then walk 2½ hours inland. The forest has three circuits of varying difficulty (1½–4hrs), costing 15,000–25,000Ar for guiding per group of up to five people. A campsite was established in 2012 with sheltered pitches and toilet and shower facilities.

THE ROAD TO MAROMOKOTRO The route northeast from Antsohihy leads to the highest mountain in Madagascar, Mount Maromokotro. A rather degraded 129km road with picturesque views runs to **Bealanana**. This town is quite high (about 1,100m) and the climate with ample rainfall allows the cultivation of potatoes and a great variety of fruit. **Faniry** *hotely* (**€€**) has simple rooms.

Heading further northeast you reach **Ambatoria** in a couple of hours. This small lively town has many shops, simple lodgings at **Vallée Rose** (**€**) and is the last stop for the taxi-brousse (and the last place with fuel).

Continuing beyond, the road gets even worse and you'll need a guide. The next 25km to **Mangindrano** could take 3 hours as there are several small rivers to ford. It has no hotels and is 'like a ghost town without the tumbleweed', reports Rory Graham. It's possible to visit the **Tsaratanana Massif** from here. Ask for Lefalle, an experienced guide who can organise porters. One of the great excursions in the area is to climb **Maromokotro** (2,876m), but it takes at least a week to reach the peak (see box, page 367).

MANDRITSARA The road southeast from Antsohihy is in fairly good condition. Taxi-brousses leave every morning, passing through **Befandriana Nord** where there is a basic hotel and continuing through beautiful mountain scenery to Mandritsara, the cultural centre of the Tsimihety people. The journey should take about 5 hours.

Mandritsara means 'peaceful' (literally 'lies down well'), and was reportedly bestowed on the town by King Radama I during his campaigns. There are several hotels here including **Hôtel Pattes**, a nice little place with excellent food.

Mandritsara also, surprisingly, has one of the best hospitals in Madagascar. They have a regular turnover of medical students on their electives from all over the world; for details contact the Friends of Mandritsara (*www.mandritsara.org.uk*).

MAINTIRANO TO MORONDAVA

MAINTIRANO This small western port is attractive for people who want to get well off the beaten track. The road from Tana (RN1) is poor and deteriorating; a taxi-brousse is likely to take at least 24 hours to travel the 630km. The town is large enough to have a bank (BOA) but is no longer served by Air Mad. Weekly flights from Tana are operated privately (**m** *034 70 013 50*). Boats leave for Mahajanga every new and full moon.

A reader points out that although it appears to be a seaside town on the map, 'it's as though the town has turned its back on the sea: virtually nothing overlooks the ocean'. On the edge of town opposite the shrimp factory is **Chalet du Rose** (✎ *65 022 52*) which has mid-range suites and bungalows with air conditioning. **Voanio** is a good budget alternative.

A reasonable road runs from Maintirano to **Antsalova**, 119km south. This town is the northern entry point for Tsingy de Bemaraha National Park. In theory there's a route through the park to the main gateway at Bekopaka.

BARREN ISLANDS This scattering of a dozen or so inhospitable coral islands and islets, none larger than about 50ha, lies 12–33km off the length of coastline stretching for about 60km southward from Maintirano. There have been recent moves to open them up to ecotourism although infrastructure for this is still in the early stages of development. As we go to press, the archipelago has been given the go-ahead to become a Marine Protected Area. It is the destination for an incredible annual migration of nomadic Vezo fishermen – see the box on page 414.

If you are interested in a visit, get in touch with Blue Ventures (m *034 76 932 03*; e *olivier@blueventures.org*).

TAR SANDS DEVELOPMENT
Kara Moses, environmental journalist

Madagascar has the world's fourth-largest deposits of tar sands – bitumen mixed with clay and sand, which can be extracted through processes that are highly energy- and water-intensive, to produce oil. Currently in operation on a huge scale in Canada, it is a relatively new and highly controversial industry; extraction and burning produces four times more greenhouse gas emissions than conventional oil and causes extensive environmental damage. It has been dubbed 'the most destructive project on earth'.

Like a dark cloud, the threat of tar sands development looms on Madagascar's horizon. If it goes ahead, it would be the largest operation outside Canada. French company Total and US-based Madagascar Oil hold licences for the huge bitumen deposits in the Melaky region, but production is not yet financially viable, and the unstable political situation has slowed progress. However, as oil prices increase, markets and technologies develop, and the political crisis passes, production will become more viable.

The local environment and communities would certainly suffer. The Bemolanga deposits sit beneath the grazing land of people who rely exclusively on cattle herding for their livelihood, and the river they rely upon for all their water needs would risk depletion and contamination.

To transport the oil to the coast for export, a pipeline would have to be built through or near Beanka Forest, where a bird was discovered in 2009 that was completely new to science, along with other previously undescribed species.

The Tsimororo extraction site, where small-scale production of heavy oil (slightly deeper deposits of bitumen) began in 2013, lies adjacent to the Tsingy de Bemaraha and Ambohijanahary protected areas, risking contamination of their water systems.

Despite the environmental and social cost of this project, Madagascar's economy stands to benefit little; after 30 years of production, the Malagasy government would see only 4% of profits. It is very difficult to see any silver lining in this dark cloud.

The annual migration of Vezo fishermen from villages on Madagascar's southwest coast is, by many accounts, among the least understood human migrations of our time. It is a mass movement of fishermen and their families, who travel many hundreds of kilometres in search of fertile fishing grounds.

For many, the ultimate goal is the remote, offshore Barren Island archipelago. There are no trees, no respite from the burning tropical sun, no vegetation at all – and no fresh water. It is easy to see how these fragmented sea-bound deserts, strung out in the vastness of the Mozambique Channel, got their name.

Yet, for as many as nine months of the year, small nomadic communities make this inhospitable land their home. Migrant families, who have sailed as far as 1,000km in dugout pirogues to reach the islands, sleep under the sails of their boats. Their most important possessions are their fishing gear.

Following the seasonal movements of favoured fish species – those that fetch the highest price in local markets – some families will spend as much as two months at sea, making the long journey from their villages in the south.

The legacy of this complex human journey can be traced in the composition of the villages along the west coast. In all of these places, migrants – old and new – have settled. There are many migrations across the entire west and southwest coast of Madagascar. But the journeys from villages north of Toliara to the Barren Islands are among the longest and most dangerous.

The Vezo pirogues are battered by the force of oceanic southwesterly winds that charge up the Mozambique Channel. For vast stretches of the coastline there are very few places to come ashore to shelter from the high winds and huge swells. Scattered safe landing places are hard to find, and days and nights can be spent at sea before it is possible to reach land. Every year there are casualties and deaths; fishermen that set sail in the morning and don't return, and divers who don't make it back to the surface alive. But while the dangers are great, the changing dynamics of this traditional migration make the risk worth taking for many Vezo.

What was once a largely subsistence-based movement to new fishing grounds has become an increasingly commercialised temporary resettlement of fishermen. The demand from Asian markets for delicacies such as shark fin and sea cucumbers is pushing many of Madagascar's seafaring Vezo to the limits.

A devastating combination of climate change, and overfishing caused by coastal population growth and industrial fishing, mean that Madagascar's fragile marine resources are in decline. The contest for what remains is tough. The Vezo now compete with mechanised trawlers – some fishing illegally in Malagasy waters.

What was once a way of relieving pressure on historic fishing grounds has become an intense and dangerous pursuit of the shark fin and sea cucumbers that are now the ocean's gold. As these resources dwindle, success for many of the younger migrants is short-lived. The sea has always provided for the Vezo, and money earned there is spent quickly on land, in the expectation that it can be earned again tomorrow. Yet many migrants now return home empty-handed – with only memories of an ocean in which sea life was once abundant and sharks so numerous that it was too dangerous to enter the water. For the Vezo, life is changing, and the very resources they depend upon for their existence are growing scarce.

TSINGY DE BEMARAHA NATIONAL PARK (↖ 22 013 96; m 034 49 401 30; e bmr@parcs-madagascar.com)

Protecting its largest area of tsingy, this 158,000ha national park is one of the wonders of Madagascar and has rightly been recognised as a UNESCO World Heritage Site. The scenery rivals anything in the country and it's a treasure trove for botanists.

The awe-inspiring grey forest of rock pinnacles is matched by the care with which walkways have been constructed to allow visitors to see this place in safety. Steps, boardwalks, ladders, cables and suspension bridges have been installed with phenomenal expertise to form a pathway allowing tourists to explore the tsingy in safety. Amid all this grey are splashes of green from the pachypodiums and other strange succulents (see box, page 416) which find footholds in the crevices. And there's plenty of wildlife too, including Decken's sifakas, red-fronted brown lemurs, chameleons, collared iguanids, crocodiles, forest rats and scops owls.

The park office and several good lodgings are to be found at the gateway town of Bekopaka, at the reserve's southwestern extremity.

Getting there and away

Access is virtually impossible in the rainy season (typically late Nov to Apr), so the park and hotels close down for this period. Even at the best times much of the road from Morondava is horrendous. Unless you are made of money and can afford to charter a plane to the dirt airstrip near Bekopaka, there are essentially three options for getting here: by 4x4 from Morondava (187km/8–10hrs); a 3–5-day descent of River Tsiribihina from Miandrivazo to Belo-sur-Tsiribihina then by 4x4 from there (94km/4–5hrs); or a 3–5-day descent of River Manambolo from Ankavandra directly to Bekopaka. Since the rivers are not easily navigated against their direction of flow, the only option for *departing* Bekopaka is the road to Morondava.

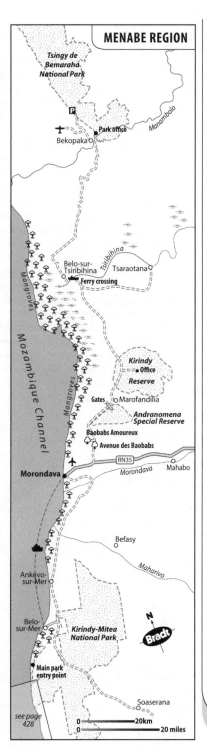

MENABE REGION

see page 428

Tsingy – the razor-sharp pinnacles produced by erosion of limestone massifs by acidic rain – are found in several parts of Madagascar, most notably Ankarana and Bemaraha national parks. The dry deciduous forests in which tsingy occur are characterised by very high endemism, and are among Madagascar's most rewarding areas for plant enthusiasts.

Pandanus and *Dracaena* species are encountered in tsingy areas and are superficially similar, with tall thin stems and long thin dark green leaves. However, *Pandanus* tend to have thicker trunks, larger leaves, spikes on the trunk and serrated edges to the leaves compared with the slender smooth leaves of *Dracaena*. *Pandanus* often feature a 'tripod' effect produced by aerial roots.

Pachypodium lamerei, common throughout Bemaraha, is a spiny columnar plant when young but has a smooth whitish surface and bulbous base when older. Towering trees of *P. rutenbergianum* and *P. decaryi*, a small plant with a smooth globular base, are common in Ankarana. *P. ambongense* has a very localised habitat on the tsingy at Namoroka.

Euphorbia viguieri, thick green stems of up to 50cm tall with long whitish thorns and prominent red and green top-knots of floral parts, and numerous tree-like euphorbias with narrow green cylindrical stems, are common in both areas; whereas *E. ankarensis*, short sticks with attractive pale green cones of cyathophylls at the top, is confined to Ankarana where thousands occur. The low-growing *E. aureo-viridiflora*, *E. herman-schwarzii* and *E. neohumbertii* and the larger *E. pachypodioides* and *E. tirucalli* also occur in this area.

Commiphora species, medium-sized trees, are common on the tsingy and are readily identified by the profuse scaling of bark, usually brown but sometimes with a greenish tinge. Eventually clumps of bark are shed to leave attractive pale-coloured plaques among the scaly bark. *Dalbergia*, *Cassia* (with pale green fine foliage appearing in October) and *Tamarindus indica* are huge trees common on the tsingy.

Adenia epigea (huge globular caudiciforms with a base up to 1m in diameter) and *A. lapiazicola* are common at Ankarana and *A. firingalavensis* occurs at Bemaraha. The latter is easily identified by the dark dull green caudex which usually tapers upwards, but is occasionally spherical. (It sometimes lacks a caudex when growing on soil, such as at Kirindy, suggesting that the harsh conditions of the tsingy may contribute to caudex formation as a survival mechanism.)

Hildegardia erythrosiphon is a medium-sized tree with a buttressed base and masses of brilliant red flowers which are easily seen above the canopy in the deciduous forest. The bright yellow flowers with dark red or purple throat of *Uncarina* are also visible from a distance in the sparse forest. *U. ankaranensis* is confined to Ankarana, but *U. peltata* and *U. sakalava* are more widely distributed.

For backpackers whose budget won't stretch to hiring a 4x4 and driver for a few days, options are limited. Occasional public transport in the form of *camion-brousses* does run from Morondava but not very often and it's extremely slow. You won't have the option of stopping at Kirindy and the Avenue des Baobabs *en route*, and then you will need to find a vehicle to transport you to the trail heads at the park anyway. So your best bet would be to ask around and try to hook up with other travellers in Morondava to split the cost of vehicle hire. One company, **Madagascar Touring** (page 427), has now taken the difficulty out of finding travel buddies by running a 12-seater truck (see box, page 418) on scheduled departures between Morondava and Bekopaka a few times per week. When there are fewer than six bookings, they use a 4x4. They also offer three-day packages for 300,000Ar per person that covers your transfer, park permit, guide and a river excursion; not included in the deal are food and accommodation.

🏠 **Where to stay and eat** All of the hotels are at Bekopaka, but quite spread out (up to 4km from the park office). There are also **campsites** with very basic facilities near to the park office and not far from the Grand Tsingy trail head, which is 17km away (1¼hrs by 4x4).

🏠 **Soleil des Tsingy Lodge** (9 bungalows)
📞22 209 49; m 033 15 719 68/034 14 719 68;
e contact@soleildestsingy.com; www.
soleildestsingy.com. New in 2013. A 15ha plot with
luxurious bungalows that have king-size beds &
spacious en-suite bathrooms. Infinity-edge pool,
large terrace & restaurant with panoramic views.
€€€€€

🏠 **Grand Hotel du Tsingy du Bemaraha
(Vazimba)** (20 bungalows) m 033 08 799
48/034 99 389 99; e contact@legrandhotel-
du-tsingy.com; www.legrandhotel-du-tsingy.
com. Opened in 2009, a Malagasy-owned hotel
with ambitions to be the largest in Bekopaka.
Nicely planted plot with pool & huge restaurant
surrounded by quaint brick bungalows for 2–6
people, attractively decorated with excellent
en-suite bathrooms; hot water & 24hr electricity.
€€€€

🏠 **Orchidée du Bemaraha** (13 bungalows)
m 032 05 714 14/032 07 596 58/032 50 898
79; e contact@orchideedubemaraha.com
or orchideedubemaraha@gmail.com; www.
orchideedubemaraha.com. En-suite dbl, twin &
family rooms. Superb food. €€€€

🏠 **Olympe du Bemaraha** (24 rooms
& 24 bungalows) m 032 05 216 05/032 07
202 46/034 07 202 46/034 07 890 05/034 49
205 03 (manager)/034 49 205 12; e info@
olympedubemaraha-madagascar.com or

reception@olympedubemaraha-madagascar.
com; www.olympedubemaraha-madagascar.
com. On a hill overlooking the river. En-suite family
bungalows with solar-heated shower & veranda.
Rooms mostly en suite. Large swimming pool;
restaurant with bar, Wi-Fi & panoramic view.
€€€–€€€€

🏠 **Camp Croco** 📞22 630 86; www.
madcameleon.com. On the south side of the river,
opposite Bekopaka. Furnished safari-style tents.
Shared toilets & showers. Bar & restaurant. €€€

🏠 **Relais des Tsingy** (6 bungalows) m 032
02 049 48; e relais.tsingy@yahoo.fr; www.tsingy-
de-bemaraha.com. A beautifully situated set of
bungalows with en-suite bathrooms, overlooking
a lake. €€€

🏠 **Tsingy Lodge** (5 bungalows) m 033 11 507
56/034 15 426 49/032 70 676 92; e tsingylodge@
yahoo.fr; www.tsingy-lodge.com. Malagasy-run
lodge near the park office. Simple, clean bungalows;
some en suite. Run by an ex-guide. €€€

🏠 **Tanankoay** (15 bungalows) m 032 02
226 62/033 13 658 45/034 18 251 93; e rj_tony@
yahoo.fr or tanankoay@yahoo.fr; www.tanankoay.
com. Small tranquil site run by welcoming
& knowledgeable English-speaking owners:
a Malagasy guide & his French wife. Simple
bungalows, some en suite with hot water, set in an
attractive botanical garden. Camping for 5,000Ar.
4x4 for transfers & excursions. €€–€€€

Visiting the park Although there are forested areas of the park with good wildlife, it is the tsingy that makes this place special. Two main areas are developed for tourism: the **Petit Tsingy** near the park office and the **Grand Tsingy** a little over an hour's drive north. There are now more than a dozen different circuits, of which the easiest is **Tantely** (2km/1hr), which gets you among the otherworldly pinnacles of the Petit Tsingy. This can be combined with the **Andadoany** forest trail to make a 4-hour walk. However, for the most dramatic views you need to do the difficult **Ankeligoa** circuit (6km/5hrs)

We were met at Tsingy de Bemaraha by a large, robust-looking truck instead of one of the ubiquitous fleets of 4x4s. I felt smug – high off the ground and twice as wide as a Land Rover, it looked like it was perfectly suited to the dusty, bumpy road. Our tour group fondly named her 'Bertha'. This 12-seater truck gives independent travellers an option to book a single seat to their destination, rather than hiring a 4x4 and private driver for a few days at great expense. It's a welcome budget option. For tours, hiring the entire thing allows groups of more than six to travel in the same vehicle and share in the experience of bird spotting and watching Malagasy life by the side of the road.

Each leather, bench-like seat is fitted with a metal handrail. When the engine jolted to a start, we saw why they were worn with use. We clung on while Bertha lurched down dusty tracks. The handrails didn't stop us knocking shoulders with every dip or lump in the road. With no air conditioning, we opened the windows and, no doubt defying any number of health and safety rules, propped open the door with an end table. The breeze was worth the price of getting covered in a film of red dust.

The journey was slow and each 4x4 that overtook us was deflating. Bertha barely ever exceeded walking pace. I stopped feeling smug. But she did have her upsides. After hours of driving, when the lactic acid built up to a fizz in our knees, we could get out and walk beside her, like going for a stroll with a friend. We spotted insects and birds in the bushes, and walked around colourful roadside tombs while 4x4s accelerated past. We saw the stretches between the towns in detail. Bertha would wait for us at the end of our walk and we didn't feel like we'd lost any journey time. Though we had to get up before dawn and arrived at hotels long after the sun had set, it felt like we had seen more on the journey than if we were going at 60kph.

Bertha was a spectacle. Villagers would crowd around her, waiting for us to descend from a couple of feet above the ground and stretch our legs. The large box on wheels transporting *vazaha* as if they were a herd of zebu caused more intrigue than a blacked-out sedan. While other vehicles had their windows rolled up to keep air conditioning in, fat green mangoes and sweet rice cakes were offered through Bertha's. We watched Malagasy kids touch the wood panels of the truck as they walked past, as if they were some ancient good luck charm.

in the Petit Tsingy and also visit the even more dramatic Grand Tsingy. For both of these you need to be fairly fit and have no fear of heights. The best circuit in the Grand Tsingy, **Andamozavaky**, is a stunning full day's excursion involving a lot of climbing and some caves (take a torch). The tsingy here is amazing, with pinnacles 50m high.

For a break from sweating in the tsingy you can take a **pirogue trip** up Manambolo River, which cuts a spectacular gorge through the limestone along the park's southern boundary, to look for fish eagles and visit a cave. There's also a lake near the park entrance with a resident pair of fish eagles and waterfowl such as white-faced whistling ducks, Humblot's herons and purple herons.

With the time and effort needed to get to Bemaraha, you should spend two full days at the very least to experience the various circuits. The optimum time to visit weather-wise is June to August, before the heat gets too oppressive, but this is also peak season with the downside that long queues can form on the via ferrata (steel cable climbing route) and they sometimes run out of safety harnesses.

Permits and guides There may be a queue in the mornings at the park office (☺ *07.00–16.00*) so to make an early start, arrange your visit and get your permit the day before. See page 73 for permit prices. Guiding rates range from 12,000Ar to 55,000Ar according to the length of the circuit and size of your group.

BELO-SUR-TSIRIBIHINA Where else can you find a royal family serving beer in a bar (see box below)? Belo is a pleasant town with several good restaurants and a lively Friday market. Located on the northern bank of River Tsiribihina, it is a natural stopping place *en route* to Bekopaka and the finishing point for boat trips downriver (page 433), so sees quite a few visitors – especially in July and August. Tsiribihina means 'where one must not dive' – apparently because of crocodiles!

To proceed south from Belo, it is necessary first to cross the river by ferry. This typically takes 25–55 minutes (depending whether you are going with or against the flow) as it involves travelling 4.5km along the river rather than just straight across.

Where to stay and eat

🏠 **Lodge de la Saline** Tsangajoly; m 034 14 599 21; e info.resa.lodge@csd.mg; www. lodgedelasaline.com. Over the other side of the river, some 15km south of town, this new lodge describes itself as 'eco-responsible' as it is built with natural/recycled materials & has solar power. Birders & botanists will be interested in the protected area, at the centre of which are the salt pans of Delta company (open to public tours).

In addition to the flora & fauna, they have a yoga centre, solarium, pool, gym & American games room. The en-suite rooms are equipped with AC & Wi-Fi; some also with sat-TV. €€€€€–👒

🏠 **Karibo** (25 rooms) m 032 51 872 13/033 01 862 53/034 20 872 13; e hotelkariborestaurant@ yahoo.fr or hotelrestaurantkaribo@gmail.com. Small functional rooms; huge restaurant. Favoured by tour groups; service can be slow. €€

FITAMPOHA AND A MEETING WITH ROYALTY   *Hilary Bradt*

You don't expect to find a prince serving beer in a hot, dusty coastal town; nor to have an audience with a princess in a bar. But Belo-sur-Tsiribihina is the home of the Menabe (Sakalava) royal family, and even royals have to make a living, biding their time until the next *fitampoha.*

Every eight to ten years the royal family receives empowerment from the ancestors through this ceremony of washing the sacred relics. The relics are called *dady*, and comprise bones, and perhaps fingernails and teeth. They are stored in an iron box in a sacred house (*zomba*) which you can see in the southern part of town, protected by a high fence of sharpened staves. In the old days the dady would be carried into battle to ensure victory.

Over a beer, Princess Georgette told me about the ceremony, bringing out a photo album from the last fitampoha in 2004 to illustrate her story. It takes place in August, on a Friday when there's a full moon. From Thursday midnight it is forbidden to wash in the river. Reeds must be collected at midday, from a special place an hour's walk from the town – accompanied by singing and dancing. Descendants of nobility wash the royal clothing and hang it on the reeds to dry. Friday is the sacred day, when the relics are washed in the river.

The princess, now 70, told us she was a direct descendant of King Toera, who fought the French in the war of independence, and chose death rather than surrender. The French agreed to educate his ten-year-old son who later became King Kamamy, governor of Menabe and the father of the princess sitting with me in that hot, dark bar. 'But there are descendants all over the world.'

🏠 **Menabe** (15 rooms) **m** 032 42 635 35; **e** hoteldumenabe@free.fr; http://hoteldumenabe. free.fr. Built by a Greek in the 1920s. En-suite dbl & trpl rooms. €€

🍴 **Mad Zebu** **m** 032 07 589 55/032 40 387 15/034 40 309 60; **e** restaurantmadzebu@yahoo. fr. Despite its name, this is the best restaurant in Belo and among the best in the country. Excellent food served on a breezy patio. See box below.

KIRINDY RESERVE (**m** *033 03 092 49/033 16 303 78*; **e** *cfpfmva20051@yahoo.fr; entry 25,000Ar pp, guiding 20,000–60,000Ar per circuit per group of up to 4*) This is one of the most rewarding natural areas in Madagascar and is part of the 125,000ha Menabe protected area. (It is not to be confused with the Kirindy-Mitea National Park, covered on page 429.) Until a few years ago its sole purpose was the sustainable 'harvesting' of trees, but despite this selective logging the wildlife here is abundant, and several habituated species now even frequent the bungalow and restaurant area.

It is one of the few places where you may see the giant jumping rat and the narrow-striped mongoose, and is also the best place in Madagascar to see the fossa. For a truly exciting experience, visit the park when the fossas are overcome with

---

MICHELIN STARS IN THE MIDDLE OF NOWHERE   *Suzy Pope*

Marking the halfway point along the dirt road from Tsingy de Bemaraha to Morondava, the town of Belo-sur-Tsiribihina is a popular lunch stop. A bowl of rice stuffed hastily into mouths while vehicles wait for their slot on the rickety old car ferry is a common sight. Belo is not the kind of town you spend any length of time in. Shacks and stalls of corrugated iron cluster around the muddy Tsiribihina River. Two-storey, concrete and wooden buildings peeling colourful paint line the main street. But it is here, a world away from the relatively metropolitan capital, that I found my favourite meal in Madagascar.

The Mad Zebu restaurant was founded by Michelle, who has always been passionate about making traditional Malagasy food. Her son, Chef Onja, learned to cook in Antananarivo before working in a 3-star Michelin restaurant in the South of France. Now running the kitchen at Belo's finest establishment, he adds a modern, sophisticated twist to traditional zebu stews and grilled river fish. The result is Michelin-standard meals in the middle of nowhere.

Starters include fat, juicy shrimp from the Tsiribihina River and fresh carpaccio of tilapia. Zebu steak that melts in your mouth and tender wild duck legs are on offer for main. Chef Onja specialised in patisserie, so leave room for dessert. Traditional African peanut brittle and soft chocolate mousse show off his skill in fusing the old with the new.

In a town where the buildings feel run-down and bone-tired, it's the care over presentation that makes each dish at the Mad Zebu truly amazing. Dramatic sweeps of *jus* curl around architecturally perfect towers of rice. Parcels of vegetables wrapped in cassava leaves stand neatly in a line. It is surreal, cutting into a perfectly cooked steak, or skewering a delicate vegetable flower while a zebu cart trundles past and bare-footed children play in the dusty street. If you were only looking at your plate you could be in one of the world's gastronomic capitals, but the ramshackle surroundings just add to the unexpected delight of dining here.

The Mad Zebu gives you a reason to linger a little longer in a town where the main aim is to get out and move on. Forget the aye-aye, or the giraffe-necked weevil, this restaurant is the biggest surprise in Madagascar.

KIRINDY: AN ISLAND WITHIN AN ISLAND   *Lennart Pyritz*

Madagascar is a separate world; an isolated island, home to countless unique species. Against this background, Kirindy is a superlative within a superlative. A number of species live nowhere else on earth but in this remnant of dry deciduous forest.

Monogamous pairs of giant jumping rats – Madagascar's largest rodents, which look like a peculiar kangaroo-rabbit crossbreed with a rat's tail – dig their burrows only in the soft, red soils of Kirindy. A second local endemic is the recently described Madame Berthe's mouse lemur. Weighing just 30g, it is the world's smallest primate. Yet another special treat of Kirindy is the fossa, the island's largest carnivore. Incredibly elusive elsewhere in Madagascar, you'd be unlucky not to see them around the campsite, always on the lookout for scraps. And if you visit in November, you may also witness their unique mating behaviour: a female spends many days in a tree copulating in turn with the several males queuing at the bottom.

Besides the fossa, jumping rats and eight lemur species (from the solitary, gnomish mouse lemurs to the troops of large sifakas), Kirindy is home to about 20 other mammals, including rodents, tenrecs, bats and the endangered narrow-striped mongoose. The majority of the lemurs are nocturnal, but they occur at exceptionally high densities, so you are guaranteed to see some. A night walk is a must! Kirindy is also a hotspot for ornithologists, with about 70 bird species, including the rare white-breasted mesite and crested ibis, vasa parrots, harrier-hawks, kingfishers, sunbirds and vangas. Some 50 reptiles and 15 amphibians, as well as an innumerable variety of colourful insects, complete the zoological spectrum.

Kirindy's plants are equally notable, including three species of baobab and the endemic *hazomalany* tree. Several marked nature trails allow visitors to explore the forest vegetation.

Right next to the tourist camp, Prof Peter Kappeler and his team from the German Primate Center have been operating a research station since 1993, where an international group of field biologists study the ecology and behaviour of Kirindy's fauna. Thus the tourist guides are constantly kept updated by the researchers, and eagerly pass on news of the very latest scientific discoveries to visitors.

Lennart Pyritz was a PhD student at the German Primate Center studying red-fronted lemurs. He now works as a science journalist in Germany.

spring fever. Jonathan Ekstrom reports: 'They mate voraciously over four days between late October and late November – but the precise timing is pot luck.'

Reptile-viewing is excellent: you may see collared iguanas seeking open sandy spots to lay their clutches of eggs, while hognose snakes eagerly sniff out these freshly laid snacks, unearthing them with their snouts and swallowing the eggs whole. See the box above for a more detailed rundown of Kirindy's wildlife.

The reserve's own accommodation is pretty basic but, even if you normally dislike roughing it, you should try to stay a night here. Day visitors see far less than those able to observe wildlife at the optimum times of dawn and dusk, and a night-time stroll is usually an exceptional wildlife experience with nocturnal lemurs and chameleons easily seen and – if you are lucky – a giant jumping rat.

On the other hand – if you're *unlucky* – you could have an experience such as readers Paul and Inbal Kolodziejski had on their honeymoon: 'An hour into the night walk our guide started to look nervous, walking back and forth. It turned out he'd lost the track. He started walking in circles and we could see he was beginning to panic – never a good sign from your guide in the middle of the night in a scary forest! After much frantic running around, he told us he must consult the spirit of his grandfather, so he crouched, covered his head, and rocked back and forth. We waited, having visions of sleeping in the forest. After he finished, he didn't look like he knew anything more than before, but at least he'd calmed down and we could talk to him!'

Eventually they stumbled across a numbered tree tag that allowed them to work out their location; perhaps grandfather had sent a signal after all.

Kirindy is about 65km (1½–2½hrs) northeast of Morondava, and 45km (1½–2hrs) south of Belo, on a road which can become impassable in the rainy season. Package tours are offered by many Morondava hotels. The reserve's lodgings are rather overpriced and quite run-down, but it's the only option for an overnight stay, unless you want to drive 20 minutes south to Camp Amoureux (see below) – which is even pricier but more justifiably so. Kirindy has 12 bungalows with en-suite cold showers and six four-bed dorms with communal bucket showers. Camping is no longer permitted, apparently owing to increasingly audacious and inquisitive fossa. A fairly expensive restaurant serves simple Malagasy meals.

MAROFANDILIA Do stop at this inspiring village an hour or so from Morondava by 4x4. The **Boutique d'Art Sakalave** is a roadside shop 19km north of the turning for the Baobabs Amoureux, and 28km north of RN35. Begun as a Peace Corps project, the boutique is now a thriving independent business. The quality of the woodcarvings for sale is excellent and only wood from trees that are already dead and collected from community-managed forests is used. The prices are fair and the profits go directly to help the local community and to conserve the remaining forest. The boutique fosters a pride among the local Sakalava for their traditional craft and culture.

Nearby is **Camp Amoureux** (m *032 07 843 44/033 15 729 35/033 37 342 13/034 29 380 60*; e *friendlycamp@madagascar-discovery.com*; €€€€), with accommodation in the form of 13 sheltered tents in the forest, with en-suite bathrooms (cold showers), and a central eating area. The site was opened by the conservation NGO FANAMBY, which also administers the nearby Avenue des Baobabs protected area. There is a 1½-hour walking circuit at Camp Amoureux, where day and night walks are possible in a forest with seven lemur species (five nocturnal). Guiding costs 10,000Ar per group, plus 10,000Ar per person for park entry.

ANDRANOMENA SPECIAL RESERVE (☎ *95 921 28*; e *arn.parks@gmail.com or krm. parks@gmail.com*) This reserve just south of Marofandilia protects 6,420ha of dense dry deciduous forest including three species of baobab. It is home to 11 species of reptile, 48 birds and seven lemurs including Verreaux's sifakas and red-fronted brown lemurs, both readily seen. The giant jumping rat is also found here and there are several lakes with accompanying waterfowl.

Guides cost 5,000Ar per circuit of 2–3 hours. For permit prices see page 73. It takes about an hour to get here by car from Morondava (hotels and tour operators there can arrange a visit). If you are planning to visit independently, make arrangements at the National Parks office in Morondava first.

BAOBABS AMOUREUX These baobab 'lovers' (*Adansonia za*), so called because they are a romantically intertwined pair, have become almost as famous as Avenue des Baobabs itself. Turn left 3.5km north of the Avenue and you will find them a further 3.5km down this track. You can see another similarly entwined pair at Camp Amoureux near Marofandilia.

AVENUE DES BAOBABS (*www.association-fanamby.org*) This cluster of towering Grandidier's baobabs (*Adansonia grandidieri*) is one of Madagascar's most famous views. In 2007 the avenue (together with about 300 baobabs of three species in the surrounding 1km) became an officially protected natural monument. There is now a car park, fee to pay to visit, souvenir shop, information office and tree nursery, with an active programme to plant saplings among the existing trees. The project suffered a setback late in 2012 when a fire engulfed 11ha of the 320ha reserve, destroying 99 of the 220 newly planted trees, but no mature baobabs were affected.

To get to the avenue turn left off RN35 about 13km from Morondava, and the baobabs are 5.5km further on. It takes about 40 minutes by car/taxi, or you can come by bike or quad. The best light for photography is just before sunset (it brings out the red hue in the bark), but sunrise is almost as good and you're much more likely to have the place to yourself.

MORONDAVA

The Morondava area was the centre of the Sakalava kingdom and their tombs (sadly now desecrated by souvenir hunters) bear witness to their power and creativity.

This was evidently a popular stopping place for sailors in the past and they seem to have treated the natives generously. In 1833, Captain W F W Owen wrote of Morondava: 'Five boats came alongside and stunned us by vociferating for presents and beseeching us to anchor.'

Today Morondava is the centre of a prosperous rice-growing area – and has successfully introduced ostrich farming to Madagascar. For tourists it is best known as a seaside resort with a laid-back atmosphere and the southern gateway to many of the attractions of the western region, including the western deciduous forest, the famous baobabs, Tsingy de Bemaraha National Park and Belo-sur-Mer.

GETTING THERE AND AWAY Morondava is 701km from Tana (via Miandrivazo) and served by a good road that takes around 10 hours nonstop in a private vehicle. By taxi-brousse (44,000Ar) it takes longer but it is not recommended to travel overnight due to road security. **Cotisse** (m *032 12 027 00/11*) runs a daily scheduled service in a comfortable vehicle leaving at 07.00 from Tana and Morondava. **Transport Première Classe** (m *033 15 488 88/034 22 588 88/033 01 588 88/032 43 588 88*; e *malagasycar@gmail.com; www.malagasycar.com*) runs a daytime service in comfortable air-conditioned vehicles (meals included); in Tana you can book at the Grand Mellis Hotel. For details of the route south to Toliara, see page 427.

Morondava is served by regular Air Mad **flights** and several **boats**, including a weekly ferry to Belo-sur-Mer.

GETTING AROUND Baobab Café Hotel rents out quad bikes and the Mada Bar has motorbikes for hire.

WHERE TO STAY
Luxury ♛
 Palissandre Côte Ouest [424 B6] (30 bungalows) Nosy Kely; ☏ 95 520 22/95 520 26; m 033 15 349 74; e palissandrecoteouest@gmail. com; www.hotel-restaurant-palissandrecoteouest. com. The most upmarket accommodation in town

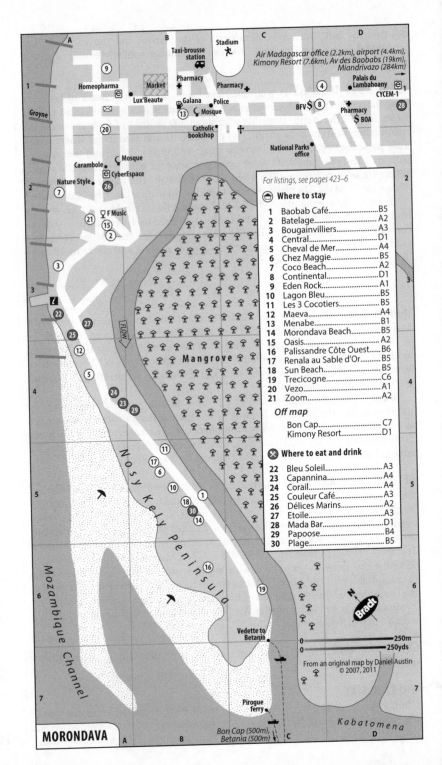

MORONDAVA

Stadium

Taxi-brousse station

Air Madagascar office (2.2km), airport (4.4km), Kimony Resort (7.6km), Av des Baobabs (19km), Miandrivazo (284km) →

Palais du Lambahoany

CYCEM-1

Homeopharma

Market

Pharmacy

Pharmacy

BFV

Pharmacy

BOA

Lux'Beaute

Galana

Police

Mosque

Catholic bookshop

Carambole

Mosque

National Parks office

Nature Style

CyberEspace

F Music

Groyne

Mangrove

Nosy Kely Peninsula

FLOW

Mozambique Channel

Vedette to Betania

Pirogue ferry

Bon Cap (500m), Betania (500m)

Kabatomena

For listings, see pages 423–6

⌂ Where to stay

1	Baobab Café	B5
2	Batelage	A2
3	Bougainvilliers	A3
4	Central	D1
5	Cheval de Mer	A4
6	Chez Maggie	B5
7	Coco Beach	A2
8	Continental	D1
9	Eden Rock	A1
10	Lagon Bleu	B5
11	Les 3 Cocotiers	B5
12	Maeva	A4
13	Menabe	B1
14	Morondava Beach	B5
15	Oasis	A2
16	Palissandre Côte Ouest	B6
17	Renala au Sable d'Or	B5
18	Sun Beach	B5
19	Trecicogne	C6
20	Vezo	A1
21	Zoom	A2

Off map

	Bon Cap	C7
	Kimony Resort	D1

✖ Where to eat and drink

22	Bleu Soleil	A3
23	Capannina	A4
24	Corail	A4
25	Couleur Café	A3
26	Délices Marins	A2
27	Etoile	A3
28	Mada Bar	D1
29	Papoose	B4
30	Plage	B5

250m

250yds

From an original map by Daniel Austin © 2007, 2011

by far. En-suite seafront bungalows with AC, sat-TV, safe, minibar & balcony. B/fast inc. Wi-Fi area, boutique, pool & spa. Excursions, fishing, boat trips, quad hire, kayaks, tennis & snorkelling gear. Credit cards accepted.

Upper range €€€€

🏠 **Baobab Café** [424 B5] (28 rooms) Nosy Kely; ➊ 95 520 12; m 032 85 034 84/034 29 113 30/034 51 120 70/034 64 229 70; e baobabtours@ blueline.mg; www.baobabcafe-hotel.net. The hotel backs on to the river on the east side of Nosy Kely (rooms overlooking the river can be smelly). AC rooms with en-suite facilities, minibar & TV. Good restaurant. Large pool. Deep-sea fishing.

🏠 **Chez Maggie (Masoandro)** [424 B5] (12 bungalows) Nosy Kely; ➊ 95 523 47; m 032 47 326 70; e info@chezmaggie.com; www. chezmaggie.com; see ad, 4th colour section. American-Malagasy-owned & firmly established as the local anglophone hang-out; a friendly place to meet fellow travellers. Spacious bungalows, all en suite with hot water & most with AC. Lovely garden setting with small pool, excellent restaurant & Wi-Fi. Organises river trips & other excursions.

🏠 **Kimony Resort** [424 D1] (2 rooms & 26 bungalows) m 034 07 202 46 (owner)/034 07 205 24/034 07 205 50/034 07 890 05 (manager); e info@kimonyresort-morondava.com or reception@kimonyresort-morondava.com; www. kimonyresort-morondava.com. Built by 3rd-generation Indian immigrant who owns a wooden furniture company & also Olympe du Bemaraha at Bekopaka. Spacious wooden bungalows with smart décor, situated nr beach north of town; en suite with AC (eve only), sat-TV, minibar & veranda. Swimming pool, children's play area, massage & zoo with lemurs & reptiles.

🏠 **Maeva** [424 A4] (7 rooms) ➊ 95 944 49; m 032 70 946 39; e maeva.hotelmorondava@ gmail.com; www.hotelmaeva-morondava. com. Built in 2007 by a Frenchman & his young Malagasy wife. Dbl, trpl & family rooms (named after different animals & plants), all en suite with safe, Wi-Fi & sea view; some with AC.

🏠 **Renala au Sable d'Or** [424 B5] (6 rooms & 13 bungalows) Nosy Kely; m 032 04 976 88/032 91 652 44 (manager); e renala.contact@blueline. mg. Wooden bungalows, surrounded by gardens, with sat-TV, Wi-Fi & en-suite facilities; most with

AC & some with balcony, minibar & safe. Trips & 4x4 hire. Cybercafé & good restaurant. Visa accepted.

🏠 **Sun Beach** [424 B5] (10 rooms) ➊ 95 924 32; m 032 07 511 75/032 40 242 75; e sunbeach. morondava@gmail.com; www.sunbeach-morondava.com. Pleasant spot near beach, just behind Philaos. Bungalows with en-suite hot-water facilities, AC & Wi-Fi. Opened as a restaurant in 2000, the bungalows were added in 2011.

🏠 **Vezo** [424 A1] (25 rooms) m 032 11 220 00/032 11 220 01/032 29 447 82; e andre. menage@vezohotel.com (manager) or infos@ vezohotel.com. Opened in 2013 in a colonial-style former bank building. Rooms with hot water facilities, sat-TV, safe, minibar & some with AC.

Mid-range €€€

🏠 **Bougainvilliers** [424 A3] (12 rooms & 8 bungalows) Nosy Kely; ➊ 95 521 63/95 921 63; m 032 04 554 12/034 49 521 63; e bvl_nd@ yahoo.fr. Wide range of rooms & prices. Becoming run-down.

🏠 **Cheval de Mer** [424 A4] (6 rooms) Nosy Kely; m 033 06 272 12/034 37 488 53/034 98 971 78. Rooms are en suite with fan, just off the beach. Wi-Fi.

🏠 **Coco Beach (Arche de Noé)** [424 A2] (7 rooms & 5 bungalows) m 032 81 438 66 (manager)/032 96 077 90 (reception)/033 29 543 53 (manager). Straightforward en-suite accommodation with hot water, right on the beach.

🏠 **Continental** [424 D1] (19 rooms) m 032 02 798 09 (manager)/032 48 687 10. Downtown 3-storey hotel with a variety of rooms: some budget & some with AC.

🏠 **Lagon Bleu (Philaos)** [424 B5] (18 rooms) Nosy Kely; m 032 66 787 31; e sica@moov.mg. En-suite rooms with hot water, some with AC & kitchenette. Massage.

🏠 **Les 3 Cocotiers** [424 B5] (10 rooms) m 034 11 100 10; e cocotiersmorondava@ yahoo.com or hotel3cocotiers@gmail.com or les3cocotiers@gmail.com. Straightforward clean rooms for a reasonable price.

🏠 **Morondava Beach** [424 B5] (16 bungalows) ➊ 95 523 18; m 032 40 213 99; e morondavabeach@yahoo.com. A wide range of en-suite bungalows, some with hot water & AC. Massage & full range of excursions.

🏠 **Trecicogne** [424 C6] (20 rooms) Nosy Kely; ➊ 95 942 13; m 032 04 687 60/034 51 636 66;

e trecicogne@moov.mg; www.hoteltrecicogne.com.
Range of rooms, mostly en suite inc a few with AC.

🏠 **Zoom** [424 A2] (9 rooms) 📞 95 520 59;
m 032 81 113 36. Trpl rooms with en-suite hot-
water facilities; a couple with AC.

Budget €€

🏠 **Batelage** [424 A2] (12 rooms & 14
bungalows) m 032 04 852 32/032 49 804 65/034
04 203 34; e batelagehotel@yahoo.fr. En-suite
dbl & trpl rooms, some with TV; no hot water in
bungalows. Car hire.

🏠 **Bon Cap** [424 C7] (3 bungalows) Betania;
m 032 41 129 66/033 89 561 60. Hotel, restaurant
& bar in Betania village, away from the hustle &
bustle of town. Owned by a piroguier. Simple dbl
bungalows with showers. Camping permitted.

🏠 **Central** [424 D1] (8 rooms) m 032 05 621
02; e hocentral@moov.mg. On the main street
Simple en-suite rooms with fan.

🏠 **Eden Rock** [424 A1] (11 rooms) m 032 40
859 45/034 68 513 18; e rejelanatacha@yahoo.
fr; www.edenrockhotel-morondava.com. Good
value; close to beach. En-suite rooms with hot
water, sat-TV & Wi-Fi; most also with optional AC
for extra fee.

🏠 **Menabe** [424 B1] (27 rooms) m 032 07
607 00 (owner)/032 07 607 02/032 46 298 78;
e hoteldumenabe@free.fr. Open since 1984.
Rooms on 3 floors, all en suite with hot water; a
few with sat-TV & AC.

🏠 **Oasis (Chez Jean le Rasta)** [424 A2] (4
bungalows) Rte de Batelage; m 032 04 931 60;
e jeanlerasta@yahoo.fr. Bungalows rather run-
down but the bar & restaurant are great. Nightly
live music, drums & reggae performed by owner
Jean le Rasta & local musicians. Bike hire.

✸ **WHERE TO EAT AND DRINK** Several of the hotels serve good food, most notably
Chez Maggie, **Sun Beach** and **Renala au Sable d'Or**. For a lively laid-back atmosphere,
try **Oasis**.

✸ **Capannina** [424 A4] m 032 04 670 90/034
05 670 90. Popular & well-located eatery with
always-reliable food & great pizza.

✸ **Corail (Chez Alain)** [424 A4] m 032 83 409
86. Splendid restaurant; seafood platters highly
recommended. Good pizzas too.

✸ **Délices Marins** [424 A2] m 034 07 205 25;
e titi250171@gmail.com; ⏰ Tue–Sun, closed
Mon. Seafood & pizza restaurant.

✸ **Etoile** [424 A3] m 032 27 288 14; e philippe.
leclech@gmail.com. New restaurant & bar,
decorated with Malagasy musical instruments.
Good range of *rhums arrangés*.

✸ **Mada Bar** [424 D1] m 032 04 703 99/034 04
194 19; e madabar69@yahoo.fr. Great ice cream
& pizza, inc take-away. Also kayak, motorbike &
mountain bike hire.

✸ **Papoose** [424 B4] m 034 04 063 17. Simple
grill eatery & bar.

✸ **Plage** [424 B5] ⏰ 06.30–22.00. Bar & grill
restaurant.

💻 **Bleu Soleil (Chez Patricia)** [424 A3]
m 033 06 010 07; e raharimalalapatricia@yahoo.
fr. Snack bar. Also kayak rental & massage.

💻 **Couleur Café** [424 A3] m 032 75 326 12;
e couleurcafe@freenet.mg. Beachfront snack bar;
great location.

NIGHTLIFE F Music [424 A2] is a bar with a nice atmosphere. Several of the hotels
and restaurants also have good bars.

MONEY AND COMMUNICATIONS There's a branch of BFV bank with an ATM on
the main street [424 C1]; BNI and BOA have branches here too. For internet, the
computers at **Homeopharma** [424 A1] are much faster than at **CyberEspace** [424
A2]. At the eastern end of town is another cybercafé called **CYCEM-1** [424 D1].

SHOPPING There are no supermarkets but **Lux'Beaute** [424 B1] is a fairly well-
stocked general store and the bustling main **market** [424 B1] is nearby. The
Carambole [424 A2] and **Nature Style** [424 A2] boutiques are worth checking out

for souvenirs. Or for a truly unique Malagasy gift, browse the huge range of *lamba* cloths at **Palais du Lambahoany** [424 D1].

TOURIST INFORMATION, TOUR OPERATORS, VEHICLE HIRE AND FLIGHTS

ℹ ORTMEN [424 A3] m 034 31 713 39/034 07 205 46; e ort_men@yahoo.fr; www. morondavatourisme.com. Regional tourist office.

✈ **Air Madagascar** [424 D1] Mamahora; 📞 95 920 22; m 032 07 222 14/034 49 422 35; e moqssmd@airmadagascar.com; ⊕ Mon–Fri 07.30–11.30 & 14.30–17.00, Sat 08.00–10.00

✈ **Madagasikara Airways** m 032 05 970 02/034 05 970 34

Baobab Tours [424 B5] Based at Baobab Café. Large selection of vehicle & boat trips inc deep-sea fishing & overflights of the tsingy. Pricey.

Francois Vahiako [424 A3] 📞 95 521 63; m 034 04 338 54. Based at Bougainvilliers. Head of the Morondava Guides Association. Also 4x4 hire.

Jean le Rasta [424 A2] Based at Oasis. Recommended by several travellers as efficient. Speaks good English & has a 4x4.

Madagascar Touring 📞 26 413 36; m 034 85 009 82/034 79 739 49/034 18 594 06/034 15 880 85; e madagascartouring@gmail.com or infos@ madagascaradventures.com; www.madagascar-touring.com or www.madagascaradventures. com. Tour operator & vehicle hire. They also run a 12-seater shuttle bus (truck) to Bemaraha and Belo-sur-Mer (page 417). See ad, page 435.

Remote River Expeditions [424 B5] 📞 95 523 47; m 032 47 326 70; e info@remoterivers.com; www. remoterivers.com. Based at Chez Maggie; highly praised. Vehicles & multilingual guides. River descents & all kinds of other specialist trips both locally and across Madagascar. See ad, 4th colour section.

MORONDAVA TO TOLIARA

Although the towns are only 345km apart as the crow flies, travelling directly between Morondava and Toliara is not easy. The roads are poor (although the inland route from Toliara towards Morombe is being improved at the time of writing) so it is easier to go by sea in some sections. If you plan to sail (rather than take a motorboat) then the wind usually favours going northwards.

Sail pirogues are easily found at each of the villages *en route*, so you can do the journey in stages using a different boat for each leg. But if you want a motorboat, then you'll have to hire a boat and boatman to stay with you all the way.

A sail *piroguier* charges 120,000Ar or so per day and, with a good wind, can cover more than 60km. But weather conditions can change quickly, so be prepared to get stuck halfway and spend one or more nights camping on the beach, or holed up in a tiny fishing village.

Based in Betania at Morondava is motor *piroguier* **Francis** (m *032 41 129 66/033 18 780 40*). In Belo-sur-Mer, **Ramaro** (m *033 18 789 75*) and **Dede** (m *033 01 863 73*) own motor pirogues. Transfers from Morondava to Belo typically cost around 500,000Ar per boat (maximum four passengers). Morondava to Morombe (at least three days) costs about 1,200,000Ar. Or to go as far as Salary it is about 2,000,000Ar (at least five days). From there to Toliara is fairly easy by road.

If you only want to go from Morondava as far as Belo, then most Belo hotels can arrange transfers, or come with the Madagascar Touring truck (see above). A Corsican former French navy commando runs a 26-seat motorboat called *Kintan'ny Maraina* ('The Morning Star') twice a week for 85,000Ar per person (3–4hrs). It leaves if there are at least six passengers. For departure dates, enquire at Renala in Morondava (or m *033 03 364 25*).

A fortnightly *camion-brousse* runs between Morondava and Toliara, going south one Thursday and returning the following Thursday – but this goes via the unexciting inland route (not via Morombe, Andavadoaka and Salary) and takes at least 18 hours. It only runs in the dry season because north of Manja the road is impassable from November due to the river crossings. *Camion-brousses* also run nightly between Morombe and Toliara (16hrs/25,000Ar).

On the coastal road there are daily taxi-brousses between Morombe and Andavadoaka (8,000Ar) but there is no public transport between Andavadoaka and Salary, although occasional private vehicles make the trip. From Antsepoka, fishing co-operative trucks run overnight most nights to Toliara. It's a stinky journey, unless you can bag a spot in the cab, but should only cost around 25,000Ar (or 15,000Ar as far as Salary). From Salary to Toliara, taxi-brousses run on alternate days. Once you get beyond Manombo Sud, it is easy to find vehicles going to Toliara.

ANKEVO-SUR-MER At this little village between Morondava and Belo-sur-Mer, a Belgian association called ADDA has set up some wonderful community-run bungalows. Families take turns being responsible for them, switching once each has generated a certain amount of income (📞 95 928 41; m 033 07 489 10; e *marcel.willems977@gmail.com*).

BELO-SUR-MER Not to be confused with Belo-sur-Tsiribihina, this is a rather colourful Vezo village famed for its shipbuilding. Large boats in all stages of construction line the seafront. Belo has only just got back on its feet after a major cyclone impact in 2009.

The Madagascar National Parks office is next to the Catholic church on the southern side of the village. Go here to buy permits for visits to Kirindy-Mitea National Park (m 033 17 672 94). Belo has Airtel cellphone coverage.

🏠 Where to stay and eat

🏠 **Tsara Belo** (9 bungalows) m 033 02 911 64; e contact@tsara-belo.com; www.tsara-belo.com. Built in 2012. En-suite (cold water) bungalows for 3–5 people, set back from the

MENABE TO TOLIARA

Belo-sur-Mer (31km)
see page 475

N

Bradt

0 — 20km
0 — 20 miles

Andranopasy

Antongo

Bemahola

Mangoky

Kirindy-Mitea Nat Park

Ambahikily

Mangolovolo

Tanandava

Ankiliabo

Morombe

Mamono

Mining concession zones

Ferry crossing

Ankoabe

Lake Ihotry

Ambiky

Andavadoaka

Tanavao

Mining concession zones

Befandriana

Lake Namonty

Ampasilava

Kililaly

Bay of Assassins

Mikea National Park

Basibasy

Antsepoka

Bedo

Antanimieva

Ambohitsabo

Ambatomilo

Seasonal lake

Bekodoy

Antampimbato

Soahazo

Salary Nord II

Ampasikibo

Salary Nord I

Ankaramifoka

Antseva

Tsiandamba

Ankililoaka

Tsifota

Milenaka

Manombo

Fiserenamasay

Manombo

Manombo Sud

Mangily

Ifaty

Ranobe-PK32 Protected Area

Fiherenana

Honko Mangrove Centre

Mozambique Channel

Toliara (Tulear)

RN7

Arboretum d'Antsokay

Grotte Sarodrano

St Augustine's Bay

Onilahy

beach. 4x4 transfers, fishing & mangrove trips. €€€€

🏠 **Entremer** (5 bungalows) **m** 033 15 472 45; **e** contact@beloentremer.com; www.beloentremer.com. Well-run hotel with spacious solar-powered bungalows with en-suite facilities. €€€–€€€€

🏠 **Corail** (1 room & 10 bungalows) **m** 033 20 326 87; **e** corailisa@yahoo.fr. Just south of village, nr the church. All rooms en suite (cold water) with balcony. Pirogue trips. €€€

🏠 **Dauphin** (6 bungalows) **m** 033 71 795 56; **e** dauphinvezo@yahoo.fr. Rebuilt in 2012 after cyclone destruction. En-suite beachfront bungalows with cold water only. Fishing, kayak & pirogue trips. €€€

🏠 **Ecolodge du Menabe** (11 bungalows) **m** 033 09 436 32; **e** info@menabelo.com; www.menabelo.com. Best rooms in town, a short walk south of village; smart but fairly simple beachfront bungalows with nice bathrooms. Boat trips, kayak hire & 4x4 excursions/transfers. €€€

🏠 **Hatea (Ampanareta Village Camp)** (1 room & 4 bungalows) **m** 033 06 951 32; **e** amparetra@gmail.com. Simple, Italian-owned place on a peaceful 3ha peninsula. Mainly a campsite but also with a few self-catering bungalows & a 7-person dorm. No hot water. €€–€€€

🏠 **Chez Lova** (4 rooms) **m** 033 19 114 43; **e** restolovabelo@yahoo.fr. Quaint bungalows with shared cold-water facilities right in centre of village. €€

🏠 **Dorotel** (8 bungalows) **m** 033 01 863 54. Basic hotel at the southern end of the village. Communal cold-water facilities. €€

🏠 **Chez Mon Ami** (4 rooms) **m** 033 01 863 73. Communal cold-water facilities. Owner Dede has a small café/shop & a motor pirogue. €–€€

NOSY ANDRAVANO AND OTHER ISLANDS Belo is the base for visiting a cluster of nine offshore islands, the largest of which is Nosy Andravano. Those to the north are mere sandbanks, but the islands to the south have vegetative cover. Nomadic Vezo fishermen live on the northerly islands for half the year. There are shark carcasses and turtle shells left to dry on the sand, and fish and shark fins are salted in troughs. Each island is fringed by coral reefs, although to view the healthy coral you may have to go up to 2km offshore. You can hire a pirogue in Belo to take you around the islands.

KIRINDY-MITEA NATIONAL PARK This park protects a great variety of habitats – including mangroves, dunes, lakes and beaches – but sees only a trickle of visitors. The entrance to the park is at **Manahy**, 15km southwest of Belo. See page 73 for permit prices. Organise your visit at the park office in Belo or Morondava.

A zone focused on the two lakes, **Ambondro** and **Sirave**, was declared a Ramsar Wetland of International Importance on World Wetlands Day in 2015. These lakes are particularly interesting since they are fady to the local people so have been undisturbed for generations. Local legend tells of many beasts said to live in Kirindy-Mitea, including a half-horse half-zebu, a mangrove swamp monster called Bahisatsy, a wild man called Hako, and a Herculean man who once ripped a gigantic *nato* tree from its roots.

The less mythological wildlife more likely to be encountered by tourists includes most of the species of lemur that can be found in Kirindy or Andranomena, as well as ring-tails (this is the northern limit of their territory). 'The park is a veritable kingdom of baobabs with three species and a density of these trees unparalleled elsewhere,' notes Mark Fenn of WWF. 'The lakes near to Manahy have over 30 species of birds (many rare) and endangered waterfowl.'

ANDRANOPASY The very small village of Andranopasy is conveniently located midway between Belo-sur-Mer and Morombe. It has just one hotel, **Djamat** (€–€€), with seven very basic bungalows. There is no cellphone coverage and only a very limited selection of food available, but the hotel can prepare meals with advance warning.

MOROMBE Morombe is a crumbling shadow of its former colonial grandeur, but after dark it becomes quite a party town no matter what the day of the week (with some particularly bold and persistent prostitutes). During the daytime there's a fairly extensive market, as well as several small shops, a post office and a branch of BOA – the only bank between Morondava and Toliara (⊕ *Mon–Fri 08.30–11.35 & 14.30–16.30*). There is good cellphone reception.

The town essentially comprises two roads running parallel to the beach. Most administrative buildings are on the landward road, while the centre of activity after dark is along the seaward road. Here you will find **Eclipse (Chez Papa Dorant)**, a restaurant and discotheque that was built for the influx of eclipse-chasing tourists in 2001. Many travellers treat Morombe as a transit town on the journey to or from Andavadoaka, but there are a couple of decent hotels if you plan to linger, as well as some very cheap ones for those on a budget.

A drive of some 22km northeast of Morombe, at Mangolovolo, is Madagascar's **fattest baobab**. For some reason it has become a particularly popular tourist site among Japanese visitors, who affectionately refer to the tree as 'Sumo'.

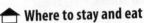 Where to stay and eat

🏠 **Pirogue d'Or (Lakana Volamena)** (12 bungalows) m 032 02 147 24/032 55 474 60; e moromberbe98@yahoo.fr; www. piroguedormoromberbe.com. South of town. Lovely bungalows with en-suite bathrooms (hot water), safe, minibar & sat-TV; but atmosphere strangely tense. **€€€–€€€€**

🏠 **Baobab** (15 bungalows) m 034 05 000 58/034 11 001 58; e nassim.tahora@gmail.com. South of town, facing the sea. En-suite with hot water. Restaurant. **€€€**

🏠 **Croix du Sud** (8 bungalows) m 032 47 855 18. North end of town. Rooms with cold-water facilities. Bar. **€€€**

🏠 **Crabe** (10 bungalows) e baynbb@yahoo.fr. North end of town. En-suite bungalows with sea view & simpler ones behind. **€–€€**

🏠 **Datier** (12 bungalows) Basic bungalows with en-suite cold shower; communal toilets. Electricity. **€**

✖ **Pyramides** Opposite Croix du Sud. Recommended for a good meal at very reasonable prices.

✖ **Sea Food** m 032 83 933 07. Tremendous *fruits de mer* near the fuel station north of town on the landward road.

ANDAVADOAKA 'This is a remote village but tremendously rewarding as a result; a very different experience from the beach resorts like Ifaty and Anakao,' writes Richard Nimmo of Blue Ventures. 'It is a place where you can truly experience local culture and see the lives of fishermen unchanged for centuries. It is one of the largest fishing communities on the southwest coast and on a calm morning the fleet of outrigger canoes sailing out to fish at dawn is a magical sight.'

The area can boast the richest marine ecosystem on the southwest coast, and has therefore become the home for many migrating fishermen, as well as a developing tourist resort. Manta rays and turtles are regularly seen, with seasonal migrations of humpback whales between June and October and phenomenal megapods of up to 500 dolphins have also been sighted in recent years. The area is the main base of marine conservation organisation Blue Ventures. They have helped train local 'eco-guides' whose services can be enlisted at Blue Ventures' research and conservation centre at the southern end of the village.

Andavadoaka has a range of hotels to suit all budgets and the village's infrastructure is improving: it now has an airstrip served weekly by Air Mad and a cellphone mast (Telma).

Coral bleaching is the parting of company of coral and the algae that give it its colour. This can happen under the stress of sustained high or low temperatures or pollution. Climate change, El Niño and the associated increases in sea surface temperatures have resulted in severe coral bleaching events in recent years and represent the greatest natural threat to these systems. Bleaching events are increasing in their frequency and severity and current estimates suggest it could become an annual event within 25–50 years. Dive operators in the tourist centres of Anakao and Ifaty have claimed almost 100% mortality of hard corals in shallow sites.

In addition to large-scale natural threats, local populations have significant effects on the health of Madagascar's coral reefs. Poor land-use practices are one of the primary anthropogenic threats to coastal biodiversity, and large areas of forest have been destroyed by rapid expansion of slash-and-burn agriculture. Wide-scale burning has exacerbated soil erosion, which now affects more than 80% of Madagascar's total land area. Raised levels of siltation on coral reefs, in particular in the west, have already been widely reported, most notably on near-shore reefs close to river mouths.

There is a critical need for better knowledge and understanding of Madagascar's marine and coastal ecosystem processes. It is essential to monitor the impacts of bleaching and the recovery rates of reefs, in order to incorporate resilience and resistance factors into future selection and management of protected marine areas.

About 1½ hours south of the village by pirogue is the **Bay of Assassins**, which makes a good excursion. You can also get there by zebu cart in about an hour (20,000Ar). Near the bay you can visit Blue Ventures' aquaculture projects (community farming of sea cucumbers and red seaweed). In the same area is a spider tortoise breeding project. Eco-guides can arrange an excursion. They can also take you to a forest of bizarrely stunted (almost spherical) Grandidier's baobabs.

Less than 5km south of Andavadoaka is the little village of **Ampasilava**. Between the two villages is Laguna Blu Resort, owned by an Italian doctor who has built a hospital nearby. It has a very good reputation locally and people come from many miles around for treatment.

🏠 Where to stay and eat

🏠 **Laguna Blu Resort** (14 bungalows) Ampasilava; m 034 05 814 10/032 05 814 11; e lagunablueresort@lagunablueresort.com; www.lagunablumadagascar.com. Classy Italian-owned bungalows. Very comfy rooms with hot water. HB & FB options. €€€€

🏠 **Coco Beach** (10 bungalows) Andavadoaka; m 034 14 001 58; e nassim.tahora@gmail.com. Seafront spot at southern end of village. Old & new stone & wooden bungalows, all en suite (cold water) with veranda. €€€

🏠 **Manga Lodge** (8 bungalows) 2km south of Andavadoaka; m 034 38 192 37; e madamangalodge1@yahoo.fr. On a beautiful bay 10mins south of the village by 4x4. Nice French-owned bungalows with cold-water facilities. Food excellent & copious. €€€

🏠 **Chez Antoine** (15 bungalows) Andavadoaka. At the top of the village, simple huts with en-suite bucket showers. €–€€

Alasdair Harris, Blue Ventures

The people of Madagascar's coastal villages are culturally, economically and spiritually tied to the sea. Villagers rely on marine resources for food, transport and trade, and often hold ceremonies and erect shrines thanking their ancestors for the bounty provided by the ocean. The Vezo are known as 'the people of the sea' because of their semi-nomadic seafaring culture.

With some 3,000km of submerged coral reefs, Madagascar's coastal areas are among the most biologically diverse and yet least-studied ecosystems on earth. However, local demand for these resources is rising as a result of population growth and immigration from arid inland regions.

It has been estimated that at least half of all tourists arriving in Madagascar each year visit a coral reef area. But these areas have been largely neglected from a conservation perspective. The people of Madagascar are now beginning to take steps to protect the marine resources they rely upon for survival.

Since 2003, the remote village of Andavadoaka has been the centre of an exciting new movement in coastal management. With the help of international marine conservation group Blue Ventures, Andavadoaka's fishing community has pioneered locally managed marine reserves and fisheries closures to improve the sustainability of the region's fisheries and protect the biodiversity underpinning the Vezo way of life. These pilot reserves have produced impressive results, improving catches and encouraging neighbouring villages to get involved.

These villages established **Velondriake**, the first community-managed marine protected area (MPA) in the country. Today, Velondriake ('to live with the sea') is one of the largest locally managed marine reserves in the Indian Ocean, spanning 670km^2 and benefiting more than 7,000 people. The MPA incorporates 24 surrounding villages and protects coral reefs, mangroves, sea grass beds, baobab forests and other threatened habitats. It is governed through a *dina* – traditional village laws governing resource use that have been legalised by the state. Malagasy law gives strong enforcement and conflict resolution powers to the local communities, allowing them to levy fines for infractions of the dina.

Since 2006, other villages have been inspired to take control of their own fisheries and locally managed reserves have since been established up and down the coast. The effectiveness of Velondriake's reserves in increasing the size and catches of octopus – the region's most economically important fishery – also caught the attention of Madagascar's government, which in 2005 passed legislation creating seasonal closures of the octopus fishery nationwide.

Samba Roger, a former teacher from Andavadoaka and Velondriake's elected president, was awarded WWF's prestigious J Paul Getty Award (2009) for conservation in recognition of his outstanding leadership in conservation.

Visitors can contact him or find out about Velondriake at the Blue Ventures information centre at the southern end of the village.

The enormous accomplishments of Velondriake today are a testament to how local management of resources can be both successful and sustainable. Through creating a sense of ownership and pride in marine and coastal resources, as well as enabling communities to take lawful actions as necessary, Velondriake is achieving the primary goal of protecting marine and coastal biodiversity and traditional livelihoods in southwest Madagascar.

ANTSEPOKA AND SOUTH TO TOLIARA Just south of the Bay of Assassins, the tiny village of **Antsepoka** has a hotel called **Chez Fidel**. The eight simple huts with en-suite bucket showers have gorgeous views over a small bay backed by dunes (m *034 15 103 46*; €). The remaining stretch of coastline between here and Toliara is covered in *Chapter 9*; see pages 235–41.

RIVER TRIPS

Descending a river by boat offers an excellent way to access remote areas of Madagascar. Combining a river journey with standard overland, biking or trekking programmes can make an ideal adventure holiday. Several tour operators offer comfortable, well-catered river trips and multi-activity itineraries suitable for all ages and interests. The most popular are floats on the lazy western rivers, five of which are detailed below.

Many of the tour operators listed in *Chapter 4* can organise river trips on comfortable vessels with good food, camping equipment and experienced guides. Particular specialists are **Remote River Expeditions** (see pages 90 and 427) who take small groups on all the main rivers of Madagascar and have pioneered several new trips.

Be aware that some boats are quite shadeless, so take adequate sun protection and plenty of water, and pack your bags to protect sensitive items – one reader's rucksack got so hot in the sun that his camera film and tent both melted inside! When camping, if you need to use a sandbank as a toilet, make sure to bury your waste properly. And be certain to take all your trash away with you.

TSIRIBIHINA RIVER This is an increasingly popular trip that can easily be organised from the base town of Miandrivazo (see page 434). The boat guides have organised themselves into a professional association, AGPM; wherever you are staying, someone from AGPM will find you. The most popular operator is Papola (owned by Pirogue Hotel) whose comfortable fleet of canvas-shaded boats has sunloungers on the upper deck and a covered dining area staffed by excellent cooks.

However, there are no toilets on board and at the time of writing no toilet tent or privacy screen is provided at the campsites. With several boatloads of campers overnighting on the same sandbanks night after night, human waste and toilet paper is very much in evidence near the bushes that provide scant privacy. This situation will hopefully improve soon.

From Miandrivazo it's a 2-hour drive to Masay Camp where you join the river. If you arrive on market day – Wednesday – you will find it hard to progress to the boat mooring against the flow of humanity. The river descent takes 3–5 days and most people love it for the wildlife seen from the boat (mainly birdlife) as well as the glimpses of rural life on the riverbanks. Tiffany Coates did it by pirogue and noted that they saw more wildlife than others who opted for (noisier) motorboats. 'The three-day pirogue trip was one of the highlights of my whole time in Madagascar,' she remarked. But the gentle simplicity is not to everyone's taste: reader Patrick Laughlin described it as 'the most boring river I have ever floated, and I have floated many rivers in many countries'.

In the dry season you will camp on sandbanks, but if you come in the rainy season you will stay overnight in villages. Being the most popular river trip can mean that you will be camping alongside several other groups. Avoid this boat journey in June, July and August if the thought of seeing lots of other tourists *en route* depresses you. The descent ends at Belo-sur-Tsiribihina, covered on page 419.

Miandrivazo Said to be the hottest place in Madagascar, the town lies on the banks of the Mahajilo, a tributary of the Tsiribihina. Legend has it that the name comes from when King Radama was waiting for his messenger to return with Rasalimo, the Sakalava princess with whom he had fallen in love. He fell into a pensive mood and, when asked if he was well, replied 'Miandry vazo aho' ('I am waiting for a wife').

The town is a typical lowland Malagasy community, the main street stretching for a couple of kilometres and lined with open-sided wooden shops providing every imaginable service or goods (including a bank with ATM). There's a WaterAid depot providing clean water, tailors, cobblers, welders and a video shack showing incomprehensible films – the whole place is great fun.

🏠 Where to stay and eat

🏠 **Princesse Tsiribihina** (13 rooms) m 032 04 828 45/034 05 828 45; e princesse-tsiribihina@ espacemada.com. Clean & comfy en-suite rooms 1km from town; lovely view over the valley. Swimming pool. €€€–€€€€

🏠 **Arc en Ciel** (9 rooms) m 032 26 700 60/033 19 541 41; e jimmica.randriakoto@gmail.com. Dbl rooms with fan & some with en-suite facilities. €€–€€€

🏠 **Mango** Pleasant rooms. Good pizza. €€–€€€

🏠 **Chez la Reine Rasalimo** Concrete bungalows on a hill overlooking the river. Dbl & trpl rooms with mosquito nets & fans; good food. €€

🏠 **Pirogue** (6 rooms & 6 bungalows) m 032 07 508 37 (manager)/032 41 333 93. Reasonable, basic hotel with great views. €€

🏠 **Gîte de Tsiribihina** A simple hotel with basic rooms. €–€€

🏠 **Laizama** Simple rooms & helpful staff. 'We often found ducks in the shower,' notes R Harris. €

MANAMBOLO RIVER This trip typically takes three days (though five allows for some rest and sightseeing), beginning at Ankavandra, west of Tana. It is a spectacular journey through the untouched homeland of the Sakalava. On the third day you pass through the dramatic Manambolo Gorge between towering limestone cliffs, and through Tsingy de Bemaraha National Park. The chances of seeing the area's special wildlife, such as Decken's sifaka and the Madagascar fish eagle, are high. The finishing point of the river descent is Bekopaka, the gateway town for visiting the park.

MANGOKY RIVER The journey of some 160km from Beroroha to Bevoay runs through an isolated region in the southwest of the island, with no roads north or south of the river for more than 100km. This calm water stretch offers expansive beaches for camping and many unexplored side canyons. The Mangoky passes through sections of dry deciduous forests which are dominated by perhaps the largest baobab forest on earth, with three species including the huge *Adansonia grandidieri*.

However, this is no longer a pristine experience as large fires to the south in recent years have forced local populations to move closer to the river; small villages are appearing and the effects of their presence are bound to become more evident.

MAHAVAVY RIVER The Mahavavy was first explored in 1998, when the rafting team from Remote River Expeditions put in at Kandreho and ended in Mitsinjo. The area is extremely rich in both lemurs and birds (including fish eagles), with large expanses of beautiful forest. Lemur-viewing is far superior to the other western rivers, with plenty of Decken's and crowned sifakas and red-fronted brown lemurs – especially around the Kasijy Forest and the riverine tamarind gallery forest between Bekipay and Ambinany.

ONILAHY RIVER With the recent establishment of Tsinjoriake and Amoron'i Onilahy protected areas, ecotourism infrastructure is being put in place, including provision for travellers wishing to descend the Onilahy from the Sept Lacs region to Toliara. See pages 233–5 for more information.

Appendix 1

HISTORICAL CHRONOLOGY

2000BC	Some recent archaeological evidence suggests humans reached Madagascar more than 4,000 years ago.
AD500	Approximate date of first significant settlement of the island.
850	First known villages in north; penetration of the interior begins in south.
1200	Establishment of Arab settlements. First mosques built.
1500	'Discovery' of Madagascar by the Portuguese Diego Dias. Unsuccessful attempts to establish permanent European bases on the island followed.
1650s	Emergence of Sakalava kingdoms.
1700s	Eastern Madagascar increasingly used as a base by pirates.
1716	Fénérive captured by Ratsimilaho. Betsimisaraka confederacy begins.
1750	Death of Ratsimilaho.
1787	The future Andrianampoinimerina declared King of Ambohimanga.
1795–96	Andrianampoinimerina established his capital at Antananarivo.
1810–28	Reign of Radama I, Merina king.
1818–20	First mission schools opened in Tamatave (Toamasina) and Antananarivo.
1823	Writing system for Malagasy established using Latin characters.
1828–61	Reign of Ranavalona I, Merina queen.
1835	Publication of the Bible in Malagasy, but Christian faith outlawed.

THE ORDEAL OF *TANGENA*   *Hilary Bradt*

James Hastie, royal tutor in 1817, described one of the more barbaric tortures that King Radama I was using on his subjects: the Ordeal of *Tangena*. *Tangena* is a Malagasy shrub with a poisonous fruit. This poison was used to determine the guilt or innocence of a suspected criminal. A 'meal' consisting of three pieces of chicken skin, rice and the crushed *tangena* kernel was prepared. The suspect was then forced to drink large quantities of water to induce vomiting. If all three pieces of chicken skin reappeared the person was innocent (but often died anyway). If the skin remained in the stomach the unfortunate suspect was killed, usually after limbs, or bits of limbs and other extremities, had been lopped off first.

One of the successes of Hastie's influence on the king was that the monarch agreed that, although the Ordeal of *Tangena* should continue, dogs could stand in for the accused. This decision was ignored by Queen Ranavalona who used it freely on the Christian martyrs she persecuted with such enthusiasm. Sir Mervyn Brown estimates that several thousand Malagasy met their deaths through the *tangena* shrub during Queen Ranavalona's long reign.

The Ordeal of *Tangena* was finally abolished by King Radama II in 1861.

KING RADAMA II'S SHAM ASSASSINATION
Hilary Bradt

The son of the 'Wicked Queen' Ranavalona, King Radama II was a gentle ruler who abhorred bloodshed. He was pro-European, interested in Christianity (although never formally a Christian) and a friend of missionary William Ellis. After Radama's death, Ellis wrote: 'I have never said that Radama was an able ruler, or a man of large views, for these he was not; but a more humane ruler never wore a crown.' With missionaries of all denominations invited back into Madagascar, intense rivalry sprang up between the Protestants sent by Britain, and the Jesuits who arrived from France. Resentment at the influence of these foreigners over the young king, and disgust at the often rash changes he instigated, boiled over in 1863, and only eight months after his coronation he was assassinated – strangled with a silken sash so that the *fady* against shedding royal blood was not infringed.

The French–British rivalry was fuelled by the violent death of the king; Ellis was even accused of being party to the assassination. But was Radama really dead? Both Ellis and Jean Laborde believed that he had survived the strangling and had been allowed to escape by the courtiers bearing him to the countryside for burial. Uprisings supposedly organised by the 'dead' king supported this rumour. Historian Raymond Delval makes a strong case that the ex-monarch eventually retreated to the area of Lake Kinkony and lived out the rest of his life in this Sakalava region.

1836	Most Europeans and missionaries leave the island.
1861–63	Reign of Radama II, Merina king.
1861	Missionaries readmitted. Freedom of religion proclaimed.
1863–68	Queen Rasoherina succeeds after Radama II assassinated.
1868–83	Reign of Queen Ranavalona II.
1883	Coronation of Queen Ranavalona III.
1883–85	Franco–Malagasy War.
1895–96	Establishment of full French protectorate; then a full colony a year later.
1897	Ranavalona III exiled (to Réunion, then Algiers); Merina monarchy abolished.
1917	Death of Ranavalona III in exile.
1942	British troops occupy Madagascar, seizing military control from French.
1946	Madagascar becomes an Overseas Territory of France.
1947	Nationalist rebellion suppressed with thousands killed.
1960	Madagascar achieves full independence with Philibert Tsiranana as president.
1972	Parliament dissolved; power handed to General Ramanantsoa who ends France's special position and establishes relations with communist countries.
1975	Lt Cdr Didier Ratsiraka named head of state after a coup. Country renamed Democratic Republic of Madagascar; Ratsiraka elected president.
1976	Ratsiraka nationalises large parts of the economy and forms AREMA party.
1980	Economy collapses and IMF called in. Market economy gradually introduced.
1984	The first Bradt Guide to Madagascar is published!
1991	Demonstrations and strikes. About 130 protestors killed by Ratsiraka's forces.
1992	Under pressure of demonstrations, Ratsiraka introduces democratic reforms replacing the socialist system, but is forced to resign.
1993	Albert Zafy elected president under new constitution. Birth of Third Republic.
1996–97	Albert Zafy impeached then Didier Ratsiraka re-elected president.
2000	Elections: AREMA wins in most cities (not Tana); only 30% turnout.

2001	Ratsiraka and Tana mayor Marc Ravalomanana both claim victory in elections.
2002	Ravalomanana recognised as president after six-month stalemate.
2003	Ravalomanana announces plan to triple size of Madagascar's protected areas.
2006	Ravalomanana wins second term and announces 'Madagascar Action Plan'.
2007	English declared an official language, alongside Malagasy and French.
2009	Ravalomanana toppled from power in a coup; 34-year-old Tana mayor Andry Rajoelina appoints himself president of the 'High Transitional Authority'.
2010	Rajoelina establishes new constitution lowering minimum age for presidential candidates from 40 to 35 (and removing English as an official language).
2013	Presidential elections finally go ahead after years of stalling.
2014	Former Minister of Finance Hery Rajaonarimampianina becomes president.

THE TWO-MAN INDUSTRIAL REVOLUTION   *Hilary Bradt*

Technology was largely introduced to Madagascar by two remarkable Europeans: James Cameron, a Scot, and Jean Laborde, a Frenchman.

James Cameron arrived in Madagascar in 1826 during the country's 'British phase' when the London Missionary Society had attempted to set up local craftsmen to produce goods in wood, metal, leather and cotton. Aged just 26, Cameron was already a skilled carpenter and weaver when he arrived, and had a broad knowledge of physics, chemistry, mathematics, architecture and astronomy. Cameron seemed able to turn his hand to almost anything mechanical. Among his achievements were setting up Madagascar's first printing press (by studying the manual, since the printer sent out with the press had died), a reservoir, an aqueduct, and the production of bricks.

Cameron's success in making soap from local materials ensured his royal favour after King Radama died and the xenophobic Queen Ranavalona came to power. But when Christian practice was forbidden in 1835, he left.

He returned in 1863, when they were once more welcome in Madagascar, to oversee the building of stone churches, a hospital, and the stone exterior to the original wooden *rova* built by Jean Laborde in Tana in 1839.

Jean Laborde was even more of a renaissance man. He was shipwrecked off the east coast of Madagascar in 1831. Queen Ranavalona, no doubt pleased to find a less godly European, asked him to manufacture muskets and gunpowder, and he soon filled the gap left by the departure of Cameron and the others. Laborde's initiative and inventiveness were amazing: in a huge industrial complex built by forced labour, he produced munitions and arms, bricks, tiles, pottery, glass, porcelain, silk, soap, candles, cement, dyes, sugar, rum... in fact just about everything a thriving country in the 19th century needed. He ran a farm which experimented with suitable crops and animals, and a country estate for the Merina royalty and aristocracy to enjoy such novelties as firework displays.

So successful was Laborde in making Madagascar self-sufficient that foreign trade was discontinued and foreigners expelled. He remained in the queen's favour until 1857 when he too was expelled because of involvement in a plot to replace the queen by her son. The 1,200 workmen who had laboured without pay in the foundries of Mantasoa rose up and destroyed everything. The factories were never rebuilt, and Madagascar's Industrial Revolution came to an abrupt end.

He returned in 1861 and became French consul, dying in 1878. A dispute over his inheritance was one of the pretexts for the Franco-Malagasy war.

Appendix 2

THE MALAGASY LANGUAGE

PRONUNCIATION The Malagasy alphabet is made up of just 21 letters (the English alphabet with C, Q, U, W and X omitted). Pronunciation is as follows:

a	as in 'hat'	j	as ds in 'pads'
e	as in 'bet'	s	between the s in 'sip' and the sh
o	oo as in 'too'		in 'ship' but varies regionally
i/y	as ee in 'seen' but shorter	ai	like y in 'my'
g	as in 'get'	ao	like ow in 'cow'
h	almost silent	eo	pronounced ey-oo

STRESSED SYLLABLES Some syllables are stressed, others almost eliminated. This causes great problems for visitors and unfortunately – like in English – the basic rules are frequently broken. Generally, the stress is on the penultimate syllable, except in words ending in -na, -ka and -tra where stress shifts forward to the preceding syllable.

Occasionally a word may change its meaning depending on how it is stressed: *tánana* means 'hand', and *tanána* means 'town'. (This phenomenon is also common in English: *desért* means 'abandon', and *désert* means 'a barren wasteland'.)

Malagasy words always end in a vowel. Usually this final vowel is virtually silent, except in the case of -e which is always stressed. That said, there is regional variation: for example, you will hear *azafady* ('please/pardon') pronounced both as 'azafad' and 'azafadee'.

GETTING STARTED The easiest way to begin to get a grip on Malagasy is to build on your knowledge of place names (you have to learn how to pronounce these in order to get around). As often noted throughout this book, most place names mean something so you have only to learn these meanings and – hey presto! – you have the elements of the language. Here are some bits of place names:

an-, am-, i-	at, the place where	*manga*	blue, good, mango
arivo	thousand	*maro*	many
be	big, plenty of	*mena*	red
fotsy, -potsy	white	*nosy, nosi-*	island
kely, keli-	small	*rano, -drano*	water
kily	tamarind	*tany, tani-*	land
mafana	hot	*tsara*	good
maha	which causes	*tsy, tsi-*	not, none
mainty, mainti-	black	*vato, -bato*	stone
maintso	green	*vohitra, vohi-, -bohi-*	hill, mountain

Thus Ambohitsara is 'the place of the good mountain': am-bohi-tsara.

VOCABULARY   Stressed letters or syllables are underlined.

Social phrases

English	Malagasy	Phonetic pronunciation
Hello	Manao ahoana	mano oown
	Salama	salam
	Mbola tsara	m'boola tsar
	Manakory/Akory	manakoory/akoory
What news?	Inona no vaovao?	inoon vowvow?
No news	Tsy misy (vaovao)	tsimeess (vowvow)

The preferred word for 'hello' varies regionally, but *manao ahoana* will be understood wherever you go. These easy-to-learn phrases of ritualised greeting establish contact with people you pass on the road or meet in a village. For extra courtesy (important in Madagascar) add *tompoko*, pronounced 'toomp'k', at the end of each phrase.

Simple phrases for conversation

English	Malagasy	Phonetic pronunciation
What's your name?	Iza no anaranao?	eeza nanaranow
My name is…	Ny anarako…	ny anarakoo
Goodbye	Veloma	veloom
See you again	Mandra pihaona	mandra pioon
I don't understand	Tsy azoko	tsi azook
I don't know	Tsy haiko	tsi haikoo
Very good	Tsara tokoa	tsara t'koo
Bad	Ratsy	rats
Please/Excuse me	Azafady	azafad
Thank you	Misaotra	misowtr
Thank you very much	Misaotra betsaka	misowtr betsak
Pardon (may I pass)	Ombay lalana	m'bay lalan
Let's go	Andao andeha	andow anday
Cheers!	Ho ela velona!	wellavell
I have nothing	Tsy misy	tsimeess
I don't need it	Fa tsy mila	fatseemeel
Go away!	Mandehana!	mandayhan

Note: the words for yes (*eny*) and no (*tsia*) are hardly ever used in conversation. The Malagasy tend to say *yoh* for yes and *ah* for no, along with appropriate gestures.

Numbers

English	Malagasy	Phonetic pronunciation
1	iray/iraika	rai
2	roa	roo
3	telo	teloo
4	efatra	efatr
5	dimy	deem
6	enina	enna
7	fito	feetoo
8	valo	valoo
9	sivy	seev
10	folo	fooloo
100	zato	zatoo
1,000	arivo	areevoh

440

Market phrases

English	Malagasy	Phonetic pronunciation
How much?	*Ohatrinona?*	*ow<u>treen</u>*
Too expensive!	*Lafo be!*	*laffbay*
No way!	*Tsy lasa!*	*tseelass*

Basic needs

English	Malagasy	Phonetic pronunciation
Where is…?	*Aiza…?*	*ayza*
Is it far?	*Lavitra ve izany?*	*<u>lav</u>tra vay<u>zan</u>*
Is there any…?	*Misy ve…?*	*mees vay*
I want…	*Mila… aho*	*meel… aa*
I'm looking for…	*Mitady… aho*	*m'tadi… aa*
Is there a place to sleep?	*Misy toerana hatoriana ve?*	*mees too ayran atureen vay*
Is it ready?	*Vita ve?*	*<u>vee</u>ta vay*
I would like to buy some food	*Te hividy sakafo aho*	*tayveed sa<u>kaff</u> wah*
I'm hungry	*Noana aho*	*noo<u>nah</u>*
I'm thirsty	*Mangetaheta aho*	*mangataytah*
I'm tired	*Vizaka aho*	*veesa<u>kaa</u>*
Please help me!	*Mba ampio aho!*	*bampeewhaa*

Useful words

English	Malagasy	Phonetic pronunciation
village	*vohitra*	*voo<u>ee</u>tra*
house	*trano*	*tran*
road	*lalana*	*lalan*
town	*tanana*	*ta<u>nan</u>*
river	*ony*	*oon*
rivulet	*riaka*	*reek*
child/baby	*ankizy/zaza kely*	*ankeeze/zaza kail*
man/woman	*lehilahy/vehivavy*	*lay<u>laa</u>/vay<u>yaav</u>*
food/meal	*hanina/sakafo*	*anee/sa<u>kaff</u>*
water	*rano*	*rahn*
rice	*vary*	*var*
eggs	*atody*	*atood*
chicken	*akoho*	*akoo*
bread	*mofo*	*moof*
milk	*ronono*	*roonoon*
fish	*trondro*	*<u>troo</u>ndr*
meat	*hena*	*hen*
pig/pork	*kisoa*	*kisoo*
duck	*gana*	*gan*
zebu/beef	*omby*	*oomby*
sugar	*siramamy*	*seera<u>mam</u>*
tea	*dite*	*deetay*
coffee	*kafe*	*kafay*
salt	*sira*	*seer*
beer	*labiera*	*labee<u>air</u>*
butter	*dibera*	*diberr*
potato	*ovy*	*oov*
beans	*tsaramaso*	*tsaramass*

Note: in Malagasy the plural form of a noun is the same as the singular form.

Appendix 3

FURTHER INFORMATION

BOOKS Madagascar's historical links with Britain and the current interest in its natural history and culture have produced a century of excellent books written in English. This bibliography is a selection of our favourites in each category. Note that many are out of print but may be found secondhand.

General: history, the country, the people

Allen, P M & Covell M *Historical Dictionary of Madagascar* Scarecrow, USA 2005 (2nd ed). A pricey (£58) but very comprehensive dictionary of important people and events in Madagascar's political, economic, social and cultural history from early times to present day.

Austin, D & Bradt, H *Madagascar Highlights* Bradt Travel Guides (UK); Globe Pequot Press (USA) 2012. A full-colour guidebook aimed at travellers on an organised or group tour.

Bradt, H *Madagascar* (World Bibliographical Series) Clio (UK); ABC (USA) 1992. An annotated selection of nearly 400 titles on Madagascar, from the classic early works to those published in the early 1990s.

Brown, M A *History of Madagascar* D Tunnacliffe, UK 1996. The most accurate, comprehensive and readable of the histories, brought completely up to date by Britain's foremost expert on the subject.

Clifford, B *Return to Treasure Island and the Search for Captain Kidd* HarperCollins 2003. The story of Captain Kidd and the author's expedition to search for his ship, the *Adventure Galley*.

Covell, M *Madagascar: Politics, Economics and Society* (Marxist Regimes series) Frances Pinter, UK 1987. An interesting look at Madagascar's Marxist past.

Croft-Cooke, R *The Blood-Red Island* Staples, UK 1953. A racy and engaging account of a somewhat unconventional officer's adventures during British occupation in 1942.

Crook, S *Distant Shores: By Traditional Canoe from Asia to Madagascar* Impact Books, UK 1990. The story of the 4,000-mile Sarimanok Expedition by outrigger canoe from Bali to Madagascar. An interesting account of an eventful and historically important journey.

Dodwell, C *Madagascar Travels* Hodder & Stoughton, UK 1995. An account of a journey through Madagascar's most remote regions by one of Britain's leading travel writers.

Donenfeld, J *Mankafy Sakafo: Delicious Meals from Madagascar* iUniverse, USA 2007. The first English-language cookbook of Malagasy cuisine (the title means 'tasty food'). Some 70 recipes interspersed with endearing tales of the author's travels in Madagascar.

Drysdale, H *Dancing with the Dead: A Journey through Zanzibar and Madagascar* Hamish Hamilton, UK 1991. An account of Helena's journeys in search of her trading ancestor. Informative, entertaining and well written.

Ecott, T *Vanilla* Penguin, 2004. The UK and US editions are subtitled 'travels in search of the luscious substance' and 'travels in search of the ice cream orchid' respectively. Among other places, the author visits Madagascar, the world's biggest producer of this fragrant pod.

Ellis, W *Madagascar Revisited* John Murray, UK 1867. The Rev William Ellis of the London Missionary Society was one of the most observant and sympathetic of the missionary writers. His books are well worth the search for secondhand copies.

Eveleigh, M *Maverick in Madagascar* (Lonely Planet Journeys) Lonely Planet, Australia 2001. A well-written account of an exceptionally adventurous trip in the north of Madagascar.

Fox, L *Hainteny: The Traditional Poetry of Madagascar* Associated University Presses, UK & Canada 1990. Over 400 beautifully translated *hainteny* with an excellent introduction to the history and spiritual life of the Merina.

Grandinetti, R *Final Solution: Germany's Madagascar Resettlement Plan* The Barnes Review, USA 2012. A little-known chapter of history: how the world might have been had Hitler stuck to his original plan to send the Jews to Madagascar.

Grehan, J *The Forgotten Invasion: The Story of Britain's First Large-Scale Combined Operation, the Invasion of Madagascar 1942* Historic Military Press, UK 2007. Detailed account of a little-known aspect of Anglo-Malagasy history by a leading military historian.

Grunewald, O & Wolozan, D *Tsingy – Stone Forest* Madagascar Editions Altus, France 2006. Stunning photography of Tsingy de Bemaraha.

Laidler, K *Female Caligula: Ranavalona, the Mad Queen of Madagascar* John Wiley, UK 2005. The fascinating tale of Ranavalona's bizarre reign.

Lanting, F *Madagascar: A World out of Time* Robert Hale, UK 1991. A book of stunning, and somewhat surreal, photos of the landscape, people and wildlife. Text by renowned Madagascar experts John Mack and Alison Jolly.

Manser, R *Around Madagascar on My Kayak* Jonathan Ball, South Africa 2012. The extraordinary tale of the author's 2009 bid to become the first person to circumnavigate the world's fourth-largest island by kayak.

McCaughrean, G *Plundering Paradise* Oxford University Press, UK 1996. Children's fiction (but good light reading for adults too) based on the story of pirate's son Ratsimilaho. An English brother and sister get caught up in real pirate adventures.

Murphy, D *Muddling through in Madagascar* John Murray, UK 1985. An entertaining account of a journey (by foot and truck) through the highlands and south.

Parker Pearson, M & Godden, K *In Search of the Red Slave* Sutton Publishing, UK 2002. An archaeological team goes in search of Robert Drury. An absorbing account which reads like a whodunit, but is equally interesting as a portrait of the Tandroy people.

Randrianja, S & Ellis, S *Madagascar: A Short History* Hurst, UK 2009. A general history of the country presented chronologically.

Rasoloson, J *Malagasy–English/English–Malagasy Dictionary and Phrasebook* Hippocrene, USA 2001. Handy local language guide for travellers.

Sibree, J *Madagascar Before the Conquest: The Island, the Country, and the People* T Fisher Unwin, UK 1896. Sibree (with William Ellis) was the main documenter of Madagascar during the days of the London Missionary Society.

Spong, C *Madagascar: Rail and Mail* Indian Ocean Study Circle, 2003. Available from Eric Hatton (*29 Paternoster Close, Waltham Abbey, EN9 3JU*). £12 plus postage. A monograph detailing the country's philately and railways.

van den Boogaerde, P *Shipwrecks of Madagascar* Eloquent, USA 2009. An overview of around a hundred notable shipwrecks off Malagasy shores.

Ethnography

Astuti, R *People of the Sea: Identity and Descent among the Vezo of Madagascar* Cambridge University Press, UK 1995. An academic exploration of what it means to be Vezo.

Bloch, M *From Blessing to Violence* Cambridge University Press, UK 1986. History and ideology of the circumcision ritual of the Merina people.

Ewins, E *Fihamy: A Living Legend* Blurb, USA 2005. An analysis of Malagasy oral tradition in a Masikoro village, centred on a banyan tree.

Haring, L *How to Read a Folktale: The Ibonia Epic from Madagascar* Open Book Publishers, UK 2013. The spellbinding first English translation of a traditional Malagasy folk epic.

Haring, L *Verbal Arts in Madagascar: Performance in Historical Perspective* University of Pennsylvania Press, USA 1992. Study of Malagasy folklore including more than a hundred translated riddles, proverbs, *hainteny* and oratories.

Lambek, M *The Weight of the Past: Living with History in Mahajanga* Palgrave Macmillan, USA 2002. The author looks at the role of history in the identity of the Sakalava.

Mack, J *Madagascar: Island of the Ancestors* British Museum, UK 1986. A scholarly and informative account of the ethnography of Madagascar.

Mack, J *Malagasy Textiles* Shire Publications, UK 1989.

Powe, E L *Lore of Madagascar* Dan Aiki (*530 W Johnson St, Apt 210, Madison, WI 53703*), USA 1994. An immense work – over 700 pages and 260 colour photos – with a price to match. This is the only book to describe in detail and in a readable form all 39 ethnic groups in Madagascar.

Ruud, J *Taboo: A Study of Malagasy Customs and Beliefs* Oslo University Press/George Allen & Unwin, UK 1960. Written by a Norwegian Lutheran missionary who worked for 20 years in Madagascar. A detailed study of *fady, vintana* and other Malagasy beliefs.

Sharp, L A *The Possessed and the Dispossessed: Spirits, Identity and Power in a Madagascar Migrant Town* University of California Press, USA 1993. Describes the daily life and the phenomenon of possession (*tromba*) in the town of Ambanja.

Sharp, L A *The Sacrificed Generation: Youth, History and the Colonized Mind in Madagascar* University of California Press, USA 2002. An academic but very readable look at the role of the younger generation in Madagascar.

Wilson, P J *Freedom by a Hair's Breadth* University of Michigan, USA 1993. An anthropological study of the Tsimihety people, written in a clear style and accessible to the general reader.

Natural history (general literature)

Attenborough, D *Zoo Quest to Madagascar* Lutterworth, UK 1961. Still one of the best travel books ever written about Madagascar, with, of course, plenty of original wildlife observations. Out of print, but copies can be found; more readily available as part of the three-book compilation *Journeys to the Past* (1981).

Durrell, G *The Aye-aye and I* HarperCollins, UK 1992. The focal point is the collecting of aye-ayes for Jersey Zoo, written in the inimitable Durrell style with plenty of humour and travellers' tales.

Goodman, S & Jungers, W *Extinct Madagascar: Picturing the Island's Past* University of Chicago, USA 2014. Impressive hardback presentation of the Malagasy fauna no longer living.

Heying, H E *Antipode: Seasons with the Extraordinary Wildlife and Culture of Madagascar* St Martin's, USA 2002. Herpetologist Heather Heying recounts her experiences studying mantella frogs on Nosy Mangabe and presents her own view of the Malagasy.

Jolly, A *A World Like Our Own: Man and Nature in Madagascar* Yale University Press, USA 1980. The first and still the best look at the relationship between the natural history and people of the island. Highly readable.

Jolly, A *Lords and Lemurs* Houghton Mifflin, USA 2004. The long-awaited sequel to *A World Like Our Own*. Alison Jolly knows Berenty better than anyone and writes about it better than anyone. This is a marvellous blend of scientific and anthropological fact in a book that reads like a novel. It's funny, engrossing and often surprising.

Jolly, A *Thank You, Madagascar* Zed Books, UK 2015. An autobiographical look back over the author's 50-year relationship with Madagascar, with extracts from her conservation diaries.

Pakenham, T *The Remarkable Baobab* Weidenfeld & Nicolson, UK 2004. A follow-up to *Remarkable Trees of the World* by the same author. This is the story of the baobab, six out of eight species of which live exclusively in Madagascar.

Preston-Mafham, K *Madagascar: A Natural History* Facts on File, UK & USA 1991. The most enjoyable and useful book on the subject. Illustrated with superb colour photos (coffee-table format), it is as good for identifying strange invertebrates and unusual plants as in describing animal behaviour.

Quammen, D *The Song of the Dodo* Hutchinson, UK 1996. An interesting account of island biogeography and its implications for nature reserves.

Thompson, P *Madagascar: The Great Red Island* UK 2004. A self-published account of travels in Madagascar by a botanist, so of particular interest to plant lovers. There's a useful appendix on plant names.

Tyson, P *The Eighth Continent: Life, Death and Discovery in the Lost World of Madagascar* Bradt Travel Guides (UK); Globe Pequot Press (USA) 2013. An American journalist's description of accompanying four scientific expeditions in Madagascar, with American, British and Malagasy scientists. Interspersed with extensive information on Madagascar's history, archaeology and natural history.

Weinberg, S *A Fish Caught in Time* Fourth Estate, UK 1999. The fascinating tale of the 1938 discovery of a live coelacanth – a fish previously believed extinct for millions of years – off Madagascar's shores.

Wendenbaum, E *Makay: A la découverte du dernier Eden* Martinière, France 2011. Stunning coffee-table book about the remote Makay Massif. The text is French but the book is mainly pictorial, including 28 3D images.

Wilson, J *Lemurs of the Lost World: Exploring the Forests and Crocodile Caves of Madagascar* Impact Books, USA 1990. Revised 1995. An amusing and lively account of British scientific expeditions to Ankarana and subsequent travels in Madagascar.

Wright, P & Larrey, F *Madagascar: Forests of our Ancestors* Biotope, France 2010. Beautifully illustrated coffee-table book about the Malagasy rainforest by the worldwide lemur expert responsible for setting up Ranomafana National Park. English or French edition.

Natural history (specialist literature and field guides)

Cribb, P & Hermans, J *Field Guide to the Orchids of Madagascar* Royal Botanic Gardens, Kew, UK 2009. Guide to Madagascar's extensive orchid flora; over 750 colour photos.

Dorr, L J *Plant Collectors in Madagascar and the Comoro Islands* Royal Botanic Gardens, Kew, UK 1997. Biographical and bibliographical information on over a thousand individuals and groups.

Dransfield, J & Beentje, H *The Palms of Madagascar* Royal Botanic Gardens, Kew, UK 1996. A beautiful and much-needed book describing the many palm species of Madagascar.

Dransfield, J, Beentje, H, Britt, A, Ranarivelo, T & Razafitsalama, J *Field Guide to the Palms of Madagascar* Royal Botanic Gardens, Kew, UK 2006. A guide to more than a hundred of the native palms with over 180 colour photos plus distribution maps for each species.

Garbutt, N *Mammals of Madagascar: A Complete Guide* A&C Black, UK 2007. This completely revised and updated guide contains photographs and distribution maps for all Malagasy mammals, including dozens of newly described species. Very comprehensive. Paperback; suitable for use as a field guide.

Garbutt, N & Austin, D *Madagascar Wildlife: A Visitor's Guide* Bradt Travel Guides (UK); Globe Pequot Press (USA) 2014 (4th ed). A photographic guide to the island's most interesting and appealing wildlife, including where best to see it.

Glaw, F & Vences, M A *Field Guide to the Amphibians and Reptiles of Madagascar* 2007. The third edition of this thorough guide to the herpetofauna gives over 700 detailed species profiles and 1,500 colour photos. Available through NHBS. Also available in Malagasy.

Goodman, S & Benstead, J *The Natural History of Madagascar* Chicago University Press, USA 2004. The most thorough and comprehensive account yet published. The island's geology, climate, human ecology and impact, marine ecosystems, plants, invertebrates, fish, amphibians, reptiles, birds, mammals and conservation written by no fewer than 281 authorities in their field. A hefty 1,709 pages.

Hawkins, F, Safford, R & Skerrett, A *Birds of Madagascar and the Indian Ocean Islands* Christopher Helm, UK 2015. Truly excellent illustrated ornithological field guide.

Hermans, J, Hermans, C, Cribb, P, Bosser, J & Du Puy, D *Orchids of Madagascar* Royal Botanic Gardens, Kew, UK 2007. A checklist of all known Malagasy orchid species, with complete bibliography, superbly illustrated with colour photos.

Hillerman, F E & Holst, A W *An Introduction to the Cultivated Angraecoid Orchids of Madagascar* Timber Press, USA 1987. Includes a good section on climate and other plant life.

Jasper, J & Gardner, C *Life Amongst the Thorns: Biodiversity & Conservation of Madagascar's Spiny Forest* John Beaufoy, UK 2015. Stunning coffee-table book on this southern habitat zone. Foreword by Sir David Attenborough.

Jovanovic, O *et al. Frogs of Madagascar: Genus Mantella* CI USA, 2008. Laminated pocket identification guide booklet.

Leuteritz, T *et al. Turtles and Tortoises of Madagascar* CI USA, 2008. Laminated pocket identification guide booklet.

Martin, J *Masters of Disguise: A Natural History of Chameleons* Facts on File (USA); Blandford (UK) 1992. Beautifully illustrated with photos by Art Wolfe; everything a chameleon aficionado could hope for.

Mittermeier, R *et al. Lemurs of Madagascar* CI USA, 2005. Laminated pocket identification guide booklet.

Mittermeier, R *et al. Diurnal and Cathemeral Lemurs of Madagascar* CI USA, 2008. Laminated pocket identification guide booklet.

Mittermeier, R *et al. Nocturnal Lemurs of Madagascar* CI USA, 2008. Laminated pocket identification guide booklet.

Mittermeier, R *et al. Lemurs of Madagascar* CI 2010 (3rd edition). An extensively updated, illustrated field guide to all Madagascar's lemurs.

Morris, P & Hawkins, F *Birds of Madagascar: A Photographic Guide* Pica Press, UK 1999. We find this well-respected guide difficult to use in the field but it is the authoritative text and photos provide serious birders with the details for reliable identification.

Pedrono, M *The Tortoises and Turtles of Madagascar* Natural History Publications, Borneo 2008. Illustrated guide to Malagasy chelonians.

Petignat, A & Cooke, B *Guide to the Succulent Plants of South-West Madagascar* Arboretum d'Antsokay, Madagascar 2016 (2nd ed). Pictorial guide to the xerophytic species in 14 plant families. Bilingual French/English.

Petignat, A & Jasper, L *Baobabs of Madagascar: Pocket Guide* 2012. Illustrated identification pamphlet for the baobab species.

Petignat, A & Jasper, L *Baobabs of the World* Struik, South Africa 2015. Authoritative guide to these fascination trees, with maps and photos.

Rauh, W *Succulent and Xerophytic Plants of Madagascar* Strawberry Press, USA 1995 & 1998. In two volumes. Expensive but detailed and comprehensive; lavishly illustrated with photos.

Rübel, A, Hatchwell, M & MacKinnon, J *Masoala: The Eye of the Forest* Theodor Gut Verlag, Switzerland 2003. A photographic book on the Masoala National Park available in English, French and German editions.

Sinclair, I & Langrand, O *Birds of the Indian Ocean Islands* Struik, South Africa 1999. The most user-friendly of the field guides to Madagascar's birds. Clear layout with a large number of excellent illustrations and distribution maps for quick reference on the trail. No photos but see next entry.

Sinclair, I, Langrand, O & Andriamialisoa, F *A Photographic Guide to the Birds of the Indian Ocean Islands* Struik, South Africa 2006. Similar to the above guide by the same authors, but with photos instead of illustrations; bilingual English/French.

Where to buy books on Madagascar

Editions Karthala (France) 22–24 Bd Arago, 75013 Paris; www.karthala.com. This French publisher specialises in Madagascar, both for new titles & reprints.

Kew Books ☎ 01768 341899; m 07764 352570; e info@kewbooks.com; www.kewbooks.com.

Specialist sellers of the botanical publications of Royal Botanic Gardens, Kew.

Mad Books (Rupert Parker) 151 Wilberforce Rd, London N4 2SX; ☎ 020 7226 4490; e rupert@madbooks.co.uk; www.madbooks.co.uk. Rupert specialises in old & rare (out-of-print) books on

Madagascar & will send out his catalogue on request. He will also search for books.

Madagascar Library (Daniel Austin) www. madagascar-library.com. Online catalogue of 4,000 books & articles. Photocopies of items from the library can be purchased (subject to copyright). The online bookstore (*www.madagascar-library.com/shop.html*) has more than 150 in-print book & CD titles for sale.

Natural History Book Service (NHBS) 2–3 Wills Rd, Totnes, Devon TQ9 5XN; ☎01803 865913; e customer. services@nhbs.com; www.nhbs.com. Specialists in wildlife books, CDs & DVDs.

MAPS   Outside of Madagascar, the only maps that are generally available are 1:2,000,000 road maps. For more detailed maps of specific regions and towns, you will need to contact FTM; see page 171 for details.

MAGAZINES   All available internationally by subscription unless otherwise stated.

Anglo-Malagasy Society Newsletter (quarterly; English) This e-newsletter is distributed to members of the Anglo-Malagasy Society (see page 137) and covers important Malagasy news, especially political and economic.

Info Tourisme Madagascar (triannual; in French and as an e-publication in English translation) www. info-tourisme-madagascar.com. Covers developments in the tourism sector. No subscription; available from ONTM in Tana.

Madagascar Magazine (quarterly; in French) www. madagascarmagazine.com. Latest news in economics, commerce, culture & tourism.

New Magazine Madagascar (monthly; in French) Malagasy music, fashion, art & events.

Revue de l'Océan Indien (monthly; in French) www.roimadagascar.net. News & features from the Madagascar region.

Vintsy (bimonthly; mainly in French & Malagasy but some articles in English) e vintsy@wwf.mg; www. wwf.mg. WWF-Madagascar's conservation magazine running since 1991.

MALAGASY PRESS

L'Express (daily; in French & Malagasy) www. lexpressmada.com
La Gazette de la Grande Ile (daily; in French & Malagasy) www.lagazette-dgi.com

Madagascar Tribune (daily; in French) www. madagascar-tribune.com
Midi Madagasikara (daily; in French & Malagasy) www.midi-madagasikara.mg

USEFUL WEBSITES
General

www.airmadagascar.com Domestic flight schedules.
www.sobika.mg Online news and more.
www.madonline.com News, chat and general information.
www.annumada.com Malagasy telephone directory.
www.anglo-malagasysociety.co.uk Anglo-Malagasy Society.
www.malagasyword.org Interactive Malagasy dictionary.
www.madagascar-library.com Detailed catalogue of books and articles on Madagascar.
www.wildmadagascar.org Madagascar's wildlife, people and history by Rhett Butler.

Natural history

www.savethelemur.org Madagascar Fauna & Flora Group.
www.durrell.org Durrell Wildlife Conservation Trust/Jersey Zoo.
www.wwf.mg World Wide Fund for Nature in Madagascar.
www.conservation.org Conservation International.
www.parcs-madagascar.com Madagascar National Parks.
http://lemur.duke.edu Duke University Primate Center.
www.sahonagasy.org Malagasy frog conservation project.
www.madagasikara-voakajy.org Malagasy bat conservation.
www.marojejy.com Marojejy National Park and Anjanaharibe-Sud Reserve.

Index

Bold indicates main entries; *italic* indicates maps; NP = national park; SR = special reserve

INDEX OF ADVERTISERS